Tyndale New Testament Commentaries

Volume 6

Romans

Tyndale New Testament Commentaries

Volume 6

Series Editor: Eckhard J. Schnabel
Consulting Editor: Nicholas Perrin

Romans

An Introduction and Commentary

David E. Garland

Academic
An imprint of InterVarsity Press
Downers Grove, Illinois

Inter-Varsity Press, England
36 Causton Street, London SW1P 4ST, England
Website: www.ivpbooks.com
Email: ivp@ivpbooks.com

InterVarsity Press, USA
P.O. Box 1400, Downers Grove, IL 60515, USA
Website: www.ivpress.com
Email: email@ivpress.com

Inter-Varsity Press, England, publishes Christian books that are true to the Bible and that
communicate the gospel, develop discipleship and strengthen the church for its mission in the world.

IVP originated within the Inter-Varsity Fellowship, now the Universities and Colleges Christian
Fellowship, a student movement connecting Christian Unions in universities and colleges throughout
Great Britain, and a member movement of the International Fellowship of Evangelical Students. That
historic association is maintained, and all senior IVP staff and committee members subscribe to the
UCCF Basis of Faith. Website: www.uccf.org.uk.

InterVarsity Press®, USA, is the book-publishing division of InterVarsity Christian Fellowship/
USA® and a member movement of the International Fellowship of Evangelical Students. Website:
www.intervarsity.org.

First published 2021

Set in Garamond 11/13pt
Typeset in Great Britain by Avocet Typeset, Bideford, Devon
Printed and bound in Great Britain by Ashford Colour Press Ltd, Gosport, Hampshire

UK ISBN: 978–1–78974–312–8 (print)
UK ISBN: 978–1–78974–313–5 (digital)

US ISBN: 978-1-5140-0353-4 (print)
US ISBN: 978-1-5140-0354-1 (digital)

British Library Cataloguing-in-Publication Data
A catalogue record for this book is available from the British Library.

Library of Congress Cataloging-in-Publication Data
A catalog record for this book is available from the Library of Congress.

CONTENTS

GENERAL PREFACE

The Tyndale Commentaries have been a flagship series for evangelical readers of the Bible for over sixty years. Both the original New Testament volumes (1956–1974) as well as the new commentaries (1983–2003) rightly established themselves as a point of first reference for those who wanted more than is usually offered in a one-volume Bible commentary, without requiring the technical skills in Greek and in Jewish and Graeco-Roman studies of the more detailed series, with the advantage of being shorter than the volumes of intermediate commentary series. The appearance of new popular commentary series demonstrates that there is a continuing demand for commentaries that appeal to Bible study leaders in churches and at universities. The publisher, editors and authors of the Tyndale Commentaries believe that the series continues to meet an important need in the Christian community, not least in what we call today the Global South, with its immense growth of churches and the corresponding need for a thorough understanding of the Bible by Christian believers.

In the light of new knowledge, new critical questions, new revisions of Bible translations, and the need to provide specific guidance on the literary context and the genre of the individual passages as well as on theological emphases, it was time to publish new commentaries in the series. Three authors have revised their commentaries that appeared in the second series. The original aim remains. The new commentaries are neither too short nor unduly long. They are exegetical and thus root the interpretation of the text in its historical context. They do not aim to solve all critical questions, but they are written with an awareness of major scholarly debates which may be treated in the Introduction, in Additional notes or in the commentary itself. While not specifically homiletic in aim, they want to help readers to understand the passage under consideration in such a way that they begin to see points of relevance and application, even though the commentary does not explicitly offer these. The authors base their exegesis on the Greek text, but they write for readers who do not know Greek; Hebrew and Greek terms that are discussed are transliterated. The English translation used for the first series was the Authorized (King James) Version, while the volumes of the second series mostly used the Revised Standard Version; the volumes of the third series use either the New International Version (2011) or the New Revised Standard Version as primary versions, unless otherwise indicated by the author.

An immense debt of gratitude for the first and second series of the Tyndale Commentaries was owed to R. V. G. Tasker and L. Morris, who each wrote four of the commentaries themselves. The recruitment of new authors for the third series proved to be effortless, as colleagues responded enthusiastically to the opportunity to be involved in this project, a testimony to the larger number of New Testament scholars capable and willing to write commentaries, to the wider ethnic identity of contributors, and to the role that the Tyndale Commentaries have played in the church worldwide. It continues to be the hope of all those concerned with this series that God will graciously use the new commentaries to help readers understand as fully and clearly as possible the meaning of the New Testament.

Eckhard J. Schnabel, Series Editor
Nicholas Perrin, Consulting Editor

AUTHOR'S PREFACE

I am especially grateful to the editor of this series, Eckhard Schnabel, for the invitation to write a commentary on Romans. I benefited immensely from his own masterful two-volume commentary on Romans. I am also indebted to the legion of interpreters of Romans who have devoted their energies and wide-ranging expertise towards bringing clarity to this letter. Unfortunately, not all their names are reflected in the footnotes. I am grateful to Philip Duce at Inter-Varsity Press for his insightful comments; he has been most gracious. My graduate assistants at George W. Truett Theological Seminary, Baylor University, have been invaluable throughout the course of this project. Tia Kim managed to hunt down hundreds of articles on Romans and checked early chapters. I am also thankful for my other graduate students, James Heikkila and Daniel Xingshi Gao; and Lisa Meister Rondina especially provided indispensable help and constructive criticism. All of these students have inspired me with their friendship, stout faith, academic acumen and dedication to ministry. I am also grateful to Dr Howard Batson, pastor of First Baptist Church, Amarillo, Texas, for his comments after reading a rough draft. Romans belongs to the gathered church and not the academy, and I was heartened by his encouragement and conviction that this commentary could be useful for those seeking to proclaim and teach Romans in their various ministerial roles and settings. I am highly indebted to Suzanne Mitchell for her careful and skilful copy-editing and to Belinda Latchford for her proofreading. Naturally, the errors that remain are mine. Finally, I am most grateful for the support of my wife, Nancy Minter, who has brightened my life in countless ways as one who is incredibly loving, gracious and generous.

Thomas Schreiner reflects that Paul 'ultimately wrote Romans as a servant of God to honor his Lord' (Schreiner, p. 26). The fondest hope of any commentator on Romans is that his or her work might also in some small way bring honour and praise to God's name.

David E. Garland

ABBREVIATIONS

General

AASF	Annales Academiae Scientiarum Fennicae
AB	Anchor Bible
ABR	*Australian Biblical Review*
ACNT	Augsburg Commentaries on the New Testament
ANTC	Abingdon New Testament Commentaries
BBR	*Bulletin for Biblical Research*
BCBC	Believers Church Bible Commentary
BDAG	*A Greek–English Lexicon of the New Testament and Other Early Christian Literature*, ed. W. Bauer, F. W. Danker, W. F. Arndt and F. W. Gingrich, 3rd edn (Chicago: University of Chicago Press, 2000)
BECNT	Baker Exegetical Commentary on the New Testament
Bib	*Biblica*
BibInt	Biblical Interpretation Series
BN	*Biblische Notizen*
BNTC	Black's New Testament Commentaries
BSac	*Bibliotheca Sacra*
BT	*The Bible Translator*
BTCP	Biblical Theology for Christian Proclamation
BTNT	Biblical Theology of the New Testament

BZ	*Biblische Zeitschrift*
BZNW	Beihefte zur Zeitschrift für die neutestamentliche Wissenschaft
CBC	Cambridge Bible Commentary
CBET	Contributions to Biblical Exegesis and Theology
CBQ	*Catholic Biblical Quarterly*
CC	Concordia Commentary
CJ	*Concordia Journal*
CSC	Christian Standard Commentary
ECC	Eerdmans Critical Commentary
ECL	Early Christianity and Its Literature
EDNT	*Exegetical Dictionary of the New Testament*, ed. H. Balz and G. Schneider, 3 vols. (Grand Rapids: Eerdmans, 1990–3)
EvQ	*Evangelical Quarterly*
EKK	Evangelisch-katholischer Kommentar zum Neuen Testament
ExpTim	*Expository Times*
FRLANT	Forshungen zur Religion und Literatur des Alten und Neuen Testaments
HBT	*Horizons in Biblical Theology*
HNTC	Harper's New Testament Commentaries
HTA	Historisch Theologische Auslegung
HTR	*Harvard Theological Review*
ICC	International Critical Commentary
Int	*Interpretation*
IVPNTC	InterVarsity New Testament Commentary
JBL	*Journal of Biblical Literature*
JETS	*Journal of the Evangelical Theological Society*
JSNT	*Journal for the Study of the New Testament*
JSNTSup	Journal for the Study of the New Testament Supplement Series
JSPL	*Journal for the Study of Paul and His Letters*
JTI	*Journal of Theological Interpretation*
JTS	*Journal of Theological Studies*
KEK	Kritisch-exegetischer Kommentar über das Neue Testament (Meyer-Kommentar)

LCL	Loeb Classical Library
LSJ	*A Greek–English Lexicon*, ed. H. G. Liddell, R. Scott and H. S. Jones, 9th edn, with rev. supplement by P. G. W. Glare (Oxford: Oxford University Press, 1996)
LXX	Septuagint (Greek translation of the Hebrew Scriptures)
MM	*The Vocabulary of the Greek Testament Illustrated from the Papyri and Other Non-Literary Sources*, ed. J. H. Moulton and G. Milligan (Grand Rapids: Eerdmans, 1930–82)
MNTC	Moffat New Testament Commentary
MT	Masoretic Text
NCBC	New Century Bible Commentary
NCCS	New Covenant Commentary Series
Neot	*Neotestamentica*
NICNT	New International Commentary on the New Testament
NIGTC	New International Greek Testament Commentary
NovT	*Novum Testamentum*
NovTSup	Supplements to Novum Testamentum
NRTh	*Nouvelle revue théologique*
NSBT	New Studies in Biblical Theology
NTS	*New Testament Studies*
OTL	Old Testament Library
OTP	*Old Testament Pseudepigrapha*, ed. J. H. Charlesworth, 2 vols. (New York: Doubleday, 1983, 1985)
PNTC	Pillar New Testament Commentary
RB	*Revue biblique*
RevExp	*Review and Expositor*
SBJT	*Southern Baptist Journal of Theology*
SBLDS	Society of Biblical Literature Dissertation Series
SBT	Studies in Biblical Theology
SGBC	The Story of God Bible Commentary
SHBC	Smyth & Helwys Bible Commentary

SIG	*Sylloge Inscriptionum Graecarum*, ed. W. Dillenberger, 4 vols., 3rd edn (Leipzig: Hirzel, 1915–24)
SNTSMS	Society of New Testament Studies Monograph Series
SNTW	Studies of the New Testament and Its World
SP	Sacra Pagina
TDNT	*Theological Dictionary of the New Testament*, ed. G. Kittel and G. Friedrich (Grand Rapids: Eerdmans, 1964–76)
Thayer	*A Greek–English Lexicon of the New Testament*, ed. J. H. Thayer (New York: American Book Company, 1889)
THKNT	Theologischer Handkommentar zum Neuen Testament
TLNT	*Theological Lexicon of the New Testament*, ed. C. Spicq, tr. J. D. Ernest, 3 vols. (Peabody: Hendrickson, 1995)
TNTC	Tyndale New Testament Commentary
TPINTC	TPI New Testament Commentaries
TTCS	Teach the Text Commentary Series
TynBul	*Tyndale Bulletin*
TZ	*Theologische Zeitschrift*
UBCS	Understanding the Bible Commentary Series
USFISFCJ	University of South Florida International Studies in Formative Christianity and Judaism
VE	*Vox Evangelica*
WBC	Word Biblical Commentary
WUNT	Wissenschaftliche Untersuchungen zum Neuen Testament
ZECNT	Zondervan Exegetical Commentary on the New Testament
ZNW	*Zeitschrift für die neutestamentliche Wissenschaft*

Ancient texts

1 En.	1 Enoch (Ethiopic Apocalypse)
1QH	Thanksgiving Hymns

1QM	War Scroll
1QS	Rule of the Community, Manual of Discipline
2 Bar.	2 Baruch (Syriac Apocalypse)
2 En.	2 Enoch (Slavonic Enoch)
3 Bar.	3 Baruch (Greek Apocalypse)
4QFlor	4QFlorilegium
4QMMT	Miqṣat Maʿaśê ha-Torah
Abr.	Philo, *De Abrahamo*
Acts Pet.	Acts of Peter
Ag. Ap.	Josephus, *Against Apion*
Agr.	Philo, *De agricultura*
Agr.	Tacitus, *Agricola*
Ann.	Tacitus, *Annales*
Ant.	Josephus, *Jewish Antiquities*
Apoc. Mos.	Apocalypse of Moses
Apol.	Tertullian, *Apologeticus*
b. ʿAbod. Zar.	ʿAbodah Zarah (Babylonian Talmud)
b. Mak.	Makkot (Babylonian Talmud)
b. Pesaḥ	Pesaḥim (Babylonian Talmud)
b. Qidd.	Qiddušin (Babylonian Talmud)
b. Yebam.	Yebamot (Babylonian Talmud)
b. Yoma	Yoma (Babylonian Talmud)
Bell. civ.	Caesar, *Bellum civile*
Ben.	Seneca, *De beneficiis*
Caus. plant.	Theophrastus, *De causis plantarum*
CD	Cairo Genizah copy of the Damascus Document
Claud.	Suetonius, *Divus Claudius*
Clem.	Seneca (the Younger), *De clementia*
Comm. Rom.	Origen, *Commentarii in Romanos*
Conf.	Philo, *De confusione linguarum*
Diatr.	Epictetus, *Diatribai (Dissertationes)*
Ep.	Fronto, *Epistulae*
Ep.	Pliny the Younger, *Epistulae*
Ep.	Seneca (the Younger), *Epistulae morales*
Fug.	Philo, *De fuga et inventione*
Gen. Rab.	Genesis Rabbah
Geogr.	Strabo, *Geographica*

Her.	Philo, *Quis rerum divinarum heres sit*
Hist.	Tacitus, *Historiae*
Jub.	Jubilees
J.W.	Josephus, *Jewish War*
LAB	Liber antiquitatum biblicarum (Pseudo-Philo)
Leg.	Cicero, *De legibus*
Leg.	Philo, *Legum allegoriae*
Leg.	Plato, *Leges*
Let. Aris.	Letter of Aristeas
Lev. Rab.	Leviticus Rabbah
m. ʿAbod. Zar.	ʿAbodah Zarah (Mishnah)
m. ʾAbot	ʾAbot (Mishnah)
m. Giṭ.	Giṭṭin (Mishnah)
m. Ketub.	Ketubott (Mishnah)
m. Mak.	Makkot (Mishnah)
m. Qidd.	Qiddušin (Mishnah)
m. Šabb.	Šabbat (Mishnah)
m. Sanh.	Sanhedrin (Mishnah)
Mart. Pol.	*Martyrdom of Polycarp*
Metam.	Apuleius, *Metamorphoses*
Metam.	Ovid, *Metamorphoses*
Mil. glor.	Plautus, *Miles gloriosus*
Mor.	Plutarch, *Moralia*
Mos.	Philo, *De vita Mosis*
Mut.	Philo, *De mutatione nominum*
Odes Sol.	Odes of Solomon
Opif.	Philo, *De opificio mundi*
Post.	Philo, *De posteritate Caini*
Praem.	Philo, *De praemiis et poenis*
Prot.	Plato, *Protagoras*
Ps.-Phoc.	Pseudo-Phocylides
Pss Sol.	Psalms of Solomon
Quint. fratr.	Cicero, *Epistulae ad Quintum fratrem*
Rab. Perd.	Cicero, *Pro Rabirio Perduellionis Reo*
Resp.	Plato, *Respublica*
Sat.	Juvenal, *Satirae*
Sib. Or.	Sybylline Oracles
Somn.	Philo, *De somniis*

Spec.	Philo, *De specialibus legibus*
T. Gad	Testament of Gad
Tg. Ps.-J.	Targum Pseudo-Jonathan
T. Naph.	Testament of Naphtali
Tusc.	Cicero, *Tusculanae disputationes*
Virt.	Philo, *De virtutibus*
Vit. beat.	Seneca (the Younger), *De vita beata*

Bible versions

ASV   American Standard Version (1901).

CEB   The Common English Bible. © Copyright 2011 by the
Common English Bible. All rights reserved. Used by
permission.

CJB   The Complete Jewish Bible. Copyright © 1998 by David
H. Stern. All rights reserved. No portion of this book
may be reproduced, stored in a retrieval system, or
transmitted in any form or by any means, without prior
written permission of the publisher.

CSB   The Christian Standard Bible. Copyright © 2017 by
Holman Bible Publishers. Used by permission. Christian
Standard Bible®, and CSB® are federally registered
trademarks of Holman Bible Publishers, all rights
reserved.

ESV   The ESV Bible (The Holy Bible, English Standard
Version), copyright © 2001 by Crossway, a publishing
ministry of Good News Publishers. Used by permission.
All rights reserved.

JBP   The *J.B. Phillips New Testament in Modern English*, published
by HarperCollins Publishers, copyright © J. B. Phillips,
1960, 1972.

KJV   Extracts from the Authorized Version of the Bible (The
King James Bible), the rights in which are vested in the
Crown, are reproduced by permission of the Crown's
Patentee, Cambridge University Press.

MSG   *THE MESSAGE.* Copyright © by Eugene H. Peterson
1993, 1994, 1995, 1996, 2000, 2001, 2002. Used by
permission of NavPress Publishing Group.

SELECT BIBLIOGRAPHY

Commentaries on Romans

Achtemeier, Paul J. (1985), *Romans*, Interpretation (Atlanta: John
Knox).
Barrett, Charles Kingsley (1971), *A Commentary on the Epistle to the
Romans*, rev. edn, BNTC (London: Continuum).
Barth, Karl (1933), *The Epistle to the Romans* (London: Oxford
University Press).
Bence, Clarence L. (1996), *Romans: A Commentary for Bible Students*,
Wesleyan Bible Study Commentary (Indianapolis: Wesleyan
Publishing House).
Best, Ernest (1967), *The Letter of Paul to the Romans*, CBC
(Cambridge: Cambridge University Press).
Bird, Michael F. (2016), *Romans*, SGBC (Grand Rapids:
Zondervan).
Black, Matthew (1973), *Romans*, NCBC (Grand Rapids:
Eerdmans).
Bruce, F. F. (1963), *The Epistle of Paul to the Romans*, rev. edn,
TNTC (Grand Rapids: Eerdmans).
Brunner, Emil (1959), *The Letter to the Romans* (Philadelphia:
Fortress).
Byrne, Brendan (1996), *Romans*, SP (Collegeville: Liturgical
Press).
Cottrell, Jack (2005), *Romans*, College Press NIV Commentary
(Joplin: College Press).

Cranfield, C. E. B. (1975, 1979), *A Critical and Exegetical
Commentary on the Epistle to the Romans*, ICC, 2 vols. (Edinburgh:
T&T Clark).

Dodd, C. H. (1932), *The Epistle of Paul to the Romans*, MNTC (New
York: Harper).

Dunn, James D. G. (1988), *Romans*, WBC, 2 vols. (Dallas: Word).

Edwards, James R. (1992), *Romans*, UBCS (Grand Rapids: Baker).

Fitzmyer, Joseph A. (1993), *Romans*, AB (New York: Doubleday).

Gignac, Alain (2014), *L'Épître aux Romains*. Commentaire biblique
(Paris: Cerf).

Godet, Frederick (1895), *Commentary on St. Paul's Epistle to the
Romans* (Edinburgh: T&T Clark).

Haacker, Klaus (1999), *Der Brief des Paulus an die Römer*, THKNT
(Leipzig: Evangelische Verlaganstalt).

Harrison, Everett F. and Donald A. Hagner (2008), 'Romans', in
T. Longman and D. E. Garland (eds.), *The Expositor's Bible
Commentary* (Grand Rapids: Zondervan), pp. 21–237.

Harrisville, Roy A. (1980), *Romans*, ACNT (Minneapolis:
Augsburg).

Heil, John Paul (1987), *Paul's Letter to the Romans: A Reader-Response
Commentary* (Eugene: Wipf and Stock).

Hultgren, Arland J. (2011), *Paul's Letter to the Romans* (Grand
Rapids: Eerdmans).

Jackson W. [pseudonym] (2019), *Reading Romans with Eastern Eyes:
Honor and Shame in Paul's Message and Mission* (Downers Grove:
IVP Academic).

Jewett, Robert (2007), *Romans: A Commentary*, Hermeneia
(Minneapolis: Fortress).

Johnson, Luke Timothy (2001), *Reading Romans: A Literary and
Theological Commentary* (Macon: Smyth & Helwys).

Käsemann, Ernst (1980), *Commentary on Romans* (Grand Rapids:
Eerdmans).

Keck, Leander E. (2005), *Romans*, ANTC (Nashville: Abingdon).

Keener, Craig S. (2009), *Romans*, NCCS (Eugene: Cascade).

Kruse, Colin G. (2012), *Paul's Letter to the Romans*, PNTC (Grand
Rapids: Eerdmans).

Leenhardt, Franz J. (1961), *The Epistle to the Romans* (London:
Lutterworth).

Lohse, Eduard (2003), *Der Brief an die Römer*, KEK (Göttingen: Vandenhoeck & Ruprecht).

Longenecker, Richard N. (2016), *The Epistle to the Romans*, NIGTC (Grand Rapids: Eerdmans).

Manson, T. W. (1962), 'Romans', in M. Black and H. H. Rowley (eds.), *Peake's Commentary on the Bible* (London: Nelson), pp. 940–953.

Matera, Frank J. (2010), *Romans*, Paideia (Grand Rapids: Eerdmans).

Michel, Otto (1963), *Der Brief an die Römer*, KEK, 12th edn (Göttingen: Vandenhoeck & Ruprecht).

Middendorf, Michael P. (2013, 2016), *Romans*, CC, 2 vols. (St. Louis: Concordia).

Moo, Douglas J. (2018), *The Epistle to the Romans*, rev. edn, NICNT (Grand Rapids: Eerdmans).

Morris, Leon (1988), *The Epistle to the Romans*, PNTC (Grand Rapids: Eerdmans).

Murray, John (1960), *The Epistle to the Romans*, NICNT, 2 vols. (Grand Rapids: Eerdmans).

Nygren, Anders (1949), *Commentary on Romans* (Philadelphia: Fortress).

Osborne, Grant (2004), *Romans*, IVPNTC (Downers Grove: InterVarsity Press).

Pate, C. Marvin (2013), *Romans*, TTCS (Grand Rapids: Baker).

Peterson, David G. (2017), *Commentary on Romans*, BTCP (Nashville: Holman).

Porter, Stanley E. (2015), *The Letter to the Romans: A Linguistic and Literary Commentary* (Sheffield: Sheffield Phoenix).

Sanday, William and Arthur C. Headlam (1902), *A Critical and Exegetical Commentary on the Epistle to the Romans*, 5th edn (Edinburgh: T&T Clark).

Schlatter, Adolf (1995), *Romans: The Righteousness of God* (Peabody: Hendrickson).

Schnabel, Eckhard J. (2015, 2016), *Der Brief des Paulus an die Römer*, 2 vols., HTA (Witten: SCM R. Brockhaus; Giessen: Brunnen).

Schreiner, Thomas R. (2018), *Romans*, rev. edn, BECNT (Grand Rapids: Baker).

Stott, John (1994), *Romans: Good News for the World* (Downers
    Grove: InterVarsity Press).

Stowers, Stanley K. (1994), *A Rereading of Romans: Justice, Jews, and
    Gentiles* (New Haven: Yale University Press).

Stuhlmacher, Peter (1994), *Paul's Letter to the Romans: A
    Commentary* (Louisville: Westminster/John Knox).

Talbert, Charles H. (2002), *Romans*, SHBC (Macon: Smyth &
    Helwys).

Taylor, Vincent (1955), *The Epistle to the Romans*, Epworth
    Preacher's Commentaries (London: Epworth).

Thielman, Frank S. (2018), *Romans*, ZECNT (Grand Rapids:
    Zondervan).

Thiselton, Anthony C. (2016), *Discovering Romans: Content,
    Interpretation, Reception* (Grand Rapids: Eerdmans).

Toews, John E. (2004), *Romans*, BCBC (Scottdale: Herald).

Westerholm, Stephen (2004), *Understanding Paul: The Early Christian
    Worldview of the Letter to the Romans* (Grand Rapids: Baker).

Wilckens, Ulrich (1978, 1980, 1982), *Der Brief an die Römer*, EKK, 3
    vols. (Zurich: Benninger; Neukirchen-Vluyn: Neukirchener
    Theologie).

Witherington, Ben (2004), *Paul's Letter to the Romans: A Socio-
    Rhetorical Commentary* (Grand Rapids: Eerdmans).

Wolter, Michael (2014, 2020), *Der Brief an die Römer*, EKK, 2 vols.
    (Neukirchen-Vluyn: Neukirchener Theologie; Ostfildern:
    Patmos).

Wright, N. T. (2002), 'The Letter to the Romans: Introduction,
    Commentary, and Reflections', in L. E. Keck (ed.), *The New
    Interpreter's Bible*, Vol. 10 (Nashville: Abingdon), pp. 395–770.

Ziesler, John (1989), *Paul's Letter to the Romans*, TPINTC (London:
    SCM).

Other commentaries, books, monographs and articles

Abasciano, Brian J. (2006), 'Corporate Election in Romans 9: A
    Reply to Thomas Schreiner', *JETS* 49, pp. 351–371.

Achtemeier, Paul J. (1990), 'Romans 3:1–8: Structure and
    Argument', *Anglican Theological Review, Supplement Series* 11,
    pp. 77–87.

Adams, Edward (1997), 'Abraham's Faith and Gentile
    Disobedience: Textual Links between Romans 1 and 4', *JSNT*
    65, pp. 47–66.
—— (2000), *Constructing the World: A Study in Paul's Cosmological
    Language*, SNTW (Edinburgh: T&T Clark).
Agersnap, Søren (1999), *Baptism and the New Life: A Study of Romans
    6.1–14* (Aarhus: Aarhus University Press).
Allen, Leslie C. (1964), 'The Old Testament in Romans I – VIII',
    VE 3, pp. 6–41.
Anderson, R. Dean (1999), *Ancient Rhetorical Theory and Paul*,
    Contributions to Biblical Exegesis and Theology, rev. edn
    (Leuven: Peeters).
Apuleius, Lucius (1989), *Metamorphoses (The Golden Ass), Volume II:
    Books 7–11*, tr. J. A. Hanson, LCL (Cambridge: Harvard
    University Press).
Aune, David E. (1991), 'Romans as a *Logos Protreptikos*', in K. P.
    Donfried (ed.), *The Romans Debate: Revised and Expanded Edition*
    (Peabody: Hendrickson), pp. 278–296.
Banks, Robert (1978), 'Romans 7.25a: An Eschatological
    Thanksgiving', *ABR* 26, pp. 34–42.
Barclay, John M. G. (1987), 'Mirror-Reading a Polemical Letter:
    Galatians as a Test Case', *JSNT* 31, pp. 73–93.
—— (2008), 'Is It Good News That God Is Impartial? A
    Response to Robert Jewett, *Romans: A Commentary*', *JSNT* 31,
    pp. 89–111.
—— (2015), *Paul and the Gift* (Grand Rapids: Eerdmans).
Barrett, C. K. (1968), *The First Epistle to the Corinthians*, HNTC
    (New York: Harper).
—— (1976), 'The Allegory of Abraham, Sarah, and Hagar in the
    Argument of Galatians', in J. Friedrich, W. Pöhlmann and P.
    Stuhlmacher (eds.), *Rechtfertigung: Festschrift für Ernst Käsemann
    zum 70. Geburtstag* (Tübingen: Mohr Siebeck; Göttingen:
    Vandenhoeck & Ruprecht), pp. 1–16.
—— (1977), 'Romans 9.30 – 10.21: Fall and Responsibility of
    Israel', in L. De Lorenzi (ed.), *Die Israelfrage nach Rom 9 – 11*
    (Rome: Abtei von St Paul vor den Mauern), pp. 99–130.
Bassler, Jouette M. (1982), *Divine Impartiality: Paul and a Theological
    Axiom*, SBLDS 59 (Chico: Scholars Press).

—— (1985), 'Luke and Paul on Impartiality', *Bib* 66, pp. 546–552.

Bauckham, Richard (1998), *God Crucified: Monotheism and Christology in the New Testament* (Grand Rapids: Eerdmans).

—— (2002), *Gospel Women: Studies in the Named Women in the Gospels* (Grand Rapids: Eerdmans).

—— (2011), 'The Story of the Earth according to Paul: Romans 8:18–23', *RevExp* 108, pp. 91–97.

Baum, Gregory (1965), *Is the New Testament Anti-Semitic? A Re-examination of the New Testament* (New York: Paulist).

Baxter, A. G. and John A. Ziesler (1985), 'Paul and Arboriculture: Romans 11:17–24', *JSNT* 24, pp. 25–32.

Beare, Francis Wright (1962), *St. Paul and His Letters* (Nashville: Abingdon).

Beck, Brian E. (1994), 'Reflections on 2 Corinthians 5:11 – 6:2', *Epworth Review* 21, pp. 85–92.

Beker, J. Christiaan (1980), *Paul the Apostle: The Triumph of God in Life and Thought* (Philadelphia: Fortress).

Bekken, Per Jarle (2007), *The Word Is Near You: A Study of Deuteronomy 30:12–14 in Paul's Letter to the Romans in a Jewish Context*, BZNW 144 (Berlin: de Gruyter).

Bell, Richard H. (1994), *Provoked to Jealousy: The Origin and Purpose of the Jealousy Motif in Romans 9 – 11*, WUNT 2/63 (Tübingen: Mohr Siebeck).

Belleville, Linda (2005), 'Ἰουνίαν . . . ἐπίσημοι ἐν τοῖς ἀποστόλοις: A Re-examination of Romans 16.7 in Light of Primary Source Materials', *NTS* 51, pp. 231–249.

Bertschmann, Dorothea H. (2014), 'The Good, the Bad and the State: Rom 13.1–7 and the Dynamics of Love', *NTS* 60, pp. 232–249.

Bird, Michael F. (2013), '"One Who Will Arise over the Nations": Paul's Letter to the Romans and the Roman Empire', in S. McKnight and J. B. Modica (eds.), *Jesus Is Lord, Caesar Is Not: Evaluating Empire in New Testament Studies* (Downers Grove: InterVarsity Press Academic), pp. 146–165.

Bjerkelund, C. J. (1967), *Parakalō: Form, Funktion, und Sinn der parakalō-Sätze in den paulinischen Briefen*, Bibliotheca Theologica Norvegica 1 (Oslo: Universitetsforlaget).

Blackwell, Ben C. (2010), 'Immortal Glory and the Problem of Death in Romans 3.23', *JSNT* 32, pp. 285–308.

Boers, Hendrikus (2001), 'The Structure and Meaning of Romans 6:1–14', *CBQ* 63, pp. 664–682.

Bornkamm, Günther (1969a), *Early Christian Experience* (New York: Harper & Row).

—— (1969b), *Paul* (New York: Harper & Row).

Bradley, Keith R. (1987), *Slaves and Masters in the Roman Empire: A Study in Social Control* (New York: Oxford University Press).

Bray, Gerald (ed.) (1998), *Romans*, Ancient Christian Commentary on Scripture, New Testament Vol. 6 (Downers Grove: InterVarsity Press).

Breytenbach, Cilliers (2005), 'The "For Us" Phrases in Pauline Soteriology: Considering Their Background and Use', in J. van der Watt (ed.), *Salvation in the New Testament: Perspectives on Soteriology* (Leiden: Brill), pp. 163–185.

Brookins, Timothy A. (2013), 'The (In)frequency of the Name "Erastus" in Antiquity: A Literary, Papyrological, and Epigraphical Catalog', *NTS* 59, pp. 496–516.

Bruce, F. F. (1991), 'The Romans Debate – Continued', in K. P. Donfried (ed.), *The Romans Debate: Revised and Expanded Edition* (Peabody: Hendrickson), pp. 175–194.

Bryant, K. Edwin (2016), *Paul and the Rise of the Slave: Death and Resurrection of the Oppressed in the Epistle to the Romans*, BibInt 143 (Leiden/Boston: Brill).

Burer, Michael H. and Daniel B. Wallace (2001), 'Was Junia Really an Apostle? A Re-examination of Rom 16.7', *NTS* 47, pp. 76–91.

Burke, Trevor J. (2006), *Adopted into God's Family*, NSBT (Nottingham: Apollos; Downers Grove: InterVarsity Press).

Byrne, Brandon (2003), 'Paul's Adam Myth Revisited', in D. Reid and M. Worthing (eds.), *Sin and Salvation* (Hindmarsh: ATF Press), pp. 41–54.

Byrskog, Samuel (1997), 'Epistolography, Rhetoric and Letter Prescript: Romans 1.1–7 as a Test Case', *JSNT* 65, pp. 27–46.

Cadwallader, Alan H. (2018), 'Tertius in the Margins: A Critical Appraisal of the Secretary Hypothesis', *NTS* 64, pp. 378–396.

—— (2019), 'Phoebe in and around Romans: The Weight of
Marginal Reception', in P. G. Bolt and J. R. Harrison (eds.),
*Romans and the Legacy of St Paul: Historical, Theological, and Social
Perspectives*, Occasional Series 1 (Macquarie Park, NSW: SCD
Press), pp. 429–452.

Caird, George B. (1977), *Paul's Letters from Prison* (Oxford: Oxford
University Press).

—— (1980), *The Language and Imagery of the Bible* (Philadelphia:
Westminster).

Calhoun, Robert Matthew (2011), *Paul's Definitions of the Gospel in
Romans 1*, WUNT 2/316 (Tübingen: Mohr Siebeck).

Calvin, John (1960), *The Institutes of the Christian Religion*, ed. J. T.
McNeill, tr. F. L. Battles, Library of Christian Classics, 2 vols.
(Philadelphia: Westminster).

Campbell, Constantine R. (2012), *Paul and Union with Christ: An
Exegetical and Theological Study* (Grand Rapids: Zondervan).

Campbell, Douglas A. (1994), 'Romans 1:17: A *Crux Interpretum*
for the ΠΙΣΤΙΣ ΧΡΙΣΤΟΥ Debate', *JBL* 113, pp. 265–285.

Campbell, William S. (1991), 'Romans III as a Key to the
Structure and Thought of the Letter', in K. P. Donfried (ed.),
The Romans Debate: Revised and Expanded Edition (Peabody:
Hendrickson), pp. 251–264.

Caplan, H., et al. (tr.) (1913–), *Cicero*, 29 vols., LCL (Cambridge:
Harvard University Press).

Casson, Sarah H. (2019), *Textual Signposts in the Argument of Romans:
A Relevance-Theory Approach*, ECL (Atlanta: SBL Press).

Chae, Daniel Jong-Sang (1997), *Paul as Apostle to the Gentiles: His
Apostolic Self-Awareness and Its Influence on the Soteriological Argument
in Romans* (Carlisle: Paternoster).

Childs, Brevard S. (1984), *The New Testament as Canon: An
Introduction* (Philadelphia: Fortress).

—— (2001), *Isaiah*, OTL (Philadelphia: Westminster John Knox).

Clarke, Andrew D. (1990), 'The Good and the Just in Romans
5:7', *TynBul* 41, pp. 128–142.

Colson, F. H., G. H Whitaker and R. Marcus (tr.) (1929–62), *Philo*,
12 vols., LCL (Cambridge: Harvard University Press).

Cosgrove, Charles H. (1987), 'What If Some Have Not Believed?
Occasion and Thrust of Romans 3:1–8', *ZNW* 78, pp. 90–105.

Crafton, Jeffrey A. (1990), 'Paul's Rhetorical Vision and the Purpose of Romans: Toward a New Understanding', *NovT* 32, pp. 317–339.

Cranfield, C. E. B. (1994), 'Romans 6:1–14 Revisited', *ExpTim* 106, pp. 40–43.

Curtis, Heath R. (2002), 'A Female Apostle? A Note Re-examining the Work of Burer and Wallace concerning ἐπίσημοι with ἐν and the Dative', *CJ* 28, pp. 437–440.

Dabourne, Wendy (1999), *Purpose and Cause in Pauline Exegesis: Romans 1.16 – 4.25 and a New Approach to the Letters*, SNTSMS 104 (Cambridge: Cambridge University Press).

Dahl, Nils A. (1977), *Studies in Paul* (Minneapolis: Augsburg).

Danby, Herbert (1933), *The Mishnah* (Oxford: Oxford University Press).

Das, A. Andrew (2007), *Solving the Romans Debate* (Minneapolis: Fortress).

Dauge, Yves Albert (1981), *Le Barbare: recherches sur la conception romaine de la barbarie et de la civilization*, Classical Antiquity 176 (Brussels: Latomus).

Davies, W. D. (1965), *Paul and Rabbinic Judaism: Some Rabbinic Elements in Pauline Theology*, rev. edn (New York: Harper).

—— (1977–8), 'Paul and the People of Israel', *NTS* 24, pp. 4–39.

Davies, W. D. and Dale C. Allison (1988), *The Gospel according to St. Matthew*, Vol. 1, ICC (Edinburgh: T&T Clark).

DeSilva, David A. (2004), *An Introduction to the New Testament* (Downers Grove: InterVarsity Press; Leicester: Apollos).

Dewey, Arthur J. (1994), '*EIS THN SPANIAN*: The Future and Paul', in L. Bormann, K. Del Tredici and A. Standhartinger (eds.), *Religious Propaganda and Missionary Competition in the New Testament World: Essays Honoring Dieter Georgi*, NovTSup 74 (Leiden: Brill), pp. 321–349.

Dixon, Thomas P. (2020), 'Judgement for Israel: The Marriage of Wrath and Mercy in Romans 9 – 11', *NTS* 66, pp. 565–581.

Doeve, J. W. (1953), 'Some Notes with Reference to *ta logia tou theou* in Romans 3.2', in J. N. Sevenster and W. C. van Unnik (eds.), *Studia Paulina in Honorem Johannis de Zwaan* (Haarlem: Bohn), pp. 111–123.

Donaldson, Terence L. (1997), *Paul and the Gentiles: Remapping the Apostle's Convictional World* (Minneapolis: Fortress).

Donfried, Karl P. (ed.) (1991a), *The Romans Debate: Revised and Expanded Edition* (Peabody: Hendrickson).

—— (1991b), 'False Presuppositions in the Study of Romans', in K. P. Donfried (ed.), *The Romans Debate: Revised and Expanded Edition* (Peabody: Hendrickson), pp. 102–125.

—— (2007), 'Paul and the Revisionists: Did Luther Really Get It All Wrong?', *Dialog* 46, pp. 31–40.

Douglass, Frederick (1846), *Narrative of the Life of Frederick Douglass: An American Slave Written by Himself*, 2nd edn (Dublin: Webb and Chapman).

Downs, David J. (2008), *The Offering of the Gentiles: Collection for Jerusalem in Its Chronological, Cultural, and Cultic Contexts*, WUNT 2/248 (Tübingen: Mohr Siebeck).

Dryden, J. de Waal (2015), 'Revisiting Romans 7: Law, Self and Spirit', *JSPL* 5, pp. 129–151.

Duncan, George S. (1934), *The Epistle of Paul to the Galatians* (New York: Harper).

Duncan, John (2015), 'The Hope of Creation: The Significance of ἐφ' ἐλπίδι (Rom 8.20c) in Context', *NTS* 61, pp. 411–427.

Dunn, James D. G. (1982), 'Salvation Proclaimed: VI. Romans 6,1–11: Dead and Alive', *ExpTim* 93, pp. 259–264.

—— (2008), *The New Perspective on Paul*, rev. edn (Grand Rapids: Eerdmans).

Du Toit, A. B. (1989), 'Persuasion in Romans 1:1–17', *BZ* 33, pp. 192–209.

Eastman, Susan (2010), 'Israel and Divine Mercy in Galatians and Romans', in F. Wilk and J. R. Wagner (eds.), *Between Gospel and Election: Explorations in the Interpretation of Romans 9 – 11* (Tübingen: Mohr Siebeck), pp. 147–170.

Edwards, James R. (2019), *Between the Swastika and the Sickle: The Life, Disappearance, and Execution of Ernst Lohmeyer* (Grand Rapids: Eerdmans).

Engberg-Pedersen, Troels (2006), 'Paul's Stoicizing Politics in Romans 12 – 13: The Role of 13.1–10 in the Argument', *JSNT* 29, pp. 163–172.

short spread

Epictetus (1926–8), *The Discourses as Reported by Arrian; the Manual; and Fragments*, tr. W. A. Oldfather, 2 vols., LCL (Cambridge: Harvard University Press).

Epp, Eldon J. (2005), *Junia: The First Woman Apostle* (Minneapolis: Fortress).

Epstein, Isidore (ed.) (1948), *The Soncino Talmud*, 18 vols. (London: Soncino).

Esler, Philip F. (2003a), 'Ancient Oleiculture and Ethnic Differentiation: The Meaning of the Olive-Tree Image in Romans 11', *JSNT* 26, pp. 103–124.

—— (2003b), *Conflict and Identity in Romans: The Social Setting of Paul's Letter* (Minneapolis: Fortress).

Fatehi, Mehrdad (2000), *The Spirit's Relation to the Risen Lord in Paul: An Examination of Its Christological Implications*, WUNT 2/128 (Tübingen: Mohr Siebeck).

Fee, Gordon D. (1994), *God's Empowering Presence: The Holy Spirit in the Letters of Paul* (Peabody: Hendrickson).

Feldman, Louis H. (1993), *Jew and Gentile in the Ancient World* (Princeton: Princeton University Press).

Feldmeier, Reinhard (2014), *Power, Service, Humility: A New Testament Ethic* (Waco: Baylor University Press).

Ferguson, John (1970), *The Religions of the Roman Empire* (Ithaca: Cornell University Press).

Feuillet, Andre (1959), 'La Citation d'Habacuc 2:4 et les huit premiers chapitres de l'Epître aux Romains', *NTS* 6, pp. 52–80.

—— (1970), 'Le Règne de la mort et le règne de la vie', *RB* 77, pp. 481–521.

Fitzmyer, Joseph A. (1993), *According to Paul: Studies in the Theology of the Apostle* (New York: Paulist).

Fowler, Paul B. (2016), *The Structure of Romans: The Argument of Paul's Letter* (Minneapolis: Fortress).

France, R. T. (1999), 'From Romans to the Real World: Biblical Principles and Cultural Change in Relation to Homosexuality and the Ministry of Women', in S. K. Soderlund and N. T. Wright (eds.), *Romans and the People of God: Essays in Honor of Gordon D. Fee on the Occasion of His 65th Birthday* (Grand Rapids: Eerdmans), pp. 234–253.

Freedman H. and Maurice Simon (eds.) (1983), *Midrash Rabbah: Genesis*, 3rd edn (London/New York: Soncino).

Fryer, Nico S. L. (1987), 'The Meaning and Translation of *Hilastērion* in Romans 3:25', *EvQ* 59, pp. 99–116.

Furnish, Victor Paul (1972), *The Love Command in the New Testament* (Nashville: Abingdon).

Gäckle, Volker (2005), *Die Starken und die Schwachen in Korinth und in Rom: Zu Herkunft und Funktion der Antithese in 1Kor 8,1 – 11,1 und in Rom 14,1 – 15,13*, WUNT 2/200 (Tübingen: Mohr Siebeck).

Gagnon, Robert A. J. (2001), *The Bible and Homosexual Practice: Texts and Hermeneutics* (Nashville: Abingdon).

Gamble, Harry, Jr (1977), *The Textual History of the Letter to the Romans: A Study in Textual and Literary Criticism*, Studies and Documents 42 (Grand Rapids: Eerdmans).

Garland, David E. (2003), *1 Corinthians*, BECNT (Grand Rapids: Baker).

—— (2015), *A Theology of Mark*, BTNT (Grand Rapids: Zondervan).

—— (2021), *2 Corinthians*, rev. edn, CSC (Nashville: Holman Reference).

Gathercole, Simon J. (2002), *Where Is Boasting? Early Jewish Soteriology and Paul's Response in Romans 1 – 5* (Grand Rapids: Eerdmans).

—— (2006), 'The Doctrine of Justification in Paul and Beyond: Some Proposals', in B. L. McCormack (ed.), *Justification in Perspective: Historical Developments and Contemporary Challenges* (Grand Rapids: Baker), pp. 219–241.

—— (2018), '"Sins" in Paul', *NTS* 64, pp. 143–161.

Gaventa, Beverly Roberts (2010), 'On the Calling-Into-Being of Israel: Romans 9:6–29', in F. Wilk and J. R. Wagner (eds.), *Between Gospel and Election: Explorations in the Interpretation of Romans 9 – 11*, WUNT 2/257 (Tübingen: Mohr Siebeck), pp. 255–269.

Gibson, Jeffrey B. (2004), 'Paul's "Dying Formula": Prolegomena to an Understanding of Its Import and Significance', in S. E. McGinn (ed.), *Celebrating Romans: Template for Pauline Theology; Essays in Honor of Robert Jewett* (Grand Rapids: Eerdmans), pp. 20–41.

Gieniusz, Andrzej (1993), 'Rom 7,1–6: Lack of Imagination? Function of the Passage in the Argumentation of Rom 6,1 – 7,6', *Bib* 74, pp. 389–400.

—— (1999), *Romans 8:18–30: 'Suffering Does Not Thwart the Future Glory'*, USFISFCJ (Atlanta: Scholars Press).

Gignilliat, Mark S. (2006), 'Working Together with Whom? Text-Critical, Contextual, and Theological Analysis of συνεργεῖ in Romans 8,28', *Bib* 87, pp. 511–515.

Glad, Clarence E. (1995), *Paul and Philodemus: Adaptability in Epicurean and Early Christian Psychagogy*, NovTSup 81 (Leiden/New York/Cologne: Brill).

Glancy, Jennifer (2011), 'Slavery and the Rise of Christianity', in K. Bradley and P. Cartledge (eds.), *The Ancient Mediterranean World*, The Cambridge World History of Slavery Vol. 1 (Cambridge: Cambridge University Press), pp. 456–481.

Goodrich, John K. (2011), 'Erastus of Corinth (Romans 16.23): Responding to Recent Proposals on His Rank, Status, and Faith', *NTS* 57, pp. 583–593.

—— (2012), *Paul as an Administrator of God in 1 Corinthians*, SNTSMS 152 (Cambridge: Cambridge University Press).

—— (2013), 'From Slaves of Sin to Slaves of God', *BBR* 23, pp. 509–530.

Gordon, Benjamin D. (2016), 'On the Sanctity of Mixtures and Branches: Two Halakic Sayings in Romans 11:16–24', *JBL* 135, pp. 355–368.

Grindheim, Sigurd (2005), *The Crux of Election: Paul's Critique of the Jewish Confidence in the Election of Israel*, WUNT 2/202 (Tübingen: Mohr Siebeck).

Gundry, Robert H. (2010), *Commentary on the New Testament* (Peabody: Hendrickson).

Gupta, Nijay H. (2012), 'Mirror-Reading Moral Issues in Paul's Letters', *JSNT* 34, pp. 361–381.

Haacker, Klaus (2003), *The Theology of Paul's Letter to the Romans* (Cambridge: Cambridge University Press).

Hall, David R. (1983), 'Romans 3.1–8 Reconsidered', *NTS* 29, pp. 183–197.

Harrington, Hannah K. (2001), *Holiness: Rabbinic Judaism and the Graeco-Roman World* (London/New York: Routledge).

Harris, Murray J. (1986), 'Appendix: Prepositions and Theology in the Greek New Testament', in C. Brown (ed.), *The New International Dictionary of New Testament Theology*, Vol. 3 (Grand Rapids: Zondervan), pp. 1117–1215.

Harrisville, Roy A., III (1994), 'Πίστις Χριστοῦ: Witness of the Fathers', *NovT* 36, pp. 232–241.

Hartwig, Charlotte and Gerd Theissen (2004), 'Die korinthische Gemeinde als Nebenadressat des Römerbriefs: Eigentextreferenzen des Paulus und kommunikativer Kontext des längsten Paulusbriefes', *NovT* 46, pp. 229–252.

Havemann, J. C. T. (1997), 'Cultivated Olive – Wild Olive: The Olive Tree Metaphor in Romans 11:16–24', *Neot* 31, pp. 87–106.

Hays, Richard B. (1985), '"Have We Found Abraham to Be Our Forefather according to the Flesh?" A Reconsideration of Rom 4:1', *NovT* 27, pp. 76–91.

—— (1989), *Echoes of Scripture in the Letters of Paul* (New Haven: Yale University Press).

—— (2002), *The Faith of Jesus Christ: The Narrative Substructure of Galatians 3:1 – 4:11*, rev. edn (Grand Rapids: Eerdmans).

Hengel, Martin (1977), *Crucifixion* (Philadelphia: Fortress).

—— (1992), 'Christological Titles in Early Christianity', in J. H. Charlesworth (ed.), *The Messiah: Developments in Earliest Judaism and Christianity* (Minneapolis: Fortress), pp. 425–448.

Heschel, Abraham J. (1968), *Who Is Man?* (Stanford: Stanford University Press).

Hill, Wesley (2015), *Paul and the Trinity: Persons, Relations, and the Pauline Letters* (Grand Rapids: Eerdmans).

Hoekema, Anthony A. (1971), 'The Christian's Self-Image', *The Reformed Journal* 20, pp. 17–20.

Holloway, Paul A. (2003), 'The Rhetoric of Romans', *RevExp* 100, pp. 113–127.

Hooker, Morna D. (2003), 'The Authority of the Bible: A New Testament Perspective', *Ex Auditu* 19, pp. 44–64.

Hurtado, Larry W. (1981), 'The Doxology at the End of Romans', in E. J. Epp and G. D. Fee (eds.), *New Testament Textual Criticism: Its Significance for Exegesis* (Oxford: Clarendon), pp. 185–199.

—— (1999), 'Jesus' Divine Sonship in Paul's Epistle to
the Romans', in S. K. Soderlund and N. T. Wright (eds.),
Romans and the People of God: Essays in Honor of Gordon D.
Fee on His 65th Birthday (Grand Rapids: Eerdmans),
pp. 217–233.

—— (2003), *Lord Jesus Christ: Devotion to Jesus in Earliest Christianity*
(Grand Rapids: Eerdmans).

Hvalvik, Reidar (1990), 'A "Sonderweg" for Israel: A Critical
Examination of a Current Interpretation of Romans 11.25–27',
JSNT 38, pp. 87–107.

Irons, Charles Lee (2015), *Righteousness of God: A Lexical*
Examination of the Covenant-Faithfulness Interpretation, WUNT
2/386 (Tübingen: Mohr Siebeck).

Jervell, Jacob (1991), 'The Letter to Jerusalem', in K. P. Donfried
(ed.), *The Romans Debate: Revised and Expanded Edition* (Peabody:
Hendrickson), pp. 53–64.

Jervis, L. Ann (1991), *The Purpose of Romans: A Comparative*
Letter Structure Investigation, JSNTSup 55 (Sheffield: JSOT
Press).

Jewett, Robert (1990), 'Paul, Phoebe, and the Spanish Mission',
in J. Neusner (ed.), *The Social World of Early Christianity:*
Festschrift for Howard Clark Kee (Philadelphia: Fortress),
pp. 142–161.

Jipp, Joshua W. (2009), 'Ancient, Modern, and Future
Interpretations of Romans 1:3–4: Reception History and
Biblical Interpretation', *JTI* 3, pp. 241–259.

—— (2015), *Christ Is King: Paul's Royal Christology* (Minneapolis:
Fortress).

Jocz, Jakob (1966), *Christians and Jews: Encounter and Mission*
(London: SPCK).

Johansen, Bjorn O. (2016), 'The "I" of Romans 7 and Confessions
in the Dead Sea Scrolls', *BN* 170, pp. 101–118.

Johnson, E. Elizabeth (2012), 'God's Covenant Faithfulness to
Israel', in J. L. Sumney (ed.), *Reading Paul's Letter to the Romans*
(Atlanta: Society of Biblical Literature), pp. 157–167.

Johnson, S. Lewis, Jr (1972), '"God Gave Them Up": A Study in
Divine Retribution (Romans 1:24, 26, 28)', *BSac* 129,
pp. 124–133.

Kadushin, Max (1938), *Organic Thinking: A Study in Rabbinic Thought*
(New York: Bloch).

Karris, Robert J. (1991), 'Romans 14:1 – 15:13 and the Occasion
of Romans', in K. P. Donfried (ed.), *The Romans Debate:
Revised and Expanded Edition* (Peabody: Hendrickson),
pp. 65–84.

Käsemann, Ernst (1965), *Essays on New Testament Themes*, SBT 41
(London: SCM).

—— (1971), *Perspectives on Paul* (Philadelphia: Fortress).

Kaye, Bruce Norman (1979), *The Thought Structure of Romans with
Special Reference to Chapter 6* (Austin: Schola Press).

Kaylor, R. David (1988), *Paul's Covenant Community: Jew and Gentile
in Romans* (Atlanta: John Knox).

Keck, Leander E. (1979), *Paul and His Letters*, Proclamation
Commentaries (Philadelphia: Fortress).

—— (2015), *Why Christ Matters: Towards a New Testament Christology*
(Waco: Baylor University Press).

Keener, Craig S. (2014), *Acts: An Exegetical Commentary, Volume 3:
15:1 – 23:35* (Grand Rapids: Baker Academic).

—— (2016), *The Mind of the Spirit: Paul's Approach to Transformed
Thinking* (Grand Rapids: Baker).

Kertelge, Karl (1991), 'The Sin of Adam in the Light of Christ's
Redemptive Act according to Romans 5:12–21', *Communio* 18,
pp. 502–513.

Kettunen, Markku (1979), *Abfassungszweck des Römerbriefes*, AASF:
Dissertationes humanarum litterarum 18 (Helsinki:
Suomalainen Tiedeakatemia).

Kim, Seyoon (1997), 'The "Mystery" of Rom 11.25–6 Once More',
NTS 43, pp. 412–429.

Kirk, J. R. Daniel (2007), 'Reconsidering *Dikaiōma* in Romans
5:16', *JBL* 126, pp. 787–792.

Kister, Menachem (2007), 'Romans 5:12–21 against the
Background of Torah-Theology and Hebrew Usage', *HTR* 100,
pp. 391–424.

Knox, John (1961), *Life in Christ Jesus: Reflections on Romans 5 – 8*
(New York: Seabury).

—— (1962), 'Galatians', in *The Interpreter's Dictionary of the Bible*
(Nashville/New York: Abingdon), pp. 338–343.

Krauter, Stefan (2009), *Studien zu Röm 13,1–7: Paulus und der politische Diskurs der neronischen Zeit*, WUNT 243 (Tübingen: Mohr Siebeck).

Kürzinger, Josef (1958), 'Συμμόρφους τῆς εἰκόνος τοῦ υἱοῦ αὐτοῦ (Rom. 8, 29)', *BZ* 2, pp. 294–299.

Lake, Kirsopp (tr.) (1920), 'The Martyrdom of Polycarp', in *The Apostolic Fathers II*, LCL (Cambridge: Harvard University Press), pp. 309–343.

Lambrecht, Jan (2000), 'The Implied Exhortation in Romans 8,5–8', *Gregorianum* 81, pp. 441–451.

Lambrecht, Jan and Richard W. Thompson (1989), *Justification by Faith: The Implications of Romans 3:27–31* (Wilmington: Michael Glazier).

Lampe, Peter (2003), *From Paul to Valentinus: Christians at Rome in the First Two Centuries* (Minneapolis: Fortress).

Lichtenberger, Hermann (2004), *Das Ich Adams und das Ich der Menschheit: Studien zum Menschenbild in Römer 7*, WUNT 163 (Tübingen: Mohr Siebeck).

Lin, Yii-Jan (2020), 'Junia: An Apostle before Paul', *JBL* 139, pp. 191–209.

Longenecker, Bruce W. (2010), *Remember the Poor: Paul, Poverty, and the Greco-Roman World* (Grand Rapids: Eerdmans).

Longenecker, Bruce W. and Todd D. Still (2014), *Thinking through Paul: A Survey of His Life, Letters, and Theology* (Grand Rapids: Zondervan).

Lowe, Chuck (1999), '"There Is No Condemnation" (Romans 8:1): But Why Not?', *JETS* 42, pp. 231–250.

Luther, Martin (1960a), 'Preface to the Complete Edition of Luther's Latin Writings: Wittenberg, 1545', in L. W. Spitz (ed.) and H. T. Lehman (gen. ed.), *Luther's Works*, Vol. 34: *Career of the Reformer IV* (Philadelphia: Muhlenberg), pp. 327–338.

—— (1960b), 'Prefaces to the New Testament 1546 (1522)', in E. T. Bachmann (ed.) and H. T. Lehman (gen. ed.), *Luther's Works*, Vol. 35: *Word and Sacrament I* (Philadelphia: Muhlenberg), pp. 357–411.

—— (1961), *Luther: Lectures on Romans, Library of Christian Classics*, Vol. 15, ed. W. Pauck (Philadelphia: Westminster).

Luz, Ulrich (1969), 'Zum Aufbau von Rom. 1 – 8', *TZ* 25, pp. 161–181.

Lyonnet, Stanislas (1965), 'Le Nouveau Testament à la lumière de l'Ancien: à propos de Rom 8, 2–4', *NRTh* 87, pp. 561–587.

McFadden, Kevin W. (2013), *Judgment according to Works in Romans: The Meaning and Function of Divine Judgment in Paul's Most Important Letter* (Minneapolis: Fortress).

Manson, T. W. (1945), 'ΙΛΑΣΤΗΡΙΟΝ', *JTS* 46, pp. 1–10.

Marcus, Joel (1988), '"Let God Arise and End the Reign of Sin!" A Contribution to the Study of Pauline Parenesis', *Bib* 69, pp. 386–395.

Marshall, Christopher D. (1989), *Faith as a Theme in Mark's Narrative*, SNTSMS 64 (Cambridge: Cambridge University Press).

Martin, James P. (1971), 'Kerygma of Romans', *Interpretation* 25, pp. 303–328.

Martin, Ralph P. (1999), 'Reconciliation: Romans 5:1–11', in S. K. Soderlund and N. T. Wright (eds.), *Romans and the People of God: Essays in Honor of Gordon D. Fee on the Occasion of His 65th Birthday* (Grand Rapids: Eerdmans), pp. 36–48.

Martínez, Florentino García (1994), *The Dead Sea Scrolls Translated: The Qumran Texts in English*, tr. W. G. E. Watson (Leiden/New York/Cologne: Brill).

Martyn, J. Louis (1997a), *Galatians*, AB (New York: Doubleday).
—— (1997b), *Theological Issues in the Letters of Paul* (Edinburgh: T&T Clark).

Mason, Hugh J. (1974), *Greek Terms for Roman Institutions: A Lexicon and Analysis*, American Studies in Papyrology 13 (Toronto: Hakkert).

Maston, Jason (2010), *Divine and Human Agency in Second Temple Judaism and Paul: A Comparative Study* (Tübingen: Mohr Siebeck).

Meeks, Wayne A. (1987), 'Judgment and the Brother: Romans 14:1 – 15:13', in G. F. Hawthorne and O. Betz (eds.), *Tradition and Interpretation in the New Testament: Essays in Honor of E. Earle Ellis for His 60th Birthday* (Grand Rapids: Eerdmans), pp. 290–300.

Melanchthon, Philip (1944), *The Loci Communes of Philip Melanchthon*, tr. C. L. Hill (Boston: Meador).

Metzger, Bruce Manning (1965), *The New Testament: Its Background, Growth, and Content* (Nashville: Abingdon).

Meyer, Paul W. (1980), 'Romans 10:4 and the End of the Law', in J. L. Crenshaw and S. Sandmel (eds.), *The Divine Helmsman: Studies on God's Control of Human Events* (New York: Ktav, 1980), pp. 59–78.

Minear, Paul S. (1971), *The Obedience of Faith: The Purposes of Paul in the Epistle to the Romans*, SBT (London: SCM).

Mininger, Marcus A. (2017), *Uncovering the Theme of Revelation in Romans 1:16 – 3:26*, WUNT 2/445 (Tübingen: Mohr Siebeck).

Mitchell, Margaret (2002), *The Heavenly Trumpet: John Chrysostom and the Art of Pauline Interpretation* (Louisville/London: Westminster John Knox).

Moltmann, Jürgen (2004), *The Coming of God: Christian Eschatology* (Minneapolis: Fortress).

Moo, Jonathan (2008), 'Romans 8.19–22 and Isaiah's Cosmic Covenant', *NTS* 54, pp. 74–89.

Morrison, Clinton D. (1960), *The Powers That Be*, SBT 29 (Naperville: Allenson).

Motyer, Steve (1989), *Israel in the Plan of God* (Leicester: Inter-Varsity Press).

Moule, C. F. D. (1963), *The Meaning of Hope: A Biblical Exposition with Concordance* (Philadelphia: Fortress).

—— (1974), '"Justification" in Its Relation to the Condition κατά πνεῦμα (Rom. 8.1–11)', in L. De Lorenzi (ed.), *Battesimo e Giustizia in Rom 6 e 8* (Roma: Abbazia S. Paolo fuori le mura), pp. 176–201.

Mukuka, Tarcisius (2012), 'Reading/Hearing Romans 13:1–7 under an African Tree: Towards a Lectio Postcolonica Contexta Africana', *Neot* 46, pp. 105–138.

Munck, Johannes (1967), *Christ and Israel: An Interpretation of Romans 9 – 11* (Philadelphia: Fortress).

Murphy-O'Connor, Jerome (1996), *Paul: A Critical Life* (Oxford: Oxford University Press).

Nanos, Mark D. (1996), *The Mystery of Romans: The Jewish Context of Paul's Letter* (Minneapolis: Fortress, 1996).

Naselli, Andrew David (2012), *From Typology to Doxology: Paul's Use of Isaiah and Job in Romans 11:34–35* (Eugene: Pickwick).

Nolland, John (2000), 'Romans 1:26–27 and the Homosexuality Debate', *HBT* 22, pp. 32–57.

Ogereau, Julien M. (2012), 'The Jerusalem Collection as Κοινωνία: Paul's Global Politics of Socio-Economic Equality and Solidarity', *NTS* 58, pp. 360–378.

Olin, John C. (ed.) (1966), *A Reformation Debate: Sadoleto's Letter to the Genevans and Calvin's Reply* (Grand Rapids: Baker).

Olson, Robert C. (2016), *The Gospel as the Revelation of God's Righteousness: Paul's Use of Isaiah in Romans 1:1 – 3:26*, WUNT 2/428 (Tübingen: Mohr Siebeck).

Oropeza, B. J. (2016), *Exploring Second Corinthians: Death and Life, Hardship and Rivalry* (Atlanta: SBL).

Ovid (1984), *Metamorphoses, Books 1–8*, tr. F. J. Miller and G. O. Goold, LCL (Cambridge: Harvard University Press).

Oyserman, Daphna, Kristen Elmore and George Smith (2012), 'Self, Self-Concept, and Identity', in M. R. Leary and J. Price Tangney (eds.), *Handbook of Self and Identity*, rev. edn (New York/London: Guilford Press), pp. 69–104.

Pascal, Blaise (2003), *Pensées*, tr. W. F. Trotter (Mineola: Dover; orig. New York: Dutton, 1958).

Paul, Shalom M. (2012), *Isaiah 40 – 66: Translation and Commentary*, ECC (Grand Rapids: Eerdmans).

Pedersen, Johannes (1926), *Israel: Its Life and Culture, I–II* (London: Oxford University Press).

Peek, Werner (ed.) (1957), *Griechische Vers-Inschriften, Band 1: Grab-Epigramme* (Berlin: Akadamie-Verlag).

Peppard, Michael (2011), *The Son of God in the Roman World: Divine Sonship in Its Social and Political Context* (New York: Oxford University Press).

Peterman, G. W. (1994), 'Make a Contribution or Establish Fellowship?', *NTS* 40, pp. 457–463.

Peterson, David G. (1995), *Possessed by God: A New Testament Theology of Sanctification and Holiness*, NSBT (Leicester: Apollos).

Pinter, Dean (2015), 'Josephus and Romans 13:1–14: Providence and Imperial Power', in B. C. Blackwell, J. K. Goodrich and J. Maston (eds.), *Reading Romans in Context: Paul and Second Temple Judaism* (Grand Rapids: Zondervan), pp. 143–150.

Piper, John (1994), '"Grace to You" and "Grace with You"',
    Desiring God, 28 August, <https://www.desiringgod.org/
    messages/grace-to-you-and-grace-with-you>.

Plautus (2011), *The Merchant, The Braggart Soldier, The Ghost, The
    Persian*, tr. W. de Mello, LCL (Cambridge: Harvard University
    Press).

Poirier, John C. (1996), 'Romans 5:13–14 and the Universality of
    Law', *NovT* 38, pp. 344–358.

Popkes, Wiard (1982), 'Zum Aufbau und Charakter von Römer
    1.18–32', *NTS* 28, pp. 490–501.

Powers, Daniel G. (2001), *Salvation through Participation: An
    Examination of the Notion of the Believers' Corporate Unity with
    Christ in Early Christian Soteriology*, CBET 29 (Leuven: Peeters).

Poythress, Vern S. (1975–76), 'Is Romans 1:3–4 a Pauline
    Confession after All?', *ExpTim* 87, pp. 180–183.

Price, James L. (1980), 'Romans 6:1–14', *Int* 34, pp. 65–69.

Prior, Michael (1989), *Paul the Letter-Writer and the Second Letter to
    Timothy*, JSNTSup 23 (Sheffield: JSOT Press).

Ptolemy (1980), *Tetrabiblos*, tr. F. E. Robbins, LCL (Cambridge:
    Harvard University Press).

Quarles, Charles L. (2003), 'From Faith to Faith: A Fresh
    Examination of the Prepositional in Romans 1.17', *NovT* 45,
    pp. 2–21.

Rabens, Volker (2013), *The Holy Spirit and Ethics in Paul:
    Transforming and Empowering for Religious-Ethical Life*, rev. edn
    (Minneapolis: Fortress).

Räisänen, Heikki (1988), 'Paul, God, and Israel: Romans 9 – 11 in
    Recent Research', in J. Neusner (ed.), *The Social World of
    Formative Christianity and Judaism: Essays in Tribute to Howard
    Clark Kee* (Philadelphia: Fortress), pp. 178–206.

Rapinchuk, Mark (1999), 'Universal Sin and Salvation in Romans
    5:12–21', *JETS* 42, pp. 427–441.

Reichert, Angelika (2001), *Der Römerbrief als Gratwanderung: Eine
    Untersuchung zur Abfassungsproblematik*, FRLANT 194
    (Göttingen: Vandenhoeck & Ruprecht).

Richards, E. Randolph (2019), 'When Is a Letter Not a Letter?
    Paul, Cicero, and Seneca as Letter Writers', in J. R. Dodson
    and D. E. Briones (eds.), *Paul and the Giants of Philosophy: Reading*

the Apostle in Greco-Roman Context (Downers Grove: IVP Academic), pp. 86–94.

Rock, Ian E. (2012), *Paul's Letter to the Romans and Roman Imperialism: An Ideological Analysis of the Exordium (Romans 1:1–17)* (Eugene: Pickwick).

Romanello, Stefano (2003), 'Rom 7,7–25 and the Impotence of the Law: A Fresh Look at a Much-Debated Topic Using Literary-Rhetorical Analysis', *Bib* 84, pp. 510–530.

Sanders, E. P. (1983), *Paul, the Law, and the Jewish People* (Philadelphia: Fortress).

—— (2016), *Paul: The Apostle's Life, Letters, and Thought* (Minneapolis: Fortress).

Schellenberg, Ryan S. (2013), *Rethinking Paul's Rhetorical Education: Comparative Rhetoric and 2 Corinthians 10 – 13*, ECL 10 (Atlanta: Society of Biblical Literature).

Schnabel, Eckhard J. (2004), *Paul and the Early Church*, Early Christian Mission Vol. 2 (Downers Grove: InterVarsity Press).

—— (2008), *Paul the Missionary: Realities, Strategies and Methods* (Downers Grove: IVP Academic).

—— (2018), *Jesus, Paul, and the Early Church: Missionary Realities in Historical Contexts; Collected Essays*, WUNT 406 (Tübingen: Mohr Siebeck).

Schnelle, Udo (2005), *Apostle Paul: His Life and Theology* (Grand Rapids: Baker).

Schreiner, Thomas R. (1993), 'Did Paul Believe in Justification by Works? Another Look at Romans 2', *BBR* 3, pp. 131–158.

—— (2006), 'Corporate and Individual Election in Romans 9: A Response to Brian Abasciano', *JETS* 49, pp. 373–386.

Schweizer, Eduard (1981), *The Holy Spirit* (Philadelphia: Fortress).

Scott, James M. (1992), *Adoption as Sons of God: An Exegetical Investigation into the Background of ΥΙΟΘΕΣΙΑ in the Pauline Corpus*, WUNT 2/48 (Tübingen: Mohr Siebeck).

Segal, Alan F. (1990), *Paul the Convert: The Apostolate and Apostasy of Saul the Pharisee* (New Haven: Yale University Press).

Seifrid, Mark A. (1992a), *Justification by Faith: The Origin and Development of a Central Pauline Theme*, NovTSup 68 (Leiden: Brill).

—— (1992b), 'The Subject of Rom 7:14–25', *NovT* 34, pp. 313–333.

—— (2007), 'Romans', in G. K. Beale and D. A. Carson (eds.), *Commentary on the New Testament Use of the Old Testament* (Grand Rapids: Baker), pp. 607–694.

—— (2010), 'The New Perspective from Paul', *SBJT* 14, pp. 20–35.

Seneca the Younger (1920–34), *Ad Lucilium, Epistulae morales*, tr. Richard M. Gummere, 3 vols., LCL (Cambridge: Harvard University Press).

Shaw, David A. (2013), 'Apocalyptic and Covenant: Perspectives on Paul or Antinomies at War?', *JSNT* 36, pp. 155–171.

Siikavirta, Samuli (2015), *Baptism and Cognition in Romans 6 – 8: Paul's Ethics beyond 'Indicative' and 'Imperative'*, WUNT 2/407 (Tübingen: Mohr Siebeck).

Smiles, Vincent M. (2002), 'The Concept of "Zeal" in Second-Temple Judaism and Paul's Critique of It in Romans 10:2', *CBQ* 64, pp. 282–299.

Snodgrass, Klyne R. (1986), 'Justification by Grace – to the Doers: An Analysis of the Place of Romans 2 in the Theology of Paul', *NTS* 32, pp. 72–93.

—— (1988), 'Spheres of Influence: A Possible Solution to the Problem of Paul and the Law', *JSNT* 32, pp. 93–113.

Stagg, Frank (1962), *New Testament Theology* (Nashville: Broadman).

—— (1976), 'The Plight of Jew and Gentile in Sin: Romans 1:18 – 3:20', *RevExp* 73, pp. 401–413.

—— (1980), *Galatians, Romans*, Knox Preaching Guides (Atlanta: John Knox).

Starling, David (2017), '"For Your Sake We Are Being Killed All Day Long": Romans 8:36 and the Hermeneutics of Unexplained Suffering', *Themelios* 42, pp. 112–121.

Stowers, Stanley Kent (1981), *The Diatribe and Paul's Letter to the Romans*, SBLDS 57 (Chico: Scholars Press).

—— (1984), 'Paul's Dialogue with a Fellow Jew in Romans 3:1–9', *CBQ* 46, pp. 707–722.

—— (1990), 'Paul on the Use and Abuse of Reason', in D. L. Balch et al., *Greeks, Romans, and Christians* (Philadelphia: Fortress), pp. 253–286.

Stuhlmacher, Peter (1986), 'Recent Exegesis on Romans 3:24–26', in P. Stuhlmacher, *Reconciliation, Law, and Righteousness: Essays in Biblical Theology* (Philadelphia: Fortress), pp. 94–109.

—— (1991), 'The Purpose of Romans', in K. P. Donfried (ed.), *The Romans Debate: Revised and Expanded Edition* (Peabody: Hendrickson), pp. 231–242.

—— (2001), *A Challenge to the New Perspective: Revisiting Paul's Doctrine of Justification with an Essay by Donald A. Hagner* (Downers Grove: InterVarsity Press).

Suggs, M. Jack (1967), '"The Word Is Near You": Romans 10:6–10 within the Purpose of the Letter', in W. R. Farmer, C. F. D. Moule and R. R. Niebuhr (eds.), *Christian History and Interpretation: Studies Presented to John Knox* (Cambridge: Cambridge University Press), pp. 289–312.

Tacitus, Cornelius (1914), *Agricola, Germania, Dialogus*, tr. M. Hutton and W. Peterson, revised by R. M. Ogilvie, E. H. Warmington and M. Winterbottom, LCL (Cambridge: Harvard University Press).

Taylor, John W. (2004), 'From Faith to Faith: Romans 1.17 in the Light of Greek Idiom', *NTS* 50, pp. 37–48.

Taylor, N. H. (2008), 'Dying with Christ in Baptism: Issues in the Translation and Interpretation of Romans 6.3–14', *BT* 59, pp. 38–49.

Thackeray, H. St J. et al. (tr.) (1926–65), *Josephus*, 10 vols., LCL (Cambridge: Harvard University Press).

Thiselton, Anthony C. (2012), *The Holy Spirit: In Biblical Teaching, through the Centuries and Today* (Grand Rapids: Eerdmans).

Thorsteinsson, Runar M. (2015), *Paul's Interlocutor in Romans 2: Function and Identity in the Context of Ancient Epistolography* (Eugene: Wipf and Stock).

Timmins, Will N. (2017), *Romans 7 and Christian Identity: A Study of the 'I' in Its Literary Context*, SNTSMS 170 (Cambridge: Cambridge University Press).

Tomlinson, Fred Alan (1997), 'Sacral Manumission Formulae and Romans 6' (PhD thesis, Southern Baptist Theological Seminary).

Tomson, Peter J. (2003), 'What Did Paul Mean by "Those Who Know the Law"? (Rom 7.1)', *NTS* 49, pp. 573–581.

Turner, Max (1994), 'The Spirit of Christ and "Divine" Christology', in J. B. Green and M. Turner (eds.), *Jesus of Nazareth: Lord and Christ* (Grand Rapids: Eerdmans), pp. 413–436.

Van der Horst, Peter W. (2000), '"Only Then Will All Israel Be Saved": A Short Note on the Meaning of καὶ οὕτως in Romans 11:26', *JBL* 119, pp. 521–539.

Van de Sandt, H. W. M. (1976), 'Research into Rom. 8,4a: The Legal Claim of the Law', *Bijdragen: Tijdschrift voor filosofie en theologie* 37, pp. 252–269.

Verbrugge, Verlyn D. (2011), 'The Grammatical Internal Evidence for *EXOMEN* in Romans 5:1', *JETS* 54, pp. 559–572.

Viard, Jean-Sébastian (2005), 'Loi, chair et libération: une solution structurelle au problème de Romains 7,1–6', *Theoforum* 36, pp. 155–173.

Wagner, J. Ross (2002), *Heralds of the Good News: Isaiah and Paul 'In Concert' in the Letter to the Romans*, NovTSup 101 (Leiden: Brill).

—— (2010), '"Not from the Jews Only, but Also from the Gentiles": Mercy to the Nations in Romans 9 – 11', in F. Wilk and J. R. Wagner (eds.), *Between Gospel and Election: Explorations in the Interpretation of Romans 9 – 11*, WUNT 257 (Tübingen: Mohr Siebeck), pp. 417–431.

Watson, Francis (2018), 'Questiones Disputae: Roman Faith and Christian Faith', *NTS* 64, pp. 243–247.

Watts, Rikki E. (1999), '"For I Am Not Ashamed of the Gospel": Romans 1:16–17 and Habakkuk 2:4', in S. K. Soderlund and N. T. Wright (eds.), *Romans and the People of God: Essays in Honor of Gordon D. Fee on the Occasion of His 65th Birthday* (Grand Rapids: Eerdmans), pp. 3–25.

Wedderburn, A. J. M. (1988), *The Reasons for Romans: Studies of the New Testament and Its World* (Edinburgh: T&T Clark).

Weima, Jeffrey A. D. (1994), *Neglected Endings: The Significance of the Pauline Letter Closings*, JSNTSup 101 (Sheffield: Sheffield Academic Press, 1994).

White, Joel R. (2014), '"Peace and Security" (1 Thess 5.3): Roman Ideology and Greek Aspiration', *NTS* 60, pp. 499–510.

Whiteley, D. E. H. (1974), *The Theology of St. Paul*, rev. edn (Oxford: Basil Blackwell).

Whittle, Sarah (2015), *Covenant Renewal and the Consecration of the Gentiles in Romans*, SNTSMS 161 (Cambridge: Cambridge University Press).

Wiefel, Wolfgang (1991), 'The Jewish Community in Ancient Rome and the Origins of Roman Christianity', in K. P. Donfried (ed.), *The Romans Debate: Revised and Expanded Edition* (Peabody: Hendrickson), pp. 85–101.

Williams, Sam K. (1980), 'The "Righteousness of God" in Romans', *JBL* 99, pp. 241–290.

Windsor, Lionel J. (2014), *Paul and the Vocation of Israel*, BZNW 205 (Berlin: De Gruyter).

Wink, Walter (1992), *Engaging the Powers: Discernment and Resistance in a World of Domination* (Minneapolis: Fortress).

Wischmeyer, Oda (2006), 'Römer 2.1–24 als Teil der Gerichtsrede des Paulus gegen die Menschheit', *NTS* 52, pp. 356–376.

Wisse, Frederik (1972), 'The Righteous Man and the Good Man in Romans V.7', *NTS* 19, pp. 91–93.

Wolter, Michael (1978), *Rechtfertigung und zukünftiges Heil: Untersuchungen zu Römer 5,1–11*, BZNW 43 (Berlin/New York: de Gruyter).

—— (2015), *Paul: An Outline of His Theology* (Waco: Baylor University Press).

—— (2017), '"It Is Not as Though the Word of God Has Failed": God's Faithfulness and God's Free Sovereignty in Romans 9:6–29', in T. D. Still (ed.), *God and Israel: Providence and Purpose in Romans 9 – 11* (Waco: Baylor University Press), pp. 27–47.

Worthington, Jonathan (2016), '*Creatio ex Nihilo* and Romans 4.17 in Context', *NTS* 62, pp. 49–59.

Wright, N. T. (1991), *The Climax of the Covenant* (Minneapolis: Fortress).

—— (2009), *Justification: God's Plan and Paul's Vision* (Downers Grove: IVP Academic).

—— (2012), 'Romans 2:17 – 3:9: A Hidden Clue to the Meaning of Romans?', *JSPL* 2, pp. 1–25.

—— (2013), *Paul and the Faithfulness of God, Book II: Parts III and IV* (Minneapolis: Fortress).

Wu, Siu Fung (2015), *Suffering in Romans* (Eugene: Pickwick).

Wuellner, William (1991), 'Paul's Rhetoric of Argumentation in Romans: An Alternative to the Donfried–Karris Debate over Romans', in K. P. Donfried (ed.), *The Romans Debate: Revised and Expanded Edition* (Peabody: Hendrickson), pp. 128–146.

Yates, John W. (2008), *The Spirit and Creation in Paul*, WUNT 2/251 (Tübingen: Mohr Siebeck).

Yinger, Kent L. (1999), *Paul, Judaism, and Judgment according to Deeds*, SNTSMS 105 (Cambridge: Cambridge University Press).

Zeller, Dieter (1973), *Juden und Heiden in der Mission des Paulus: Studien zum Römerbrief*, Forschung zur Bibel 1 (Stuttgart: Katholisches Bibelwerk).

Ziesler, John A. (1972), *The Meaning of Righteousness in Paul*, SNTSMS 20 (Cambridge: Cambridge University Press).

INTRODUCTION

It is unnecessary to remind readers of the importance of Romans, but Luther's oft-quoted tribute in his preface to Romans is still relevant:

> This epistle is really the chief part of the New Testament, and is truly the purest gospel. It is worthy not only that every Christian should know it word for word, by heart, but also that he should occupy himself with it every day, as the daily bread of the soul. We can never read it or ponder over it too much; for the more we deal with it, the more precious it becomes and the better it tastes.[1]

Origen, however, in his preface to his commentary on Romans, notes that Romans is harder to understand than all of Paul's other letters and stirs up questions that the heretics distort (*Comm. Rom.*). Nevertheless, Romans has had an enormous impact on the lives of

---

1. Luther, 'Prefaces to the New Testament', p. 365.

many (Augustine, Luther, Wesley and Barth) who in turn influenced Christian history. John Chrysostom (AD 350–407), a prolific commentator on Paul's letters, exuberantly praises him in seven homilies (*De laudibus sancti Pauli apostoli*) that express his profound love for Paul.[2] Paul receives less than glowing appraisals among some modern laity and scholars. Talbert summarizes these critiques and rightly concludes, 'A fresh reading of this seminal document holds the promise of life' (Talbert, p. 5). A 'fresh reading' is what Luther did. He initially 'hated Paul' with all his heart because when he read in 1:17 that the righteousness of God is revealed in the gospel he thought that 'this righteousness was an avenging anger, namely, the wrath of God' that would punish him for his sins. But later he said,

> At last, by the mercy of God, meditating day and night, I gave heed to the context of the words, namely, 'In it the righteousness of God is revealed, as it is written, "He who through faith is righteous shall live."' There I began to understand that the righteousness of God is that by which the righteous lives by a gift of God, namely by faith . . . Here I felt that I was altogether born again and had entered paradise itself through open gates. There a totally other face of the entire Scripture showed itself to me.[3]

A fresh reading need not entail discarding older interpretations as necessarily inferior because they come from an earlier era. The gadflies of Athens were guilty of the logical fallacy of the appeal to novelty (Acts 17:21), which assumes something is better simply because it is innovative and seemingly more relevant.

1. The audience of the letter

When Paul wrote this letter, the city of Rome was the capital of the Mediterranean world, and Nero had become emperor at the age of sixteen in AD 54. With Nero being guided by advisors such as

---

2. Cf. Mitchell, *Heavenly Trumpet*, pp. 440–487.
3. Luther, 'Latin Writings', p. 337.

Seneca, his tutor, most were hopeful that Nero's rule would bring peace. Rome was certainly the foremost place in the empire to receive Paul's reflection on his gospel, but the destination of this letter is tied to his apostolic calling that drives his planned trips to Jerusalem, Rome and then Spain. The letter assumes that a Christian community is firmly established in Rome since Paul has for many years wanted to come to them and their faith is renowned throughout the world (1:8). He is mindful that he did not found this community. They have been obedient 'to the form of teaching to which you were entrusted' (6:17) that came not from Paul but from others. Therefore, he cannot say that they have obeyed him, as he says the Philippians have (Phil. 2:12). He also cannot call them his 'beloved children' (1 Cor. 4:14; 2 Cor. 12:14; Gal. 4:19; 1 Thess. 2:7, 11) or expect them to imitate him, as he expects the churches he evangelized to do (1 Cor. 4:16–17; 11:1; Phil. 3:17; 4:9; 1 Thess. 1:6; 2 Thess. 3:6–9). His frequent resort to the diatribe style in this letter in which he answers an imaginary interlocutor to make his points (2:1–5, 17–24; 9:19–21; 11:17–24; 14:4, 10) and to respond to objections and false conclusions (3:1–9; 3:31 – 4:2a; 6:1–3, 15–16; 7:7, 13–14; 9:14–15, 19–20) 'is particularly appropriate in a letter to a church which he does not know, for elsewhere he can argue directly with his readers'.[4]

It is unknown when or by whom the faith communities in the city of Rome were founded, but the church was not established by Peter as the later legend has it. Neither Acts nor Paul makes any mention of Peter (or any other apostle) having any connection to Rome. Luke does assert that 'visitors from Rome' were present in Jerusalem during Pentecost (Acts 2:10). It is likely that some of them were converted by the disciples' preaching, particularly that of Peter (Acts 2:14–40), and shared the gospel when they returned to Rome. Anonymous Christian merchants and business people such as Aquila and Prisca also would have brought the gospel. Perhaps Sergius Paulus, the proconsul of Cyprus who heard the word of God from Paul and Barnabas and believed (Acts 13:6–12), was another example of those who spread

---

4. Wedderburn, *Reasons*, p. 16.

the gospel upon their return to the city. The community of faith
that had Jewish origins swelled with Gentile converts. Tacitus
describes Nero unleashing a ferocious persecution of Christians
to shift blame onto them for the massive fire that consumed
Rome in AD 64. He says that a vast multitude was convicted (*Ann.*
15.44). This note, even if an exaggeration, suggests that the
believers had experienced a marked growth in numbers, which
had caught the unwanted attention of the authorities.

Paul does not address them as 'the church' in Rome (cf. 1 Cor.
1:2; 2 Cor. 1:1; 1 Thess. 1:1) but as 'all God's beloved in Rome,
who are called to be saints' (1:7). One can infer that the Roman
Christians did not meet together as one gathering but in a number
of different house churches distributed throughout the various
quarters of the city. Paul greets five separate households (16:5, 10,
11, 14, 15) where believers gathered, and there may have been
more. Scholars disagree as to whether the primary audience was
composed of Jewish or Gentile Christians. The disagreements in
interpreting the data suggest that Paul viewed his audience as
mixed. He assumes that they know the Old Testament. He
mentions Adam, Abraham, Sarah, Isaac, Rebecca, Esau, Jacob,
Pharaoh, Moses, Elijah, David and Zion without clarifications.
He includes frequent citations of or allusions to the Hebrew
Scriptures in their Greek translation (LXX). He addresses Jews by
referring to Abraham as 'our ancestor according to the flesh' (4:1)
and when he says 'I am speaking to those who know the law' in
7:1. Specific references to the Gentiles/nations (*ethnē*) appear
twenty-nine times in the letter, and he addresses them directly in
11:13: 'Now I am speaking to you Gentiles.' This phrase that
singles out Gentiles to take notice implies that Paul does not
think that he has been addressing *only* Gentiles previously. Paul
maintains that 'all have sinned' (3:23), that Christ's 'act of righteousness leads to justification and life for all' (5:18), that God 'did
not withhold his own Son, but gave him up for all of us' (8:32) so
that God might 'be merciful to all' (11:32) and 'all the peoples'
might 'praise him' (15:11). It is reasonable to conclude that Romans
is not aimed at a particular ethnic group in a community of faith
but is concerned with the church universal composed of Jews and
Gentiles.

2. Date and provenance

Paul states that he has completed his missionary work among the eastern part of the Roman Empire from Jerusalem to Illyricum (15:19, 23) and writes this letter prior to his journey to Jerusalem with the collection for the poor among the saints there (15:25–26). The scenario in Acts fits this setting. After Paul's relatively long ministry in Ephesus, probably from AD 52 to 54, Acts 20:1–3 records Paul journeying through the regions of Macedonia and coming to Greece, where he stayed three months before embarking for Syria, which may include a reference to Jerusalem since it was a Roman territory attached to the province of Syria. To avoid a Jewish plot against him, he instead went back through Macedonia. Acts identifies his travel companions as Sopater from Beroea, Aristarchus and Secundus from Thessalonica, Gaius from Derbe, and Timothy, Tychicus and Trophimus from Asia (Acts 20:4). They are presumably representatives from the churches who contributed to the collection for Jerusalem and who will accompany him there. Paul probably wrote this letter in Corinth, the capital of Achaia. He commends Phoebe, a Christian deacon from the church in Cenchreae, the eastern seaport of Corinth, who almost certainly delivers the letter (16:1–2). He also sends greetings from Gaius, one of his early converts in Corinth (1 Cor. 1:14), who Paul says is host to him and to the whole church (16:23). Erastus, who sends greetings, is probably the same person identified in a Latin inscription in Corinth from the mid first century: *ERASTVS. PRO. AED. S. P. STRAVIT* ('Erastus, in return for his aedileship, laid [the pavement] at his own expense'; cf. the comments on 16:23).

Dates are difficult to pin down precisely, and the time frame for when Romans was written is based on the dating of Paul's encounter with Gallio, the brother of Seneca and the proconsul of Achaia (Acts 18:12–17). An inscription found at Delphi (*SIG* II, p. 801) shows that Gallio was proconsul of Achaia in AD 52. Paul probably was brought before Gallio early in the latter's governorship since the Jews would have been attempting to win a new governor to their side, which would have been from mid 51 to mid 52. The proposals for when Paul wrote Romans vary. Some contend that Paul wrote during the winter of AD 56/57 (Jewett, Moo, Schnabel);

others contend that he composed the letter in AD 55/56 (Cranfield, Dunn).

3. The integrity of the letter

The arguments so far assume the integrity of the letter. The differing placements in the manuscript tradition of the doxology in 16:25–27 that marks the end of the letter raise questions. The majority of the earliest and most reliable copies of Romans place it at the end of the letter.[5] Some manuscripts place the doxology at the end of chapter 14. Papyrus 46, a valuable, slightly mutilated collection of Pauline epistles that dates from between AD 175 and 225, places the doxology between 15:33 and 16:1. No extant Greek manuscript of Romans omits 15:1 – 16:23, but scholars have offered various theories to explain the differing locations of the doxology in 16:25–27.

Origen claimed that Marcion expunged this doxology and cut out everything after 14:23 resulting in a fourteen-chapter version of Romans.[6] One might guess that Marcion was less than pleased with Paul's assertions that the Old Testament Scriptures were 'written for our instruction' (15:4) and that 'Christ has become a servant of the circumcised on behalf of the truth of God in order that he might confirm the promises given to the patriarchs' (15:8). Later scholars theorize that Paul made two copies of the letter, one without chapter 16 that he sent to the Romans, and one that added the greetings in chapter 16 that he sent to Ephesus. Others contend that chapter 16 was a separate letter sent originally to Ephesus that for some reason was appended to Romans. Ephesus becomes the primary nominee as a possible recipient of this hypothetical letter because of the mention of Prisca and Aquila (16:3–4) who had lived there (Acts 18:19) and the identification of Epaenetus as the first convert of Asia (16:5), the name of the Roman province in which Ephesus was located.

---

5. Hurtado, 'Doxology', pp. 185–199, and Moo, p. 952 n. 341, provide a technical discussion of the textual history of the passage and argue that it concluded the letter here.

6. Bray, *Romans*, pp. 379–380.

No extant manuscript of Romans, however, contains any reference to Ephesus, and the Ephesian theories have not won the day. Prisca and Aquila may have returned to Rome, where they still had business connections and could have maintained their residence during their exile. Paul does not send personal greetings to individuals in his letters to the churches where he had lived and worked for some time. Why risk omitting someone's name and hurting feelings? The Ephesians also would not need to be informed that Prisca and Aquila risked their lives for Paul (16:4) or that Epaenetus was the first convert. Those details are more likely included for the benefit of those outside Asia.

No Romans manuscript ends with chapter 15, which clearly is intended for Rome (15:22–29), and its concluding phrase, 'The God of peace be with all of you. Amen' (15:33), is not Paul's normal way of terminating a letter (cf. 16:20; 2 Cor. 13:11; Phil. 4:9; 1 Thess. 5:23; 2 Thess. 3:16). It is implausible that chapter 16 was an independent letter to commend Phoebe that is composed mostly of greetings. An important word that modern translations often do not translate is the Greek word *de* ('and' [or 'now']) in the opening phrase of 16:1. When it is translated 'Now I commend to you Phoebe', it suggests a continuation of the letter rather than the beginning of a new one. It is also hard to explain why anyone would have wanted to remove the prescript and the normal thanksgiving section of this imagined letter that commended Phoebe to the Ephesians and attach it to Romans.

The unusually long list of greetings in 16:3–16 is best explained by the unusual circumstances of his letter to the Romans. Since Paul has never visited Rome, it is more likely that he would want to boost his standing among the Romans and their receptiveness to his gospel by associating himself with a sizeable number of people whom they know and respect. The persons Paul lauds in this list can serve as his character references. They would also be likely to endorse his planned missionary enterprise to Spain and encourage others to do so.

One might ask how Paul knows so many in a place he has never visited. Only five of the names are clearly Jewish, so it does not seem to be the case that these are persons formerly exiled from Rome by Claudius who have now returned with the reign of

Nero (see below). Christians travelled widely, which is why hospitality was high on the list of Christian virtues. We might assume that Paul encountered these persons in his and their many travels.

While it is possible that Marcion caused the manuscript confusion, the most likely explanation for the possible shortened form of Romans was a later desire to abbreviate the letter to make it more universal.[7] This wish for a more generic version of Romans relevant for any Christian community is intimated by the omission of the phrase 'in Rome' in 1:7 in some Latin versions.[8] If the phrase was deliberately deleted, it may also be connected to the abridged edition of Romans that omitted 15:1 – 16:23. The conclusion that Romans was originally sixteen chapters appropriately remains the predominant view.

4. The occasion for the letter

Romans contains the reflections of one who has hammered out his theology in proclaiming the gospel in the eastern part of the Graeco-Roman world in synagogues (Acts 9:20; 13:5, 14, 43–44; 14:1; 17:1–2, 10, 17; 18:19; 19:8), marketplaces (Acts 17:17), lecture halls (Acts 19:9–10) and house church gatherings (Acts 18:7). He says that he laid out the gospel he proclaimed among the Gentiles before the pillar apostles in Jerusalem (Gal. 2:2), not to have them check it out but to try to stop interlopers from going out from Jerusalem and insisting that circumcision was a requirement for salvation (Acts 15:1; Gal. 2:12). Paul received his understanding of the gospel he preached 'through a revelation of Jesus Christ' (Gal. 1:11–12) and would not compromise or concede any of its fundamentals 'so that the truth of the gospel might always remain with' the churches he had founded (Gal. 2:5, 14). Romans contains key elements of that gospel, and Luther went so far as to assert that Paul 'wanted in this one epistle to sum up briefly the whole

---

7. Gamble, *Textual History*, pp. 115–116.

8. G 1739[mg] 1908[mg] it[g] Origen. 'In Rome' is also omitted by G in 1:15, which is unlikely to have been accidental.

Christian and evangelical doctrine and to prepare an introduction to the entire Old Testament'.[9]

While many still consider Romans to be, as Beker describes it, 'a well-ordered theological composition' and 'in some sense a "dogmatics in outline"',[10] most now regard it to be a genuine letter that addresses particular circumstances. The particular circumstances that prompted Paul to write this letter have sparked much debate. Why is the letter so unlike his earlier correspondence with the Thessalonians, Galatians and Corinthians, having the character of a summary of his teaching? Many passages take up and develop thoughts and motifs that Paul had already used in his earlier letters (Lohse, p. 46). Why did Paul think an extended presentation of his gospel was necessary? Did he write to address problems related to the recipients' circumstances, as he does in other letters, or is Romans unique in that Paul's own circumstances prompted this letter?

Jervis sorts the main proposals as to the purpose of Romans into three categories: 'theological', 'missionary' and 'pastoral'.[11] Since we learn more about Paul's circumstances as apostle to the Gentiles and little about how things stand with the Roman house churches, the description of his plans regarding trips to Rome, Jerusalem and Spain most likely convey the purposes behind the letter. Paul normally writes in lieu of a visit *after* he has been with a church. Romans is written in preparation for a visit to a group of believers he mostly has never met, and Paul declares three times that he hopes finally to make his long-desired visit to Rome (1:10, 11, 13). It is more likely, then, that his purposes in writing primarily relate to his aspiration to create a base from which to extend his proclamation of the gospel beyond Rome. Paul does not seek to intervene in any imagined problems in the Roman faith community, except, perhaps, for 14:1 – 15:13. Instead, he offers a theological résumé that will encourage them to support his mission further west. He lays out ethical guidelines that not only would

---

9. Luther, 'Prefaces to the New Testament', p. 380.
10. Beker, *Paul*, p. 77.
11. Jervis, *Purpose*, pp. 14–28.

pre-empt problems that have arisen in his churches in the East but that also remain valid for all believers struggling to live out God's reconciliation in their communal life and in a pagan society. In my view, Dahl is right:

> It is not the problems of a local church but the universal gospel and Paul's own mission which in this letter provide the point of departure for theological discussion. This is made very clear by the way in which Paul introduces the theme of the letter [1:8–15, 16–17].[12]

a. The frame of the letter as the key for unlocking the purposes of Romans

Since Paul's practice is to express his most important concerns in the opening and closing remarks that encase a letter, his comments in 1:1–17 and 15:14–33 provide the most important clues for understanding the letter's purposes.[13] In this frame, Paul reveals more about his own situation and apostolic commission to preach the gospel among the Gentiles and to bring about their obedience of faith (1:5; 15:28) than in any other letter. 'I' predominates in both sections as he focuses on himself and his plans.

i. The letter's opening (1:1–17)

The salutation in 1:1–7 is notable for being about ten times longer than his other letter openings, and 'no other known ancient letter from the Graeco-Roman or traditionally Jewish environment contains such an extensive letter opening'.[14] Verses 1 and 7 would comprise the usual greeting of a Hellenistic letter that consisted of the sender, the recipients and a greeting (cf. Acts 23:26; 1 Thess. 1:1). Though Paul identifies Timothy as the co-sender in other letters (2 Cor. 1:1; Phil. 1:1; Col. 1:1; 1 Thess. 1:1; 2 Thess. 1:1; Phlm. 1), he is mentioned only as his co-worker who sends greetings in 16:21 and not as the co-sender of Romans. The focus falls solely on Paul, who introduces himself with three distinctions – 'slave of

---

12. Dahl, *Studies*, p. 78.
13. Kettunen, *Abfassungszweck*, p. 50.
14. Byrskog, 'Epistolography', p. 38.

Jesus Christ' (NRSV mg.), 'called to be an apostle', 'set apart for the gospel of God' (1:1) – instead of the usual one in his address to churches who know him well. He expands the prescript in 1:2–4 by utilizing what many assume to be confessional material to sum up his gospel. He emphasizes his divine calling, having received from God the grace of apostleship (implied by the passive voice) 'to bring about the obedience of faith among all the Gentiles for the sake of his name'. He notes that the Romans also fall into this orbit, 'including yourselves' (1:6), which can warrant his boldness (15:15) in writing to them. His description of the recipients in 1:7 is cordial but not intimate. They are 'all God's beloved in Rome, who are called to be saints'.

Paul's thanksgiving for the Romans also varies from that in his other letters to churches he has founded. 'Because your faith is proclaimed throughout the world' (1:8) could apply to many Christian groups. After mentioning his unceasing prayers for them, he centres on his long-cherished hope of coming to Rome that so far has been impeded (1:9–15). Paul's vagueness about having wanted to share with them 'some spiritual gift to strengthen you' and his qualification 'or rather so that we may be mutually encouraged by each other's faith, both yours and mine' (1:11–12) reflect his decision not to appear overbearing but also his lack of intimate familiarity with the recipients. Paul next reviews his indebtedness to preach the gospel to Gentiles, 'both to Greeks and to barbarians, both to the wise and to the foolish' (1:14–15), and concludes in 1:16–17 with another summary of the gospel he preaches that serves as the letter's theme statement (1:16–17). The thanksgiving section diplomatically reveals that he has not purposefully neglected them, and intimates that a primary purpose behind the letter is to pave the way for a future visit as part of his apostolic mandate to preach the gospel to the Gentiles.

ii. The letter's closing (15:14–33)

Paul takes up his desire to come to Rome again in 15:14–33 and is more specific in outlining his current plans. The parallels with 1:1–15 are noteworthy:

1. The grace of apostleship given to him (1:5; 15:15–16);
2. Obedience of faith among all the Gentiles (1:5; 15:18);
3. The universal, impartial extent of salvation (1:5, 14–15; 15:19–24);
4. His service to God described using verbs (*latreuein/ hierourgein*) and a noun (*leitourgos*) that are related to priestly service (1:9a; 15:16);
5. Offering prayers for one another (1:9b–10; 15:30);
6. The hindrances that have prevented him from coming to Rome (1:13; 15:22);
7. Reliance on God's will for him to succeed in coming to Rome (1:10; 15:32);
8. The anticipation of mutual encouragement/refreshment when he comes (1:11–12; 15:29, 32);
9. Proclaiming the gospel to the Gentiles (unbelievers; 1:13; 15:18–20);
10. Indebtedness to others: Paul, a debtor to Gentiles (1:14); Gentile believers, debtors to the Jerusalem church (15:27);
11. A reference to 'fruit' (*karpos*), reaping 'fruit' (NRSV 'harvest') among the Romans (1:13), presenting ('sealing') the 'fruit' of his ministry among the Gentiles to the church in Jerusalem (15:28);
12. Peace (1:7; 15:33).

An apparent contradiction surfaces between his statements in 1:15, 'hence my eagerness to proclaim the gospel to you also who are in Rome', and in 15:20, 'I make it my ambition to proclaim the good news, not where Christ has already been named, so that I do not build on someone else's foundation.' The latter statement speaks of his pioneer evangelism and church planting. He has no intention of planting churches where others already exist (15:18–22; cf. 2 Cor. 10:15–16). He does not mean that he will never proclaim or explain the gospel in cities in which churches planted by others already exist. He understands preaching the gospel more generally here. While Rome fits well the transnational scope of Paul's calling as apostle to the Gentiles, with its mingling of nationalities from all over the world,[15] and he is ever ready to evangelize unbelievers and to instruct believers, he has no intention of settling down in Rome and becoming their resident apostle. His statement in 1:12 perhaps should be translated 'to be mutually encouraged by our faith in [faithfulness towards] one another'. 'Faith' in this instance refers to 'trust or reliability in a business partnership'.[16] His goal is not to evangelize Rome but to form a partnership with the Roman Christ-followers that will yield a harvest of converts in climes further west. Paul, however, diplomatically does not disclose until the letter's closing that his objective is for them to send him on to preach in Spain (15:24).

b. The Romans' circumstances as the occasion for the letter

Donfried insists that the first methodological principle of any study seeking to determine the purposes of Romans 'should proceed on the initial assumption that this letter was written by Paul to deal with a concrete situation in Rome'. He bases this principle on 'the fact that every other authentic Pauline writing, *without exception*, is addressed to the specific situations of the churches or persons involved'.[17] The problem Romans presents is that it is not like every other letter, and the evidence of the specific situation of the church is 'tantalizingly scanty', to use Wedderburn's phrase.[18] The tantalizing part invites interpreters to fill in what is scanty with imaginative speculation primarily directed by mirror-reading. This approach assumes that Paul always writes in reaction to something in the recipients' context, and that what he says is a mirror reflection of an issue confronting the church. While mirror-reading can help clarify a text, it can also be misused to patch holes in theories spun from gossamer-thin evidence. An obvious hazard exists in correlating every imperative, every admonition, every warning and every positive teaching in a letter to a community's particular situation. Attempts to construe the purpose of Paul's letter from the

---

15. Haacker, *Theology*, p. 17.
16. DeSilva, *Introduction*, p. 602 n. 11; LSJ, p. 1408.
17. Donfried, 'False Presuppositions', p. 103.
18. Wedderburn, *Reasons*, p. 54.

imagined circumstances of the Romans are particularly prone to error. Nevertheless, Paul's lengthy admonition in 14:1 – 15:13 for the strong to practise tolerance towards the weak is the usual starting point for conjectures about the situation in Rome that Paul supposedly addresses. The primary problem with this approach is the circular nature of the argument.[19] Interpreters construct a hypothetical setting and then interpret the text to match that life setting.[20] Minear reflects an extreme example of this method in assuming that several congregations in Rome are 'separated from each other by sharp mutual suspicions' and claims that five different factions or theological positions existed.[21]

The speculation about the Romans' circumstances is also based on meagre historical evidence. Wiefel conjectured that the expulsion of the Jews from Rome by the Emperor Claudius because of their riots, in Suetonius's words, at 'the instigation of Chrestus' (*impulsore Chresto*) in AD 49 dramatically affected the character of Christianity in Rome.[22] He claims that a community of believers founded by Jews shifted its composition when Gentile converts

---

19. Bruce, 'Romans Debate', p. 181.

20. For example, cf. Campbell, 'Romans III', p. 264.

21. Minear, *Obedience*, pp. 8–15. The first faction, the 'weak in faith' group, condemned the second, the 'strong in faith' group, who in turn ridiculed and despised the first group. Minear identifies the third group as 'the doubters'. The fourth and fifth groups he sees as composed of 'weak in faith' and 'strong in faith', respectively, but distinguished from the first and second groups by the fact that they did not condemn or despise the others. In my view, this represents an overstrained parsing of the text.

22. Suetonius, *Claud.* 25.4. Chrestus was a customary slave name, meaning 'useful' or 'beneficial', and since Christos, meaning 'anointed', might not have made sense as a name, it would have been an understandable mistake. It also was politically convenient to attribute the disruption to a slave. It is unlikely that he was a Jewish rabble-rouser since no evidence exists that Jews bore that name or that he was the one who persuaded Claudius to expel the Jews since the grammar does not support this reading. Tertullian belittles opponents of Christians who do not even know how to pronounce the name they purport to hate,

suddenly became the majority. When the Jews returned to Rome after Claudius's death, they found themselves relegated to a disenfranchised minority, and the church became ensnared in disputes over the relevance and application of the Jewish law. Wiefel alleges that Paul writes Romans 'to assist the Gentile Christian majority, who are the primary addressees of the letter, to live together with the Jewish Christians in one congregation, thereby putting an end to their quarrels about status'.[23]

Barclay dismisses this reconstruction as a 'tissue of speculation, based on flimsy evidence and ungrounded supposition' that is 'best abandoned'. He states,

> There is no evidence, either internal or external, that the expulsion of some Jews from Rome in 49 CE, or their subsequent return, had any effect on the development of the Christian churches in the city: Paul gives no hint of changes in leadership, in the ethnic composition of the communities, or in relations with synagogues.[24]

Claudius did act against the Jews in Rome, as Acts attests. Paul met in Corinth 'a Jew named Aquila, a native of Pontus, who had recently come from Italy with his wife Priscilla, because Claudius had ordered all Jews to leave Rome' (Acts 18:2). 'All Jews' could be hyperbolic since the entire Jewish population was estimated to be around 40,000–50,000. Dio Cassius (*Roman History* 60.6.6) reports that Claudius wanted to ban Jews from the city in AD 41. No reason is given as to why; one may presume it was because of his fear of religious influences from the East corrupting Roman religious practices. Claudius did not follow through with this because the Jews had grown in such numbers that expelling them would have caused a tumult. Instead, he forbade them from assembling. Suetonius's reference raises these questions: 'How many and which Jews did Claudius expel? In what year did the expulsions occur?

(note 22 *cont.*) pronouncing it 'Chrestianus' (*Apol.* 3.5). Tacitus correctly spelled his reference to Jesus as 'Christus' (*Ann.* 15.44).

23. Wiefel, 'Jewish Community', p. 96.
24. Barclay, 'Is It Good News?', p. 93.

Who was this Chrestus, and what were the controversies surrounding him?'[25]

It is most likely that the expulsion of Aquila and Prisca occurred
in AD 49, and that it was set off by intra-Jewish turbulence over
Jewish Christians preaching Christ to their fellow Jews.[26] From
archaeological evidence, however, Keener concludes,

> It is hard to imagine that the Jewish sections (known from archaeology)
> remained deserted after their absence; yet it is even more inconceivable
> that Jews recovered their property after returning if it had been seized by
> others; therefore it is unlikely that all would have left, despite the edict.[27]

It is possible to construe Suetonius's statement to mean that
Claudius expelled only those who were causing habitual disturb-
ances or perhaps only 'the key leaders'.[28] How many is unclear, but
Luke indicates it was a large number. When Claudius died, his
stepson Nero ignored many of his decrees as ludicrous (Suetonius,
Nero 33.1). Many Jews could then return to Rome, which may
explain Prisca and Aquila's presence there (16:3–5). Did all this
turmoil reshape the ethnic make-up of the Christian community
in Rome in the late 50s when Paul writes?

Paul's exhortations in 14:1 – 15:13 do not provide clear-cut data
for identifying the weak and the strong. Some think Paul refers
to Jewish and Gentile believers; some, Gentile believers and Jews;
and some, only Gentiles. Theories about the occasion of the letter
based on the identity of the weak are on shaky ground. Murphy-
O'Connor's analysis of the edict of Claudius leads him to
conclude, 'The Jewish vacuum, which is essential to the theory
that the content of Romans was determined by a unique feature
of Christianity in the Eternal City, is a myth.'[29] Wedderburn's
description of the Romans as embroiled in 'the maelstrom of the

---

25. Keener, *Acts*, pp. 2697–2698.
26. Ibid., pp. 2705–2711.
27. Ibid., p. 2704.
28. Lampe, *From Paul to Valentinus*, p. 14.
29. Murphy-O'Connor, *Paul*, p. 333; cf. pp. 9–15.

disputes'[30] and Wright's supposition that 'Christian Gentiles and Christian Jews find themselves in uneasy coexistence' (Wright, p. 406) seem unjustified. Such bold assertions must assume that Paul's friends have kept him informed about problems in Rome. Paul, however, makes no mention of having received reports of quarrels or letters raising questions (contrast 1 Cor. 1:11; 7:1; 8:1). This reconstruction of the Roman context flies in the face of Paul's expression of full confidence in the Roman believers as 'full of goodness, filled with all knowledge, and able to instruct [admonish] one another' (15:14). While different evaluations of the rhetoric Paul employs in Romans have reached different conclusions, Wuellner's contention that the letter affirms 'the communal values which Paul and the Romans share in being agents of faith throughout the world', and seeks to increase the strength of their devotion to these values, is on target.[31] Paul's statement that he writes rather boldly 'to remind', not to exhort or to correct (15:15),[32] confirms this assessment.

If 14:1 – 15:13 is not the key for understanding the occasion of this letter, why does Paul include it? Meeks surmises, 'Paul takes up the topic [of clean and unclean food] out of his experience, not theirs, because it is well suited to show in behavioral terms the outworking of the main theses of the letter.'[33] In comparing Philippians with Romans, Hartwig and Theissen make the case that the circumstances of the place where Paul writes made an imprint on the letter. Paul writes from Corinth, and his continuing written and oral interchanges with the Corinthians have been embedded in the letter to the Romans.[34] The issue of food offered to idols in 1 Corinthians 8 – 10 is quite different from Paul's discussion in 14:1 – 15:13.[35] To promote unity, Paul extrapolates basic principles from his arguments in 1 Corinthians 8 – 10 and issues commands that

---

30. Wedderburn, *Reasons*, p. 80.

31. Wuellner, 'Paul's Rhetoric', pp. 134, 139–140.

32. Kettunen, *Abfassungszweck*, pp. 152–154.

33. Meeks, 'Judgment', p. 292.

34. Hartwig and Theissen, 'Die korinthische Gemeinde', pp. 229–252.

35. Garland, *1 Corinthians*, pp. 358–360.

are generally applicable to any situation in which humans have diverse views over matters of indifference.[36] For Paul, idol food is *not* a matter of indifference.[37]

Neither can one infer from Paul's theological declarations in dialogue with an imagined Jewish opponent (2:17; 3:1–31; 4:1; 7:7, 13; 9:30–32; 11:11) and perhaps with a libertine opponent (6:1, 15) that Paul clashes with challengers in Rome. While similar themes to those in Galatians emerge in Romans, it is misleading to use the conflict in Galatians as a template for interpreting the Romans' situation. Knox is correct: 'Romans was written in a quiet and reflective mood; Galatians in the heat of battle.'[38] Paul is not engaged in a battle in Romans. It is wrong to interpret his statement that he 'is not ashamed of the gospel' to imply that he feels he must defend his gospel from those in Rome who might discredit it. In 1:16–17, Paul is not reacting to some criticism of his gospel but emphasizing that its power does not and will not fail. It has the power to lead both Jew and Greek to salvation, and one's trust in it will not prove to be in vain (cf. 9:33).

c. Paul's circumstances as the occasion for the letter
i. Taking the gospel to Spain
Morris asserts that Paul's statement in 15:14 means that the Roman believers are in good shape. He then asks, if so, 'why write?' (Morris, pp. 509–510). When Paul composes Romans, he is poised to embark on a new stage in his apostolic career. He has preached the gospel from Jerusalem to Illyricum (15:19) and avoided building on another's foundation (15:20). Paul's focus is on proclaiming the gospel where Christ has not been named in the western perimeter of the empire (15:23–24). Rome is only to be a stopover as he passes

---

36. Karris, 'Romans 14:1 – 15:13', pp. 73–75.
37. Furnish, *Love Command*, p. 115, contends, 'Romans is addressed to a church of which Paul has no firsthand knowledge, and his discussion of "the strong" and "the weak" in 14:1 – 15:13 reads like a generalized adaptation of a position he had earlier worked out respecting an actual, known situation in Corinth.'
38. Knox, 'Galatians', p. 343.

through (*diaporeuomenos*). The letter to the Romans is intended to lay the groundwork for his objective to go on to Spain from there with their support.[39] This purpose may explain the reference to the 'barbarians' as among those to whom Paul believes he is indebted to preach the gospel (1:14). Jewett notes,

> Spaniards were viewed as barbarians par excellence because so large a proportion continued to resist Roman rule, to rebel with frightening frequency, and to refuse to speak Latin or to use the Roman names for their cities, streams, or mountains.
> (Jewett, p. 131)[40]

This assertion is an overstatement since Seneca the Elder came from Córdoba, Spain, and his sons Gallio, mentioned in Acts 18:12 as the proconsul of Achaia, and Seneca the Younger, who was a well-known Stoic philosopher, statesman, dramatist and Nero's tutor, were born there but raised in Rome. This general impression of Spaniards as barbarians applies to those residing in Spain and resisting Roman cultural influence.

We can infer from what Paul writes that his desire to go to Spain would result in bringing in a harvest that would add to 'the full number of the Gentiles' (11:25) and would discharge his calling to present them as an offering to God that is 'acceptable, sanctified by the Holy Spirit' (15:16). Such a goal tallies with Jesus' promise to 'the apostles whom he had chosen' that when the Holy Spirit comes upon them, they will be witnesses to 'the ends of the earth' (Acts 1:2, 8). The city of Gades, modern Cádiz, in Spain was viewed as the end of the earth.[41]

The verb 'to send on' (*propempein*) in 15:24 refers to providing persons to accompany or escort someone on a journey, and to assist

---

39. Zeller, *Juden und Heiden*, pp. 38–77; Dewey, '*EIS THN SPANIAN*', pp. 321–349; and Morris, pp. 16–17.

40. Jewett cites Cicero, *Quint. fratr.* 1.1.27; Livy, *History of Rome* 25.33.2; 27.17.10; 28.33.2–4; Florus 1.33–34; Caesar, *Bell. civ.* 1.38.3; 1.44.2; and Pliny, *Ep.* 8.24.4.

41. Strabo, *Geogr.* 3.1.8; cf. 1.2.31; 2.5.14; 3.1.4.

in making a journey possible by providing food, money and means of travel.[42] Paul needs more than just financial support. The verb signals that he 'hopes to gain logistical and tactical support from Rome for his mission to Spain' (Jewett, p. 130). In Spain, for the first time in his ministry Paul 'would encounter strong linguistic and cultural barriers'.[43] The Romans could furnish persons to help him navigate these new waters. Prior asserts, 'Had this mission not been uppermost in his mind, and had he not needed the help of the Romans, he would neither have written to them, nor intended to pass through.'[44] Paul uses the word *karpos* ('fruit') in 15:28 for the financial offering, which is translated variously as 'what has been collected' (NRSV), 'contribution' (NIV) or 'funds' (CSB), for the Jerusalem saints. He could be making a play on words in 1:13 when he refers to the 'fruit', translated as 'harvest', that Paul hopes to gain from going to Rome. It may not simply refer to a harvest of converts but could also have a financial connotation. It could refer subtly to his hope that the Romans would provide financial backing for spreading the gospel among the Spaniards in the western reaches of the empire. If so, Paul wants them to take ownership of this mission in the same way that Antioch, under the guidance of the Holy Spirit, had set Paul and Barnabas apart and sent them off to preach the gospel in the West (Acts 13:1–3).[45] Later, when churches had been established in Ephesus and Corinth, they served as bases for evangelizing in the provinces of Asia and Achaia. Accordingly, Bruce asks, 'where would he find a base for the evangelization of Spain if not in Rome?'[46]

Paul is a good administrator planning diligently ahead (12:8). He

does not wait until he gets to Rome to put this idea in their minds. He is thinking several steps ahead. With this letter to the Christians in Rome,

---

42. BDAG, p. 873. Cf. Acts 15:3; 1 Cor. 16:6, 11; 2 Cor. 1:16; Titus 3:13; 3 John 6; 1 Macc. 12:4.

43. Crafton, 'Paul's Rhetorical Vision', p. 327.

44. Prior, *Paul the Letter-Writer*, p. 131.

45. Ibid., p. 135.

46. Bruce, 'The Romans Debate', pp. 187–188.

he starts the ball rolling, in order to benefit from its momentum when he arrives.[47]

Since Phoebe has helped many, including Paul, in the East (16:1–2), he may be sending her to Rome with the letter to help organize his campaign to the West, which is the 'matter' (16:2, CSB) he asks them to help her 'in whatever she may require' (Jewett, pp. 945–948). Paul would need Rome 'as at least a springboard if not an operational base for his missionary plans in the West' (Käsemann, p. 404). He expresses any request for help cautiously and generally because he had no prior relations with the recipients (Schnabel, I, p. 39). He is in no position to make demands as he does of the Corinthians (1 Cor. 16:1–4) but must use discreet diplomacy. He first 'needs to clarify the theological foundations of his mission before suggesting the nature of the desired cooperation' (Jewett, p. 130).

ii. The letter as a self-introduction through an introduction to Paul's gospel
Wedderburn maintains that an adequate explanation of Romans must account for Paul's impending visits to Jerusalem, Rome and Spain mentioned in the frame of the letter and the detailed exposition of the gospel of God's righteousness in the body of the letter.[48] If preparation for a venture to Spain is a primary purpose behind the writing of this letter, why does Paul include such an extended theological discourse (1:18 – 11:36) as well as the lengthy ethical exhortations (12:1 – 15:13)?

Paul must establish a rapport to win their support. In the letter's frame, he turns his hand to the sensitive task of recommending himself to an audience he has never met.[49] He asserts his divine commission as an apostle set apart 'to bring about the obedience of faith among all the Gentiles for the sake of his name' (1:1–6; 11:13; 15:15–16). It makes him 'a debtor both to Greeks and to barbarians, both to the wise and to the foolish' (1:14). He summarizes the success of his work in the East (15:15–19), and the roll call

---

47. Longenecker and Still, *Thinking through Paul*, p. 169.
48. Wedderburn, *Reasons*, p. 5.
49. Holloway, 'Rhetoric', p. 114.

of twenty-four named persons and two unnamed women whom he asks them to greet (16:3–16) serves, in effect, as a list of those who can vouch for Paul's trustworthiness and the effectiveness of his gospel.[50]

In the letter's central section, Paul presents his gospel that he has preached in the East (cf. Gal. 2:2). He cannot announce his decision to come to Rome and be sent on by them to Spain 'without further ado' and 'assume that they will receive him as [a] legitimate preacher of the gospel or even as an apostle, or that they will forthwith be ready to identify with him and with his evangelistic enterprise in the West'.[51] He could expect unstinting support for this endeavour only *after* they have a full grasp of his gospel. He hints that they may have heard defamatory distortions of it (3:8), and the body of the letter displays the soundness and authority of his gospel through his interpretation of Scripture (chs. 3–4) and examples from human experience (chs. 5–6). He shows that his gospel was anticipated in the Scripture (1:17; cf. Hab. 2:4) and does not invalidate the law (3:31; 7:12, 14; 10:5–13; 13:8–10) but is its climax (10:4). The believers' experience of the Holy Spirit further confirms the truth of his gospel (ch. 8). If the letter is a 'reminder' (15:15), it also serves as 'Paul's calling card' that he hopes will ensure the Romans' support for his mission to Spain (15:24) since they 'will know fully who and what they are supporting' (Dunn, II, p. 859). Holloway adds that Paul's adept use of rhetoric presents him as a teacher and 'person of culture worthy of their sponsorship'.[52]

iii. The return to Jerusalem weighing on Paul's mind
Leenhardt contends, 'When Paul writes to Rome his mind is full of his Spanish scheme' (Leenhardt, p. 14). That is not entirely true. Paul's plans to come to Rome must be postponed once again as he heads east to Jerusalem with the collection (15:25). What awaits him

---

50. Since Paul never distinguishes persons in chapter 16 by their secular status, identifying Erastus as 'the city treasurer' would seem to be intended to heighten their regard for Paul.

51. Du Toit, 'Persuasion', p. 200.

52. Holloway, 'Rhetoric', p. 121.

there looms worryingly over him, which might explain other features in the letter's body.

Paul mentions the collection for the first time only fleetingly in 1 Corinthians 16:1–4. He is forced to explain its purpose in greater depth in 2 Corinthians 8 – 9 when he needs to bolster the Corinthians' flagging enthusiasm for the project. Finally, his last mention of the collection occurs in Romans 15:25–28 as he prepares to depart with it for Jerusalem.[53] Earlier, the pillar apostles had agreed that God had entrusted him with the gospel for the uncircumcised and was working through him in sending him to the Gentiles (Gal. 2:7–8). Paul reports that they asked only that 'we remember the poor, which was actually what I was eager to do' (Gal. 2:10). The collection for 'the poor among the saints at Jerusalem' (15:26) may have been a fulfilment of that eagerness. Paul originally thought he would send emissaries from the contributing churches to take the gift to Jerusalem and that he would go only 'if it seems advisable' (1 Cor. 16:3–4). Paul now has determined that it is indeed advisable, if not imperative, for him to accompany the emissaries to interpret the gift.

Paul feels compelled to go in person because, as apostle to the Gentiles, he needs to interpret for the recipients what this gift means theologically about the unity of Jewish and Gentile Christians. Only once does he use the secular business term 'collection' (*logeia*, 1 Cor. 16:1), because it is not simply an offering to help the poor. He primarily refers to it in spiritual terms (author's translations): 'grace', 'privilege' (*charis*, 2 Cor. 8:4, 6, 7, 19); 'partnership', 'sharing' (*koinōnia*, Rom. 15:26; 2 Cor. 8:4); 'service', 'ministry' (*diakonia*, Rom. 15:25, 31; 2 Cor. 8:4; 9:1, 12, 13); 'earnestness' (*spoudia*, 2 Cor. 8:8); 'love' (*agapē*, 2 Cor. 8:7, 8, 24); 'willingness' (*promythia*, 2 Cor. 8:11, 12, 19; 9:2); 'generosity' (*haplotēs*, 2 Cor. 8:2; 9:11, 13); 'abundance' (*perisseuma*, 2 Cor. 8:14); 'liberal gift' (*hadrotēs*, 2 Cor. 8:20); 'undertaking' (*hypostasis*, 2 Cor. 9:4); 'blessing', 'generous gift' (*eulogia*, 2 Cor. 9:5); 'good work' (*ergon agathon*, 2 Cor. 9:8); 'the yield of your righteousness' (*ta genēmata tēs dikaiosynēs*, 2 Cor. 9:10); '[priestly] service', 'ministry' (*leitourgia*, 2 Cor. 9:12); 'fruit' (*karpos*, Rom. 15:28).

---

53. Acts remains curiously silent about the collection except for a hint that Paul brought 'alms' to his nation (Acts 24:17).

Since Paul did not organize collections for other churches that
suffered persecution and poverty, he apparently saw special spiritual
significance in this offering for Jerusalem as the culmination of his
work in the East.[54] By bringing the fruit from the harvest of his proclamation of the gospel among Gentiles back to Jerusalem, Paul
reverses the course that took him from Jerusalem around to Illyricum
(15:19). He thinks it so important that once again he postpones
travelling to Rome and knowingly risks his life (Acts 20:22–24, 36–38;
21:4, 10–14) to deliver and interpret this gift. He envisions it as a
concrete symbol that the 'Christian faith overcomes the deepest racial
barriers that formerly separated Jews from Gentiles'.[55] If successful,
the collection manifests that for those who are in Christ the dividing
wall of hostility between Jews and Gentiles has been torn down. The
two groups have been made one and are united in the bond of peace
in Christ Jesus (Eph. 2:14–18). For Paul, it demonstrates that 'there is
one body and one Spirit, just as you were called to the one hope of
your calling, one Lord, one faith, one baptism, one God and Father
of all, who is above all and through all and in all' (Eph. 4:4–6).[56]

Because Paul is not asking the Romans to contribute to this gift,
he does not delve into its theological rationale here as he does in 2
Corinthians 8 – 9. Instead, he makes a striking prayer request:

> I appeal to you, brothers and sisters, by our Lord Jesus Christ and by
> the love of the Spirit, to join me in earnest prayer to God on my behalf,
> that I may be rescued from the unbelievers in Judea, and that my
> ministry to Jerusalem may be acceptable to the saints.
> (15:30–31)[57]

---

54. Holloway, 'Rhetoric', p. 77.
55. Garland, *2 Corinthians*, pp. 418–419.
56. The collection is not a type of temple tax (Matt. 17:24–27). Though
    Gentile Christians are indebted to the Jerusalem church for having
    shared their spiritual blessings (Rom. 15:27), paying a tax would only
    reinforce a Jewish supremacy over the Gentiles.
57. Paul uses the same word 'acceptable' (εὐπρόσδεκτος) in 15:16 to describe
    the goal of his 'priestly service of the gospel of God' as a minister of
    Christ to the Gentiles that they might be an offering.

Why ask the Romans to pray that poor people will accept a gift of money?[58] What would make this gift unacceptable? The obvious problem was that it was Gentile money. Paul worries that the bitter controversy over the acceptance of uncircumcised Gentiles, ostensibly settled at the Jerusalem conference (Acts 15), continued to endanger the church's unity. Those who insisted, 'Unless you are circumcised according to the custom of Moses, you cannot be saved' (Acts 15:1) and the false brothers he mentions in Galatians 2:4 may still haunt the Jerusalem church. Jewish believers, zealous for the law, might not accept this tangible sign of gratitude because it also entailed accepting Gentiles as their brothers and sisters in Christ, children of Abraham and fellow heirs to the promises to Israel.[59]

Therefore, it is not surprising that this letter, written on the eve of his departure for Judea, deals with issues that might deter Jewish believers from accepting Gentile believers: the validity of the law for salvation (7:7–25); the justification of humans before God apart from works of the law (3:27 – 4:6; 9:32; 11:6); Abraham as the father of both the circumcised and the uncircumcised who have faith like his (4:12); God's remedy for the sin of all humans (5:12–21); and the election of Israel and how their hardening in unbelief relates to the inclusion of Gentiles (9:1 – 11:36). These issues addressed in the letter's central section would be of 'particular concern to Jerusalem'.[60] Acts records that when Paul arrived in Jerusalem and visited James and the elders, he 'related one by one the things that God had done among the

---

58. A past famine prompted an earlier relief effort (Acts 11:28). Persecution (Gal. 1:22–23; 1 Thess. 2:14–15) probably deepened their poverty.

59. Cf. the many references to the inclusion of Gentiles (1:5–6, 13; 3:29; 4:16–18; 9:24, 30; 10:12–13; 11:11, 25; 15:7–18; 16:4, 26).

60. Jervell, 'Letter', pp. 58–59. Dahl, *Studies*, p. 77, writes, 'It is easy to find reminiscences of the conflicts in which he had recently been involved and of which we have evidence in his letters to the Corinthian and Galatian Christians. It is also possible to read the letter as a draft of the "collection speech" which Paul intended to deliver in Jerusalem.' Cf. also Wilckens, I, pp. 43–46.

Gentiles through his ministry'. They responded with praise but expressed apprehension that 'thousands of believers' among the Jews who are 'zealous for the law ... have been told about you that you teach all the Jews living among the Gentiles to forsake Moses, and that you tell them not to circumcise their children or observe the customs' (Acts 21:18–21). Paul's comments about the value of circumcision in 2:25 – 3:2 would be particularly relevant in this context. This context also explains the inclusion of 9:1 – 11:36. Moo asserts, 'For their part, Jewish Christians need to understand that salvation history has moved on from the days in which God's people were mainly restricted to Israel' (Moo, p. 922). Accepting the gift from the Gentile believers would reveal their acceptance of the new situation.

It is too much to say that Romans is 'a brief drawn up by Paul in anticipation of the renewed necessity of defending his gospel in Jerusalem',[61] or that Paul formulates a theological defence of the understanding of the gospel that he will present in Jerusalem when he delivers the collection.[62] This letter is not simply a dress rehearsal for Jerusalem. Knowing that he might face challenges when he presents this offering from Gentile Christ-followers may explain why Paul includes so many passages that refute a Jewish interlocutor raising objections and drawing false inferences about his gospel.

Paul also implores the Romans to pray that he might be delivered from the unbelievers in Judea. The revival of militancy and nationalistic fervour among fellow Jews and the rise of fanatics who believed that Jews who fraternized with Gentiles were traitors presented serious dangers. Dunn writes, 'Such nationalistic feeling would tend to view the offering of Gentiles with increased suspicion' (Dunn, II, p. 880). He cites Josephus's account that the later Jewish revolt against Rome became inevitable when the firebrand captain of the temple, Eleazar, son of the high priest Ananias, persuaded the temple officials to 'accept no further gift or sacrifice from a foreigner' (*J.W.* 2.409–410 [Thackeray, LCL]). The believers in Jerusalem might be intimidated by a radical

---

61. Suggs, 'Word', p. 295.

62. Bornkamm, *Paul*, pp. 93, 95–96.

element of non-believers and fear accepting anything from uncircumcised Gentiles.

Paul must also explain why he is postponing his visit to Rome. Some might wonder why an apostle to the Gentiles continues to bother with the Jews in Jerusalem. Wiefel documents that strong anti-Jewish sentiments existed in Rome at the time of Nero and before, and reasonably contends that 'the positive statements regarding all of Israel appear for the first time in Paul's letter to the Romans and must be seen against this background'.[63] Paul informs the Romans that a 'hardness' has overtaken the Jews, but it is not final (11:2). His deep belief that God has not given up on Israel means that neither will he give up on his 'kindred according to the flesh' (9:3). Paul's return to Jerusalem is not love's labour lost that squanders more promising evangelistic opportunities in the West. Paul believes that it is futile to go to Rome or Spain with a gospel of reconciliation while leaving behind an unreconciled church in which Jews and Gentiles refuse to accept one another. He is convinced that the salvation of Jews and the salvation of Gentiles are intertwined (11:25–32). Since Israel's stumbling has meant 'riches' and 'reconciliation' for the world, how much more will their acceptance of the gospel bring for the world (11:12, 15)!

iv. Giving the Romans Paul's gospel so that they might proclaim it themselves Jervis contends that Paul writes Romans out of his apostolic obligation to them so that they 'may hear his particularly powerful and effective presentation of the gospel' and 'become part of his "offering" of "sanctified" and "obedient" Gentiles' to God.[64] The letter, then, serves as a preliminary sharing with them of his 'spiritual gift to strengthen' them (1:11), but to strengthen them in what way? Since his recipients are already believers, he is not writing to add them to his harvest of Gentiles. Paul instead wants in this lengthy letter to brace up theologically their understanding of and witness to the gospel, which he self-assuredly identifies as 'my gospel' (2:16; 16:25).

---

63. Wiefel, 'Jewish Community', p. 100.

64. Jervis, *Purpose*, pp. 163–164.

Reichert proposes that Paul instructs the recipients of the letter in his gospel to enable them to proclaim it on their own should his plans fall through and his coming to Rome continue to be thwarted. The letter is therefore a 'balancing act'. The Romans are not simply the recipients of his gospel (2:16; 16:25) but also those who are to broadcast his gospel.[65] On the one hand, since they have Paul's gospel in this letter, they should be able to fend off interlopers 'who cause dissensions and offences' (16:17–20; cf. 2 Pet. 2:1; 2 John 7), the legalists who would amend it, the libertines who would pervert it, and the hot-air merchants who would twist it to glorify themselves. On the other hand, they share a calling from God (1:1, 6–7) that imposes the obligation to preach the gospel to others who remain in bondage to sin.[66] They have in Paul's gospel a theological wellspring from which to evangelize others, both Jew and Greek.

Melanchthon's oft-quoted pronouncement that the letter is 'the compendium of Christian doctrine'[67] is unsatisfactory because Paul does not touch on or deal systematically with many vital Christian doctrines. The arguments in this letter, however, draw on Paul's long experience as a teacher and preacher, and they lay out central facets of his gospel that are the theological foundation for bringing Jews and Gentiles to the obedience of faith, for helping them recognize their solidarity in Christ and how it is part of God's purpose to bring wholeness and order through Christ to a disordered and broken world. Sympathetic mutuality should emerge from the recognition that Jews and Gentiles are one in Christ. It expresses Paul's missionary vision for all churches everywhere, not just Rome.

This focus also explains the lengthy ethical section. While it may 'provide examples of the kind of concrete moral behavior expected of Christians',[68] most importantly, it teaches how

---

65. Reichert, *Der Römerbrief*, pp. 77–91. Wedderburn, *Reasons*, p. 71, uses the balancing act image to a different end, referring to Romans as 'a diplomatic tightrope'.

66. Schnabel, *Paul and the Early Church*, p. 1472.

67. Melanchthon, *Loci Communes*, p. 69.

68. Aune, 'Romans', p. 296.

Christians are to live in a pagan society and how they as a diverse body of believers are to handle in-house differences. It diminishes the effect of Romans to read it as if it were addressed only to a particular church with a particular problem. 'The gospel of God' (1:1) that Paul presents in this letter is intended to bring about the obedience of faith for the entire world, including the Romans 'who are called to belong to Jesus Christ' (1:6). It 'is directed to the human problem and therefore includes all local problems'.[69] For humans who are religiously wired and prone to quarrel, Paul's admonitions in 14:1 – 15:13 present a model of Christian reconciliation that assumes that the community's life must reflect the reconciliation worked by God in the lives of believers. Since God has saved Gentiles and adopted them into the people of God on the same grounds as Jews, through faith in Christ, Jews and Gentiles must accept one another and live together in harmony. This truth also applies to any Christian group that might divide over indifferent matters. An unreconciled church impedes the preaching of the gospel of reconciliation.

Mindful of the tensions and misinterpretations his gospel has provoked and fully aware that he will have to defend it when he arrives in Jerusalem, Paul fully expounds his gospel for the Roman believers. His hope is that they might affirm its universal scope, live in harmony with one another, walk according to the Spirit, and share in his commitment to bring about 'the obedience of faith' among the Gentiles in every nation for the glory of God (16:25–27) by sending him on to proclaim the gospel in Spain.

5. The nature of the letter

Richards notes that the average length of over 14,000 private papyrus letters that have been discovered is eighty-seven words. Aside from Romans, Paul's letters average around 2,495 words. That far exceeds the average number of words in the epistles of the notable literary letter writers Cicero and Seneca. Cicero's letters averaged 295 words, with his longest letter consisting of 2,520

---

69. Martin, 'Kerygma', p. 303.

words. Seneca averaged 972 words, with his longest letter (*Ep*. 95) consisting of 4,201 words. The 7,114 words in Paul's letter to the Romans make it exceptional. Richards estimates the cost for producing such a long letter to be equivalent to $2,275.[70] Paul was not a frequent letter writer, but his outsized letters were intended to reach a wide audience since they were not written to one recipient but were addressed to a community of believers, including Philemon (Phlm. 2).

Paul shaped the letter form to serve his own purposes, but the various theories attempting to identify the genre and rhetorical categorizations of the letter have not reached a consensus.[71] These differing conclusions suggest that Romans cannot be pressed into any one particular genre, and 'these resemblances mean nothing more than that Paul has effectively utilized various literary conventions of his culture to get his message across' (Moo, p. 14). The assumption that Paul received a formal rhetorical education is uncertain. Schellenberg finds no evidence that Paul 'evinces familiarity with the specific conventions of formal Greco-Roman rhetoric'.[72] Romans may simply be described as a very long 'letter–essay' containing 'instructional material set out within an epistolary frame' (Longenecker, p. 14).

6. Theological themes in Romans

a. God

The frequency of Paul's references to God (*theos*) in the letter, 153 times, reveals that it is 'fundamentally about God' (Morris, p. 20), but more precisely, about God's power through Jesus Christ to save humanity from destruction (1:3–4, 16–17). Paul asserts that God is 'one' (3:30), 'immortal' (1:23), 'eternal' (16:26), and with unfathomable knowledge and wisdom (11:33; 16:27). God is the God of both Jews and Gentiles (3:29), and 'from him and through

---

70. Richards, 'Letter', pp. 87–89.
71. The multiple proposals concerning the character of Paul's rhetoric in Romans reveal that judgments about it are not conclusive.
72. Schellenberg, *Rethinking*, p. 240.

him and to him are all things' (11:36). Paul does not simply identify God by God's attributes. God is best and most fully known from what God has done in Christ. The gospel of God (1:1) is the power of God for salvation (1:16), and it is God's power alone that saves humans (11:23). The gospel reveals the righteousness of God (1:17): God's saving action on behalf of his people that is unleashed on the world, God's justice in inflicting wrath and judging the world (3:3–6), and God's gift to humans in declaring those who have faith to be righteous (4:3–11, 22–25; 5:17; 8:33). God is faithful and can do, and does, all that he has promised (4:21; 11:29), and God's sovereign will cannot be prevented from being accomplished (9:11–24) so that all things will accrue to God's glory (11:36; 16:27).

While the righteousness of God brings salvation without distinction to all who believe (3:21–25, 29–30; 14:3, 18), the wrath of God's righteous judgment on sinful humanity is made plain in history (1:18–31) and will be meted out at the end of time when all will stand before God's judgment seat (2:1, 5; 3:4–6; 9:22; 12:19; 14:10). God impartially condemns (2:11) all who wickedly oppose his will. Yet God is kind and forbearing (2:4). God saves believers from the wrath that is due to sinful humankind (5:9) because God is merciful (9:16; 11:30; 15:9) and justifies the ungodly (8:33). God's wrath and God's mercy are not in opposition to each other but are interdependent (Isa. 60:10).

The God of Israel also shows grace to Gentiles and intends to include them in the people of God based on their confession of faith, not their Jewish ancestry or conversion that comprises undergoing Jewish rites of passage. Since the law was not intended to bring salvation, God reckons humans to be righteous apart from works (4:6). Justification by faith is the theological counterpart to Jesus' pronouncements in the Gospels that a person's sins are forgiven (Matt. 9:2; Mark 2:5; Luke 7:47–48). Jews also need the gospel of grace. It is only by God's grace (5:15, 20) that God cancels the wages of sin and freely offers the gift of eternal life (6:23). In doing so, 'God has done what the law, weakened by the flesh, could not do: by sending his own Son in the likeness of sinful flesh, and to deal with sin, he condemned sin in the flesh' (8:3). God has put forward Christ as a sacrifice of atonement by his blood to save Christ-followers who have faith in what God has done (3:25). God gives life to the dead and calls into existence the things that do not exist (4:17) and raised Christ from the dead (4:24; 10:9). God loves us and 'proves his love for us in that while we still were sinners Christ died for us' (5:8). Believers are beloved of God (1:7) and as God's children can intimately address God as 'Abba! Father!' (8:15). Nothing can separate believers from God's love (8:35–39), whether they be supernatural powers that God rules or the earthly powers that God has appointed (13:1), because God has predestined believers to be glorified with Christ (8:29–30).

b. Jesus Messiah

Paul utters a cry of desperation, 'Wretched man that I am! Who will rescue me from this body of death?' (7:24). This cry raises the issue: how do humans living in a world of chaos, under God's wrath and under the tyranny of sin, death (5:12–21) and the law, which human sin corrupts (7:7–25), enter a right relationship with God? He asks *who* will deliver him, not *what* will deliver him, and the answer comes in the next verse: 'Thanks be to God through Jesus Christ our Lord!' (7:25; cf. 11:26). Paul identifies Christ as the Son of God (1:3, 4, 9; 5:10; 8:3, 29, 32), and in 9:5 goes much further. He is the Messiah according to the flesh, but more: he is God over all (see commentary). He has died and been raised by God to live again so that he might be Lord of both the dead and the living (14:9).

Paul emphasizes that the abundance of grace in which believers stand (5:17) comes from Christ's act of obedience in dying for the ungodly (5:6) and sinners (5:8). It leads to the possibility that many will be made righteous. Christ's atoning death countered Adam's trespass that led to the plight of death and condemnation that burdens all humanity (5:12–21). Through Christ, believers receive 'redemption' (3:24) and have 'peace with' God (5:1) and receive 'reconciliation' (5:11). In Christ, they are set free from the law of sin and of death and no longer stand condemned (8:1–2). Christ Jesus has not left them to fend for themselves but is at the right hand of God interceding for them (8:34). In Christ, they 'walk in newness of life' (6:4). It is the great hope of believers that they will be raised with Christ from death (6:5–9; 8:11) and conformed to the image of God's Son. Through Christ Jesus, they will receive the gift of eternal life (5:21; 6:22–23).

Grace and peace become the keynotes for those who live under Christ's lordship in the new age of salvation (1:7; 8:6; 14:19; 15:13). Consequently, those welcomed by God in Christ are to pursue peace with other believers (14:19) and, as far as possible, to live peaceably with all (12:18). The grace and peace that come through Christ have made possible the universal, impartial reach of salvation to both Jews and Gentiles. Gentiles who believe in the gospel (1:5–6; 4:16–18; 9:24, 30; 10:12–13; 11:11, 25; 15:7–18; 16:26) have been incorporated into God's people, but Paul insists that they do not displace Israel. While Israel according to the flesh does not constitute the true people of God (9:6) and has been cut down to a remnant (9:27–29; 11:5), God has a grander purpose to save a full number of Israel (11:26). Despite appearances to the contrary, mainstream Israel's present faithlessness in rejecting the gospel will not nullify God's faithfulness (3:3).

c. The Holy Spirit

'The Spirit' figures prominently in the letter. Paul refers to 'the Spirit' fifteen times (2:29, cf. CSB; 7:6; 8:4, 5, 6, 9, 13, 14, 16, 23, 26, 27 [2x]; 15:19, 30), 'the Holy Spirit' five times (5:5; 9:1; 14:17; 15:13, 16) and 'the spirit of holiness' once (1:4). He also uses the terms 'the Spirit of God' (8:9, 11 [2x], 14) and the 'Spirit of Christ' (8:9). Paul states that Christ 'was declared to be Son of God with power according to the spirit of holiness by resurrection from the dead' (1:4). The Spirit creates true circumcision of the heart (2:29) because the written code only kills. Where the law brings death, the Spirit gives life (7:6; cf. 2 Cor. 3:6). The Spirit continuously pours God's love into believers' hearts (5:5) and sets them free from the law of sin and death (8:2).

The same Spirit at work in the resurrection of Jesus Christ from the dead (1:4) is at work here and now to make the newness of the resurrected life a reality in the lives of believers. Living under the power of the Spirit enables Christ-followers to fulfil the just requirement of the law (8:4) and to put to death the deeds of the body (8:13). The mind that is sold into sin's slavery in the everyday marketplace of the flesh is transformed by the Spirit and brings life and peace (8:5–8). The Spirit does not simply convey the mysteries of the Spirit (1 Cor. 14:2) but also enlightens and renews the darkened, reprobate mind that fosters indecent behaviour (1:28), and directs believers to live ethical lives that are well pleasing to God (12:2). The mind that is set on the things of the Spirit and led by the Spirit is no longer hostile to and alienated from God (8:7). When the Spirit of God dwells in a believer the result is a healthy, intimate relationship with God (8:9) and a wholesome relationship with others (cf. Gal. 5:19–24).

The Spirit as 'the spirit of adoption' affirms that believers are the children of God (8:15–16), intercedes for them in their creaturely weakness in communicating to God when they do not know what to pray in times of suffering (8:26–27), and, consequently, inspires their hope (15:13). Believers' experience of the first fruits of the Spirit (8:23) anticipates the full blessings that will come at the end of the age. Believers aglow in the Spirit (12:11) and filled with the Spirit's love (15:30) convey the joy (14:17) that wins others to Christ. The Spirit also gave power to Paul's ministry through the signs and wonders that accompanied his proclaiming the good news of Christ (15:19).

d. Scripture

The Scriptures of Israel are authoritative for Paul as the word of God, and more than half of the scriptural quotations in Paul's letters are to be found in Romans. They are a witness to the gospel (1:2; 3:21; 4:23–24a; 15:3–4, 8–9; 16:26) and reveal that God's promises to Israel are fulfilled in Christ (4:13–17; 9:4–5; 15:8). Consequently, Paul *reads the Old Testament christologically approaching it with the question of how it bears witness to the Christ event*.[73] The crucified and risen Messiah becomes the foundation of a new perspective on the law and the key for unveiling the mystery of God's plan in Scripture to save both Jews and Gentiles that heretofore was not fully recognized or understood. The Old Testament remains relevant for Christians who understand that it 'was written for our instruction, so that by steadfastness and by the encouragement of the scriptures we might have hope' (15:4; cf. 4:23–24).

Throughout Romans Paul cites the Scriptures to show how the gospel, as compared with the law, contends with the weakness of

---

73. Schnelle, *Apostle Paul*, p. 323 (emphasis original).

the flesh, the plague of sin and the power of death. He clinches his case that no one on earth, including Jews, is righteous (3:10 = Eccl. 7:20) and that all humankind is in bondage to sin (1:18 – 3:10) with a cluster of texts from the Psalms and the Prophets (3:11–18). His argument that Abraham was justified by faith and not works and that he is the father of all who believe (4:1–25) is based on his interpretation of Genesis 15:6 and Psalm 32:1–2. Paul draws on Genesis 3 to compare Adam, 'a type of the one who was to come' (5:14), to Christ to illustrate that 'just as sin exercised dominion in death, so grace might also exercise dominion through justification leading to eternal life through Jesus Christ our Lord' (5:21). To cap his argument that the suffering of believers in a hostile world does not mean that God has abandoned them or that it negates God's purpose to glorify them, Paul cites Psalm 44:22 (8:36). Though they may be led to the slaughter like sheep, they will be more than conquerors since nothing can separate them from the love of God in Christ (8:37–39). Paul cites Scripture at least forty times in chapters 9–11 to prove that Gentiles can be included in the people of God, that God remains faithful to Israel, and that the salvation of Gentiles and the salvation of Israel are interconnected. He wraps up this long argument by citing Job and Isaiah (11:33–36). In 15:9–12, Paul also concludes his exhortations of chapters 12–15 by citing texts from the Psalms, Deuteronomy and Isaiah – the Law, the Prophets and the Writings – to seal his argument that God has willed the inclusion of Gentiles in salvation so that they together with Jews 'may with one voice glorify the God and Father of our Lord Jesus Christ' (15:6).

ANALYSIS

1. THE LETTER OPENING (1:1–17)

A. Salutation (1:1–7)

B. Thanksgiving and Paul's indebtedness to preach the gospel (1:8–15)

C. Theme statement: the gospel as the revelation of God's righteousness (1:16–17)

2. HUMANITY'S REBELLION AGAINST GOD THAT ROUSES GOD'S WRATH (1:18 – 3:20)

A. God's wrath against pagans who dishonour God (1:18–32)

B. God's wrath against Jews who dishonour God (2:1–29)

    i. The censurer of others who is no less guilty (2:1–11)

    ii. God's impartiality in judgment (2:12–16)

    iii. Jewish boasts in the law and physical circumcision do not grant immunity from God's judgment (2:17–29)

C. The credibility of God (3:1–8)

D. All are under sin's power (3:9–20)

3. GOD'S SOLUTION FOR ALL: CHRIST'S ATONING DEATH AND JUSTIFICATION THROUGH FAITH IN CHRIST (3:21 – 4:25)

A. God's righteousness disclosed in Christ's atoning death (3:21–26)

B. Justification through faith, not by works (3:27–31)

C. Abraham, an illustration of justification by faith and a model for God's people (4:1–25)

    i. Abraham justified by faith apart from works (4:1–5)

    ii. David accredited righteous apart from works (4:6–8)

    iii. Abraham was justified by faith prior to circumcision so he could be father of both the circumcised and the uncircumcised (4:9–12)

    iv. God fulfilled the promise to Abraham through faith apart from the law (4:13–22)

    v. Abraham's unwavering faith in God's promise as the model for every believer (4:23–25)

4. JUSTIFICATION BY FAITH BRINGS PEACE AND RECONCILIATION WITH GOD, A RENEWED LIFE AND THE HOPE OF GLORY (5:1 – 8:39)

A. The results of God's love through Christ's death: peace and reconciliation with God (5:1–11)

B. Eternal life and righteousness brought by God's victory in Christ cancels out the condemnation and death brought by Adam's transgression (5:12–21)

    i. The action of one placed the future destiny of others under sin and death (5:12)

    ii. Excursus on the law and sin in relation to death (5:13–14)

    iii. Contrast between the universal effects of Adam's trespass and of Christ's righteous act (5:15–17)

    iv. The reign of grace overcomes the dominion of sin and death (5:18–21)

C. Freedom from the dominion of sin and the law to live in service to righteousness (6:1 – 7:6)

    i. The believer is dead to sin to walk in newness of life (6:1–14)

ii. The believer is freed from sin to become a slave of
righteousness (6:15–23)

iii. The believer is discharged from the law to live the new
life of the Spirit (7:1–6)

D. The law's inability to check sin and generate the obedience
it demands (7:7–25)

i. How sin manipulates the law (7:7–12)

ii. Why the law fails to surmount human sin (7:13–25)

E. Life in the Spirit (8:1–30)

i. The Spirit as the fountainhead of obedience
(8:1–17)

ii. The Spirit as the source of hope in the midst of
suffering (8:18–30)

a. The groaning of creation (8:18–22)

b. The groaning of believers (8:23–25)

c. The groaning of the Spirit (8:26–27)

d. The certainty of salvation: all things work to the
good for those whom God has called (8:28–30)

F. The assurance of victory through Christ's love (8:31–39)

5. GOD'S FAITHFULNESS TO ISRAEL AND THE INTERLOCKING DESTINY OF ISRAEL AND THE GENTILES IN SALVATION (9:1 – 11:36)

A. God's sovereign freedom in dealing with Israel and the
nations: hardening and mercy (9:1–29)

i. Paul's grief over his Jewish kindred's failure to believe
the gospel (9:1–5)

ii. God's word has not failed (9:6–13)

iii. God alone determines who is elect (9:14–26)

iv. God has saved a remnant in Israel and added Gentiles
to the people of God (9:27–29)

B. Righteousness through faith for Jew and Gentile has been
made known to all Israel (9:30 – 10:21)

i. Gentiles have obtained righteousness by faith; Israel
has not because it seeks to establish its own
righteousness (9:30–33)

ii. Christ has brought an end to the law as the basis for a
righteous standing before God (10:1–4)

iii. Christ, the model of believers' relationships with
others (15:1–6)

iv. The unity of diverse believers praising God together
(15:7–13)

7. THE LETTER CLOSING (15:14 – 16:27)

A. Paul's calling as a minister of Christ Jesus to the Gentiles
and his travel plans (15:14–33)

   i. Paul's calling as a minister of Christ Jesus to the
   Gentiles (15:14–22)

   ii. Paul's plans to visit Jerusalem, Rome and Spain
   (15:23–29)

   iii. Request for prayers for Paul's safety and the success of
   the Jerusalem offering (15:30–33)

B. Final greetings (16:1–27)

   i. Commendation of Phoebe (16:1–2)

   ii. Greetings to various individuals and groups (16:3–16)

   iii. Concluding admonitions and a blessing (16:17–20)

   iv. Greetings from those with Paul (16:21–24)

   v. Benediction: glory to the God of wisdom through
   Jesus Christ (16:25–27)

COMMENTARY

1. THE LETTER OPENING (1:1–17)

A. Salutation (1:1–7)

Context

The Greek epistolary greeting was normally short: sender, recipients, greeting (Acts 15:23; 23:26; 1 Thess. 1:1). Verses 1 and 7 would constitute this usual greeting, but Paul freely modifies epistolary conventions. He expands the prescript to include a profile of his credentials as a divinely called apostle and a concise summary of the gospel he preaches. Though Timothy is identified as the co-sender in other letters (2 Cor. 1:1; Phil. 1:1; Col. 1:1; 1 Thess. 1:1; 2 Thess. 1:1) and is mentioned as Paul's co-worker who sends greetings in 16:21, he is not identified as the co-sender of Romans. The focus falls solely on Paul, his divine call as an apostle, his divine message, and his divine commission to bring the gospel to the Gentiles. He does not introduce this information because he is on the defensive, as he was in Galatians with its extended greeting (Gal. 1:1–5). Paul had never visited Rome but knows some of the letter's recipients (16:3–15). He is confident that he will receive a sympathetic hearing for his message and that they will support his mission to Spain (15:23–29). This sender formula, which is ten times longer than is typically found in Paul's other letter openings, reveals his concern to present his credentials for writing this letter to the Christians in Rome. They were not converted by him and may have heard negative rumours about him (cf. 3:8; 6:1, 15), but he wants them to view with favour both him and the gospel he presents in this letter.

The Greek word translated as 'gospel' (*euangelion*) frames the entire letter. It appears three times in the letter opening (1:1–17; in 1:1, 9, 16) and three times in the letter closing (15:13 – 16:27; in 15:16, 19; 16:25), six out of the nine occurrences in the letter (cf. 2:16; 10:16; 11:28). The gospel proclaims what God has done in keeping the promises to Israel and in raising Jesus from 'the domain of death' (Keck, p. 46). The gospel about God's 'Son, who was descended from David according to the flesh' (1:3) is not only good news for Israel. That he was 'declared to be Son of God with power according to the spirit of holiness by resurrection from the dead' (1:4) means that he is more than Israel's Messiah; he is Lord over all. In fulfilling the promises to Israel and raising Jesus from the dead God reveals 'the riches of his glory for the objects of mercy, which he has prepared beforehand for glory', and these include those 'whom he has called, not from the Jews only but also from the Gentiles' (9:23–24). The letter unfolds the gospel's implications for Israel and for the Gentile world.

Comment

1. In identifying himself to his recipients, Paul cites three credentials rather than limiting them to just one as he usually does in his greetings. First, he is a *servant* ['slave', *doulos*] *of Jesus Christ*. In the Greek, Paul refers to him as 'Christ Jesus' rather than Jesus Christ, which makes it clear that he does not understand *Christ* to be part of a double name but a title. He is Messiah Jesus, anointed by God. Rendering it 'servant of Christ Jesus' is conducive for hearing an echo of the title 'the servant of the LORD' that is used of Abraham (Ps. 105:42), Moses (2 Kgs 18:12; Ps. 105:26; Dan. 9:11), Joshua (Josh. 24:30 [LXX]; Judg. 2:8), Jonah (Jon. 1:9 [LXX]), David (2 Sam. 7:5; Ps. 78:70; 89:3), the prophets (2 Kgs 17:23; Amos 3:7; Zech. 1:6) and even Israel (Isa. 41:8–9). Paul would use this term to represent his

ministry in terms of the Isaianic 'servant of the LORD' as the herald of salvation to the nations (Isa. 42:1–6; 52:7, 10; 61:1).[1] It is estimated that one in five persons in Rome was a slave,[2] so it is more likely that Paul intends to conjure up for the original audience images from their familiarity with slavery (6:6–22; cf. Matt. 6:24; 1 Cor. 7:21) rather than from their knowledge of the term's use in Scripture. He does not intend to exalt himself with this title since he uses the language of slavery also to speak of all believers who have been acquired by Christ (1 Cor. 6:20; 7:22–23; Eph. 6.6; Col. 4:12). A slave is under the complete authority of the master who bought him or her and has no right to self-determination (Schnabel, I, p. 83). Paul understands himself to be in bondage to Christ, wholly owned by him and no more than his tool (Wolter, I, p. 80; cf. Luke 17:7–10), which raises the spectre of dishonour. He reminds the Philippians that Christ took the form of a slave, humbling himself and dying the slave's death on the cross. To read this

> metaphor in the context of political or social advancement is to misunderstand Paul's humility in subordinating himself to one who has already lowered himself to the point of dying a slave's death. As Jesus embraced dishonour, so Paul, in calling himself a slave of Christ, embraces dishonour.[3]

Being Christ's slave is not analogous to being Caesar's slave, with its lofty status and privileges. As the slave of Christ who 'did not please himself' (15:3), Paul understands himself to be the 'slave of all' (1 Cor. 9:19; 2 Cor. 4:5; cf. Mark 10:44; Gal. 5:13), indebted to Greeks and barbarians and to the wise and foolish (1:14).

Second, Paul introduces himself as a *called … apostle*, an ambassadorial agent. The unspoken agent in this calling is God,

---

1. Windsor, *Paul*, pp. 99–112.
2. Lampe, *From Paul to Valentinus*, p. 183, maintains that from the list of those to be greeted in 16:3–15, nine of the thirteen persons about whom it is possible to draw conclusions have names that indicate a slave origin.
3. Glancy, 'Slavery', p. 459.

not others. Paul did not volunteer for this role or arrogate this title to himself, nor did he rise in the ranks to be elected an apostle by others. Nor did God invite him to consider becoming an apostle. He is an apostle by 'God's sovereign action, God's deliberate choice' (Keck, p. 40).

Third, Paul underscores that God chose him for this special task. He was *set apart for the gospel of God*, which draws on imagery used by the prophets Isaiah (Isa. 49:1) and Jeremiah (Jer. 1:5) to imply that he could not resist God's sovereign choice in conscripting him (cf. Gal. 1:15–16). Similarly, in 2 Corinthians 5:14, he asserts that the love of Christ constrains and sustains him in this call.

The *gospel* also receives a threefold qualification in these opening verses. Paul identifies it first as *the gospel of God*, which may imply both that it has been initiated and sent by God and that it is about God. Cranfield contends that most of the inhabitants of the Roman Empire would have associated 'gospel' with Roman imperial propaganda and the announcements of such events as the birth of an heir to the emperor, his coming of age and his accession to the throne, as glad tidings or gospels with the emperor cult (Cranfield, I, p. 55).[4] The emperor cult, however, was promoted in the provinces and not in the city of Rome, and the Greek noun for 'gospel' (*euangelion*) and its verb form were also used for good tidings in everyday life and need have no political overtones (Wolter, I, p. 83). Paul distinguishes the one gospel from everyday good news or imperial good news by asserting that it is the gospel from the one God about 'Messiah Jesus'. It is true that the gospel proclaims that Jesus is Lord and King, not Caesar, but it is universally true that the gospel is far more than word of something pleasant, fortunate or otherwise positive. It is news about God's reign that brings eternal salvation.

2. Second, Paul affirms that this gospel was promised beforehand *through his prophets in the holy scriptures* (3:21; 4:3, 6–8; 16:26; cf. Gal.

---

4. Fronto (*Ep.* 4.12) claims that images of the emperor were found 'anywhere and everywhere' so that 'the emperor – especially Augustus' could be called 'the only Empire-wide god in the Roman pantheon'. Cf. Peppard, *Son of God*.

3:8). Three inferences may be drawn from this assertion. (1) God has been faithful to fulfil the promises of old (4:13–25; 15:8). The term 'gospel', as Paul understands it, germinates from the soil of Isaiah (cf. 10:14–16 where Paul cites Isa. 52:7) where the verb form is associated with announcing the good news that God has come (Isa. 40:9), reigns (Isa. 52:7) and brings liberation (Isa. 61:1), and that the nations will proclaim the praise of the Lord (Isa. 60:6). (2) The Scriptures are read correctly only when it is recognized that 'the gospel is the fulfilment, not the negation, of God's word to Israel'.[5] The gospel neither nullifies the law (3:31) nor negates the promises but celebrates their fulfilment. (3) The gospel is not the contrivance of a new religion but the good news heralding that God's promises to Israel and engagement in their history have reached their climax, quite surprisingly, in the crucifixion and resurrection of the Messiah.[6] The message of the cross and resurrection must be understood through the Old Testament 'categories of sacrifice, atonement, suffering, vindication' (cf. 1 Cor. 15:3–4).[7]

3–4. Third, the gospel reveals that God's plan for humanity's salvation centres on his Son, Jesus Christ. Paul's summary of the basic content of the gospel reflects the consensus among believers. Whether Paul adopts or adapts an existing Christian confession, as many contend, is immaterial.[8] Breytenbach asserts: 'Paul cites or alludes to tradition because he agrees to it.'[9] Moo therefore is correct: 'The meaning of these verses ... is to be determined against the background of Paul and his letters, not against a necessarily hypothetical traditions-history' (Moo, pp. 43–44).

The phrase *descended from David according to the flesh* refers to Jesus' genealogical descent as an actual man. The *flesh* in this context has a

---

5. Hays, *Echoes*, p. 34.

6. Beker, *Paul*, p. 341.

7. Barrett, *First Epistle*, pp. 338–339.

8. The deeply entrenched opinion that Paul cites an early confession is refuted by Calhoun, *Paul's Definitions*, pp. 85–142; Poythress, 'Romans 1:3–4'; and Scott, *Adoption*, pp. 221–244. This confession accords with how Luke portrays the gist of Paul's first sermon in Acts 13:33–35.

9. Breytenbach, '"For Us" Phrases', p. 177.

neutral (cf. 4:1; 9:3, 5; 11:14; 1 Cor. 10:18), not a negative, meaning. In the incarnation, Jesus met the Jewish expectation that the Messiah would be David's descendant (cf. 9:5; 15:12, 'the root of Jesse'; 2 Tim. 2:8). His Davidic ancestry confirms God's fidelity in fulfilling the covenant with David (2 Sam. 22:51; Ps. 18:50)[10] and substantiates the fact that the gospel is firmly anchored in Israel's history.

That he was *declared to be Son of God* does not mean that Jesus *became* the Son of God for the first time at his resurrection. The phrase *with power* modifies the title *Son of God* and not the verb *declared*. Before his resurrection he was the Son of God in weakness. The incarnation that reached its climax in the crucifixion veiled his all-powerful lordship (2 Cor. 13:4, 'For he was crucified in weakness'; cf. Acts 2:31–36). The resurrection manifested Jesus' glory and demonstrated that he was the *Son of God with power*.[11] It revealed him to be 'the power of God and the wisdom of God' (1 Cor. 1:24) to whom 'all things' are subjected (1 Cor. 15:20–28). Paul does not understand the gospel to be limited to Jesus' birth and resurrection, which is what many nominal church attenders might assume from making their appearance only at Christmas and Easter. For the sake of brevity, Paul uses a literary device (synecdoche) in which a part of something is substituted for the whole. Jesus' entire life and ministry is encapsulated with the reference to its beginning, birth, and its end, *resurrection*. On 'two axes' of 'flesh' and 'Spirit', Paul 'captures the whole of the Son through his parts'.[12] The middle part of Jesus' life, his ministry and crucifixion, is assumed also to be part of the gospel.

The phrase *spirit of holiness* appears only here in the New Testament and reflects a Hebraic idiom, an adjectival genitive that means 'the Holy Spirit'.[13] Paul is not talking about Jesus' nature or essence

---

10. Cf. also 2 Sam. 7:12–14; Isa. 11:1–5, 10; Jer. 23:5–6; 33:14–16; Ezek. 34:23–24; 37:24–25.

11. Paul does not develop here the idea that as the first raised from the dead (Acts 26:23), Jesus' resurrection makes possible the resurrection of others (1 Cor. 15:21).

12. Calhoun, *Paul's Definitions*, p. 133.

13. Cf. 1QS 3:7; 4:21; 8:16; 9:3; 1QH 7:6–7; 9:32.

but events in his life. The *spirit of holiness* refers to the Holy Spirit 'who raised Christ from the dead' (8:11) after the 'spirit of Satan' killed him with the complicity of the Jewish leaders and the Roman imperial system.

5–6. Since Paul does not mention a co-sender, the plural pronoun *we* refers only to himself as he highlights his singular calling. He understands himself to be especially entrusted with the duty of bringing the gospel to the Gentiles (15:16, 18; Acts 9:15; Gal. 2:7–9). *Grace and apostleship* is a turn of phrase in which the two words express more emphatically the same notion (a hendiadys). As the phrase 'sound and fury' more compellingly expresses the meaning 'furious sound', *grace and apostleship* means 'the grace [or gift] of apostleship'. It more compellingly conveys his conviction that he was set apart by God solely because of God's grace (cf. 1 Cor. 15:9–10; Eph. 3:2, 7–8). God's grace gave him the power and authority that he did not possess on his own to carry out his apostolic ministry. This divine grace is also the authority behind this letter: 'I have written to you rather boldly by way of reminder, because of the grace given me by God' (15:15; cf. 12:3; 1 Cor. 3:10; Gal. 2:9).

The goal of his ministry is to engender the *obedience of faith* among the Gentiles (15:18–20; 16:25–26).[14] This phrase may refer to 'faith' that produces 'obedience' (subjective genitive), but it more likely means 'faith that consists in obedience' as an epexegetical genitive (Cranfield, I, p. 66). It refers to the obedient response to the gospel's call to believe in Christ since faith is only sufficiently evidenced through obedience. Paul believes that God has commissioned him and others to evangelize the whole known world. Obedience is also a vital issue for Paul because, unlike many other religions at the time, the Christian faith is intent on guiding daily behaviour. Therefore, he wants to bring converts to obey from the heart the gospel (6:17, 'the pattern of teaching' they received [NIV]; 10:16–17); the truth (2:8; cf. Gal. 5:7); righteousness

---

14. Paul uses the term *ta ethnē* in Romans to denote 'the Gentiles' rather than 'the nations' in general, with the one exception of 4:17–18 where he refers to the 'many nations'.

(6:16–19); Christ (2 Cor. 10:5); and God (11:30–32). If they obey, it means that they are in a right relationship with God. If they do not, they are destined to experience divine vengeance with fiery flames (2 Thess. 1:8).

Another goal of Paul's preaching to the Gentiles is *for the sake of his name*, for them to 'glorify God for his mercy' (15:9). God intends for his name to be proclaimed 'in all the earth' (9:17), but unfaithful Jews have caused it to be 'blasphemed' among the Gentiles (2:24). He hopes that the obedience of the Gentiles who now receive mercy from God (11:31) will provoke the Jews to jealousy (11:11, 14) and cause them to obey the gospel, receive God's mercy and bring glory to God (11:31–36).

The phrase 'among whom you also are' (NASB) could mean that the audience resides in a city that is a vast, multi-ethnic melting pot. It is more likely that it means that they are predominantly Gentiles (1:13; 11:13).[15] His point is that as he is an apostle to the Gentiles, the Romans fall under the scope of his commission since they belong to *all the Gentiles* to whom he has been sent (11:13–14; Gal. 2:8–9). Jervis comments, 'They are part of his mission not because Paul has chosen them but because God has chosen them for Paul.'[16] Though he had not founded the church, he does not overstep any bounds in writing to them (cf. 15:20–21; 2 Cor. 10:13–16) since they too belong to the nations that he has been graced by God to bring to the obedience of faith.

7. Paul does not identify the recipients as 'the church in Rome' (cf. 16:5; 1 Cor. 1:2; 2 Cor. 1:1; Gal. 1:2; 1 Thess. 1:1) but as *all . . . in Rome* who are differentiated from others as *God's beloved*. He does not identify them as 'Romans' but as those *in Rome* because his audience comprises people from a variety of ethnic and national backgrounds. Identifying them as *beloved* is significant since 'as regards election' Israel is 'beloved, for the sake of their ancestors' (11:28; cf. Deut. 10:15). Regardless of their ethnic heritage, all those who are 'called to belong to Jesus Christ' (1:6) are *also* beloved by

---

15. The phrase 'among whom also' (*en hois kai*) appears in Mark 15:40 and Acts 17:34 and means 'including'.

16. Jervis, *Purpose*, p. 77.

God because of their trusting response to what God has done in Christ. The designation *beloved* points forward to the citation of Hosea 2:23 in 9:25 prophesying the inclusion of Gentiles:

> Those who were not my people I will call 'my people',
> and her who was not beloved I will call 'beloved'.

He then cites Hosea 1:10 in 9:26 that declares,

> And in the very place where it was said to them, 'You are not
>   my people',
> there they shall be called children of the living God.

Paul applies another term, *saints* ('holy ones'), that was used to characterize Israel (cf. Lev. 11:44; 19:2; 20:7, 26) to the believers in Rome. He is 'called to be an apostle', and they are *called to be saints*, consecrated to God. Daniel 7:18, 21–22, 27 and Joel 2:16 provide the background for the idea that they are sanctified as the end-time people who will triumph with God and 'receive the kingdom and possess it forever'.[17] Beloved by God, they are called to be holy, which gives them the task of presenting their 'bodies as a living sacrifice, holy and acceptable to God' (12:1). These affirmations unveil Paul's conviction that, in Christ, former heathens have been grafted into Israel's rich heritage (11:17). In what follows, Paul will unpack how it is that membership in the people of God no longer has anything to do with one's birthright or ethnicity but only the obedient response to God's initiative in Christ. He also will clarify why the gospel is so desperately needed by humanity that is mired in sin, why some in Israel, who had the advantage of receiving 'the oracles of God' (3:2), 'the adoption, the glory, the covenants, the giving of the law, the worship, and the promises' (9:4), are cut off from God, and why Gentiles, the unbeloved (9:25) 'who did not strive for righteousness', have attained 'righteousness through faith' (9:30).

---

17. Oropeza, *Second Corinthians*, p. 54. Cf. also 1 En. 62:8; 100:5; 1QM 3:5; 10:10; 12:7; 1QH 7:10; 1QS 5:18; CD 4:6.

Paul modifies the traditional Greek salutation by changing the Greek *charein* ('greetings'; cf. Acts 15:23; 23:26; Jas 1:1) to the similar-sounding *charis* (*grace*) and adding the Semitic *peace*. Grace through Christ is God's response to sin (5:20). It results in peace between God and reconciled sinners, and peace of mind (8:6) in the security of God's acceptance. It also results in peace in their midst because they are cemented together by their common bond to *our Father and the Lord Jesus Christ*. The reference to peace is particularly pointed in a letter to Romans. Augustus's rise to power put an end to civil war and bloodshed by establishing a military dictatorship. 'Peace' became a prominent propaganda mantra: Caesar as peacemaker.[18] When Nero came to power, he seemed to have no ambition to establish himself by achieving military victories, and many who continued to long for peace thought he would bring a new age of universal peace and the end of all wars. His reign did not turn out the way people hoped, which only confirms that humans apart from God do not know the ways of peace (3:17; cf. Isa. 59:7–8). How different the peace of God is (5:1–11; 8:6; 15:13, 33; 16:20). The Romans talked about peace. In contrast to military kingdoms that reign through terror, injustice and oppression, God's kingdom brings the reality of 'righteousness and peace and joy in the Holy Spirit' (14:17).

Theology

The letter opening asserts that Paul has been called to serve a higher cause under the highest authority, Jesus Christ our Lord, who is mentioned four times in 1:1–7. That Paul puts God and Christ side by side in his greeting in 1:7 manifests his belief in Christ's full divinity. No Jew would send greetings from God and Moses. The confession about Christ in 1:3–4, however, is the theological epicentre of this opening. In the recent history of the interpretation of these verses, the focus has fallen on the attempt to reconstruct the Christology of the early confession that Paul presumably cites. It is argued that the adoptionist tenor of the text is a fossil of the early church's lower Christology that later developed

---

18. Rock, *Paul's Letter*, pp. 177–182.

into a higher Christology: the earthly Son of David became the heavenly Son of God only at the resurrection.[19]

This interpretation is mistaken. If Paul cites this piece of liturgical confession to summarize his gospel, he must concur with it. He would not have understood it to convey the idea that Jesus was elevated to Son of God at his resurrection. Had 'Son of David' been intended to be antithetical to 'Son of God', 'we would have expected the particle *de* ['but'], which usually implies contrast'.[20] Instead, the two titles are not antithetical but complementary. Paul declares that God sent 'his Son, born of a woman, born under the law' (Gal. 4:4), and he does not envision a time when Jesus was not God's Son. Why then would the Son be appointed Son? The summary of the gospel reaches the high point with the declaration that the Son is 'Jesus Christ our Lord'. It accords with the implication of Jesus' challenge in Mark 12:35-37 that he is more than the son of David; he is also David's Lord. The confession for Paul means that Jesus who comes from David's stock is not simply the Messiah of Israel but has a status as Lord over the entire universe that transcends earthly history. This interpretation matches the trajectory more poetically rendered in Philippians 2:6-11.

While the confession is primarily describing a two-stage progression in the manifestation of Jesus as the Son of God, the explanation of the patristic interpreters should not be ignored. The Church Fathers used this passage to legitimate the two natures of Christ but mainly to reinforce the real humanity of Christ.[21] This reading remains valid in that Jesus' Davidic descent does affirm his humanity, a theme that surfaces in 8:3: God sent his Son 'in the likeness of sinful flesh'. The pre-existent Son of God entered fleshly existence so that God might condemn 'sin in the flesh' – the frail, corrupted nature of Adamic humanity – and accomplish redemption. In the next stage, Christ became the prototype for the resurrection

---

19. Bauckham, *God Crucified*; Hengel, 'Christological Titles'; and Hurtado, *Lord Jesus Christ*, document the church's high Christology from early on.

20. Hurtado, 'Jesus' Divine Sonship', p. 227.

21. Jipp, 'Ancient, Modern, and Future', pp. 241-259.

when the Spirit raised his mortal body from the dead (8:11). The difference is that when he was raised by God he was also enthroned to share God's rule, which is expressed by the image of him sitting at God's right hand (8:34). God's promise to David to 'raise up your offspring after you' (2 Sam. 7:12) is given a new interpretation. It does not refer to David's heirs coming into existence and reigning but to the singular event of Jesus' resurrection. In these opening verses, Paul previews these two vital soteriological features that are developed in chapter 8.[22] Paul's apostolic calling to take the gospel to the Gentiles is embedded in this Christological confession with Davidic roots:

I will make the nations your heritage,
    and the ends of the earth your possession.
(Ps. 2:8)

It matches Paul's citation from Isaiah 11:10 in 15:12:

The root of Jesse shall come,
    the one who rises to rule the Gentiles;
in him the Gentiles shall hope.[23]

B. Thanksgiving and Paul's indebtedness to preach the gospel (1:8–15)

Context
Paul's letters normally contain a formal expression of thanksgiving. As does the salutation, this thanksgiving section differs from those in his other letters. It contains only a brief, rather generic note of thanks (1:8). He does not focus on the recipients of the letter and what he prays God will accomplish for them, as he does in other letters where he knows well his audience and their situation. Instead, he addresses only what he prayed God would do for him.

22. Ibid., pp. 256–257.
23. Jipp, *Christ Is King*, p. 178.

He draws attention to his enduring wish to come to Rome, hindrances that have prevented him from doing so thus far, the scope of his mission and his indebtedness to preach the gospel to Greeks and barbarians. Since the thanksgiving section provides an abstract of the contents and purpose of the letter, it hints at the letter's primary purpose to pave the way for a future visit. With three explanatory remarks he justifies and enlarges on this purpose, which may be outlined as follows (adapted from Byrne, p. 48):

1. Thanksgiving: their faith is proclaimed throughout the world (1:8).
2. Intention: Paul's constant prayer that he might succeed by God's will in coming to them (1:9-10). Reason: to strengthen them and to impart some spiritual gift so that they may be mutually encouraged by their trust in one another (language from the arena of business relationships; 1:11-12).
3. Past intention: Paul's abiding but thwarted ambition to visit them (1:13a). Reason: to reap some harvest among them as he has done among the rest of the Gentiles to whom he is indebted to preach the gospel (1:13b-14).
4. Reiteration of his past intention: his eagerness to preach the gospel also to those who are in Rome (1:15). Reason: because of the gospel's power that reveals God's righteousness that saves both Jew and Greek through faith (1:16-17).

After the cursory thanksgiving in 1:8, Paul seeks to capture the goodwill of an audience he has not met in person and cause them to be kindly disposed to what follows (*captatio benevolentiae*). He broaches the subject of his prospective visit to Rome that will fulfil a long-held desire but postpones until the close of the letter his hopes of securing their support for a mission to Spain when he finally does arrive in Rome (15:14-32). He lays the groundwork for this visit, however, by explaining his indebtedness to preach the gospel to all. He then gives a brief statement about the powerful effect of the gospel that saves everyone who has faith. The statements in 1:3-4 and 1:16-17 about the gospel express the theme of the letter. The gospel is the medium by which word of God's righteous regime will reach all peoples throughout the world. Faith responds to hearing the gospel preached (10:13–17). Its matchless power has driven Paul to proclaim the gospel among the Gentiles throughout the East and drives him to want to proclaim the gospel in Rome and beyond.

Comment

8. That Paul begins with *first* does not mean he intends a 'second'. It basically means 'Let me begin' (NEB). This thanksgiving is not as fulsome as those written to churches that he founded and tended (cf. Phil. 1:3–11; 1 Thess. 1:2–10). That Paul gives thanks for *all* of them in Rome suggests that he has 'no quarrel with anyone in the community' (Kruse, p. 59). There is no hint that he writes to address problems among the Romans that he may have heard about. He salutes them because others have spread word of their faith *throughout the world* (cf. 16:19). Paul employs hyperbole because those in Spain have not yet heard the gospel, but it gives evidence of the gospel's unstoppable power to expand throughout the world. Believers elsewhere can take heart that the faith has taken root in the very capital of the Roman Empire.

9–10. Paul appeals to God as his witness, since God knows his internal thoughts, that he constantly remembers them in his prayers. This statement also reiterates the fact that he serves God. The word translated *serve* (*latreuō*) is connected to worshipping in 1:25 (cf. Phil. 3:3). The use of the cognate noun *latreia* in 12:1 reveals that any ritual understanding of worship has been modified so that the believers' daily lives in giving themselves completely over to God are understood as a sacrificial offering (12:1–2). Paul serves God with his whole being, and serving God *with [in] my spirit* is probably a reference to his prayer life (cf. Luke 2:37), 'the inward side of his apostolic service contrasted with the outward side consisting of his preaching' (Cranfield, I, p. 77).

He twice attests that he has long wanted to come to them but has not as yet succeeded. God directs his mission agenda (cf. Acts 16:7–10), hence his prayers that God might open the way for him to come to Rome. In 15:20–22, he explains that his work in proclaiming the gospel in the eastern regions where Christ has not been named has prevented him from venturing to Rome. He writes that he is now ready to head west, and that also means west of Rome.

It is noteworthy that Paul connects these verses to his thanksgiving with the use of *for*. The Romans' faith is proclaimed throughout the world, but parts of the world have yet to hear the gospel. A subtext underlies this thanksgiving. If they will support his intended mission to Spain (15:24), the Christian faith and the renown of their faith will extend even further.

11–12. *Longing to see you* is the language of friendship and signifies Paul's desire to solidify a friendship that he implies already exists. Paul's expectation that sharing some spiritual gift with them will serve to *strengthen* them may hint that the church suffers afflictions for its faith. The same verb appears in the Thessalonian correspondence in the context of bracing the church to face bitter persecution (1 Thess. 3:2, 13; 2 Thess. 2:17; 3:5; cf. 1 Pet. 5:10). Paul does not specify the spiritual gift he might impart, but it certainly involves 'ministering', 'teaching' and 'exhortation', gifts he lists in 12:6–8. He also would expect that 'my gospel' (2:16), which he expounds in this letter, will strengthen the Roman believers when he comes to them 'in the fullness of the blessing of Christ' (15:29; cf. 16:25). Later, he implies that his preaching from Jerusalem to Illyricum has brought 'spiritual blessings' to the Gentiles (15:19, 27).

Paul seems to back-pedal by stating his expectation that they will be mutually encouraged by each other's faith. He is not worried that he might have sounded presumptuous or patronizing. He does not wish to imply that they are hampered by some deficiency in their faith but recognizes that successful ministry is not a one-way street. He wishes to come alongside them, knowing that ultimately God is responsible for strengthening them through his gospel (16:25). Paul's extensive list of persons in 16:1–23 testifies to his belief in the reciprocity between the minister and those with whom he or she ministers. DeSilva translates it, 'to be mutually encouraged by our faith in [or trust in, or faithfulness toward] one another', in which 'faith' refers to 'trust or reliability in a business partnership'.[24]

---

24. DeSilva, *Introduction*, p. 602 n. 11.

While the faith of believers inspires and buttresses the faith of other believers, Paul is making another point. He hints at his anticipation of forming a partnership with them (cf. Phil. 1:5; 4:15–16). In the Graeco–Roman world, gifts 'entail the expectation and obligation of return'.[25] Paul assumes from a policy Jesus instituted that sowing spiritual gifts should reap material benefits from the recipients, though he makes no use of the right (1 Cor. 9:11–14). He is confident, however, that in return for the spiritual gift he shares with them (cf. 15:27) they will see fit to offer him 'tactical and logistical support' for his mission to Spain (15:24; Jewett, p. 130).

13. Driven by the divine necessity compelling him to preach the gospel to the Gentiles (1 Cor. 9:16; Gal. 1:16), Paul had intended to come to Rome to *reap some harvest among you* (literally, 'that I might have some fruit in you', ASV), that is, conversions from his missionary preaching (Col. 1:6), as he had elsewhere among the Gentiles. His original intentions, however, were derailed. Stuhlmacher asserts, 'This verse in no way indicates that Paul is still intending to come as a missionary to preach the gospel in Rome.'[26] Paul states unequivocally that his goal is 'to proclaim the good news, not where Christ has already been named, so that I do not build on someone else's foundation' (15:20). His sights are set elsewhere, and he only wants to assure the Roman believers that he has not deliberately ignored them.

He expects a different kind of *harvest* (fruit) from his future visit. The Greek word translated as *harvest* ('fruit', *karpos*) appears in 15:28. It is translated there as 'what has been collected' to refer to the financial contribution from Gentile churches that he will deliver to the poor among the saints in Jerusalem. In Philippians 4:17, the word refers to the Philippians' gifts towards supporting his missionary work in Thessalonica (Phil. 4:16). If Paul is to preach the gospel in Spain, he will need 'the fruit' of the Romans' material support for this missionary venture, evangelizing 'still unconverted Gentiles in northern Italy, southern Gaul, and the Iberian

---

25. Barclay, *Paul*, p. 63.
26. Stuhlmacher, 'Purpose', p. 237.

Peninsula'.[27] His ultimate goal is to set off for Spain with Rome as the launching platform.

14. *Greeks* and *barbarians*, the 'non-Greeks', along with the *wise*, the intelligentsia who are astute in their own eyes (12:16), and the *foolish*, the coarse and uncultivated, are classifications derived from human evaluations. The Greeks labelled people benighted *barbarians* because of their want of Greek language, culture and education. The onomatopoetic word suggested to Greek ears that their language sounded like stammering gibberish ('bar, bar, bar'). The term has a less derogatory connotation in the New Testament, used to describe those who speak an unfamiliar language (Acts 28:2, 4; 1 Cor. 14:11). Philo, a Greek-educated Jew, even describes the law of Moses as written in the language of 'barbarians', which some felt needed to be translated into Greek (*Mos.* 2.27 [Colson, LCL]). Those who considered themselves innately superior to others, however, applied the term contemptuously to outsiders judged to be 'wild', 'crude', 'fierce' and 'uncivilised'.[28] From a Roman perspective, the Spaniards, whom Paul plans to evangelize, fit both categories of *barbarian* in the negative sense of being *foolish* and as those who speak a language foreign to Greeks (Jewett, pp. 130–132).

15. Paul is always eager to win new converts through the preaching of the gospel and rejoices when others 'dare to speak the word with greater boldness and without fear' (Phil. 1:14). He essentially fulfils his long-held hope to preach the gospel to the Romans by providing them with an advanced instalment of his gospel in this letter.[29]

Theology
The gospel challenges the human predilection to dishonour those who are different in three ways. First, it erases human barometers

---

27. Ibid.

28. H. Windisch, 'βάρβαρος', *TDNT* I, p. 548. Roman evidence examined by Dauge, *Le Barbare*, pp. 472–473, typifies barbarians as 'inhuman, ferocious, arrogant, weak, warlike, discordant . . . unstable', the antithesis of the enlightened Roman (noted by Jewett, p. 131).

29. Dahl, *Studies*, p. 77.

that sort people into castes. All are sinners (3:23); all are without excuse (1:20; 2:1); and God makes foolish all the world's wisdom with its specious labelling of persons (1 Cor. 1:20). Second, the gospel reveals that God is impartial towards all (2:9–11) and has no intention of turning barbarians into Greeks, Gentiles into Jews, or Jews into Gentiles. God's impartiality is the theological grounds for the mission to the Gentiles. Third, Paul's claim to be indebted to preach the gospel to all differentiates him from Greek philosophers who courted only the educated and refined and shunned those regarded as ignorant and stupid (Michel, p. 50).

The gospel lays an obligation upon Paul (1 Cor. 9:16). Instead of saying he is duty-bound to Greeks and barbarians, however, he says he is indebted to them. How could he be indebted to those he has never met and who have given him nothing? As Minear explains it, 'Obligation to him who died [Christ] produces obligation to those for whom he died.'[30] That obligation imposes a duty on all Christians, not just Paul. Minear writes: 'Those who belong to Christ are debtors whose every act of obedience is an expression of an obligation which simultaneously includes the Lord and those whom the Lord has welcomed.'[31] The Roman Christians are no less indebted to those they might be tempted to dismiss as 'foolish' and 'barbarians'.

C. Theme statement: the gospel as the revelation of God's righteousness (1:16–17)

Context
The word 'for' (*gar*) connects this thesis statement to what precedes and starts a chain that explains why Paul fervently wanted to preach the gospel in Rome and why the aim of his pilgrim witness is 'to bring about the obedience of faith among all the Gentiles' (1:5). He is not ashamed of the gospel. Why? Because it is 'the power God for salvation to everyone who has faith' (1:16). Why? Because the gospel reveals God's righteousness and progresses 'from faith to

---

30. Minear, *Obedience*, p. 104.
31. Ibid., p. 105.

faith' (CSB). The gospel does not simply deliver information about God; it saves those who respond in faith and gives them life.

Comment

16. Paul's declaration that he is not ashamed of the gospel is not an ironic understatement in which he expresses an affirmation through a negative statement (litotes). He does not mean, 'I am mighty proud of the gospel' (contra Jewett, p. 136). The expression *I am not ashamed* makes an assertion about something that is contrary to prevailing standards and values (Wolter, I, pp. 114–115).[32] The gospel proclaims that a man who suffered crucifixion, the most shameful of deaths, was raised and exalted by God. This message is 'a stumbling-block to Jews and foolishness to Gentiles' (1 Cor. 1:23) because it turns human wisdom upside down. Jews might be chagrined by how this gospel seems to nullify Israel's priority and sacred institutions and to scatter God's grace indiscriminately among other supposedly less-deserving nations.[33] Gentile believers then displace the disobedient in Israel instead of Israel triumphing over Gentiles. To Gentiles, the gospel represents the quintessence of foolishness and weakness. Jewett comments,

> A divine self-revelation on an obscene cross seemed to demean God and overlook the honor and propriety of established religious traditions, both Jewish and Greco-Roman. Rather than appealing to the honorable and righteous members of society, such a gospel seemed designed to appeal to the despised and the powerless . . . There were powerful, social reasons why Paul should have been ashamed of this gospel; his claim not to be ashamed signals that a social and ideological revolution has been inaugurated by the gospel.
> (Jewett, p. 137)

He goes on: it 'shatters the unrighteous precedence given to the strong over the weak, the free and well-educated over the slaves

---

32. Cf. Plato, *Prot.* 341b. It does not imply that Jewish Christian critics of his gospel have put him on the defensive.

33. Watts, 'Not Ashamed', pp. 22–23.

and ill-educated, the Greeks and Romans over the barbarians' (Jewett, p. 139). It makes the preacher seem contemptibly weak (1 Cor. 4:9–11), submitting to the mortification of being clapped in chains (2 Tim. 1:8, 12, 16; 1 Pet. 4:16). The gospel radically transforms the meaning of honour and shame as it was understood in the ancient world. The only honour that matters is the honour that God ascribes to humans according to canons completely foreign to human standards. If Paul does not allude to a saying of Jesus (Mark 8:38), his words resonate with it. Not being ashamed of the gospel guards against the more calamitous fate of being put to shame before God at the end of the age (Mark 8:38; Luke 9:26).

The verb *aischynō* can also mean being put to shame for pinning one's hope on the wrong things. Paul's citation of Isaiah 28:16 in 9:33, 'See, I am laying in Zion a stone that will make people stumble, a rock that will make them fall, / and whoever believes in him will not be put to shame', has a compound form of the verb 'to be disappointed', 'to be put to shame' (*kataischynein*), to refer to the let-down that puts one to shame when one's faith and hope are shown to be misplaced (cf. 10:11; 1 Pet. 2:6). He affirms in this verse his conviction that the gospel is not a mirage and that the hope it offers will not 'disappoint' (*kataischynei*, 5:5). Therefore, devoting his life to proclaiming the gospel will not be for naught because divine power infuses it (2 Cor. 4:7; 1 Thess. 1:5) and has produced his ministry success (15:19). In the context of his mission objectives introduced in this section, not being ashamed of the gospel also characterizes his conviction that it will ultimately triumph over all the seen and unseen powers of this world that afflict human existence (8:38).

In these opening verses, Paul provides a supplementary defin-ition of the gospel.[34] In 1:3–4, he describes what it is. It is the fulfilment of what God promised in the Scriptures concerning his Son. In 1:16–17, he describes what it does. It is God's power for salvation (1 Cor. 1:18; 2:5) and reveals God's righteousness. This additional definition discloses the fact that the gospel is more than a plan of salvation but is a power that brings about salvation. In the rest of the letter, he reveals that salvation encompasses being

---

34. As argued by Calhoun, *Paul's Definitions*.

rescued from the wrath of God (5:9), being delivered from the dominion of sin (6:1–14), living in the Spirit (8:9) that will culminate in an acquittal in the divine law court (8:1), and receiving eternal glory with Christ at the end of the age (13:11).

The statement *to everyone who has faith* has pivotal importance in Romans. Faith in this instance refers to trust in the good news of salvation that God has accomplished in Christ (3:21–31). Paul does not understand faith to be 'a leap in the dark' but 'a deliberate response to the convincing and persuasive light of truth'.[35] It is the diametrical opposite of suppressing the truth about what can be known about God by deliberately choosing to remain in the dark (1:18–19).

The pattern of *to the Jew first and also to the Greek* accords with Jesus' announcement, 'I was sent only to the lost sheep of the house of Israel' (Matt. 15:24; cf. 10:5–6). The gospel had been promised through the Jewish prophets long beforehand (1:2–3), and the Jews have been divinely privileged (9:4–5) and are elect and beloved of God 'for the sake of their ancestors' (11:28). Naturally, the gospel would come to them first. Since anyone can have faith, however, the advantage of the Jews over Gentiles is only 'chronological' (Ziesler, p. 70). Paul's elucidation of the gospel reveals that God shows no favouritism in offering salvation to Jew *and* Greek based on the sole criterion of faith. Paul divides humanity into these two ethnic groups (cf. 1 Cor. 1:22–24; 12:13; Gal. 3:28; Col. 3:11), and the issue of Jew and Greek, circumcised and uncircumcised, emerges as a main theme in the letter (2:9–11; 3:9, 29–30; 4:9–18; 9:23–33; 10:12; 11:17–32). Jews and Greeks are also divided into those who are believers and those who are not. The divine power behind the gospel has brought members from both groups together in Christ to become 'saints', 'God's holy people' (1:6–7), who are now identified as 'the church [assembly]' that belongs to God (1 Cor. 10:32). No distinction exists between them in the community of the called, but since they retain their ethnic and cultural differences, give and take is required for navigating their new identity and life together as siblings in Christ (14:1 – 15:7).

---

35. Keener, *Mind of the Spirit*, p. 6 n. 22.

17. What Paul means by the *righteousness of God* is much debated. In Romans, the righteousness of God can be revealed and confirmed (3:5), disclosed and attested (3:21) and shown (3:25), and is something to which one must submit (10:3).

(1) The genitive '*of* God' (*tou theou*) may be interpreted as a genitive of source or origin. It could refer to God's conferral of the status of righteousness on believers as a gift of grace apart from works of the law (cf. 2 Cor. 5:21).[36] In 10:3, Paul contrasts God's righteousness with that which humans seek to attain by their own efforts. Paul's hope of attaining the resurrection of the dead is based on 'not having a righteousness of my own that comes from the law, but one that comes through faith in Christ, the righteousness from God based on faith' (Phil. 3:9). Cranfield argues that this view agrees best with the structure of the epistle's argument: Paul expounds the words 'the one who is righteous by faith' in 1:18 – 4:25 and expounds the promise that 'the one who is righteous by faith will live' in 5:1 – 8:39 (Cranfield, I, pp. 97–98). The problem with this view is that when Paul specifically refers to righteousness conferred by God, as he does in Philippians 3:9, he adds the preposition 'from' (*ek*).

(2) The righteousness of God may be interpreted as a possessive genitive that refers to an aspect of God's nature, God's 'justice' or 'moral integrity' (cf. 3:5).[37] God's righteous character is revealed in God's actions, the salvation of sinners who respond with faith and the retribution against sinners who do not. Some propose that Paul specifically has in mind God's fidelity to his covenant promise to Abraham and to Israel. The promises 'focus upon the eschatological gathering of all the nations into the people of God'.[38] God keeps his promise to Abraham by making all those who believe, both Jews and Greeks, children of Abraham, children of God and joint heirs with Christ (8:16–17). This interpretation is supported by the congruence of the phrase 'the justice [righteousness] of God' (3:5) with 'the faithfulness of God' (3:3) and 'God's truthfulness'

36. Irons, *Righteousness*, most recently defends this view.

37. Keck, *Paul*, p. 117.

38. Williams, 'Righteousness', p. 270.

(3:7). Seifrid shows, however, that the words 'justice [righteousness]' and 'covenant' seldom appear together in the Old Testament.[39]

(3) The righteousness of God may be a subjective genitive in which God is the subject of the verbal idea. Jewett argues that the passive voice of the verb *is revealed*

> assumes that God is the agent behind this revelation of his righteousness. It does not simply refer to one of God's attributes but designates God's redemptive action that saves those who have faith, establishes new communities of faith, and ultimately will restore the whole creation.
>
> (Jewett, p. 142)

In the Hebraic tradition, the phrase refers to God's saving activity in history (cf. Ps. 98:1–2).[40] The missional context makes this reading most likely. It also mates well with 'the power of God' (1:16) and the 'wrath of God' (1:18), which are both subjective genitives. As the wrath of God is 'revealed' (1:18) in what God does (1:24, 26, 28), it follows that the righteousness of God is also 'revealed' in what God does. God does justice on the earth because God is just; as Paul says in 3:26, he is both 'just' and 'justifier' (ASV). On the other hand, Paul may not have intended to limit the meaning of the phrase to only one aspect but deliberately chosen to be imprecise. God's righteousness in the Old Testament

> can denote God's character as that of a God who will always do what is right, God's activity of establishing right, and even, as a product of this activity, the state of those who have been, or hope to be, put right.
>
> (Moo, p. 92)

God is righteous, acts righteously in relationships, and deigns to bestow a righteous standing on humans.

The phrase 'from faith to faith' (CSB; NRSV, *through faith for faith*) has also prompted multiple interpretations. Many accept the view

---

39. Seifrid, *Justification*, pp. 214–219.
40. Ziesler, *Meaning*, p. 186.

reflected in the translation 'by faith from first to last' (NIV). This interpretation emphasizes the cardinal importance of faith alone and reinforces that faith is the only way God's righteousness is recognized and accepted.[41] The preposition 'from' is understood not as a starting point ('received by faith and leading to greater faith') but as identifying faith as the sole foundation.[42]

Another view recognizes that the idiom 'from something to something' expresses a progression (cf. 2 Cor. 2:16; 3:18). The immediate context that refers to the progression of faith from the Jew first and then to the Gentile suggests that Paul may have in mind the progression of the revelation of God's righteousness from 'the faith of the Old Testament believer to the faith of the New Testament believer'.[43] This interpretation accords with Paul's commentary on Abraham's faith in chapter 4, where he identifies him as 'the ancestor of all who believe without being circumcised and who thus have righteousness reckoned to them' (4:11). The promises were made first to the Jews as God set them apart to be a light to the nations (Isa. 42:6; 49:6; 60:3; Acts 13:47). The gospel then comes to Gentiles through the witness of believing Jews. Once again, it is difficult to limit Paul's meaning to one aspect to the exclusion of all others.[44]

Another view reads the preposition from a theocentric perspective to refer to God's or Christ's faithfulness, to which believers respond with faith.[45] If this interpretation is correct, then

41. 'Faith' appears forty times in the letter; the verb 'to believe/trust', nineteen times.

42. Harris, 'Prepositions', p. 1189.

43. Quarles, 'From Faith to Faith', p. 21.

44. Taylor, 'From Faith to Faith', claims that the Greek idiom *ek* ('from') + an abstract noun + *eis* ('to') + an abstract noun denotes either progression or increase, and that it reflects Paul's enthusiastic description of the increasing number of believers in the Gentile world.

45. Campbell, 'Romans 1:17', p. 281, contends that Paul refers to the 'faithful obedience of Christ through Calvary that revealed God's salvation and also created the possibility of individual salvation through belief and perseverance until the eschaton'.

Paul could have made it clearer by citing the Septuagint rendering of Habakkuk 2:4, 'The one who is righteous will live by my
faith [faithfulness]', which includes the pronoun 'my' faith. While
faith in Greek can mean 'faithfulness' and 'trust', one might
expect, for clarity's sake, that Paul has only one meaning in mind
for *faith* in the four references to it in these two verses. That
would be 'human trust'. Paul's emphasis on revelation sounded in
verse 17, however, has too often been ignored. Mininger contends
that Paul 'describes how God's own attribute of righteousness
(content) is presently revealed in the gospel (location), which is
more likely to be understood as coming about from divine
faithfulness (source) to human faith (destination)'.[46] Humans may
not know 'the mind of' God (11:34) from their own resources, but
God has revealed in history 'the depth' of his 'riches and wisdom
and knowledge' and his 'unsearchable' judgments and 'inscrutable'
ways (11:33) in the gospel. Humans can respond to 'the power of
God for salvation' (1:16) only with faith. That this compressed
phrase refers to God's faithfulness to which humans respond
with faith is confirmed by the letter's opening in verses 1–7. Paul
moves from God's faithfulness in fulfilling the gospel, 'which he
promised beforehand through his prophets in the holy scriptures'
(1:1–2), to human response, 'the obedience of faith among all the
Gentiles' (1:5).

Paul cites Habakkuk 2:4 to confirm the truth of this statement
from the Scripture. He cited this passage in Galatians 3:11 in the
context of his assertion that Abraham 'believed God, and it was
reckoned to him as righteousness' (Gal. 3:6). Does Paul intend the
phrase *by faith* to be taken adjectivally, modifying persons as *righteous*, or adverbially, describing how righteous persons *will live*? The
first option is represented by the RSV: 'He who through faith is
righteous shall live'; the second, by the NRSV: 'The one who is righteous will live by faith.' The context leads one to expect the citation
to substantiate that one can conform to God's righteous standards
and come into a right relationship with God only through faith.
Paul says this explicitly in 5:1: 'we are justified [made righteous] by

---

46. Mininger, *Uncovering*, p. 61.

faith'.[47] The first option tallies with the central argument of Galatians. One cannot get right with God based on obedience to the law (Gal. 2:16; 3:11) since the law imparts neither life nor righteousness (Gal. 3:21). As Gentiles 'receive the promise of the Spirit through faith' (Gal. 3:14), so Gentiles are justified 'by faith' (Gal. 3:8). Paul makes this same point in Romans 4:13–16. Interpreters may be trying to draw too fine a distinction in trying to narrow Paul's meaning (Dunn, I, pp. 45–46). Schreiner asserts, '"To be righteous by faith" and "to live by faith" are alternate ways of expressing the same reality' (Schreiner, p. 82).

Will live may refer to receiving 'eternal life' and being delivered from God's wrath. That requires that the righteous live differently from those who are subjected to God's wrath and 'deserve to die' (1:18–32). Being justified by faith is not the end of the story. Faith is also to govern one's continuing life, as the ethical exhortations in 6:1–21 and 12:1–15 make clear.

Theology

The noun 'righteousness' occurs thirty-four times in Romans, its verbal cognate 'to justify' occurs fifteen times, and the adjective 'righteous' occurs seven times. Kruse helpfully identifies five different aspects of Paul's references to the righteousness of God in Romans. Paul uses it (1) to speak of God's *'distributive justice'* by which 'God recompenses humanity in accordance with its response to his revelation' (1:18–32; 2:2–11; 3:1–20); (2) to defend God's *'covenant faithfulness'* (3:3–9; 9:1–29; 11:1–10); (3) to expound on God's *'saving action'* in providing redemption through Christ's sacrificial death (3:21–26); (4) to expound on it as God's 'gift *of justification and a right relationship with himself'* (4:1–25; 5:17; 9:30 – 10:4); and (5) to explain how that gift 'leads to *righteousness of life* in believers' (6:1–23; 8:4) (Kruse, pp. 79–80). Kruse contends, 'All these aspects of God's

---

47. It is less likely that Paul understands this passage to be a messianic prophecy and that the 'righteous one' refers to Christ. 'Righteous one' is used as a title for Christ in Acts 3:14; 7:52; 22:14; 1 Pet. 3:18; 1 John 2:1, but never by Paul, and nothing in the context points to this meaning.

righteousness can be included under the one umbrella of *God acting in accordance with his own nature for the sake of his name*' (Kruse, p. 80 [all emphasis original]). In the context of 1:17, it seems most likely that Paul has in mind two of these aspects, which are expressed most clearly in 3:25–26, namely, 'God's saving action in Christ whereby he brings people into a right relationship with himself' (Kruse, p. 81). The gospel and the response to it reveal God's righteousness that produces salvation, faith, life, and the elimination of the chasm between Jew and Greek. Bird masterfully manages to include the whole spectrum of views in his conclusion:

> The righteousness of God signified the fidelity and justice of God's character, the demonstration of his character as the judge of all the earth, and his faithfulness toward Israel in Jesus Christ. The righteousness of God, then, is the character of God embodied and enacted in his saving actions. It is a saving event that is comprehensive, and it involves vivification, justification, and transformation.
> (Bird, p. 43)

Paul will make clear that humans cannot earn credits towards righteousness through obedience to the law. Checking one's righteousness quotient as if it were a credit score manifests a wrong attitude that vitiates any claim to righteousness. Righteousness comes only from God and not from ourselves. Faith confesses one's total inadequacy to attain righteousness on one's own, trusts God's enterprise to provide salvation solely through Christ and accepts a new identity in Christ. Marshall observes,

> Faith alone can penetrate the ultimate paradox of the gospel: that the kingly power of God is manifest in the suffering and death of Jesus on the pagan cross, transforming the cross into a power that is infinitely greater than any human power.[48]

---

48. Marshall, *Faith*, pp. 207–208.

2. HUMANITY'S REBELLION AGAINST GOD THAT ROUSES GOD'S WRATH (1:18 – 3:20)

The thematic statement in 1:16–17 parallels the statements in 3:21–29. God's righteousness 'is revealed' (1:17) and 'has been disclosed' (3:21), and God has acted to bring salvation to all who believe in Christ (1:16; 3:22). These two passages wrap around 1:18 – 3:20, which presents the incriminating evidence of humanity's multiple ways of dishonouring God. Paul indicts the Gentile first (1:18–32) and then the Jew (2:1 – 3:20).

The gospel recounts what Jesus did as the Son of God and chronicles what rebellious humanity did to him (Acts 13:26–39). Preaching the gospel, then, cannot avoid unmasking human unrighteousness that rampages through the world and passes itself off as wisdom. In 1:18 – 3:20, Paul levels the ground by showing that all humans are in a vice-laden, doom-laden situation that cannot avoid God's wrath. Both Gentiles and Jews are without excuse (1:20; 2:1). This registry of universal defiance of God prepares for Paul's disclosure of God's solution to this human wickedness (3:21–31). Those who have faith in Christ are freely justified and live no longer in the shadow of God's wrath that would blot them out, but under God's grace that redeems them in Christ (3:24).

A. God's wrath against pagans who dishonour God (1:18–32)

Context

The opening salvo in Paul's indictment of humanity reveals how pagans have triggered God's wrath through their idolatry. From a Jewish perspective, the Gentiles' sinful rebellion is taken as a given. 'Gentile' and 'sinner' are almost synonymous (Gal. 2:15). Paul does not specifically identify the culprits as Gentiles. His division of humanity into Jew and Greek (1:16) and the resonance of his accusations with traditional Jewish censure of Gentile immorality, however, make it most likely that Gentile sinners are Paul's first target.[1] Hebrew tradition assumes that idolatry – worshipping what is not God, venerating the creation rather than the Creator – is the vice that leads to all vices:

> For the worship of idols not to be named
> is the beginning and cause and end of every evil.
> (Wis. 14:27)

Idolatry is the breeding ground for perverse religious distortions about God, moral depravity and social chaos. Since Israel also lapsed into idolatry in its history, Paul can easily apply to Gentiles the invectives in Scripture levelled against Israel for rejecting the glory of God and provoking God's wrath in handing them over to their stubborn hearts and moral corruption (Pss 81:12; 106:20; Jer. 2:11; Ezek. 8:12; cf. Acts 7:42). Humans have opposed the truth that God made available to them. The emphasis in 1:18–32, however, is not on the human condition but on God's wrathful reaction to human unrighteousness (Schnabel, I, p. 205). God's wrath is provoked by the deliberate despising and perversion of the truth about God that God has made accessible to all (Wis. 13:1–9).

---

1. Paul's arguments have striking parallels with Wis. 11:15; 12:1–11, 24; 13:1 – 14:31.

Comment

18. God's righteousness entails both grace and judgment (cf. 11:22), and God's *wrath* is the judgment side of this righteousness as God's punitive reaction to the evil that manifests itself as impiety towards God and in humans degrading themselves and others. Paul never uses the verb 'to be angry' (*orgizein*) with 'God' as its subject. God's wrath is not the same as the fits of temper so characteristic of the irascible Greek gods who arbitrarily and petulantly punish the ill-starred objects of their fury.[2] Zeus (Jupiter), for example, whose vengeance is visualized by the thunderbolt, was easily roused to anger by petty insults, as were all the gods of Greek mythology. They were known for capriciously inflicting torments on humans.[3] God's wrath differs in that it is directed against wicked actions. The two nouns *ungodliness* and *wickedness* express the same reality in red letters. *All ungodliness and wickedness* includes both Jewish and Gentile ungodliness and wickedness, but Paul starts with what is easiest to verify from a Jewish perspective: the stereotypical sins of Gentiles that occasion God's retribution.

Since God's wrath is revealed *from heaven*, it has inescapable cosmic consequences. The use of the present tense *is revealed* means that it operates within history to punish human corruption and perversions. It is also future in that it will culminate on 'the day of wrath' when God, who has the power to destroy both body and soul in hell (Matt. 10:28; Luke 12:5), will judge and mete out the final punishment (2:5, 16).

19–20. Humanity can infer the invisible God's existence from the created universe (Acts 14:17) because, as Paul asserts, God purposefully has made *plain* his existence (cf. Job 12:7–9; Ps. 19:1).

---

2. This divine fury is manifest in the opening invocation of Homer's *Iliad* 1.1.

3. H. Kleinknecht, 'ὀργή', *TDNT* V, p. 390, notes that the divine wrath (*ira deum*) that falls on those who despise the gods was well established in Roman cults and myths and their understanding of their history (Livy, *History of Rome* 2.36.5; 9.29.11; Tacitus, *Ann.* 14.22). The Old Testament also is filled with manifestations of God's wrath upon Israel, reflections on its motives and counsel on how to turn it aside.

The implication is that humans can see the fingerprints of the Creator's majesty and matchless power from the grandeur of creation even without direct revelation. Such evidence does not provide a saving knowledge of God, however. Reason and observations from nature may reveal that God exists, but they lead only to a fuzzy and incoherent understanding of God's essence. Paul understands that persons can fully see God only in Christ, who is 'the image of the invisible God' through whom 'all things in heaven and on earth were created' (Col. 1:15–16). He asserts, however, that God's *eternal power and divine nature* are knowable to anyone from mere glances at creation because God has willed it and has given humans the capacity to make sense of them. Paul has no interest in unpacking how God is disclosed in creation. Instead, he makes the case that humans wilfully disregard what they know of God from creation.[4] To be sure, they may gawk in wonder at creation, but they refuse to glorify, obey and give thanks to the Creator. They substitute the glory of God for something they have fabricated and deified, and they bow down to their own artifices.

Calvin's statement that the human mind is 'a perpetual factory of idols' is apropos. He asserts,

> Man's mind, full as it is of pride and boldness, dares to imagine a god according to its own capacity; as it sluggishly plods, indeed is overwhelmed with the crassest ignorance, it conceives an unreality and an empty appearance as God.[5]

By fashioning idols and concocting divine myths to prop them up, humans concede that a greater power exists beyond themselves. They prefer, however, the counterfeit gods of their own devising that might smile upon their delusions that they are the centre of the universe. The problem, then, is not their lack of knowledge of God, but their failure to acknowledge God (Edwards, p. 47). Humans wilfully reject God's claim on their lives and twist what they know of God into beggarly falsehoods. Paul will contend also that 'the

---

4. Bornkamm, *Early Christian Experience*, p. 59.
5. Calvin, *Institutes*, 1.11.8 (I, p. 108).

righteousness of God has been disclosed [made plain], and is attested by the law and the prophets' (3:21) and that his 'gospel' (16:25) 'is now disclosed [made plain], and through the prophetic writings is made known to all the Gentiles, according to the command of the eternal God, to bring about the obedience of faith' (16:26). The rejection of the righteousness of God that is made evident in the gospel also provokes God's wrath.

21–22. The awareness of God, however embryonic it might be, has not led to honouring or giving thanks to God. Paul focuses on this refusal to return thanks and to give glory to God and the predisposition to turn up their noses at God's wisdom and benevolence as humanity's deeply rooted sin. As Jesus was unhappy about the healed but ungrateful lepers (Luke 17:11–19), God is unhappy with humans' lack of appreciation for the manifold blessings in creation. Ingratitude causes them to tumble further into the darkness. Gundry notes, 'Such thanksgiving would have kept them from deifying themselves and those other creatures in the form of ridiculous images.'[6] It would also have kept them from exalting their own empty wisdom and helped them to recognize that 'the wisdom of this world is foolishness with God' (1 Cor. 3:19). Because they are self-confident in their idolatry and wise in their own eyes (cf. 1 Cor. 1:21), their concepts of God and their philosophies are not simply partial, they are utterly wrong from beginning to end.

When humans mutiny against the known Lord of creation, dark shadows drape their minds, giving rise to unbridled wickedness. In the verses that follow Paul gives three examples of offences that precipitate God handing the wrongdoers over to their sins, with its ravaging consequences. Exchanging the glory of the immortal God for idols (1:23) results in God delivering them to impurity and the degradation of their bodies (1:24). Exchanging the truth of God for a lie (1:25) results in God delivering them to sexual perversions (1:26–27). Refusing to acknowledge God in their moral decision-making results in God delivering them to a vice-prone mind and ensuing social bedlam (1:28–31).

---

6. Gundry, *Commentary*, p. 575.

23. The verb *exchanged* (*allassō/metallassō*) is repeated three times (1:23, 25, 26) and designates 'perversions of the God-given possibilities of life' (Schnabel, I, p. 200, author's translation). People prefer idols that nurture their hearts' cravings instead of the true, living God who confutes them as leading to utter futility. The plethora of idols in Paul's world, where people paid homage to all manner of false gods and godlings, fetishes, charms, superstitions and ideologies, illustrates his point. They traded the immortal God for counterfeit images of mortal beings, including fowls of the air, grass-eating, cud-chewing bovines, and crawling reptiles. Ironically, humans created in the image of God worship images of creatures over which God intended them to have dominion (Gen. 1:26). The Romans believed in many spirits that presided over various but limited spheres of activity and had 'no existence apart from that operation'.[7] Worshippers would utilize a kind of organizational flow chart for the various gods to discern which ones had charge of what they desired to get, and then venerate them to get it. Harrington observes,

> The Greeks and Romans had no commitment to a particular belief system or even to any particular one of the gods. Multiple shrines could be attended by the same individual. Even the mystery cults allowed continuing devotion to one or another of the other cults . . . it was common belief that many powers existed in the world.[8]

Refashioning God into a pantheon of deities may have seemed to give them more control over the divine, but they created a hellish host of powers that only enslaved them (cf. Gal. 4:8).

Idolatry seems to be endemic to the human species, but it was pandemic among the Greeks (cf. Acts 17:16). Those familiar with Scripture, replete with its scorn for idolatry (cf. Ps. 106:20; Isa. 44:9–20), would know that Paul's imagery draws on Jewish history that was also riddled with idolatrous phases (Deut. 4:16–20; 2 Kgs 17:15; Ps. 106:20; Jer. 2:5, 11; Wis. 13:1). They would also know that

---

7. Ferguson, *Religions*, p. 68.
8. Harrington, *Holiness*, p. 24.

God does not tolerate idolatry and punishes it severely (cf. Exod. 32:31–35).

24. God does not sit passively by, frowning on sin. The phrase *God gave them up* (or 'delivered them over') is repeated three times to describe God's reaction. The meaning of this verb in this context lends itself to three interpretations. (1) God leaves them to themselves and allows the toxic repercussions of their sin to cause them to self-destruct, in effect, 'to stew in [their] own juice' (Fitzmyer, p. 272). (2) God does not restrain the evil consequences of their actions but abandons them to their fate: 'God is simply letting happen what their own choices have set in motion' (Johnson, p. 35). If one chooses chaos for one's life, God allows it to work itself out. (3) In a deliberate act of judgment, God delivers people over to be punished (cf. Acts 7:42; 1 Tim. 1:20).[9] God hands them over to passions that are never satiated, and they dishonour their bodies with their shameful, self-degrading conduct. All three interpretations bear elements of the truth and need not be mutually exclusive. The multiple uses of the verb in the LXX for God handing Israel over to the hands of their enemies to punish them for their transgressions (*paradidōmi*; cf. Lev. 26:25; Judg. 2:14; 2 Chr. 6:36; Ps. 105:40–41 [LXX]; Mic. 6:16), as well as punishing the wicked nations (Isa. 34:2), argue for this last meaning as primary.

The genitive articular infinitive *to the degrading of their bodies among themselves* may convey either purpose ('in order that') or result ('with the result that'), or, more likely, it clarifies the nature of the 'impurity' or 'uncleanness' as sexual.[10] They become consumed with lustful passion (cf. 1 Thess. 4:5) that knows no restraint. In worshipping the unlimited indulgence of sexual desires, they become like that which they worship, hollow replicas of what God intended humans to be.

25. Paul restates what he says in 1:23 for emphasis. Revering the creature rather than the Creator makes something that is finite something that is absolute. Paul, by contrast, can hardly mention the Creator without breaking into doxology (cf. Ps. 106:48). Doxology

---

9. Johnson, 'God Gave Them Up', pp. 126–129.
10. Cf. 2 Cor. 12:21; Gal. 5:19; Eph. 5:3; Col. 3:5.

affirms that we rely solely on God, who determines what we must hope for, what we must fear and how we must live. Barrett comments,

> The immediate result of this rebellion was a state of corruption
> in which men were no longer capable of distinguishing between
> themselves and God, and accordingly fell into idolatry, behind which,
> in all its forms, lies in the last resort the idolization of the self.
> (Barrett, p. 37)

26. God's reaction, handing them over to *degrading passions*, is not capricious but a righteous judgment. The phrase 'for indeed' (*te gar*) before *their women* is often left out of English translations, but it introduces what Paul considers to be appalling examples of degrading passions and concrete evidence that a culture that worships idols ruptures the created order. He is not specific about what females are doing. The parallel with what males are doing, having sexual relations with other males ('and in the same way', 1:27), suggests that females engage in a similar reversal of natural sexual roles. In both verses, Paul uses the nouns 'females' (*thēleiai*) and 'males' (*arsenes*) rather than 'women' and 'men', which is a deliberate allusion to the creation account in Genesis 1:27, 'male and female he created them'. *Natural intercourse* is assumed to be intercourse between a male and a female, and *unnatural* intercourse is between female and female or male and male. *Natural* refers to what Paul considers to be visibly obvious from human anatomy: that males and females were created with differentiated sexual organs that complement one another to make procreation possible. *Unnatural* or 'contrary to nature' (ESV) refers to using the sexual organs in ways that conflict with 'the anatomical and procreative complementarity of male and female'.[11]

Paul's use of the verbs *exchanged* and 'giving up' in 1:27 assumes that they chose same-sex partners of their own volition. He regards this same-sex object choice as another manifestation of human idolatry and a perversion of God's intention evident in the created order. He reflects the Jewish tradition that viewed homosexual

---

11. Gagnon, *Homosexual Practice*, p. 254; cf. Plato, *Leg.* 636 a–c.

practices as a clear example of the shameful consequences of suppressing God's truth.[12]

27. While heterosexual relationships can also be marred by shameless acts, those sins are denounced elsewhere in Paul's letters. Here, he zeroes in on the way male same-sex object choice 'runs counter to the way God has designed human sexuality'.[13] Paul's reference to nature, *natural intercourse*, does not refer to an individual's nature but to God's established order of creation. Same-sex intercourse is 'in essence a misuse of God's creation, whatever the personal inclinations of an individual'.[14] Paul does not limit the *shameless* same-sex acts of males only to certain categories of actions, such as pederasty, male prostitution, homosexual promiscuity, heterosexuals performing same-sex acts or the exploitative abuse of slaves. He applies the term to all male same-sex acts. His point is that perverting the relationship humans are to have with God leads to the perversions of God's intention for human sexual relationships.[15]

The phrase translated 'received in themselves the due penalty for their error' (NIV) interprets the verb 'what was necessary' (*edei*) in the Greek. This penalty is grounded in God's judgment as the warranted punishment for the sin. One pays an unexpectedly high price for rebelling against God's truth. Paul does not believe that humans have an inalienable right to express their sexuality in any way they choose. Their lusts so darken their minds that they are easily seduced into imagining that perversions of the created order are normal and therefore acceptable.

---

12. Cf. Philo, *Spec.* 2.50; 3.37; *Abr.* 26.133–136; Josephus, *Ag. Ap.* 2.199; 2 En. 10:4; 34:2; Ps.-Phoc. 190–192; Sib. Or. 3:185–187, 595–600; T. Naph. 3:1–5.

13. France, 'From Romans', p. 249.

14. Ibid.

15. Jesus alludes to the proverbial unnatural lust of Sodom (cf. 2 Pet. 2:6; Jude 7) in affirming the judgment on them (Gen. 19:1–29), though he uses hyperbole to warn that it will be more tolerable for Sodom on the day of judgment than for those who reject his messengers and the gospel (Matt. 10:14–15; 11:23–24; Luke 10:11–12).

Paul does not specify what they *received in their own persons*. It could refer to sexually transmitted diseases, increased femininity in men (cf. Philo, *Spec.* 3.37), increased mannishness in women, and/or the degradation of the soul that results from committing indecent acts.

28. Paul employs a play on words, which I translate, 'They did not see fit [*edokimasan*] to have God in their knowledge so God gave them up to an unfit [*adokimon*] mind' (cf. Barrett, p. 39). The verb *see fit* is used, for example, for testing coins to see if they ring true or are fake, and for testing persons to see whether they are qualified for an office or not. *Mind* represents 'the sum total of the whole mental and moral state of being' (BDAG, p. 689). Paul says that God was the object of human scrutiny and received a thumbs down. Humans fool themselves, however, if they think that they dispose of God when they try to depose God from the divine throne. The result is an unfit (or *debased*) mind that is so corrupted it can no longer think straight. Because it cannot think straight, it does not properly direct thanks to God (1:21). Because it is not appreciative of God's lordship over creation, its capacity for moral discernment is nil, so that it is rebellious, easily hoodwinked, and prone to causal illusions that block it from being corrected.

29–31. Same-sex acts are the most obvious perversions of the created order that incite God's punishing wrath, but they are not the only sins. God's wrath flames forth against 'all ungodliness and wickedness' (1:18). The inevitable price of trying to have one's way with God is spiritual poverty and social chaos. The broken relationship with God leads to the breakdown of morals and the break-up of society. Paul catalogues examples of the latter in this list of twenty-one vices. Bence summarizes, 'Paul indicates that the unrighteous eventually lose their moral bearings (senseless), their integrity (faithless), their capacity for love (heartless), and their ability to respond to those in need (ruthless)' (Bence, p. 41). In a letter directed to believers in Rome, the vices of being *insolent, haughty, boastful, heartless* and *ruthless* particularly apply to the imperialistic sins of a Roman Empire that deifies itself by deifying its emperors. The indictment, however, applies to all nations. Schlatter concludes, 'The revelation of the divine wrath is evident in a religion that feeds on lies, in a body that is profaned, and in a community in which hatred and war are native' (Schlatter, p. 45).

32. Paul delivers the summary judgment and implicates those who encourage and promote wrongdoing. They know God's decree and admit that those who violate it deserve death. This concession acknowledges that God's wrath is not unjust and that their condemnation is merited. When they applaud or sympathize with those who commit these sins, they are complicit in building a society brimming with vice. Cranfield comments that 'those who condone and applaud the vicious actions of others are actually making a deliberate contribution to the setting up of public opinion favourable to vice, and so to the corruption of an indefinite number of other people' (Cranfield, I, p. 135). Paul's conclusion means, 'The insistence upon the "package deal" by which one must approve another's lifestyle else he is guilty of rejecting the other person will not stand up.'[16]

Theology

Paul's discussion of the wrath of God is not a vestige from the Old Testament that has regrettably slipped into the New Testament that predominantly portrays God as a God of love and grace (cf. 1 John 4:16). Käsemann recognizes that 'God has always exercised his claim to dominion over creation by meeting the disobedient with retribution' (Käsemann, p. 35). God may be kind and forbearing (2:4), but if God were indifferent to evil, God would condone it and would not be righteous. The wrath of God is the inevitable reaction to human rebellion against God and God's purpose in creation. It is 'not God's attitude toward us but the effect which God's holiness has upon those who are against him' (Brunner, p. 167). Humanity's 'No' to God is answered by God's 'No' to them. The gospel reveals both God's righteousness and 'the abysmally deep sinfulness of the world', which, as Paul presents it, is a manifestation of God's wrath that 'points forward to the full manifestation at the end'.[17] Idolatry

---

16. Stagg, 'Plight', p. 406. Nolland, 'Romans 1:26–27', provides a powerful rebuttal to those who would argue that Paul's statements have no relevance for modern Christian sexual ethics or that Paul condemned different kinds of homosexual practices that differ from what moderns might consider acceptable.

17. G. Stählin, 'ὀργή', *TDNT* V, pp. 441–442.

exposes a ruptured relationship with God, who will not be mocked. Sexual sins expose the fractured relationships humans have with others that bring their own deadly repercussions.

Paul does not portray God's wrath as smiting sinners with extraordinary natural events such as pestilence, violent tempests and blazing fires. As a kind of hidden judge (Harrisville, p. 37), God does what seems to be nothing. Sinners are not captive to an impersonal law of the universe, 'an inevitable process of cause and effect in a moral universe', as Dodd contends (p. 23). Nor is 'the principle of retribution built into the structure of God's ordered universe', as Caird asserts.[18] Paul's view accords with that of the Old Testament that the source of wrath is not 'an obscure or indeterminate power, but the personal will of Yahweh with which it is necessary to come to terms'.[19]

Cause and effect coalesce so that the degrading passions, the debased mind and being filled with every kind of wickedness are the punishment (Käsemann, pp. 38, 47). Moral perversion is the result of God's wrath, not simply the reason for it. Dabourne writes, 'God gives the sinners up to what they have made of themselves.'[20] They are punished by the very sins they sin, creating a vicious cycle. This principle is found throughout Jewish literature. Chasing after false idols makes them false in all that they do (2 Kgs 17:15). Worshipping what is worthless makes them worthless (Jer. 2:5). People reap whatever they sow (Gal. 6:7).[21] They also become like the gods they worship. By worshipping the images of beasts, their morals become beastly. Later in Romans, Paul identifies 'Sin' as a power. Paul's picture of the effects of God's wrath

---

18. Caird, *Paul's Letters*, p. 85.

19. J. Fichtner, 'ὀργή', *TDNT* V, p. 397.

20. Dabourne, *Purpose*, p. 194.

21. Cf. Wis. 11:15–16: 'In return for their foolish and wicked thoughts, / which led them astray to worship irrational serpents and worthless animals, / you sent upon them a multitude of irrational creatures to punish them, / so that they might learn that one is punished by the very things by which one sins.' Cf. also Jub. 4:34; T. Gad 5:10; 1QS 4:11; m. 'Abot 4:2.

when humans seek to break free from God shows them handed over to a power that claps them in the irons of bondage that they cannot break by their own strength.

This understanding of God's wrath corrects a common misunderstanding that sin is something to be dreaded only if it is detected. There is no getting away with sin. It is like a cancer that destroys. With cancer, the deadly thing is not its detection but the disease running its course. The problems come when the disease goes undiscovered, and even when it is diagnosed it may be too late. If the rebellion that suppresses God's truth and exchanges it for monstrous lies marches on unchecked, ruination ensues in this life and damnation in the next.

God's wrath is ultimately redemptive in intention. Being under God's wrath is not intended to be an unending condition. It is provisional. The translation 'God gave them up' (1:24, 26, 28) may wrongly imply that God writes them off. The better translation is 'God gave them over' (NIV). While God may 'hate all evildoers' (Ps. 5:5), God does not intend to abandon them for ever. Instead, God allows sinners to go their own way in the hope that their subsequent wretchedness will cause them to snap out of it before it is too late and there is no turning back. Delivering them over to their sin is 'a deliberate act of judgement and mercy on the part of the God who smites in order to heal (Isa 19.22) . . . throughout the time of their God-forsakenness God is still concerned with them and dealing with them' (Cranfield, I, p. 121).

Jesus' parable of the prodigal son who made his own choices and wound up in a pigsty provides an example. The son 'came to himself', arose and, filled with contrition, returned to his father, who received him with open arms (Luke 15:12–24). God must work in this way, allowing persons to hit rock bottom in the hope that they will come to themselves and repent, because God gave human beings free will. They are not machines. When an engine does not work, it can be fixed, even if it means putting in a whole new set of parts. Human evil, covetousness and malice cannot be so easily fixed. When humans are already deeply mired in the muck of their own making, like Christian, the central character in John Bunyan's *Pilgrim's Progress*, who sinks under the weight of his sins and sense of guilt into a cavernous bog, the Slough of Despond, they cannot escape by pulling themselves up by their own bootstraps. The statement attributed to Martin Luther is true: 'Sin is a knot which only God can untie.' Redemption from sin that leads to knowing and worshipping God as the Father of the Son through the Spirit will be costly.

The perpetrators of the acts Paul lists 'deserve to die' (1:32) and cannot inherit the kingdom of God (1 Cor. 6:9–10), but this verdict is not final while they still live. God bears with patience the objects of his wrath (9:22) and has provided a solution through Christ to humanity's insolvent condition. Believers are 'justified by his blood' and will 'be saved through him from the wrath of God' (5:9). They may have been guilty of these things, but 'you were washed, you were sanctified, you were justified in the name of the Lord Jesus Christ and in the Spirit of our God' (1 Cor. 6:11; cf. Rom 3:24).

B. God's wrath against Jews who dishonour God (2:1–29)

Paul has said that the wrath of God is poured out on 'all ungodliness and wickedness' (1:18). He then sketched the sins of the Gentiles who deliberately reject the revelation of God they have received. He now draws a bead on the Jews in 2:1–29. They also are entrapped by sin's merciless power, and, despite their posturing as God's unassailable elect, they will be subject to God's impartial scrutiny at the judgment. Paul intends to destroy the props that enable Jews to imagine that they could be reckoned righteous before God 'on any basis other than that offered in the gospel: the righteousness of God made accessible through faith' (Byrne, p. 79). They too are guilty of ungodliness (11:26) and wickedness (2:8; 3:5) and therefore also evoke God's wrath. Paul's argument in 2:1–29 headlines two basic principles: God judges all humanity 'in accordance with truth' (2:2), and God will disregard everyone's ancestry and judge each according to his or her obedience to the law – the written law or the law written on their hearts (2:12).

i. The censurer of others who is no less guilty (2:1–11)

Context

Paul adopts a diatribe style in this section.[22] He brusquely answers and exposes mistaken presuppositions and conclusions framed as the questions of the fictional dialogue partner. He also poses his own counter-questions. The purpose is 'to expose error so that the auditor can more clearly see the truth'.[23] The indefinite 'whoever you are' (2:1) means that the dialogue partner could be anyone who believes he or she is morally superior to those involved in the decadence described in 1:18–32: a Gentile moral teacher, a Jew, or even a Jewish Christian. The majority opinion that Paul directs his censure against 'Jewish despisers of Gentile (im)morality' is correct (Ziesler, p. 81).[24] Paul initially cloaks his dialogue partner's identity simply as one who judges others, but in 2:17 the partner is clearly identified as a Jew. The following list of allusions to Jewish texts and themes throughout verses 1–29 indicates that this person is a representative of Israel who believes himself to be an advantaged member of the elect people of God.

(1) The preceding indictment of idolatry and debauchery in 1:19–32 reflects the typical Hellenistic Jewish polemic against Gentile sins (though the term 'Gentiles' never appears). What follows in 2:1–11 challenges the Jewish sense of moral superiority and privilege that assumes God will condemn the Gentiles for their sins but will give his chosen people a special indulgence. Wisdom 12:22 gives voice to this attitude:

---

22. The diatribe style imitates the informal conversation between a teacher and his students; cf. Stowers, *Diatribe*, pp. 85–118. The dialogue partner in the letter may be 'fictional', but that does not mean that Paul does not have in view those who held the views he exposes as false.

23. Stowers, *Diatribe*, p. 177.

24. Wischmeyer, 'Römer 2.1–24', pp. 356–376. Neither does Paul defend himself against some Christians in Rome who have slandered his gospel. Nor is he censuring a Gentile Christian who claims to be a Jew. The ones accused are those who were 'entrusted with the oracles of God' (3:2), a passage that answers any objections to what he says in 2:1–29.

So while chastening us you scourge our enemies ten thousand
    times more,
so that, when we judge, we may meditate upon your goodness,
and when we are judged, we may expect mercy.

(2) Paul utilizes the tradition of the 'day of wrath' in the Old
Testament (e.g. Zeph. 1:15; cf. 1 Thess. 1:10). Such a reference would
be a mystery to a pagan dialogue partner (cf. Acts 17:30–34; 24:25).
The idea of 'storing up wrath for yourself' (2:5; cf. Deut. 32:34–35)
is akin to its opposite of laying up treasures in heaven (Matt. 6:19–
20; Tob. 4:9–10; 2 Esd. 6:5; 7:77).

(3) The citation of Psalm 62:12 (61:13, LXX) in 2:6 confirms that
Paul chides a Jew who acknowledges that God will repay persons
according to what they have done and therefore is impartial.

(4) Other themes that recur throughout Jewish literature emerge:
the danger of and punishment for a 'hard heart' ('stubbornness',
Deut. 9:27); the riches of God's kindness, forbearance and patience;
the conviction that they expire on the day of wrath when it will be
too late to repent. In Romans, 'riches' (9:23; 11:12, 33), 'kindness'
(11:22), 'patience' (9:22) and 'forbearance' (3:25) are all connected to
God's dealings with Israel (Schnabel, I, p. 265).[25]

(5) The presumption that Israel enjoys a privileged status in the
judgment is reflected in Wisdom 15:1–3:

But you, our God, are kind and true,
patient, and ruling all things in mercy.
For even if we sin we are yours, knowing your power;
but we will not sin, because we know that you acknowledge us
    as yours.
For to know you is complete righteousness,
and to know your power is the root of immortality.

Paul's primary purpose in this section is 'to prove that the
Jews are guilty before God, for they have transgressed the reve-

---

25. This praise of God's mercy surfaces frequently in the Psalms (Pss 25:7;
    69:16; 86:5; 100:5; 106:1; 109:21; 136:1; 145:8–9).

lation they have received, just as the Gentiles have rejected the revelation they have received (1:18–32).[26] Jews have been 'entrusted with the oracles of God' (3:2), but they have turned away from this *special* revelation God has given them that points to Jesus as their Messiah (Luke 24:25–27, 44; 2 Cor. 3:14–15).

Paul's rhetorical strategy may be likened to that in Amos 1 – 2 in which the prophet castigates Damascus, Gaza, Tyre, Edom, the Ammonites and Moab for their multiple transgressions (Amos 1:3 – 2:3) and suddenly pivots to attack the sins of Judah and Israel (Amos 2:4, 6).[27] A Jewish audience likely would utter 'Amens' all the way through 1:18–32, but Paul is not through. He next impeaches the Jews in four stages:

(1) The special position of the Jews in relation to God does not confer on them the right to sit in judgment on the rest of humankind (2:1–11). God alone sets the criteria for the judgment and gets to say who is and who is not acceptable.

(2) Election implies partiality, and Paul's point is that God will be impartial. Jews may not presume that because of their election they will receive preferential treatment and will be unscathed by God's retribution against sinners in the final judgment. The law's criterion for vindication by God's judgment is not the possession or knowledge of the written law but obedience to its commands. Obedience decides one's eternal destiny. Those who obey the law that is only written on their hearts will shame those who know but disobey the written law (2:12–16).

(3) Knowing the law, teaching it to others and taking pride in it are all useless if one violates its commands (2:17–24).

(4) Physical circumcision, the ground of Jewish confidence as the seal of the covenant, is meaningless unless it also signifies a cleansed heart (2:25–29). This indictment of Jews prepares for the gospel's accusation against all humanity (3:20).[28]

---

26. Schreiner, 'Justification by Works?', p. 140.

27. Popkes, 'Zum Aufbau', p. 499.

28. McFadden, *Judgment*, p. 153.

Comment

1. *Therefore (dio)* has its typical inferential force and continues the thought – but what thought? If Paul is no longer talking about the Gentiles but about Jews when he switches to the second-person singular, the 'therefore' refers to 1:18, 'the wrath of God is revealed from heaven against all ungodliness and wickedness'. The Jews' ungodliness and wickedness is also under indictment. God's wrath is poured out on three categories of persons: those 'who *practice* the vices listed in the preceding section'; those 'who *approve* of what they do' (1:32b); and 'those who *disapprove*, in the sense that they sit in judgement upon the previous two classes (2:1, 3)' (Byrne, p. 83). It falls on everyone.

Whoever you are translates 'O man' found in the Greek in 2:1, 3 (cf. 9:20). Paul may seem to attack the general human proclivity to pass judgment on others' sins while paying no regard to one's own. Jewett contends that he targets the arrogant, pretentious 'bigot' to overturn all group exceptionalism of whatever stripe (Jewett, p. 14). 'O man' underscores that the one addressed is a mere human being, not God who is the one and only transcendent judge. Dunn notes, 'The contrast between human and divine judgement becomes a key theme in the remainder of the indictment (2:1–3, 12, 16, 27; 3:4, 6–8)' (Dunn, I, pp. 79–80). While his reproaches may apply to anyone who smugly judges others, Paul specifically has in mind the Jew who judges Gentiles. His sin is not that he condemns Gentiles but that he does *the very same things*, which in the context can only refer to the sins itemized in 1:19–32. Since God condemns those who practise such things (1:32), the accusations in 1:18–32 establish a common ground. Both Gentiles and Jews are 'without excuse' (1:20; 2:1).[29]

This censurer of others is also 'without excuse' (csb) or 'without defence'. His judgment of others turns back on himself (cf. Matt. 7:1–5). He pronounces his verdict on others that ricochets back and condemns him as well. He may not commit exactly the same sins, but he is no less wicked and is without excuse. His religious pride is a type of idolatry that blinds him to his own wickedness.

---

29. Ibid., p. 55.

2. Paul declares what is self-evident to Jews: God is a righteous judge who makes true judgments (Pss 96:13; 98:9; Jer. 11:20; Acts 17:31; Rev. 16:7; 19:2).[30] *In accordance with truth* asserts that God's judgment is objective and impartial. The dialogue partner's crucial mistake is not that he dares to mount the judge's throne or to gloat haughtily over God's condemnation of others. Instead, he fails to recognize that he is also guilty of sins that incite God's wrath and fury. He possesses the truth in the law (2:20) but does not obey it (2:8). He knows the truth about God's judgments, but he does not repent. He compares himself favourably with Gentile sinners and deceives himself into believing that he is exempt from God's condemnation because God will judge him by a different standard.

3. The rhetorical question *Do you imagine . . . that . . . you will escape the judgement of God?* goes unanswered. Paul assumes the answer is obvious: no-one who does the same things he condemns others for doing will escape God's judgment. The question implies that the dialogue partner imagines that he *will* escape. Paul's aim is to establish Israel's sinfulness and explode the myth that Israel's status at the judgment is impregnable. Dunn cites a parallel statement in the Psalms of Solomon: 'And those who do lawlessness shall not escape the judgement of the Lord' (15:8) (Dunn, I, p. 81). The author of the psalm continues by asserting that Jews are the righteous who bear God's mark of salvation and live by God's mercy while the sinners have the mark of destruction and will perish for all time. This notion also appears in the Wisdom of Solomon 11:9–10, which praises Wisdom for disciplining the wilderness generation with mercy and testing them as a father does in giving a warning. By contrast, the ungodly 'were tormented when judged in wrath' and 'examined . . . as a stern king does in condemnation'. Election by God does not automatically free the Jews from the potential of eternal punishment. When brought before the bar of the all-knowing judge, they will not be exonerated because of a favoured-nation clause in the covenant. God's impartiality results in universal condemnation according to the standards laid out in the law.

---

30. The future judgment is 'according to truth' (m. 'Abot 3:16).

4. The fictional dialogue partner is sadly mistaken if he thinks God deals out only retribution to Gentiles and only kindness to Jews. Generous *kindness* refers to a divine characteristic of God in dealing with sinners (Mic. 7:18; Wis. 11:23; 12:19, 22), but Paul also connects it to God's 'severity': God will cut off those in Israel who disobey (11:22). *Forbearance* relates to God passing over sins (3:25). God has held back in punishing sinners, but Paul ties God's *patience* to enduring 'the objects of wrath that are made for destruction' to show the riches of his glory for the 'objects of mercy' who are 'not from the Jews only but also from the Gentiles' (9:22–24). Misconstruing God's present kindness as approval that assures of divine clemency at the final judgment is a fatal error. God is forbearing and patient only to provide time for repentance (2 Pet. 3:9). The opportunity to repent expires at the last judgment (2 Bar. 85:1–2).[31] Pious Jews of Paul's day would agree, as evidenced by Sirach 5:4–7:

> Do not say, 'I sinned, yet what has happened to me?'
>   for the Lord is slow to anger.
> Do not be so confident of forgiveness
>   that you add sin to sin.
> Do not say, 'His mercy is great,
>   he will forgive the multitude of my sins',
> for both mercy and wrath are with him,
>   and his anger will rest on sinners.
> Do not delay to turn back to the Lord,
>   and do not postpone it from day to day;
> for suddenly the wrath of the Lord will come upon you,
>   and at the time of punishment you will perish.[32]

What Jews might not acknowledge is that God is kind, forbearing and patient to allow time for Gentiles *also* to repent (cf. Acts

---

31. The conative force of the verb 'leads' (*agei*, present tense) is captured in the translations *is meant* [intended, supposed] *to lead*. Versions that translate it as 'leads you to repentance' mislead.

32. Cf. also Wis. 12:10.

17:30–31). Repentance, however, is a gift of God (Acts 5:31), and Paul will argue that God is impartial not only in judgment but also in bestowing gifts.

5. Paul controverts theological assumptions like those found in 2 Maccabees 6:12–16. The author seeks to explain the calamities that have befallen Israel:

> In the case of the other nations the Lord waits patiently to punish them until they have reached the full measure of their sins; but he does not deal in this way with us, in order that he should not take vengeance on us afterwards when our sins have reached their height.

The author regards it as 'a sign of great kindness not to let the impious alone for long, but to punish them immediately', and it means that God 'never withdraws his mercy from us' and 'does not forsake his own people'.[33] Deuteronomy 32:34–35 contains the reassurance that Israel's enemies will meet with God's retribution:

> Is not this laid up in store with me,
>   sealed up in my treasuries?
> Vengeance is mine, and recompense,
>   for the time when their foot shall slip;
> because the day of their calamity is at hand,
>   their doom comes swiftly.

A promise that, by contrast, God will have compassion and vindicate the people follows (Deut. 32:36). Paul insists instead that

---

33. Pss Sol. 7:5–10 expresses the same sentiment: 'For you are kind, and will not be angry enough to destroy us. While your name lives among us, we shall receive mercy and the gentile will not overcome us. For you are our protection, and we will call to you, and you will hear us. For you will have compassion on the people Israel forever and you will not reject them; And we are under your yoke forever, and (under) the whip of your discipline. You will direct us in the time of your support, showing mercy to the house of Jacob on the day when you promised (it) to them' (Wright, *OTP* II, p. 658).

his dialogue partner, like Israel's enemies, is amassing a warehouse full of sins that will be avenged on the day of wrath (cf. 1 Thess. 2:14–16). Paul debunks the idea that the world will be divided 'into virtuous Jews and wicked pagans' (Ziesler, p. 85).

A theme Paul develops later forms the theological basis for his assertions in this unit. It is that the law has failed to solve the problem of a *hard and impenitent heart*,[34] and human volition fails to bring about the required obedience. The law may be spiritual, but humans are 'of the flesh, sold into slavery under sin' (7:14). Therefore, they can never perfectly fulfil the law. The law is impotent to create obedience but quite potent in pronouncing judgment on disobedience. Zealous pursuit of the law (10:2) cannot be the means to escape God's wrath. Bullishness for the law ironically has resulted in bull-headed disobedience of God. Jewish disdain for Gentiles has resulted in discrediting God's audaciousness in choosing Israel to be God's witness to the world. The human heart's bent towards sin affects both Jews and Gentiles. It needs a more effective remedy than the law. Humans need a new basis for establishing their righteousness before God.

6. That God will *repay according to each one's deeds* pervades Jewish literature.[35] Paul's point, however, is to stress that God rewards and punishes impartially, and one's race or heritage will not factor into this reckoning. Paul's remarks on God's impartiality form a chiasm:

A God will repay according to each one's works (2:6)
  B Those who do good will receive eternal life (2:7)
    C Those who do not obey the truth will receive wrath
      and fury (2:8)
    C' Those who do evil will suffer trouble and distress
      (2:9)

---

34. A hard and unrepentant heart (cf. 9:18; 11:25) plagued the rebellious wilderness generation (Deut. 9:27; Ps. 95:8).

35. Cf. Job 34:11; Ps. 62:12; Prov. 24:12; Eccl. 12:14; Isa. 3:10–11; Jer. 17:10; Ezek. 33:20; Hos. 12:2; Matt. 7:21; 16:27; John 5:28–29; Jas 1:22–25; Rev. 20:12–13; 22:12; Sir. 16:12. Cf. Yinger, *Paul, Judaism, and Judgment*, pp. 19–142.

B' Those who do good will receive glory, honour and peace
(2:10)
A' God is impartial (in judgment) (2:11)

Pate comments that the

> contrast in destinies recalls Deuteronomy 27 – 30, especially 30:15–20
> and the 'two ways' tradition specified there: if Israel obeys the
> stipulations of the Torah, they will experience the blessing of the
> covenant, which is life, but if they disregard the Torah, they will
> experience the curse of the covenant, which is wrath in the form of
> exile (cf. 30:4–5).
> (Pate, p. 43)

Paul's emphasis on 'the Jew first and also the Greek' (2:9–10)
expands this tradition to apply also to Gentiles.

7. In verses 7 and 8 Paul spells out two axioms related to God's
judgment according to one's deeds: doing good will reap an eternal
reward (cf. Gal. 6:9); doing evil will reap wrath and fury. The phrase
literally translated 'patience of good work' refers to persevering in
good work, consistent action and not the occasional deed.

Seeking *glory and honour* has nothing to do with seeking self-
exaltation. Paul's linking of these two words with *immortality*
(*aphtharsia*, 'not being subject to decay') means that he refers to a
state of being in the afterlife when God has resurrected mortal
human beings. Humans do not innately possess immortality, as the
Greek view of the immortality of the soul presupposes. Only God
bestows imperishability along with the glory and honour that befits
eternal life (1 Cor. 15:51–54). Seeking glory, honour and immortality
means doing what pleases God so that one is no longer destined to
the corruption of death but is accounted worthy of the resurrection
and a place in the age to come (Luke 20:35), namely, *eternal life*. For
believers who are in Christ, it means being conformed to the
glorious image of his Son (8:29; 1 Cor. 15:49; Phil. 3:21). But this
comment jumps ahead of Paul's argument.

8. Zephaniah 1:14–18 and 2:2–3 picture the wrath and fury
unleashed on the day of the Lord enveloping disobedient Israel,
and Paul believes that Israel is gravely disobedient in rejecting

Christ (10:21; 11:31). Those who do not obey the truth are no different from those who suppress the truth (1:18). One of the root causes of this disobedience is *self-seeking* (*eritheia*), which can be defined as 'pursuing one's own importance, guarding and increasing one's power, and grasping for the gains inspired by this craving' (Schlatter, p. 53). It has evoked God's *wrath*, and the addition of the word *fury* (*thymos*) suggests that this wrath is God's personal and 'deeply felt' indignation (Dunn, I, p. 87).

9. *For everyone* correctly translates 'for every soul of man' in the Greek text and refers to every person's life (Fitzmyer, p. 302). The Jews may be first in privilege, but they also will be first in punishment (Amos 3:2). Greater privileges bring greater accountability. God will administer the judgment according to the principle enunciated by Jesus: 'From everyone to whom much has been given, much will be required; and from one to whom much has been entrusted, even more will be demanded' (Luke 12:48).

10. God will separate the good from the evil in the judgment. The division is not between the Jew and the Greek but between those who have consistently done what is good and those who have done what is evil. Paul's statement reflects John the Baptist's warning to those who might be blasé about the wrath to come because of their false confidence in having Abraham as their forefather. They cannot ignore bearing 'fruits worthy of repentance' (Luke 3:7–9). At this stage in his argument, Paul is interested only in establishing that if Jews fail to do good works, they are liable to God's harsh judgment and cannot expect to be grandfathered in based on their long-standing covenant with God and the merits of the patriarchs. Schreiner summarizes, 'The main reason Paul introduced the issue of repayment according to works is to show the Jews that God is impartial, that there will be no special favoritism for them' (Schreiner, p. 122).

11. That *God shows no partiality* reinforces the statement in 2:6 that 'he will repay according to each one's deeds', Jews and Gentiles alike.[36] It underpins the basic premise that salvation comes to

---

36. Cf. Deut. 10:17–18; 2 Chr. 19:7; Job 34:19; Eph. 6:9; Col. 3:25; 1 Pet. 1:17; Wis. 6:7; Sir. 35:12–16; 2 Bar. 13:8; 44:4; 2 En. 46:3; Jub. 5:16.

everyone who has faith, to the Jew first and also to the Greek, and wrath comes to everyone who suppresses the truth, Jew or Gentile (1:16–18).

Theology

Paul argues that his dialogue partner cannot divorce himself from the morass of evil plaguing the world simply by expressing his indignation over it. At the judgment, one will not be asked, 'What or whom did you condemn?' but 'What did you do?' The problem in judging others is that the measuring rod humans use to judge others and themselves is fundamentally twisted by the sins listed in 1:30: insolence, haughtiness (arrogance) and boastfulness, which makes their judgments hopelessly biased. Humans 'unhappily possess an inbred proclivity to mix ignorance of themselves with arrogance toward others'.[37] One cannot judge others as if they were the only ones guilty. God did not call Israel to be the moral watchdogs of the world but a light to the Gentiles.

Paul is not merely condemning the judgmentalism of a pretentious and arrogant person.[38] He does not call for his dialogue partner to repent of his judgmental attitude or to be more prudent in judging (contrast 14:4, 10–13). He will not stand condemned before God because he turned up his nose at others' decadence. Paul expects him to concur that such sins are abhorrent and deserving of wrath (Schnabel, I, p. 270). He is condemned instead for committing the same sins. (Schreiner, pp. 115–116). By affirming that God rightly judges sins (2:2), he acknowledges that God rightly judges (Wilckens, I, p. 256). He too will be the object of God's wrath for his sins.

God administers judgment with impartiality. Many do not mind if God is partial as long as God is partial towards them and not others. In chapter 2, Paul debunks the view that Jews will get off more lightly for their sins because of their inherited covenant relationship with God. He lays the groundwork for describing Israel's persistent failure to obey God's word. None can rely on the

37. Davies and Allison, *St. Matthew*, p. 673.
38. Stowers, *Diatribe*, p. 177.

kindness of God and expect to get a free pass at the judgment. God is also severe (11:22). Since God's judgment is in accordance with the truth, God does not grade on a curve to absolve those who suppose themselves to be God's favourites. Since God is righteous, God does not treat sin as lightly as humans often hope. The ones who are outwardly pious are even more susceptible to taking for granted their blessed assurance. But God destroys security based on human categories and human religiosity. While God is patient, the end-time judgment awaits everyone, including those belonging to Israel and to the church. If they know the truth but have not allowed God to change their hearts, they will be condemned for treating God's bountiful goodness and patience with contempt.

Paul's statements in 2:7–9 may seem to teach that salvation can be attained by virtue of works. Since this view contradicts his main argument in Romans that salvation comes by faith alone, this inference cannot be his intent. It is important to recognize that 'for the moment he is considering, not what man can plead, but what God requires. He has yet to show that the works God rewards spring from faith' (Taylor, p. 27). He spells out 'a universal principle concerning God's righteous judgement' (Hultgren, p. 115). Ziesler summarizes Paul's point: 'God requires the practice of righteousness, and not just assent to it' (Ziesler, pp. 80–81).

One should be careful not to read too much into what Paul says in this unit. Wolter recognizes that Paul presents a fictive situation from the perspective of the Jew who judges. He has yet to present the perspective of the judgment from the Christian vantage point (Wolter, I, pp. 183–184). His point is that God judges all according to their works with no distinction. He does not yet make clear that all fall short. When they are weighed in the balance, their good works will never tip the scale towards righteousness. Justification is unattainable through works.

It is therefore important to interpret these statements in the light of Paul's entire argument. As Hultgren avers,

> He seeks to show that there is no hope of salvation for anyone apart from the redemptive work of God in Christ . . . God's judgement, Paul says, is fundamentally according to works. On *that* basis alone, some are

found righteous, others guilty – in principle, if not in fact. This entire
diatribe concerns judgement apart from Christ, whom Paul mentions
only once, and that is at the end of the section (2:16).
(Hultgren, p. 112)

On that basis, any hope of salvation requires absolute obedience.
He pulls the rug out from under those in Israel who think they will
be justified before God from their fulfilment of the law. This unit
provides the rhetorical framework for what follows: 'The only hope
for anyone is the grace of God extended in the redemptive death
of Christ. God is impartial, and that is fundamental to understanding both his judgement and his grace' (Hultgren, p. 113).

ii. God's impartiality in judgment (2:12–16)
Context
This unit expands on the statement that God shows no favouritism
and spells out why. Those who have sinned without the law will
perish. Those who have sinned under the law will be judged by the
law (2:12). What Paul leaves unsaid but assumes is that the law is an
exacting taskmaster: 'Cursed is everyone who does not observe and
obey all the things written in the book of the law' (Gal. 3:10; cf.
Deut. 27:26). He is building up to his conclusion that all have
sinned (3:23), and all will be held responsible before God for their
sin (3:19). Disobedience leads to death and destruction.

The thought expressed in 2:12 is completed in 2:16:

> All who have sinned apart from the law will also perish apart from the
> law, and all who have sinned under the law will be judged by the law . . .
> on the day when, according to my gospel, God, through Jesus Christ,
> will judge the secret thoughts of all.

In between, 2:13–15 parenthetically explains how God can judge
Jews and Gentiles on equal terms. In the case of Jews, the law
decrees that only the doers of the law are righteous, and merely
hearing the law will not lead to their acquittal. Gentiles may be
without the written law, but by virtue of instinctively doing what
the law commands, they reveal that they experience the tug of the
divine will in their lives. The written law condemns the Jews for

failing to be doers of the law; the Gentiles' consciences condemn them for their failure to do what they know is right. The conclusion in 2:16 asserts that, through Christ, God will judge impartially the actions and secret thoughts of all humankind (cf. 14:10, 12).

Comment

12. The verb 'sin' (*hamartanō*) and an explicit reference to the Mosaic law appear for the first time in Romans. Paul refers to the *law* nineteen times in 2:12–19. Being 'without the law' (*anomōs*) appears twice in 2:12 (cf. 7:9). Paul takes for granted a central tenet of Judaism that God favoured Israel over all the nations by giving them the law. An answer to why God gave the law only to such an insignificant nation appears in a widespread rabbinic tradition that explains that God had offered it also to the Gentile nations but they declined, rejecting the commands not to murder, commit adultery or steal. Sipre §343, a later rabbinic commentary on Deuteronomy, cites Micah 5:15 as God's response to this rebuff:

And in anger and wrath I will execute vengeance
on the nations that did not obey.

Of all the nations, only Israel was willing to accept the yoke of the law.[39] This tradition reinforced Israel's sense of superiority over the nations. Possession of the law, however, does not make for virtue. Paul's point is that whatever one's ancestry and privileges, sin evokes God's wrath and fury and incurs condemnation, anguish and distress (2:9). Human sin therefore creates parity (cf. 3:9). Being without the written (Mosaic) law does not excuse Gentiles when they sin. Possessing the written law does not exempt Jews when they sin.

Snodgrass points out that Paul adopts 'a Jewish view of judgement, but one that is radicalized and applied to both Jew and Gentile'. He also notes that Judaism did not require one to be perfect for salvation. Jews also believed in mercy: 'Mercy was

---

39. Cf. also Mekilta Baḥodesh 1 on Exod. 19:2 and Baḥodesh 5 on Exod. 20:2; Sipre Deut. §343; LAB 11:1–2; b. ʿAbod. Zar. 2b–3a.

viewed as the lot for the righteous (usually the Jews) and judgement according to works was the lot for the evil (usually the Gentiles).'[40] Paul rejects that distinction to contest a misinterpretation of the significance of Israel's election. He sets up his position that if God did not justify sinners by faith, none would be saved, since all are sinners. If the criteria for the divine judgment were based solely on their deeds according to the law's requirements, all humans would fall short. The righteousness that God requires is far more than membership of the covenant community; it is doing what God demands of those within the covenant (Exod. 24:7; Deut. 27:26).[41]

13. *Hearers of the law* echoes Deuteronomy 6:4–5, 'Hear, O Israel', and alludes to the Jewish custom of hearing the Law and the Prophets read every Sabbath (Acts 13:27; 15:21). What truly matters in God's sight is obedience to the law, not simply familiarity with it (cf. Matt. 7:21; John 13:17; Jas 1:22). As Ezekiel 18:5–9 makes crystal clear, one must follow God's statutes to become righteous. The rabbis concurred (m. 'Abot 1:17). Gentiles also understood the principle of proving 'your words by your deeds' (Seneca, *Ep.* 20.1).

Paul's statement that the *doers of the law* will be justified seems to contradict flatly what he says in 3:20a: 'For "no human being will be justified in his sight" by deeds prescribed by the law' (literally, 'by works of law'). What Paul says in 2:13 should not be isolated from his entire argument. In this phase of it, he intends only to undercut any mistaken assumption that possession of the law spares one from God's judgment. That only doers of the law will be justified states a basic premise of the old dispensation. It should not be taken as Paul's understanding of the sole criterion in the final judgment that Paul envisions will be through Christ. The old dispensation judged according to the unyielding standard of complete obedience to the law. No-one is able to measure up to that standard. Consequently, no-one will be exonerated. For this reason, Paul elsewhere characterizes the old dispensation, which requires doing the law to receive life (Gal. 3:12; cf. Lev. 18:5), as 'the ministry of condemnation' (2 Cor. 3:9). It explains why he says that 'the law

---

40. Snodgrass, 'Justification', p. 78.
41. Gathercole, 'Justification', p. 237.

brings wrath' (Rom. 4:15), since 'all who rely on the works of the
law are under a curse; for it is written, "Cursed is everyone who
does not observe and obey all the things written in the book of the
law"' (Gal. 3:10; cf. Deut. 27:26). The new dispensation, by contrast,
makes divine grace 'universally available to Jews and Greeks apart
from merit'.[42]

14–15. The majority of versions interpret the Greek word
translated 'by nature' or *instinctively* (*physei*) as modifying the verb
'do': *When Gentiles, who do not possess the law, do instinctively what the law
requires* (literally, 'the things of the law'). *What the law requires* in 2:15
interprets the phrase that reads literally in Greek 'the work of the
law'.[43] The implication is that Gentiles carry out God's commandments without having been instructed by the written law.
This statement forestalls any objection that might be inferred from
Paul's assertion in 5:13: 'sin is not reckoned when there is no law'.
One might ask how the Gentiles without the law can be held
accountable for their sin if they did not know it was sin. That their
deeds correspond with what the written law requires reveals that
they are not ignorant of divine law. Paul has already declared that
they know God's decree and that defiance of God's decree deserves
death (1:32).

By saying that Gentiles do what the law requires, Paul does not
refer to all Gentiles, nor does he mean to imply that some Gentiles
perfectly obey all of God's law.[44] If that were so, why were the Jews
the only ones who needed the revealed law? He simply asserts that
evidence exists that some Gentiles have experienced the transcendent claim of the divine moral law written on their hearts and
live virtuous lives (for example, Cornelius, according to Acts 10:1–2).

---

42. Bassler, 'Luke and Paul', p. 551.

43. Paul uses the plural 'the works of the law' only in a negative sense as
    something irrelevant for establishing one's righteousness (3:20, 28; Gal.
    2:16; 3:2, 5, 10). He abbreviates the phrase to 'by works' in 4:2 and 'of
    the law' in 4:16.

44. This view accords with the assertion in 2 Esd. 3:36, 'You may indeed
    find individuals who have kept your commandments, but nations you
    will not find.'

That they are *a law to themselves* means that while they might not be able to recite the Ten Commandments, 'they are capable of a high moral standard that coincides with the teachings set forth by the moral commandments'.[45] This assertion explains how some Gentiles live morally principled lives without the written law and how, when they fail to do so, their consciences serve as their accuser.

Conscience is conceived here to be a judge of actions, not a guide that directs actions.[46] That *their conflicting thoughts* accuse or excuse them has no connection to God's final judgment. The verdict of one's conscience does not clear one before God. In defending his conduct to the Corinthians, Paul attests that he is unaware of anything against himself, but he is not the final judge. He is 'not thereby acquitted' because the Lord will judge his conscience and 'will bring to light the things now hidden in darkness and will disclose the purposes of the heart' (1 Cor. 4:4–5; cf. Acts 24:16).

16. This verse completes the thought of 2:12 after the parenthetical explanation about the criterion of God's judgment that levels the playing field. The term *day* refers to the court where the ultimate judgment takes place. This meaning for 'day' is found in 1 Corinthians 4:3, when Paul says, 'It is a very small thing that I should be judged by you or by any human court ['day' in Greek].' As the supreme judge, God is all-knowing and can detect what humans think is safely hidden, their secret deeds and private thoughts. Paul makes the theologically astounding statement that God will carry out this judgment through Jesus Christ who will be the cosmic judge of all.[47]

According to my gospel does not mean that Paul's message is his idiosyncratic take on the good news about Christ. It is 'the proclamation of Jesus Christ, according to the revelation of the mystery that

---

45. Donaldson, *Paul*, pp. 146–147.

46. Seneca illustrates this notion: 'Therefore, as far as possible, prove yourself guilty, hunt up charges against yourself; play the part, first of accuser, then of judge, last of intercessor. At times be harsh with yourself' (*Ep.* 28.10 [Gummere, LCL]).

47. Matt. 25:31–33; John 5:22, 27; Acts 10:42; 17:31; 1 Cor. 4:5; 2 Cor. 5:10; 2 Thess. 1:7–10; 2 Tim. 4:1; Rev. 22:12.

was kept secret for long ages' (16:25). In this context, he conveys that his gospel does not eliminate accountability in the judgment, as some have maligned it as doing (3:8). Doing good is not superfluous and now irrelevant,[48] but by identifying Jesus Christ as the final judge, Paul introduces another criterion for the judgment that he will develop later. Only those who belong to Christ and have been transformed by his power will withstand his judgment (8:37–39).

Theology

The separation at the final judgment will not divide along strictly ethnic lines, but who are these morally principled Gentiles who 'will condemn you [a Jew] that have the written code and circumcision but break the law' (2:27)? When Paul uses the term 'Gentiles' (*ethnē*), he usually has in mind non-Christian Gentiles (2:24; 3:29). Many reasonably conclude that he refers to Christians as those who fulfil the law (Cranfield, I, p. 156; Jewett, p. 213; Kruse, p. 132; Schnabel, I, pp. 295–297; Wright, p. 441). Paul refers to Christians simply as 'Gentiles' in 11:13 and 15:9. In my view, however, 'by nature' or 'instinctively' (2:14) does not allude to the fulfilment of Jeremiah 31:31–32 in the lives of Christians and does not refer to the reborn nature. Believers have the written law (1 Cor. 10:11), and they certainly are not 'a law to themselves' but are under 'the law of Christ' (1 Cor. 9:21; Gal. 6:2). Believers do not obey 'by nature' ('instinctively') but do so only through the power of the Spirit (8:4, 14; Gal. 5:22–25). Paul resorts here to the Stoic concept of natural law to make his case that Jews are not the only ones who can know God's will (Fitzmyer, pp. 310–311). His comments are consistent with Philo's explicit statements about Abraham, who lived long before the law was given to Moses on Mount Sinai. Citing Genesis 26:5, Philo writes that Moses makes

> this crowning saying, 'this man did the divine law and the commands'.
> He did them not taught by written words, but unwritten nature gave
> him the zeal to follow where wholesome and untainted impulse led
> him . . . Such was the life of the first, the founder of our nation, one

---

48. Cf. 1 Cor. 3:13–15; 2 Cor. 5:10; 11:15; Gal. 6:7–9; Eph. 6:8–9; Col. 3:24–25.

who obeyed the law . . . himself a law and an unwritten statute.
(*Abr.* §275 [Colson, LCL])[49]

Gentiles 'show that what the law requires is written on their hearts, to which their own conscience also bears witness' when 'their conflicting thoughts . . . accuse or perhaps excuse them' for their actions (2:1). That they struggle within themselves over right and wrong reveals that they have an acquaintance with what is right and wrong.

Paul's overall rhetorical purpose should be kept in mind before mining these statements for theological doctrine. He mentions the moral Gentiles to puncture Jewish pride that assumes Jews have an advantage over the Gentiles because they possess the law and the Gentiles do not. His goal is not to commend the Gentiles but to show that God will judge both Gentiles and Jews impartially by the same universal standard that the law enjoins. Ziesler is correct: 'At this stage in the letter Paul is still dealing with the human situation apart from God's gracious action in Jesus Christ, which he will not reach until 3:21' (Ziesler, p. 81).

Paul's validation of moral Gentiles who have the law written on their hearts does not mean that they will be acquitted by passing some moral test. They are not saved by their works any more than Jews are. By highlighting that God's judgment is based on deeds, not birthright or possession of the law, Paul reinforces his point that God's judgment on the disobedient in Israel who possess the law is richly deserved. The case of the moral Gentiles forces the question: how will it stand for the Jews who have the written law if they do not do what it requires? The theological point to take away from this passage is that the gospel is 'the power of God for salvation' that delivers *us* from God's wrath that is directed against *our own* sin (1:16–18) and not simply aimed at the 'ungodliness and wickedness' of others.

---

49. This view is also found in m. Qidd. 4:14: 'And we find that Abraham our father had performed the whole Law before it was given, for it is written, "Because that Abraham obeyed my voice and kept my charge, my commandments, my statutes, and my laws"' (Danby, *Mishnah*, p. 329).

Another question arises: 'How can Paul say that the doers of the law will be justified (2:13) and then affirm that no one will be justified before God on the basis of doing the works of the law (3:20)?' (Matera, p. 67). The former statement does not nullify the fact that all are guilty of sin and under the power of sin and will not be saved except by faith. Paul will make it clear that no-one can rely on 'works of the law' or an imagined innate goodness for salvation. All will appear before God's tribunal at the final judgment and will be subjected to God's penetrating probing that exposes the secrets of the heart. Paul warns that possessing God's special revelation does not give anyone an advantage if one does not heed it. Jesus' parable of the dialogue between the rich man, consigned to Hades, and Father Abraham underscores the point. Abraham's final word declares, 'If they do not listen to Moses and the prophets, neither will they be convinced even if someone rises from the dead' (Luke 16:31). For Christians, the bar will be even higher, since in addition to Moses they have the commands of Christ who was raised from the dead, and they know him to be their judge.

Consequently, Christians should understand that at the Judgment Day they will be held accountable for what they have done in the body (2 Cor. 5:10; cf. 1 Cor. 3:12–15; 2 Cor. 11:15; Eph. 6:8–9; Col. 3:24–25). Käsemann comments,

> The danger of the pious person is that of isolating God's gifts from the claim which is given with them, and of forgetting to relate forbearance and patience to the Judge of the last day. Humans always crave security. They seek to obtain it through moralism, worshiping the gods, or trusting the divine goodness. The Lord who is known as Judge, however, does not ensure security, he destroys it.
> (Käsemann, p. 55)

Therefore, one cannot avert God's condemnation by staking claim to 'the moral high ground' (Bird, p. 74). Snodgrass avers, '"Works righteousness" is excluded, but saving obedience in response to God's grace is not.'[50] Christians no longer live under the shadow of

---

50. Snodgrass, 'Justification', p. 84.

being judged by their works. They are justified only by being in Christ (8:10–11). Their salvation comes as a gift and not as a reward for good deeds (Gal. 2:21; Eph. 2:8–9). Those who are in Christ can trust that their salvation is secure, because everything good that Christians do stems from God working in them (Phil. 2:13) as the Holy Spirit brings forth the fruit of the Spirit (Gal. 5:16–25). That security does not mean that they need not work out their 'salvation with fear and trembling' (Phil. 2:12)

iii. Jewish boasts in the law and physical circumcision do not grant immunity from God's judgment (2:17–29)

Context

Paul addresses his Jewish dialogue partner to answer the question: how does God's impartiality tally with the status of the Jews as God's chosen people? He shatters any notion that the Jews' special entitlements provide an escape clause that allows them to skirt God's judgment. His argument turns on the second half of the principle laid out in 2:12: 'all who have sinned under the law will be judged by the law'. Jews may have the truth contained in the written code of the law, but that advantage does not give them immunity from punishment stipulated by the law. God's wrath does not fall only on Gentile sinners. If Jews transgress the law, they face the same condemnation.

The term 'Jew' in 2:17 and 2:29 brackets this unit as Paul redefines who is truly a Jew. His description of his dialogue partner is like Josephus's portrayal of the Pharisees as 'a group of Jews priding itself on its adherence to ancestral custom and claiming to observe the laws of which the Deity approves' (*Ant.* 17.41 [Marcus and Wikgren, LCL]; cf. 1QM 10:8b–11). Paul's attack on this proud Jew resembles Jesus' assault on the scribes and Pharisees as hypocrites in Matthew 23. In 2:17–24, Paul accentuates the hypocrisy of the Jew who boasts of his reliance on the law that he believes makes him a beacon of light for others but whose manifold transgressions of the law lead Gentiles to disdain rather than to glorify God's name. In 2:25–29, Paul argues that being a true Jew has nothing to do with bearing the name 'Jew', tracing one's bloodline or having physical markings. Instead, the true Jew is marked by an internal circumcision of the heart in the Spirit that brings obedience to the law. This is the only thing that counts before God. Fleshly circumcision that distinguishes the Jew from the Gentile becomes irrelevant. Paul is leading up to the climax of his argument that *all* are sinners and enemies of God (3:23). The last stroke is his conclusion that since 'no one will be declared righteous in God's sight' (3:20, NIV; cf. Ps. 143:2), only God can remedy the problem of sin and bring about reconciliation and redemption. God has done so in Jesus Christ.

Comment

17. The one addressed proudly designates himself *a Jew*, as Paul himself does in Galatians 2:15 where he contrasts being a Jew with being a 'Gentile sinner'. Paul also boasted in his Jewish bona fides in Philippians 3:4–6 as one who was 'circumcised on the eighth day, a member of the people of Israel, of the tribe of Benjamin, a Hebrew born of Hebrews'. He believed that his relationship with God was secure because of a righteousness based on his obedience to the law. Therefore, Paul is not presenting a snide distortion of his opponent. It is Judaism as he experienced it. The series of boasts are not ironic but serve as legitimate grounds for confidence in and gratitude towards God when accompanied by obedience. The problem is that the entitlements Paul lists fill his Jewish dialogue partner with false assurance and a breezy conceit. The *if* makes his comparison of a Gentile who does what the law requires without having been instructed by the written law (2:14) and a Jew who boasts in the law but dishonours God by breaking it (2:23) a hypothetical situation to clarify his point. The obedient Gentile represents a best-case scenario; the disobedient Jew, a worst-case scenario.

'Reliance on the law' had long defined Jewish identity. The psalmist delights that God's law is in his heart (Ps. 40:8). Often cited is the boast in 2 Baruch 48:22–24:

> In you we have put our trust, because, behold, your Law is
>   with us,
> and we know that we do not fall as long as we keep your
>   statutes.
> We shall always be blessed; at least, we did not mingle with the
>   nations.

> For we are all a people of the Name;
> we, who have received one Law from the One.
> And that Law that is among us will help us,
> and that excellent wisdom which is in us will support us.[51]

The catch is that Israel must do more than rely on the law; they must keep the law's statutes to be blessed by God and to avoid falling.

To *boast* in God can be good (1 Cor. 1:31; 2 Cor. 10:17), but it becomes tainted when it turns into a boast about oneself, that is, when one boasts about one's election by God and unduly assumes that one belongs to the only group that will be vindicated in the judgment because of that special relationship to God. Paul is not merely condemning a puffed-up sense of superiority over others. Instead, he decries boasting that encroaches on God's sovereignty and impartiality. The references in the immediate context to those who will and will not face God's righteous judgment in 2:1–5 and the outline of the criteria of God's judgment in 2:6–16, 25–29 confirm that the boasting Paul has in mind refers to assurance related to God's final judgment. In 3:27–30 and 4:2, Paul excludes the boasting that assumes that God is only the God of the Jews or that justification is based on the works of the law. He argues that the 'hope of sharing the glory of God' is based only on faith (5:2). He reproaches here the presumptuous boast that Jews alone will be saved from God's wrath.

18. God's law teaches the difference between righteousness and iniquity, the right and wrong way to live. Through its lens Jews can test and discern *what is best* among differing things. In practice, however, Paul accuses his interlocutor of acting as if he were oblivious to the distinctions. His point is that while the Jew may be instructed in the law, knowledge is useless without obedience. What one does, not what one knows, reveals one's true character.

19–20. Knowing God's law is not simply a privilege to be used for one's selfish ends but brings with it the obligation to teach others, as Moses did (Deut. 4:5–8). The dialogue partner

---

51. Klijn, *OTP* I, p. 636.

understands himself to be *a guide to the blind* and *a light to those who are in darkness*. That is Israel's calling. Enlightened by the law, they are to be a light that shines for a world that dwells in darkness (Isa. 42:6–7; 49:6; cf. Wis. 18:4), not simply a light that shines 'on the face of the Many', the members of one's sect. The light is snuffed out when words do not correspond to deeds. One then becomes a blind guide (Matt. 15:14; 23:16, 24). Those without inner light from God (cf. 2 Cor. 4:6) cannot be a guiding light for others. Those who are morally rudderless cannot steer others in the right direction.

21–22. Switching to biting accusatory questions, Paul indicts his dialogue partner for breaching the very law upon which he relies.[52] The reproaches disclose why he can accuse this Jew of doing 'the very same things' as the Gentile sinners (2:1). The stock list of sins appears in the same order in Philo (*Conf.* 163), and Seneca logs the identical three sins in an inventory of monstrous acts (*Ep.* 87.22–24). The conclusion to a listing of sins, which includes adultery and stealing from God's sanctuary, in Psalms of Solomon 8:8–13 comports well with Paul's point: 'There was no sin they left undone in which they did not surpass the gentiles' (Pss Sol. 8:13 [Wright, *OTP* II, p. 659]). This Jewish sinner is no better than a Gentile sinner and has no grounds for boasting.

While the first two accusations, stealing and adultery, stem from the Decalogue in reversed order (Exod. 20:14–15; Deut. 5:18–19), it is less clear what the verb translated as *rob temples* (*hierosyleō*) denotes. This charge may be literal and relevant to the situation of the Romans. Josephus recounts an incident of a Jew who lived in Rome and professed to instruct men in the wisdom of the laws of Moses. He gathered a group who persuaded a woman convert named Fulvia to send purple and gold to the temple in Jerusalem. Instead of delivering the gifts to the temple, the group absconded with them. When Fulvia's outraged husband informed Tiberias, the emperor, the ensuing investigation resulted in the order to banish

---

52. Paul raises six questions in 2:21–29 that are followed by nine questions in 3:1–8.

Jews from Rome (Josephus, *Ant.* 18.81–84). On the other hand, the charge may refer to the hypocrisy of abhorring idols while trafficking in idolatrous paraphernalia from pagan temples. The questions recall Jeremiah's diatribe:

> Will you steal, murder, commit adultery, swear falsely, make offerings to Baal, and go after other gods that you have not known, and then come and stand before me in this house, which is called by my name, and say, 'We are safe!' – only to go on doing all these abominations? (Jer. 7:9–10)

The charge of robbing temples is therefore more likely a general reference to sacrilege (cf. Acts 19:37).[53]

23. Three times Paul accuses his dialogue partner of transgressing the law (2:23, 25, 27). The law was not given so that Jews could flaunt their ascendency over others. Paul contends instead that it was added to identify sin as wilful transgression (Gal. 3:19; cf. Rom. 4:15; 5:14). The law should silence this man's boasting. His sinful disobedience dishonours God and makes him no better than the pagan Gentile who does not honour God (1:21).

24. Paul caps off his accusations against his Jewish interlocutor with a slightly altered citation from Isaiah 52:5. Isaiah identifies Israel's lowly estate in exile as emboldening the rulers of the nations to despise God's name. Schreiner notes that in the context of Isaiah's theology (Isa. 64 – 66) 'the people are in exile because of their sin (40:2; 42:24–25; 43:22–28; 50:1)' (Schreiner, pp. 143). Paul draws on this context and Ezekiel's emphasis that Israel's sinfulness has also caused the Gentiles to discredit God's name. Because Israel has profaned God's holy name, God must act to sanctify his name. The prophet Ezekiel particularly emphasizes God's promises to sanctify his name:

---

53. Josephus's use of the term is broad: 'Let no one blaspheme those gods which other cities esteem such; nor may anyone steal what belongs to strange temples; nor take away the gifts that are dedicated to any God' (*Ant.* 4.207 [Thackeray, LCL]).

I will sanctify my great name, which has been profaned among the
nations, and which you have profaned among them; and the nations
shall know that I am the LORD, says the Lord GOD, when through
you I display my holiness before their eyes.
(Ezek. 36:23; cf. Ezek. 20:41; 28:22, 25; 38:16, 23; 39:27; 2 Bar. 21:25)

25. Paul takes for granted that Jews esteem circumcision as the
divinely ordained outward sign of their special covenant relationship with God and of belonging to this holy covenant people. The
'for' (*gar*) is often omitted in translations. It introduces not a new
line of thought but 'strengthening premises' to substantiate what
precedes – that the one who boasts in the law dishonours God by
transgressing the law (2:23).[54] Circumcision is no longer the
outward certification that one belongs to God's covenant people.
It can become instead a sign of hypocrisy when one who is merely
circumcised fails to honour the obligations it entails (Exod. 15:26;
Lev. 25:18; Deut. 4:40; 6:1–6). If the covenant requirements are
disobeyed, then the mark of the covenant is meaningless. Circumcision is no different from uncircumcision, and Jews, like this
dialogue partner, become like Gentiles, 'excluded from citizenship
in Israel and foreigners to the covenants of the promise' (Eph.
2:12a, NIV). Paul does not go so far as to say that they are 'without
hope and without God in the world' (Eph. 2:12b, NIV). His
assertions in 11:17–32 make it clear that is not true. Paul's point is
this: Jews may believe circumcision set them apart as *the* people of
God, but it is not 'a certain passport to salvation' (Barrett, p. 58).
    26. Paul's phrasing of his question in Greek with the negative
interrogatory particle (*ouch*) expects the answer 'Yes': *if those who are
uncircumcised keep the requirements of the law, will not their uncircumcision
be regarded as circumcision?* Most devout Jews would disagree, but
Paul's use of the passive voice (*be regarded*, 'be reckoned') assumes
that God is the subject of the verb. God will regard them so, which
means that circumcision of the flesh is irrelevant to God when it
comes to eternal life. Paul steadfastly maintains elsewhere, 'Circumcision is nothing, and uncircumcision is nothing; but obeying

---

54. Casson, *Textual Signposts*, pp. 128–131.

the commandments of God is everything' (1 Cor. 7:19; cf. Gal. 5:6; 6:15).

27. Paul now cites the case of Gentiles who do not receive physical circumcision because they do not have the Mosaic law as their birthright (cf. Gal. 2:16) but who have kept what the law requires. To assume that someone who is uncircumcised keeps the law, Paul must have in mind only the moral commands in the law (cf. 13:8–10). Obedience to the moral law is decisive for being considered spiritually circumcised. Uncircumcised Gentiles who keep the law could be presented at the final assizes as damnatory evidence against Jews who transgress the law.

The written code (literally in Greek 'the letter', *to gramma*) refers to the law that is external, that which is chiselled on stone tablets or written with ink in books (2 Cor. 3:3). It contrasts with what is internal and written by 'the Spirit of the living God . . . on tablets of human hearts' (2 Cor. 3:3; cf. Rom. 7:6). The problem with 'the letter' as something that is only external is that it has no more power to make someone obey its commands than a traffic stop sign has the power to make a driver come to a complete stop. It simply makes running a stop sign a deliberate transgression. Committing deliberate transgressions places one under a curse: 'Cursed be anyone who does not uphold the words of this law by observing them' (Deut. 27:26; Gal. 3:10; cf. 2 Cor. 3:6–7). The letter not only does not solve the problem of sin but can even make it worse by arousing sinful passions (7:5–11). Even if we obey the commands, we do so like maladroit piano students who memorize the piece, hold their hands correctly, play all the right notes, but fail to make music because the main concern is to avoid making a mistake.

28–29. Paul switches from the second-person singular in addressing his dialogue partner to the third person to comment on two representative individuals, the public Jew and the secret Jew. He draws the astounding conclusion that 'the public Jew with his circumcision is not the true Jew. The secret Jew whose heart is circumcised by the Spirit is the real one.'[55] Outward displays of piety often serve only to cover up inner corruption. Jesus condemns

---

55. Gathercole, *Boasting*, p. 208.

the scribes and Pharisees who 'do all their deeds to be seen by others' by making 'their phylacteries broad and their fringes long' (Matt. 23:5). They are like 'whitewashed tombs, which on the outside look beautiful, but inside they are full of the bones of the dead and of all kinds of filth' (Matt. 23:27). Righteousness is not something that is only external, a surface whitewash, and the true Jew is not someone who is only conspicuously Jewish in following outward customs. That person is simply a Jew according to the flesh (4:1; 9:3; 11:14). The true Jew is identified by an inward disposition that manifests itself in being 'obedient from the heart' (6:17). Paul is not yet referring, at least explicitly, to regenerate Gentile Christ-followers and their spiritual circumcision (Phil. 3:3; Col. 2:11) under a new covenant. His sole purpose at this point in his argument is to expose 'the failures of his contemporaries in order to convince them of their need for that inner renewal that only the Spirit of God can effect' (Matera, p. 77). Bodily circumcision is no prophylactic against God's judgment. *Praise . . . from God*, namely, God's positive verdict in the judgment (1 Cor. 4:5), results only from a thoroughgoing spiritual makeover that affects one's behaviour.

Theology
Josephus lauds the law of Moses as superior to the laws of all other nations, including the wisest of the Greeks. He claims the law is 'the most excellent and necessary form of instruction' (*Ag. Ap.* 2.175 [Thackeray, LCL]) that regulates the entire life of Jews (*Ag. Ap.* 2.156) and boasts, 'So then, learning the laws by heart from our first perception, we have them engraved, as it were, in our hearts, and rare is the one who transgresses them; plea bargaining to escape punishment is impossible' (*Ag. Ap.* 2.178 [Thackeray, LCL]). Paul would agree with the last part of this statement but would challenge the assertion that Jews have the laws so engraved on their hearts that they rarely transgress them. He argues that while they may possess the law and have intimate knowledge of it, that privilege has not resulted in the required obedience. Instead, it has fostered only unjustified overconfidence about how they will fare in God's judgment (cf. Jer. 9:23–26). This is the problem. Their boasting keeps repentance at bay and keeps them from believing

in Jesus as Lord. Paul will argue that all are in need of salvation from damnation for failing to keep the law. Judgment is based on what one does irrespective of one's background. Not every Jew commits the cardinal sins listed, but every Jew is guilty of sin and is liable to God's condemnation despite the Jews' advantaged heritage and their circumcision as the seal of their covenant with God. McFadden concludes, 'The theme of judgement according to works lays a foundation for justification in Romans by developing the context in which justification by faith is to be understood.'[56]

Christians also need to hear Paul's message of judgment. In a world that is filled with those who talk loudly, Paul argues here that actions are what define us. By radically underscoring the problem of human transgression that will lead to God's judgment even for God's chosen people, Paul's message of justification by grace through faith has greater impact. Owning a Bible and memorizing its contents does not save Christians today any more than possessing and studying the law saved the Jew in Paul's day. God never asks what one knows about the law or whether one had good intentions to obey it. One cannot glory in an identity that is not shown to be authentic by one's obedience. Bragging about one's special standing before God is a sure way to lose it. Eternal life comes only through the grace offered in Jesus Christ.

Receiving God's grace does not jettison God's expectation of righteous behaviour. Paul says that while 'neither circumcision nor uncircumcision counts for anything' (Gal. 5:6), what does count is 'faith working through love' (Gal. 5:6), 'a new creation' (Gal. 6:15) and 'obeying the commandments of God' (1 Cor. 7:19). Heschel declared, 'I am commanded, therefore I am',[57] but Paul will argue later that God requires more than obedience that answers a command. God could have created robots to mimic obedience to the law. Jesus required obedience that claims a person wholly for God, and Paul also understands that keeping the commandments of God (1 Cor. 7:19) means an obedience to the will of God that is far more radical than fussy observance of an external code.

---

56. McFadden, Judgment, p. 122.
57. Heschel, Who Is Man?, p. 111.

Paul does not explain how an uncircumcised Gentile might be able to obey the law when his Jewish interlocutor could not. In my interpretation, he does not refer to Gentile Christians becoming spiritual Jews in this passage. He makes a case about Jewish identity. If an uncircumcised Gentile fulfils the intention of the law, even without submitting to Jewish ritual traditions, that person becomes a better representative of what it means to be a Jew than a Jew who does obey these traditions but violates the intention of the law summed up in loving your neighbour as yourself (13:9). At this stage in his argument, Paul aims only at puncturing Jewish pride that assumes the Jews are the only people who interest God and that they alone will be saved because of their birthright and superior heritage. After reading all of Romans, however, Christians understand this text differently and recognize that with the advent of Christ the only Gentile who could possibly meet this benchmark is a Gentile Christ-follower who is justified by faith (3:26) and lives under the promised new covenant (Jer. 31:31–34; Ezek. 36:25–27).

In Deuteronomy 10:16, Moses exhorts Israel to circumcise the foreskin of their own hearts (cf. Jer. 4:4), but in 30:6, he asserts that God will perform this heart circumcision: 'Moreover, the LORD your God will circumcise your heart and the heart of your descendants, so that you will love the LORD your God with all your heart and with all your soul, in order that you may live' (cf. Ezek. 11:19–20; 36:26–27; Jub. 1:23; Odes Sol. 11:1–3). Paul will argue later that the Holy Spirit is the renewing force behind this spiritual operation. Paul is yet to make the case that Christians fulfil the law only by being in Christ. It is therefore dangerously mistaken to take this text to mean that one can become righteous by fulfilling the law through one's own power. Moo comments,

> Like John the Baptist (Matt. 3:7–10) and Jesus (cf. Matt. 21:28–32) before him, Paul denies that belonging to the covenant people per se ensures acceptance with God. Neither possession of the law nor circumcision marks a person as truly belonging to God. Only repentance (2:4) and an inner, heartfelt commitment to God (2:28–29) – in a word, faith – ultimately count before the Lord. (Moo, p. 136)

That Paul's dialogue partner has convinced himself that he is a guide to others may reflect his lack of self-awareness, like those who 'may be clever enough to teach many, / and yet be useless to themselves' (Sir. 37:19). It is Israel's calling, however, to teach others and to glorify God's name among the nations. The problem is that their conduct does not draw the nations to God but instead repels them. Those who teach others but do not practise what they teach are condemned across all cultures. Paul expresses his fear of this failure: 'I punish my body and enslave it, so that after proclaiming to others I myself should not be disqualified' (1 Cor. 9:27). Paul expects that the faith and obedience of Christ-followers will radiate throughout the world (1:8; 16:19).

C. The credibility of God (3:1–8)

Context
In this unit, Paul corrects the possible mistaken inference that God's impartiality in judging both Jew and Gentile means that God has revoked the covenant promises to Israel. Paul does not discount Jewish pre-eminence but asserts that simply possessing the 'words of God' does not mean that one will obey them. Being physically circumcised does not ensure that one's heart has been circumcised – that is, having a pure heart devoted to God. What is decisive is doing God's will as spelled out in God's divine utterances.

To make his position clearer, Paul shifts his rhetorical strategy. The questions in this unit do not originate from an imaginary protester. They develop from the internal logic of Paul's argument in 2:1–29 and clarify major propositions. The questions he asks, then, are not intended to refute outside opponents but to lead believers to a deeper understanding and commitment of their lives to the gospel he preaches.[58] He assumes that his audience will concur with both the answers and the reasoning behind them.[59] He uses the questions to present a historical or theological fact in his

---

58. Achtemeier, 'Romans 3:1–8', p. 83.
59. Stowers, 'Paul's Dialogue', p. 711, cites Quintilian and Teles as examples of this method of argument.

answer. If some were unfaithful (3:3), God remains true (3:4). God's righteousness does not hinge on the faithfulness of his people. If my unrighteousness highlights God's faithfulness, which abounds to God's glory (3:7), is it unfair for God to judge me and inflict wrath on me for being a sinner (3:5, 7)? Absolutely not. God rightfully is the judge of the world.

This unit affirms God's integrity in keeping promises and in both saving and judging. The answers to the questions raised derive from God's words (3:2), God's faithfulness (3:3), God's truth (3:4, 7), God's righteousness (3:5), God's judgment (3:6) and God's glory (3:7). The questions raised here are taken up again and answered in greater depth in chapter 9: he addresses God's truthfulness and faithfulness to his promises (3:3–4, 7) in 9:7–13; God's justice/injustice (3:5) in 9:14–18 (10:2–3); God's judgment (3:6) in 9:22; and God's glory (3:7) in 9:23. Paul also takes up the question whether one should sin so that more grace might abound (3:8) in 6:1 and 6:15. There he does more than condemn the slanderous suggestion that his gospel of grace encourages persons to continue to do what is evil to evoke even more grace from God and augment God's glory as all-merciful. He discusses the power that Christians have through the Spirit to live righteous lives.[60] Paul cites Psalm 51:4 in 3:4, but the whole psalm informs Paul's theological assumptions in the context of his arguments (Jackson W., pp. 70–72). God desires truth in one's inner self (Ps. 51:6), which accords with what Paul says in 2:28–29. God does not delight in shallow, outward works such as sacrifices and burnt offerings (Ps. 51:16), which accords with what Paul says in 3:20, 27–28; 4:1–6; 9:12, 32; and 11:6. Instead, God requires 'a broken spirit . . . a broken and contrite heart' (Ps. 51:17), and then God forgives. God's forgiveness blots out the guilt of sins yet does not solve the problem. David pleads for God to create a clean heart for him and to renew in him a steadfast spirit (Ps. 51:10). Paul shows how God does this for believers through the Spirit (8:1–13; cf. 2:29).

---

60. Wright, 'Romans 2:17 – 3:9', p. 7.

Comment

1–2. The first question reprocesses the Jewish boasts highlighted in 2:17–20 that denote the distinctive advantages Jews have over others. The second question takes up the theme of circumcision raised in 2:25–29. Those who have read Galatians might assume that Paul's answer to the second question about the benefit of circumcision would receive a resounding 'Nothing' (Gal. 5:6; 6:15; cf. 1 Cor. 7:19). He pulls the rug out from under this false supposition by saying that circumcision has *much* value, *in every way*. The issue of God's credibility lies at the root of the two questions. If the Jew has no advantage and circumcision has no value, then either the Scriptures are a false witness or God has reneged on the promises – in particular, the promise made to Abraham in Genesis 17:1–7 that is tied to the requirement of circumcision. God declares it an 'everlasting covenant'. Paul argues from the basic assumption that God is always faithful (Deut. 7:9; 32:4; Ps. 33:4; Isa. 49:7). Israel's primacy is not illusory. The Jews' priority, however, may mislead them to think that God will treat them differently from the rest of the world's sinners. God's covenant with Abraham does not include a non-punishment clause. God's righteousness will not exempt Israel from receiving the same impartial judgment meted out to all sinners (Cranfield, I, pp. 176–177).

Most Jews viewed circumcision as an indispensable mark that signified obedience to God's commands (Deut. 30:15–20).[61] Since one could break the Sabbath to circumcise a boy on the eighth day (m. Šabb. 19:2), Jews regarded circumcision as foremost among the biblical commands. Jubilees calls it an 'eternal ordinance':

> anyone who is born whose own flesh is not circumcised on the eighth day is not from the sons of the covenant, which the Lord made for Abraham since (he is) from the children of destruction. And therefore there is no sign upon him so that he might belong to the Lord because

---

61. According to a late rabbinic Midrash, when a Roman official asked R. Oshaya why God had not made man as he wanted him, he replied that it was in order that man should perfect himself by the fulfilment of a divine command (Gen. Rab. 11:6).

(he is destined) to be destroyed and to be annihilated from the earth
and to be uprooted from the earth because he has broken the covenant
of our Lord God.

(Jub. 15:26)[62]

Paul, however, has defined circumcision's value in terms of obedience to the law (2:25). Circumcision turns into a meaningless physical
mark if it does not reflect what it is intended to signify, namely,
obedience to God in one's heart and soul. Jews therefore can squander their advantages, and their circumcision can become uncircumcision when they are unfaithful to God.

The Jews are truly privileged because they were entrusted with
the oracles of God (cf. Deut. 4:8; Ps. 106:12; 147:19–20), which most
likely refers to God's revelation in Scripture.[63] Paul may have in
mind particular revelation related to the scriptural promises related
to Christ. He comments in 3:21–22 that God's righteousness has
been disclosed apart from the law, is attested by the Law and the
Prophets, and comes only through faith in Christ. Since he also
declares, 'For whatever was written in the past was written for our
instruction, so that we may have hope through endurance and
through the encouragement from the Scriptures' (15:4, CSB), it is
likely that he has in mind the oral utterances of God 'promised
beforehand' that became 'the gospel of God' (1:1–2). Paul emphasizes God's promises to Abraham in 4:13–14, 16, 20 (cf. 15:8).

The verb *entrusted* implies that God spoke to Israel for the benefit
of others. Paul uses the same verb to state his conviction that God
entrusted him with a stewardship of the gospel that God willed to
save all peoples by faith so that he would pass it on to others (1 Cor.
9:17; Gal. 2:7; 1 Thess. 2:4; 1 Tim. 1:11). In the same manner, God
did not call Israel to be the curator of the divine words to be safely
locked up in some holy, tamper-proof museum. Being the trustee
of the divine words obligated Israel to be labouring in the world as
'a guide to the blind, a light to those who are in darkness' (2:19–20;
cf. Isa. 42:6; 49:6; 60:3).

---

62. Wintermute, *OTP* II, p. 87.

63. Doeve, 'Some Notes', p. 122.

3-4. The beginning of verse 3 is best translated, 'What if some did not trust [believe]?' Paul refers to the Jewish refusal to recognize that the promises to Abraham were now being fulfilled in Jesus as the Messiah (10:14-21).[64] He later laments that many of his fellow Jewish have rejected Jesus as the Messiah and have stumbled over the stumbling stone because they have sought a righteousness based on works and not on faith (9:31-33; cf. 1 Pet. 2:6-8). By refusing to believe in Jesus they repeat Israel's past rebellion (cf. 1 Cor. 10:7-10). For Paul, this failure to believe in Christ (11:23) is equivalent to 'unfaithfulness to the covenant'.[65] Using the word *some* allows for a faithful remnant (11:5), but the refusal by other Jews to believe the gospel places them on the same level as unbelieving Gentiles.

The faithfulness of God implies God's fidelity to promising salvation for Israel (cf. Num. 23:19; Deut. 7:9; Isa. 49:7). Nehemiah 9:7-8 affirms that God is righteous for fulfilling the promise to Abraham. The rub is that according to Paul's gospel the fulfilment of the promise to Abraham accords salvation to foreskinned Gentiles who believe in Christ, while excluding Jews who are duly circumcised and faithful to the law but who do not believe in Christ. Paul poses a leading question expecting the answer 'No': *What if some were unfaithful? Will their faithlessness nullify the faithfulness of God?* Paul regards the premise behind the question as unthinkable,[66] and it receives an emphatic *By no means!* God's faithfulness is bound to God's character, and Paul considers it axiomatic that God is true, always faithful in keeping promises, and always doing what is right. The unfaithfulness of some Jews will not cause God to renounce the pledge to be faithful to Israel.

Let God be proved true translates a third-person imperative which has no equivalent in English. Like the third-person imperatives we

---

64. Cosgrove, 'What If', p. 105 n. 38, notes that Paul uses the substantive adjective form (*apistos*) of the verb (*apisteō*) for 'unbelievers' (1 Cor. 6:6; 7:12-15; 10:27; 14:22-24; 2 Cor. 4:4; cf. 6:14-15).

65. Hall, 'Romans 3.1-8', pp. 185-186.

66. This and the following questions in this chapter anticipate fuller answers that Paul expounds in chapters 9-11 (cf. 9:14).

find in the Lord's Prayer ('Your kingdom come. Your will be done', Matt. 6:10), Paul prays for divine action, for God to manifest (once again) God's fidelity true to the covenant. The prayer alludes to Psalm 116:11 (115:2 LXX) in which the psalmist indicts everyone as a liar while God has remained true despite dealing with a fickle and untrustworthy Israel. The citation from Psalm 51:4 (50:6 LXX), *So that you may be justified in your words, / and prevail in your judging*, confirms Paul's line of reasoning. Being true to the covenant also entails that God execute judgment on Israel when their sin warrants it. The *words* of God do not only record promises and blessings. They also include warnings of God's judgment, stories of God regularly carrying out that judgment, and the recognition that God was just to do so. In the cited psalm, the contrite David confesses his sin before God (presumably for sexually assailing Bathsheba and orchestrating her husband Uriah's death) and acknowledges that God was right in severely punishing him for his sin. The full story of David reveals, however, that God remains true to the covenant promises even when God inflicts dire punishment. David proved unfaithful, but God's judgment on his sin did not rescind God's truthfulness in making the promises to David that his offspring would reign for ever (2 Sam. 7:13–14; Ps. 89:24–37). God remained faithful in fulfilling the promises made to David (cf. Rom. 1:3).

Paul's context imagines a court scene at the end of time in which God wins the verdict over Israel. Only at the end of time will it become evident to all that God has triumphed.[67] Despite allegations that God has jilted the chosen people, God will stick to the course that has been mapped out to offer salvation to all humans, and God will be proven to have been true, faithful, righteous and merciful even when God judges.

5–6. The phrases *what should we say?* and *I speak in a human way* indicate that Paul is not responding to an imagined objector but seeks to reinforce his teaching point that God remains righteous when bringing wrath on the Jews' wickedness just as God is righteous in bringing wrath on the Gentiles' wickedness (1:18). All

---

67. Williams, 'Righteousness', pp. 269–270.

those who are 'self-seeking and who obey not the truth but wickedness' will face God's 'wrath and fury' (2:8). Despite their great advantage in being entrusted with 'the oracles of God', the Jews have been unfaithful to God (cf. 2 Kgs 17:18–19; Neh. 9:13–30). This is not an anti-Jewish comment since Paul uses the first-person plural pronoun in *our injustice* (or 'our unrighteousness') to express his union with the Jews (cf. 9:3–4). Throughout Israel's history, God demonstrated his righteousness when he poured out mercy on Israel after they sinned (Neh. 9:31) and when he poured out his wrath after they sinned (Jer. 32:30–33). The suggestion that God might be *unjust* in inflicting wrath on the Jews therefore receives a ringing 'No!' God's saving power does not suspend God's judging power. When God inflicts punishment for unrighteousness, it is in harmony with God's righteousness that also brings salvation to the unrighteous. Scripture affirms that God is the judge of the world (Gen. 18:25) and, as Psalm 51:4 makes clear, also affirms God's fairness in meting out punishment. Denying God the freedom to condemn the Jews is equivalent to denying God the freedom to be the judge. God's integrity entails that God will judge all, including Israel, fairly. Since God is even-handed in judging, God is not underhanded in condemning Israel, particularly those Jews who give lip-service to their reliance on the law yet thumb their noses at God by transgressing it. Paul rejects cheap grace for Israel. If God were to waive expressing wrath on the Jews in history, then God would be unfair, inconsistent and unrighteous in judging the world at the end-time assizes.

7. God is the judge of the world, and Paul reduces any objection to this obvious point to an absurdity with his last question: why should God hold him accountable for his sin when it is God's forgiveness that amplifies God's glory as a gracious Saviour? Translating it as 'someone might argue' (NIV) is most misleading. The *I* refers to himself since Paul sees himself as a sinner (cf. 1 Cor. 15:9–10) who 'also' (*kagō*; CSB) is being judged by God. He speaks of himself as a representative of all Jews who claim allegiance to the law and mistakenly assume that they deserve a bye in the judgment (Phil. 3:4–6) and that God's truthfulness and faithfulness to the promises will be manifested when God will

bail them out despite their sins. When read in the light of Galatians 2:15, the question contains a deeper bitterness. Jews conventionally differentiated themselves from Gentiles who were sinners. The question asks, 'Why am I, a Jew, judged as if I were on the same level as a lawless Gentile?' Implicit in this question is another: 'How could this about-turn by God in which Jews are liable to the same judgment as unrighteous Gentiles possibly bring glory to God?' One can see why Paul offers the forewarning in verse 5 that he speaks 'in a human way' (*kata anthrōpon*). This all-too-human viewpoint that assumes special privilege and expects leniency from God that even someone like Paul might entertain must be totally rejected. Jews are in the same position as Gentiles and all humanity when it comes to God's judgment of sinners.

8. Memories of opponents' criticism that Paul's gospel asserts that believers are no longer under any obligation to obey God's law and that it consequently fosters sin probably trigger this parenthetical outburst. The opponents may be Christian Jews (Acts 15:1, 5; 21:21) or Jews outside the church.[68] If the detractors are unbelieving Jews, they falsely reason that if God does not differentiate between Jews and Gentiles, then God has abandoned differentiating between the righteous and the sinner. Any idea that a divine moral order presides over the world goes up in smoke. If those who misrepresent his gospel are Christians, they falsely reason that it serves no purpose to knock oneself out trying to obey God's law. It is more likely that Paul still has in mind Jewish opponents to the gospel. The question assumes that the greater the human evil, the greater God's grace must be to forgive it. Displays of such amazing grace blazon God's glory all the more. God therefore has no right to judge Jews for their faithlessness to the covenant since it only serves to enhance God's glory. Paul's strong denunciation of those who make such untenable inferences conveys

---

68. The opponents are unlikely to be Roman Christians since Paul phrases his question to expect the answer 'No!', expecting his audience to agree with him that such an inference is ridiculous.

his conviction that rejecting or distorting his gospel brings divine condemnation.

Paul's answer to the question anticipates his arguments in chapter 11. He maintains that Israel's 'stumbling' (11:11), 'defeat' (11:12), 'rejection' of the gospel (11:15), 'hardening' (11:25), enmity towards the gospel (11:28) and 'disobedience' (11:30) have opened the door for Gentiles to receive 'salvation' (11:11), 'riches' (11:12) and 'reconciliation' (11:15). God's mercy on sinners has made 'known the riches of his glory' (9:23), and Paul concludes the argument in chapters 9–11 with a doxology, 'To him be the glory for ever' (11:36). Israel's persistence in their sinful rebellion against the gospel, however, does not bring greater glory to God. Only their acceptance of it (11:15) will magnify God's glory when God takes away their sins (11:27) and miraculously grafts them back 'into their own olive tree' (11:24).

Theology

The issue of God's righteousness is central to Romans (1:17; 3:21; 9:6; 9:30 – 10:4; 11:29–32). In this unit, Paul grapples with the question as to how God remains righteous after promising to prosper Israel in an everlasting covenant (Gen. 17:1–7) only to condemn them for refusing to believe in Christ. Paul's fundamental belief that God is right and humans are wrong governs his argument. Gentiles face the wrath of God because they reject the light given in nature. Some Jews face the wrath of God (1 Thess. 2:14–16) because they reject the light given in the 'oracles of God' and deny that God's promises are being fulfilled by Christ's coming into the world. He argues from passages from the Psalms that humans, in this context applied to the Jews, are unfaithful (3:3), liars (3:4), unrighteous (3:5) and unabashed sinners (3:7). They are neither true to God nor true to their calling. God's righteousness, however, remains constant, unaffected by human corruption. God is faithful (3:3) and true (3:4) and demonstrates righteousness in judging sin (3:5), not just in showing mercy. God's wrath on sin is not waived for the Jews because of their special covenantal status. As judge of the world, God judges all sinners alike. God also shows mercy on all sinners alike who believe in Jesus.

Paul addresses the concern that if God's impartial judgment accepts Gentiles who have faith in Jesus and rejects law-obeying Jews who do not, then the world is no longer governed by the fruit of good deeds.[69] Why put oneself out trying to do good deeds?[70] Grace does not make sin any less loathsome to God. Paul insists that God does not overlook sin simply to be touted as a kindly benefactor. Penitent sinners, such as David (Ps. 51:4), recognize that God is their judge and that God's punishment for their sin is fully warranted. Paul adopts the same posture in acknowledging that God also judges him as a sinner. Penitent sinners own up to their state of abject deficiency and also plead for salvation and hope that God will be merciful. The psalmist knows that God also demonstrates his righteousness in pardoning the sin of unrighteous humans (Ps. 143:2, 11).[71]

The solution to humans' sin problem, however, is far more complex than God simply cancelling the debt and whitewashing the sin. Paul knows that there can be no forgiveness or salvation outside of trusting in Christ. Consequently, not believing in Jesus, whether one is faithful to the law or not, epitomizes unrighteousness. Jews have an advantage because of their history with God, but they have no advantage when it comes to making a claim on God by virtue of their own merit. They have none, and God will not handicap the final verdict in their favour. This point is important for what follows. If God makes no exception for the Jews, then all humankind must stand condemned before God.

Paul acknowledges the magnitude of the Jews' privilege. The gospel has not voided the attendant benefits and obligations that come from being God's chosen people. Instead, they are intensified. Having 'the oracles of God', 'the law and the prophets', entrusted to them (3:2, 21) gave the Jews an advantage, a preview of God's intentions in a new covenant. From Paul's perspective, possessing the 'oracles of God' is an advantage only if they are interpreted as

---

69. Bassler, *Divine Impartiality*, p. 47.

70. Paul addresses the vital importance of ethical behaviour for Christians in chs. 6–8.

71. Cosgrove, 'What If', p. 95.

signposts pointing to the gospel revealed in Jesus Christ. They also steer Israel to fulfil its vocation in the world. The 'oracles of God' are not to be turned into a legal codebook of behaviour that bolsters Jewish boasts and countenances their exclusion of others who fail to measure up to their standards rather than God's.[72] Israel's superiority, therefore, is based solely on its weighty responsibility to be a light to the world. As Cranfield comments, Israel had an inside track, but those who stood the nearest to the working out of God's saving purposes were 'blind, deaf, and uncomprehending'. The reason was that 'they fundamentally misunderstood their special position when they thought of it as a ground for complacency and all too human glorying' (Cranfield, I, p. 178). They turned the 'oracles of God' into ethnic rituals that cordoned themselves off from others. They bowed their knees before the altar of their imagined ethnic superiority. That attitude will result only in self-exclusion from salvation.

D. All are under sin's power (3:9–20)

Context
After insisting that God is always reliable and upholds the covenant promises, while the chosen people have been unfaithful, untruthful and unrighteous, Paul corroborates this accusation with the testimony of Scripture. Since the Scriptures are addressed to the Jews (3:19), they should see themselves as the object of these denunciations. The chain of quotes cataloguing a gamut of sins is probably Paul's own creation.[73] They quash any Jewish boast to be morally superior to others. Paul's aim, however, is to make the case that if Jews are under the power of sin, then all people, both the self-acclaimed righteous and infamous sinners, are also in its unrelenting clutches. Jews and Gentiles are united in this human morass.

The Scripture passages in their original contexts denounced Israel's enemies and the wicked in Israel. Since Paul believes that

---

72. Caird, *Paul's Letters*, pp. 136–137.
73. Seifrid, 'Romans', p. 616.

Scripture 'has imprisoned all things under the power of sin, so that
what was promised through faith in Jesus Christ might be given to
those who believe' (Gal. 3:22), these passages are examples of Scripture consigning everyone under the power of sin. They obliterate
the distinctions between the righteous and the unrighteous. All are
without excuse and store up wrath for themselves for 'the day of
wrath, when God's righteous judgement will be revealed' (2:5).

Paul sets out the dire situation in which all, both Jews and
Gentiles, are mired as a prelude to his discussion of God's
resolution of the problem (3:21–26). God's solution shines an even
harsher light on the severity of the human predicament and makes
it fully known. The cross of Christ reveals humanity's inborn,
inveterate and intractable rebellion against God. Only faith in
Christ changes one's life.

Comment

9. Paul's question is normally rendered, 'Do we have any advantage?' or *Are we any better off?*, which takes the verb (*proechometha*) as
a middle voice with an active meaning. Since no lexical examples
for this usage have been found, the verb has also been read as a
middle voice in which the subject acts in his own interest. The *we*
would refer to Paul, who asks if he is putting forward a pretext or
an excuse to defend himself.[74] It also could be read as a passive
verb: 'Are we surpassed?', that is, 'Have we (Jews) lost our advantage and are we now in a worse position than they (Gentiles)?'
Neither of these readings makes sense from what follows, where
Paul asserts that all humans are equally guilty. The usual translation
is the best option as Paul picks up his argument from 3:1 and
moderates his assertion in 3:2 that Jews have an advantage, 'much,
in every way'. He now says, *No, not at all*, which might be better
translated as 'not entirely' (CJB) or 'not altogether'. The acknowledged Jewish advantages in receiving special revelation do not
shield them from the power of sin nor from God's wrath because
of their sins. All are under the law. The Jews are under the Mosaic
law; the Gentiles, under the universal moral law (2:15–16). Being

---

74. Literally, the Greek verb means 'to hold something before oneself'.

under the law means that both Jews and Gentiles are under the power of sin that seizes the commandment, perverts it, blurs the distinction between right and wrong, and generates cravings that violate God's law (7:8–11) and ensnare them in the web of death.

The noun *sin* (*hamartia*) makes its first appearance in Romans. Paul conceives of sin here as something far more fearsome than individual sinful acts. It is a power that takes captive and enslaves every person, Jew and Greek (7:14).

10–12. The first scriptural proof in verse 10 comes from Ecclesiastes 7:20 and states the main theme: 'Surely there is no one on earth so righteous as to do good without ever sinning' (cf. Isa. 24:5). For Paul, this indictment would also include David, whom God declares to be 'a man after my heart, who will carry out all my wishes' (Acts 13:22; cf. 1 Sam. 13:14). The quotes from Psalm 14:1–3 (Ps. 53:3) in verses 11–12 contain charges similar to those Paul makes against the Gentiles in evoking God's wrath. While God seeks humans long before humans seek God, humankind failed to respond to God's overtures and chose to go after their own gods. A darkened mind, useless from its moral depravity, and a complete lack of understanding of one's proper place in creation (cf. 1:21, 28) are the results of not seeking God. Human relationships deteriorate (cf. 1:29–32). Kindness dies, and with it every shred of goodness. If these accusations are true of Jews and their failure to seek God, then Israel's reason for being a light to the nations has been extinguished. God will have to rebuild Israel (cf. Acts 15:15–18) to accomplish that calling.

13–17. The citations in these verses from Psalm 5:9; 140:3; 10:7; and Isaiah 59:7–8 (Prov. 1:16) spell out how sin affects everything in a human's life: throat, lips, mouth and feet. Throats that have become *opened graves* vividly pictures an inner corruption that manifests itself in speech marked by treachery, malice, blasphemy and hostility. Evil speech – *'Their throats are opened graves; / they use their tongues to deceive.' / 'The venom of vipers is under their lips.' / 'Their mouths are full of cursing and bitterness'* – results in acts of human cruelty. Such corrosive speech destabilizes peace by further alienating persons from one another as they lurch down deadly paths of destructive horror, shedding blood without hesitation and sowing widespread misery. All human history reflects the repeated breakdown of peaceful accord as individuals and nations are bent on conquering others so that they might be known as conquerors (cf. Rev. 6:2).

18. The last passage cited, from Psalm 36:1, presents the principal reason why humans do not seek God. *Fear of God* does not refer here to reverential awe. It refers instead to dread of God's final judgment (cf. 13:3). John Calvin, defending his break from the Catholic Church as leaving false worship for true worship in his discovery of the Scriptures, wrote:

> Being exceedingly alarmed at the misery into which I had fallen, and much more at that which threatened me in view of eternal death, I, duty bound, made it my first business to betake myself to your way, condemning my past life, not without groans and tears.[75]

Calvin came to appreciate that believers need not fear God's sentence of eternal death.

19. As a promise, the law witnesses to Christ (Luke 24:27, 44), but Paul highlights another function of the law. It provides objective and decisive proof of humankind's guilt. Jews are *under the law* (1 Cor. 9:20; Gal. 4:5), but the law will not come to the Jews' defence as a character witness in God's judgment. It is their accuser, exposing their unrighteousness and sin (7:7–25), and their jury, imposing the death sentence for their failures to obey. When that sentence is read at the final judgment, every mouth uttering hollow complaints, allegations and excuses will be throttled.

20. Paul sums up his argument with a final quote from Psalm 143:2 indicting all humanity: *no human being will be justified in [God's] sight* (cf. Gal. 2:16). Translating it as *no human being* or 'no-one' to refer to human beings in general misses a subtle theological point. Paul altered the psalm's 'no one living' to read 'all flesh'. Paul chooses the word 'flesh' because for him it denotes

> man in his weakness and corruptibility, man in his dependency on this world. It is precisely man in his independence from God, choosing to

---

75. Olin, *Reformation Debate*, p. 90.

live on his own terms, for himself, man the creature of his appetites, subservient to his mortality, man taking his sense of value from this world, its society and its standards, man, in a word, as 'flesh', who can have no hope of acquittal on the day of judgment.

(Dunn, I, p. 159)

Paul may echo Genesis 6:12: 'And God saw that the earth was corrupt; for all flesh had corrupted its ways upon the earth.' Being 'in the flesh' means that all humans are incapable of altering their corrupted state through works of the law.

Paul also adds that 'all flesh' will not be justified by 'works of the law' (CSB). 'Works of the law' (cf. 3:28; Gal. 2:16; 3:2, 5, 10) refers to those ceremonial commands in the Mosaic law that serve as boundary markers dividing Jews from Gentiles, such as the observance of the Sabbath, feast days, food restrictions and circumcision. Observing them means that one lives 'like a Jew' and not 'like a Gentile' (Gal. 2:14). Adherence to these boundary markers displays the Jews' exclusive covenant relationship with God, which can feed pride and become tangible grounds for boasting. Dunn originally contended that 'works of the law' functioned as a means 'to retain one's status as a member of the people of God', and that Paul regarded them as 'more superficial, at the level of "the letter" (2:27, 29), an outward mark indicative of ethnic solidarity (2:28), something more limited than "the patient perseverance in good work" (2:7)' (Dunn, I, pp. 158–159). Dunn has since clarified that he views 'works of the law' as referring to 'what the law requires, the conduct prescribed by the Torah' that must be performed.[76] It is argued that Paul refers to the emphasis placed on laws that distinguished Jews from Gentiles as a way to consolidate their superior status and to exclude Gentiles. Certainly, many Jews feared losing that which made them special in their eyes, and so they magnified the importance of these laws.

This view that 'works of the law' applies primarily to boundary markers in the law fails to take into account the full orb of Jewish religion in this era that could affirm that salvation came by grace

---

76. Dunn, *New Perspective*, pp. 23–28.

and also righteousness came by works without trying to harmonize the different conceptions.[77] It also garbles Paul's view of justification by faith.[78] Gathercole comments, 'The problem for the Jew is not their attitude that exploits their privileges, possession of the law and circumcision, but their transgressing the law which makes their circumcision uncircumcision.'[79] Since Paul says that 'works of the law' fail to achieve justification for (literally) 'all flesh' (*no human being*), he does not think that 'works of the law' applies only to Jewish boundary markers. It also applies to Gentiles who do not possess the law but instinctively do what the law requires (2:14–17). The problem with 'works of the law' is not that they are a distinctively Jewish means of excluding others but that 'they are "works" that humans under sin's power (3:9) are unable to produce in adequate measure to secure righteous standing with God' (Moo, p. 220).

The traditional view that Paul understands 'works of the law' to refer to the attempt to establish one's righteousness by means of doing the works commanded in the Mosaic law remains valid.[80] 'Works of the law' are not to be limited only to Jewish boundary rituals that separate Jews from Gentiles and oppose the gospel's universality that transcends the distinction between Jew and Gentile.[81] They refer to all the commands in the *law*, and 'works'

---

77. 2 Bar. 51:7 refers to 'those who are saved because of their works' (Klijn, *OTP* I, p. 638). Cf. 1 En. 99:10.

78. For a summary and critique of this 'new' perspective(s) on Paul, see Gathercole, *Boasting*; Seifrid, 'New Perspective'; and Stuhlmacher, *Challenge*.

79. Gathercole, 'Justification', p. 239.

80. Cf. Deut. 27:26; 28:58; 29:29; 32:46. Seifrid, *Justification*, pp. 56–57, 71–81, finds a clear emphasis on the importance of works for eventual salvation in Pss Sol. and 1QS. Talbert, pp. 91–99, documents how Palestinian Judaism was far more 'legalistic' than the new perspective on Paul allows.

81. 4QMMT is a composite reconstruction of a letter written by the leaders of the Qumran sect to anonymous addressees, portions of which survive in different fragments. The letter outlines interpretations of Mosaic precepts that distinguish what is pure and impure in the

implies that these commands require obedience. Paul sees the Jews' primary problem as seeking to establish their own righteousness by striving to do what Moses commanded in the law, and not submitting to God's righteousness that comes only through Christ (10:3, 5). Ephesians 2:8–10; 2 Timothy 1:8–10; and Titus 3:4–7 explicitly reject the belief that one can be saved by works of righteousness. Even if one does not believe that Paul wrote these letters, the reactions of some first-century Jews to this confidence are evidence that they did hold this view. If one believes that Paul did write these letters, it is evidence that he sought to counter the view that one can earn salvation through works. The prayer of Ezra in 2 Esdras 8:33, 'For the righteous, who have many works laid up with you, shall receive their reward in consequence of their own deeds', reflects this view. God rebuffs Ezra's plea to be 'merciful to those who have no store of good works', even though it would declare 'your righteousness and goodness' (2 Esd. 8:36–41). God declares instead that 'a great number' will perish because 'they despised the Most High, and were contemptuous of his law, and abandoned his ways', knowing full well that doing so meant that 'they must die' (2 Esd. 8:55–58).

Paul also links the phrase 'works of the law' to *the law* in 3:20. In Galatians 3:10–11, he equates 'works of the law' with 'all the things written in the book of the law'. In Galatians 2:21, he argues, 'If justification [righteousness] comes through the law, then Christ died for nothing', which parallels his statement in 2:16: 'no one will be justified by the works of the law'. The problem is that the law cannot

---

(note 81 *cont.*) administration of the temple cult. It is the only ancient Jewish text that contains the phrase 'some works of the law'. It appears in a context of warnings for transgressing the author's interpretation of certain precepts in the law with the promise that it will be 'reckoned to you as justice [righteousness] when you do what is upright and good before him' (Martínez, *Dead Sea Scrolls*, p. 79). The verdict of righteousness proceeds from doing the works of the law. Fitzmyer's interpretation of the phrase given shortly after the document's publication remains compelling. It refers to 'things prescribed or required by the Mosaic law' (*According to Paul*, pp. 18–20).

break the power of sin, but sin breaks the power of the law, rendering it incapable of helping humans surmount sin. According to Romans 5:20 and Galatians 3:19, God added the law to make obvious the moral and religious situation of the world by clarifying the nature of sin as a deliberate violation of God's will. It makes clear that humans not only violate God's will when they sin, but they do so fully aware that it is a violation of God's will. With the law, their defiance now becomes conscious and deliberate rebellion against God.

The phrase 'works of the law' is equivalent to the use of 'works' by itself in 4:2–6 (cf. 9:32). It refers to anything that a person does expecting that it will 'bring him or her into favor with God' (Moo, p. 220).[82] Paul was convinced that he was blameless when it came to righteousness commended by the law (Phil. 3:6). Sin seizes every opportunity to distort the law (7:7–23) and causes humans, for example, to modify the law's requirements to make them more attainable and thus create the mirage that one has fulfilled its intentions. In 10:21, Paul cites Isaiah 65:2 to counter any delusion that Israel has dutifully submitted to God. They have consistently been disobedient and contrary. Banking on their obedience to the law to win an acquittal at the final judgment is misguided and will derail the salvation they so zealously pursue (10:1). Sin, the refusal to honour God and the exaltation of oneself, existed before the law. Paul asserts that God did not give the law as a guide on how to attain salvation, nor as a legacy to elevate Jews over Gentiles, but as a divine informer that brings *knowledge* of one's sinfulness. The evident inability of Jews to keep the whole law brings Jews down to the same level as Gentiles as sinners before God. The battery of sins in 3:10–18 provides an example of how the law functions in specifying evil deeds. It convicts both Jews and Gentiles. All are without excuse and, when confronted with the incontrovertible evidence of their sins in God's court of law, they can only remain silent. Attempts to obey the law to set oneself right with God are futile, since the law only heightens an awareness of failure. Worse,

---

82. McFadden, *Judgment*, pp. 90–91, notes, 'Paul uses the word "work" together with its cognates and synonyms to refer to good or evil works throughout the accusation.' Cf. 1:32 – 2:3, 7–10; 13, 15, 25–26, 27.

the law offers no permanent antidote to sin. The priests must offer the law's prescribed sacrifices for sin continually, day after day, year after year (Heb. 7:27; 9:6, 25). This repetition was a perpetual reminder that they never completely remove guilt and never cleanse from sin 'once for all' (Heb. 10:1–3). The need for atonement persists. Consequently,

> God has bypassed the Law altogether in the eschatological manifestation of his righteousness. Nevertheless, the Law retains its capacity to convict man of unrighteousness and, now that its testimony can finally be comprehended through Christ (cf. 2 Cor. 3:14–16), it serves also as a witness to the righteousness of God (Rom 3:21b).[83]

Paul understands that forgiveness, righteousness and redemption come only through Christ's atoning sacrifice and through faith in Christ.

Theology
It is not provocative for a Jew to say that all have sinned. It is asserted in 2 Esdras 8:35: 'For in truth there is no one among those who have been born who has not acted wickedly; among those who have existed there is no one who has not done wrong.' It is provocative, however, for a Jew to imply that obedience to the law is not the way to salvation and that those who follow that path are hopelessly doomed. The reason is that all humankind is under the power of sin. The root problem is not Israel's misuse of the law that leads to self-righteous boasting about their superiority over others, nor their thinking that they are safe from God's judgment because of their unique status as God's chosen people. The problem is that Jews are under the same power of sin and guilty of the same wickedness that galvanizes God's wrath against the Gentiles. Paul personifies sin as a cosmic power. Sin is not simply an infraction of God's law but a force that manipulates humans as if they were mere puppets. Persons do not have control over their sin; sin controls them. It corrupts everything they do and think, including their

---

83. Williams, 'Righteousness', p. 271.

learned meditations and best intentions. Consequently, all attempts to obey the law ultimately fail.

The law has no power to defuse the power of sin. It only raises awareness of human sinfulness. Paul portrays the law as a kind of investigating officer, prosecutor, and judge and jury. It consigns all humankind to death row in the dungeon where sin serves as a cruel jailer. Barrett expresses well the human plight that Paul describes:

> As long, therefore, as God's righteousness is manifested and understood in terms of the law it must spell wrath. The only hope for man is that God should find some other means, beyond law and religion, of manifesting his righteousness. (Barrett, p. 30)

The law offers no remedy and no reprieve. Only God has the power to enable the great escape from sin's clutches and eternal death.

Paul's statement in 3:20, 'by the works of the law shall no flesh be justified in his sight' (ASV), modifies what he wrote in 2:13 that only 'the doers of the law' will be 'righteous in God's sight'. In principle, Paul grants that final vindication may be attained by doing what is good (2:7, 10). While the phrase 'no flesh' in Greek essentially means 'no human being', the more archaic, literal rendering is a reminder that the problem is that flesh can never do what is good because it weakens the law (8:3) and is hostile to God (8:7).[84] The human incapacity to fulfil God's demands in the law means that no-one can ever achieve a right standing with God based on his or her works. No-one has sufficient resources to give anything to God that could ransom his or her soul (Ps. 49:8; Mark 8:37). Repeated repentance and mournful appeals for God to show mercy do not suffice to receive acquittal before the bar of God's unyielding justice. Because of sin, humans find themselves in such a hopeless quagmire that it requires God to create some other measure by which they can be justified. Otherwise, all inevitably will be condemned. Therefore, Paul amends the warnings in the

---

84. Gathercole, 'Justification', p. 239.

Old Testament that keeping the ordinances of God is the way to life and disobeying them is the way to death (Lev. 18:4–5; Deut. 4:1; 5:32–33; 11:8–9; 30:15–20). They may be the way to live life as a Jew, but they are not the way to eternal life.

Consequently, continuing to rely on works of the law to achieve justification before God is not only futile, it reflects a sinful stubbornness to submit to the way that God now provides for humans to become righteous through faith in Christ. 'Works of the law' do not simply lead to a dead end; they hurtle one over a cliff of destruction. This theological tenet applies to all forms of human religious expression that tend towards legalism and imply that redemption can be won by one's own resources and efforts. For example, in Mithraism, a mystery religion particularly popular with Roman soldiers, redemption was viewed as something a man could automatically win when he did certain things, being ritually cleansed, submitting to ordeals and living up to an ethical code. Christians too may think that God will reward them for being virtuous – that is, virtuous as they define it according to human standards. If virtue is set up as the goal to which persons must strive to make themselves worthy of salvation, then they have embarked on a lifelong enterprise of keeping books with God. When persons hold up what they have done for God to admire and applaud, the spiritual ground on which they claim to stand caves in like an unexpected sinkhole.

Paul's conclusion about the futility of the works of the law to achieve righteousness is based on his conviction that after Jesus' atoning death and his resurrection we now live in a new eschatological age that has superseded the old Mosaic covenant. The day of the Mosaic covenant has passed, and a new covenant is in force that includes Gentiles and Jews. This radical shift is underscored by Paul's statement, 'To the Jews I became as a Jew, in order to win Jews. To those under the law I became as one under the law (though I myself am not under the law) so that I might win those under the law' (1 Cor. 9:20). Paul, a former Pharisee, zealous for the law (Gal. 1:14), now understands himself to be under a different covenantal arrangement so that his righteousness does not come from the law but from being in Christ (Phil. 3:9).

3. GOD'S SOLUTION FOR ALL: CHRIST'S ATONING DEATH AND JUSTIFICATION THROUGH FAITH IN CHRIST (3:21 – 4:25)

A. God's righteousness disclosed in Christ's atoning death (3:21–26)

Context

Paul has shown how the righteous wrath of God against sin is being revealed from heaven (1:18 – 2:11; 2:12–29; 3:1–20). All are condemned as transgressors of God's law and are destined to face the brunt of God's wrath. Nevertheless, all is not lost. Paul shifts from his description of humanity's dismal state under sin to sketch briefly God's solution. Jesus Christ's atoning death, God's grace and the human response of faith in Christ afford redemption. God has manifested his saving righteousness through Christ's atoning sacrifice that vanquishes sin and offers salvation as a gift. Romans 3:21 – 4:25 is the counterpart to 1:18 – 3:20 that portrays humanity under God's wrath, its wretchedness and its condemnation. All those who respond to God's initiative with faith in Christ Jesus join themselves to him and can receive a reprieve: atonement, reconciliation and a right standing before God at the final judgment. The law detects sin and pronounces a death sentence; grace alone liberates one from sin and offers righteousness by faith for all (3:27 – 4:25).

Comment

21. Only God can counteract the wrath of God, and God has acted, apart from the law, to liberate humans from the power of sin and deliver them from divine wrath (5:9; 1 Thess. 1:10). The phrase *but now* is more than a verbal transition. It refers to 'the present time' (3:26; cf. 5:9–11; 7:6; 8:1) when God has ushered in a new epoch in history that offers every person access to a new standing before God before it is too late. In 2 Corinthians 6:2, Paul interprets Isaiah's words about 'an acceptable time' ('a time of [God's] favour'; Isa. 49:8) to refer to the present day as 'the day of salvation'.

Irrespective of law means that the establishment of a right relationship with God is no longer based on obedience to the law, something that has proven impossible for humans to attain. The law does not absolve the guilty or declare the unrighteous to be righteous. It does not waive distinctions between people, the clean and unclean, sinners and righteous, or Jews and Greeks. In what follows, Paul declares that a right relationship with God can be grounded only in faith in Jesus Christ. Acts 13:38–39 provides an apt commentary on what Paul means: 'through this man forgiveness of sins is proclaimed to you; by this Jesus everyone who believes is set free from all those sins from which you could not be freed by the law of Moses'. Paul makes clear in Galatians 3:16–26 that God intended the law to be only provisional. It was not the ultimate expression of God's redemptive will. Although Paul focuses on the negative function of the law as a divine, public prosecutor, charging humans with sin, he does not thrust it aside in this new era of grace. The Law and the Prophets remain the authoritative expression of God's revelation as they bear witness to this new development of God's design for saving humans. Habakkuk 2:4, as cited in 1:17, represents the Prophets in proclaiming, 'The one who is righteous will live by faith.' Genesis 15:6, as cited in 4:3, represents the Law with its testimony that Abraham 'believed God, and it was reckoned to him as righteousness'.

22. Paul reprises the main theme of the letter introduced in 1:16–17 that the righteousness of God is revealed through faith for

faith. Paul omits the verb, and the verb chosen for an English translation depends on how one renders the Greek phrase that reads,
literally, 'faith of Jesus Christ'. As with the English phrase 'the love
of God', in which God could be the subject of the verbal idea with
the meaning 'God's love' for us, or the object of the verbal idea with
the meaning our 'love for God', Paul's intention here has recently
sparked a vigorous debate. The phrase appears seven other times in
Paul's letters (3:26; Gal. 2:16 [2x], 20; 3:22; Phil. 3:9; Eph. 3:12) and
could refer to the faith/faithfulness that Jesus Christ demonstrated
(subjective genitive) or to our faith in Jesus Christ (objective
genitive). If interpreted as a subjective genitive, God's righteousness
'is disclosed' through Jesus Christ's faithfulness. If interpreted as an
objective genitive, it is 'given' or 'comes' through faith in Jesus
Christ.

The subjective genitive assumes an underlying narrative about
Jesus Christ, namely, that Jesus obeyed God's will by taking the
form of a slave and submitting himself to death and trusting that
God would be faithful to deliver him.[1] This interpretation may
best explain the use of the perfect tense 'has been disclosed' in
verse 21. His atoning death has demonstrated God's righteousness.
If Paul refers to human faith in Christ, some find it hard to see how
it would display the righteousness of God. Instead, they view that
it more likely is displayed in what Christ has done. Christ's
faithfulness to God in his death is the basis on which those who
believe receive justification. What Paul says in 5:19 would support
this idea: through the disobedience of one man, Adam, many were
made sinners, and through the obedience of the one man, Christ,
the many will be made righteous. Others also argue that Paul distinguishes 'the faith of Christ' by using the verb 'to believe' for
'faith in Christ' (Gal. 2:16; 3:22). Idiomatic Greek is said to express
the object of faith in the dative case, as in 4:3, 'Abraham believed
God' (cf. Gal. 3:6), or with the prepositions *epi* or *eis*, as in 4:24;
Galatians 2:16; and Colossians 2:5, not with the objective genitive.[2]

---

1. Hays, *Faith*, pp. 119–162; Wright, *Paul*, pp. 836–851.
2. Grammatical arguments are inconclusive since examples of the
   objective genitive surface in Mark 11:22 ('faith in God'); Acts 3:16

A similar grammatical construction occurs in 4:16 where 'the faith of Abraham' clearly refers to Abraham's faith and not faith in Abraham. This passage, however, refers to Abraham's personal faith in God's promise, not his faithfulness to God.

The traditional reading that Paul refers to *faith in Jesus Christ* is nevertheless still to be preferred, for the following reasons.[3] (1) The importance of faith saturates Romans (1:5, 8, 12; 3:27–28, 30; 4:5, 9, 11–20; 5:1–2; 9:30, 32; 10:6, 8, 17; 11:20; 16:26). It is unlikely that Paul abruptly switched the meaning of the noun 'faith' (*pistis*) that refers to the believers' personal faith elsewhere in Romans, and particularly in chapter 4 that immediately follows, to mean 'faithfulness' when it comes to Christ Jesus (Schreiner, p. 193). (2) Jesus is never the subject of the verb 'to trust' (*pisteuein*) in the New Testament, and Paul never refers to him as 'faithful' (Dunn, I, p. 166; Schnabel, I, p. 383). (3) The structure of Galatians 2:16, where the phrase 'faith of Jesus Christ' occurs, indicates that it denotes believing in Christ Jesus:

A a person is justified
    B not by the works of the law
        C but through faith [of] Jesus Christ.
        C′ And we have come to believe in Christ Jesus
    A′ so that we might be justified by faith in Christ,
        B′ and not by doing the works of the law.

The key phrase is 'And we have come to believe in Christ Jesus.' The objection that the translation 'through faith in Jesus Christ' makes the next phrase 'we have come to believe in Christ Jesus' redundant misses the point. Paul repeats the idea of faith in Christ Jesus to emphasize that justification is for 'all who believe', both Jews and Gentiles, with no discrimination (Kruse, p. 181). The

---

(note 2 *cont.*) ('faith in his name'); and Jas 2:1 ('believe in our glorious Lord Jesus Christ').

3. It should be said that salvation is 'presented' (3:25, CSB) through God's faithfulness and Christ's faithfulness that summon our faith in response (cf. Barth, p. 42).

account of Abraham that immediately follows this passage reinforces Paul's point that faith is the basis for justification. Christians are recognized as 'descendants of Abraham' because they have faith as Abraham did (Gal. 3:6–9), not because of Christ's faithfulness. (4) The context of the phrase in Romans 3:22 concerns how sinners who fall short can never attain righteousness through the works of the law but are accounted righteous only through their faith. (5) Finally, no early Christian interpreters understood 'faith of Christ' as Christ's faith, nor did they debate its meaning.[4]

Not only do Gentiles gain a right standing before God through their faith in Jesus, but Jews do so also since sin blankets all humanity without distinction (3:9, 23). As God judges all without distinction (2:9), so God offers grace to all without distinction, including the barbarians of Spain. The phrase introduced by *gar*, *For there is no distinction* ('no difference', NIV), strengthens the assertion that the righteousness of God through faith in Jesus Christ is for all who believe. The cross shatters the accepted partition between the righteous and sinners, but now divides humankind between those who believe in Christ and those who do not, those who are being saved and those who are perishing (1 Cor. 1:18), and those who are freed from God's wrath and those who are not.

23. Unlike the Pharisee who pigeonholed as a 'sinner' only the woman who washed Jesus' feet with her tears and wiped them with her hair (Luke 7:36–39), and the conventional Jewish view that labelled the mass of Gentiles as 'sinners' (Gal. 2:15), Paul brands everyone (*all*) a sinner (cf. Isa. 64:6; Gal. 2:17). What does it mean that they all *fall short of the glory of God*? Is *the glory* (1) that which clothed Adam when he had direct fellowship with God but which

---

4. Harrisville, 'Πίστις Χριστοῦ'. Donfried, 'Paul', pp. 34–35, comments, 'Although widely separated chronologically and geographically, one finds a remarkable concurrence in such diverse authors as Origen (Alexandria, ca. 185–254), Chrysostom (Constantinople, ca. 347–407) and Ambrosiaster (perhaps fourth century)', and cites their interpretations.

was ruined by his sin and consequent estrangement from God;[5] (2) the approbation that comes from God (John 5:44; 12:43); (3) the glory that should be given to God but which was exchanged for idolatrous images (1:23); (4) the transcendent ethical likeness to God; or (5) the eternal destiny in glory at the end time?

While the first option would seem to have support from Jewish texts, Blackwell comments,

> If Adam's experience is in the background here, it is not *Adam's* glory that humans lack, but rather *God's* glory. Accordingly, the future experience of glory is not a return to Adam's glory but a participation in God's glory through Christ (8.17–30).[6]

In 5:2, 'sharing the glory of God' is 'our hope', having obtained access to God's grace. In 8:17–18, believers share in Christ's 'sufferings in order that we may also share in his glory' (NIV), and 'the sufferings of this present time are not worth comparing with the glory about to be revealed to us'. In 8:21, all creation 'will be set free from its bondage to decay and will obtain the freedom of the glory of the children of God'. It is most likely that Paul understands 'the glory of God' to be 'an eschatological state of being' that one hopes to receive at the end of the age. Righteousness is the condition for receiving it.[7] All fail to make the grade because sin makes all unfit to receive it. Paul affirms, however, that God has 'prepared in advance for glory' 'the objects of his mercy' (9:23, NIV; cf. 2 Cor. 3:18; 4:17). For believers, it means that this mortal flesh, sown in dishonour, will be raised in glory (1 Cor. 15:43). Blackwell connects *glory* to justification that is mentioned in the next verse:

> In the same way that justification leads to new life (e.g., 1.17; 5.17, 18, 21; 8.10), it also leads to glorification, which is a life of incorruption (5.1–2; 8.30). Thus, the righteousness–glory association provides further

---

5. Cf. Apoc. Mos. 20:1–2; 21:6; 3 Bar. 4:16; Gen. Rab. 12:6; Tg. Ps.-J. Gen. 2:25; 3:7.

6. Blackwell, 'Immortal Glory', p. 291.

7. Ibid., p. 294.

evidence that Paul understands justification as the means for rectifying human mortality arising from sin, as well as rectifying the broken relationship arising from guilt and characterized by shame.[8]

24. In verses 24–25, Paul employs three different metaphors to describe what God has done through Jesus Christ to rectify humanity's dire situation. The first comes from the courtroom. *Justified* is a legal term that means 'acquitted'. Paul has argued that sin has ensnared all humanity, and God owes them nothing but condemnation. An acquittal can come only as an unanticipated gift, because the guilty have nothing to offer to gain a favourable ruling. Justification differs from forgiveness in that it 'is a once-for-all declaration of God on behalf of the believing sinner' (Harrison and Hagner, p. 71). What is startling is that God declares this final verdict in advance, not at the end of a person's life (Bruce, p. 102).

Job asked, 'How can a mortal be just before God?' (Job 9:2). Paul only says here that it comes 'freely' (NIV), that is, undeservedly, apart from any merit or acts of piety. Later in the letter, he will explain that acquittal, 'no condemnation', comes only to those who are in Christ Jesus (8:1; cf. Phil. 3:8–9).

Redemption is the second metaphor, and Paul draws it from the social world, where it 'was associated with the release of captured prisoners of war and the manumission of slaves from service (e.g., Exod. 21:8; Lev. 25:25; Let. Aris. 12:35; Josephus, *Ant.* 12.27)' (Bird, p. 117). For the audience, the image would naturally conjure up the notion of a ransom payment. Jesus employs this picture when he says that the Son of Man came 'to give his life a ransom for many' (Mark 10:45). The assumption is that humans are set free from their captivity to sin by the ransom of Christ (6:17–18; Eph. 1:7). The emphasis falls only on the result, liberation from servitude, not on the one whom the ransom buys off. The enemy is to be destroyed, not paid off. The redemption applies only to those who are 'in Christ' (cf. 6:11, 23; 8:1–2; 12:5)

25–26. Only God can effectively counteract the wrath of God. The first verb translated *put forward* (NRSV), 'presented' (NIV) or

---

8. Ibid., p. 303.

'displayed publicly' (NASB) would correspond well with Paul's dumbfounded question to the Galatians, 'Who has bewitched you? Before your very eyes Jesus Christ was clearly portrayed as crucified' (Gal. 3:1, NIV). It also fits the context of disclosing (3:21) and demonstrating (3:25) God's righteousness. 'The righteousness of God has been disclosed' (3:21), and all can see it exhibited in Christ's death on the cross. The verb (*protithēmi*), however, can also mean 'intended' or 'purposed'. Paul uses it in 1:13 to tell the Romans how many times he 'intended' to come to them (cf. Eph. 1:9, 'the mystery of his will . . . which he purposed in Christ' [NIV]). The cognate noun appears in 8:28 to refer to those called according to God's 'purpose' and in 9:11 to refer to the 'purpose' of God's election (cf. Eph. 1:11; 3:11; 1 Tim. 1:9). This translation of the verb explains why God has *passed over* sins committed in the past (cf. 2:4; 9:22; Acts 14:16; 17:30), and letting sins go would be incompatible with God's righteousness, since it would imply that God turns a blind eye to sin and pretends it never happened. Cranfield explains:

> God has in fact been able to hold His hand and pass over sins without compromising His goodness and mercy, because His intention has all along been to deal with them once and for all, decisively and finally, through the cross.
>
> (Cranfield, I, p. 212)

The cross reflects God's eternal purpose, and it was 'not some sudden new idea or impulse on God's part' (Cranfield, I, p. 210). *In his divine forbearance* answers the question of how God can pass over sins and remain holy and just. God's purpose all along was for redemption to come through Jesus Christ as the *sacrifice of atonement*. Both translations of the verb, *put forward* and 'purposed', are germane.

Paul's third metaphor describing God's initiative in solving the human problem of sin derives from the Jewish cult. The word *hilastērion* can be interpreted as referring to the means of expiation (of sin) or the place of propitiation (of God's wrath). Translations vary, rendering it as *sacrifice of atonement* (NIV, NRSV), 'sacrifice for reconciliation' (NJB), 'expiation' (RSV), 'propitiation' (KJV, ESV), 'mercy seat' (NET) or 'the place of sacrifice where mercy is found'

(CEB). The Septuagint uses this noun twenty-one times to translate the Hebrew word *kappōret* for the gold-plated cover with cherubim at either end that covered the ark of the covenant in the Holy of Holies. The only other time the word occurs in the New Testament is in Hebrews 9:5 where it refers to the cover of the ark. It marked the place where God told Moses, as the representative of Israel, 'I will meet with you and give you all my commands for the Israelites' (Exod. 25:22, NIV). It occupied the most sacred space where the high priest entered once a year on the Day of Atonement to sprinkle the front of the mercy seat seven times with the sacrificial blood of a slain bull on and before it, and, at the culmination of the ritual, to sprinkle the blood of a slain goat presented as a sin offering on and before it (Lev. 16:14–15). When combined with sin offerings for the high priest (Lev. 16:6, 11, 17, 24), the people (Lev. 16:10, 17, 24) and the holy place (16:20), the people's sins on this day were cleansed before the Lord (Lev. 16:30).

In choosing this word rich with atonement associations in the Septuagint, Paul employs metonymy to describe something strongly associated with a particular thing or concept as if they were synonyms, but each retains its distinct area of meaning. For example, when Paul says, 'May I never boast of anything except the cross of our Lord Jesus Christ' (Gal. 6:14), he is not talking about the literal cross but the historical reality of Jesus' crucifixion and its manifold theological message. The cross is an inanimate object, as is the mercy seat, but from their associations with God and the forgiveness of sins, both words convey so much more. By using metonymy, writers intend to capture readers' attention with vivid imagery that suggests those broader and deeper meanings. It also expresses these meanings more succinctly,[9] and its poetic effect can stir deep emotions. One can imagine that for many Jews a reference to 'the mercy seat' could rouse the same deep emotions

---

9. For instance, Paul uses the picturesque word 'sword' in 8:35 to refer to something that threatens Christians but does not separate them from the love of Christ, instead of saying 'violent death at the hands of enemies of the gospel'. Heb. 4:16 uses metonymy in referring to 'the throne of grace' with all of its theological associations.

that a reference to 'the old rugged cross' might awaken in some today. Philo described the *hilastērion*, which he translates as 'the mercy seat', as 'a symbol in a theological sense of the gracious power of God' (*Mos.* 2.95–96 [Colson, LCL]; cf. *Fug.* 100).

Translations such as 'propitiation', 'expiation' and *sacrifice of atonement* muffle the imagery of the mercy seat and only partially capture its meaning, in the same way that the full impact of Jesus' parables is abridged when they are reduced to one point. 'Mercy seat' might have been a foreign image to Gentiles in the audience who were not familiar with the LXX. Others more familiar with the Scriptures could elucidate its meaning for them by pointing to its connection to the accounts of God's mercy in the Scriptures. Given the Old Testament background of this word, Paul conveys that the place where our sins are atoned for has shifted from what was hidden behind a curtain in the temple to the cross where Jesus' blood was poured out for all to see. The cross of Christ is 'the mercy seat' where we see the gracious power of God displayed.

By his blood reinforces the sacrificial imagery (cf. Matt. 26:28/ Mark 14:24; Luke 22:20; 1 Cor. 10:16; 11:25). It is not the blood of a sacrificial animal that makes atonement (Lev. 17:11) but Jesus' own blood that he willingly shed for others (5:9). The image includes both the idea of expiation, the cleansing of sin (cf. Isa. 53:10) or 'not counting people's sins against them' (2 Cor. 5:19, NIV), and the idea of propitiation, turning away God's wrath against sin, which is a theme that began in 1:18. Christ's crucifixion has supplanted the mercy seat in the Holy of Holies where God's presence and mercy were supremely manifested. The substitutionary sacrifice of Christ represents the blood of the people condemned to die and atones for their sin. Bird comments,

> Jesus' death . . . turns out to be a vicarious sacrifice and a penal
> substitution whereby God 'condemned sin in the flesh' of Jesus
> as a 'sin offering' (Rom 8:3) and 'God made him who had no sin to
> be sin for us' (2 Cor 5:21).
> (Bird, p. 120)

Christ's sacrificial death was meant *to prove* ('show', 'demonstrate') God's righteousness both in judging sin and in showing mercy to sinners. God is righteous in punishing sin through Jesus' death, and God is the one who justifies in making believers, who have no righteousness of their own, righteous through their faith in the efficacy of Jesus' death and resurrection to redeem them from their sins.

Theology

God has a record of passing over sins. Due for extermination for violating God's specific command, Adam and Eve received only expulsion. Reuben, guilty of intercourse with his father's concubine (Gen. 35:22), the punishment for which was death (Lev. 20:11) and being cut off from the people (Lev. 18:29), received mercy instead: 'May Reuben live, and not die out' (Deut. 33:6). God's seeming tolerance of the wicked caused consternation for Jews during times when the Gentiles oppressed Israel and prospered. Why did God deal with Israel's sins immediately and seem to let the Gentiles off scot-free? One answer is provided in 2 Maccabees 6:12–17. God did not let Israel's sins pile up but punished them promptly as an act of mercy 'in order that he should not take vengeance on us afterwards when our sins have reached their height' (2 Macc. 6:15). God did not love the impious Gentiles and consequently waited until their sins reached the full measure before lowering the boom of a desolating judgment. Paul refutes this view. Instead of planning some terrible destruction for the Gentiles when their sins had reached the full mark, God dealt with them patiently because he planned to address their sins through Christ's atoning death and to provide the same access to righteousness that Jews have, namely, through their faith in Christ. God could not simply wipe the slate clean by pardoning sins. That would be seen as condoning sin. Christ's death on the cross shows how seriously God in his righteousness takes sin, how costly forgiveness is, and how much love underlies God's grace.

Paul's use of metonymy in the image of the mercy seat compares Jesus' death on the cross to the place where the sacrificial rite on the Day of Atonement for the forgiveness of sins was carried out. Significant differences between the two show how Jesus' death supersedes the Day of Atonement and the mercy seat as the place where one finds God's presence, grace and mercy, because it far transcends them.

(1) The mercy seat was the holiest spot in the Holy of Holies and hidden in sacred isolation behind the veil. Only the high priest might venture into this area, and that only once a year on the Day of Atonement. Even then, the mercy seat was shrouded by the cloud of incense that protected the high priest from viewing God's presence (Lev. 16:2, 12–13). By contrast, Jesus' crucifixion occurred in public for all to see. Manson comments,

> The mercy-seat is no longer kept in the sacred seclusion of the most holy place: it is brought out into the midst of the rough and tumble of the world and set up before the eyes of hostile, contemptuous, or indifferent crowds.[10]

It is at the cross on Golgotha, the place of the skull, not at the mercy seat in the Holy of Holies, that the decisive sacrifice for the forgiveness of sins has occurred.

(2) The high priest conducted the atonement ritual before the mercy seat after ritually cleansing himself. In Paul's account, God is the subject of the verbs and is the one who initiates Christ's sacrifice. God demonstrated his righteousness and purposed and presented Christ (3:25–26; cf. 8:3, 32) to appease his wrath and cleanse believers of all their sins.

(3) Jewish atonement rituals in the sanctuary had to be repeated day after day, year after year (Heb. 9:25; 10:1), which testifies to their ineffectiveness. Christ's death was once for all (6:10; Heb. 9:12), not to be repeated.

(4) The old mercy seat was sprinkled with the blood of sacrificial animals as the cleansing agent. The new mercy seat is sprinkled with Christ's own blood (3:25; 5:9).

(5) The atonement ritual only temporarily cleansed the sins of the faithful in Israel, but only *their* sins. Christ's sacrifice cleanses all the sins of all sinners who have faith in Christ (cf. 5:6, 8).

(6) In the Graeco-Roman pagan context, the word *hilastērion* and its cognate verbs were used for a supplicatory offering to placate the anger of a temperamental deity, to make the deity gracious and thus

---

10. Manson, 'ΙΛΑΣΤΗΡΙΟΝ', p. 5.

to ward off any punishment. By contrast, God in his gracious mercy takes the initiative, not humans. God offers up Christ as a sacrifice to deal with sin and avert the consequences of divine wrath. The initiative is entirely with God. 'The cross proceeds from God's grace, and it does not make God gracious' (Peterson, p. 197). God is already gracious.

As Paul writes in 8:3, God 'condemned sin in the flesh' 'by sending his own Son in the likeness of sinful flesh to be a sin offering' (NIV; cf. 4:25; 8:32). Brunner comments,

> The atoning sacrifice of Christ does not overcome God's wrath in the same way as an angry tyrant is placated and favourably influenced by gifts. God does not receive a gift. He bestows Christ on us and in him he gives himself (8:32). The reconciliation does not overcome God's enmity but ours (Eph. 2:14).
>
> (Brunner, p. 167)

Humans cannot make atonement through their ritual acts. All they can do is respond to God's action in Christ with a confession of faith, as did the Gentile centurion who, facing Jesus on the cross, witnessed how he died and declared, 'Truly this man was God's Son!' (Mark 15:37–39). Those who make this confession no longer stand against God but can stand under God's grace.

(7) Paul underscores the fact that divine retribution for sin is real, and humans had better not discount the reality of God's wrath against sin. The cross both expresses God's wrath and satisfies it (Peterson, p. 197). Stählin comments, 'Only he who knows the greatness of wrath will be mastered by the greatness of mercy. The converse is also true: Only he who has experienced the greatness of mercy can measure how great wrath must be.'[11]

The dramatic conclusion is that Paul presupposes that Christ's death on Golgotha has replaced the sacrificial cult of atonement in the temple. Atonement and escape from God's wrath come only through Christ's death. It is 'effective once for all time and procures for those who believe the forgiveness of their sins, new

---

11. G. Stählin, 'ὀργή', *TDNT* V, p. 425.

life before and with God, and consequently the righteousness of
God which sinners lack (cf. 1 Cor. 6:20; 2 Cor. 5:21)' (Stuhlmacher,
p. 61).

B. Justification through faith, not by works (3:27–31)

Context
In 3:27–31, Paul draws out the consequences of God's justification,
redemption and atonement of sinners with a series of four
questions and answers. What of boasting? It is excluded. On what
principle (or law)? Works? No; on the principle (or law) of faith. Is
God a tribal deity only? No, God is the God of Jews and Gentiles.
Is the law discarded? No; it is upheld, but upheld by faith, not by
works.

Comment
27. The first rhetorical question that asks, literally in the Greek,
'Where is *boasting*?' assumes that the grounds for boasting have
vanished (cf. 1 Cor. 1:20). Paul is not referring to pride in general
but the particular Jewish *boasting* that is represented in 2:17–23, the
boasting that 'exhibits a confidence in the rightness of one's relationship with God, a sense of security, or even privilege, that is
based on one's faithful adherence to the demands of the law of
Moses'.[12] The statement *It is excluded* concludes that argument. The
boasts in Jewish privileges, obedience to the law and identity
badges belie the truth that Jews are no less guilty of sin than are
Gentiles.

Paul's second question essentially asks, 'What is the basis for
excluding boasting? Does not the law require works?' Paul's answer
is, 'No, the law requires faith.' The *law* could refer to a principle,
but in the context more probably refers to the Mosaic law because
of the contrast between 'works prescribed by the law' and 'faith'
(3:28). The verb *is excluded* is in the passive voice, suggesting that
God is the agent of the action who has shut down all human
boasting through the demonstration of God's righteousness apart

12. Lambrecht and Thompson, *Justification*, p. 17.

from the law. The law of Moses requires a person to obey all that is in the law to be counted righteous (10:5, citing Lev. 18:5). Paul has shown that one can never attain righteousness through obedience to the law. The law also points to a righteousness that comes by faith. In 10:6–8 (NIV), Paul interprets Moses' declaration 'The word is near you; it is in your mouth and in your heart' (Deut. 30:12–14) to point to the sinner's confession of faith in Christ that leads to salvation. Faith recognizes that the best that humans can do is all too often at odds with the best that God can do and submits to God's unmerited grace. Paul's next section shows that, as a matter of fact, the account of Abraham in the Law testifies to justification by faith (4:3, 9, 17–18; 10:5–6)

28–30. *Works prescribed by the law* refers to doing what the law prescribes, not limited simply to boundary markers that separate Jews from Gentiles. In Paul's opinion, Jews, including himself, fail to win divine favour because one who strives to do so always falls short in the attempt. A focus on works invariably imports a mercenary spirit into religion and results in a cold smugness, a fondness for negatives, a lack of empathy for others. If justification and salvation were based on works of the law, only Jews or, tenuously, Jewish proselytes could meet the requirements, and it would make God the *God of Jews only*. Jews confess, however, that *God is one* (Deut. 6:4) and God of all. God is also *the God of Gentiles* (cf. Zech. 14:9). Since sin ensnares all humanity, no grounds exist for any group to boast of its imagined superiority over others. Since God is one, God offers only one way to salvation. Salvation is available to all solely through faith in Jesus Christ. Faith in Christ wipes away any discrimination between Jews and Gentiles.

Two corollaries follow from this reality. First, to gain Christ through whom they receive salvation by faith, Jews must count as forfeit their privileges (9:4–5) and their supposed righteousness that they seek to establish on their own through their obedience to the law (10:3), as Paul himself once did (Phil. 3:5–8). Second, because of their faith in Messiah Jesus, Gentiles are counted as righteous before God as Gentiles and do not need to become Jews to receive salvation. If it were required for Gentile believers to become Jews and to keep the law to be saved and to be counted as equal to Jews, it would imply that God is the God of the Jews only (3:29).[13]

31. Paul's final question in this series asks if justification by faith, apart from the law, calls into question the law's validity. It receives another resounding 'No!' The Law and the Prophets testified to this gospel (3:21). The story of Abraham found in the law of Moses and the testimony of David that immediately follows prove this assertion. Neither does faith make void the law and its demands. In 4:9–12, Paul shows how faith upholds the law concerning circumcision. Circumcision receives its true meaning by showing faith. As for obeying its legal demands, Paul argues in 8:4 that 'the righteous requirement of the law' is 'fully met' in believers 'who do not live according to the flesh but according to the Spirit' (NIV). In Galatians 3:13 (ESV), Paul cites the law: 'Cursed is everyone who is hanged on a tree' (Deut. 21:23). God, however, transformed the cursedness of Christ's crucifixion when God raised him from the dead. The result is that 'in Christ Jesus the blessing of Abraham might come to the Gentiles, so that we might receive the promise of the Spirit through faith' (Gal. 3:14).

Theology

Jesus' parable about the Pharisee and the tax collector praying in the temple (Luke 18:9–14) vividly illustrates Paul's declaration that 'a person is justified by faith apart from works prescribed by the law' (3:28). The problem is that in contemporary sermons, the tax collector cries out for mercy in a confession and walks out of the temple justified with no indication that he changed his life. The story needs further context in other sermons to prevent the impression that all one needs to do to receive a halo is to confess one's sins again and again. What Paul says here complements the parable. God's justification is a creative work that does not simply absolve the guilt. In justifying sinners, God places them in a redemptive relationship that sets them on the path to being cured. God does more than acquit them of their sin; God unfolds a new way of life for them. The cross is not simply a transaction that

---

13. Cf. Nanos, *Mystery*, p. 183.

clears the debt of sin. It is saving when it touches human hearts and changes their existence.

Faith is so prominent in this passage because

> Faith alone can penetrate the ultimate paradox of the gospel: that the kingly power of God is manifest in the suffering and death of Jesus on the pagan cross, transforming the cross into a power that is infinitely greater than any human power.[14]

What God has done in Christ's atoning sacrifice on the cross, the new mercy seat, meets with the world's derision and resistance (1 Cor. 1:22–23). As Pascal memorably wrote, 'There is enough light for those who only desire to see and enough obscurity for those who have a contrary dispositon.'[15] Consequently, faith is not a refuge from the uncertainties and insecurities of the world. The present participle in verse 22, 'for all who believe', implies steadfast belief (Schnabel, I, p. 385) that must endure through times of tribulation (8:18, 35–39).

Faith accepts the guilty verdict of the law, recognizes that one can never tote up enough merits to rectify the situation of one's sin, and accepts God's offer of salvation in Christ by grace as the only alternative. It is a response to what God has done in Christ and not a work itself that an individual exchanges for works of the law to earn God's favour. Faith is an act of acceptance that pleases God rather than a slavish attitude that seeks to please God. Harrison and Hagner note that Paul never says that people 'are saved *on account of* their faith in Christ, a construction that might encourage the notion that faith makes a contribution and has some merit'. Instead, one appropriates salvation through faith. 'Faith is simply a mode of receptivity ("the hand of the heart", as Frédéric Godet puts it). Faith receives what God bestows but adds nothing to the gift' (Harrison and Hagner, p. 70).

Faith in Christ is not simply passive assent that mouths doctrinal statements heard in church. Nor is it a hollow assurance without

---

14. Marshall, *Faith*, pp. 207–208.
15. Pascal, *Pensées*, p. 118.

self-committal. Paul will show that justification by faith does not mean that obedience to the law is no longer necessary. Faith produces work (1 Thess. 1:3) because grace transforms believers and the Holy Spirit empowers them (8:3–14). Luther wrote, 'It is impossible to separate works from faith, quite as impossible as to separate heat and light from fire.'[16] Obedience to God summed up in the command to love your neighbour as yourself (13:8–10; 15:2; cf. Mark 12:31; Gal. 5:14) is the empirical evidence that one has been justified by faith.

C. Abraham, an illustration of justification by faith and a model for God's people (4:1–25)

Context
God no longer shows forbearance towards human sin but has resolved it decisively through Christ Jesus' sacrificial death (3:25). In so doing, God provides the way for humans to break away from sin's grip and come into a right relationship with him through faith in Christ (3:26). In this section, Paul expands on his answers to the questions raised in 3:27–31 and drives home points from his previous arguments. (1) The examples of Abraham and David show how the Law and the Prophets testify that faith does not nullify the law (3:31). The Abraham story comes from the Law, and David was considered a prophet (Acts 2:29–31). (2) Paul focuses on Abraham with an expanded interpretation of Genesis 15:6, 'Abraham believed God, and it was reckoned to him as righteousness.'[17] The scriptural proofs confirm that persons are justified by faith apart from the law (3:21) and not by works of the law (3:28). On the contrary, if the law were the criterion for being an heir to the promise, it would nullify faith (4:14). (3) Being justified by faith, given a right standing with God, means that no-one has any grounds for boasting about achievements or birthrights (3:27; 4:2–5). Abraham obediently left his heathen

---

16. Luther, 'Prefaces to the New Testament', p. 371.
17. Gen. 15:6 is cited three times (4:3, 9, 22), with the first and last citations framing the passage.

milieu at the behest of God. Nevertheless, he could make no claim on God as one who still belonged to the category of the ungodly justified by God's grace (4:5). (4) While Abraham is the archetype of one reckoned righteous solely on the grounds of his faith in God, he 'points beyond himself and beyond the whole dispensation of the Law to the future justification by faith of Jew and Gentile alike'.[18] God 'will justify the circumcised on the ground of faith and the uncircumcised through that same faith' (3:29–30), so that all who trust in what God has done in Christ have equal standing before God (4:24–25). Paul makes this point by stating in 4:16–18 that Abraham is 'the father of all of us'. Abraham's children consist of those who 'share the faith of Abraham'. The result is that God's people includes all those who exhibit this faith, which fulfils God's promise that all the nations would be blessed through Abraham (Gal. 3:8). This fact buttresses the purpose of the letter. If God's promise to Abraham did not extend to all, what would be the point of taking the gospel to others?

Comment
i. Abraham justified by faith apart from works (4:1–5)

1. The opening sentence of this section presents translation problems. Does the phrase *according to the flesh* go with *Abraham* or with the verb *gained*, also translated as 'found' (CSB)? Does Paul ask one question or two? Hays divides the sentence into two questions and contends that *according to the flesh* goes with the verb. He translates it: 'What then shall we say? Have we found Abraham to be our forefather according to the flesh?'[19] The CEB adopts this interpretation with its translation, 'So what are we going to say? Are we going to find that Abraham is our ancestor on the basis of genealogy?' Elsewhere in the letter, the question 'What then are we to say?' introduces another question making a false inference that provokes a sharp denial (3:5; 6:1; 7:7; 9:14).[20] If this second question

---

18. Allen, 'Old Testament', p. 19.

19. Hays, 'Abraham'; followed by Bird, pp. 140–141; Wright, p. 489.

20. In 8:31 and 9:30, the subsequent rhetorical questions are accurate and are not contradicted.

raises an issue that is false – that Abraham was our ancestor according to the flesh – one would expect it to be answered with a strong denial, but this is absent. Instead, what follows in 4:2–8 addresses the question whether Abraham was justified by works. Paul breaks his normal pattern in his use of the question 'What then are we to say?' by following it with a description of what Abraham discovered. The rendering 'What then will we say that Abraham, our forefather according to the flesh, has found?' (CSB) remains the best alternative.[21] The answer is that Abraham 'found grace', favour with God (Gen. 18:3), and discovered that he was justified by faith and not works (Michel, p. 115).

The phrase *according to the flesh* in this instance refers to lineage (cf. 1:3; 9:3, 5; 11:14) and introduces the vital issue that Paul wishes to settle. As Abraham's natural offspring, Jews took for granted that he was *their* 'forefather' (NIV; Ps. 105:6; Isa. 41:8), which made them, as God's chosen ones, the rightful heirs of God's promises to him. *According to the flesh*, however, 'implies that there are other children who belong to Abraham in a different way' (Cranfield, I, p. 227). Paul argues that spiritually Abraham is also the forefather of uncircumcised Gentiles who demonstrate the same faith he did when he was uncircumcised. They are grafted into Abraham's family tree (11:17, 24) through their faith. On the other hand, not all of Abraham's physical descendants according to the flesh are true children of Abraham (9:7–8). Many of Paul's 'kindred according to the flesh' (9:3) have become branches lopped off from the spiritual family tree because of their unbelief (11:17, 21).

This chapter answers the question: what is the criterion that allows believers to be counted as the true children of Abraham and heirs of God's promised blessings? The decisive factor is not fleshly

---

21. Barclay, *Paul*, p. 483 n. 88, notes that Hays' interpretation misconstrues 'forefather' as a predicate ('Have we found Abraham *to be* our forefather according to the flesh?'). The predicate would not have a definite article, but 'forefather' has an accusative definite article in this sentence. 'Abraham', not an inferred 'we', must be the subject of the infinitive 'to have found'. Paul summons Abraham as a witness, and what follows concerns what he found, not what we discovered.

descent but faith. Paul's answer transforms how Abraham's father-hood is to be understood. Abraham's true descendants, whether they are circumcised or uncircumcised, follow the trail of footprints Abraham made when he trusted God (cf. Gal. 3:6–9).

This section contains a more developed exposition of Abraham's story than that found in Galatians 3:6–18. Duncan contends that Paul's sudden appeal to Abraham in Galatians 3:6 was not because he opened up 'a new subject of controversy; rather it is that his op-ponents have already based their case on an appeal to the case of the patriarch, and Paul now sets himself to refute them'.[22] The troublemakers in Galatia seemed to have Scripture on their side by arguing that one had to become circumcised to become a son of Abraham (Gen. 17:23–26). When Jews thought of Abraham, they thought of the covenant of circumcision in the flesh and his obedience when he was tested to sacrifice Isaac. James, for example, cites Genesis 15:6 to make the point that 'our ancestor' Abraham was 'justified by works when he offered his son Isaac on the altar' (Jas 2:21–24; cf. Gen. 22:2, 9, 16–17). Hebrews 11:17 relates Abra-ham's faith to his readiness to offer up Isaac. Stephen's synopsis of the highlights of Jewish history associates Abraham with the divine promise of an inheritance to his posterity, the covenant of circumcision and the birth of Isaac, who became the father of Jacob, who became the father of the twelve patriarchs (Acts 7:2–8). He makes no mention of his faith. Sirach 44:19–21 summarizes this traditional Jewish view:

> Abraham was the great father of a multitude of nations,
>   and no one has been found like him in glory.
> He kept the law of the Most High,
>   and entered into a covenant with him;
> he certified the covenant in his flesh,
>   and when he was tested he proved faithful.
> Therefore the Lord assured him with an oath
>   that the nations would be blessed through his offspring;
> that he would make him as numerous as the dust of the earth,

---

22. Duncan, *Galatians*, p. 83; cf. Barrett, 'Allegory'.

and exalt his offspring like the stars,
and give them an inheritance from sea to sea
and from the Euphrates to the ends of the earth.[23]

Backed into a biblical corner, Paul radically reinterprets the story
of Abraham's faith in the Genesis narrative by reading it se-
quentially. Abraham did nothing to earn any recognition from
God. Before Abraham was circumcised or prepared to sacrifice
Isaac, God reckoned him righteous. Paul argues from this fact that
God can also accept Gentiles as Abraham's heirs when they exhibit
the same faith in God that Abraham did. Paul draws on his
previous argument from his theological fracas with the Judaizers
and expands on it to make new points.

2. The Jewish picture of Abraham as 'perfect in all his deeds
with the Lord, and well-pleasing in righteousness all the days of his
life' (Jub. 23:10) would lend itself to boasting, were it true. It would
mean that Paul could not say that all boasting is eliminated (3:27).
Abraham's boasts, however, appear only in Jewish legend that
venerates his obedience. Human renown carries no weight with
God. In God's presence, Abraham can hardly pat himself on the
back.

3. Paul begins a lengthy interpretation of Genesis 15:6 to make
his case that Abraham was credited with righteousness by God
merely because 'he believed the LORD'. The word *righteousness*
(*dikaiosynē*) occurs eight times in this chapter, and the cognate verb,
translated 'to justify' (*dikaioō*), occurs twice. The verb translated

---

23. Cf. Neh. 9:7–8; 1 Macc. 2:50–52; Jub. 17:18; 18:16; 21:2–3; 23:10; Philo,
    Her. 90–99. Jewish writings extolled Abraham as the first proselyte
    to convert from heathen ways (Jub. 12:1–8, 12–14; Philo, *Virt.* 219;
    Josephus, *Ant.* 1.155) and for keeping the whole law even before it was
    given (2 Bar. 57:1–2; CD 3:1–3). To explain how God could say that
    Abraham 'obeyed my voice and kept my charge, my commandments,
    my statutes, and my laws' (Gen. 26:5), it was assumed that God gave
    him a preview of the law (m. Qidd. 4:14; b. Qidd. 82a; b. Yoma 28b;
    Gen. Rab. 64:4; Lev. Rab. 2:10). Paul claimed instead that God gave
    Abraham a preview of the gospel (Gal. 3:8).

reckoned or 'credited' (*logizomai*) occurs eleven times in this chapter. While it can have the broader meaning 'to consider' (2:3; 6:11; 8:18; 9:8; 14:14), in this context it has a mercantile connotation of crediting to someone's account. To be *reckoned* is an accounting term, and the passive voice points to God as the bookkeeper. God credited Abraham as righteous in the divine ledger. When God did so, Abraham had performed no religious duties and had no religious accomplishments. He only trusted in God who promised that his descendants would be too many to count. For Paul, what is important is that God reckoned that trust as *righteousness* in an act of sheer grace.[24] Because he believes that humans cannot attain righteousness out of their own resources, he does not read Abraham's later willingness to sacrifice his son Isaac (Gen. 22) into this passage, as many Jewish interpretations did to explain why God would have accounted him as righteous (e.g. Jas 2:21; 1 Macc. 2:52).

Paul also believes that being reckoned righteous does not bestow the quality of righteousness on the sinner but enables a relationship with God. Whiteley illustrates this point well:

> A man may have a weight in relation to the earth, but the weight is always dependent on the gravitational pull of the earth, and does not belong to the man as such. In the same way, a man has not righteousness in himself, even a righteousness given gratuitously by God: What God has gratuitously conferred upon men is a right relationship with Himself.[25]

4–5. Paul unpacks the meaning of the verb 'was reckoned' in verses 4–8. As an artisan working in the leather trade, he knows that workers receive compensation for what they have done based on a contractual agreement. Since 'all . . . are under the power of

---

24. Jesus provides a picture of this grace in the parables in which, out of sheer generosity, a king writes off an insurmountable debt (Matt. 18:23–35) and a landowner pays farmhands far more than they have earned from their work (Matt. 20:1–15).

25. Whiteley, *Theology*, p. 160.

sin' (3:9) and have no works that earn God's favour, God owes them nothing. Being credited as righteous comes as 'an undeserved gift', which is something 'surrounded by sentiment, not subject to law, and unpredictable in its timing or quantity'.[26]

Paul implies that when God reckoned Abraham righteous, Abraham belonged to the category of *the ungodly* who have no grounds to make demands of God. The *ungodly* are not to be mistaken for hardened reprobates who could not care less about God. Keck sagely comments, 'Paul sees that only the *un*godly trust such a God; the godly trust the God who counts their godliness as righteousness' (Keck, p. 121). The blueprint for being reckoned righteous, then, is found in what happened to Abraham when he trusted God. Therefore, Abraham becomes a prototype of the salvation of ungodly Gentiles whom God also has no reason to reckon righteous. God incongruously does so only because they trust God as Abraham did. Paul also applies this model to how Jews become righteous. For Paul to make 'the pattern of Gentile righteousness by faith normative for Jewish righteousness, rather than the reverse', is world-shattering for Jews who are confident that one can become righteous and receive God's blessing through works of the law (Johnson, p. 75). It completely upends this presupposition about how salvation works.

ii. David accredited righteous apart from works (4:6–8)

6–8. In developing the meaning of Genesis 15:6, Paul employs a common Jewish method of interpretation (*gezerah shewah*) in which one text is explained by another text that shares a key word.[27] The term *reckon* (*logizesthai*) is also found in Psalm 32:2 (LXX 31:2) where David, another venerated figure in Israel's history, speaks of God not reckoning his sin.

In Psalm 32:1–2 as quoted by Paul, David counts *blessed* the one *whose iniquities are forgiven, whose sins are covered, the one against whom the Lord will not reckon sin.* By combining the two biblical texts, Genesis

---

26. Barclay, *Paul*, p. 485.
27. The method (*gezerah shewah*) is the second of Rabbi Hillel's seven canons of interpretation.

15:6 and Psalm 32:1–2, Paul expands the meaning of God reckoning one righteous to include also having one's sins forgiven. This reality reinforces the point that Abraham had no exceptional merits that prompted God to justify him. Since the psalm brings up only David's confession of his transgressions (Ps. 32:5) and says nothing about his works, Paul glosses the quotation by adding 'apart from works' (NIV) to underscore his point.

David would have been hopelessly condemned had God only reckoned his sins. The context of the psalm reveals that God did not merely acquit David and leave him as a justified sinner still captive to sin. God's forgiveness of iniquities, covering of sins and not reckoning sin does more than simply wipe the slate clean; God responds to humans marred and broken by sin with a new, transformative act that seeks to make things right. God's powerful word creates results (Ps. 33:9). God acts to restore the breach of the relationship caused by human sin. Not reckoning David's sins did not make David good but it set him free from the past and in a right relation with God so 'good can follow' (Keck, p. 124).

iii. Abraham was justified by faith prior to circumcision so he could be father of both the circumcised and the uncircumcised (4:9–12)

9–12. Paul takes for granted that Abraham is the forefather of the Jews (4:1) but he intends to prove that Abraham is also the spiritual forefather of the uncircumcised. The words *circumcised* and *uncircumcised* dominate these verses. Paul notes that in the Abraham story, faith comes first (Gen. 15:6), then circumcision (Gen. 17:9–27). He emphasizes three times that Abraham was in an uncircumcised state when God declared him righteous.[28] Therefore, Abraham was equivalent to a Gentile, without circumcision and without the law. God could not have reckoned Abraham righteous because he had obeyed the law and performed Jewish rites. God reckoned Abraham apart from the law, and he was righteous only because of his faith. Consequently, God does not restrict

---

28. The NIV correctly interprets the word *how* (*pōs*) in v. 10 to mean 'under what circumstances'.

salvation, which comes from being declared upright, only to those who are circumcised and live under the law. Since God can count as righteous those who have a foreskin, God can be the God of both the circumcised and the uncircumcised (3:29–30), and Abraham can be the forefather of all who believe as he did (4:11).

The Genesis sequence, as Paul interprets it, reveals that Abraham is first the father of the uncircumcised. Only much later did he become the father (*the ancestor*) of the circumcised (4:12) when he himself was circumcised (Gen. 17). What was the purpose of circumcision if it was not an indispensable prerequisite for being reckoned righteous by God? Circumcision did not confer righteousness but served only as a visible mark, a *sign* and *seal* that confirmed Abraham's *righteousness that he had by faith* (4:11).[29] Keener likens it to 'the rainbow in Gen 9:12–13, 16–17, a reminder of the deliverance that God had established, not the deliverance itself' (Keener, p. 65). One might ask: what seal do uncircumcised Christians have if they remain uncircumcised? Paul answers elsewhere that all Christians are 'sealed' with the Holy Spirit (2 Cor. 1:22; Eph. 1:14; 4:30), something that is visible only in changed lives and behaviour (8:1–17).

Paul concludes that God intended all along for Abraham to become the point of union for circumcised Jews and foreskinned Gentiles who walk in his footsteps and are saved by faith alone. Since he was later circumcised, Abraham is the father of the circumcised who follow in his footsteps and are saved by faith (Cranfield, I, pp. 236–237). Since he was justified when he was uncircumcised, Abraham is the father of the uncircumcised who

---

29. This rendering of the phrase in Greek 'the righteousness of faith' interprets it as a genitive of source. Abraham's righteousness had its source in his faith as opposed to a faux righteousness that originates in one's boast to have obeyed the law (Phil. 3:5).

Paul deliberately avoids the phraseology of Genesis 17:11 that refers to God's command to 'circumcise the flesh of your foreskins' as 'a sign of the covenant between me and you'. That phrase would shore up the presumption of Israel's preeminence as God's sole covenant partner because of circumcision.

are also saved by faith. This conclusion essentially eliminates the category of 'proselyte', 'a second class of insiders within the Jewish and Christian assemblies' (Bird, p. 139).

iv. God fulfilled the promise to Abraham through faith apart from the law (4:13–22)

13. That God declared Abraham righteous is not the whole story. God promised to bless Abraham and to make his descendants a great nation (Gen. 12:2) with offspring as numerous as the dust of the earth (Gen. 13:16), the stars in the heaven (Gen. 15:5) and the sand on the seashore (Gen. 22:17). God also promised to give his descendants a vast expanse of land (Gen. 13:15–17; 15:18; 17:8). Since God promised that all the families of the earth would be blessed in him (Gen. 12:2; 18:18; 22:18) and that he would become the father of a multitude of nations (Gen. 17:5), God did not intend to restrict these blessings to Abraham's biological heirs; they also were to embrace the nations. The phrase *not . . . through the law* is placed first in the Greek, and the phrase *but through the righteousness of faith* is placed last for emphasis. With this key point Paul explains how the multitude of nations without the law could be included in the promise. Abraham did not receive the promise as a reward for his obedience to the law, 'which came four hundred and thirty years later' (Gal. 3:17). He received it as one who believed what he heard from God. The multitude of nations can receive the blessings of the promise in the same way: through believing the gospel (1:16; 10:4, 9–12; 15:13). *Righteousness of faith* is a subjective genitive that should be translated 'the righteousness that comes by faith' (csb). By deliberately wrapping these phrases around the reference to the promise to Abraham and his *descendants* ('seed'), Paul accentuates that the fulfilment of the promise is appropriated *only* through faith. Later, in chapters 7–8, he will explain more fully the role of the law and why the promise not only does not but *cannot* come 'through the law'.

Jewish interpretation over time expanded the inheritance of 'the land' to apply to the whole *world*.[30] In the New Testament, the

---

30. Cf. Sir. 44:21; 2 Esd. 6:59; 2 Bar. 14:13; 44:13; 51:3.

promises are spiritualized and given eschatological import (Matt. 5:5; 25:34). Paul understands the *world* (*kosmos*) in this context to refer to the future eschatological world that the faithful will inherit.[31] The fulfilment of the promise also means 'inheriting' 'the kingdom of God' (14:17; 1 Cor. 4:20; 6:9–10; 15:50; Gal. 5:21; Eph. 5:5), receiving 'eternal life' (2:7; 5:21; 6:22–23; Gal. 6:8), being glorified with Christ (8:17) and receiving the gift of the Spirit (Gal. 3:14), a present reality 'guaranteeing what is to come' (2 Cor. 5:5, NIV).

14–15. 'Those who are of the law', the literal rendering of the phrase translated *the adherents of the law* or those 'dependent on the law', are not Abraham's legitimate heirs if they presume that their acceptance by God depends on the works of the law. Paul revises the question posed in 3:31 by contending that faith does not nullify the law. The law empties faith of any value and nullifies the promise. If the law were the governing principle for determining righteousness, faith would be irrelevant. Worse, the law utterly fails to lead to righteousness. In an aside, Paul explains that the law raises the stakes by revealing that sin is the wilful transgression of what persons know to be God's law. Wilful rebellion against God spawns God's wrath. The problem with the law is that, like a radar gun that catches speeders, it only identifies infractions. It does not resolve the heart of the problem by transforming the offender into a non-speeder who will now always obey speed limits, nor does it spare the offender the punishment due for violating the law. Only faith rescues the ungodly from wrath.

16–17. Paul summarizes his argument thus far: the promise depends entirely on the response of faith to God's initiative of extending grace. Since God did not mediate the promise to Abraham through the law, it has no role in certifying who Abraham's heirs are. The recipients of the promise, or the inheritance (4:14), are only Christian believers, Jews and Gentiles who have faith as Abraham did. Since faith is no different for the Jew than it is for the Gentile, it means that Abraham is the father of all who have faith. This statement is corroborated by Genesis 17:5: *I*

31. Adams, *Constructing*, p. 168; cf. Sir. 44:21; 1 En. 5:7; Jub. 17:3; 22:14; Philo, *Mos.* 1.155; Philo, *Somn.* 1.175.

have made you the father of many nations. What is remarkable about this
declaration is that it affirms that God had *already* accomplished this
purpose (*I have made you*) long before Abraham's promised child was
even born. The promise can be spoken of as already realized
because God has the absolute power to give life to the dead (cf.
John 5:21; Rom. 8:11; 2 Cor. 1:8–9) and to call into existence things
that do not exist.[32]

The mention of giving *life to the dead* prepares for the reference
to Jesus' resurrection (4:25). Calling *into existence the things that do not
exist* need not refer to *creatio ex nihilo,* creating out of primordial
nothingness, though this idea does surface in Jewish sources (cf. 2
Macc. 7:28–29; 2 Bar. 21:4; 48:8; 2 En. 24:2). *The things that do not exist*
(literally, 'the nothings') probably refers in this context to the *many
nations* mentioned in verses 17 and 18, what God called them when
they did not yet exist.[33] The 'nations' are specifically identified in
2 Esdras 6:56–57a as 'nothing':

> As for the other nations that have descended from Adam, you have
> said that they are nothing, and that they are like spittle, and you have
> compared their abundance to a drop from a bucket. And now, O Lord,
> these nations, which are reputed to be as nothing . . .

Paul's later citation of Hosea 2:23 in 9:25, 'Those who were not my
people I will call "my people"', captures the gist of what he means
here.

18. Paul next describes how Abraham's faith played itself out.
Abraham did not base his trust in God on the cold hard facts.
Humans with their befogged and fragmentary knowledge can grasp
only through faith the fact that God's creative power does what is
utterly impossible. In a hopeless situation, Abraham anchored his
hope in divine, not human, possibilities and trusted that God's word
packed the power to accomplish what God promised.

---

32. Unlike those who evoke God's wrath by snubbing their Creator (1:20,
    25), Abraham directed his faith to the one 'from' whom 'and through'
    whom 'and to' whom 'are all things' (11:36).

33. Worthington, *'Creatio ex Nihilo',* p. 59.

The opening phrase with the Greek preposition *epi* is usually translated *hoping against hope*. It may be better to translate it 'piling hope upon hope' with the idea that 'Abraham kept putting more "hope" in place of previous "hope", wanting to see what was not yet visible' (Porter, p. 109). Each step of the way led him to new vistas of hope.

19–22. Abraham believed that he would become the father of many nations when the prospect that he would become the father of a single child seemed highly unlikely. Abraham could see and *considered* how hopeless it was. He and Sarah were both *as good as dead*; but weak in body, Abraham did not grow weak in faith. He believed that God could revive his virility and revitalize Sarah's womb. It was a miracle when Isaac, the promised son, was born. Abraham was about one hundred and had a corpse-like body. Sarah had always been barren (Gen. 11:30) and, at ninety (Gen. 17:17), was long past menopause and had a corpse-like womb.[34] God keeps promises, but not always according to our timetable.

It is a bit disconcerting, however, to read Paul's interpretation that Abraham did not weaken in faith beside portions of the Genesis narrative. In Genesis, Abraham protests to God (Gen. 15:2–3), twice allows Sarah to be taken into a king's harem (Gen. 12:11–20; 20:1–18), tries to procure the promised heir through Hagar instead of Sarah (Gen. 16:1–6) and laughs at God's promise of a son (Gen. 17:15–17). Paul notes, however, that Abraham 'was strengthened in his faith' (NIV), a divine passive which refers to God as the agent of strengthening. Abraham cannot take credit for this strengthening of his faith. *Being fully convinced* that God would do what he had promised is also in the passive voice. With the clock ticking and time running out for him and Sarah, Abraham did not convince himself that God would be faithful and fulfil the promise. God convinced him. What Paul says of his own experience, that 'the Lord stood by me and gave me strength', enabling him to carry out his charge to proclaim the gospel to the Gentiles despite harrowing obstacles (2 Tim. 4:17), also applies to Abraham's struggles during long years of waiting. When Abraham was dogged

---

34. The English word 'necrosis' transliterates the Greek word Paul uses.

by misadventures, God made his faith dogged, relentless. As a result, Abraham gave to God the glory that the Gentiles had withheld (1:21, 23).

v. Abraham's unwavering faith in God's promise as the model for every believer (4:23–25)

23–25. Paul reads the Scriptures looking back from what God has done in Christ and asserts that the story of God reckoning Abraham righteous applies to current believers (cf. 15:4; 1 Cor. 10:11). Allen comments, 'Christian faith is Abraham's all over again, faith in the same God of miraculous life who had now demonstrated His power afresh in the wonder of the resurrection.'[35] Christians will be reckoned righteous because of their faith in Jesus. In 4:24, Paul refers to being reckoned righteous as something that will happen to us in the future, but he uses the past tense in 3:24 and 5:1 to refer to Christians having been justified through faith, something that has already occurred. There is no contradiction. From the perspective of Genesis 15:6 and the Abraham saga, the justification of believers was something that would happen in the future.

The difference between Abraham's theocentric faith and the Christocentric faith of Christ-followers is that the latter faith is placed in something even more mind-boggling than the promise of God ushering life from a seemingly dead womb: Christ-followers believe that God brought to life one who was dead and buried in a tomb. It is not enough to believe that Jesus' resurrection happened, however. Paul carefully specifies that Christians *believe in* him *who raised Jesus our Lord from the dead*. To be made right with God, one needs to entrust one's life entirely to God, who makes promises to those who are in Christ. To those who are dead because of sin, God will give new life (8:10). To those whose mortal bodies succumb to death, God will give eternal life (8:11).

Paul must assume that his audience knows the details of Jesus' passion, since this verb *was handed over* is so prominent in Gospel accounts of it (Matt. 26:2, 15–16; 27:26; Mark 15:15; Luke 22:6; 24:7;

---

35. Allen, 'Old Testament', p. 19.

John 19:16; 1 Cor. 11:23). He must also assume that they would hear echoes of Isaiah 53:5, 11–12 in the phrase *for our trespasses* and would agree with what Paul writes in 5:6–11. God addressed the problem of sin through the atoning efficacy of Jesus' sacrificial death, and the believer's justification was the outcome of Jesus' resurrection. The two events should not be separated such that Jesus' death did one thing and the resurrection another. The cross and the resurrection represent a single mighty act of the Father that cannot be disjoined.[36]

Theology

Paul must untangle a theological knot. God promised Abraham that 'all peoples on earth / will be blessed through you' (Gen. 12:3, NIV; 18:18; 22:18). The nations have dishonoured God and done things deserving the curse of death (1:32) rather than blessing. Furthermore, Israel's unfaithfulness has caused God's name to be blasphemed among the Gentiles (2:23–24). Worse, Israel has rejected the call to be a means for God to bless the world by limiting salvation to themselves alone. They presume that God will reckon righteous only those who are circumcised. If Gentiles must become circumcised to receive salvation, it means that they must become Jews, which means that God is the God only of Jews. Paul argues from the Abraham account in Genesis that Abraham is the father of both Jews and Gentiles who believe. He also infers that being declared righteous depends entirely on the sovereign act of God. Righteousness is totally divorced from human performance and depends entirely on one's faith in response to God's promises. Paul draws a further inference from the Genesis account: *all* who trust in God's promises as Abraham did can be reckoned righteous. This truth explains why Paul has proclaimed the gospel from Jerusalem to Illyricum (15:19), is eager to proclaim it in Rome (1:15) and intends to proclaim it in places where Christ has not been named, such as Spain (15:20, 28). It is why Paul concludes that Genesis 15:6 was also written for a contemporary audience (4:23–24a). Paul understands

---

36. For example, Paul says of the resurrection, 'If Christ has not been raised, your faith is futile and you are still in your sins' (1 Cor. 15:17).

that God's promises to Abraham are *now* being fulfilled with Gentiles coming to faith.

For Abraham, faith entailed placing trust in God's spoken word even though the promise would be fulfilled in an indefinite future and there was no observable verification that the realization of the promise was remotely possible given the seeming hopelessness of his and Sarah's human condition. Brunner comments that faith is not a work, 'a virtue outshining all other virtues'. It is 'to surrender oneself unconditionally' to God's hand, giving 'God his place' to work in one's life, and 'expecting everything from him' (Brunner, p. 38).

Abraham's faith did not mean an intellectual assent to propositions about some remote divine force. His faith was quite different from Philo's interpretation that he 'first grasped a firm and unswerving conception of the truth that there is one Cause above all' (*Virt.* 216). Rather, his faith 'was directed toward a God of whom he had a direct and personal knowledge'.[37]

Acting upon his trust in God turned Abraham's life upside down and brought a change in the way he lived. Faith meant his life was governed by a sustained hope in God who gives life to the dead, which made perseverance possible in moments of despair. He held on to God's promise in the midst of his fleshly demise with a body as good as dead and a wife who was beyond childbearing years and barren even in her youth. God did not change his condition and make him miraculously virile. Abraham remained weak and impotent but trusted that God could and would work a miracle regardless of human weakness and impotence.

Despite setbacks that would seem to quash the promise from ever becoming a reality, Abraham's faith resulted in his continuous glorification of God. He acknowledged his personal incapacity, which is intrinsic to the human condition and not limited to getting old. It is often said that being old means you now need someone to help you, but that is true of all humans whatever their age. Abraham turned to God for help and gave glory to God even when that help seemed remote.

---

37. Adams, 'Abraham's Faith', pp. 61–62.

Abraham's faith did not count as a work for which he accrued merit with God. Genesis 15 recounts Abraham obeying God's command to go outside to gaze at the heavens (Gen. 15:5). Abraham is completely passive, 'merely ... listening and looking' and accepting God's word that his descendants would be as numerous as the stars in the sky (Harrisville, p. 64). Abraham was not 'especially virtuous' but was someone who was 'in himself without hope'.[38] Faith simply responds to God's gracious initiative that may seem to come out of the blue.

Abraham did not strengthen his faith over the years of disappointment by straining ever harder to believe. God, the author of faith, strengthened his faith. God is the primary actor, initiating the promise, fortifying the one who responds to the promise, and following through in fulfilling the promise.

Paul identifies God as the one who justifies the ungodly (4:5), the one who gives life to the dead and calls into existence the things that do not exist (4:17), and the one who handed Jesus over to death for our trespasses and raised him from the dead for our justification (4:24–25). Hill writes, 'The identity of the God of Abraham – who God was in the past, for Abraham – is bound up with the identity of God as the God of Jesus – who God is as the one who raised Jesus.'[39] This identity shows how in saving humans God brings salvation where there are few prospects for it – for a wandering Aramean, for a deceiver named Jacob, for a no-name, stiff-necked throng of slaves working in an Egyptian brick factory, for shepherds at a Bethlehem manger, for a thief on a cross, and for an anonymous Roman executioner at Golgotha. God begins with nothing because humans lack any capacity to save themselves and any merit worth mentioning that God can use to their advantage. Salvation is like God standing before a dark void and creating the world (4:17), standing before Sarah's withered womb and bringing forth a child (4:18–21), and standing before a dank tomb and raising Jesus from the realm of the dead (4:24). Humans can receive God's salvific work *only* by faith. Laden with sin, humans can only trust

---

38. Timmins, *Romans 7*, p. 183.
39. Hill, *Paul*, p. 56.

that such a God makes fit those who are unfit for a relationship with God. Beleaguered by mortality, those who are in Christ can only trust that such a God will also raise them from the dead. Those who are in Christ recognize that such a God has broken down the barriers that divide persons into races, tribes, clans and castes, and through their shared faith has joined them together into a single, spiritual family. As a result, the world is not divided into Jews and Gentiles, but into 'those who give allegiance to Christ and those who do not' (Jackson W., p. 94).

4. JUSTIFICATION BY FAITH BRINGS PEACE AND RECONCILIATION WITH GOD, A RENEWED LIFE AND THE HOPE OF GLORY (5:1 – 8:39)

Paul introduces a new section in 5:12 – 8:39 with a hinge passage in 5:1–11. That unit closes 1:18 – 4:25 with its emphasis on justification – 'Therefore, since we are justified by faith' (5:1) – and lists its results: peace and reconciliation with God and the hope of glory. It also launches what follows with its emphasis on what justification by faith entails for the lives of believers who now have the assurance of a new life freed from the dominion of sin and the sin-corrupted law. This next section also develops their hope of glory as joint heirs of Christ with the assurance of God's final victory over all evil powers intent on terrifying believers and cutting them off from Christ's love. The emphasis on life, newness of life and eternal life, appears throughout this section (5:17, 18, 21; 6:4, 11, 13, 22, 23; 8:2, 6, 10, 12, 13). Paul refers to 'Christ' twenty-four times in this section, compared to twice in the previous section, and 'through' or 'in our Lord Jesus Christ' (and its variants) occurs at key structural points (5:1, 11, 21; 6:23; 7:25; 8:39). The striking number of parallels in vocabulary and concepts between 5:1–11 and 8:18–36 suggests that these passages serve as literary markers that frame the entire section. Words or phrases that appear in 5:1–11 reappear in 8:18–36: 'justified' (5:1, 9; 8:30, 33); 'sufferings' (5:3; 8:18, 35–36); 'hope' (5:2, 4, 5; 8:20, 24–25); giving of the Spirit (5:5; 8:23); 'glory'/'glorify' (5:2; 8:18, 21, 30); 'endurance' (patience) (5:4; 8:25); 'God's love' (5:5, 8; 8:37, 39); 'the death of [God's] Son' (5:10; 8:32); and being 'saved' (5:9–10; 8:24) occur throughout this section.[1]

A. The results of God's love through Christ's death: peace and reconciliation with God (5:1–11)

Context

In 3:21–26 and 4:23–25, Paul laid out the theological principles of justification by faith that are concisely stated in 3:22: 'This righteousness is given through faith in Jesus Christ to all who believe. There is no difference between Jew and Gentile' (NIV). With 'therefore' (5:1), he summarizes the results for believers as recipients of God's grace that he has stressed in 3:21–31 and 4:1–25. For the first time in the letter, Paul identifies himself with his audience by using 'we', not as an authorial plural (3:8) but to denote himself and his readers. In the short span of these eleven verses 'we' occurs sixteen times, and '*our* Lord Jesus Christ', the tie that binds believers together in a common union, brackets this unit (5:1, 11). Paul has established that no difference exists between Jews and Gentiles 'since all have sinned and fall short of the glory of God' (3:23). This unit forms a bridge to the rest of the letter that will move forward under the theological conviction that no difference exists between Jews and Gentiles who believe in the God 'who raised Jesus our Lord from the dead, who was handed over to death for our trespasses and was raised for our justification' (4:24–25). Jewish and Gentile believers share a common faith in God's Son as their Lord and have had the love of God poured into their hearts through the Holy Spirit given to each of them.

The word translated 'boast' (*kauchaomai*) in 5:2–3 and 11 also brackets this unit. Instead of snubbing the glory of the immortal God (1:23), boasting falsely in God as a means of validating and glorifying themselves (2:17) or boasting in the law (2:23), believers

---

1. Cf. Dahl, *Studies*, pp. 88–90; and Luz, 'Zum Aufbau', p. 178.

boast in their 'hope of sharing the glory of God'.[2] That hope of glorification in the life to come (8:18) is made possible because of God's love, demonstrated in the death of Christ (5:6, 8) and poured out into the hearts of believers through the Holy Spirit (5:5; cf. Joel 2:28; Acts 2:17). It has made justification and reconciliation possible, opened access to God, and provides deliverance from God's wrath. The peace we have 'with God through our Lord Jesus Christ' (5:1) is the result of the reconciliation we have received 'through our Lord Jesus Christ' (5:11).

Comment

1. Most ancient texts read 'let us have peace' (*echōmen*, present active subjunctive) instead of *we have peace* (*echomen*, present active indicative), which is less strongly attested. Internal evidence, however, weighs heavily in favour of the indicative. In the context, Paul states facts: 'we have obtained access to this grace' (5:2); 'we were reconciled to God . . . having been reconciled' (5:10); 'we have now received reconciliation' (5:11). It is unlikely that he believes reconciliation with God has already happened but peace with God is so uncertain that he must enjoin his audience to have it. Therefore, Paul does not begin by saying, 'Let us have peace with God . . . and let us boast in the hope of the glory of God', but 'We have peace with God through our Lord Jesus Christ . . . and we boast in our hope of sharing the glory of God.'[3] He does not exhort his audience in this unit but describes a present reality they have through being justified by God based on faith.

---

2. Paul's use of the first-person plural throughout this unit shows that God has bonded together Christ-followers, as the offspring of Abraham, 'father of all of us' (4:16), in this peace.

3. Verbrugge, 'Internal Evidence', p. 569, provides grammatical evidence ruling out the hortatory subjunctive reading. While the similar pronunciation of the two verbs may have caused confusion, it is possible that the later church's concern to encourage peace among members influenced the variant. For example, Origen comments on this verse, 'Peace reigns when nobody complains, nobody disagrees, nobody is hostile and nobody misbehaves' (Bray, *Romans*, p. 126).

Peace does not refer to inner serenity but to an end to being 'estranged and hostile in mind, doing evil deeds' (Col. 1:21). Those in a harmonious fellowship with God may feel tranquillity as the weight of sin and a troubled conscience is lifted (Isa. 32:17), but Paul himself admits to feeling 'utterly, unbearably crushed', despairing of life (2 Cor. 1:8), feeling 'perplexed' (2 Cor. 4:8) and having 'fears within' (2 Cor. 7:5), suffering from anxiety for all his churches (2 Cor. 11:28) and having sorrow upon sorrow (Phil. 2:27). Therefore, peace of mind is different from having peace with God. Having peace with God means that Christ-followers, unlike the wicked (3:17), no longer stand under God's wrath (5:9; cf. 1:18) but have security, well-being and wholeness from an intimate relationship with God and living in step with God's will.

The priestly benediction 'the LORD lift up his countenance upon you, and give you peace' (Num. 6:26) and Isaiah's prophecy 'Peace, peace, to the far and the near, says the LORD; / and I will heal them' (Isa. 57:19) have been fulfilled. Isaiah asserts,

> The effect of righteousness will be peace,
>   and the result of righteousness, quietness and trust for
>   ever.
> (Isa. 32:17)

What God has done through Christ, however, goes beyond what was imagined. Isaiah also declares that there is no peace for the wicked (Isa. 57:21), but 'now' (Rom. 3:21), even the wicked who put aside their brazen defiance of God along with their smug pretensions and accept God's offer of grace are made right with God and have peace with God.

2. Paul may use secular imagery to assert that through our faith in Christ we obtain *access* to God's royal audience chamber (Bruce, p. 123; cf. Eph. 2:18; 3:12).[4] It is more likely that he employs cultic imagery from Scripture. He imagines 'unhindered access to the sanctuary as the place of God's presence' (Käsemann, p. 133; cf. Heb.

---

4. Cf. Xenophon, *Cyropaedia* 7.5.45; Plutarch, *Themistocles* 28.

4:15–16; 10:19–22).[5] This access was possible only for those who were pure and unblemished, and that has now been made possible for sinful believers through Christ's atoning death that embodies God's grace. Paul accentuates God's grace by saying that we have access not to God but to *this grace*. Under the law, sinners who dared approach the divine presence were in peril of being obliterated by a consuming fire (cf. Lev. 10:1–3; 16:1–21). Now, believers, enfolded by divine favour, need have no fear when Christ ushers them into God's presence.

Käsemann comments, 'The basic understanding of existence comes to expression in boasting. In this, a person tells to whom he/she belongs. In a fallen state the person boasts of himself and his powers' (Käsemann, p. 133). Consequently, Paul excluded boasting based on works of the law (3:27) since it holds up what one has done, expecting God to approve and applaud it. Having been lifted up from the depths of degradation to stand on the ground of grace, Christ-followers have a different ground for boasting. They can boast only about what God has done in their lives (1 Cor. 1:31; 2 Cor. 10:17; citing Jer. 9:24), not what they have done themselves. Because believers place their trust in Christ, they exult in a new destiny, the *hope* of *the glory of God*. They will be made fit for heaven and will be glorified as joint heirs of God with Christ (8:17). Believers are saved not merely from the punishment of God's wrath, but for glory (Jackson W., p. 110).

3. Peace with God does not lead to peace with the world, which continues its rebellion against God. Christians openly confess faith in a crucified Messiah. In a world hostile to God, obedience to Christ puts them in danger, and Christ-followers must anticipate persecution. Suffering is a harsh reminder that Christ-followers still live in the interim before the end-time consummation. If one were to look at Paul's own body, one would see that as Christ's apostle he had endured multiple hardships that left him branded with scars from many beatings (2 Cor. 4:7–12; 6:4–10; 11:21–33; Gal. 6:17). The sufferings Paul has in mind, then, are not the afflictions that can assail any human but those that result specifically from believers

---

5. Cf. Exod. 29:4, 8, 10; Lev. 4:14; 21:18–19; Num. 8:9–10.

living out their devotion to Christ. Open commitment to Christ results in suffering for Christ's sake (Mark 4:17). Christians faced ostracism and rejection from their families and acquaintances and prosecution and execution from governmental authorities because their faith was perceived as a harmful superstition. It was feared as anti-religious for renouncing the worship of all other deities and arousing their ire that would then lead to local disasters and social disorder. Jews perceived Christians as blasphemous for worshipping a man as God and as dangerous because their aggressive evangelism among Gentiles without requiring them to come under the law eradicated Jewish religious integrity. Those who value the approval of the ones with power and influence in this world more than God's approval are unlikely to suffer for Christ. The only reason rejoicing in afflictions makes any sense is because believers have the hope of the resurrection. The gospel does not offer our best life now, free from tough times, but eternal life in the world to come.

Neither are setbacks in Satan's arena crushing blows for believers, since the school of suffering can prepare them to persevere in ever more extreme battles. External pressure does not reduce them to dust but strengthens them as those refined by fire (1 Pet. 1:6–7). Therefore, believers do not boast only in sharing future divine glory, but also in their present afflictions, because they can provide greater confidence in the sufficiency of God's grace and the power of Christ dwelling in them (2 Cor. 12:9–10). Christians who pile hope upon hope (4:18) in the face of suffering and persecution (8:18, 35–39) face life with greater fortitude. The Greek word translated *endurance* (*hypomonē*) refers to the capacity to hold out or bear up in the face of difficulty and can also be translated as 'fortitude', 'patience', 'steadfastness' or 'perseverance'. The quality of intrepid staying power Paul intends is best rendered by 'fortitude' (Jewett, p. 354). How one responds during grim times – whether one cracks under persecution or not – reveals one's character. Paul admits that he is an earthenware vessel 'afflicted in every way', 'perplexed', 'persecuted' and 'struck down', which produces sundry chinks and cracks (2 Cor. 4:7–12). He recognizes that through his suffering he conveys to the world the treasure of the gospel that shines through the cracks in this fragile clay pot. Always carrying in his body the dying of Jesus proclaims

the wisdom of the cross for the salvation of the world. It also reveals
that the power does not derive from him but from God alone.
Because of his assurance of God's power he can endure anything,
knowing that 'the one who raised the Lord Jesus will raise us also
with Jesus, and will bring us with you into his presence' (2 Cor. 4:14).

4. Suffering also produces *character* from being tested by the
ordeal and proved faithful. Suffering met with fortitude demonstrates that our confession of faith in Christ is not empty talk. Paul
sees a believer's character growth progressing amid suffering along
the route of *endurance*. It produces *hope*, which might seem strange
since it would seem more likely that one's hope would produce the
endurance that leads to character. Paul understands, however, that
growth in spiritual maturity and Christian character results from
learning that sharing in Christ's sufferings will result in sharing in
his glory (8:17), that 'all things work together for good for those
who love God, who are called according to his purpose' (8:28), and
that nothing is 'able to separate us from the love of God in Christ
Jesus our Lord' (8:39). Paradoxically, those who pass these fiery
tests become rich in character and richer in hope.

5. The centrality of the Christian *hope* is prominent throughout
the letter (cf. 5:2, 4, 5; 8:20, 24, 25; 12:12; 15:4, 12, 13, 24). When Paul
speaks of *hope*,

> it has less to do with the future than with the present. Hope is a
> perception of the present based on the premise of God's presence
> and power. Hope is that which enables us to move into the future
> because of the reality of God's presence in the 'now time'.
> (Johnson, p. 80)

Because they have taken refuge in God, hope gives Christ-followers
assurance that they will not be 'ashamed' (1:16). It means that they
will not experience disappointment caused by the failure of their
hope that God will vindicate them, and that they will not feel
shame from their current afflictions that cause others to hold them
in contempt (cf. Pss 22:5; 25:2–3, 20; 31:1; 71:1; 119:116; Isa. 28:16).

The 'love of God' (the literal translation) refers to God's love for
believers that is poured into their hearts through the Holy Spirit

(cf. Acts 2:17–18, 33; Titus 3:6).[6] The image of pouring out implies that believers fully experience this love and that nothing is held back. God's love for humans comes into clearest focus in Christ's cross[7] as the divine power that overcomes enmity between 'the Creator and the creature' (Käsemann, p. 135). It involves dying for others to justify, reconcile and save those who are unworthy of such love. It differs dramatically from the portrayal of the goddess Isis's redemption of one Lucian in Apuleius's second-century novel *The Golden Ass* (*Metamorphoses*). Lucian had foolishly dabbled in magic and was turned into an ass. At the end of the story, Isis speaks to him in a dream:

> And if I perceive that thou art obedient to my commandment and addict to my religion, meriting by thy constant chastity my divine grace, know thou that I alone may prolong thy days above the time that the fates have appointed and ordained.
> (Apuleius, *Metam.* 11.6.24 [Hanson, LCL])

In contrast to this perspective, God's love for us is totally undeserved, and God's power will do far more than prolong earthly life. God promises us eternal life through the resurrection when our body sown in dishonour will be raised in glory (1 Cor. 15:43).

For the first time in the letter, Paul mentions the *Holy Spirit*, a transcendent power given to us that moves our spirit. Suffering led the Israelites to grumble against God when they were tested in the wilderness, but God gives us the Spirit to assure us of his love, 'that we are no longer left to ourselves and the world' but 'already set in the kingdom of freedom' (Käsemann, pp. 135–136). The Holy Spirit also fills the vacuum of our human powerlessness. If we are to be like a fountain in which God's love poured into us flows out into others, the Spirit is the pump that powers this fountain of love. The Spirit, not the law, becomes 'the decisive mark of the people of

---

6. It may be a plenary genitive that also includes our love for God. God's love for us and the outpouring of the Holy Spirit in our hearts should stir our love for God in response.

7. Martin, 'Reconciliation', p. 39.

God' (Schreiner, p. 256). The love that the Spirit pours into our hearts leads to regenerated hearts.

6–8. As a demonstration of God's love, 'when the fullness of time had come, God sent his Son, born of a woman, born under the law' (Gal. 4:4) to die for *the ungodly*. Human calendars did not determine the timing, nor did human worthiness. His death also did not transform those who are weak into those who are strong. 'Weakness' refers to a lack of merit and the incapacity to save oneself. Believers remain weak even after turning to Christ (8:26; 2 Cor. 11:30; 12:5, 9–10). A popular motto going back to Sophocles has it that 'God helps those who help themselves.' The gospel has it that God helps those who are altogether helpless. Human weakness is the place where God demonstrates infinite power. Our powerlessness meant that Christ had to die 'for us' (*hyper*, 'on behalf of'), 'both as our representative and as our substitute' (Schreiner, p. 268).[8] God decided to take our sin upon himself in the person of Jesus, who took our place in dying for us. Paul reiterates this point in 8:32: God 'did not withhold his own Son, but gave him up for all of us' (cf. 14:15; 2 Cor. 5:14–15, 21; Gal. 2:20; 1 Thess. 5:10).

Paul underscores the magnitude and astonishing nature of this sacrificial death by pointing out how it goes against all common sense: *rarely will anyone die for a righteous person*, though it is possible that someone might dare to die *for a good person*. Multiple interpretations seek to explain the relationship between the substantival adjectives *righteous* (*dikaios*) and *good* (*agathos*). They may be equivalent and placed in parallel for rhetorical effect. 'The good' may be read as neuter in gender to refer to some 'good cause', such as the law or one's nation, rather than as masculine in gender to refer to a 'good person'.[9] It could also refer to the one who has imperium, a person the state has invested with power to do what is best for the state.[10] An example might be dying for a divinized leader. Clarke contends

---

8. Powers, *Salvation*, p. 233, argues that Christ's death on behalf of others should be understood in terms of representation instead of substitution.

9. Wolter, *Rechtfertigung*, p. 331.

10. Rock, *Paul's Letter*, p. 188.

that 'the good' might also refer to a patron or benefactor to whom
one is indebted. He argues,

> It is not unthinkable in the first century that someone – because of the
> ties of patronage – would give up their life for their benefactor . . . Yet
> Christ gave up *his* life *for us* – when we were yet sinners without any
> claim on him.[11]

If it is difficult to decide who or what 'the good' is meant to
represent, the gist is clear: 'dying for shameful, unworthy people
is unprecedented' (Jewett, p. 360). Paul develops the meaning
of Christ's death for sinners first broached in 3:21–26. If it is
highly exceptional for one to die for a righteous person, it is far
more exceptional for one to die for unrighteous persons. Christ
did not give his life for those who were worthy but for sinful
humankind, revealing that 'God's love is far greater in its magnitude and dependability than even the greatest human love'
(Moo, p. 333). According to 2 Peter 2:5, in the days of Noah God
sent the flood on the ungodly to destroy them. God's incompar-
able love has now sent Jesus to save the ungodly.

9. Paul moves from the past, *we have been justified by his blood*, to
the present, *now*, to the future, *will we be saved through him from the
wrath of God.*[12] *Blood* (cf. Eph. 1:7; 2:13; Col. 1:20) draws on the
sacrificial imagery of Christ dying as an atonement for our sins
(3:24–25). *Justified by his blood* also draws attention to the gravity of
the human sinful condition from which all need redemption, and
underscores that justification received freely came at enormous
cost. Paul's point is this: if God went to such an extraordinary
extreme as to sacrifice his Son to make humans right with God,
how much more should believers be assured that God will complete their salvation and save them from divine wrath in the age to
come (cf. 1 Thess. 1:10; 5:9).

Paul conceives salvation as being worked out in two stages. The
first stage is justification by and reconciliation to God through the

---

11. Clarke, 'The Good', p. 142.
12. Wisse, 'Righteous Man', p. 93.

death of Christ, by which God mends the broken relationship, making us right and providing a new identity that befits God's vision for humanity. When believers respond with faith, they change from enemies of God to God's servants. The second stage, which is denoted by the future tense of the verb 'we will be saved' in 5:9–10, is the culmination when God's glory is revealed at the end of the age and believers share in it (5:2; 6:4; 8:18, 21, 30; Phil. 3:21; 2 Thess. 2:14).

10–11. Paul changes metaphors from 'justification' to 'reconciliation', which takes what God has done through Christ a step further. Justification is a judicial term from the law courts. A judge may acquit accused persons without ever entering a personal relationship with them. The judge only announces the verdict, in this case, 'not guilty'. The accused hardly expects to be invited over for dinner by the judge after this ruling, but probably hopes never to see the judge again. Wright points out,

> In the lawcourt, the point is not that the defendant and the judge have fallen out and need to re-establish a friendship. Indeed, in some ways the lawcourt is more obviously fair and unbiased if the defendant and the judge have no acquaintance before and no friendship afterwards.[13]

God as our judge does not simply alter the books by dropping the charges against us. God gives himself to us in friendship. This next step of reconciliation is necessary because the judge is the one who has been sinned against as the object of human hostility (Cranfield, I, p. 259).

Saved by his life refers to the risen life of Jesus. It means 'we are saved by being brought into the life of the risen Lord'.[14] Paul explains what he means in 6:4 with the paradox that 'we have been buried with him [Christ] by baptism into death, so that, just as Christ was raised from the dead by the glory of the Father, so we too might walk in newness of life'. He will also explain that Christ died for the ungodly not simply to save them from the wrath, but to make them godly.

---

13. Wright, *Justification*, p. 226.
14. Stagg, *New Testament*, p. 127.

Theology

The centrality of Christ in Paul's theology is evident in this section. Paul describes the saving work that has been done *through* Christ (5:1, 2, 9, 10, 11, 17, 18, 19, 21; cf. 3:24) *for* us (5:6, 8; 6:10).[15] Through Christ's death, believers are transformed from those who were 'powerless' (5:6, NIV), 'ungodly' (5:6), 'sinners' (5:8), 'enemies' (5:10) and worthy of divine wrath (5:9) into those who are now justified (5:1, 9), reconciled to God (5:10), at peace with God (5:1), standing in grace (5:2), saved from God's wrath (5:9) and exulting in the hope of sharing God's glory (5:2). Since God initiated this transformation while believers were still enemies, God expected them to respond to this grace with faith. When one does so, being *with* Christ (6:4, 5, 6, 8) and *in* Christ (6:11, 23) makes it possible to live a new life. Consequently, thanks are due to God 'through Jesus Christ our Lord', who died for us to bring our deliverance (7:25).

Gibson notes that 'dying for others' was a phrase that appeared in the writings of 'cult leaders, politicians, testamentarians, war memorial eulogists, hard-pressed battlefield commanders, beleaguered soldiers, and epigraphers'. His analysis concludes that the formula was employed

> to inculcate, confirm, or enforce the values that stood at the very heart
> of Greco-Roman, Imperial ideology – values that were accepted by
> Jews, Greeks, and by those whom Paul called 'the rulers of this age' as
> essential for maintaining 'peace and security' – namely, that the warrior
> is the ideal citizen; that war is 'glorious'; that violence is a constructive
> force in the building of civilization; and that 'salvation' from that which
> threatens to harm or destroy a valued way of life is ultimately achieved
> only through the use of brute force.[16]

---

15. Christ dying for us is a central tenet of Paul's theology (cf. 4:25; 8:32; 14:15; 1 Cor. 8:11; 11:24; 15:3; 2 Cor. 5:14–15, 21; Gal. 2:20; 3:13; 1 Thess. 5:9–10; 1 Tim. 2:6; Titus 2:14).

16. Gibson, 'Dying Formula', p. 38.

Jesus' death for others turns these secular beliefs upside down. Jesus did not die in battle, did not grasp for glory (Phil. 2:6–8), and died not for his own people but for his enemies.[17]

Christ dying for the ungodly also turns the common view about benefactions upside down. The Roman patronage system presupposed that the beneficiaries of gifts must be worthy of them since gifts created reciprocal obligations. One therefore did not want to give gifts indiscriminately and become tied to one who was 'disreputable, ungrateful, or otherwise worthless'. The donor therefore 'must judge the *worth* of the recipient' before bestowing a gift.[18] Through Christ's death, God bestows righteousness, peace and reconciliation on those who are helpless, unable to save themselves in any form or fashion. From a worldly perspective, none of us is worth saving. Yet God delivers us from our shame and degradation that would destine us for wrath. God saves us not in spite of our sinful condition but because of it, because we are in desperate need of saving. Schweizer comments, 'God loves us no less if we come to him with dirty hands than if we have achieved perfection in the sight of the law.'[19] Paul considers the latter to be impossible, so God loves us despite our failures in life.

Emperor Augustus's rise to power put an end to civil war and bloodshed in Rome, and he used the resulting peace as a propaganda tool to identify himself as the peacemaker. The Pax Romana that brought an end to the political instability and ushered in economic prosperity and comparative security for Rome was won and enforced by military conquests that desolated adversaries so that they could no longer resist. Tacitus has the British general Calgacus attempt to rally his troops before battle with the Romans by giving a rousing pep talk: 'To plunder, butcher, steal these things they misname empire: they make a desolation and call it peace' (Tacitus, *Agr.* 30.5 [Hutton and Ogilvie, LCL]). Haacker calls attention to the first blush of the young Nero's promising rule when the praise of Roman 'peace'

---

17. Ibid., p. 39.
18. Barclay, *Paul*, p. 39.
19. Schweizer, *Holy Spirit*, p. 83.

had 'a second heyday'.[20] Nero was lauded for bringing a final and
universal peace and the end of all wars, which appealed to a
universal longing for peace. White contends that Paul coined the
phrase 'When they say, "There is peace and security"' in 1 Thessalonians 5:3 to sum up 'the ancient world's widely shared hope
for a stable and undisturbed life free from fear of loss of life or
limb'. Paul chose two familiar terms, 'peace' (*pax*), celebrated in
Roman society, and 'security' (*asphaleia*), evoking Greek conceptions of well-being, 'to describe the greatest common good
that both Greek and Roman civilisation claimed to offer'.[21] Paul
warns the Thessalonians that those who look to Rome to ensure
a peaceful existence, undisturbed by threats from outside, and to
provide stability and welfare are inevitably destined to meet with
disappointment. The promise of peace and security will be shred-
ded by the apocalyptic deluge that Paul expects will soon break
in on the world.

In the modern era, everybody still longs for peace. Paul con-
sciously appeals to this longing but subverts the imperial ideology
that the gods were on Rome's side and Roman rulers brought peace
on earth when he cites Isaiah: 'and the way of peace they have not
known' (3:17).[22] The peace of God is something quite different.
Outside of Christ there is no hope (1 Thess. 4:13) and no peace, only
social chaos (1:29–31) and 'alienation and separation from God'.[23] In
this letter, Paul frequently mentions the peace that the gospel brings
(1:7; 2:10; 3:17; 5:1; 8:6; 14:17, 19; 15:13, 33; 16:20; cf. 12:18). 'Peace with
God', however, appears only here in the New Testament. The Roman
peace came at the end of a gun, so to speak, but more significantly it
did not bring peace with God. God's sacrifice of Jesus on a Roman
cross alone brings peace with God and alone offers salvation to the
world under the reign and law of Christ.

The human condition is beset by two problems. Humans are
ravaged by sin and death, and their relationship with God has gone

20. Haacker, *Theology*, p. 117.
21. White, 'Peace and Security', pp. 506–507.
22. Haacker, *Theology*, pp. 116–119.
23. Martin, 'Reconciliation', p. 38.

awry. Christ's death on the cross both exposes human sin and reveals God's loving resolution to these problems. Martin asserts, 'Human need is the dark canvas against which the divine love shines brightly.'[24] Our justification, peace with God and reconciliation came at an extraordinary cost. It shows God's determination to reconcile those he loves to himself. Reconciliation, however, is not a one-sided process. There can be no real reconciliation 'when one side is willing to put the past behind them and the other side merely takes advantage of it'. Both must acknowledge the wrong, and the injured party must release the pain caused by the wrong.[25] Human responsibility for Christ's death might seem to exacerbate the estrangement from God, but God has used Christ's death to redeem us from sin's control and does not count our trespasses against us. It then remains for us to accept our guilt and accept God's offer of friendship. Sometimes the phrase 'getting right with God' is used to refer to being saved. Since there is nothing that believers can do to make things right with God, it is God who makes persons right with God. Humans can only accept God's love expressed in Christ's death for them through faith. Only then does God's Spirit fill with God's love human hearts that were formerly filled with sin (2:5).

B. Eternal life and righteousness brought by God's victory in Christ cancels out the condemnation and death brought by Adam's transgression (5:12–21)

Context

Having established that one becomes righteous only by faith, Paul now clarifies *how* the righteous are to 'live' (1:17) as those now justified by faith, reconciled to God, dead to sin and animated by the Holy Spirit.[26] First, however, he must address the problem of sin and death, the two main enemies that endanger righteous living and imperil believers' hope of glory. Paul expands on his

---

24. Ibid., p. 48.
25. Beck, 'Reflections', pp. 85–92.
26. Cf. Feuillet, 'La Citation', pp. 52–80.

brief statement in 1 Corinthians 15:21–22: 'For since death came through a human being, the resurrection of the dead has also come through a human being; for as all die in Adam, so all will be made alive in Christ.' The concept of 'one human being' shaping the destiny of all those bound to him forms the basis of the comparison between Adam and Christ.[27] The comparison parries a potential Jewish objection: how could one man's death on a cross influence the lives and destinies of all people? Paul articulates what was a given in Jewish circles, that what Adam did *had* universal repercussions for all humankind, to make the case that what Christ did *has* universal repercussions for all humankind. The similarity between Adam and Christ ends there. The two are equivalent only in the universal effects of their actions. Adam, whom Paul identifies in 1 Corinthians 15:45, 47 as 'the first man', a 'living being' and 'a man of dust', was disobedient to God and returned to dust at his death (Gen. 3:19), as do all who are in Adam. Christ, whom Paul identifies in 1 Corinthians 15:45–47 as 'the last Adam', 'a life-giving spirit' and 'the second man . . . from heaven', was obedient to God, and God raised him from the dead, as God will raise all who are in Christ. Through the obedience of the one man, Christ, God overthrew the dominion of sin and death that the transgression of the one man, Adam (5:12), produced. God inaugurated the reign of grace that leads to eternal life through Christ (5:21). The refrain 'through ['in'] Jesus Christ our Lord' rings out at the beginning or end of major units in this section (5:11, 21; 6:3; 7:25; 8:39).[28]

The concept of sin figures prominently in this unit.[29] It can be read as a summary of the human condition under sin delineated in 1:18–31 and God's solution to sin through Christ elucidated in 3:21 – 5:11 (Schnabel, I, p. 545). Paul personifies sin as a power that

---

27. 'One' (human) occurs eleven times in 5:12–19 as the counterpoint to 'all', which occurs four times.

28. Tomlinson, 'Sacral Manumission', p. 87.

29. 'Sin' appears in 5:12, 14, 16; 'sinner', in 5:19; 'transgression' (*parabasis*), in 5:14; and 'trespass' (*paraptōma*), in 5:16, 17, 18, 20. The word 'sin' appears thirty-six times in chs. 6–8.

'came into' the world (5:12) and 'exercised dominion' (5:21). Later, he says that it makes persons 'slaves' (6:20), pays 'wages' (6:23), seizes 'opportunity' (7:8, 11), 'deceives' (7:11), 'kills' (7:11) and 'dwells' within persons (7:20). Since Paul does not mention here the serpent tempting Eve, as he does in 2 Corinthians 11:3 (cf. 1 Tim. 2:14), his primary interest in this unit is not to identify sin's origin or who should get the blame for it. His focus is on how sin and death secured their dominant foothold in human lives and how God has decisively dethroned them.[30] The succeeding units in this section establish that believers now are dead to sin (6:1−14), are freed from sin (6:15−23) and are discharged from the law (7:1−6) that sin has commandeered (7:11). He then shows why freedom from the law is necessary because it is incapable of generating the obedience it demands and, impaired by sin, whets the appetites of sinful passions in humans (7:7−25). Only the indwelling Spirit enables believers to fulfil the law's just requirement (8:1−17), inspires their hope (8:18−30) and assures their victory through Christ (8:31−39).

Comment
i. The action of one placed the future destiny of others under sin and death (5:12)

12. *Therefore* (*dia touto*) introduces Paul's comparison between Adam and Christ in which he presents Christ's redemptive work as the ground for believers' hope (5:2). In chapter 4, Paul creatively interpreted the classic biblical story of Abraham to show that God will credit righteousness to all those who have faith in Christ. He now draws on the classic biblical story of Adam (Gen. 2 − 3) to show that the universal influence of Christ's redemptive death on the cross has overturned the universal influence of Adam's transgression that resulted in humanity living in subjection to sin and death.[31]

Adam's sin incurred fatal consequences because God's decree imposed the sentence of death as the punishment for transgressing

---

30. Feuillet, 'Le Règne', pp. 494−495.

31. Kertelge, 'Sin of Adam', pp. 506−507.

the command not to eat of the tree of the knowledge of good and evil (Gen. 2:17). *Death* does not refer only to the termination of life. Adam may not have died immediately after violating God's command (Gen. 2:17; 3:3–4), but he immediately became estranged from God (Gen. 3:8–10). Therefore, *death* also entails spiritual death that separates one from God, and that separation can be eternal.

The prepositional phrase *eph' hō* has elicited numerous interpretations,[32] but the translation *because* ('inasmuch as', 'seeing that', 'for the reason that') has become the predominant rendering of the phrase (cf. 2 Cor. 5:4; Phil. 3:12; 4:10). Paul harks back to his description of sin in the opening chapters that concludes with the declaration that *all have sinned* (3:23). He assumes that all die because all sin, not because they inherit Adam's sin as a birthday present as the result of their parents' sexual union.[33] The logic is this:

one sinned (Adam) → he died
because all sin ← death spread to all humans

Nevertheless, Adam's sin had social consequences since his sin started a snowball rolling down the mountain that became an avalanche. To use the metaphor found in 4 Ezra 4:31–33, a grain of evil seed has produced much fruit of ungodliness. Adam's transgression also revealed the connection between sin and death (1:32; 6:16, 21, 23; 7:9–11, 13; 8:6, 13; cf. 2 Bar. 56:5–6). His progeny arrive in a world already fractured by sin. Accordingly, they are inescapably subject to sin's powerful undertow that dashes them against the rocks of death. Most important for Paul's argument, Adam is 'a representative figure' of humankind 'whose story is re-enacted in every human being . . . the corporate entity to which all individual men and women inescapably belong'. Humans are related to Adam 'by inheritance, imitation, and involvement'.[34] Though Adam's

---

32. Cranfield, I, pp. 274–281, outlines six different interpretations of the clause. Fitzmyer, pp. 413–417, identifies eleven and argues for the meaning 'with the result that'.

33. Cf. 2 Bar. 54:15, 19.

34. Caird, *Language*, p. 136.

descendants did not yet exist, they were in his loins, in the same way that Hebrews asserts that Levi was in Abraham's loins when Abraham paid a tithe to Melchizedek (Heb. 7:9–10; cf. Gen. 14:20). As Harrison and Hagner put it, 'Sin is part of the natural makeup of the children of Adam, and they cannot escape living out their Adamic nature' (Harrison and Hagner, p. 97).

The later rabbis were quite flexible in explaining death's origins, depending on the assumptions governing the point they wished to make. In one case, they argue that Adam's sin was responsible for the presence of death based on the principle of collective justice. In another case, they argue that each person dies because each person sins based on the principle of 'measure for measure'. In still another case, they argue that death is a moral purgative for the world based on the principle of divine chastisement.[35] Paul is also quite flexible in explaining death's origins and can argue that all people die because they sin on their own account and that they die because of Adam's sin (Moo, p. 354). The foundational principle behind Paul's argument here and his primary interest is that what *one* man has done determines the existence of all those bound to him. Adam's sin had deadly consequences for all since he was a prototype who manifested the typical qualities of humanity. God did not scrap the prototype, however, when it failed its first test in the Garden of Eden, nor did God seek to work out the bugs through steady improvements over the years. Instead, God planned a complete overhaul of humanity, offering a new possibility through the gift of grace through a life-giving union with Christ. Grace comes as a gift, but it needs to be received, unwrapped and applied in one's life.

ii. Excursus on the law and sin in relation to death (5:13–14)

13–14. Some translations insert a dash at the end of verse 12 to indicate that Paul breaks off his thought for a moment to counter anyone who might raise the objection: 'How can God charge one's account with sins that violate God's law and warrant death when the law did not exist until Moses?' He responds with

---

35. Kadushin, *Organic Thinking*, p. 209.

a brief excursus. God may not have posted violations in the divine ledger balance since legal rules did not yet exist. Nevertheless, death as the penalty for sin was in force during this time. Since death was universal, sin was universal. Paul argued in 1:18–32 that those without the law still know God's righteous decrees from creation (1:32; cf. 2:14–15). God's decrees, then, are found not only

> on tablets, as in the Mosaic dispensation, but also in the created order, as in the Adamic dispensation . . . Israel's special revelation is *not* the debut of law in the universe, but merely a privileged expansion of what God had made known to the nations through their inventory of nature.[36]

Humans sinned apart from the law and perished apart from the law (2:12), because they violated God's will by engaging in practices that deserved death, continually 'spitting in God's face' (1:32, MSG). Those who lived between the time of Adam and that of Moses may not have transgressed a direct commandment as Adam had, but death, sin's consequence, held an iron grip on humanity because of their dishonouring God.

Adam is the *type* or 'pattern' of *the one who was to come*, Christ, 'the last Adam' (1 Cor. 15:45), because his disobedience had an impact on all humanity just as Christ's obedience has an impact on all humanity.[37] Adam set the stage for humanity's ruination through his disobedience. Christ sets the stage for humanity's salvation through his obedience. Adam stands at the head of the old order of humanity corrupted by sin and death. Christ stands at the head of the new order of humanity renewed by grace and life. Adam had lethal consequences for the destiny of humans who came after him. Christ has far greater life-giving consequences for human destiny.

---

36. Poirier, 'Romans 5:13–14', p. 351.
37. Paul uses the word translated *type* quite differently elsewhere to refer to an exemplary (Phil. 3:17; 1 Thess. 1:7; 2 Thess. 3:9; 1 Tim. 4:12) or a cautionary (1 Cor. 10:6) model.

iii. Contrast between the universal effects of Adam's trespass and of Christ's righteous act (5:15–17)

15. The phrase *much more* rings throughout this chapter (5:9, 10, 17). In this verse and in verse 17, Paul assumes that the influences of Adam and Christ are similar because they both have universal consequences for humans. The consequences of the *trespass* and the *free gift* of grace (*charisma*) are, however, drastically different. Adam's transgression flung open the floodgates for sin and death to engulf the world.[38] Christ's atoning death on the cross reversed the ravages of sin and death. Those who are in Christ are delivered from these twin curses, flourish in God's grace and will be raised from death with Christ (6:4–8; 8:11). It is noteworthy that Paul does not yet specifically contrast Adam's transgression with Christ's obedience. Instead, he contrasts Adam's action with *God's action* in Christ, namely, the redemption graciously bestowed by God's power to give life and to raise the dead (cf. 3:24; 4:24–25; 6:4, 9; 7:4; 8:11, 34). Schnabel notes that Paul thereby highlights 'the incorporation of the Messiah Jesus in the identity of the God of Israel (cf. 1:3–4)' (Schnabel, I, p. 564, author's translation). God's superabundance of grace[39] does not just counterbalance the trespass. It overwhelmingly tips the scales. God's power to save overwhelms the power of sin and death to destroy. It is not what Christ did in faithfulness to God, but what God did in Christ (2 Cor. 5:19).

16. The one trespass led to *judgment* (*krima*) and the *condemnation* (*katakrima*) of all. *The free gift* (*charisma, dōrēma*) from God counteracted the *many trespasses* (*paraptōma[tōn]*) that have been committed by all humans, not just by one man, and it led to *justification* (*dikaiōma*). The word *dikaiōma* is rendered as *justification* here and in 5:18 in some translations. Paul uses the noun elsewhere in Romans,

---

38. In the phrase *For if the many died through the one man's trespass, the many* is a Semitism for 'all', which Paul uses in the parallel statement in 11:32 (cf. 5:12).

39. The Greek phrase that translates literally as 'the grace of God and the gift' is a hendiadys, expressing a single idea through two words connected by 'and' that means 'the gracious gift of God'.

however, to refer to God's 'righteous decree' or the law's 'just requirements' (1:32; 2:26; 8:4; cf. Luke 1:6). Many interpreters claim that Paul chose this noun instead of the one he normally uses for 'justification' (*dikaiosynē*) to continue the assonance of the series of five other nouns ending with the *-ma* suffix. He alters the normal meaning of the noun in the context to express the result of a verbal action, the acquittal of righteousness that overturns the sentence of *condemnation*. The noun normally signifies 'reparation', an action 'that satisfies the court' and clears one from condemnation.[40] It evokes 'the reparation demanded by God in the face of transgression and further connotes a demanded death – a demand met in the cross of Christ'.[41] This interpretation is confirmed by the use of the noun in 5:18: 'one man's act of righteousness [*dikaiōma*] leads to justification [*dikaiōsis*] and life for all'. The noun has the same meaning in both verses and refers to Christ's sacrifice that bore the iniquities committed by the mass of humanity and removed the grounds for their condemnation (3:25). It is best, then, to translate the noun in this verse as 'righteous deed' to refer to the righteous act of Christ's dying for sinners (5:6, 8), and not as 'justification' or 'acquittal', the resulting verdict of Christ's act.

17. The death sentence pronounced on sinners was not irrevocable (cf. 8:33–34). God's abundant provision of grace through Christ's death overturned the verdict so that sinners can now receive *the free gift of righteousness*, namely, *life*. *Righteousness* may denote that believers are not simply acquitted and let off the hook, but they are put right and given a new life in Christ (Gal. 2:20; cf. Rom. 6:6). Paul contrasts being made 'sinners' with being made 'righteous' in 5:19. The gift of righteousness reigns over believers' lives instead of sin. As the objects of divine grace, they will reign with God.

iv. The reign of grace overcomes the dominion of sin and death (5:18–21)

18. With the word *therefore* Paul returns to the comparison of Adam with Christ that he began in 5:12. The emphasis falls on 'how

---

40. Kirk, 'Reconsidering *Dikaiōma*', p. 787.
41. Ibid., p. 791.

much more' glorious are the ramifications of Christ's righteous action for humanity than the disastrous ramifications of Adam's sin. *Justification and life for all* translates the Greek phrase that can be rendered 'justification of life'. It is best rendered as an objective genitive, 'justification that leads to life'. *Life* embraces both the transformed life in the here and now, and life in the hereafter for those who are bound to Christ. *For all* does not entail universal salvation. While 'none can escape the consequences of Adam's act', 'Christ's act has no inevitable result; the gift of grace and righteousness can only be received through faith in Christ' (Schnabel, I, p. 571, author's translation). Justification may come as a gift, but it must be 'received', as Paul maintains in verse 17. Humans have the freedom to choose against Christ and to reject God's merciful offer of reconciliation (11:32). As a result, they will remain under sin's regime. God is also free to reject them for their refusal to accept God's grace. Righteousness, justification, salvation come only to those who believe (3:22, 26, 28, 30; 4:24; 10:4, 9). Those who do not believe perish (1 Cor. 1:18; 2 Cor. 2:15; 4:3; 2 Thess. 2:8–9). The phrase *for all* means that 'the gift which comes through the grace of the one man Jesus Christ' is available to all 'without ethnic distinction'.[42]

19. *The many* is interchangeable for 'all' since all *were made* sinners through Adam's disobedience. The verb translated *were made* (*katesthēsan*) means 'to cause someone to experience something' (BDAG, p. 492) or 'to show one to be something'. Adam's defiance of the first divinely given commandment plunged all who came after him under the thraldom of sin and death. By contrast, Christ's obedience, which was lifelong, manifested the power of God's grace that overflows in abundance. Its effects are utterly opposite to the results of Adam's transgression. In Adam, all were constituted sinners. In Christ, God constitutes a new identity for all believers as those who will be righteous at the final judgment (cf. Isa. 53:11).[43]

---

42. Rapinchuk, 'Universal Sin', p. 433.

43. Since believers are already reckoned righteous, *will be made* (*katastathēsontai*) should be read as a 'logical' future (so Cranfield,

20. The introduction of the written law did not solve the problem. Paul uses the same verb in the phrase *law came in* to describe the Judaizing false brothers who 'infiltrated' Paul's private meeting with the acknowledged leaders of the church in Jerusalem with designs to 'enslave us' (Gal. 2:4). He does not wish to imply in this verse that the law was an intruder like sin and death, 'squatters who entered the estate and now ruled its inhabitants' (Keck, p. 149). The coming of the law fulfils a divine purpose. Paul does not say it was added to increase 'transgressions' (plural) but to increase '*the* transgression' (singular), namely, Adam's transgression that violated a revealed commandment (5:15, 17, 18). The word *sin* in secular Greek usage was related to missing the mark, the failure to achieve a standard. This Greek word becomes in Jewish religious texts something more than missing the mark, and when the law enters it becomes a deliberate defiance of God. The promulgation of the law resulted in the *one* transgression mushrooming into *many* transgressions as humans sinned in the same way that Adam did by deliberately rebelling against God's commands (4:15; 7:7; Gal. 3:19).[44]

The law failed to produce the holiness God required (Lev. 11:44) but fostered instead a penchant to rebel (7:8) or to boast of one's righteousness and superiority over others (2:23; cf. Phil. 3:4–6). Since it imposed death for disobedience, the law ushered in the age of sin and death, not salvation. The giving of the law was not, however, God's futile attempt to bring about the renewal of Adamic humankind. Instead, the law abetted God's purpose to bind everyone over to disobedience so that God might have mercy on all (11:32; cf. Gal. 3:22). In raising the consciousness of sin, it also could serve to lead individuals to realize their need for forgiveness and deliverance. Paul's citation of Psalm 32:1–2 in 4:7–8 shows how it could work. Confronted with his guilt, David confessed his transgressions and was forgiven his sin (Ps. 32:5). This awareness

---

(note 43 *cont.*) I, p. 291; Fitzmyer, p. 421; Lohse, p. 182; Schnabel, I, p. 576; Wolter, I, pp. 357–358).

44. In a sermon, Rabbi Simlai tallied the commands that humans could break as 613 (b. Mak. 23b).

of sinfulness and the inability to atone for it can make one more receptive to God's offer of grace through Jesus Christ. Only Christ's expiatory death overcomes humans' predicament created by their transgressions (5:6, 8; 1 Cor. 15:3; 2 Cor. 5:18–19; Gal. 1:4; Col. 1:14).[45]

Davies asserts,

> It was a postulate in Rabbinic thought that a man by his obedience
> to the Torah could obtain merit. In fact, according to some of the
> Rabbis the Torah had been expressly given in order that Israel might
> be given the opportunity of gaining merit . . . These merits . . . benefited
> not merely the person who by his obedience acquired them, but also his
> contemporaries, and in addition, because of that solidarity of all the
> members of the community both past, present and future . . . they
> would also avail for those who preceded him and those who would
> follow him both here and hereafter.[46]

Kister develops this statement by comparing 5:12–21 with Sifra (Hova 12:12).[47] Both passages refer to the ruinous effects of one

---

45. Gathercole, 'Sins', counters the various assertions of scholars who
    claim that Paul did not view Christ's death as having to do with the
    forgiveness of sins.

46. Davies, *Paul and Rabbinic Judaism*, pp. 268–269.

47. Kister, 'Romans 5:12–21', pp. 391–424. Sifra is a commentary on
    Leviticus, connected to the school of R. Akiba (*c.* AD 50–235), that
    draws legal tenets and clarifications from the text. The relevant
    passage, as translated by Kister, reads: 'Rabbi Yose says: If you wish to
    know the reward [that will be] given to the righteous in the Age to
    Come you may learn this from Adam [i.e. from Adam's punishment]:
    He was given only one commandment, a prohibition, which he
    transgressed, and see how many deaths Adam was condemned [to
    suffer as a result]: his own and those of all his descendants and his
    descendants' descendants to the end of all generations. Now, which
    (divine) measure is greater, the measure of (divine) benevolence
    or the measure of (divine) punishment? Certainly, the measure of
    benevolence is greater. If, then, the lesser measure, that of punishment,

man's (Adam's) sin on all humans and also contend that 'one man' can be the source of merit by which many others receive blessings from God. They differ concerning the identity of the positive figure. Paul identifies the one man as Jesus Christ. The Sifra identifies the one man as any Jew who refrains from doing things prohibited by the Torah and who does things required by the Torah (on the Day of Atonement). It reflects the view that 'good deeds in general outweigh sin' and that a 'righteous person' gains merit for generation after generation by that person's righteous deeds.[48] Paul maintains that all such attempts are doomed to miscarry. Sin and death are powers that are far beyond a human's meagre abilities to overcome with attempts to obey the law. He insists that *only* Jesus' atoning sacrifice prevails over sin and brings God's gift of righteousness to every generation of believers.

Paul has a grim view of the effect of sin and death on human lives. They engender degradation and despair, wipe out peace and hope, and breed soulless wretches. The opening piece in 1:18 – 2:24 makes it clear that humans' deliberate choices to commit sinful actions cause them to be delivered over to dishonourable passions and debased minds so that they are without excuse. The quotations from Scripture in 3:10–18 'show, not that man is under a demonic power, but that men do wicked and sinful things'.[49] The fallen human situation is not because the whole creation is 'trapped,

---

(note 47 *cont.*) resulted in Adam and his descendants and descendants' descendants being condemned to so many deaths [for a single transgression], someone who refrains from eating *piggul* or *notar* and who fasts on the Day of Atonement, how much more does such a person acquire merit for himself and for his descendants and all his descendants' descendants to the end of all generation.' *Piggul* ('foul thing', applied to unclean sacrificial flesh) is a sacrifice that is unfit to eat because of an improper intention to eat it outside the appointed time limit, and *notar* ('leftover') refers to portions of sacrifices left over beyond the legal time when they may be eaten and must be burned (Lev. 7:15–18; 19:5–8).

48. Kister, 'Romans 5:12–21', pp. 401–402; cf. Sir. 3:14–15; b. Yoma 87a.
49. Kaye, *Thought Structure*, p. 40.

enslaved under the power of the present evil age'.[50] Sin and death
are not on an equal level with 'the cosmic powers of . . . darkness'
(Eph. 6:12). In 5:20, *sin* and *trespass* are regarded as equivalent. Sin
runs riot in human lives because of humans' sinning. No magical
charms, no human-devised battlements, no happy thoughts, no
internal light, no obedience to the law can ward off or vanquish the
guilt of sin and the fear of death that have taken control of one's
life. Only the power of God's grace exhibited in the cross and
resurrection suffices to forgive sin and to defeat its inevitable
outcome of death. Now that God has 'presented Christ as a
sacrifice of atonement, through the shedding of his blood' (3:25,
NIV), 'the rules have changed, so to speak, from divine judgment
to grace'.[51]

21. Paul concludes this unit with references to sin's reign that
leads to *death* (cf. 5:12, 14) and the counterstroke of *grace* (cf. 5:15, 17)
that leads to 'righteousness' (NIV; cf. 5:17) and *life* (cf. 5:17–18).
Grace now reigns through the redemptive work of *Jesus Christ our
Lord* (cf. 3:24) and has broken sin's reign of terror enforced by
death's sharp-edged sickle. Since Jesus' act of obedience is far
greater than Adam's act of transgression, the reward from Jesus'
sacrifice, life, now identified as *eternal life*, is also far greater. The gift
of *eternal life* after physical death to which believers still must
succumb denotes a future reward that awaits being raised with
Christ when death, the last enemy, is vanquished (1 Cor. 15:21–26,
51–57).[52]

Theology
Dodd gives voice to the difficulty Paul answers in this passage:

> You say, 'We are saved by what Christ did. But, granted that He lived
> a wonderful life, and died a death of perfect self-sacrifice, we can
> understand that He has thereby given an inspiring example, yet, after

---

50. So Martyn, *Galatians*, p. 105. Shaw, 'Apocalyptic and Covenant', and
    Gathercole, 'Sins', offer significant challenges to this view.
51. Kister, 'Romans 5:12–21', p. 402.
52. Cf. 6:22–23; Gal. 6:8; 1 Tim. 1:16; 6:12; Titus 1:1–2; 3:7.

all, He was an individual person in history: how can *His* conquest over sin and *His* achievement of the human ideal be effective for other individuals?'

(Dodd, pp. 78–79)

It may be hard to 'think of our actual participation in a single person at the head of the line' if we believe that we are autonomous individuals who think and act independently of others and should not be held accountable for others' actions.[53] To grasp Paul's point, however, it is necessary to do so. He draws on the story of Adam's sin to apply the notion that one man's action affects all others who are bound to him. Adam's transgression launched dire and inescapable consequences for all who came after him (5:12, 15–16, 18–19), as expressed in the lament in 2 Esdras 7:118: 'O Adam, what have you done? For though it was you who sinned, the fall was not yours alone, but ours also who are your descendants.' Paul argues that Christ's obedience has the same effect on all who are bound to him and develops the contrast between solidarity with Adam and solidarity with Christ. Solidarity with Christ turns lament into celebration (see Table 1 below).

Table 1: Solidarity with Adam or solidarity with Christ

In Adam	In Christ
Condemnation (5:16)	Justification (5:18)
The reign of death (5:17)	The reign of believers in life (5:17)
The disobedience of one that makes others sinners (5:19)	The obedience of one that makes others righteous (5:19)
The increased transgressions (5:20)	The increased abundance of grace (5:20)
The reign of sin bringing death (5:21)	The reign of grace bringing eternal life (5:21)

---

53. Keck, *Paul*, p. 57

Humans are born into a world where a sea of collective sinfulness encircles and engulfs them. History exposes the truth
that humans all share a dark side, a predisposition to do wrong
and to invent new ways of destroying the lives of others and
themselves. They cannot solve the problem of sin and elude the
shadow of death through their own wisdom or willpower, and the
law offers no remedy either. Sin and death invade to reign over
the world as tyrannical powers when given the slightest opening.
Therefore, it took the greater power of God to atone for sin and
to destroy death's fearsome stranglehold. God vanquished the
universal plague of sin and death through the universal remedy
of Christ's obedient sacrifice of his life. Those who are incorporated in Christ, becoming subject to him as 'Lord' (5:21), get off
death row. The phrase 'in' or 'through Jesus Christ our Lord'
figures prominently in chapters 5−8. We receive 'peace' (5:1);
'reconciliation' (5:11); 'eternal life' (5:21; 6:23); being 'alive to God'
(6:11); deliverance from 'this body of death' (7:24−25); and
safekeeping in the 'love of God' (8:39) through Jesus Christ our
Lord. Paul asserts that through Christ's death on the cross the
enduring sin of Adam from the past has been rectified and
believers will be saved from God's wrath at the future judgment
(5:9).

Bruce points out that in Scripture,

> When one man fails in the accomplishment of God's purpose (as, in
> measure, all did), God raises up another to take his place − Joshua to
> replace Moses, David to replace Saul, Elisha to replace Elijah. But
> who could take the place of Adam? Only one who was competent to
> undo the effects of Adam's sin and become the inaugurator of a
> new humanity.
> (Bruce, p. 125)

Paul is fully aware that the analogy between Christ and Adam
breaks down (5:15). Christ is not simply Adam's replacement. First,
Adam began with a clean slate and started a contagion − something
that is easy to do. Christ came into the world to reverse the effects
of sin when the pandemic was in full swing − something far more
difficult to do. It was so difficult that it required the sacrifice of his

own blood. Second, Adam's act was one of deliberate disobedience because he lent a willing ear to the whispered suggestion that God was withholding the fullness of life and happiness. He believed that he was better off doing what God told him not to do. Rather than entering a brighter paradise through his disobedience, he entered the murky prison of sin and death. Jesus was sufficiently like us to reach us but sufficiently different from us to save us, and he made a deliberate decision to be obedient unto death (Heb. 2:17–18). Through Christ's death God poured out an 'abundant provision of grace' and bestowed 'the gift of righteousness' (5:17, NIV) to all joined to Christ. Third, Adam grasped at equality with God and attempted to exalt himself (Gen. 3:5–6). Jesus emptied himself and humbled himself, taking the form of a slave to die a slave's death on a cross to save others. As a result, God highly exalted him (Phil. 2:6–11).

C. Freedom from the dominion of sin and the law to live in service to righteousness (6:1 – 7:6)

Paul has declared that the righteous are justified by faith (5:1), reconciled to God (5:10), living in the abundance of God's grace (5:17–18) and assured of eternal life (5:21). If no human is justified by works of the law (3:20), and the righteousness of God has been disclosed apart from the law (3:21), as Paul insists, does that mean that believers can now safely pay no heed to God's requirement to live holy lives? Paul's answer to that question is a resounding 'No!' That would mean that they remain in bondage to sin. Also, while individuals are saved by faith alone, 'the faith that saves is not alone – it is followed by good works which prove the vitality of that faith'.[54] In 6:1 – 7:6, Paul insists that the old way of life before their conversion to Christ cannot continue for believers. He does not simply insist that believers must live moral lives. He employs various metaphors – baptism, growing together, crucifixion, slavery, and the law of marriage – to elaborate on how their justification by God and their hope of eternal life must shape their

---

54. Metzger, *New Testament*, p. 254.

perspective on their real identity and how they are to live. They are now dead to sin because they are united with Christ in his death and resurrection. They are no longer in a hopeless situation due to the vulnerability of their mortal flesh that is so easily taken over by sin, because they have been freed from sin's enslavement. They have been discharged from the law, which is also easily taken over by sin. Their new identity in Christ means that believers can no longer accept sin in their lives as if it were not out of the ordinary or treat it as if it were only a trivial matter (Schnabel, II, p. 20).

Paul adopts a pedagogical question-and-answer style to respond to the potential and real objections that his gospel opens the door to sinning and frees believers from the fear of facing God's judgment. In this section, he introduces two units with rhetorical questions: 'What then [are we to say]? Should we continue in sin in order that grace may abound?' (6:1). Should we sin because we are no longer under law but are now lavished with grace? (6:15). He responds to both questions with a vehement No! 'By no means!' Paul fleshes out his responses to these questions with metaphors introduced by the question, 'Do you not know?' 'All of us who have been baptized into Christ Jesus were baptized into his death' (6:3); 'we have been united with him in a death like his' (6:5); 'our old self was crucified with him' (6:6); 'you are slaves of the one whom you obey, either of sin, which leads to death, or of obedience, which leads to righteousness' (6:16); 'the law is binding on a person only during that person's lifetime ... Thus a married woman is bound by the law to her husband as long as he lives; but if her husband dies, she is discharged from the law concerning the husband' (7:1–2). The metaphors add force to Paul's insistence that the believer's old self was put to death when the believer was joined to Christ. Formerly some of them were 'sexually immoral people, idolaters, adulterers, or males who have sex with males ... thieves, greedy people, drunkards, verbally abusive people, or swindlers' (1 Cor. 6:9–10, CSB). To continue committing these and multifarious other sins is contrary to the believer's new identity in Christ.

i. The believer is dead to sin to walk in newness of life (6:1–14)

Context

Paul has noted that some slander him by claiming that he advocates, 'Let us do evil so that good may come' (3:8). In 6:1–14, he refutes those who might twist his statement that 'where sin increased, grace abounded all the more' (5:20) into the perverse notion that if God's grace overflows to forgive sin, why not sin all the more to receive more grace? If the answer to the hypothetical question 'Should we continue in sin in order that grace may abound?' (6:1) were 'Yes', then nothing has changed in believers' lives. Sin and its co-conspirator, death, still rule. Paul uses three metaphors here to support his argument that they 'must consider' themselves 'dead to sin and alive to God in Christ Jesus' (6:11): immersion into Christ (6:3–4), fusion with Christ (6:5) and crucifixion with Christ (6:6). The believer's destiny is tied to Christ's destiny. The believer who has been buried with Christ (6:4), united with him in a death like his (6:5), crucified with him (6:6) and has died with him (6:8) will also be raised with him (6:5) and live with him (6:8). Those joined to Christ have died to sin and therefore cannot continue to live in sin because they have been absorbed into a divine spiritual reality that overcomes the spiritual reality of sin and death.[55]

Comment

1. Paul concludes this unit with the assertion that we live under grace, not law (6:14). That reality, however, can prompt misconceptions about the necessity for believers to live morally upright lives. His declaration in 5:20 does not mean that sinning all the more will result in believers luxuriating in a superabundance of grace. Therefore, he revisits the question posed in 3:7–8:

> But if through my falsehood God's truthfulness abounds to his glory, why am I still being condemned as a sinner? And why not say (as some people slander us by saying that we say), 'Let us do evil so that good may come'? Their condemnation is deserved!

---

55. Schnabel, *Jesus, Paul*, p. 277.

Paul cautions anyone against thinking: if my sin magnified God's glory as a gracious saviour, can God's glory be magnified even more by giving God ever tougher cases to crack that receive ever greater instalments of grace? Paul bitterly condemns this crude parody of his gospel. Justification by faith does not boil down to justification for sinning.[56] He has stated that the goal of his apostleship is to engender the 'obedience of faith' among the Gentiles (15:18; 16:26). Obedience of faith involves leaving behind 'a "lifestyle" of sin – a habitual practice of sin, such that one's life could be said to be characterized by that sin rather than by the righteousness God requires' (Moo, p. 383). Being 'united with him in a death like his' and being 'united with him in a resurrection like his' (6:5) creates a partition between the believer's former life in bondage to sin that leads to death and his or her new life in Christ that leads to eternal life (5:21).

2. Paul's answer to this misinterpretation of his gospel is: justification, yes, grace, yes, but redemption is a divine gift that also carries with it a moral demand. Barclay comments, 'A gift that is given without regard to the worth of its recipients certainly threatens to undercut the moral order.'[57] God may shower sinners with utterly undeserved grace. But it is not utterly gratuitous. It comes with the expectation of a return. The divine gift of salvation in Christ 'was *unconditioned* (based on no prior conditions) but it is not *unconditional* (carrying no subsequent demands)'.[58] God expects more than a nod of thanks or a perfunctory confession of faith in return. Käsemann asserts, 'There is no divine gift which does not bring with it a task, there is no grace which does not move to action. Service is not merely the consequence but the outward form and realisation of grace.'[59] God expects changed behaviour, which is why God will assess the believer's behaviour in the final judgment (14:10, 12; 1 Cor. 4:5; 2 Cor. 5:10). Obedience flows from faith because God's grace is transformative, recreating those who accept it into the image of Christ (2 Cor. 3:18), and generating holiness.

---

56. Price, 'Romans 6:1–14', p. 65.
57. Barclay, *Paul*, p. 496.
58. Ibid., p. 500.
59. Käsemann, *Essays*, p. 65.

Paul first uses indicatives to describe the believer's situation and how God pulls justified believers into holiness when they are united with Christ. Then he issues imperatives. Paul does not command Christians to stop sinning. Instead, he argues that for them to continue to live under sin's dominion is incompatible with their new status as those who in Christ have died to sin.

God's grace releases believers from their former slavery to sin, and this break with the old life can only be described as going through death. Cranfield lays out four diverse ways in which Paul employs the concept of death (Cranfield, I, pp. 299–300).[60] (1) 'Death' has a forensic or juridical sense. God ruled that those who are in Christ died to sin when Christ died on the cross and took their sins upon himself (6:2; 7:4; 2 Cor. 5:14). (2) 'Death' has a baptismal sense. The believers' baptism is God's seal and pledge that Christ's death and resurrection affected them personally (6:3–5; Col. 2:12). Dying with Christ in baptism signifies their acceptance of Christ's death for their sins as their death. (3) 'Death' has a moral sense. Believers put sin to death in their mortal bodies (6:6–7, 11). (4) 'Death' has an eschatological sense. Believers die to sin permanently when they, like Christ, breathe their last (6:10). They will then experience a resurrection like his (6:5, 8).

3. Most assume that Paul refers to the ceremonial rite of baptism in verses 3–4, which Cranfield assumes is the case in his second category of Paul's use of death – dying with Christ in baptism (see commentary on 6:2). As a result, this passage has been a magnet for those seeking to work out a sacramental theology of water baptism.[61] The verb 'to baptize' in English, however, is not a translation of the Greek word (*baptizein*) but a transliteration. It predisposes the English reader to think of it as a technical term that refers to the baptismal rite. In Hellenistic Greek, the verb commonly means 'to immerse, to plunge or to dip' into a substance such as water (cf. Mark 1:8; 7:3–4; Luke 3:16; 11:37–38; John 1:26). It could also be used figuratively to refer to being incorporated into

60. Cranfield 'Romans 6:1–14', pp. 40–43.
61. Matt. 28:19; Acts 2:38, 41; 8:12, 38; 9:18; 10:48; 16:15, 33; 18:8; 19:5; 1 Cor. 1:13–17; 12:3; Gal. 3:27; 1 Pet. 3:21.

something. For example, Paul uses it in this sense when he describes Christians being immersed into 'one body' (1 Cor. 12:13) or the people of Israel being immersed into 'Moses' (1 Cor. 10:2). It could also be used figuratively to mean 'being overcome or overpowered' by some intangible or abstract reality – for example, being baptized in the Spirit, in which the Spirit permeates one's life and exerts control over it (Matt. 3:11; Mark 1:8; Acts 1:5). Jesus speaks of his impending death as an immersion (baptism) in which a destructive deluge will engulf him on the cross (Mark 10:38–39; Luke 12:50; cf. Ps. 69:2). Schnabel's exhaustive study shows that the word had not yet become a technical term that routinely denoted water baptism, and this was true even into the Patristic period. The figurative usage of the word best fits Paul's meaning in this context, rather than a reference to the rite of baptism.[62] Paul does not expound on water baptism in this passage but uses the verb 'baptize' and the noun 'baptism' in 6:4 with a metaphorical nuance.

While Paul often uses the question *Do you not know . . . ?* to broach a shared tradition he assumes the audience understands (Johnson, p. 102),[63] here it introduces additional teaching that does not refer to something they already know. Paul introduces what should become obvious to them from the argument (Dunn, I, p. 308). He does not reflect on the initiatory rite for converted believers but uses immersion as a metaphor that pictures believers being plunged into Christ and into Christ's death (Schnabel, II, p. 32). The chiastic structure of the literal word order in the Greek displays that emphasis:

> All of us who have been baptized (immersed)
>> into Christ Jesus,
>> into his death
> were baptized (immersed).

In this statement Paul bundles together ideas that he expresses separately elsewhere. Believers are immersed (*baptized*) into Christ

---

62. Schnabel, *Jesus, Paul*, pp. 238–255.
63. Rom. 11:2; 1 Cor. 3:16; 5:6; 6:2–3, 9, 15–16, 19; 9:13, 24.

(Gal. 3:27), and, having been immersed into Christ, they are 'cruci-fied with' or die with him (Gal. 2:19; cf. 2 Cor. 4:10–11). The agent behind the passive voice of the verbs *have been baptized* and *were baptized* is not someone officiating the baptismal rite. It is God who joins believers to Christ. This immersion into Christ and into Christ's death occurred *before* their water baptism. Believers do not rise up out of Christ as they do out of the baptismal waters. They remain submerged in Christ Jesus.

4. Paul stresses the believers' union with Christ by repeatedly using the preposition 'with' in compound verbs and adjectives throughout this unit: *we have been buried* [placed in the tomb] *with him* (6:4), 'united with him' (6:5), 'crucified with him' (6:6) and 'will . . . live with him' (6:8). The statement *we have been buried with him* affirms three things. First, the passive voice means that God is the agent behind the action of being buried with Christ. Second, being placed in the tomb with Christ means that our old Adamic way of life, presided over by sin, death and estrangement, has been put out of its misery and laid to rest. By this means 'sin has received what it requires – the death of the sinner'.[64] Third, it means that the believer has been transported 'symbolically to that state of exist-ence that Christ entered through his death on the cross'.[65] Burial is not the end of the story. The Old Testament frequently mentions the location of the grave where someone was buried, but it is pointless to do so with Christ. Christ was not left in a tomb to which his followers could make pilgrimage to pay him homage. Nor was he abandoned to Hades but was raised up by God (Acts 2:22–35). In like manner, believers are not left to lie mouldering in the tomb. They too are raised to a new life, one that begins and ends in Christ (Col. 2:12). As Christ was buried and raised (1 Cor. 15:4) and lives by the power of God, so too with Christ-followers (2 Cor. 13:4; Col. 2:12). They no longer live under the shadow of death or the threat of God's wrath.

Paul consistently uses the metaphor to *walk*, which is often rendered 'to live', to refer to religious–ethical conduct. Because an

---

64. Wolter, *Paul*, p. 141.
65. Taylor, 'Dying', p. 47.

end-time reality has broken into the present, believers are guided to walk in the right direction on the only path that leads to eternal life. Paul clarifies in 8:4–17 that the Spirit is the indwelling guide who both leads and prods us along the way. In 6:4, he simply asserts that being immersed into Christ represents a transformation of the course of a believer's life. That change is so radical that believers can now deem themselves to be new creations (2 Cor. 5:17; Gal. 6:15). It also signifies that the same glorious power that raised Jesus from the dead has entered believers to enable them to live close to God as resolutely committed to holiness.

5. Paul spells out in 6:5–10 the implications of his assertion that believers have been immersed in Christ's death. It may be structured as shown in Table 2 below.[66]

Table 2: Dying with Christ and dying to sin

	6:5–7	6:8–10
The condition in the conditional sentence	*For if we have been united with him in a death like his (6:5a)*	'But if we died with Christ' (6:8a)
The logical consequence of the condition	*we will certainly be united with him in a resurrection like his (6:5b)*	'we believe that we will also live with him' (6:8b)
Assertion of the end result	'We know that our old self was crucified with him so that the body of sin might be destroyed, and we might no longer be enslaved to sin' (6:6)	'We know that Christ, being raised from the dead, will never die again; death no longer has dominion over him' (6:9)
Basis for the assertion	'For whoever has died is freed from sin' (6:7)	'The death he died, he died to sin, once for all; but the life he lives, he lives to God' (6:10)

---

66. Adapted from Boers, 'Structure', p. 670.

Paul introduces a second metaphor with the adjective translated *united* (*symphytoi*). It stems from the verb *symphyein*, 'to grow together' or 'to fuse together'. The perfect tense of the verb, *we have been united*, denotes something that has happened in the past with continuing results. It pictures the new life of believers as being inseparably linked to Christ. Planted together and growing together with him gives them a new identity and a new future. It will lead to their resurrection with him. Paul understands the *death* of the believer as a present reality. The believer's *resurrection* is a future event, which makes it difficult to see death/resurrection as the metaphorical element of water baptism. Rising out of baptismal waters is not what Paul means by resurrection.

What it means for us to be united 'in the likeness of his death' (CSB) 'denotes not merely the abstract idea of "likeness", but the concrete image that is made to conform to something else' (Fitzmyer, p. 435; cf. Exod. 20:4; and Deut. 4:16–18; 5:8 [LXX]). The noun 'likeness' (*homoiōma*) implies both similarity and difference (cf. 5:14). The believers' death is different from Christ's death because it is not a physical death by crucifixion as Christ's was but a metaphorical death. The similarity is this: when believers *have been united with him in a death like his* through their faith in him, it signifies the end to their old life and their participation in the results of Christ's death.[67]

If the future tense *we will certainly be united with him* is interpreted as a logical future, it 'describes a share in the risen life of Christ that the justified Christian already enjoys, as a result of the Christ-event' (Fitzmyer, p. 435). It is more likely, however, that the future tense refers to 'the redemption of our bodies' (8:23) when 'the trumpet will sound, and the dead will be raised imperishable, and we will be changed' (1 Cor. 15:52). It may be labelled 'the certainty future'.[68] The Greek text reads literally, 'we shall be also of his resurrection'. Translations render it *we will certainly be united with him in a resurrection like his* to balance it with the previous clause and to clarify the sense. The 'likeness' of the believers' resurrection is different from

---

67. Agersnap, *Baptism*, p. 288.
68. Ibid., p. 293.

Christ's in that they have yet to die a physical death, and when they do and are raised, they will not appear to others who are still alive (1 Cor. 15:5–8). It is the same as Christ's resurrection in that believers will experience a new manner of existence that results in their being 'conformed to the image of [God's] Son' (8:29; 1 Cor. 15:49; Phil. 3:21).

Understanding the likeness of his resurrection as something in the future implies that it 'is the goal of the state or process of the believers' assimilation to Christ's death'.[69] Since we do not sever all links to this world, the ultimate victory over sin awaits our physical death and resurrection, and that dying with Christ is 'a life-long process'.[70] The assurance of this future hope brings with it a present obligation. According to Luke 9:23, disciples are to take up their cross *daily* and follow Christ. Paul expresses how this reality works out in his own life in 2 Corinthians 4:10–11:

> always carrying in the body the death of Jesus, so that the life of Jesus may also be made visible in our bodies. For while we live, we are always being given up to death for Jesus' sake, so that the life of Jesus may be made visible in our mortal flesh.

He does this 'because we know that the one who raised the Lord Jesus will raise us also with Jesus, and will bring us with you into his presence' (2 Cor. 4:14).

6. The *old self* (literally, 'old man') who was crucified with Christ is the unregenerate self, which Paul defines as being 'in Adam' and ruled by sin and death (5:12–21; cf. Eph. 4:22–24; Col. 3:9–10). The term *the body of sin* does not denigrate the body as something inherently sinful but refers to our creaturely existence that is owned by sin (cf. 6:17).

Paul uses metaphors that his original audience would have understood but that modern auditors might miss. A line from a first-century novel illustrates how the phrase 'old man' was used to refer to a slave: 'he will hang me up [crucify] as an old man [= old

---

69. Dunn, 'Salvation Proclaimed', p. 263.
70. Ibid.

rogue slave] as Marsyas from a pine' (Longus, *Daphnis and Chloe* 4.8).[71] *Body* (*sōma*) was also used as a common term for a slave. In Revelation 18:13, the last item in the lengthy list of cargo that the merchants of the earth will be unable to peddle because of the fall of 'the mighty city of Babylon' (Rome), is 'bodies, that is, souls of men' (author's translation). The NIV correctly interprets this phrase as 'human beings sold as slaves'. The *body of sin* refers to the slave owned by sin and 'ruled by sin' (NIV).

'To continue in sin' (6:1) is to remain under sin's ownership as a slave of sin. How could one break that ownership? In the Roman world, being released from slavery through manumission did not mean gaining total freedom. Bradley writes:

> when slaves were set free they did not in consequence find themselves absolved of all responsibilities towards their former owners, now patrons. Instead, as a condition of release from servile status the freedman might find himself bound to his patron by a nexus of obligations, summed up in the legal term *operae*, as a result of which he continued to discharge various services for the patron for a certain length of time.[72]

Only death abolished a master's claim over a slave or former slave. Death becomes a slave's liberator. The funerary commemoration of a slave named Kiburas bears out this truth:

> Now Death (Hades) has overshadowed and he has snatched my hands from the reins of the horses of the fatherland and he has desired that the longed-for servile Kiburas look into the sacred land and after (Kiburas) having creeped on the cradle-grave, he has emancipated (this) slave-body of death. Hierax, being a fellow-slave, erected this stele.[73]

---

71. Tomlinson, 'Sacral Manumission', p. 98. According to one version of a Greek myth, Marsyas challenged Apollo to a flute-playing contest and lost, and had his flayed skin nailed to a pine tree.

72. Bradley, *Slaves*, p. 81.

73. Tomlinson, 'Sacral Manumission', p. 102, translating Peek, *Griechische Vers-Inschriften*, p. 161, text no. 651.2–7.

When Paul said that he was 'crucified with Christ' (Gal. 2:19), an ancient auditor would have thought of it as 'the typical punishment for slaves'.[74] This background explains why Paul emphasizes dying with Christ (6:3–5) and being *crucified* with Christ, because it terminates sin's title to a believer's life. Undergoing a slave's death with Christ means that believers have been set free from sin's control. The body of sin needed to be crucified so that it *might be destroyed* and annul sin's claim to ownership.

7. Paul cites as self-evidently true that one who has died *is freed from sin*. The verb translated *freed* (*dedikaiōtai*) has a forensic character elsewhere in the letter that means to 'justify', 'acquit' or 'declare righteous' (2:13; 3:20, 24, 28; 4:2, 5; 5:1, 9; 8:30, 33). It can retain the forensic sense here in the context of legal proceedings in which claims about who owns a slave or whether a slave is free or not are in dispute. In this case, Paul asserts that the slave who has died is vindicated and certified as freed from the master,[75] which is the background to his assertion that the one who has died has been set free from sin (cf. also Acts 13:38–39).

8. Dying with Christ and being buried with him is not some momentary event in the past. It is something that is 'everlasting'[76] and guarantees a new future. Many in Paul's world imagined that at death our disembodied souls would be packed off to dwell in a

---

74. Hengel, *Crucifixion*, p. 51. Cicero said that the very word 'cross' should be 'far removed from not only the bodies of Roman citizens but even from their thoughts, their eyes, and their ears. The results and suffering from these doings as well as the situation, even anticipation, of their enablement, and, in the end, the mere mention of them are unworthy of a Roman citizen and a free man' (*Rab. Perd.* 5.16 [Hodge, LCL]). Few elite Roman authors mention crucifixion, but it does appear in 'the comic-philosophical tradition' represented by Plautus (Bryant, *Paul*, p. 81). In Plautus's comedy *The Braggart Soldier*, a slave laments, 'I know the cross will be my grave: that is where my ancestors are, my father, my grandfathers, great-grandfathers, and great-great-grandfathers' (*Mil. glor.* 372–374 [de Mello, LCL]).

75. Tomlinson, 'Sacral Manumission', pp. 106–112.

76. Agersnap, *Baptism*, p. 327.

desolate twilight sphere or would be extinguished altogether. For Christians, neither will happen. Belief in the resurrection defies our common-sense intuition about life and death. We know that those who are dead and buried do not return to bodily life, but Christ-followers believe that 'Jesus did so, and we too shall rise bodily when he comes in glory with the clouds, manifesting a lordship over all things that at present remains hidden'.[77] The faith that God has destined Christ-followers for the future glory of the resurrection should change their perception of how they are to live as a result of whose they are and who they are in this present life.

9. Paul's declares, *We know that Christ, being raised from the dead, will never die again; death no longer has dominion over him.* The Gospel of John conveys this truth through allusive imagery in the narrative: 'Simon Peter . . . went into the tomb. He saw the linen wrappings lying there, and the cloth [*soudarion*] that had been on Jesus' head, not lying with the linen wrappings but rolled up in a place by itself' (John 20:6–7). The same word for 'cloth' occurs in John's account of Jesus raising Lazarus from the dead: 'The dead man came out, his hands and feet bound with strips of cloth, and his face wrapped in a cloth [*soudarion*]. Jesus said to them, "Unbind him, and let him go"' (John 11:44). Whereas Lazarus needs help to be fully released from the vestiges of the grip of death, Jesus did not. The burial wrappings left behind are a sign of the triumph over death by the power of God. Whereas Lazarus was raised but eventually will die again, John wishes to convey that Jesus' resurrection from the dead is everlasting. Paul goes further. Believers who 'have died with Christ' have the assurance that they 'will also live with him' (6:8) and will live with him for ever since his resurrection from the dead vanquished death through a greater, divine power.

10. Jesus' dying *to sin* does not mean that he formerly lived in sin. He was born in the likeness of sinful flesh (8:3; cf. Phil. 2:7) and lived on the battlefield where Satan launches endless assaults. He was subject to temptation but never succumbed. Nevertheless, Jesus experienced the full penalty of death, which is the punishment of sinners, 'on behalf of humanity' (Hultgren, p. 251). Sanday and

---

77. Watson, 'Questiones Disputae', p. 244.

Headlam write, 'The sin which hung about Him and wreaked its effects upon Him was not His own but ours' (Sanday and Headlam, p. 160). Through Christ's death, God, *once for all*, decisively condemned sin in the flesh, delivered a death blow to its power, and swallowed up death in victory by raising him from the dead.

The *life . . . he lives to God* refers to Christ being 'obedient to the point of death – / even death on a cross' (Phil. 2:8). Because God raised him from the dead and highly exalted him, believers are able to receive the rewards of his living to God.

11. Paul draws an inference from all that precedes (*So, houtōs*). Believers who are plunged into Christ's death should assess the evidence and recognize that their entire being and identity has been reformatted in Christ and that they must live in conformity with that transformation (cf. 12:2). Since Christ died to sin, they also have died to sin. Since they are fused with Christ and he lives to God, they also live to God. Living to God means living with openness to God so that one lives for God's benefit and God's glory, not one's own (cf. 14:8; 2 Cor. 5:14–15; Gal. 2:19).

Dying 'with Christ' results in being 'in Christ' which will result in being raised 'with Christ'. The phrase *in Christ*, a common idea in Paul's letters, makes its first appearance here in this letter (cf. 8:1; 12:5; 16:3, 7, 9, 10). In this context, it means that morality does not derive from knowing what God commands but knowing that God has transferred believers to a new power domain, in Christ, that fights off sin (8:9–11). Believers can say with Paul that 'I no longer live, but Christ lives in me' (Gal. 2:20, NIV).

12. Verses 12–14 form another chiasm:

A ¹² Let not sin have dominion . . .
    B ¹³ᵃ Do not present your members . . .
    B' ¹³ᵇ Present yourselves . . . and your members . . .
A' ¹⁴ᵃ Sin will have no dominion over you . . .[78]

The translation *do not let sin exercise dominion* assumes that Paul uses a second-person singular imperative. The verb, however, is a

---

78. Marcus, 'Let God Arise', p. 387.

third-person singular imperative (*basileuetō*). 'Sin', not 'you', is its
subject. Since English has no grammatical equivalent, it can only be
rendered, 'Let not sin therefore reign in your mortal body' (KJV) or
'sin must not reign' (NAB). The use of the third-person imperative is
at home in the language of prayer, as in the second and third petitions
of the Lord's Prayer (Matt. 6:9–10 / Luke 11:2): 'Let your kingdom
come, let your will be done.'[79] This subtlety suggests that 'Paul is not
issuing a general exhortation, but calling for the overthrow of an
entity that is presently reigning'.[80] Translating the opening phrase as
a command for believers to stop sin from exercising dominion in
their mortal bodies implies that they are somehow able to overthrow
sin's tyranny on their own. They cannot. It is best, then, to read this
as a plea for God to stop sin from exercising power over them.
Marcus paraphrases it, 'Let God arise and end the reign of sin!' The
only way sin can be dethroned as the ruler of our bodies is by our
dying with Christ and yielding to the power of God.

13. Paul uses the second-person plural imperative in this verse.
The two imperatives can be paraphrased 'You, for your part, are
forbidden from putting yourselves at sin's disposal as your "old
self" did'; 'you, for your part, are to put yourselves at God's disposal
as "alive to God in Christ Jesus"'.

Three interpretation issues arise in this verse. First, versions
normally render the first command as 'no longer present your
members'. 'Your members' are not to be limited to the physical
members of the body since this command is followed by a second
'present *yourselves*'. 'Members' refers to one's whole person (Ziesler,
p. 165). The NIV captures this nuance with the translation 'Do not
offer any part of yourself'. Paul refers to the many members of the
body, the foot, hand, eye and ear, with their divergent functions in
1 Corinthians 12:14–26. Eve's encounter with the serpent in the
garden shows how our bodily members are enlisted in the service
of sin (Gen. 3:1–6). She heard with her ears the serpent's craftily
phrased lies. She walked to the tree on foot, saw that the tree 'was
a delight to the eyes', and took with her hands the fruit, ate it, and

79. Ibid., p. 389.
80. Ibid., p. 392.

gave it to her husband (Schnabel, II, p. 56). It was her will, driven by her desires, that directed her members. Therefore, what one does with one's bodily members reveals one's will and to whom one's heart belongs.

Second, Paul consistently uses the noun that is translated *instruments (hopla)* in the context of warfare with reference to weapons (cf. 13:12; 2 Cor. 6:7; 10:4). Translating the word as 'weapons' presumes that an individual can be deployed either as a weapon for sin or as a weapon for righteousness. Paul makes a call to arms in which believers are to join the battle against wickedness 'on God's side'.[81] It is important to note that, with the opening prayer, 'Let God arise and end the reign of sin!', believers are not sent out to wage war alone. Marcus asserts, 'Paul does not deny the idea of obedient human action ... but rather indicates the only context in which it can take place: as part of God's own eschatological battle against the power of cosmic evil.'[82] The battle imagery reminds Christ-followers that because their mortal bodies remain vulnerable to sin's old dominion, living the Christian life is a continuing struggle. Paul assures them, however, that the fight is not a tug of war in which the opponents are evenly matched. Believers have God's strength on their side and can win the battle only through God's power that comes from outside of themselves.

Third, 'weapons of wickedness' and 'weapons of righteousness' should be taken as possessives, meaning that either wickedness or righteousness possesses the weapons.[83] Like the slaves in the next unit's example (6:15–23), our bodily members (ourselves) are under the control of a master. Either sin deploys them to further wickedness, or God deploys them to further righteousness. In the service of sin, they are headed for defeat and the punishment of eternal death. In the service of God, they are destined for victory and the reward of eternal life. The duty of believers is to put themselves completely – not partially or half-heartedly – at the disposal of God (cf. 12:1) so that sin cannot breach their defences.

---

81. Agersnap, *Baptism*, p. 367.
82. Marcus, 'Let God Arise', p. 395.
83. Ibid., p. 393.

14. Paul again insists that believers must recognize that sin does not have dominion over them because they live under grace, not law – that is, under the control of grace. He has already connected sin and the law in 5:12–21 and will develop more fully the law's inability to free one from sin's stranglehold in 7:7–25. The law is not only powerless to douse sin's flames, but sin can use it to stoke the embers of our unholy cravings into a blazing inferno.

The emphasis on being *under grace* wraps up his refutation of those who contend that his gospel encourages sin. Grace, Paul argues, does not mean that God now tolerates sin, nor does it release believers from the obligation to obey the moral law. Being under grace means that believers are no longer manacled within sin's fortified prison walls and subjected to its power that pummels them into submission. They have been set free and now live under grace outside sin's domain. Grace does not simply mean that God looks favourably upon us; it is also a power that transforms us and makes obedience possible. That is why Paul can say, 'By the grace of God I am what I am, and his grace to me was not without effect. No, I worked harder than all of them – yet not I, but the grace of God that was with me' (1 Cor. 15:10, NIV; cf. 2 Cor. 12:9).

Theology
Edwards comments,

> Authentic Christian existence always stands with one foot in the old life
> and one in the new. The Christian life is one of tension between Adam
> and Christ, sin and grace, flesh and spirit, death and life. Fallen human
> nature, which is with us from birth to death, pulls in one direction,
> and the regenerated life in Christ, which extends from conversion to
> eternity, pulls even more powerfully in the other. Christian life is hence
> life between the times and between two worlds: it is not yet free from
> the old nature, and not fully at home in the new.
> (Edwards, p. 162)

While it is true that because we live in a mortal body sin continues to buffet us with temptations that exploit our appetites, this does not mean that we have a split self-image that includes both the old self still chained to sin and the new self set free from sin. Paul's point in this unit is this: 'When we slip into an *old man* way of living, we are living contrary to our true self; we are denying our true self-image.'[84]

While believers will always need the pardon of grace for their sins, they have a new identity in Christ. When believers confess that Jesus is the Lord and Saviour of their lives, they are transferred into the sphere of Christ. They are fused with Christ and infused with Christ's power. The oracle in the Septuagint version of Isaiah 21:4 reads, 'lawlessness overwhelms me'. The word translated 'overwhelms' (*baptizei*) is the word normally transliterated as 'baptize'. Paul understands being 'baptized into Christ Jesus' in an analogous way. Believers have been overwhelmed by Christ, integrated with him, and, consequently, are able to overwhelm lawlessness. Paul uses the image of immersion into Christ's death and resurrection to show how it has an inevitable impact on the believers' moral conduct. The old life in Adam is set under the judgment of the cross, dies, and is buried with Christ. Dying with Christ brings liberation from servitude to sin. It means that 'those who belong to Christ Jesus have crucified the flesh with its passions and desires' (Gal. 5:24). Being raised with Christ means that 'it is no longer I who live, but it is Christ who lives in me. And the life I now live in the flesh I live by faith in the Son of God, who loved me and gave himself for me' (Gal. 2:20). It marks the beginning of a new life inundated by the power of his Spirit.

ii. The believer is freed from sin to become a slave of righteousness (6:15–23)

Context

In 6:15–23, Paul again refutes any suggestion that grace does not require believers to live morally and that they can safely disregard the law's moral commands because they are saved by grace. The first question in 6:1, 'Should we continue in sin?', is grounded in a misconception of what God's grace entails. Paul argues that

---

84. Hoekema, 'The Christian's Self-Image', p. 18.

because God has responded to human sin with grace, it does not mean that believers can continue to wallow in sin and expect to receive more grace. The second question in 6:15, 'Should we sin?', is grounded in a misconception of what it means for believers to be free from the law. Believers are not under the law, but that does not mean that they can now disregard any law, whether scriptural, civil or moral. They have changed masters. They are no longer enslaved to sin but now have become slaves to God and as such are under 'the law of Christ' (1 Cor. 9:21; Gal. 6:2). If Christians continue to live in sin, it means that they remain in the throes of their slavery to sin (cf. 1 Tim. 1:9–10). What has changed in their lives?

Paul's brief mention of not being under the law in 6:14–15 requires elaboration, and he takes up the issue of *how* Christians could be discharged from the law and joined to Christ in 7:1–6, and why it was necessary for Christians to be discharged from the law for their salvation in 7:7–25. Being discharged from the law does not mean that God has set believers adrift in a sea of moral depravity. Paul presents God's solution for dealing with sin in a believer's life in 8:1–17. As is common throughout Romans, it is necessary to follow the thread of Paul's extended arguments all the way to the end to grasp his meaning fully.

Comment

15. Paul forcefully rejects the false inference contained in the question *Should we sin because we are not under law but under grace?* Not being under the law does not unlock the door to 'anything goes' since there is nothing to restrain sin. Nor should it foster moral indifference and mean that 'Everything is permissible for me' (1 Cor. 6:12, CSB) or that 'All things are lawful' (1 Cor. 10:23).

Paul avoids resorting to vapid moralism with a list of dos and don'ts for Christians. Instead, he seeks to reinforce the identity of believers as those set free from sin's thrall who now belong only to God as slaves to righteousness (6:18, 22). Modern psychological experts contend that one's self-concept determines behavioural choices that are congruent with the perception of one's identity – what one believes is true of oneself in the past or the present, or what one wishes to become, or fears one might become, in the future.[85] Paul seeks to reinforce his audience's self-concept as those who are loved by God and called to be his holy people (1:7). This unit contains a series of contrasts to highlight the disparity between their past identity and their current one as believers: being *under grace* as opposed to being *under law* (6:15); being obedient to God, 'which leads to righteousness', as opposed to being obedient to sin, 'which leads to death' (6:16); becoming 'slaves of righteousness' as opposed to being slaves to sin (6:18–19); becoming slaves of God and being set free from sin (6:20, 22); becoming sanctified and destined for 'eternal life', as opposed to being awash in shame and destined for 'death' (6:21–22); and receiving a 'free gift' as opposed to earning 'wages' (6:23). Their behaviour is consequently to match their new self-identity. Right thinking about God and how God sees believers in Christ as justified, sanctified, dead to sin and alive to God leads to right behaviour, particularly one's behaviour towards one's neighbour (13:8–10).

16. Paul again draws on features of domestic slavery, with which all his audience would have been familiar, as the governing metaphor to explain that believers have been emancipated from sin's lordship and brought under the lordship of Christ and must obey only him.[86] The typical estimate is that slaves made up one-third of the Roman population. The rest were divided between freedmen and those who were freeborn. Though the slavery metaphor might dredge up a painful reality for some in his audience, it would hit home. All would recognize that the centurion's riposte to Jesus when he pleads with him to heal his slave reflects the real world of slavery: 'I say . . . to my slave, "Do this", and the slave does it' (Luke 7:8). Masters expect unconditional obedience from the slaves under their proprietorship.

17–19. Paul encourages positive thinking and offers thanks to God that his audience is no longer enslaved to sin (cf. 7:25). His aim is to reinforce their new identity in Christ that should shape their behaviour. They are no longer the old person, the slave to sin, but

---

85. Oyserman, Elmore and Smith, 'Self', p. 69.
86. Goodrich, 'Slaves of Sin', pp. 509–530.

the new person set free in Christ. He personifies sin as a slave master, and now also personifies *righteousness* as a slave master. Freedom from slavery to sin means slavery to righteousness. In verse 19, Paul adds a parenthetical statement seemingly apologizing for using the worldly and unsavoury analogy of slavery to explain holy matters. He explains, however, that it is because of the 'weakness of [their] flesh' (CSB), which translations interpret to mean their *natural* or 'human' *limitations*. This may be a reference to their limited intellectual capacity to understand. Paul never uses 'flesh' elsewhere, however, to refer to one's thinking capacity. It is more likely that he refers here to his audience's human impotence rather than their limited understanding. The expression conveys the idea that 'fallen, Adamic humanity does not have the *capacity* to carry out the new life of obedience to God'.[87] Because flesh can use 'grace as a license for sin', Paul describes 'the character of obedience' as slavery to God who becomes their slave master.[88]

The slavery metaphor, however unpleasant it might be to our moral sensitivities, gets the point across. The slave's impetus to obey the master does not come from his or her inclination to do so. Slaves are compelled to obey. The metaphor allows Paul to note how the two slaveries, slavery to sin and slavery to righteousness, differ. First, slavery to righteousness prompts eager service from a transformed *heart* (6:17). Slaves of righteousness do not obey resentfully or only when they are watched, to avoid punishment or to gain a reward. They obey wholeheartedly. Obedience *from the heart* is evidence of the divine hand in renewing the human heart that Jeremiah says is 'devious above all else' and 'perverse' (Jer. 17:9) and that Paul says can be 'foolish and darkened' (1:21, NIV) and 'hard and unrepentant' (2:5, NIV). Slaves of righteousness respond to God as Jesus did in Gethsemane: 'not what I want, but what you want' (Mark 14:36).

Second, slavery to righteousness differs dramatically in its results. Paul reminds them that when they were slaves to moral *impurity* their *iniquity* ('lawlessness', *anomia*) steadily worsened ('lawlessness leading to [more] lawlessness'). Being owned by

---

87. Timmins, *Romans 7*, p. 87.
88. Ibid., p. 88.

righteousness, by contrast, leads to 'holiness' (NIV), the antithesis of *impurity* (1 Thess. 4:7). 'Holiness' (*sanctification*) is used in Scripture to refer to 'God's action in consecrating his people for his possession and purposes'.[89] Peterson defines it this way: 'With regard to God himself, holiness implies transcendence, uniqueness and purity. With regard to God's people, holiness means being set apart for a relationship with the Holy One, to display his character in every sphere of life.'[90] Balz avers, 'Holiness or sanctification is, then, the comprehensive acceptance by believers of the holiness of God in order that they may enter into communion with God, not a gradual progression toward religious-ethical perfection.'[91] It is not an aspiration but what believers are called to be (1 Cor. 6:11).

Since Paul emphasizes that believers live under grace, this passage cannot be interpreted to suggest that he encourages believers to achieve their sanctification as if it could be attained as a meritorious work. Holiness is a status granted to us by God. Recognizing and absorbing this status into one's self-concept affects one's behaviour. Any transformation in the Christians' lives is, however, entirely the work of God, as Paul says in 2 Corinthians 3:18: 'And all of us, with unveiled faces, seeing the glory of the Lord as though reflected in a mirror, are being transformed into the same image from one degree of glory to another; for this comes from the Lord, the Spirit.'

The phrase *to the form of teaching to which you were entrusted* is difficult. The word *typos* is variously translated as 'form', 'pattern' or 'standard'. In 16:17, the 'teaching' refers to the authoritative tradition of faith they have learned. Fitzmyer argues that the *teaching* does not refer to some fixed catechetical formulation or creed but to 'the proclamation about God's work in Christ Jesus' and 'the "pattern" according to which Christians are to live' (Fitzmyer, p. 450).[92] The word *typos* could be used to refer to 'a mark made as

---

89. Siikavirta, *Baptism*, p. 149.

90. Peterson, *Possessed by God*, p. 24.

91. H. Balz, 'ἅγιος . . .', *EDNT* I, p. 16.

92. Paul alludes to Christ's death, burial, resurrection and his living to God in 6:1–11, assuming his audience's familiarity with these facts.

the result of a blow or pressure' (BDAG, p. 1019) or the shape that comes from a mould, '*the pattern in conformity to which a thing must be made*' (Thayer, p. 632 [emphasis original]). Being 'in Christ' means for believers that Christ makes an imprint on their lives and moulds their behaviour. Paul uses the word in Philippians 3:17 to mean 'example' or 'model': 'Brothers and sisters, join in imitating me, and observe those who live according to the *example* you have in us' (emphasis added). Those who constitute the 'us' are valid models to follow only if they closely model Christ Jesus (Phil. 2:5–8; cf. 1 Cor. 11:1; 1 Thess. 1:6). In this context, Paul may be saying that believers have been imprinted by the teaching about Christ so that their lives are formed by it and they can emulate his example, as Paul later instructs them to do (15:1–4).

This interpretation explains why the teaching was not delivered *to them*. This teaching was not *entrusted* to their care so that they become its custodians. Instead of being handed over to their sins and to the consequences of their iniquities (1:24, 26, 28), they are handed over to the *teaching* to be controlled by it.[93] The passive voice is a divine passive. God delivers them over to the teaching that leads to eternal life.

20. Their being enslaved to sin in their pre-conversion life meant they had no obligation to behave in an upright manner. Their lifestyle under sin's mastery represents the exact opposite of what Psalm 45:7 praises. Instead of hating wickedness and loving righteousness, they loved wickedness and hated righteousness. The governor Felix provides an example of one who prefers wickedness to righteousness. When Paul, his prisoner, spoke to him of 'righteousness, self-control and the judgment to come', he became afraid and told him to go away (Acts 24:25, NIV).

21. The word *advantage* ('benefit', NIV, NASB) is an interpretation of the word 'fruit' in Greek (*karpos*). It is best to punctuate this

---

93. The verb *paradidōmi* in v. 17 is consistently translated 'delivered' or 'handed over' elsewhere in the letter (1:24, 26, 28; 4:25; 8:32), and 'delivered' (ASV) is the better translation here, rather than *entrusted* (NRSV), 'has . . . claimed your allegiance' (NIV), 'committed' (ESV) or 'introduced' (NJB).

verse as Moo does: 'Therefore, what fruit did you have then? That
of which you are now ashamed. For the end of these is death' (Moo,
pp. 432–433). The shame is not connected to being demeaned as
slaves, barbarians, uneducated or weak (1 Cor. 1:27–29). It arises
from their shameful behaviour, being guilty of the litany of evils
that Paul lists in 1:29–31 and 3:10–18. Since Paul assumes that
people have a conscience with a moral capacity (2:15), it is possible
that before their conversion they felt flickers if not floods of shame
– the painful feeling of mortification and sorrow caused by the
consciousness of how dishonourable, unworthy and foolish their
behaviour was. Becoming slaves of righteousness, however, gives
converts the moral discernment to recognize their former lifestyle
and the societal structures they took for granted in a different light
– as shameful weapons that sin used to inflict death.

Paul uses the imperfect tense, 'you were having' (*did you . . . get*),
in 6:21 to indicate continuous action in past time. One might infer
that the stench of the rotten fruit clung to them.

22. The fruit of being enslaved to righteousness is *sanctification*
('holiness'). Again, holiness is not a process of moral betterment to
which believers are tasked but a sanctified status that God gives to
us through Christ (cf. Heb. 2:11; 10:10, 14, 29; 13:12).[94] Paul makes
this clear in 1 Corinthians 6:9–11:

> Do you not know that wrongdoers will not inherit the kingdom of
> God? Do not be deceived! Fornicators, idolaters, adulterers, male
> prostitutes, sodomites, thieves, the greedy, drunkards, revilers, robbers
> – none of these will inherit the kingdom of God. And this is what some
> of you used to be. But you were washed, you were sanctified, you were
> justified in the name of the Lord Jesus Christ and in the Spirit of our
> God.

Sanctification, then, is similar to justification in that believers are
not justified by their efforts nor sanctified by their efforts. They also
do not become *more* sanctified by their efforts any more than they
become *more* justified by their efforts.

---

94. Siikavirta, *Baptism*, p. 147.

23. Paul used military imagery in insisting that believers cannot allow sin to deploy them as weapons in the war against God (6:13). This imagery may be reflected in the word *wages* (*opsōnia*), which originally was used for soldiers' pay (cf. Luke 3:14; 1 Cor. 9:7; 1 Macc. 3:28; 14:32; 1 Esd. 4:56). Paul emphasizes that death is the pay cheque one earns from serving sin (1:32; 5:12, 14, 17, 21; 6:16, 21; 7:5). By contrast, *eternal life* (mentioned twice in vv. 22–23) comes as a *free gift*, largesse that cannot be earned.

The gift of eternal life is imparted through allegiance to Jesus Christ as Lord. Attaching the title *Lord* to *Christ* in this context has biblical resonances that are related to God's deliverance of Israel from their slavery in Egypt: 'I am the LORD your God, who brought you out of the land of Egypt, out of the house of slavery' (Exod. 20:2; cf. Exod. 6:6–7; 13:3; Deut. 6:12–13; Ps. 81:10). Freedom from the bondage of sin comes only from being in Christ.

Theology
Paul assumes that humans do not have the freedom to be their own masters – as Adam and Eve wanted to be, with such catastrophic results. The only freedom we have is to choose which master we will serve. Either sin or God will have the title deed to our souls. One cannot be dually aligned or unaligned. Harrison and Hagner assert,

> There is no middle ground, no place in Christian experience where one is free to set one's own standards and go one's own way. So, it is idle to object that on becoming a believer one is simply exchanging one form of slavery for another. There is no alternative . . . life cannot be lived in a vacuum.
>
> (Harrison and Hagner, p. 111)

That to which one gives one's deepest allegiance determines one's behaviour. In John 8:34, Jesus declares, 'Very truly, I tell you, everyone who commits sin is a slave to sin' (cf. 2 Pet. 2:19).

Paul understands sin to be a pattern of life that is the opposite of obedience to God. Rebelling against the divine will and succumbing to sinful passions (7:5) results in sinners becoming mired in a bog from which they cannot extricate themselves. The more they sin, the more stuck they become. Even when they attempt to avoid sin and obey the law by their own power, they only sink deeper in the mire (7:7–25). Therefore, Paul's analogy of being enslaved to sin is fitting. While it is fair to say that he personifies sin as a dark power that believers must resist, it does not absolve sinners from their accountability for their sinful actions. It is wrong to assume that the human plight is caused by enslavement to sin – 'Sin' with a capital S, a power that is 'out there' and at large in the world – rather than by something within the human heart that causes us wilfully to do wicked things (cf. 3:10–18).[95]

Interpreters should not play down individual sin as the cause of our human plight and claim that this plight is not self-caused or addressed by God's forgiveness of sin. One should consider Paul's frequent use of the plural 'sins' in the epistles indisputably written by him (Rom. 4:7; 7:5; 11:27; 1 Cor. 15:3, 17; Gal. 1:4; 1 Thess. 2:16) and in the so-called disputed epistles (Eph. 2:1; Col. 1:14; 1 Tim. 5:22, 24; 2 Tim. 3:6). Also, in several cases the noun 'sin' in the singular clearly refers to 'a human act rather than a personification or a power'.[96] Humans are responsible before God for their condition. God's solution is to offer forgiveness of sins and the power of the Holy Spirit to liberate believers from sin's power.

The two slaveries, slavery to sin and slavery to righteousness, are totally different in their results. Those who become sin's slave soon discover that it is a harsh taskmaster that claps them in irons, fastens a slave collar around their necks, tattoos its ownership on their foreheads, and cracks a deadly whip to keep them bowing and scraping before their master. Sin seems to promise freedom but instead robs persons of it. Sin dehumanizes them as their lives go skidding and careening towards inescapable destruction. Slavery to sin has a domino effect by entangling its victims in ever more sin, increasing their shame and intensifying their spiritual numbness that makes them less prone to respond to God's initiative of grace. Slavery to righteousness sets the victim free, removes the shame and offers life. Humans cannot escape sin's bondage by their own

---

95. Shaw, 'Apocalyptic', p. 160; cf. Kaye, *Thought Structure*, pp. 39–40.
96. Gathercole, 'Sins', p. 154.

willpower since sin has corrupted it. Mere repentance and regretting that one is enslaved to sin also is not enough to break its power. Sanders states,

> If plain ordinary old-fashioned repentance coupled with a plea for God's forgiveness would solve human wickedness, God need not have sent his Son. Paul's downplaying of repentance, the usual cure for transgression, is determined by his prior conviction that salvation is provided only by Christ.[97]

Feeling sorry for sinning does not preclude sin from holding sway over our mortal body. What is needed is a saving power from outside of oneself to overcome sin's domination. When one dies with Christ Jesus and is united with him, one also is placed in the hands of God who defeated sin on the cross, who raised Christ Jesus from the dead, and who will raise the believer with the assurance of eternal life.

iii. The believer is discharged from the law to live the new life of the Spirit (7:1–6)

Context

In 7:1–6, Paul utilizes the metaphor of the Jewish law of marriage regarding a wife who is widowed to argue that, just as a widow is no longer bound to her husband after he dies, so believers who have died in Christ are discharged from the law and are free to belong to another. Paul uses the phrase 'Or do you not know' (NASB, ESV) in 6:3 and 7:1 as a kind of bracketing device to clamp the three analogies in 6:1 – 7:6 together. He argued that believers have been definitively removed from the dominion of sin, death and the law that bears the fruit of death (6:21). They have been transferred to the dominion where the Spirit rules, enabling them to live a new life (6:4) that will bear the fruit of holiness (6:22). He stated that believers have been set free from the law (6:14), and in this next analogy he seeks to illustrate how that is possible and how they are now free to be joined to Christ (6:3, 8, 11, 23). The

---

97. Sanders, *The Apostle's Life*, p. 626.

conclusion in 7:5–6 that those living under the law are more prone to have their sinful passions aroused than those living under grace and enjoying the new life in the Spirit also serves as the segue into his next topics. His declaration 'While we were living in the flesh, our sinful passions, aroused by the law, were at work in our members to bear fruit for death' (7:5) delivers the thesis statement for 7:7–25 in which he delineates the law's failure to master human fleshliness that is so easily captured by sin. His declaration 'But now we are discharged from the law, dead to that which held us captive, so that we are slaves not under the old written code but in the new life of the Spirit' (7:6) provides the thesis statement for (8:1–30) that devotes attention to the new life in the Spirit.[98] What complicates things is that Paul understands himself as still 'fleshly' (7:14). God's eschatological 'now' of salvation has broken into the present order, but Christians still experience fleshliness.

Comment

1. In this new illustration, Paul addresses his audience more intimately as *brothers and sisters* (cf. 1:13). He concedes that only some of them might comprehend his argument because it stems from the fine points of the Jewish law regarding marriage. The Jewish law regarding marriage binds a wife to her husband for life. If he gives her a bill of divorce, she is free to marry another without being accused of adultery (Deut. 24:1–4). The same would be true if he were to die (cf. 1 Cor. 7:8–9; 1 Tim. 5:14).

2–3. Paul gleans a principle from a wife's legal status as *married* (literally, 'under a man') that all can understand. The law binding her to her husband is in force only while the husband is alive. His analogy, however, is more complicated. In Jewish law, marriage transferred a woman from her father's authority to her husband's authority, and a wife was under her husband's authority and subject to him. This statement that she *is bound by the law to her husband as long as he lives,* however, did not apply in Roman law, since the wife could divorce her husband at any time. Also, according to Roman

---

98. Timmins, *Romans 7*, p. 167.

law, a widow was not immediately free to remarry after her husband's death but was required to wait one year before remarrying or forfeit any right to inheriting her husband's estate (Dunn, I, p. 360). In Jewish law, the command 'You shall not covet your neighbour's house; you shall not covet your neighbour's wife, or male or female slave, or ox, or donkey, or anything that belongs to your neighbour' (Exod. 20:17) assumes that wives belong to their husbands like any other chattel, which explains why only the husband had the right to dissolve the marriage. The law required only that he give her a writ of divorce (Deut. 24:1–4). The essential formula in the bill of divorce is, 'Lo, thou art free to marry any man' (m. Giṭ. 9:3).[99] With a bill of divorce, she could remarry without fear of being accused of adultery with its prescribed penalty of death (Lev. 20:10; Deut. 22:22; John 8:4–5). The rabbis did make provision for a wife to initiate proceedings that would compel her husband to divorce her when his defects made him unbearably odious – such as one smitten with boils, polyps or a disgusting odour, a gatherer of excrement, a coppersmith or a tanner (m. Ketub. 7:10). Therefore, in Roman and Jewish law the husband did not need to die for the wife to be free to marry another.

Jesus, however, interpreted the rule concerning the bill of divorce far more stringently by rejecting the husband's right to divorce for any reason (Matt. 5:31–32; 19:9; Mark 10:11; Luke 16:18). Paul cites Jesus' interpretation of divorce in 1 Corinthians 7:10–11 and extrapolates a corollary in 1 Corinthians 7:39 that matches what he says here: 'A wife is bound as long as her husband lives. But if the husband dies, she is free to marry anyone she wishes, only in the Lord.' Paul must assume that some, but not all, in his audience would know Jesus' interpretation of the law. Divorce is not an option for the husband or the wife because God intended marriage to be a lifelong relationship.[100] This interpretation of the wife's legal status under the law of marriage assumes that she can be set free from her husband's authority only by his death.

---

99. Danby, *Mishnah*, p. 319.
100. Tomson, 'What Did Paul Mean', pp. 573–581.

4. *In the same way* ('for this reason', *hōste*) draws an inference from this example. Christ died, and believers *died to the law through the body of Christ*, with the result that they are now freed from sin and can *belong to another.* The verb *died* is in the passive voice and is better translated 'we were put to death', in which God is the agent (Schnabel, II, pp. 106–107). It assumes that Christians died to sin when they believed in Jesus and were immersed in his death and buried with him (6:2–11).

Commentators are wont to point out that Paul's argument from the analogy is faulty. If the woman is compared to the believer, she is freed from the law because of her husband's death, not her own death. If the husband is compared to the law, the law does not die. Instead, the believer dies to the law (Bruce, p. 145). The law, however, does not come to an end in the analogy. It binds the wife to her husband during his life and would condemn her as an adulteress were she to decide to leave him and marry another. Only her husband's death sets her free to marry another. But the law then protects her from being branded an adulteress if she does remarry. When she marries another, the law of the husband is reinstated. One might add that since Christ was raised from the dead never to die again (6:9; cf. 4:24; 6:4; 8:11; 10:9), the bond between Christ and believers is never to be broken.

This lack of precision in the application of the example is unavoidable 'because of the absolute and paradoxical novelty of the Christian experience which contradicts any comparison and escapes any illustration'.[101] The analogy should be interpreted as illuminating the believers' situation from the perspective of both characters, the husband and the wife. Death, like the death of a husband, frees one *from* something – in this case, a previous binding relationship. The husband's death changes the wife's legal status and frees her *for* a new relationship. The analogy, then, lays out the principle that explains how believers are no longer under the authority of the law *and* its condemnation. They have been released from it by their death with Christ. This unit addresses 'the Christian's moral life in the absence of the law' (author's

---

101. Gieniusz, 'Rom 7,1–6', p. 400.

translation).[102] Having been released from the law, believers now come under the authority of Christ and are transferred from the sphere of flesh to that of the Spirit. The Spirit directs and generates ethical actions, which the law cannot.

5. Paul refers to the plight of being under the law and dominated by the power of living in the flesh. *Flesh* in this instance does not signify one's mortal body. It refers to an orientation that is anti-Spirit (Gal. 5:16–17) and incapable of pleasing God (8:8). Paul personifies *flesh* as he does sin. It is a power that sets sinful passions ablaze. The law did not create this problem, but it was unable to solve anything by restraining sinful passions. Instead, it added fuel to the fire when sin used it to inflame the passions that proliferated and resulted in death (6:21). Paul's point simplified is this: Not being under the law does not open the door to immorality. Instead, not being under the law means that one of the main tools that sin manipulates to work death in us and to do evil (7:19) has been eliminated from the believer's life.

6. Paul returns to the metaphor of slavery he used in 6:15–23 with the verb 'to serve' (*douleuein*). The translation *so that* we are slaves *not under the old written code but in the new life of the Spirit* captures this meaning. It is a given for Paul that one is either a slave to sin (6:20) or a slave of God (6:22). Consequently, freedom from the law does not mean freedom to do as one pleases. For believers, it means that they have been turned over from the law to a new master, the Spirit.

Paul does not denigrate the law with the term *the old written code* (literally, 'the oldness of the letter'). The 'letter' could refer to 'what the legalist is left with as a result of his misunderstanding and misuse of the law' (Cranfield, I, p. 339), particularly when it is distorted into requiring works to earn salvation.[103] It is better, however, to understand *the old written code* as referring to the law from the perspective of its visible form. It is the law perceived as only lifeless letters etched on tablets or inscribed with ink on scrolls that has no power to transform hearts. Paul contrasts the letter

---

102. Viard, 'Loi', p. 169.
103. Käsemann, *Perspectives*, pp. 138–166.

with the Spirit whose living, transforming power dwells in believers (8:9) to fulfil in them 'the just requirement of the law' (8:4) and to conform them 'to the image of [God's] Son' (8:29; cf. 2 Cor. 3:18). Under sin's domain, the written code is easily twisted and garbled so that it leads to death. Under the Spirit's domain, everything leads to life.

Theology
The law may be 'spiritual' (7:14), but it is not the Spirit. It functions in the domain of the flesh because we are 'of the flesh' or 'fleshly' (7:14) and 'groan inwardly while we wait for adoption, the redemption of our bodies' (8:23). Consequently, it arouses the sinful hungers lurking within us instead of arousing obedience. The Spirit, however, operates internally to produce a spiritual inner transformation that makes possible the new life (new creation) that is entirely oriented towards God so that it bears fruit for God with moral behaviour (6:22). That we are fleshly does not mean that we do not participate 'in the newness of the Spirit'. The 'newness' (ASV), 'new life' (NRSV) or 'new way' (NIV) of the Spirit (7:6) 'has arrived in the confines of the old order . . . not all associations with the flesh are broken'.[104] Therefore, Paul argues that this situation demands that one must constantly seek to live according to the Spirit (8:4–13) to have any hope of bearing fruit for God (7:4). It is futile to try to serve God through the law that is 'unable to effect the obedience which it demands'.[105]

D. The law's inability to check sin and generate the obedience it demands (7:7–25)

A primary aim in this letter is to build up the Roman believers' confidence in the truth of Paul's gospel that discloses the righteousness of God apart from the law (3:21). If his gospel upholds the law, as he insists it does (3:31), he has yet to explain fully why believers not only are discharged from the obligations in the old written

---

104. Timmins, *Romans 7*, p. 179.
105. Ibid., p. 180.

code (7:6) but must be released from the law if they are to bear fruit for God (7:4). He expands on his earlier statements that the law brings knowledge of sin (3:20), brings wrath (4:15), multiplies trespasses (5:20) and arouses sinful passions (7:5) to clarify that the law can have no role in a believer's salvation. But he does so delicately, so as not to disparage the law or imply that it led Israel up a blind alley. Seifrid recognizes this:

> Paul here defends his Gospel against the potential Jewish objection that it compromises the holiness of *Torah* . . . In Rom 7, therefore, he is attempting to persuade his audience of the validity of this exclusion of the Law from God's saving purpose.[106]

This passage leads into his argument in 8:1–30 that the Spirit is 'God's alternative to the Law and the antidote to the flesh'.[107] From chapter 6, we learn that

> Paul locates participation in the new aeon of salvation *in the midst of ongoing solidarity with the old*. Believers have died with Christ but still have a death to die. They participate in Christ's risen life before their own bodily resurrection.[108]

It means that they still live in a pre-resurrection fleshly body. This eschatological framework makes more understandable and reasonable the older view that the condition of the 'I' in 7:9–25 is 'that of a believer in Christ who is expressing an ongoing solidarity with the old life "in the flesh" . . . Although he is no longer "in the flesh", he is nevertheless still "fleshly"'.[109] This condition explains why Paul concludes this unit with the statement 'So then, with my mind I am a slave to the law of God, but with my flesh I am a slave to the law of sin' that interpreters so often want to expunge since it seems to contradict the joyful exclamation in the same breath,

---

106. Seifrid, 'Subject', p. 324.
107. Fee, *Empowering*, p. 515.
108. Timmins, *Romans 7*, p. 168.
109. Ibid., p. 169.

'Thanks be to God through Jesus Christ our Lord!', that precedes it (7:25). It also explains why Paul says, 'we ourselves, who have the first fruits of the Spirit, groan inwardly while we wait for adoption, the redemption of our bodies' (8:23). Paul's purpose in

> delineating the eschatological antithesis is not to locate his readers within the new aeon, nor simply to explain that there is a manner of living that corresponds to the new sphere of existence, but to underline that the life of the new age cannot come to fruition within the legal parameters of the old.[110]

To make this case as forcefully as possible, Paul writes auto-biographically. While some have dismissed reading 7:7–25 as autobiographical as something 'relegated to the museum of exegetical absurdities', it is the most natural way to understand this section and the 'arguments against it are not conclusive' (Bruce, p. 151). Paul's use of 'I' with the intensive reflexive pronoun 'I myself' (*autos egō*; cf. NIV) in 7:25 substantiates this view since he uses this phrase elsewhere *only* to refer to himself (9:3; 15:14; 2 Cor. 10:1; 12:13).[111] Therefore, Paul writes of his own experience to show how the law offers no answer to the human predicament menaced by sin. It leads him to conclude that only 'the law of the Spirit of life in Christ Jesus' can and 'has set you [believers] free from the law of sin and of death' (8:2). Since the law spells out the way of life that delights God, some might fret that abandoning it in the slightest way invites God's wrath. Paul assuages this apprehension in 8:18–39 by asserting that believers who have received the first

---

110. Ibid., p. 170.
111. Banks, 'Romans 7.25a', p. 41. He notes (p. 42 n. 25) that the 'I' by itself occurs fifty-four times, not counting Rom. 7; Gal. 2:19–20, and the seven occurrences in the Pastorals. It *always* refers to Paul himself except twice where a scriptural quotation has God speaking (Rom. 12:19; 14:11), twice in Corinthian slogans (1 Cor. 1:12; 3:4), once where an imaginary Gentile speaks (Rom. 11:19) and once in Tertius's greeting (Rom. 16:22).

fruits of the Spirit are fully secure in Christ. Because of God's steadfast love manifested in Christ (8:3–4), no power on earth or in heaven can break the believers' union with God or cut them off from God's love (8:31–39). Believers, however, still reside in the land of hope awaiting 'the redemption of our bodies' (8:23) and must patiently await the glory to be revealed in them (8:24–25). During this interim, they will continue to experience sufferings (8:18, 35), groanings (8:23) and the futility of creation (8:20).

This section divides into two units that begin with questions raising potential objections concerning the law's role and receive an emphatic rejection. The question 'Is the law sin?' begins 7:7–12 and receives the answer 'Absolutely not.' What follows is an explanation of the relation of sin to the law. The question 'Did what is good become death to me?' begins 7:13–25 and receives the answer 'Absolutely not.' What follows is an explanation of why the law cannot control sin.

i. How sin manipulates the law (7:7–12)

Context

This unit begins with the fourth in a series of rhetorical questions (cf. 6:1, 15; 7:1): 'What then should we say? That the law is sin?' This question is prompted by Paul's assertion in 7:5, 'While we were living in the flesh, our sinful passions, aroused by the law, were at work in our members to bear fruit for death.' It seems that the Mosaic law is the villain that abetted our bondage to sin. Such an inference is completely out of the question (7:12) for Paul, and he again answers a question with a vehement 'No!' (cf. 6:2, 15). The law is not sin, but it is related to sin. He explains how this is so in 7:7–11. The key characters of this unit appear in a chiastic pattern:

The law (7:7a)
    Sin (7:7b–8)
        'I' (in relation to the law and sin, 7:9–10)
    Sin (7:11a)
The law (7:11b–12)

Comment

7. Paul begins by explaining: *if it had not been for the law, I would not have known sin. I would not have known what it is to covet if the law had not said, 'You shall not covet'* (cf. Exod. 20:17; Deut. 5:21; Rom. 13:9). His citation of the command omits the specific list of items in Exodus and Deuteronomy that one is not to covet ('your neighbour's house . . . wife, or male or female slave, or ox, or donkey, or anything that belongs to your neighbour') and makes the commandment applicable to 'every kind of coveting' (7:8, NIV). To covet is to set one's heart on possessing for oneself something forbidden and not one's own, which leads to actions detrimental to one's neighbour. Covetousness is connected to the longings of the body and can be considered the root of all sin (Dunn, I, p. 380). It puts the self at the centre. Byrne defines it as 'radical selfishness: the consuming desire to turn all things other than myself – God, other human beings, other creatures – to the service of my own interest regardless of their own autonomy'.[112] This commandment of all the Ten Commandments is particularly apt as an example of how sin takes one captive. One might, for example, meticulously keep the Sabbath holy (Exod. 20:8), but come to grief trying to keep covetousness (which, in Greek, can also mean 'lust') in check.

8. Paul continues to personify sin as something that deceives (7:11) and breeds death (7:13). When he learned from the law that coveting was a sin, sin took over and conjured up every desire within him. *All kinds of covetousness* covers the gamut of desires. Mindfulness of the commandment's prohibition does not curb fleshly urges since the flesh is a spawning ground for all manner of desires and envies. These cravings usher in sin and enable it to set up a base of operations in the flesh that then takes command of a person's life (cf. also 7:11). Sin operates like a virus that hijacks living cells to replicate, spread and ransack the body. As a virus can camouflage itself to hide from as well as sabotage a cell's antiviral defences, so sin can mask itself as innocuous, disable any resistance mechanisms such as the conscience, and throw open all the doors for every manner of evil to enter (7:17, 20). Sin's stratagems are

---

112. Byrne, 'Adam Myth', p. 46.

multifarious, and the symptoms of its infection are manifold, but its results are always the same: death.

The commandment is not to blame for awakening sin from its dormancy. It is sin that incites disobedience by taking advantage of our creaturely condition and our vulnerability to its enticements. Sin may seem to be a coercing dark power behind our actions, but individuals do not escape culpability by pinning their plight on demon 'Sin'. Eve blamed the serpent for deceiving her, but God did not absolve her for violating the commandment (Gen. 3:13, 16). Adam and Eve succumbed to temptation from a deep spiritual pride that made them want to be equal with God. History reveals the dark side of human nature that leads persons to commit hor-rifically evil acts or to stand by in silent consent. It is not the law's fault that it is incapable of changing human nature or controlling its infatuations and furies. What the law can do, however, is expose our unrestrained desires for what they are: the self-absorbed, self-seeking, cut-throat desire for more and more (cf. 3:20).

9. Paul's sustained use of the pronoun *I* that begins with the first-person singular verb in verse 7 and the pronoun 'me' in verse 8 and continues in 7:10, 14, 17, 20 (2x), 24 and 25 makes this passage stand out from the rest of Romans and his other writings. It would seem obvious that Paul refers to himself, but many find it problematic that he would describe himself, a believer, as such a miserably insolvent sinner. It appears to controvert his assurances that believers have died to sin (6:2), are no longer enslaved by it (6:6), are freed from it (6:7) and are dead to it (6:11). He has claimed that those who live under grace no longer live under sin's dominion (6:14), are obedient from the heart (6:17), and have become slaves of righteousness (6:18) and slaves of God (6:22). Therefore, inter-preters offer other options for who is speaking in this passage and whether the speaker refers to the present or the past.[113]

Some contend that Paul speaks about his experience under the law before becoming a Christian. If Paul were speaking auto-biographically about his earlier life in Judaism, he would seem to

---

113. For an extensive history of research, see Lichtenberger, *Das Ich*,
    pp. 13–106; and for a briefer summary, Timmins, *Romans 7*, pp. 1–8.

contradict his statements in Galatians 1:13–14 and Philippians 3:3–7. In these passages, he does not say that he felt despair over his inability to fulfil the law – just the opposite. He surpassed others in zeal for the traditions of the fathers and considered himself to be 'blameless' when it came to righteousness under the law (Phil. 3:6). Others argue that after turning to Christ Paul possessed a clearer view of the law's inherent problems (cf. 2 Cor. 3:14–16), God's purpose in giving it (Gal. 3:19–24) and the dangers of unenlightened zeal (Rom. 10:2), so that he now assesses his former life differently. But why does he not make it clearer that he is speaking here about his former life in Judaism, as he does in Philippians and Galatians? This view founders on the statement that he *was once alive apart from the law*. Growing up a Jew, there was never a time when Paul was apart from the law. One could quibble that Paul refers to the time before he reached the age of accountability and that he became a son of the commandments when he would have undertaken the demands of the law. But he does not describe his childhood innocence.

Perhaps Paul uses the vivid *I* for rhetorical effect as he adopts the persona of Israel and reflects retrospectively on their condition, struggling to obey the law apart from Christ. If the *I* refers to Israel's experience under the law and the commandments first given at Mount Sinai (Moo, pp. 454–456), however, it is hard to imagine that Paul would say that Israel *was . . . alive apart from the law*, and sin only 'sprang to life' (NIV) after they received the law from Moses' encounter with God on Mount Sinai. This claim 'is only true of Adam before the divine commandment resulted in Adam's expulsion from the garden when he transgressed it' (Käsemann, pp. 196, 206). It is also unlikely that Israel in their current state of unbelief (10:1; 11:14) would offer thanks to 'God *through Jesus Christ our Lord*' for their future deliverance (7:25, emphasis added).

An allusion to the Edenic story of Adam may best explain Paul's use of the past tense in verses 7–13. When Paul reflects theologically, he tends to theologize out of the storied world of biblical narratives and then apply it to current situations. When he talks about faith, as he does in chapter 4, he thinks of Abraham, who epitomized faith. When he talks about law, as he does in 2 Corinthians 3:1–18, he thinks of Moses, who epitomized the law. When he talks about sin, as he does in 5:12–21, he thinks of Adam, who epitomized sin. Paul harks back to the archetypal Adam story to reflect on the characteristic human response to a divine commandment. At least four echoes from the Edenic story emerge in verses 7–11 that support this reading.

First, the *commandment*, which is singular (7:8, 9, 10, 11, 12), recalls Genesis 2:16; 3:11, 17. Adam and Eve sinned only after God gave Adam the commandment not to eat of the fruit of the tree of life. Otherwise, sin would have remained dead because there was no command for them to disobey (7:8–9). Second, the image of sin 'seizing an opportunity' in 7:8, 11 recalls the serpent's (sin's) sudden appearance immediately after God issued the commandment (Gen. 3:1, 4). Third, the statement that sin 'deceived me' in 7:11 echoes Eve's excuse for breaking the commandment when she says, 'The serpent tricked me' (Gen. 3:13). Fourth, the connection between the sinful deed and death in 7:9–11 recalls the penalty God stipulated for violating the commandment (Gen. 2:17; 3:3).

Some interpreters claim that the true-to-life feature of the 'I' narrative stems from Paul's use of 'speech in character' (technically known as *prosōpopoeia*, 'making a mask') as he impersonates Adam (or Eve) throughout the whole unit. The ancient rhetorical theorists, however, are unanimous that the speaker whose character is being represented must always be identified, which does not happen in this speech.[114] Therefore, it is better to see Paul reflecting in verses 7–13 on 'his own encounter with the Mosaic law as a recapitulation of the primeval sin of Adam in the garden', which explains the 'Adamic cast to the experience of life under Torah' that shapes these verses.[115] Dunn maintains, 'Adam is the one whose experience of sin typifies and stamps its character on everyone's experience of sin within the epoch he began' (Dunn, I, p. 378). In Adam's sin, Paul sees himself and his own experience with sin when confronted with God's command. In his own sin, he sees Adam, the representative of all sinful humankind. The 'I' = Adam

---

114. Anderson, *Ancient Rhetorical Theory*, pp. 201–205; and Timmins, *Romans 7*, pp. 12–34.

115. Timmins, *Romans 7*, pp. 133–134.

= Paul = humankind, every human who rebels against God and comes under death's grip, expelled from God's presence and the tree of life, riddled with moral corruption and facing the inevitable end, which is death (Dunn, I, p. 383).

10–11. The *commandment* need not refer only to the one commandment given Adam in the garden but can represent the whole law. The Scriptures attest that the law was given as a way of life that leads to life (Lev. 18:5; Deut. 6:24; Prov. 6:23; cf. Sir. 17:11; 45:5). In providing a standard for what is right and wrong, the commandment dispels moral indifference. Knowing what to do and what not to do, however, does not enable one to obey. Sin is so powerful that it manipulates the law and, like a parasite, sucks the air out of the law's life-giving function so that it yields only a suffocating death. While Adam and Eve did not immediately die after transgressing God's commandment, their immediate alienation from God points to a spiritual death. After their expulsion from the garden, life east of Eden turned into a train wreck as sin and death pervaded all human existence (5:12).

12. Paul does not want his Roman audience to think that he scorns the law or teaches 'all the Jews living among the Gentiles to forsake Moses', as was rumoured among some Jewish believers in Jerusalem (Acts 21:20–21). The law is *holy*, as are all the Scriptures (1:2). *Holy* means that it is pure, perfect and consecrated to the service of God (cf. Ps. 19:7). The law is *just*, reflecting the divine canons of what is virtuous and evil, and presenting the divine criteria for how we will be assessed at the final judgment (2:16; 14:10–12; 2 Cor. 5:10). It is *good*, meeting the highest possible standards.

Theology

Sin is notoriously deceitful (Heb. 3:13), and the phrase 'sin . . . deceived me', as noted, echoes Eve's self-justification for eating from the forbidden tree (Gen. 3:13; cf. 2 Cor. 11:3; 1 Tim. 2:14). Not everyone's sin is like the transgression of Adam (5:14), but the conflated story of Adam and Eve mirrors everyone's experience of being beguiled by sin. The serpent (sin), introduced as the craftiest of animals (Gen. 3:1), conned Eve in three ways that characterize sin's enduring ploys (Schnabel, II, pp. 140–141). First, it cited only the one negative command God issued: 'Did God say, "You shall not eat from any tree in the garden"?' (Gen. 3:1). It deliberately ignored God's gracious beneficence: 'You may freely eat of every [other] tree of the garden' (Gen. 2:16). Second, it cajoled Eve into believing that God would not punish disobedience by death: 'You will not die' (Gen. 3:4). It claimed that God was only bluffing and would be blasé about any disobedience. Third, it used the commandment to sow seeds of doubt about God's goodwill. It claimed that God issued the command not to eat from the tree of the knowledge of good and evil (Gen. 2:17) because God did not want humans to become godlike. The serpent sweet-talked Eve into believing that she could be like God if only she were bold enough to rebel (Gen. 3:5). The ruses worked because the forbidden tree was 'a delight to the eyes' (Gen. 3:6). The serpent used the command to awaken covetousness – in this case, wanting to be like God.

The echoes from the Genesis account admirably serve to reveal how sin so easily seduces our fleshly nature, since the flesh finds so many things in the world eye-catching and alluring (1 John 2:16). As a result, fleshly humans continue to be taken in by sin's web of lies and ensnared in sin's web of death. In the sphere of the flesh, sin easily undermines the law so that it provokes rather than prevents sin and becomes its accomplice in inflicting death. The commandment directs us to God, but sin erects diversions and roadblocks. It exploits the commandment to goad inward passions into action because it makes inroads through our swarm of desires. It convinces one to dismiss the commands as unreasonable, as requiring needless abstaining from what is pleasurable, and as oppressively curtailing our freedom to do as we please.

ii. Why the law fails to surmount human sin (7:13–25)
Context
This sub-unit begins with another rhetorical question – 'Did what is good, then, bring death to me?' – that receives another strong, negative rejoinder: definitely not! The adjective 'good' applies to the 'commandment' but also summarizes the character of the whole law. The law's holiness is indisputable, but when sin

establishes a foothold in the flesh, it twists what was given for Israel's well-being[116] into a tool that churns out evil. The law is 'spiritual' (7:14) in what it prescribes, but it is not the Holy Spirit. It packs no spiritual punch to animate the behaviour it prescribes. It 'unmasks sin, gives it recognizable definition, removes ambiguity from the sinful act' and exposes sin's true character (Dunn, I, p. 386). In other words, it reveals humanity's plight but is powerless to change it. It cannot break sin's stranglehold. Sin manipulates the law to exploit the weakness of the flesh, but the law turns the tables on sin. It makes sinners accountable to God (3:19–20) and reveals that sin's final outcome is only death (6:23). Since the law only shows sin to be utterly sinful, it follows that God did not intend for the law to be sin's remedy or the path to salvation. That fact is Paul's main point in this entire section.

Comment

13. Since 'our sinful passions, aroused by the law, were at work in our members to bear fruit for death' (7:5), and 'the very commandment that promised life proved to be death to me' (7:10), one might reasonably ask if the law is not a Trojan Horse, something aligned with sin and slipped in to bring death to us. Since the law is good, this inference is wrong. It is also wrong to infer that God miscalculated in giving the law since the results are so ruinous. The purpose clause, *in order that [hina] sin might be shown to be sin* in *working death in me through what is good*, and the result clause, 'so that [hina] through the commandment, sin might become sinful beyond measure' (CSB), imply that God foresaw what would happen. Paul hints that 'a quiet Providence is at work' as God's purpose was to bring knowledge of sin through the law (3:20; 5:13).[117] One can construe that purpose as ultimately redemptive.[118] Recognizing sin for what it is can strip away the thin make-up of fake righteousness that humans daub themselves with to dupe both themselves and

---

116. Cf. Deut. 4:40; 5:16, 29; 6:3, 18; 10:13; 12:25, 28; 22:7.

117. Timmins, *Romans 7*, p. 112.

118. Cf. the comments on the wrath of God in the *Theology* section on 1:18–32.

others that they are holy. When their sin sickness is fully exposed by the law and they acknowledge that they are in a desperate situation from which they cannot extricate themselves, it can make them more receptive to God's remedy that comes only through what God has done in Christ and through the power of the Holy Spirit.

14. Paul leaves the Edenic echoes that surface in 7:7–11 and switches to the present tense in verses 14–25 to link 'the narrative to the present which Paul shares with his readers'.[119] He has discussed how sin took control and manipulated the law, and now shifts to how sin can take control of a person's willpower so that he or she does its bidding.

The law is not only 'holy and just and good'; Paul now says that it is also *spiritual*. The problem is that he is *of the flesh*, 'fleshly' (*sarkinos*), as are all humans. The translation that he is 'unspiritual' (NIV) is misleading. The adjective 'fleshly' refers to the substance out of which he is made.[120] He describes his anthropological condition (cf. Gal. 2:20; Phil. 1:22). He is made of flesh and blood and, therefore, is 'congenitally at odds with God's law', which is 'spiritual'.[121] Paul recognizes that we are all creatures of clay with physical needs and appetites. Even when one's existence is in Christ, existence in an earthly body can levy an unavoidable encumbrance. In Gethsemane, Jesus rebuked his frail disciples who failed to watch as he had commanded them, and conceded, 'The spirit is willing, but the flesh is weak' (Mark 14:38, NIV). Fleshly humans are intrinsically weak, susceptible to being lured into walking 'according to the flesh' (8:4), and therefore sit perilously on the powder keg of sin that can explode at any time.

Paul does not describe the anguish of humans in general who, apart from Christ, try to live by the law but whose inner passions

---

119. Seifrid, 'Subject', p. 318.
120. 'Made of flesh' (*sarkinos*) is the original reading, instead of 'belonging to the order of earthly things' (*sarkikos*), though they are roughly synonymous. He is speaking of himself only in the physical sense (Longenecker, p. 648).
121. Timmins, *Romans 7*, p. 143.

drive them to act against their better judgment. Unregenerate persons do not delight in the law of God and desire to do it (7:18, 22), since they neither seek God (3:11) nor fear God (3:18). Such people are 'creature[s] of flesh and blood' (NJB) who fall prey to sin. Being 'fleshly' is part and parcel of an earthly existence. This is the problem for the law. It may be spiritual, but it operates in a 'fleshly' realm where humans easily skid off its guiding rails into a quagmire because of their innate frailty. In addressing the Corinthians as 'fleshly' ('of the flesh', *sarkinos*) rather than as those who are 'spiritual' (1 Cor. 3:1), Paul does not mean that they are entirely without the Spirit. Instead, he addresses them as Christians who as humans are 'weak, corruptible people, and, therefore, liable to sinful patterns of behavior' and who remain 'infants in Christ'.[122]

Even those who might be regarded as mature in Christ, however, can be found lacking. In speaking about himself, Paul speaks for every believer who yearns to do God's will and falls short. Paul confesses to his past sin of violently persecuting the church and trying to destroy it (Gal. 1:13), which made him the least of all the apostles (1 Cor. 15:9), but he does not say that since becoming a Christ-follower all sin is now behind him. The 'I' in 1 Corinthians 13:1–3 represents a believer speaking, and Paul recognizes that this 'I' can become loveless and reduced to a clanking chunk of bronze or a clamorous cymbal. In Romans 7, Paul's 'I' is a 'representative, paradigmatic "I", the Apostle Paul speaking as an exemplar on behalf of the "we" to whom he writes'.[123] He is speaking to fellow believers who are the only ones who can fully grasp what he is saying. He does not stand apart from his addressees and lecture them on sin. Instead, he identifies with them in encountering the distress that sin in their lives causes. The 'you' in 8:2 ('the law of the Spirit of life in Christ Jesus has set *you* free from the law of sin and death'; emphasis added) reveals that he understands his experience to be their experience as enfleshed human beings. Manson's observation that 'here Paul's autobiography is the biography of Everyman' (Manson, p. 945) is not correct. It is the life of a

---

122. Ibid., p. 140.
123. Ibid., p. 135.

Christian who in this mortal frame seeks to obey God's will and is frustrated upon miserably failing.

Interpreters who dismiss this autobiographical interpretation, however, ask how Paul could possibly say that he, as a believer, is *sold into slavery under sin*? The paradox of being freed from sin and yet sold under sin reflects the tension between the 'already' and the 'not yet'.[124] Being *sold . . . under sin* refers to the circumstance of his mortal flesh. The verb *sold* is in the Greek a perfect passive particle that refers here to his human condition as fallen and corrupt that continues after becoming a believer. Paul has not sold himself into this slavery (contrast Lev. 25:39; 1 Kgs 21:20, 25; 2 Kgs 17:17); he was born into it. The psalmist laments,

> Indeed, I was born guilty,
>   a sinner when my mother conceived me.
> (Ps. 51:5)

His 'history has been determined by Adam'.[125] As a mortal human being, he is damaged to the very core of his being. One does not become de-fleshed and transported to another dimension of existence upon becoming a believer. Participating in the new life offered in Christ does not mean that Paul fully possesses it.[126] It lies in the future. Schreiner affirms, 'The struggle with sin continues for believers because we live in the tension between the already and the not yet' (Schreiner, p. 389).

Consequently, sin continues to assault Paul as a believer even though he is in the body of Christ (7:4), and his human flesh serves as sin's ally in the daily bout between good and evil. This reality explains why Paul says, 'I punish my body and enslave it, so that after proclaiming to others I myself should not be disqualified' (1 Cor. 9:27). Paul may be encouraged that 'though our outward man [our creatureliness] is decaying, yet our inward man is renewed day by day' (2 Cor. 4:16, ASV), but full deliverance from sin and its

---

124. Dryden, 'Romans 7', p. 136.
125. Timmins, *Romans 7*, p. 145.
126. Ibid., p. 97.

mortal sting awaits the resurrection. It will take place 'when this perishable body puts on imperishability, and this mortal body puts on immortality', when 'Death has been swallowed up in victory' (1 Cor. 15:54). Until then, even after receiving 'the first fruits of the Spirit', believers 'groan inwardly while we wait for adoption, the redemption of our bodies' (8:23).

15. The *I* now becomes an active agent who wills to do what is good but ends up doing what it hates (7:19, 25). This tension does not depict the unregenerate person's conflict since the will of the 'I' aligns itself with God's law (7:12, 16) and 'the good' (7:16, 19, 21, 25). Paul is talking about himself and his quandary. He does not understand why he wills one thing and does another. Yet it happens. The fleshly *I* is not the master of its actions. Sin captures the will to do what is 'good' and provokes one to commit actions that are at odds with what one knows to be good. Paul knows not to covet and does not want to covet, but his actions reveal a deep-seated covetousness. As a fleshly human, he veers towards satisfying bodily appetites that lead to death as if sin exerted some pre-ternatural gravitational pull. This tension exposes the law's power-lessness to slay dragon sin and to convert its 'thou shalt's and 'thou shalt not's into obedience.

16–17. Paul's recognition that his actions do not correspond to his good intentions, however, testifies to the goodness of the law. The problem is that sin still has a branch office in his flesh that makes him incapable of obeying the law, an assertion he repeats in verse 20. Sin has colonized the will and then, like a puppeteer, pulls the strings of the body's members to perform what is morally wrong on life's stage.

18. Since Paul asserts that nothing good dwells in him, the whole *I* is implicated in sin. Paul does not believe that humans have a lower nature that sins and a higher nature that is capable of goodness. Fleshliness affects all human nature, and the law does not acquit anyone simply for willing to do what is right. It requires full obedience (Gal. 3:10), and good intentions to obey do not meet the requirements.

19–20. Paul does not allude to the unbeliever's dilemma as Epictetus expressed it: 'What he wills he does not do; what he does not will he does' (*Diatr.* 2.26.3–4 [Oldfather, LCL]); nor as Ovid complained: 'I approve the better course, and yet I choose the worse' (*Metam.* 7.19–21 [Miller and Goold, LCL]). Instead, he refutes a Jewish confidence that if one willed to do the law, one could do it. Sirach insists,

> If you choose, you can keep the commandments,
>   and to act faithfully is a matter of your own choice.
> He [God] has placed before you fire and water;
>   stretch out your hand for whichever you choose.
> Before each person are life and death,
>   and whichever one chooses will be given.
> (Sir. 15:15–17)

The Testament of Asher 1:5–7 articulates the same assurance:

> The two ways are good and evil; concerning them are two dispositions within our breasts that choose between them. If the soul wants to follow the good way, all of its deeds are done in righteousness and every sin is immediately repented. Contemplating just deeds and rejecting wickedness, the soul overcomes evil and uproots sin.[127]

This view also is found in Psalms of Solomon 9:4a: 'Our works (are) in the choosing and power of our souls, to do right and wrong in the works of our hands' (Wright, *OTP* II, p. 660). In 4 Maccabees 2:4–6, the writer assumes that reason can master covetousness:

> Not only is reason proved to rule over the frenzied urge of sexual desire, but also over every desire. Thus the law says, 'You shall not covet your neighbour's wife or anything that is your neighbour's.' In fact, since the law has told us not to covet, I could prove to you all the more that reason is able to control desires.
>   Just so it is with the emotions that hinder one from justice.

Paul refutes this optimistic view that an individual in the flesh has the power to obey the law. Even with knowledge from the law

---

127. Kee, *OTP* I, p. 817.

of what is good and the desire to do it, he still does what is wrong. The law may inform the will, and his mind may decide it is good to fulfil it, but a dark impulse within him leads him to transgress it. The will is captive to sin and needs a greater power beyond itself and beyond reason to be able to fulfil the law.

21. Paul's references to *a law*, 'another law' (v. 23), 'the law of sin' (v. 23) waging war against the spiritual 'law of God' (v. 22), and 'the law of my mind' that delights in God's law (v. 23) may seem confusing. The recurrence of the word 'law' (*nomos*) in these verses suggests to some that Paul resorts to *antanaclasis*, a rhetorical device in which the writer repeats a key word but changes its meaning. Paul is said to use 'law' in two ways: to refer to the Mosaic law and to refer to an operative principle or procedure. Dunn argues instead that Paul uses the word 'law' consistently to refer to the Mosaic law (Dunn, I, p. 392), but he portrays it as operating in the spheres of two different powers. In the one case, the law of God is under the mastery of the Spirit, who directs it to work for what is good. In the other case, the law is under the mastery of sin, which directs it to work for what is evil.[128] The tension created by wanting to do *what is good* and then not doing it means the sin operating in his flesh thwarts his good intentions. What he finds when he seeks to do the good prescribed by the law is that *evil* is always *close at hand*. This is what he finds about the law (Wright, pp. 569–570). He cannot obey it but winds up doing what is iniquitous even when trying to obey it. This conclusion sets up the solution to this cleft stick that will follow in the next unit.

22. In his letters, Paul qualifies the law as *the law of God* only here and in 7:25 and 8:7. This qualification emphasizes the law's divine origin and authority, which distinguish it from 'another law', the law that sin has commandeered and that causes him to mutiny against God's law. His *inmost self* ('inner being') refers to what he 'should be, in distinction from what he actually is'.[129] It is Paul at his rational best. As a believer, his 'inmost self' understands, subscribes to, delights in and desires to do what the law says (cf. 1

---

128. Snodgrass, 'Spheres'; and Wright, *Climax*, p. 198.
129. N. Walter, 'ἔσω', *EDNT* II, p. 64.

Cor. 2:10–16; Gal. 5:17–18). His joyful agreement with the law (7:16) echoes that of the psalmist:

> My lips will pour forth praise,
>   because you teach me your statutes.
> My tongue will sing of your promise,
>   for all your commandments are right.
> Let your hand be ready to help me,
>   for I have chosen your precepts.
> I long for your salvation, O LORD,
>   and your law is my delight.
> (Ps. 119:171–174)

The problem is that being at one's rational best is never sufficient. Paul is unable in his fleshly condition to turn his delight in the law into obedience.

23. It is important to parse Paul's wording carefully when he says that he is *captive to the law of sin that dwells in my members*. Paul does not understand himself to be captive

> to sin *per se*, but 'to the law of sin which is in my members' . . . This 'law' of sin wages a war . . . *within*, where it has so infiltrated the person of ἐγώ [*egō*], that 'the law of my mind' is overpowered.[130]

Paul understands sin as 'an operative law' that runs 'his (Adamic) bodily state'. But this is not 'an unqualified description of his being'.[131] *The law of my mind* refers to 'the Law of God *as accepted* by my conscious self'.[132] Paul understands that his corporeality makes him still vulnerable to sin's cancerous, metastasizing progression. It means that 'freedom from slavery which believers have been gifted in Christ is not yet possessed as an anthropological phenomenon'.[133] Why else does he exhort the audience to pray to God

---

130. Timmins, *Romans 7*, pp. 145–146.

131. Ibid., p. 147.

132. Moule, 'Justification', p. 182.

133. Timmins, *Romans 7*, p. 147.

not to let 'sin exercise dominion in your mortal bodies, to make you obey their passions' (6:12, as interpreted above)? Why else command, 'No longer present your members to sin as instruments of wickedness, but present yourselves to God as those who have been brought from death to life, and present your members to God as instruments of righteousness' (6:13)?

24. Paul lays bare his profound anguish over his helpless fleshly condition. He is *wretched*. He inhabits a *body of death*. This phrase is a genitive of quality, denoting 'the deathly character of this body' that 'is totally subject to the power of death in this world'.[134] He finds himself incapable of obeying the law as he wants to, and the law offers no solution, creating what would seem to be a fatal impasse. Dunn comments,

> Here certainly Paul speaks for himself, and not merely as a
> spokesperson for humanity at large; this is not the stylized formulation
> of one who is long since removed from the situation in question. The
> one who cries for help so piteously cries from *within* the contradiction;
> he longs for deliverance *from* the endless war and frequent defeat.
> (Dunn, I, p. 410)

Caught in the overlap of the two ages, Paul pleads for deliverance from *this body of death* and its congenital weakness. His lament parallels what he says in 2 Corinthians 5:2: 'For in this tent we groan, longing to be clothed with our heavenly dwelling.' Paul and other Christians 'have not yet experienced full liberation from sin' and consequently 'are conscious of the continuing presence of sin in their lives' (Schreiner, p. 390). It produces the vexation Paul expresses here for his failure when he wills what is right but cannot

---

134. Ibid., pp. 152–153. While I do not believe Paul is speaking about the
    Jew apart from Christ, what he says resonates with deep piety reflected,
    for example, in 1QS 11:9–10: 'I belong to evil humankind, to the
    assembly of unfaithful flesh; my failings, my iniquities, my sins,
    [illegible] with the depravities of my heart, belong to the assembly of
    worms and of those who walk in darkness' (Martínez, *Dead Sea Scrolls*,
    p. 18; cf. Johansen, 'Romans 7', pp. 101–118).

do it (7:18–20). He is totally helpless under the law, but in the next unit Paul shows that believers are not totally helpless when the Spirit of Christ dwells within them (8:10–11) and not sin (7:2).

It is important to note that Paul does not ask, '"What will rescue me?" but "Who" . . . ?' (Harrison and Hagner, p. 124). Holloway asserts, 'The tyranny of desire is not a philosophical problem to be solved by the application of a rational therapy, nor is it a problem of moral ignorance to be solved by instruction in Torah.'[135] The law offers no deliverance from this fallen condition and only metes out death as the punishment for transgressions. If the law were able to justify and to save, then what was the purpose of Christ's death (Gal. 2:21)? What humans need is a divine Saviour, and a divine power to overcome sin's stranglehold and to harness mutinous impulses and transform them into obedience (8:2). That deliverer is Christ (11:26; 1 Thess. 1:10; 2 Tim. 4:18).

25. Paul exults that, thanks to God's gracious initiative, deliverance will come through Jesus Christ. The thanksgiving in 1 Corinthians 15:56–57 provides a close parallel. Paul mentions the 'sting of death', 'sin', and 'the law' as 'the power of sin', and then rejoices, 'But thanks be to God, who gives us the victory through our Lord Jesus Christ.' The 'victory' in 1 Corinthians 15:57 clearly refers to the future deliverance of believers in the resurrection, so it follows that the reference to being rescued in 7:24–25 is also to the believer's future deliverance from this present 'body of death'. Banks comments,

> Weighted down as he is with the sense of his own wretchedness as he lives in constant tension between what he is *kata sarka* ['according to the flesh'] and what he is *en Christō* ['in Christ'], he throws his gaze forward to the decisive event which alone can bring the tension to an end.[136]

Through Jesus Christ our Lord means that this deliverance will transpire only for those who by the grace of God are joined to Christ and his resurrection (5:21; 6:4; 8:11, 17, 19, 23). It is only the

135. Holloway, 'Rhetoric', p. 116.
136. Banks, 'Romans 7.25a', p. 39.

'wretched' person who fully understands and appreciates God's grace in Christ.

Since an unexpected negative statement about his current state follows this thanksgiving, many commentators assume that it is out of place or was added later as a gloss. No textual evidence, however, exists to support these suppositions. The text must be interpreted as it stands. It reinforces the point that full deliverance awaits the future. In the meantime, Paul recognizes that he still lives in the shadow of Adam in a body of death. The second half of this verse serves as a delayed conclusion to what precedes. 'I myself' (NIV) or 'I dependent on myself alone' (*autos egō*) am fundamentally in need of help to obey the law and to please God. Dunn comments,

> Paul *is* speaking of life in the old epoch of Adam in this section, but since that epoch runs through till death (5:12–21; 1 Cor. 15:21–26) believers perforce still belong to it, 'in the flesh', 'mortal bodies'. The balance of v 25b therefore is not an expression of salvation still to begin, but of the process of salvation under way and still to be completed. (Dunn, I, p. 399)

Having shown that none can obey God's commands in their own power and that the law is powerless to help, Paul will show in the next section that believers can do so through the Spirit's power and only through the Spirit of God dwelling in them (8:11). Therefore, Paul makes an implicit command that believers must live in the sphere of the Spirit of Christ, who alone counteracts the flesh that causes humans to fall into the clutches of sin and death (Gal. 5:16–18).

Theology

This section offers evidence why 'the letter kills' and why what is 'chiselled in letters on stone tablets' (cf. Exod. 24:12; 31:18) can be fairly described as 'the ministry of death' (2 Cor. 3:6–7). It also explains why the gospel must be law-free. The law does not and cannot offer redemption from our bondage to sin. Instead, it 'turned sin into transgression, increased the trespass, and produced wrath' (Peterson, p. 41), which is what Paul means when he writes cryptically that 'the power of sin is the law' (1 Cor. 15:56). Sin uses the law to stimulate open disobedience and leads even the law's most ardent devotees to bend the rules to their advantage. The law can never make happen what God demands in it because humans exist in a physical body, and sin seductively and maliciously uses the old written code to stoke the flames of desires. As a written code, it has the power only to reveal how utterly sinful sin is (7:13), twisting what is holy to produce evil ends. As a written code, it hands down the sentence of death and justifies God's contention against us, so that we cannot possibly win the case when we stand before God's judgment seat (3:4; Ps. 51:4).

The problem with the law is directly related to anthropology. The law is powerless to defeat the power of sin because of the intrinsic weakness of human flesh. The law is not sin (7:7) but 'holy and just and good' (7:12), but with the coming of Messiah Jesus it is no longer God's vehicle for salvation. The law founders because it operates in the sphere of fleshly weakness where humans are helpless against the deadly drag of sin and death. The law cannot renovate, let alone perfect, human existence in the flesh. Paul vividly describes his own experience as a fleshly person who longs to fulfil God's law and fails. In the unit that follows, Paul proclaims that God sent his Son to share the human condition and to condemn sin. The pouring out of the Spirit into the hearts of believers means that they are no longer disabled by their fleshly condition. Paul's main argument is that the law is incapable of producing the obedience it requires, and therefore salvation comes only 'through faith in Jesus Christ for all who believe' (3:22).[137] It is only when believers live out their new identity in Christ because the Holy Spirit indwells them that they can fulfil the just requirement of the law (8:3–4). Believers must be constantly reminded of, embrace and enact the reality that they are 'slaves not under the old written code but in the new life of the Spirit' (7:6). Timmins comments, 'Believers are no longer in the flesh. But since the new age has arrived within the confines of the old order, not all associations with the flesh are broken.'[138]

---

137. Romanello, 'Rom 7,7–25', pp. 526–527.
138. Timmins, *Romans 7*, p. 179.

Being fleshly and inhabiting a mortal body means we are subject to weaknesses because of our Adamic humanity, but it says nothing about our existence in Christ whereby we live only by faith and will be saved only by grace. Timmins compares Paul's description of himself in this passage to Abraham,

> an example of faith in the midst of bodily death . . . He is a believer, but someone whose faith brings not a reformation of the fallen bodily condition but a reorientation of existence around God, whose power alone brings life to the dead (4:23–25; 8:1–11).[139]

Those who are justified, consecrated believers are the most vexed at being unable to escape completely the tug of their Adamic flesh, so that they fail to do what is right but do what they hate. Consequently, many believers find in this passage a telling description of their own struggles. We are still mortal beings not yet freed from the ravenous maw of covetousness, no matter how much we try to deny, whitewash or repress it. Luther's comment remains apropos: 'Indeed it is a great consolation to us to learn that such a great apostle was involved in the same grievings and afflictions in which we find ourselves when we wish to be obedient to God.'[140] Others have chimed in: 'How can we doubt that this is true for Paul when it is so true for us?'[141] These comments capture why Paul uses the 'I' in this section. He wants to confess to his audience that he is like them and 'stands amongst them as a sinner'.[142]

Dunn points out that it is a paradox that the law can have both positive and negative functions at the same. It has a negative function as 'the glue which binds sin to death' and a positive function 'because it leaves the sinner no alternative to death other than the death of Christ' (Dunn, I, p. 401). It is also a paradox that the believer, as one living in the flesh, is both freed from sin (7:1–6; 8:1–4) and at the same time 'sold . . . under sin' (7:14). It is because

---

139. Ibid., p. 185.

140. Luther, *Lectures*, p. 208.

141. Knox, *Life*, p. 67.

142. Timmins, *Romans 7*, p. 209.

we have not been completely removed from the fray. Sin's stubborn virus can lie dormant but revive and cause a relapse. As a result, all will face the inescapable sting of death. However, Paul will insist in the next unit, in 8:1–11, that while sin may 'remain' it need not 'reign' (Moo, p. 383, citing John Wesley's sermon 'Repentance of Believers'). He can give thanks to God at the conclusion of this unit (7:25) that though Christians 'do not escape the death which is the fruit of their sin, they are able to survive it because Christ has endured it with them and for them' (Dunn, I, p. 401).

E. Life in the Spirit (8:1–30)

Paul's chief concern is not that believers receive forgiveness and relief from the feeling of moral culpability, but rather that they can be delivered from the sinful flesh that makes inevitable the repeated swerving away from the will of God. Forgiveness that does not include some way to neutralize the cause of the transgressions fails to solve the dilemma. Paul would have believers recognize that in their new life in Christ they have both new moral obligations and new divine resources to fulfil them. They can now live in the sphere of the Spirit of God's activity in the world. The Spirit's role now becomes prominent as enabling the believer's obedience of faith. The Spirit is the channel by which God's love is poured into the hearts of believers (5:5) and the agent who empowers them to work 'signs and wonders' (Acts 4:30; 5:12; 14:3; Rom. 15:19; 2 Cor. 12:12; Heb. 2:4) and to bear ethical fruit in their lives (Gal. 5:22–25). The Spirit who abides in believers is also the agent of their resurrection (8:11). This reality solidifies their hope and security in God's love amid their 'sufferings of this present time' (8:18) in a world in 'bondage to decay' (8:21). Moule writes, 'If the whole Bible blew away except this one chapter, we should still have a priceless treasure left – and a great deal of light on what a Christian means by hope.'[143] Since it is still possible that one who is in a corruptible body can return to a life of sin, Paul's discussion also contains implied admonitions. The Spirit has given believers a new identity

---

143. Moule, *Hope*, p. 3.

as the children of God, adopted as heirs (8:14–17). They are therefore to live as those destined for glory with their minds governed by the Spirit who, with the help of the Spirit, have put to death the deeds of the body.

i. The Spirit as the fountainhead of obedience (8:1–17)

Context

What remedy do believers have when they exist in a forlorn 'body of death' that is continually assaulted by the power of sin? The sense of failure now fades as Paul resumes the confident tone of 5:1–6. God does not save and declare believers to be righteous (5:19) only to leave them as they are, weak, ungodly and enemies (5:6, 10). Paul introduced God's solution in a summary manner in 7:6: 'But now we have been released from the law, since we have died to what held us, so that we may serve in the newness of the Spirit and not in the old letter of the law' (csb), and now expounds on what that means. The law is no longer the definitive authority that orders religious–ethical life since it is compromised by sin.[144] The religious–ethical life of those who are in Christ Jesus is now formed and regulated by the Spirit.

The process of forming a new humanity in Christ 'so that the just requirement of the law might be fulfilled in us' (8:4) begins when believers cross the threshold into the domain of God's Spirit. In this outline of God's continuing work in the lives of Christ-followers, the Spirit comes to the fore and is cited twenty-one times in 8:1–27, compared to five times in chapters 1–7 and eight times in chapters 9–15. The Spirit gives us life by setting us free from the law of sin and death that plagues our mortal bodies (8:2, 11), enables us to fulfil 'the just requirement of the law' (8:4), brings peace (8:6), gives evidence that we belong to Christ (8:9) and are God's children (8:14, 16), enables us to 'put to death the deeds of the body' (8:13), and helps us in our weakness to know what to pray and intercedes for us in accordance with God's will (8:26–27).

---

144. Gäckle, *Die Starken*, p. 334.

Comment

1. The *now* recalls 7:6, 'but now we are discharged from the law', and the 'new stage in salvation history, which moves beyond that of the law and the promises' (Fitzmyer, p. 343; cf. 3:21; 5:9, 11; 6:22; 7:6; 11:30; 16:26). Christ's death and resurrection have changed the direction of history. Under the old epoch when sin, death and the law reigned unrestrained, a curse fell on 'everyone who does not observe and obey all the things written in the book of the law' (Gal. 3:10, citing Deut. 27:26). In the new epoch of the Spirit, Christ has borne the condemnation that all deserve and 'redeemed' believers 'from the curse of the law by becoming a curse for us' (Gal. 3:13). Christ was raised from the dead, sits at the right hand of God and intercedes for believers (8:34). Accordingly, all those who are in Christ Jesus will escape the death sentence fated for all those in Adam (5:18) because they have been crucified with Christ and will share his destiny of being resurrected and living to God (6:6–11). No-one else is entitled to bring charges against God's chosen (8:33) who are justified/ acquitted by faith (5:1).

Though the highest court has reversed the death sentence for their sins, sin's onslaught on this carnal frame that Paul dramatically portrays in 7:14–25 is not over. In what follows he develops what being *in Christ* entails for this struggle. God does not leave believers alone to do battle with sin in their frail, wayward and mortal bodies. In Christ, they can serve in newness of Spirit (7:6), which means they draw on divine power to accomplish the work that God has begun in them (Phil. 2:12–13).

The *condemnation* that belongs to the law's era is only one of several contrasts between the two epochs of sin, death and the law and of the Spirit that Paul highlights in 8:1–17 (see Table 3 on p. 259).

2. Paul confirms the truth of the previous statement. In the new epoch inaugurated by the sending of God's Son and the outpouring of God's Spirit, the Spirit acts on human hearts to bring about obedience to the law and engender life. Many commentators regard the word *law* (*nomos*) in the phrase *the law of the Spirit* to refer to a 'principle' (cf. 7:21). Paul uses the word 'law', however, in 8:3 to refer to the Mosaic law and presents it as coming under the control of

Table 3: Contrasts between the epoch of sin, death and the law
and the epoch of the Spirit

The epoch of sin, death and the law (7:5)	The epoch of the Spirit (7:6)
Condemnation (5:16, 18)	No condemnation (8:1)
The law of sin and death (8:2)	The law of the Spirit of life in Christ Jesus (8:2)
What the law could not do weakened by the flesh (8:3)	What God did in Christ to condemn sin in the flesh (8:3)
Walking, living and setting the mind on the things of the flesh (8:4–5)	Walking, living and setting the mind on the things of the Spirit (8:4–5)
Death (8:6, 13a)	Life and peace (8:6, 13b)
Inability to please God (8:8)	Fulfilling the just requirement of the law (8:4)
Sin (8:10)	Righteousness (8:10)
Slavery (8:15)	Adoption as children of God and heirs (8:15–17)

either the flesh or the Spirit.[145] He does not intend his original audience to guess whether the word *nomos* refers to the Mosaic law or a principle. He uses the word seventy-plus times in the letter consistently to refer to the Mosaic law. Here he describes it under the influence of different force fields. *The law of the Spirit . . . in Christ Jesus* refers to the Mosaic law in the power sphere of the Spirit that makes the believers' fulfilment of the law possible. *The law of sin and death* refers to the Mosaic law in the power sphere of the flesh where sin warps and exploits it (7:11) so that it produces condemnation and eternal death.[146] Since the law is 'spiritual' (7:14), it only operates as God intended it in the sphere of the Spirit. Living in the force field of the Spirit frees believers from the law that is engraved on stone and in the sphere of the flesh is so easily forged as a tool of

---

145. Snodgrass, 'Spheres', p. 107.
146. Casson, *Textual Signposts*, pp. 71–72.

sin.[147] 'The obedience of faith among all the Gentiles' that Paul
understands to be the objective of his apostleship (1:5; 15:18; 16:26)
is possible only through the operation of the Spirit who does not
work 'on tablets of stone but on tablets of human hearts' (2 Cor.
3:3).

Paul's argument is this. Sin worms its way in through the portal
of the flesh and distorts the law and deforms humanity. The Spirit's
power re-forms those who are in Christ and transforms them so
that they can fulfil 'the just requirement of the law' (8:4) and be
conformed to the image of God's Son (8:29). Freedom does not
come from trying to conform to a written code but only from
surrendering oneself completely to the control of God's Spirit. Paul
asserts that under the Spirit's power the external Mosaic law
develops into an interior law (Jer. 31:33) – in this case, as argued
below, the Christian law of love.[148]

3. Paul touches on Christ's pre-existence (*sending*), his incarnation (*in the likeness of sinful flesh*) and his atoning sacrifice ('to be a
sin offering', NIV) to summarize what God has done to redeem
believers from their fleshly circumstances. The law in the sphere
of the flesh could not supply the power to surmount the fleshly
predisposition to rebel against God. Conquering sin required
more than God simply writing it off and reducing our debt to
zero. God had to do something more radical to eradicate it. Since
the flesh is the field of battle which sin has occupied and where it
has set up headquarters, God must send his Son (John 3:16; Gal.
4:4; 1 John 4:9) in the likeness of sinful flesh to vanquish the
invader. Dunn comments, 'God did not redeem flesh by an act of
incarnation; he destroyed flesh by an act of condemnation'
(Dunn, I, p. 440). God made attainable in the new life in Christ
Jesus what was completely unattainable in the old life under the

147. The KJV and ASV read 'made *me* free' rather than '*you*'. It is likely that
the word 'me' was introduced to harmonize with Paul's cry in 7:24,
'Who will rescue me from this body of death?' It is possible that 'you'
was introduced by the unintentional repetition of the last two letters of
the previous word in Greek.

148. Lyonnet, 'Rom 8, 2–4', pp. 583–586.

law, namely, fulfilment of 'the just requirement of the law' (8:4).

In the likeness of sinful flesh means that Christ 'assumed human nature' (Cranfield, I, p. 381). He was fully human, identical to enfleshed humans (Phil. 2:7). As the NJB renders the phrase, Christ had 'the same human nature as any sinner'. He shouldered what all humans experience, including death that is the result of sin. *Likeness*, however, also implies difference. Christ was completely different from other humans with respect to sin, and it is a fundamental Christian tenet that he knew no sin (2 Cor. 5:21; Heb. 4:15; 1 Pet. 2:22, 24; 1 John 3:5).

Paul does not believe that humans can overcome sin's power if they would only follow Christ's example. God did what humans could not do for themselves by sending his Son *to deal with sin*, a translation of the phrase that reads literally in Greek 'concerning sin' (*peri hamartias*). This translation does not specify how sin would be dealt with, and the rendering 'to be a sin offering' (NIV, NASB) is more accurate. That phrase appears in Leviticus 9:2; 14:31 (LXX); Psalm 40:6 (39:7, LXX); and Isaiah 53:10, among many other passages, to refer to the 'sin-offering' sacrifice.[149] Paul's use of it harks back to the image of Christ's 'blood' in 5:9, which, he says, 'justified' us. The sin offering was the sacrifice for sins committed unintentionally or in ignorance. The sin offering that covers unintentional sins fits the situation of the 'I' in 7:15 who does not sin defiantly but unwillingly.

In the Old Testament, humans present the sin offering *to* God. In the sin offering of God's Son, God is the one who offers it *for* humans. Christ's solidarity with humans meant that he took upon himself our sinfulness, endured the curse of the law when he was hanged on a cross (Gal. 3:13), and redeemed us from law's death sentence. God shattered sin's rule through Christ's death, pulling off what Dunn terms 'the most dramatic reversal of all time'. God converted death, which had been 'sin's ally and final triumph

---

149. Cf. Lev. 5:6–8, 11; 6:25, 30; 7:7; 9:7, 10, 22; 10:17, 19; 14:13, 19; 16:3, 5, 9, 25; Num. 6:16; 7:16; 29:11; 2 Chr. 29:23–24; Neh. 10:33; Ezek. 42:13; 43:19.

(5:21)', 'into sin's own defeat and destruction' (Dunn, I, p. 422). Sin had run riot through the flesh, but God triumphed and brought sin under judgment through his Son sent in the likeness of sinful flesh.

4. The *just requirement* [*dikaiōma*] *of the law* is singular, which can assume that 'the law's requirements are essentially a unity' (Cranfield, I, p. 384). Paul uses the plural 'the requirements of the law' in 2:26, and he may have chosen to use the singular here to point to the love commandment, which he regards as the moral essence of the law.[150] In Galatians 5:14, he maintains, 'The whole law is summed up in a single commandment, "You shall love your neighbour as yourself"' (cf. Mark 12:28–31; Gal. 6:2). This statement occurs in a similar context where Paul contrasts the Spirit and the flesh. He commands the Galatians to 'live by the Spirit', with the promise that they then will 'not gratify the desires of the flesh' (Gal. 5:16). This interpretation is strengthened by his declaration in Romans 13:8–10,

> Owe no one anything, except to love one another; for the one who loves another has fulfilled the law. The commandments, 'You shall not commit adultery; You shall not murder; You shall not steal; You shall not covet'; and any other commandment, are summed up in this word, 'Love your neighbour as yourself.' Love does no wrong to a neighbour; therefore, love is the fulfilling of the law.

Paul is not speaking of the observance of the law but its fulfilment. The love command becomes the hermeneutical touchstone for deciding what commands to keep and how to keep them to fulfil the law's intentions.

The passive voice in *might be fulfilled* or 'fully met' (NIV) *in us* in 8:4 places the emphasis on what God does in us and not on what we might accomplish on our own (cf. Gal. 2:20). To use the language of Galatians, the fulfilment of the law comes as the 'fruit of the Spirit' for those who live by the Spirit and are guided by the Spirit (Gal. 5:22–25), and not as a work that believers accomplish.

---

150. Van de Sandt, 'Research', pp. 268–269.

The participial phrase *who walk not according to the flesh but according to the Spirit* may be translated as introducing a condition instead of making a statement of fact: 'provided we live not according to the flesh'. This reading 'insinuates ... that Christian living is not something that flows automatically from faith and baptism; co-operation with God's Spirit is required' (Fitzmyer, p. 488). Paul introduces the flesh–Spirit antithesis 'not as mutually exclusive conditions, but more as an exhortation, as contrasting and opposed alternatives' (Dunn, I, p. 425). As human beings, Christians still live in the flesh. That fact does not mean that they are controlled by the flesh that has become a power field that is anti-Spirit (Gal. 5:17). Paul responds to opponents in Corinth who think 'we live by the standards of this world' (2 Cor. 10:2, NIV), literally, that 'we walk according to the flesh'. He states, 'For though we walk in the flesh, we do not war according to the flesh' (2 Cor. 10:3, ASV). He means that though 'we live in the world' (NIV) or 'we live as human beings' (NRSV), he does not allow the standards of the flesh that sin has corrupted to determine his responses in this conflict. Living *according to the flesh* means that the world's patterns of behaviour that are hostile to God surround us. Living *according to the Spirit* means that we allow a personal divine power to abide in us who gives us the willpower and strength to resist these sinful influences and to behave in accordance with God's will. The law that is so ineffective in the sphere of the flesh becomes renewed in the sphere of the Spirit when God gives believers a spiritual heart transplant. Paul does not cite God's promises in Ezekiel 36:26–27 and Jeremiah 31:33; nevertheless, they inform his views (cf. 2 Cor. 3:3, 6):[151]

> A new heart I will give you, and a new spirit I will put within you; and I will remove from your body the heart of stone and give you a heart of flesh. I will put my spirit within you, and make you follow my statutes and be careful to observe my ordinances.
> (Ezek. 36:26–27)

---

151. Yates, *Spirit*, p. 145.

> This is the covenant that I will make with the house of Israel after those
> days, says the LORD: I will put my law within them, and I will write it on
> their hearts; and I will be their God, and they shall be my people.
> (Jer. 31:33)

Paul assumes that these promises that once were understood to be
limited to Israel have been universalized to include Gentile believers, since all believers receive the Spirit.

5–6. While righteous living springs forth naturally as the fruit
of the Spirit, walking according to the Spirit is not something that
arises involuntarily. Because the flesh is so prone to sin in this
terrestrial realm, living according to the Spirit requires determination on the believer's part. That fact explains Paul's exhortations
to live – that is, to be guided – by the Spirit in Galatians 5:16, 25 (cf.
Rom. 13:14; 1 Pet. 2:11).

To *set the mind* on the flesh or on the Spirit refers to an established orientation that determines one's aspirations and behaviour. The *flesh* is not the body in contrast to the soul. It is a
force field (like an electromagnetic force field) where the power
of sin surrounds a human's existence, aligns it in a direction that
is diametrically opposed to God's will, and produces the self-
absorption, self-indulgence, self-reliance and venal disregard of
others that stubbornly defies God. The *Spirit* creates a force field
that mediates Christ's presence, aligns believers' innermost
commitments with God's will, empowers them to carry it out and
sets up a shield to defend against an invasion by sin. These two
mindsets oppose each other: 'For what the flesh desires is
opposed to the Spirit, and what the Spirit desires is opposed to
the flesh; for these are opposed to each other, to prevent you
from doing what you want' (Gal. 5:17). Each mindset exercises
exclusive control: 'there is no middle ground here, no possibility
of successfully combining these contrary orientations' (Jewett,
p. 488). Those who are flesh-minded become its prisoners and
cannot escape its captivity except through their faith in God's
redemption that places them in the force field of the Spirit's
greater power. The outcomes of each mindset also are completely
opposite. The flesh delivers only *death*. The Spirit engenders *life
and peace*. The *death* that results from a flesh disposition does not

refer simply to the irreversible cessation of all vital functions. One can experience spiritual death while one is still alive. The deadly alienation from God in this life foreshadows an eternal death and separation from God. Believers' experience of *life and peace* in this life is a foretaste of what comes to full realization in the life to come (Edwards, p. 205). *Peace* refers to peace from God (1:7; 15:13) and with God (5:1), and it leads to peace with others (14:19). Believers who rest in God's peace differ radically from those living in the power field of the flesh, with its addiction to enmity (8:7), cursing, bitterness and blood-shedding that leads to ruin and misery.

7–8. Paul explains why living according to the flesh inevitably results in death. Flesh-mindedness habitually revolts against God because it is inherently *hostile to God*. Paul numbers 'enmities' among the works of the flesh (Gal. 5:20), and enmity towards God is deadly.

9. Does Paul offer assurance in saying, 'But you do not exist in flesh but in Spirit, *since* indeed God's Spirit dwells among you' (Jewett, pp. 474, 489)? Or does he offer a proviso: 'Yet you are not in the flesh; you are in the Spirit, *if in fact* God's Spirit dwells in you' (Fitzmyer, pp. 479, 488)? The conjunction (*eiper*), which can be translated 'since' or 'if in fact', appears again in 8:17 where it clearly introduces a stipulation: 'if children, then heirs, heirs of God and joint heirs with Christ – if, in fact [*eiper*], we suffer with him so that we may also be glorified with him'. What follows in verses 9–10 using 'if' (*ei*) strengthens the interpretation that Paul introduces a stipulation in verse 9. Edwards recognizes that 'the purpose of these statements is hortatory, and their effect resembles an orchestra's crescendo, or climactic finale' (Edwards, p. 206). In the defence of the gospel apart from the law, Paul warns that the *only* way that believers can overcome the disposition of the flesh that is beset by sin and live a life pleasing to God is to walk *in*, *by* and *through* the Spirit who unleashes a new power that enables believers to do what the law was too weak to do.

This assertion implies that the criterion for determining whether persons truly belong to Christ is evidence that they have allowed the Spirit to galvanize their faith into discernible differences in

thinking and behaviour and not simply their assent to a series of
doctrinal faith statements. The Spirit puts an end to the works of
the flesh and empowers believers to manifest Christlike qualities
(Gal. 5:17–25).

10. Paul recaps what he wrote in 7:8–11 and 24. This mortal
body, under the sentence of death, will die physically because we
still have one foot in this present evil age. Our physical demise is
not, however, the final word. Christ's presence in believers' lives
through the indwelling Spirit is life-giving. Being in Christ and
Christ being *in you* through the Spirit means that believers live
within the sphere of divine power whose lines of force align all
the aspects in its force field to make righteousness possible.
Opposition to God produces death, but righteousness produces
life. Righteousness and life are possible only as gifts from God
that we receive.

11. Paul lamented the 'sin that dwells within me' (7:17, 20) but
now declares that when the Spirit *dwells in you*, sin is driven out. He
offers another but complementary answer to his question 'Who
will rescue me from this body of death?' (7:24). The deliverer is
the Spirit who mediates the presence of the risen and exalted
Christ and enables believers to bear fruit for God (7:4). What is
remarkable is that the immortal, divine Spirit of God comes to
dwell in our sin-afflicted, mortal bodies. This affirmation dramatically differs from the assumptions of others in Paul's and later
eras that the solution to the human plight requires our spirits to
take flight from our mortal bodies for an ecstatic union with the
Spirit in some other-worldly realm. The Spirit, however, 'is not
confined to a spiritual realm divorced from the material and social'
(Dunn, I, p. 445). The Spirit has boundless freedom to go wherever
there is a need to bring life and comes into the heart of mortal
humans who are open to receiving the outpouring of this divine
gift.

Paul establishes that the Spirit gives life to sinners who are as
good as dead (8:10), shepherds them into righteous living (8:10) and
is the force in raising them to eternal life. God who raised Jesus
from the dead will not leave our bodies in the grave and allow
sin and death to have some semblance of victory over us. The
Spirit does not only function as a guarantee of believers' future

resurrection but serves as the agent of that resurrection.[152] This point connects Jesus' glorification as the Son and believers' glorification as 'children of God' (8:14, 16). Through the Spirit of holiness Jesus was appointed the Son of God in power by his resurrection from the dead (1:4). In the same way, 'believers will be resurrected through the Spirit who raised Jesus from the dead', and they too will be 'revealed in glory (8:18) as sons of God (8:19, 21, 23)'.[153]

12–13. The mention of the resurrection reminds the audience that believers' salvation is not yet complete. Their future life is the resurrected life; their present life is one of indebtedness. Paul uses a metaphor from accounting to make the point that for the present they remain debtors who must repay their creditor. Believers no longer owe a debt to the flesh but 'to God and his Spirit' (Fitzmyer, p. 492). They can repay it only through obedient service. Paul assumes that obedience is necessary for salvation and implicitly admonishes his audience again to live by the Spirit and to kill off *the deeds of the body* (13:12; cf. Gal. 5:24; Col. 3:5). The present tense of the Greek verb translated *put to death* may signify something that they must do repeatedly. It conveys that 'the battle with sin is not a momentary event, no matter how sincere, but a lifetime commitment' (Edwards, p. 207). *Put[ting] to death the deeds of the body* is the result of a two-way collaboration between the Spirit and the believer.[154] When believers submit to the Spirit's control (8:14), the Spirit is the executioner who destroys the deeds of the body.

Paul uses the term *body (sōma)* here rather than 'flesh' *(sarx)*. The two terms can overlap and be used interchangeably. The body, however, can either be committed to sin (1:24; 6:6) and its members used as instruments of wickedness (6:13), or it can be committed to God (12:1) and its members used as instruments of righteousness

---

152. Textual evidence divides on whether the phrase after the preposition
        dia is in the accusative case, meaning '*because* of his Spirit who lives in
        you' (NIV), or in the genitive case, meaning '*through* his Spirit that dwells
        in you' (NRSV). Cranfield's arguments for the genitive are the most
        persuasive (Cranfield, I, pp. 391–392).
153. Hurtado, 'Jesus' Divine Sonship', p. 231.
154. Maston, *Divine and Human Agency*, p. 178.

(6:19). It is more likely that Paul understands the term *body* here as having been taken over by sin so that it is oriented to do what is evil.

14. The law only points the way; the Spirit leads the way. Godet describes this leading as the Spirit dragging persons 'where the flesh would fain not go' (Godet, p. 309). Käsemann describes it as being 'driven by the Spirit' (Käsemann, p. 218), which implies forceful coercion in which one has no choice but to follow. In the context, however, the verb *agontai* refers to leading or guiding morally or spiritually (BDAG, p. 16), which is done by persuasion rather than by force. One can resist (cf. 2:4). Therefore, being *led by the Spirit* implies that one has consented to the Spirit taking control of one's life. The compulsion to follow comes from hearing the Spirit's voice calling and recognizing it as a divine beckoning (cf. John 10:16) to a manner of life that leads to glory.

Those led by the Spirit become *children of God*, a distinction enjoyed only by Israel, even when they were rebellious (Exod. 4:22–23; Deut. 14:1; Isa. 1:2–4), as the only nation to experience a close intimacy with God. As children they are also heirs of God destined for glory (8:21). By contrast, sin leads its vassals down the road to enslavement and perdition (6:16–20). Believers become children of God based solely on their faith (Gal. 3:26), regardless of their biological descent.

This embrace of believing Gentiles as children of God was something else that the law was unable to do (8:3), since it divided humankind between Israel and those branded as 'the uncircumcision' (literally, 'the foreskins'). Paul says that Gentiles by birth were formerly regarded as 'aliens from the commonwealth of Israel, and strangers to the covenants of promise, having no hope and without God in the world' (Eph. 2:11–12). Now the indwelling Spirit makes believing Gentiles along with believing Jews the children of God. This is not a meaningless honorific status with few or no duties. Being children of God brings with it the weighty responsibility to conduct oneself in accordance with God's moral requirements.[155]

---

155. Burke, *Adopted*, p. 147.

15. Most recognize that *Abba!* was Jesus' distinctive direct address to God in prayer, though it appears only in Mark's account of Jesus' agonized prayer in Gethsemane (Mark 14:36).[156] As God's Son cried out to God, 'Abba, Father', using a reverent but child's term of endearment, so the Spirit, who mediates the presence of Christ in believers, enables them to cry out intimately to God as *Abba! Father!* That God, whom the psalmist identifies as 'awesome', 'the Most High' and 'a great king over all the earth' (Ps. 47:2), and whom Paul identifies as the One 'from [whom] and through [whom] and for [whom] are all things' and who is owed 'glory for ever' (11:36), would allow believers to address him so warmly is an astounding truth of the Christian faith. The cry attests to their new, intimate relationship to God as their Father and that they understand that God loves them and has adopted them into the family. It is emblematic of a transformed self-identity that also transforms behaviour. The use of the particle *for* in verse 15 explains that 'it is the Spirit-shaped experience of being adopted by God as a loving Father that empowers the Roman Christians to put to death the works of the body'.[157] Interpreting the image of adoption against an Old Testament background yields another insight. Paul lists 'adoption' in 9:4 as one of the privileges of Israel (Exod. 4:22; Deut. 14:1; Hos. 1:10). Applying this honour to include Gentile believers is based on the adoption formula in 2 Samuel 7:14 that later was applied to the Messiah in both Jewish and Christian traditions: 'I will be a father to him, and he shall be a son to me' (cf. 4QFlor 1:10-13). If this declaration is true of Christ, Paul reasons it must also be true of those who are in Christ. In 2 Corinthians 6:18, Paul applies the declaration made to David specifically to believers:

I will be your father,
     and you shall be my sons and daughters,
says the Lord Almighty.[158]

---

156. Garland, *Mark*, pp. 234–235.

157. Rabens, *Holy Spirit*, p. 204.

158. Jub. 1:24–25 applies 2 Sam. 7:14 and the title 'sons of God' only to the Israelites who will have returned to God in all uprightness.

It is striking that Paul uses the transliteration of the Aramaic *Abba* in a letter addressed to a Greek-speaking audience. He also uses the phrase 'Abba! Father!' in Galatians 4:6 and must assume that Gentile Christians were familiar with this distinctive address. The Roman Christians may have become familiar with this tradition from the preaching of Palestinian Christians who came to Rome before Paul. The verb *cry* (*krazomen*) is in the present tense, which implies that the Spirit of God's Son (8:9) continues to stir them to cry out 'Abba! Father!' when they invoke God's name in their prayers. Its repetition serves as a constant reminder of their close relationship to God as children of God.

If the audience were familiar with the Markan tradition of Jesus praying passionately in Gethsemane as he faced the cross, 'Abba, Father, for you all things are possible; remove this cup from me; yet, not what I want, but what you want' (Mark 14:36), this cry may purposely replicate Jesus' prayer. If so, the cry may remind them that as God's children they must also submit to God's will and share the suffering of Jesus, the Son of God (8:17).[159] The Spirit thereby turns the rebellious enmity that crucified God's Son into the loving trust of a child who submits to the benevolent Father's will. While sin causes one to quail in fear of death, the Spirit produces in believers a profound and intimate trust that their Father will bring them through suffering and through death to resurrection.

16–17. Does the Spirit testify '*with* our spirit that we are children of God', as many translations have it, or '*to* our spirit' (so Cranfield, I, p. 403; NET)? While we may need to hear the Spirit's reassurance that we are indeed God's children, the compound verb means 'to testify with' (*symmartyrei*), which argues for the first translation. Believers are in such close communion with the Spirit that the Spirit-inspired cry of 'Abba! Father!' offers joint testimony that they genuinely are God's children (cf. John 1:12).

Adoption as children of God brings with it the legal right to inheritance. Believers become co-heirs with Christ of God's blessings, but Paul now adds conditions that contain an implicit exhortation: 'if indeed ['provided that', NJB] we share in his

---

159. Burke, *Adopted*, pp. 95–96.

sufferings' (NIV). Christ shares his inheritance with believers, but to share his inheritance of glory they must also share his suffering. The reintroduction of the theme of suffering recalls 5:2–5, the beginning of this entire section. Paul affirms that suffering is the necessary prelude to the fulfilment of the hope of sharing in God's glory. The indwelling Spirit does not remove believers from this world to delight in heavenly joys but directs them to serve in the way of the Lord that brings suffering in its wake (Mark 8:34; 1 Thess. 3:2–3). Believers are still under assault from powers hostile to God, and suffering comes as 'a necessary component of identifying with Christ's death'.[160] Becoming partners of Christ in suffering in this life promises partnership with Christ in the glory of the next life.

Theology
The new age has come, but the old age of sin and death lingers so that our Christian faith is lived out in the context of trial and suffering. Believers live under a new lordship, but while they live on earth, they 'are still involved in a struggle to manifest this new life' (Käsemann, p. 176). Paul presents the two orientations of setting one's mind according to the flesh or according to the Spirit as irreconcilable alternatives. In the Scriptures Israel is often challenged with 'either–or' conditions: 'either God is Lord or not – Israel cannot limp between two options; either Israel is faithful or faithless – a mixed response to God's call is a negative response'.[161] The purpose behind such language

> is not to describe individual or group behavior so much as to prescribe what the community of faith should be. The language is that of the prophetic call, which is intended to result in decisive commitment that leads into a future of increased faithfulness.[162]

---

160. Wu, *Suffering*, p. 118.
161. Kaylor, *Paul's Covenant Community*, p. 147. He notes, 'Jesus' teaching is filled with either/or statements; there are two gates, two ways, two masters, two treasures between which one must make a decisive choice.'
162. Ibid., p. 148.

This insight suggests that one should interpret the antithesis between flesh and Spirit in verses 4–8 as an implied exhortation. The parallels between these verses and Galatians 5:16–18, a passage that urges a course of conduct, corroborate this view. Believers have been liberated by Christ from sin and the law but live 'in the overlapping of the ages' and 'are still tempted by the flesh'.[163] The imperative in Galatians 5:16 implies that the danger always lurks that believers might choose the flesh and its toxic alloy of sin, death and the law (cf. 1 Cor. 3:1–4; Col. 3:1–4). Therefore, Paul warns that the unavoidable outcome of a flesh-oriented life is death. Schweizer describes this flesh orientation as being 'constrained to live' by one's 'money . . . physical strength or sexual prowess [or attractiveness] . . . learning, art, and poetry, and . . . moral superiority and . . . special piety'.[164] This fact explains Paul's urgent ethical exhortations in his letters. Believers need repeated reminders of their liberation from sin. Paul asserts that with the indwelling Spirit they are no longer pitiable and defenceless slaves to sin. The history of human slavery and colonization reveals that even when set free, the mind often remains tethered psychologically to the past servitude. Paul encourages his audience by affirming that the Spirit gives them the power to overcome their old master and to prevail over sin. Believers may not be able to control the toxic emotions and urges that flood their minds, but the indwelling Spirit of Christ helps quell them and control what they do in response to them. We are still desiring beings, but the Spirit deadens the egotism that covets, which can lead to a profusion of other sins. Edwards helpfully reminds us, 'The idea is one of direction, not perfection; orientation toward a goal if not yet attainment of it' (Edwards, p. 204). The command to the Corinthians, 'Examine yourselves to see whether you are living in the faith. Test yourselves. Do you not realize that Jesus Christ is in you? – unless, indeed, you fail to pass the test!' (2 Cor. 13:5), applies to all believers. Sin can be defeated only under the dominion of the Spirit.

In a short space in 8:9–11, Paul speaks of 'the Spirit of God' living in you (8:9), having 'the Spirit of Christ' (8:9), 'Christ' being

---

163. Lambrecht, 'Implied Exhortation', p. 449.
164. Schweizer, *Holy Spirit*, p. 122.

in you (8:10) and 'the Spirit of him who raised Jesus from the dead' living in you (8:11). This language reveals that Paul thinks of Christ as divine, and it provides the seeds for the later development of trinitarian theology. Paul understands that God sent the Son (8:3; Gal. 4:4), gave him up for all of us and raised him up from the dead (4:25; 8:32; 2 Cor. 5:21), and supplies the Holy Spirit (5:5; 6:19; 2 Cor. 1:22; 5:5; Gal. 3:5; 4:6; 1 Thess. 4:8). The references to the Spirit in this unit make clear that Paul does not think of the Spirit as some featureless, shadowy force. The Spirit is intensely personal. The Spirit is the 'I' of God meeting the 'I' of humans (7:9–25) and transforming their sinful orientation and making a new creation (2 Cor. 5:17). The Spirit and Christ are closely related, but they are not one and the same. In the Old Testament, 'the Spirit of God' 'refers to God himself when he comes to act upon his creation and among his people' and dwell among them.[165] Turner asserts, 'The Spirit is now also thought to act as the dynamic extension of the risen Christ's personality, and activity, as formerly he had been thought to act as God's.'[166] The work of the Spirit is Christ-centred and not only mediates Christ's presence to believers but also frees them from sin's power and delivers and vindicates them in trials (Phil. 1:19).

Paul does not characterize the working of the Spirit's divine power by its astounding ecstatic manifestations but simply as the prime mover in believers' moral lives rather than the prime mover in their ecstatic experiences. It is difficult to describe what an electric charge is, but we are well acquainted with what it does when it interacts with other charges and fields in making possible the electric motors, generators and transformers that underpin modern technology. In the same way, it is difficult to describe the Holy Spirit, but we can see the effects of the Spirit's power in the transformation of our lives that is particularly manifest in the fruit of the Spirit (Gal. 5:22–23).

---

165. Fatehi, *Spirit's Relation*, p. 212.
166. Turner, 'Spirit of Christ', p. 432.

ii. The Spirit as the source of hope in the midst of suffering (8:18–30)

Context

In this unit Paul switches from the positive outlook of the Spirit-empowered life and the promise of being glorified as co-heirs with Christ to the sufferings of this present time. The switch jolts the audience back to the reality of their current circumstances. If Christ has become the heir of all things and God's plans for the world's salvation have reached their pinnacle in his exaltation, Paul must address why believers are still oppressed and dishonoured. If they are saved from God's wrath (5:9), why do they still face so much suffering? Is their suffering God's retribution for their sins? Paul's answer is 'no'. He does not explain why the innocent and faithful suffer. Instead, his answer is that, as incomprehensible and threatening as their suffering is, it does not negate God's purpose to glorify Christ-followers.

Paul supports his assertion in 8:17 that sharing in Christ's suffering ensures sharing in Christ's glory with the thesis statement, introduced by 'for' (*gar*), for the next unit (8:18–30): the present suffering that Christians face because of their faith in Christ does not thwart the future glory that God will reveal in them.[167] Paul develops this thesis through small units that describe the threefold groaning of creation (8:19–22), of believers (8:23–25) and of the Spirit (8:26–27). Believers may live in the realm of the Spirit (8:9), but they still live in physical bodies in a creation that remains in bondage to futility and decay where groaning and travail abound (Godet, p. 313). The conclusion in 8:28–30 affirms that God has set in motion an irrevocable chain of events that will lead to believers' glorification. God has predestined, called, justified and glorified them. Since that chain cannot be broken, the believers' glorification is certain despite appearances when suffering weighs them down.

---

167. Gieniusz, *Romans 8:18–30*, pp. 90–100.

Comment

a. The groaning of creation (8:18–22)

18. Many translations omit the word 'for' (*gar*) that connects this verse to what precedes and serves as a marker that what follows gives support to the previous statement. Paul also repeats the concepts of *sufferings* and *glory*. That believers share Christ's sufferings in the present does not mean that they will not also share his glory in the future. The verb *I consider* (*logizomai*) introduces a proposition that is not obvious. It suggests that after careful evaluation of the matter from the perspective of his faith in Christ Paul has drawn this conclusion and expects that his audience will affirm it after following his argument. He is not saying that the present sufferings are not worth comparing to the future glory that will be revealed in us. That would be obvious. Paul seeks to establish what is not evident by contrasting rather than comparing the present suffering with the future glory. Gieniusz's analysis of the usage of the Greek word *axia* (plural) that normally is translated 'are not worth' concludes that it means instead 'not to have weight *to oppose*'.[168] Paul means that the sufferings that Christians endure in this present age do not have the power to foil the promised glory that is yet to be revealed. The Christian hope of glory is secure.

Suffering can include, among many other things, the pain and fatigue from bodily infirmities and privations, the grief over the deaths of loved ones, and the heaviness that setbacks inflict on the spirit. These things naturally happen to those who are part of the created order that is subject to 'futility' (8:20) and the 'bondage to decay' (8:21). The suffering that Paul has in view, however, is what happens to Christians *because* of their faith in Christ and solidarity with Christ. It is not despite their faithfulness to Christ that they suffer; they suffer because of their faithfulness to Christ. First Peter provides some examples of these afflictions that can beset believers: suspicious slander (1 Pet. 2:12); the ignorance of foolish persons who seek to cause harm (1 Pet. 2:15; 3:13); intimidation (1 Pet. 3:14); accusations and constant challenges to defend their faith (1 Pet.

---

168. Ibid., pp. 90–100.

3:15–16); vilification by former associates (1 Pet. 4:4, 14–16); and ridicule (1 Pet. 4:14, 16). Paul can add many other threats, including the 'sword', the danger of suffering the death penalty (8:35–36). It was not uncommon for people to regard suffering as evidence of God's retribution for some sin (John 9:2), as most clearly demonstrated by the charges levelled against Job by his friends Eliphaz (Job 4:7–8), Bildad (Job 8:20) and Zophar (Job 11:14–17). Outsiders may demean believers because of their suffering, and suffering may cause believers to waver and think that it renders suspect their hope of future glory. Therefore, Paul must assure his audience that their continuing suffering neither signals God's displeasure with them nor dashes their hope of future glory (cf. Col. 3:4).

Paul does not advocate stoic indifference to suffering, because he confesses elsewhere to feeling 'so utterly, unbearably crushed that we despaired of life itself' (2 Cor. 1:8). The suffering that causes such despair requires and receives consolation (2 Cor. 1:3–11). In this passage, however, he is not consoling those who suffer that all will be better in the life to come. Instead, Paul makes the case that believers should not think that their suffering in this life is an ominous sign that forebodes that the glory to come somehow might be denied them. Those who share Christ's sufferings in this life will also share the blessedness of Christ's glorious, resurrected state (Phil. 3:21). God promises to transform their bodies and to reveal their radiant splendour as God's children. This promise is sure and unaltered by their sufferings on earth.

19. The certainty of this hope of glorification remains concealed (8:24), as is evident from the groaning of all creation. Creation is subject to futility and groans in travail (8:20, 22). Paul personifies creation as craning its neck with fervent longing *for the revealing of the children of God*. The word translated *eager longing* is used of those whose circumstances are troublesome and painful.[169] That creation looks ahead to the revealing of God's children and their vindication implies that 'the destinies of humanity and creation are interlocked'.[170]

---

169. Ibid., pp. 176–183.
170. Wu, *Suffering*, p. 137.

What Paul means by *creation* is debated. Interpreters identify it as non-human creation both animate and inanimate, non-human creation plus unbelievers, all humanity, unbelieving humanity alone, or believing humanity alone. The last option can be ruled out since the groaning of creation and of believers are contrasted in 8:22 and 8:23. It cannot refer to all humanity since it cannot be said that the plight is not by their own choice (8:20). Therefore, most interpreters opt for the first meaning, non-human creation (cf. Wis. 2:6; 5:17; 16:24; 19:6). It means that God is not only concerned with the salvation of individuals; God also intends to renew creation.

20. The *futility* of creation can refer to its disorder or inability to fulfil its purpose, making everything seem empty and pointless. *Futility* refers to the dissonance between the way we perceive things should be and the way they really are. 'Vanity of vanities, says the Teacher, / vanity of vanities! All is vanity' appears at the end and beginning of Ecclesiastes (Eccl. 1:2; 12:8) and means that all is not right with God's world but should be. Creation did not come to this state by chance. One has subjected it to futility. The passive voice *was subjected* combined with the phrase *the one who subjected it* points to God as the agent behind this futility. God subjected all things to humans (Gen. 1:28–30; Ps. 8:6–8; 115:16; Heb. 2:5–8), and human rebellion led to the cursing of the ground (Gen. 3:16–17; 5:29). Adam's fall had cosmic consequences (Bruce, p. 169), and its effects continue to be played out in the relationship between God and his rebellious human creatures and the earth itself.[171] Isaiah 24 – 27 provides the primary source for Paul's description of creation's decay and groaning as it suffers the consequences of God's judgment on persistent human sin:

> The earth lies polluted
> > under its inhabitants;
> for they have transgressed laws,
> > violated the statutes,
> > broken the everlasting covenant.
> Therefore a curse devours the earth.
> (Isa. 24:5–6a; cf. 2 Esd. 7:11)

---

171. Moo, 'Romans 8.19–22', pp. 74–89.

The situation is not hopeless. The phrase *in hope* modifies the verb 'to wait with eager longing' that appears in 8:19. Paul's comment *for the creation was subjected . . . by the will of the one who subjected it* is a parenthetical observation inserted between the assertion that creation waits with 'eager longing' 'in hope'. It describes creation's current condition, why it longs eagerly for the revealing of the children of God, and why it groans.

21. As groaning believers have a hope (8:24–26), so does groaning creation.[172] The phrase 'in hope' (8:20) is completed in this verse with a word that is either to be treated as a marker beginning an explanatory clause, 'that', or as a subordinating conjunction marking causality, 'because'. Most translations render it 'in hope that', so that what follows is the content of the hope: *that the creation itself will be set free from its bondage to decay.* 'Because' is the better rendering (KJV, RSV) since the hope refers to God's future action. Because of God's sovereignty there is no doubt that this hope will be realized. Hope in God does not disappoint (5:5). As Thielman insists, 'This is not a hope "that" God will set creation free; it is a firmly grounded hope "because" God will certainly set creation free' (Thielman, p. 404). Captive to corruption and decay, creation longs for liberation and to experience the fulfilment of the hope when God redeems the children of God and reveals their glory. Then, futility (vanity) will become vitality.

22. 'For we know' (CSB) introduces what is accepted as a well-known fact, and Paul uses it to conclude his observations about creation's situation. Two compound verbs, 'groaning together' and 'suffering agony together', are frequently translated as one verb: *groaning in labour pains* (NRSV) or 'groaning as in the pains of childbirth' (NIV).[173] The sense is that creation 'with one accord' groans, which means that every part of creation suffers (Cranfield, I, p. 417). The childbirth experience was conventionally regarded as the most intense pain, and it reads too much into the text to interpret this suffering as giving birth to glory or 'a new heaven and

---

172. Duncan, 'Hope', pp. 411–427.
173. Creation's groaning is reminiscent of the land in 'mourning' (Isa. 24:4, 7; Jer. 4:28; 12:4).

a new earth' (Rev. 21:1). Birth pangs do not always promise a joyous outcome. They could and often did result in stillbirth or the mother's death (1 Sam. 4:19–20; Jer. 4:31). Paul's point, then, is not that suffering gives birth to glory. Instead, he asserts that creation will experience the glory that accompanies the revelation of the children of God *despite* its prolonged suffering. God certainly will set creation free from its bondage, which implies that suffering 'not only does not thwart the future but it cries out for a hope and indeed does not happen without a future view'.[174]

b. The groaning of believers (8:23–25)

23. Even believers who have *the first fruits of the Spirit* groan in this present age. The image of *first fruits* implies that more is to come.[175] Believers have the first portion of the Spirit's pledge guaranteeing their redemption and future glory (cf. 2 Cor. 1:22; 5:5), which is a reminder that their glorification is not yet fully realized. Therefore, they must wait expectantly (8:25; 1 Cor. 1:7; Gal. 5:5; Phil. 3:20; Heb. 9:28) like creation (8:19). Moo comments, 'It is *because* we possess the Spirit as the first installment and pledge of our complete salvation that we groan, yearning for the fulfillment of that salvation to take place' (Moo, pp. 542–543). The groaning is a derivative of hope.

Paul uses the verb 'to groan' in 2 Corinthians 5:2, 4 to refer to groaning to be clothed with the resurrection body ('with our heavenly dwelling'). It is in the context of Paul's catalogue of afflictions where he says that he is 'always being given up to death for Jesus' sake' (2 Cor. 4:8–11). Nevertheless, he does 'not lose heart' because he knows that 'this slight momentary affliction is preparing us for an eternal weight of glory beyond all measure' (2 Cor. 4:16–17). In

---

174. Gieniusz, *Romans 8:18–30*, p. 161.

175. The word *first fruits* could also mean 'birth certificate' (BDAG, p. 98), which would complement the statement 'The Spirit himself testifies with our spirit that we are God's children' (8:16, NIV; cf. *TLNT* I, pp. 148–150). Paul uses the word six other times, however, to refer to the first fruits of the harvest (cf. 11:16; 16:5; 1 Cor. 15:20, 23; 16:15; 2 Thess. 2:13).

the context of believers in the Graeco-Roman world, the frustration and suffering that mark life for persecuted Christians in this present age also incite the groaning that longs for the promised redemption. Groaning refers to involuntary sounds made under the weight of aching distress that serve as a wordless supplication to God for deliverance. Such groaning does not arise from hopelessness, misgivings or creaturely angst, but from a sure hope that longs to reach the state of perfect redemption.

24–25. Believers can endure their suffering only in *hope*. Hope does not focus on things that 'occupy the present' but trusts in 'the One who holds the future' (Edwards, p. 216). Their suffering does not mean that believers are not the children of God, as the casual observer might presume. The natives of Malta, for example, falsely assumed that when a viper sank its fangs into Paul, it must be because he was a murderer. He had escaped peril on the sea, but 'justice has not allowed him to live' (Acts 28:4). The true status of Christ-followers cannot be 'seen' from empirical observations. Only the eyes of faith see what others cannot see – Jesus being glorified in his suffering on the cross; the glory of God shining through the cracks of clay jars that have been buffeted by afflictions (2 Cor. 4:6–18). Käsemann captures the gist of what Paul is driving at: 'Assurance of salvation is not salvation secured. Faith always remains hope, even when earth seems to offer no hope' (Käsemann, p. 238). The statement *if we hope for what we do not see, we wait for it with patience* contains an implicit exhortation that Paul articulates in 12:12: 'Rejoice in hope, be patient in suffering, persevere in prayer.' Their salvation is secure, and it is nearer to them now than when they first believed (13:11). Yet the darkness that cloaks the world has not completely faded.

c. The groaning of the Spirit (8:26–27)

26. *Likewise* means that just as hope upholds believers undergoing suffering, so the Spirit also helps them. Creation groans, believers groan, and the Spirit groans with sighs that defy articulation in intelligible human words. Paul pictures a situation in which believers try to pray but only emit groans because of the pain of suffering that has no vocabulary to describe its intensity. They are helpless even in praying to God for help. Since the Spirit dwells in believers (8:9–11), they have a divine intercessor who comes to their aid. The verb translated *helps* means to take hold together with another (cf. Luke 10:40). The image means that believers do not sit on the sidelines while the Spirit does all the work. The Spirit aids us *in our weakness* by imparting a power that we do not have so that we can carry a share of the load. Nevertheless, the Spirit does get the short end of the stick, so to speak, and does the heavy lifting.

Not knowing what to pray as we ought has nothing to do with not knowing the right words or techniques. It is not that believers do not know *how* to pray, but they are in situations where they do not know *what* to pray. *Our weakness* refers to the limited capacity to understand (6:19) since we know only in part and see through a mirror indirectly (1 Cor. 13:9, 12). We do not understand the whys and wherefores of what God intends for us as we go through suffering. The purpose of suffering seems inscrutable, since none of us has a transcendent observation post. Consequently, we cannot discern what to pray *as we ought*. Believers do not know what they need and also are prone in their ignorance of God's will to try to impose their will on God. Jesus' response to the request of James and John to sit at his right hand in glory, 'You do not know what you are asking' (Mark 10:37–38), would be an appropriate response to many of our prayer requests. Paul himself learned from God's answer to his anguished prayers for the thorn in his flesh to be removed that God's purpose for him was quite different (2 Cor. 12:7–10). To those encountering suffering because of their commitment to Christ and who do not know what to pray, Paul assures them that their sighing and groaning is sufficient. The Spirit becomes the translator of their sighs and cries before God. The Spirit does not convey what believers think they need, since they do not know what to pray, 'but what they really need' (Thielman, p. 408).

27. Paul asserts that the Spirit takes anguished groans and expresses the cry for help far more effectively than an articulated prayer.[176] The Spirit knows the thoughts (1 Cor. 2:11) and the will

---

176. Cf. John 14:16, 26; 15:26; 16:7; 1 John 2:1.

of God and intercedes for us in accordance with God's will. It is not a one-way prayer, however, from the believer through the Spirit to God. A reciprocal interaction transpires. Through the Spirit who dwells in the believer's innermost being, God can communicate his will to the believer. When we stop our attempts at eloquence in prayer and listen to the Spirit praying in us, a new doorway opens between heaven and earth that allows us to receive what God has to say and to give to us. Paul's primary aim is not to theologize about the nature of prayer. In the context, he wants to communicate to his audience that 'our sufferings in the present time . . . are neither a penalty for nor proof of our ungodliness but only an occasion in which we experience the presence and the assistance of God's Spirit himself'.[177] Lamentation can be transformed into the assurance of security in God's eternal love.

Since Paul writes from Corinth, it is tempting to see in 'wordless groans' a reference to glossolalia and praying with the spirit and not with the mind (1 Cor. 14:14–15).[178] If so, Paul would not regard glossolalia as a sign that one had reached a higher spiritual plane but as a sign of one's weakness. Glossolalia is not 'groans' but 'speech that is not intelligible' (1 Cor. 14:9). Also, in this context, Paul does not have in mind a charismatic gift that only some believers might possess. He is speaking of the circumstances of suffering that can unsettle afflicted believers so that they produce only agonized groans as stammered prayers. Furthermore, the Spirit's groanings are in the divine sphere. They do not need the believer's voice box, and they are understood only by God, not by a human interpreter (1 Cor. 14:27).

d. The certainty of salvation: all things work to the good for those whom God has called (8:28–30)

28. Christians may not know what to pray in times of severe stress, but they can know that all things work together for good. Plato claimed,

---

177. Gieniusz, *Romans 8:18–30*, p. 220.
178. Cf. Fee, *Empowering*, pp. 575–586.

> This must be our notion of the just man, that even when he is in
> poverty or sickness, or any other seeming misfortune, all things will in
> the end work together for good to him in life and death: for the gods
> have a care for any whose desire is to become just and to be like God.
> (*Resp.* 10.613; cited by Edwards, p. 217)

Paul does not apply this statement to 'the just man', nor does he apply it to any person. It is not a trite cliché that means we should not despair because every cloud has a silver lining, or that every sad or unpleasant thing that might happen to one ultimately results in something good. This statement is valid only *for those who love God* (Exod. 20:6; Deut. 5:10; 6:5; 7:9; 1 Cor. 2:9) and *are called according to his purpose*, which is a description of those who belong to the people of God. What needs clarification is what Paul means by *work together*, *all things* and *good*.

One can read the subject of the verb *work together* as 'he works together', referring to God. A textual variant with significant support adds 'God' as the subject.[179] While most reject it as the original reading, it represents an early interpretation that God is the one who causes all things to work together for good (NIV, NASB, NJB) since God has sovereign power over all things, and God achieves his purpose in all things. Since the verb *work together* implies collaboration, one can interpret Paul to mean that God directs all things to work conjointly towards our good. The collaborator also could be the Spirit, who not only intercedes for 'the saints' (8:26–27) but also works together with God for their good.[180]

The word order in the Greek, however, suggests that the subject of the verb is *all things* (a neuter plural taking a third-person singular verb): *all things work together for good* (NRSV, ESV, CSB). *All things* in the context refers not to everything that may happen to a person but specifically to the sufferings of those who love God (8:18, 35–39; cf. 5:3–4). It would include all the terrifying things cited in 8:35 — hardship, distress, persecution, famine, nakedness, peril and the

---

179. P⁴⁶ A B 81 cop^{sa} Origen^{gr2/5}.
180. Gignilliat, 'Working', pp. 511–515.

sword – that can endanger believers because of their faith. The statement assures believers who withstand 'the sufferings of this present time' (8:18) that the evil that others intend for them cannot sabotage the *good* that God has predestined for them (cf. Gen. 50:20).

The *good* does not refer to what humans conventionally regard as good – the things they may believe make for happiness, such as health, wealth and comfort. The *good* refers to the believers' final redemption so that they might be glorified with Christ (8:17–18, 21, 30). Paul assures his audience that even the most harrowing and heart-rending things that can happen to believers do not jeopardize the glory that God promises them as co-heirs with Christ. Their suffering produces 'endurance', which produces 'character', which produces 'hope', which will not fail (5:3–5). As they are co-sufferers with Christ, their sufferings only draw them nearer to God (cf. Phil. 1:12–14, 19–24) and to ever closer conformity to the image of his Son (8:29; 2 Cor. 4:8–18; Phil. 3:10–11; 1 Pet. 4:13).

29. The word 'because' (*For*) presents the basis for the assurance that all things work together for good. God's foreknowledge means that God had a blueprint of what was to be accomplished (Isa. 37:26; cf. 2 Esd. 6:1–6). This predetermined plan (Acts 2:23) is 'the mystery that was kept secret for long ages' (16:25; cf. 1 Cor. 2:7; Eph. 3:9; Col. 1:26; Titus 1:2–3) that has now been revealed in Christ. Here, foreknowledge refers to God's knowledge of individual believers before the foundation of the world (Dunn, I, pp. 482–483). The word 'highlights God's covenant love and affection for those whom he has chosen' (Schreiner, p. 445).

Predestined refers to God's eternal power to accomplish this foreordained plan. While being 'called according to [God's] purpose' (8:28) suggests that salvation does not hinge on our choosing God but on God's choice of us (Eph. 1:4–5, 11–12; 1 Thess. 5:9; 1 Pet. 1:2), it has nothing to do with whether individuals have been predestined for heaven or hell. It means that they have been marked out as God's children to grow into the image of God's Son (Bruce, p. 176). Believers in a situation of suffering and persecution need encouragement. *Predestined* here refers to God knowing something in advance and affirms that God 'always had a plan to get believers to the finish line, working all things together for good' (Witherington, p. 228). It means that their glorious destiny 'is firmly set' in God's purposes (Wright, p. 602), and no power on earth or in the heavens can dislodge it.

Our deformed humanity will experience a radical transformation and will be reformed into those conformed to Christ. Our hope is that God predestined us to enjoy in the future the glory of resurrected and transformed bodies like that which Christ now has. Being *conformed to the image of [God's] Son* also is relevant for this earthly life (12:2). To 'know Christ and the power of his resurrection' does not mean that one can now escape trouble; just the opposite. It means sharing 'his sufferings by becoming like him in his death' (Phil. 3:10). Being 'conformed', then, does not mean 'being like' Christ but being united with Christ in sharing his experiences (8:17) and being immersed into his death and 'united with him in the likeness of his death' (6:4–5, CSB).[181] *Firstborn* signifies Christ's pre-eminence over all creation (Col. 1:18), his authority as God's preferential heir, and, here, his solidarity with the large company of believers who will be glorified with him.

30. At the end of his argument Paul affirms that his opening proposition in 8:18 is proven. Despite their current suffering, the believers' glorification is certain. He repeats the last word of a clause as the first word of the next clause (anadiplosis) to create a powerful rhetorical progression that underscores how God directs the process of salvation to bring his people to their final glory with Christ that God had determined beforehand. God foreknew, predestined, called, justified (considered righteous) and glorified believers. The aorist tense of the verb *he . . . glorified* represents a future act as something that is already accomplished since God has already determined that this glorification will happen.

Theology
Bauckham contends, 'For just as creation waits, so do believers; just as creation is to be set free, so will believers; just as creation groans,

---

181. J. Kürzinger, 'Συμμόρφους', *TDNT* V, pp. 294–299.

so do believers. The two are bound up together in the same story.' However, an imbalance between these two characters exists in that 'creation . . . is the innocent victim of human wrongdoing'.[182] Creation was not made wrong but went wrong when humans brought creation down with them with their sin. Humans continue to debase creation when they use it for purposes for which it was not made. God did not create the chemical and physical properties of the elements listed in the periodic table so that humans might create bombs to blow people up, to poison others, or to degrade the environment with acid rain, deforestation and the warming of the oceans. This degradation of creation affects all living things. Creation's future, however, is tied to the future revelation and glorification of the children of God. Paul asserts that God is faithful to the whole of creation and is as concerned with the redemption of creation as with the redemption of human beings. God will not abandon creation on the last day but will redeem it by reconciling everything, whether things on earth or things in heaven, to himself through Christ (Col. 1:20).

Moltmann is on target in stating that 'there is no fellowship with Christ without fellowship with the earth. Love for Christ and hope for him embrace love and hope for the earth.'[183] If God placed the first humans in the Garden of Eden 'to work it and take care of it' (Gen. 2:15, NIV), then Christians are to be engaged in caring for creation as well as being engaged in God's purpose to redeem humanity. Both tasks seek to make the world a healthier place in which God can be glorified.

Paul's primary purpose in this unit, however, is to encourage and comfort believers trying to navigate their lives in the shoal waters of persecution and suffering. Being in Christ does not diminish the misery caused by suffering, but it 'makes it infinitely more bearable' (Dunn, I, p. 435). It is important to note that believers do not pray to whatever power might be out there that cares about their situation, but to one they can address intimately as 'Abba, Father'. Since prayer is believers' communication with the

---

182. Bauckham, 'Story', p. 93.
183. Moltmann, *Coming*, p. 279.

divine realm, they have a direct communication channel through the Spirit who knows their mind and God who knows the Spirit's mind. 'We do not know how to pray' (8:26) does not refer to prayers of praise, thanksgiving and repentance, but to prayers when we are in a desperate situation.

The situation of suffering from persecution causes Christians to pray with groans and sighs (8:23, 26). These prayers remain under the yoke of not knowing, of weakness and poverty, so that even in our prayers we live only by God's justification of sinners (Cranfield, I, p. 422). Many times, however, believers use prayer as if it could automatically summon the ruler of the universe to alleviate suffering or ill-health. The prayer that Jesus taught his disciples to pray contains no plea for God to change the adverse situations in the petitioner's life. We pray that God's kingdom might come. At other times, believers in times of stress might pray for strength to endure as if God could dispense a magic pill that immediately imparts strength. Such a prayer ignores the fact that one builds up strength only from a regular regimen of struggling against hurdles. In Gethsemane, Jesus did not pray for strength to face what lay before him but for God's will to be done.

Times arise in the lives of believers when they do not know what to pray except to cry out with deep, inarticulate sounds. Frederick Douglass (1818–96) escaped from slavery and fled to the northern area of the USA where he became famous for his eloquence as a national leader of the abolitionist movement. He describes in his autobiography the groaning of slaves under the burden of suffering. He recalls the slaves selected to go to 'the Great House Farm' to receive the monthly allowance for themselves and their fellow slaves. The woods would 'reverberate with their wild songs, revealing at once the highest joy and the deepest sadness'. He continues:

> I did not, when a slave, understand the deep meaning of those rude and apparently incoherent songs . . . They told a tale of woe which was then altogether beyond my feeble comprehension . . . they were tones loud, long, and deep; they breathed the prayer and complaint of souls boiling over with the bitterest anguish. Every tone was a testimony against slavery, and a prayer to God for deliverance from chains. The hearing

of those wild notes always depressed my spirit, and filled me with
ineffable sadness. I have frequently found myself in tears while hearing
them.[184]

Paul assures believers that God hears their prayers uttered in
crushing distress. The Spirit interprets these groans to God, but
the communication is two-way. The Spirit also communicates
God's will to us. Wink contends, 'We learn to pray by stopping the
attempt and simply *listening* to the prayer already being prayed in us.
And what we hear is a strange kind of help. The Spirit groans in us
inarticulately, wordlessly.'[185] While answers may vary for different
believers according to their different circumstances and God's
purposes, one answer from God is constant whatever their situation. God promises a greater deliverance than they know how to
pray for or could even imagine. Believers will be conformed to the
glorious image of God's Son (8:29; cf. 1 Cor. 15:49). In the resurrection, God promises that 'the body of our humiliation', subject
as it is to the slings and arrows of this mortal life, will be transformed 'so that it may be conformed to the body of his [Christ's]
glory, by the power that also enables him to make all things subject
to himself' (Phil. 3:21).

F. The assurance of victory through Christ's love (8:31–39)

Context

The conclusion to this large section contains parallels with the
bridge passage in 5:1–11 with its mention of justification (5:1; 8:33);
suffering (5:3; 8:35–37); God's/Christ's love (5:5; 8:35); Christ's death
(5:6, 10; 8:34); being saved from wrath/condemnation (5:9; 8:33–34);
Christ's resurrection (5:10; 8:34); and boasting in the Lord (5:11;
8:37). Paul raises four questions whose answers recapitulate the
chief implications of what precedes. 'If God is for us, who can be
against us?' (8:31, NIV). 'Who will bring any charge against God's
elect?' (8:33). 'Who is to condemn?' (8:34). 'Who will separate us

---

184. Douglass, *Narrative*, pp. 13–14.
185. Wink, *Engaging the Powers*, p. 305.

from the love of Christ?' (8:35). With a grand flourish, Paul catalogues the gamut of powers and afflictions that might seem able to set believers adrift from God's love and to thwart the glory that God has determined to bestow on them, to press home the point that nothing in all creation can do so.[186] The answers to the questions, which he expects his audience would be able to provide themselves, is intended to evoke an uplifting emotional response. Though believers may face the depths of suffering in the present, they can boast in God from whom they have received peace, reconciliation and the fullest outpouring of God's love through Jesus Christ their Lord that assures them that their hope of the glory of God is secure (5:1–11). God's love has conquered all things through Jesus Christ, and through Jesus Christ will give believers all things.

Comment

31. *Who is against us?* Persecuted Christians might answer, 'There is no shortage of enemies who have risen up against us.' A vast array of earthly foes and cosmic arch-enemies are deployed to strike down Christ's followers. Believers, however, need not fear them. When Elisha's ministering servant quivered in terror at the sight of the Syrian army surrounding them, the prophet responded, 'Be strong and of good courage. Do not be afraid or dismayed before the king of Assyria and all the horde that is with him; for there is one greater with us than with him' (2 Chr. 32:7). Paul goes further. God is the creator of all things through Christ (11:36; 1 Cor. 8:6; Eph. 3:9; Col. 1:16), and all things are subject to God (1 Cor. 15:28; Phil. 3:21). The phrase *if God is for us* might better be translated 'since God is for us'. Whoever or whatever it is that might wage war against God's people makes no difference. No matter how powerful or terrifying the enemies might seem to be, they cannot mobilize enough forces to defeat them. God our redeemer (Ps. 34:19) will deliver us, because God's love for us, manifest in sending Christ

---

186. Scholars often note that Greek and Latin moralists also catalogue things that can impede one from following the path of virtue, but Paul's answers to these threats is distinctively Christian.

Jesus to die for us, and God's power, manifest in raising him from
the dead, assure our salvation.

32. Paul reiterates what God has done on behalf of believers.
First, God did not spare his Son, the greatest imaginable sacrifice
a father could make. The word *withhold* ('spare') also occurs in
Genesis 22:12. Some think that Paul alludes to Abraham's willingness not to spare his son Isaac. If Paul does so, it is only to make
the case that giving up one's cherished son is the supreme act of
sacrifice. What God did with his Son, however, was significantly
different from what Abraham was willing to do. Isaac was not to
be sacrificed *for* others, and the idea of vicarious atonement is not
to be found in any interpretations of the biblical account of this
story in pre-Christian Judaism (Fitzmyer, p. 531). According to 4
Maccabees 13:12, Abraham was willing to sacrifice Isaac for the
sake of 'godliness' or 'piety', not to atone for anyone's sins. Also, no
ram, caught in a thicket, suddenly appears as a substitute sacrifice
to save God's Son from death as it does in the Isaac story (Gen.
22:13). 'The blood of bulls and goats' or rams and calves is
insufficient 'to take away sins' (Heb. 10:4). Paul has written that
God sent his Son as a sin offering (8:3) and put him 'forward as a
sacrifice of atonement by his blood' (3:25) to effect eternal redemption for believers.

Second, God gave Christ Jesus up, presumably, to the powers of
sin and death (4:25; 1 Cor. 2:8; Col. 2:14–15) to bring about their
defeat. Paul's conclusion from this action leads to his third point.
The extreme cost of not sparing his own Son from death and
handing him over *for all of us* provides convincing evidence that
God will follow through on what is far less costly, giving us 'all
things' (NIV). 'All things' refers to 'all that is necessary for our salvation' (Sanday and Headlam, p. 219) and our glorification (8:30).
One should not connect 'all things' to so-called material blessings.
In the context, 'all things' refers to what God has done '"for us" *in
the present* because of what he has already done "for us all" through
the work of Christ *in the past*' (Longenecker, p. 755).

33–34. One could punctuate the answers to the two questions
in these verses also as questions: 'Who will bring any charge against
God's elect? Is it God?' 'Who is to condemn? Is it Christ Jesus?'
(Barrett, pp. 172–173). Answering questions with questions is a

common trait of rabbis. In this case, the counter-questions would dismiss the first questions as totally absurd. It is more likely, however, that Paul's responses to the questions follow the pattern in Isaiah 50:7–9. Isaiah answers the questions 'Who will contend with me?' and 'Who are my adversaries?' with an assertion about God, not with another question. Paul does the same thing here. He responds to the questions with theological assertions. If any would raise accusations against God's elect (cf. Rev. 12:10), God, the final judge, has already acquitted them (5:1). If any, such as Satan (Job 1 – 2; Zech. 3:1), would try to condemn God's elect, Christ Jesus has already died for them and sits enthroned at God's right hand (Ps. 110:1) interceding on their behalf (cf. Isa. 53:12; Heb. 9:24; 1 John 2:1). The answers to the questions reaffirm the opening statement in 8:1, 'There is therefore now no condemnation for those who are in Christ Jesus', and make it clear that none could ever dare to stand up before God's throne to condemn those who have died with God's Son.

35. Since none can accuse and none can condemn God's elect, Paul insists that nothing, not even suffering, can separate believers from Christ's love. He itemizes seven afflictions that may cause some in the hollows of momentary despair to believe that God has abandoned them (cf. Ps. 22:1–2). The list of adversities serves to reinforce the case that nothing ultimately imperils God's promise to glorify them with Christ. The list is not hypothetical. Paul and many other Christians have faced *persecution* (1 Thess. 3:2–4; 2 Thess. 1:4) that led to *famine* (being 'without food', 2 Cor. 11:27); *nakedness*, which is an example of utter poverty (Matt. 25:36; Jas 2:15; 2 Cor. 11:27); 'afflictions' that cause inward *distress* (2 Cor. 6:4; 12:10); ever-present *peril* or 'danger' (1 Cor. 15:30; 2 Cor. 11:26); and the ultimate penalty, the *sword*, a metonym for execution (Acts 12:2; Heb. 11:37).

The later Mishnaic tractate 'Abot 5:8–9 lists seven kinds of retribution for seven classes of transgressions (cf. Sir. 39:28–31; LAB 3:9). It claims that three different levels of 'famine' cause drought and tumult because of the failure to pay various prescribed tithes. 'Pestilence' comes from the failure to bring death-penalty cases before the court. The 'sword' comes from delaying justice. Horrible 'beasts' afflict the world because of false swearing and profaning the sacred name Yahweh that it was forbidden to pronounce. 'Captivity' (exile) comes from idolatry, incest and bloodshed. The assumption behind these assertions is that various forms of suffering are God's proportionate punishment for sins. Paul's theological perspective on suffering is starkly different. First, he insists that the afflictions believers might face are *not* punishments for sin. Second, he insists that nothing that might happen to believers can terminate Christ's love for them or exclude them from participating in Christ's glory to be manifest at the end of the age. Christians are not to ask if they have done something that has brought such misfortune upon them. What has brought about their suffering is publicly living out their faith in Christ. That faith also gives them the assurance that Christ's love for them is unwavering and everlasting.

36. Paul supports this last assertion with a quote from Psalm 44:22 (43:23, LXX). The sheep of God's pasture (Ps. 100:3) are being slaughtered (Zech. 11:4, 7). The psalmist protests loudly against the suffering of those who have not forgotten God and have not been false to God's covenant (Ps. 44:17). It seems so inexplicably undeserved since God knows the secrets of their hearts and that these victims are innocent (Ps. 44:21). Why did Paul think that this text was apropos? First, it affirms the innocence of believers. Their unrelenting suffering (*all day*) has not come upon them as punishment for their sin. Why they are *accounted* ('reckoned') as sheep to be slaughtered is not answered because the answer resides in God's purposes that remain hidden and beyond human understanding. All that can be said is that the sufferings manifest solidarity with the sufferings of Christ, who also suffered as one who was innocent (8:17; cf. Isa. 53:7; Luke 23:41, 47; Acts 8:32–35).

Second, the psalm's 'function is not to assert that the people of Christ suffer, but rather (presupposing that this is the case) to ask whether those sufferings can have the effect of separating Christ's people from his love'.[187] Allen asserts,

The psalmist's despairing note of complaint is replaced by the Apostle's exultant tones of assurance. Persecution does not obstruct God's

---

187. Starling, 'For Your Sake', p. 115.

purposes, but [is] His appointed way for His people. As for the Servant of the Lord, so for His followers, the Cross is but the precursor of the crown.[188]

37. Paul wraps affirmations of God's love that will transform tribulations into the greatest victory around the list of the most ruinous things that can happen to us in this earthly life. Paul coins a novel word in Greek to describe it: 'super-conquering' (*hypernikōmen*). The victory does not occur by smashing the enemy through violent means but through the giving of life in love. Such love that so values sinners to forgive them and promises to raise them in glory is not something that Paul's audience, especially the slaves, had ever experienced. Consequently, they must be continually reminded of it.

38–39. Paul lists contrasting pairs to cover a range of threats to and enemies of God's elect that are weaponless when set against God's steadfast love. *Death*, the tool of sin, may still plague humanity, but it will be defeated as the last enemy (1 Cor. 15:26, 51–55). *Life* encompasses everything that happens to us in our daily existence, the cares of the world and its lures (Mark 4:19), or the problems that weigh us down and bring grief upon grief that sometimes make people wish for death. *Angels* are not the messengers of glad tidings but refer to the spiritual forces of evil in the heavenly realms (cf. 1 En. 6 – 8) who deceive and torment. Paul says that Satan can disguise himself as an angel of light (2 Cor. 11:14; cf. 2 Cor. 12:7). *Rulers* may refer to 'the powers of this dark world' (Eph. 6:12, NIV) against whom believers must contend. Paul affirms that Christ will conquer these angels and rulers (1 Cor. 15:24; cf. Eph. 1:21; 1 Pet. 3:22) and promises that God will shortly crush Satan, however he is manifested, under the believers' feet (16:20; cf. 1 Cor. 15:25, 27; Eph. 1:22; Heb. 1:13). *Things present* and *things to come* reflect the volatility of the present and the unpredictability of the future.

Height (*hypsōma*) and *depth* (*bathos*) could be spatial terms encompassing the whole universe (cf. 10:6–7). The same terms appear in Isaiah 7:11, 'Ask a sign of the LORD your God; let it be deep as

---

188. Allen, 'Old Testament', pp. 22–23.

Sheol or high as heaven', representing the outermost limits. As he refers to differences in time, so Paul may now refer to differences in place, as the psalmist says:

> If I ascend to heaven, you are there;
> if I make my bed in Sheol, you are there.
> (Ps. 139:8)

Paul may mean that there is no physical limit to the reach of God's love in Christ Jesus. In the context, however, Paul itemizes things that might seem to pose a threat to believers on earth. It is difficult to see how height, what is high in relation to the earth, and depth, what is low in relation to the earth, pose a threat to God's love. Christians are not raised to the heights and do not fear being cast into the abyss. It is possible, therefore, that Paul utilizes the terms *height* and *depth* in the Roman context to refer to the highest point and lowest point in the movements and relative positions of celestial bodies that the pseudoscience of astrology presumed influenced human affairs. Some dismiss this reading because Paul does not use the precise terminology found in the astrological texts (*hypsōma/tapeinōma*). One can argue, however, that it is unlikely that Paul had read such texts. The term he uses for *height* was related to the stars gaining altitude in their courses as an astrological sign (Plutarch, *Mor.* 149a). Paul may have deliberately avoided the astrological term for the celestial space below earth's horizon from which the stars arise (*tapeinōma*), because he uses the cognate terms (*tapeinos*, 12:8; 2 Cor. 10:1; and *tapeinosophrynē*, Eph. 4:2; Phil. 2:3; Col. 3:12) with the positive connotation of humility. Paul does not assume that the powers that rule the motions of the stars in the heavens really have any power over human life, but he must have been aware that many were persuaded that astrological powers did determine their fate. Marcus Manilius, a first-century Roman poet and supposed author of *Astronomica*, describes how the twelve sections of the heavens governed twelve sections of human life: home, war, business, law, marriage, wealth, dangers, social class, children, character, health and success (Book 2). Robbins asserts in his introduction to *his translation of Tetrabiblos* by Claudius Ptolemy, 'With few exceptions, everyone, from emperor to the lowest slave, believed in it [astrology]."[189] Since Julius Caesar ignored the augers warning him not to enter the senate on the ides of March, his successors, Augustus, Tiberius, Claudius and Nero, took the portents of the zodiac and the rising and setting of constellations outside the zodiac far more seriously. It is still quite possible that Paul wants to allay the fears of those who believed that astrological powers controlled their fate and could separate them from God's love by insisting that the destiny of believers is determined only by God, not by the celestial bodies God created.

In case he missed something that humans might deem threatening, Paul finishes by discounting the threat of *anything else in all creation*, whatever humans might imagine that power to be. Nothing can separate *us* from God's love that has been revealed through Christ Jesus our Lord. Paul mentioned God's love first in 5:5, 8 at the beginning of this section, and he now appeals to it at its conclusion. This last statement affirms that God's love cannot be known apart from Christ, and it is only the cross that shows what God's love really is (Morris, p. 342).

Theology

From a human vantage point, life seems so fragile. All will be touched by the pain of losing loved ones and must face the reality of their own deaths and the anguish of suffering. Paul responds to this reality from God's vantage point. God's love and power overcome death and will glorify believers with Christ whom he raised from death. Therefore, he assures Christ-followers that they have a sure hope even in the thick of suffering when others might think all is hopeless. Paul does not dismiss suffering as a mere trifle compared with the glory to come. The afflictions are not trifling. Paul argues instead that God has not promised believers immunity from suffering in this age, and when they suffer for their faith in Christ they should not let the shadows of world-weariness darken their hope in God.

The unwarranted suffering of the faithful can create personal and communal crises even for believers. Everything that used to

---

189. Robbins, in Ptolemy, *Tetrabiblos*, p. xi.

make sense of life collapses and casts doubt on their sense of having a secure relationship with God. Is it as secure as they believed? The context of Paul's assertions in this unit seems to be the futility under which all existence on earth has been placed since the fall (8:20). Scientific and technological advances that deal with problems only in a piecemeal fashion are not the answer. The only cure is God's renewal of the earth and glorification of the redeemed at the end of the age (8:19, 23). In the meantime, the worst earthly trials cannot break the bond of love between God and his children. Even when God's sheep suffer,

> The LORD is good and his love endures for ever;
>   his faithfulness continues through all generations.
> (Ps. 100:5, NIV)

John on Patmos sees Jesus enthroned in heaven as a 'slaughtered' lamb who is worthy 'to receive power and wealth and wisdom and might and honour and glory and blessing' (Rev. 5:6, 9, 12). In sharing Christ's humiliation and suffering, believers will certainly share in his glory.

5. GOD'S FAITHFULNESS TO ISRAEL AND THE INTERLOCKING DESTINY OF ISRAEL AND THE GENTILES IN SALVATION (9:1 – 11:36)

Some interpreters have found chapters 9–11 to be a burdensome addition to an otherwise fine epistle. Beare expresses this negative sentiment:

> We cannot feel that the apostle is at his best here, and we are inclined to ask if he has not got himself into inextricable (and needless) difficulties by attempting to salvage some vestige of racial privilege for the historic Israel – Israel 'according to the flesh' – in spite of his own fundamental position that all men are in the same position before God.[1]

Others try to get rid of what they think is a curious aside and an anomalous reversion to Jewish-Christian thought that is not an integral part of the main argument by dismissing it as an excursus or later interpolation. Such readings of this section are wrongheaded.

---

1. Beare, *St. Paul*, pp. 103–104.

Since chapters 9–11 contain one-third of the theological body of the letter, it is unlikely that Paul is going off on a tangent. This section carries over terms from the previous chapter and develops them as they pertain to Israel. References to the 'children of God' (8:14, 19, 21; 9:7–8, 26), 'adoption' (8:15, 23; 9:4), God's calling (8:28, 30; 9:7, 12, 24–26), God's election of a people (8:33; 11:5, 7, 28), God's love (8:35, 37, 39; 9:13, 25; 11:28) and being saved (8:24; 9:27; 10:9, 13; 11:14, 26) all resurface. What makes this section unique among Paul's letters is the extensive (nearly forty) citations of Scripture passages. They cover the broad sweep of Israel's history, from the celebrated narrative of their creation and election, to their deliverance from Pharaoh, to their persistent rebellion against God, to God's preservation of a remnant among them, to their present hardening and refusal to believe the gospel about Christ, to their ultimate salvation.

Paul's acknowledgment of his heartache over Israel's unbelief (9:1–5) and his ardent desire that his Jewish kindred who have stumbled so badly be saved reveals that these chapters do not contain his dispassionate analysis of Israel's fate. He is emotionally invested. In lamenting the current unbelief of his kinfolk, he wishes that his brothers and sisters in the flesh might become his brothers and sisters in the Spirit. He finds comfort in the Scriptures where he finds revealed God's plan for the salvation of humankind. He sums it up in 11:32: 'For God has imprisoned all in disobedience so that he may be merciful to all.'

At the beginning of the letter, Paul connects the gospel to what God 'promised beforehand through his prophets in the holy scriptures' (1:2). At the end of the letter, he states that 'the revelation of the mystery', which he has unveiled in what precedes, 'was kept secret for long ages but is now disclosed, and through the prophetic writings is made known to all the Gentiles, according to the command of the eternal God, to bring about the obedience of faith' (16:25–26). Therefore, his interpretation of the Scriptures drives and supports his arguments that Israel remains God's people despite being reduced to a remnant. It also substantiates that God planned for Gentiles to be included in the people of God. The present and future status of Israel, however, is the main topic of this section, which centres on answering three vexing questions. If

Israel is lost and in need of salvation (10:1), has the word of God failed (9:6)? Why did Gentiles who did not pursue right-eousness obtain it, while Israel zealously pursued the law of righteousness and did not obtain it (9:30–32)? Has God rejected his people (11:1)?

A. God's sovereign freedom in dealing with Israel and the nations: hardening and mercy (9:1–29)

Context

The statement in 9:6a, 'It is not as though the word of God had failed', introduces the pressing issue that is addressed in this first unit and one of the central themes of chapters 9–11. Paul raised a similar question in 3:3. Did the unfaithfulness of 'some' Jews call into question the reliability of God's promises? 'Will their faithlessness nullify the faithfulness of God?' Paul answered with a resounding 'No!' and cited Psalm 51:4 to buttress this response:

> So that you may be proved right when you speak
> and prevail when you judge.
> (3:4, NIV)

He fleshes out this answer and his substantiation of God's right-eousness, faithfulness and integrity in chapters 9–11. The word of God *has not failed*.

The shift from the extended list of Israel's privileges in 9:4–5 to the list of grievances that follows suggests that something has gone terribly wrong for Israel. His discussion of the remnant in 9:6–29 discloses that when he referred in 3:3 to 'some' Jews who have been unfaithful he did not have in mind only a few. He regards most Jews in his day to be unfaithful because of their current rejection of God's Son. The majority refuse to submit to God's righteousness (10:3), persist in disobedience (10:21; 11:30–31) and stumble about in a spiritual stupor (11:8). They are so hardened in their disobedience (11:25) and unbelief (11:20, 23) that they have become enemies of God (11:28). Nevertheless, God has preserved a remnant in Israel, and much to the chagrin of many Jews zealous for the law, God incongruously has shown mercy to the Gentiles. Gentiles who have accepted by faith the offer of salvation in the death and resurrection of Christ have been incorporated into God's people without meeting the prerequisites of being circumcised and coming under the law.

In 9:6–29 Paul trains his sights on those Jews who claim that God has chosen them from among the nations to be the elect and that their election is irrevocable. They assume that if Israel should be unfaithful, God will certainly grant them amnesty since they are God's chosen people. Paul repudiates this presumption of security by redefining Israel. God's people are called and established solely by God's inscrutable grace. Paul stresses God's sovereignty in making what may from a human perspective seem to be mystifying choices throughout history. Human cultural norms and traditions do not influence God. God constituted Israel by fulfilling the promise to Abraham only through Isaac (9:7–9) and by choosing only Jacob, the younger son, over Esau, the elder son (9:10–13). God shows mercy on anyone God chooses and hardens anyone he chooses (9:15–18). Depending on God's purposes, he makes vessels destined for destruction and vessels destined for glory (9:20–23). Humans are God's creation and have no right to question God's sovereignty that is manifested in these choices.

Comment

i. Paul's grief over his Jewish kindred's failure to believe the gospel (9:1–5)

1. Paul begins this new section with a solemn oath from one who can be trusted as a believer in Christ that what he writes is the truth. He can assume that his audience has experienced the Holy Spirit's witness in their lives (cf. 8:6), so he adds that what he says also is confirmed by the witness of his inner consciousness that is moulded by the Holy Spirit. Why he feels the need to affirm the truth of what he says about his sorrow and anguish over Israel is not clear. It is unlikely that he needs to prove that being an apostle to the Gentiles has not minimized his love for or connection to his Jewish kindred. Instead, he may intend to validate his emotional assertion in 9:3 that, were it possible, he would forfeit his salvation if it would bring salvation to Israel. He also intimates that the Holy

Spirit guides his reflections on Israel's current condition and their future.

2. Paul's grief for Israel resonates with Jeremiah's mourning over the disaster that had overtaken the rebellious and reckless Israel of his day (Jer. 4:19–22; 2 Esd. 8:15–17) and with Jesus' mourning over the impending destruction of Jerusalem because of the refusal to accept him and their choosing instead the way of the sword (Luke 19:41; cf. Jer. 9:1; 13:17; 14:17). That those who first heard the gospel have turned their backs on God by rejecting God's Son, their Messiah, intensifies Paul's heartache. He understands that God has used their rejection to make possible the conversion of Gentiles and to deliver on the promise to Abraham that he would become 'the father of many nations' (4:16–18). It does not lessen the pain of seeing his kindred who style themselves as the people of God being so blind to the salvation offered to all people in Christ. Their unceasing spiritual dullness causes him unceasing sadness.

3. Paul resorts to hyperbole to express his profoundest grief over the Jews' continuing unbelief. He could wish that he might become a thing *accursed* (cf. Gal. 1:8–9) on behalf of his 'brothers and sisters' (CSB), his own race of people. His poignant longing mirrors Moses' plea for God to forgive Israel for worshipping the golden calf or, if God should not forgive them, to blot him out of the book God has written (Exod. 32:30–34). Paul's statement 'presupposes that his kinsmen are for the moment outside the sphere of salvation'.[2] Their lack of faith in Christ makes them guilty of great sin and, like the Israel of old, worthy of condemnation. Paul knows that God refused Moses' moving petition. His use of the imperfect tense of the verb, which expresses an unfulfilled action and is best translated as 'I could almost wish', reveals that he also knows that God would refuse his supplication, too. He cannot atone for his people's sin by becoming accursed as Christ did (Gal. 3:13; cf. 1 Cor. 1:13). He also knows that nothing can separate him from the love of God in Christ Jesus our Lord (8:39), but he expresses his willingness to make the supreme sacrifice to save his people were it possible. That he submitted 'five times' to the punishment of the forty lashes

---

2. Räisänen, 'Paul', p. 180.

prescribed in Deuteronomy 25:1–3 (2 Cor. 11:24), presumably for his deviant beliefs regarding a crucified Messiah and his insistence that Gentiles could be included into the people of God without being circumcised, testifies to his commitment to his kindred. According to the rabbinic interpretation of this punishment, before the flogging, a man is regarded as wicked and deserving of being cut off from the people of God. After the flogging, he is called 'your brother' (m. Mak. 3:15).³ Paul could have left the synagogue for ever and shaken the dust from his feet. Instead, he accepted this synagogal discipline to maintain his connections with the synagogue and the opportunities to preach the gospel to save his fellow Jews. He also knows that he risks his life by returning to Jerusalem with the financial contribution for the poor among the saints, and therefore asks the Romans to pray that he 'may be rescued from the unbelievers in Judea' (15:31). He is willing to do so because it might result in saving some of his own people (11:14).

4–5. Paul asked earlier, 'Then what advantage has the Jew?' (3:1). His answer is, 'Much, in every way', but he mentions only one advantage: 'the Jews were entrusted with the oracles of God' (3:2). He now tallies eight additional advantages that God granted them during the old covenant era (2 Cor. 3:1–18). (1) They are *Israelites*. Paul has used the term 'Jews' exclusively in chapters 1–8 but switches to 'Israel' in chapters 9–11, where eleven of the seventeen occurrences of this name in Paul's letters appear. The name recalls the ancient history of the people when God renamed Jacob 'Israel' for having struggled and prevailed with God and obtained God's blessing (Gen. 32:28). The name was then applied to his descendants. It evokes God's election of them, a small and seemingly insignificant people, to bear witness to an eternal God who invades history, and they did so in ways that arose nowhere else in the world. (2) *Adoption* recalls God's choice of Israel out of all the peoples of the earth (Deut. 14:1–2) to enter a filial relationship with God as God's firstborn son (Exod. 4:22–23). (3) Israel experienced the divine *glory* that appeared in the wilderness (Exod. 16:10), that covered Mount Sinai (Exod. 24:16–17), that filled the tabernacle

---

3. Cf. Garland, *2 Corinthians*, pp. 496–498.

(Exod. 40:32–38) and that filled the temple (1 Kgs 8:10–11). (4) Israel also received God's irrevocable *covenants*. These include the covenants with Abraham, Isaac and Jacob (Lev. 26:42), and the covenant that Israel would be God's most treasured possession of all the nations, a kingdom of priests and a holy nation particularly stands out (Exod. 19:1–8). Moses ritually demonstrated this covenantal relationship with God when he took the blood of the sacrifice and sprinkled it on them as 'the blood of the covenant that the LORD has made with you in accordance with all these words' (Exod. 24:8). It also includes the covenant with David in which God promised to raise up his descendant and establish David's kingdom for ever (2 Sam. 7:8–16). God also promised to establish a new covenant with Israel in which God would put the law within them and write it on their hearts (Jer. 31:31–34). (4) 'The receiving of the law' (NIV; Exod. 20:1–17; Deut. 5:1–22) distinguished Israel from all other nations.

(5) God also gave Israel the *worship*, which included the multi-faceted feasts and sacrificial observances in the tabernacle and then the temple (1 Chr. 28:13) that continually reminded Israel of God's presence with them (Josh. 22:27) as the one true God willing to forgive their sins (1 Kgs 8:11, 30). (6) Israel inherited the *promises* made to Abraham (Gen. 12:7; 13:14–17; 17:4–8; 22:16–18; Rom. 4:13, 16, 20) and that God repeated to Isaac (Gen. 26:3–4) and to Jacob (Gen. 28:13–14) to make them as numerous as the stars of heaven and that 'all the families of the earth shall be blessed in you and in your offspring'. God also promised David that his royal throne would be established for ever (2 Sam. 7:11–16; 2 Chr. 7:18; 21:7; Ps. 132:11–12; Isa. 9:6–7), and through Jeremiah promised a new covenant in which God would write the law on their hearts (Jer. 31:31–34).

(7) The principal *patriarchs* are Abraham, Isaac and Jacob, who presumably constitute the 'rich root' in the metaphor of the olive tree (11:17). Jacob's sons became the patriarchs of the twelve tribes, and Paul maintains that Israel is primarily loved 'on account of the patriarchs' (11:28, NIV). (8) The climactic privilege of Israel is *the Messiah* who, according to the flesh, is the descendant of Abraham, Judah and David (Matt. 1:1–17; Rom. 1:3). The Messiah is the fulfilment of the 'promises given to the patriarchs' (15:8). In Paul's mind,

however, the Messiah is not simply God's gift to Israel. He is to become Israel's gift to the entire world, and he will realize humanity's universal hope, not just Israel's.

There are three main options for punctuating the last part of 9:5. (1) The first option treats the whole clause as applying to Christ and boldly asserts his divine nature: from the patriarchs 'comes the Messiah who is over all and God blessed for ever'. (2) A second option inserts a period after Christ 'who is over all', followed by a doxology to God: 'God be blessed for ever.' (3) A third option applies the whole clause to God and offers praise to God for giving the privileges listed: 'God, who is over all, be blessed for ever.'

The first option is preferable since it reflects the natural word order in Greek and accords with what Paul says elsewhere about Christ as Lord over all (14:9; 1 Cor. 15:28; Eph. 1:20–23; Phil. 2:9–11; Col. 1:15, 17–18) and as equal with God (Phil. 2:6). If the doxology were an independent clause referring to God, one would expect the adjective *blessed* to precede *God* in the Greek word order (cf. 1 Cor. 1:3; Eph. 1:3; 1 Pet. 1:3) or for a reference to God to precede it in the context (cf. 1:25; 11:36; 2 Cor. 11:31). By saying that Christ is God over all, Paul amends the traditional understanding of the Messiah. Who he is *according to the flesh*, that is, according to his 'human ancestry', is not the full story. There is more to be said. He is equal with God (cf. 1 Cor. 8:6; 2 Cor. 4:4; Phil. 2:6; Col. 1:15, 19; 2:9; Titus 2:13) and Lord (10:9, 13; 14:9). This theological assertion is a major sticking point for Jews who think that it perverts their confession that God is one. From Paul's perspective, it heightens the seriousness of Israel's rejection of Christ as the Messiah sent by God for the salvation of the world. To reject Christ is equivalent to rejecting God.

The list of Israel's benefits drives home the theological dilemma Paul must address. Israel is the original legatee of God's promises, but Paul applies these same privileges to believers who include Gentiles. As those who are in Christ, they are adopted as children of God (8:15, 23; Gal. 4:5; Eph. 1:5). They have received the hope of glory (5:2; 8:18, 21). They are participants in a new covenant (1 Cor. 11:25; 2 Cor. 3:6; Gal. 4:24). As for the law, they can fulfil the requirement of the law through the Spirit and only through the Spirit (8:4). They now offer true, spiritual worship by offering their bodies to God as a living sacrifice (12:1; cf. Phil. 3:3). They are also considered children of Abraham through their faith (4:12; Gal. 3:7–9, 29). Finally, they are in Christ, belong to Christ and have been made co-heirs with Christ (8:9–11, 17). Since these privileges now also apply to Gentile Christians, and Paul will shift in chapter 10 to a list of God's grievances against Israel, it suggests that something has gone seriously awry for Israel that requires an explanation.

ii. God's word has not failed (9:6–13)

6. Following the list of Israel's privileges, someone might be prompted to ask Paul, 'If, according to your gospel, Israel is lost for not believing in Christ, does that mean that God's promises are like withered flowers that have fallen to the ground?' (cf. Jas 1:11; 1 Pet. 1:24). Could Israel bring a breach of promise suit against God and claim that God has been a duplicitous custodian of the promises? With other biblical writers, Paul regards as outrageous any suggestion that God's word could founder (cf. Josh. 21:45; 23:14; 1 Kgs 8:56; Ps. 119:89–91; Isa. 40:8; 55:10–11). He firmly insists, 'It is certainly not that God's word has failed' (author's translation). God is righteous, and God's word is utterly reliable (cf. 3:4; 15:8).

7. To support this point, Paul clarifies the meaning of God's 'word'. He limits it here to God's promise to Abraham that Sarah would bear a son (Gen. 18:10, 14, cited in 9:9) and the declaration that Abraham's descendants will be recognized ('called') only through Isaac (Gen. 21:12). Therefore, he delimits the definition of Israel by insisting that God does not certify all of Abraham's 'seed' ('descendants') as 'children of Abraham'. God earmarked Abraham's children for separate destinies (cf. Gal. 4:23, 29–30). The implication is that parentage, racial descent, a distinctive Jewish way of life (4:14, 16) or geographical borders do not define who Israel is in God's eyes since Israel 'is created not by blood and soil, but by the promise of God' (Barrett, p. 169). The translation *shall be named* loses the nuance of the verb Paul uses. That they 'shall be called' (*klēthēsetai*) implies that being 'children of the promise' (9:8) and rightly called 'Israel' depends entirely on God's calling (4:17; 8:28, 30; 9:12, 24–26). It is not based on the ability to trace one's bloodline back to Abraham.

8–9. Paul stresses that God's *promise* applied only to Sarah giving birth to a son at the appointed time (Gen. 18:10, 14). Abraham had eight sons: Ishmael by Hagar, Isaac by Sarah, and six sons by Keturah (Gen. 25:1–2). Of these eight, only Isaac is the child of the promise. Since Abraham and Sarah were well beyond the age for procreation and Sarah was barren, Paul acclaims this birth as miraculous – God giving 'life to the dead' and calling 'into existence the things that do not exist' (4:17). His point is 'that *the only Israel that exists is the one God brought into being through promise and call*'.[4] Tracing one's lineage back to Abraham does not confirm that one belongs to *the children of the promise*, only that one belongs to Abraham's *children of the flesh*. The two are not the same. It follows that being circumcised and claiming Abraham as one's father does not guarantee salvation.

The citation from Genesis 18:10 and 14 introduces another wrinkle in the fulfilment of God's promises: they will be fulfilled at an 'appointed time' (NIV; cf. Gal. 4:4). Believers cannot always discern how God is working out his eternal purposes in the present and because of their limited vantage point should not despair that God's word has somehow failed. They should also recognize that God's timetable is not our timetable.

10–12. Paul advances his argument that being children of the promise depends entirely on God's prior choice. Though Rebecca is not prominent in the Genesis narrative, he cites her because her story provides further proof that God takes the initiative in election without regard to merit or how human criteria might grade someone's status. After citing how God chose only one of the sons whom Abraham conceived by different wives, he now cites how God chose only one of the sons born from the same mother from one act of intercourse. God chose Rebecca to be Isaac's wife (Gen. 24:7, 14–15, 48), and, like Sarah, she had been barren and became pregnant with twins only after God granted Isaac's prayer request regarding her childlessness (Gen. 25:21). Like Sarah, she received a promise from God, who told her,

---

4.   Gaventa, 'Romans 9:6–29', p. 260.

Two nations are in your womb,
    and two peoples born of you shall be divided;
one shall be stronger than the other,
    the elder shall serve the younger.
(Gen. 25:23)

Paul offers no explanation why God chose Jacob over Esau who, as the firstborn of the twins, would have been Isaac's primary heir according to human conventions. He only plays up the fact that God made this choice *before* the twins *had been born or had done anything good or bad.*

Some Jews sought to justify this puzzling choice by attributing it to God's foreknowledge of Esau's waywardness (cf. Jub. 19:13–18; 35:13; Philo, *Leg.* 3.88–89). By contrast, Paul cites the passages from Genesis to stress that God's election derives solely from God's sovereign and prior decision (cf. Isa. 14:24). Esau and Jacob shared the same parents and the same lack of distinctive achievements, but they were assigned different destinies. Being a child of the promise has nothing to do with one's parentage or one's *works.* Wolter writes, 'God's election is always and only God's antecedent *action* and never *re-action.*'[5] The thrust of Paul's argument is expressed in verse 11 with the phrase 'so that God's purpose according to election might stand' (CSB). The implication is that 'the continued existence of the chosen people through the birth of new sons of promise is always dependent on God'.[6] God's purposes are achieved through God's gracious selection of persons without regard to their worthiness. They can never claim that their election was merited, nor should they look down on those they perceive not to be elected.

Acts refers to Paul as a 'chosen instrument' (*skeuos eklogēs*, Acts 9:15, NIV). The use of the word 'instrument' (or 'vessel') clarifies that God chooses persons and groups to implement his purposes (cf. 8:28). Paul understands himself to have been chosen by God before he was born to proclaim God's Son among the Gentiles

---

5. Wolter, 'God's Faithfulness', pp. 35–36.
6. Munck, *Christ*, p. 37 n. 32.

(Gal. 1:15–16). Yet he understands himself also to be the 'least of the apostles' (1 Cor. 15:9), 'the very least of all the saints' (Eph. 3:8) and simply a 'servant' working in God's field seeking to fulfil the tasks assigned to him (1 Cor 3:5–9; Eph. 3:7; Col. 1:25).

13. The citation from Malachi 1:2–3, *I have loved Jacob, / but I have hated Esau*, perhaps reflects Semitic hyperbole (cf. Matt. 10:37; Luke 14:26). To love Jacob and to hate Esau means that God preferred Jacob over Esau (cf. Gen. 29:30–31; Deut. 21:15–17). This blunt pronouncement further emphasizes God's freedom in election. It also reinforces the point that receiving God's promise does not come as an inalienable birthright through physical descent (cf. Eph. 1:11; 2 Tim. 1:9). That no explanation is offered as to why God loves Jacob and hates Esau assumes that God's elective purposes often are hidden from humans and that God does not need to defend the choice. The constancy of God's promise to Abraham follows unexpected paths that go against the grain of what humans assume to be appropriate. In the case of Jacob and Esau, favouring Jacob over Esau overturned human convention that considers the firstborn child to be the rightful heir and therefore the one who should have received the blessing of the promise. While the choice of Jacob implies Esau's rejection, in this context his rejection meant only that God did not intend to use Esau as the instrument for fulfilling God's elective purposes in history. It did not mean that he was excluded from Isaac's blessing (cf. Heb. 11:20) despite selling his birthright (Heb. 12:16–17). The two brothers born from the same mother and father would become separate nations, Israel and Edom (Gen. 36:1–43). Edom's later miserable condition (Obad. 1–2, 18) is simply a fulfilment of another of God's promises to Abraham: 'whoever curses you I will curse' (Gen. 12:3, NIV).

iii. God alone determines who is elect (9:14–26)

14. Paul forestalls a challenge by asking another question that expects 'No' as the answer: 'There is no injustice with God, is there?' This question has arisen before in the letter: 'God is not unjust to inflict wrath on us, is he?' (3:5). The 'No' in both cases is emphatic. One might think it unfair that God has picked the winners and losers before the race even begins without any regard to their meritorious performance. From a human perspective, it seems completely unjust. When Job reproachfully questions God's justice, he receives a long and sharp rebuke from God (Job 40:6 – 41:34). How could Job ever presume that he could gird up his loins to take on God? Job must admit that nothing humans do can thwart God's purposes and that he was wrong to question God about wonders far beyond his capacity to comprehend (Job 42:2–3). Paul would concur.

15. God's declaration to Moses, *I will have mercy on whom I have mercy, / and I will have compassion on whom I have compassion* (Exod. 33:19), occurs after the grievous golden calf incident (Exod. 32:1– 35). Israel justly deserved severe punishment for its sin but received God's mercy instead. This citation from Moses about God showing mercy on whomever God chooses underscores that there are no preconditions for receiving mercy. God can shower mercy on whomever God wants without having any obvious reason to do so. That means, 'To be a people that belongs to this God is to be a people that lives by God's mercy.'[7]

16. Paul rules out that God shows mercy on the strength of the human desire to obey (cf. 7:15–21) or on human 'running', that is, striving to reach the goal of obeying the commandments (cf. Ps. 119:32). He has already insisted that 'a person is justified by faith apart from works prescribed by the law' (3:28) and that God credits righteousness to a person 'apart from works' (4:6, NIV). Since humans always fall short in both their intentions and their exertions and never can do anything to make themselves worthy of God's blessing, this divine mercy is the only reason why humans can be saved. Psalm 147:10–11 expresses well God's perspective on human effort:

> His delight is not in the strength of the horse,
>   nor his pleasure in the speed of a runner;
> but the LORD takes pleasure in those who fear him,
>   in those who hope in his steadfast love.
> (Noted by Schnabel, II, p. 323)

---

7. Eastman, 'Israel', p. 157.

Everything depends on God's mercy, which is always unmerited.

God has not adopted a new mode of dealing with humans with the advent of Jesus. Paul contends that God has always been merciful. God showered undeserved mercy on the people of Israel in creating them and forgiving them time after time through the centuries. God's showing incongruous mercy throughout Israel's history should make it less surprising that God could and would also shower unexpected and undeserved mercy on Gentiles by grafting in these wild olive branches to share in the rich root of the cultivated olive tree (11:17). God's mercy is not casual, however. God's mercy is poured out on believers through Christ's atoning death, which preserves God's righteousness in clearing the guilty who deserve wrath (Thielman, p. 436).

17. Paul shifts from God's freedom to show mercy on whomever God chooses to God's freedom to harden whomever God chooses. The two coexist and are dispensed according to God's purposes. Pharaoh serves as the classic example of hardening. Paul cites Exodus 9:16 and equates God speaking with *the scripture* speaking. He replaces the original phrase in the text 'this is why I have let you live' with 'I raised you up for this very purpose' (NIV) to stress that God raised up Pharaoh for a special historical role. God used the stubbornness of the nameless Pharaoh to abet his plans in creating Israel.[8] This divine intervention was a defining moment in Israel's history. How Pharaoh bears responsibility for his hardening is not at issue. The sequence of the many references in Exodus to Pharaoh's hardening suggests that God hardened one who was already hardened (Exod. 3:18–20).[9] God did not force Pharaoh to do what he was not already predisposed to do, did not hatch brand-new sin in his heart, and did not change him from one who was sweet and compassionate into one who was cruel and vicious. Pharaoh was already inclined towards heartlessness as one who arrogantly blustered, 'Who is the LORD, that I should heed him and let Israel go? I do not know the LORD, and I will not let Israel go'

---

8. Gaventa, 'Romans 9:6–29', p. 264.
9. Exod. 4:21–23; 7:3, 13, 14, 22; 8:15, 19; 9:7, 12, 35; 10:1, 20, 27; 11:10; 13:15; 14:4, 8, 17.

(Exod. 5:2). God punishes people like Pharaoh, who already rebel against God, by 'calcifying this rebellion' and hardening already 'resistant hearts' (Thielman, p. 458). What happened to Pharaoh matches Paul's description of what God's wrath does. God hands people over to their sins (1:24, 26, 28), and God handed Pharaoh over to his defiance. That means that God allowed his defiance to harden him so thoroughly that he became ever more defiant. Paul's point, however, is that God can use human stubbornness to achieve his purposes. Pharaoh's hardened refusal to free the people of Israel revealed that he and Egypt's gods were no match for God's power. It resulted in God's *name*, not Pharaoh's, being *proclaimed* both to Israel (Exod. 10:1–2; 13:14–16) and throughout *all the earth* (Exod. 9:16; 14:17–18; cf. Ps. 106:7–8). The demonstration of God's power to save his people resulted in God's name being glorified in the whole earth (cf. 11:36; 15:7; 16:27).

18. God's hardening and mercy are part of God's elective purpose that leads to a positive end. Paul broadens the principle that God can show mercy or harden whomever God wants to prime the audience to accept his assertion that God hardened the majority of Israel so that God could have mercy on the Gentiles. As God used a hardened Pharaoh to show his power in redeeming Israel from Egypt, so God will use the hardened majority of Israel to bring the offer of salvation to the Gentiles (11:7–11). This view undergirds Paul's contention that everything depends on God's mercy rather than on human will or striving.

19. Paul again adopts the question-and-answer device to reinforce his teaching point. If God hardened Pharaoh's heart to display his power, someone might cavil: 'How can God blame humans for sin, since they cannot resist God's will, which might entail hardening them so that they sin?' A similar objection to God's dealings with humans arose in 3:7: 'But if through my falsehood God's truthfulness abounds to his glory, why am I still being condemned as a sinner?' The question *who can resist his will?* sets up what follows (cf. Job 9:19, LXX: 'who can resist his judgment?'). Humans, whether they like it or not, cannot contest God's sovereign will. They certainly deceive themselves if they think they could run the world better or be more merciful and just than God is.

20. Paul does not respond to these questions with a theoretical discussion but instead upbraids anyone for asking them. He first alludes to Isaiah 29:16 to emphasize God's absolute sovereignty and to confront the creature with the Creator who formed the first man 'from the dust of the ground' (Gen. 2:7). Humans have no right to call God on the carpet for whatever might displease them. God is free to act however God wills, even if, from a human perspective, it seems to be unfair. Humans may not like the way God works in history, which may seem to them to be capricious, but they cannot demand that God act according to their wishes. They were created to serve God's purposes, and they can only accept God's will as it works itself out in their lives and in history. Paul points out how ridiculous it would be for an object made by a craftsman to complain about how it has been crafted or how it is to be used. In the same way, Israel cannot impudently talk back to God, its Creator, and ask why God has done this or that in its history. God does not need to explain himself to them for anything he does (cf. Job 9:12; Dan. 4:35).

21–23. Paul develops this idea of God's sovereignty with the image of a potter. Israel as a lump of clay in the hands of God the potter was a familiar analogy in Scripture (Isa. 45:9; 64:8; Jer. 18:1–12; cf. Wis. 12:12–13; 15:7; Sir. 33:13). Who are humans to question the potter's purposes or wisdom? As the potter, God can fashion the clay into any kind of object depending on its needed purpose. The clay has no intrinsic value. Its value depends entirely on what the potter does with it.

God chose to use *objects of wrath* for a certain purpose. In the context, these 'objects' would probably be unbelieving Israel, who, like Pharaoh, are ripe for judgment and destruction because of their sinful rebellion. Though they are destined for destruction after they have become useless, God does not immediately destroy them. Instead, God endures *objects of wrath* with *much patience* (cf. 2:4) *in order to make known the riches of his glory for the objects of mercy, which he has prepared beforehand for glory.* The point is not that God created some people for destruction, who are forever barred from God's mercy and destined for perdition, and others as the recipients of God's mercy, who are forever blessed and destined for glory. Paul's thought is that God as Creator has the sovereign freedom to fashion objects from the same clay for different purposes. God can raise up those like Pharaoh and raze them to the ground to show his power to make his name 'resound through all the earth' (Exod. 9:16).[10] This revelation of God's wrath (1:18; 2:8; 3:5) becomes a necessary foil that makes the riches of God's mercy both more noticeable and more glorious. While God is free to do whatever he wishes with the objects he creates, Paul asserts that God uses that freedom redemptively by showing mercy to all who deserve destruction (cf. 11:32).

24–25. The objects of God's mercy, the *us* whom God has *called* and 'prepared beforehand for glory' (9:23), are believers. They do not come *from the Jews only but also from the Gentiles*. Paul presents this as a question whose answer his audience knows is 'yes'. He is talking about them, the children of God (5:2; 8:21, 30). To support this answer, Paul applies the prophecy from Hosea 2:23 (2:25 in the LXX) that originally pertained to Israel to include also Gentile Christians. In Hosea's context, *not my people* refers to God's judgment on the Northern Kingdom. Calling them *my people* envisions their restoration. Paul applies the oracle in his context to the Gentiles (cf. 1 Pet. 2:10) who are, from a Jewish assessment, classic examples of those who are 'no people' (cf. 10:19). This bias is expressed, for example, in 2 Esdras which asserts that God created this world only for Israel, the people God had chosen (2 Esd. 6:54–55). It continues, 'As for the other nations that have descended from Adam, you have said that they are nothing, and that they are like spittle, and you have compared their abundance to a drop from a bucket' (2 Esd. 6:56). The passage from Hosea establishes the principle that God in his mercy and love can redeem those who seemed to have been thrust aside and disowned because of their disobedience (Schnabel, II, p. 341). Since Israel was called into being purely by God's grace and once was *not my people* and *not beloved*, Paul reasons that God can broaden the recipients of the promises to those outside Israel who also were not God's people and not beloved. God's mysterious mercy that was evident in Israel's early

---

10. Examples of God raising up persons to realize his objectives abound in the Old Testament (cf. Deut. 18:15; 1 Sam. 2:35; 1 Kgs 14:14).

history (9:6–18) has now manifested itself in the inclusion of
Gentiles. Gentile believers who formerly were *not my people* have
been transformed into *my people* and been merged into the assembly
of the saved by being in Christ.

Paul makes this correlation applicable to Gentile believers by
slightly altering Hosea's wording from 'I will say' to *I will call*. The
verb 'call' appears in 9:7 where Paul asserts that Abraham's
descendants 'shall be named' ('shall be called') through Isaac, and
in 9:12 where Paul asserts that being children of Abraham and of
the promise depends entirely on God's call. The principle that
God's promise to Abraham is fulfilled only through those whom
God freely calls (9:11–12) allows Paul to connect the dots. He takes
as fact that God has *also* called Gentile believers.[11] In the same way
that God *called* Israel into being, purely by unmerited grace, God
has also *called* Gentile Christians to be a part of the elect and to be
'justified' and 'glorified' (8:30). God has the power to call 'into existence the things that do not exist' (4:17), is free to have mercy on
whomever he wants, and is also free to call whomever he wants.
God's track record shows him to be consistent in extending this
call. It goes out to those one would least expect to be called, the
nobodies. By changing Hosea's 'I will have pity on Lo-ruhamah
['Not pitied']' to *I will call . . . her who was not beloved . . . 'beloved'* Paul
links the choice of Gentiles to the unconventional decision to love
Jacob instead of Esau (9:13). Neither had done anything to deserve
God's love.

The upshot is that being members of the people of God now
depends entirely on having faith in Christ Jesus. In the next section,
Paul makes it clear that God's people are only those who confess
'Jesus is Lord' and believe in their 'heart that God raised him from
the dead' (10:9). This reality explains why Paul's citation of Hosea
2:23 stops short of including the people's response to God's mercy:
'You are my God.' More is required: confessing Jesus as Lord.

26. The second citation from Hosea (Hos. 1:10; 2:1 in the LXX)
provides further proof that God's word has not failed. The

---

11. Cf. Rom. 1:6–7; 8:28, 30; 1 Cor. 1:2, 9, 24; Gal. 1:6; 5:8; Eph. 4:1, 4; Col.
      3:15; 1 Thess. 2:12; 4:7; 5:24; 2 Thess. 2:14.

inclusion of Gentiles as *children of the living God* (8:14, 17, 21; Gal. 3:26) fulfils the promise God made to Abraham that he would be the father of many nations (4:17; Gen. 17:5). As the living God, God can give life to Gentiles who were 'dead in your transgressions and sins' (Eph. 2:1, NIV) and 'excluded from citizenship in Israel and foreigners to the covenants of the promise, without hope and without God in the world' (Eph. 2:12, NIV). They are manifestly children of God when they are led by the Spirit to cry out, 'Abba! Father!' (8:14–15). Not only is it the case that not all the children of Abraham are his 'descendants' (9:7), but it is also the case that not all 'the children of Israel' qualify as *children of the living God.*

iv. God has saved a remnant in Israel and added Gentiles to the people of God (9:27–29)

27–28. Paul introduces a composite quote from Isaiah 10:22–23 and 28:22b with the prophet Isaiah crying out in sorrow over Israel's gloomy future. In the contexts of both passages, Isaiah prophesies that God has decreed destruction and will turn away from Israel because of Israel's disobedience. Isaiah's prophecy underscores the present threatening situation for Israel. How best to translate the quotation, however, is uncertain. The Greek text refers to the Lord carrying out (his) 'word' (*logos*), which is translated as *sentence.* The difficulty for interpretation is determining what this 'word' denotes and how to translate the combination of participles that follows. The first participle (*syntelōn*) means 'to finish', 'to accomplish', 'to bring to fulfilment'. The second participle (*syntemnōn*) means 'to cut short' or 'to limit'. (1) If the 'word' refers to God's promise, it means that the promise will be cut short and fulfilled only to a limited degree. This reading is unlikely since it would imply that God revised the promise and would suggest that God's word partly fails. (2) If the 'word' refers to the fulfilment of God's promise to show mercy to those who believe and to punish those who do not, it refers to the completeness and finality with which it will be carried out. (3) If the 'word' refers to the time when God will execute this judgment or sentence, it means that God will not prolong indefinitely the period of divine patience (2:4–6; 3:25; 9:22; 2 Pet. 3:9) but has cut down the time left. (4) If the 'word' refers to God's 'sentence' on the Israelite nation, it means that God decisively has cut back Israel (cf. 'cut off' [*ekkoptein*] in 11:22, 24). From the great number of born Jews, God has diminished Israel to a remnant.

This last reading of the text best fits the context. Paul makes the point that even if the people of Israel are as numerous as *the sand of the sea*, it does not mean that they all are numbered among 'the children [sons] of the living God' (9:26). The combination of Hosea's and Isaiah's testimonies reinforces the opening thesis in 9:6 that 'not all Israelites truly belong to Israel' (Wilckens, II, p. 207). From the very beginning and throughout Israel's history God determines who Israel is. God's condemnation has fallen severely upon the disobedient people, and now only a remnant remains.[12]

The Hebrew text of Isaiah has a remnant that 'will return' (Isa. 10:22), but Paul cites the LXX version that reads only a remnant *will be saved*. Being *saved* fits his concern about the status of Israel's salvation (10:9, 13; 11:14, 26) that is in doubt because of their current hardened condition (11:7, 25; cf. 2 Cor. 3:14). Sin has so deeply estranged all humans, including Israel, from their Creator that they need more than a return from exile. They need to be saved from their sins, which can transpire only through their trust in Christ (5:9–11; 10:9, 13). Paul understands that Isaiah's oracle has been fulfilled, and the remnant now consists of those Jews, chosen by grace, who believe in Christ (11:5). God now carries out his purposes through a shrunken Israel.

29. Paul takes his audience to the very brink of Israel's destruction and now in this verse slams on the brakes. Israel will not plunge over the precipice into annihilation. The idea of a remnant connotes judgment on the majority and salvation for the few.[13] The prophecy from Isaiah 1:9, however, offers a ray of hope for the majority in their current condition of unbelief. God has not judged Israel so harshly that it will become like Sodom and Gomorrah

---

12. The community at Qumran considered themselves to be the faithful remnant of Israel awaiting God's vindication and the destruction of the wicked from the earth (CD 1:4–5; 3:12–13; 1QM 13:8; 14:8–9).

13. Grindheim, *Election*, p. 150.

who were wiped off the face of the earth for their wickedness (Gen. 19:24; 2 Pet. 2:6). God *left* . . *to us*, that is, the rest of unbelieving Israel, *survivors*. The Greek word translated *survivors* (NRSV), 'descendants' (NIV, NASB) and 'offspring' (ESV, CSB) is 'seed' (*sperma*). Paul uses the word in 9:7–8 in God's promise to provide Abraham with 'seed'. Translating the word as 'descendants' or 'offspring' in 9:29 accurately conveys that God faithfully fulfils that promise even in the dire circumstances of Israel's disobedience. Nevertheless, this translation fails to do full justice to the image of seed that promises to 'germinate, sprout and blossom into a renewed Israel'.[14] The 'seed' is like a 'freshly plucked olive leaf' (Gen. 8:11) that keeps alive the promises to Israel. As Isaiah declares,

> The surviving remnant of the house of Judah shall again take root downwards, and bear fruit upwards; for from Jerusalem a remnant shall go out, and from Mount Zion a band of survivors. The zeal of the LORD of hosts will do this.
> (Isa. 37:31–32 = 2 Kgs 19:30–31)

The seed will germinate into a great, and perhaps, from a human perspective, unexpected, harvest.

Paul contends that God has acted justly (9:14) in displaying wrath (9:22) on Israel's rebellion (Isa. 1:2–5), but God also has acted mercifully in preserving a remnant. Otherwise, Israel would have been laid waste. The preservation of a seed offers proof that God's word, the promise to Abraham, has not failed. It also offers the certain hope that it will not fail.

Theology

If one treats chapters 9–11 as separate, disconnected arguments, then one can find support for belief in double predestination in 9:13: 'I have loved Jacob, but I have hated Esau'; for belief that one's destiny rests on one's own free response to God's grace in 10:13: 'Everyone who calls on the name of the Lord shall be saved'; and for belief in universalism in 11:32: 'For God has imprisoned all in

---

14. Wagner, *Heralds*, p. 116.

disobedience so that he may be merciful to all.' Before drawing such theological conclusions from Paul's statements, it is vital to follow his argument all the way to the end in 11:36. Failing to do so and cherry-picking particular portions of his argument that might fit one's inclinations will cause one to miss the bigger picture of what Paul intends.

Paul's purpose in chapters 9–11 is to reveal how God's mercy and judgment are being worked out to achieve the larger purpose of the salvation of Jews and Gentiles. In 9:1–29, Paul tackles the current problem of Israel's unbelief. He contends that members of the chosen people, Israel, *can be* and *are* lost. They do not have security from their ancestry, their circumcision, their zealous pursuit of the law or their own imagined righteousness. As Munck colourfully states, 'The Jew has no right to wave his pedigree in God's face.'[15] Paul believes that the majority in Israel is lost because they have failed to believe in Christ who, as God's anointed one, fulfils the hopes of Israel.

If Israel is lost, Paul must then address the problem that this fact raises. God made promises to Israel. If Israel is lost, does that suggest that God has defaulted on these promises and call into question God's reliability? Does God vacillate? Paul has just asserted that nothing in all creation 'will be able to separate us from the love of God in Christ Jesus our Lord' (8:39). But if Israel could be lost, does that mean God's love does not endure for ever? Paul traces the pattern of the fulfilment of God's word through Scripture to show that God is creative, unrestricted and dumb-founding. God is the one who elects (9:11, 12, 25), shows mercy (9:16, 18), endures with much patience (9:22) and takes away sin (11:27). God is also the one who hardens and causes people to stumble (9:18; 10:19; 11:7–10, 25), but God has imprisoned all in disobedience so that no-one has any claim on God and God may be merciful to all (11:32).

In this unit, Paul primarily wants to deflate Jewish audacity that thinks it can dictate to God. Instead, it is God who dictates. Paul maintains that pots do not argue with their potter about how they

---

15. Munck, *Christ*, p. 108.

were made or for what purpose they are to be used. In the same way, God is totally free to say who God's people are, and Paul proves it from Israel's Scriptures. Paul insists that 'Israel is always and only God's creation', and his main contention is 'that God created Israel and that Israel's past as well as its future depends entirely on God's own saving power and glory'.[16] Therefore, the Jew does not tell God. God tells the Jew.

Paul's statements regarding individuals – God loved Jacob and hated Esau (9:13) 'even before they had been born or had done anything good or bad' (9:11), and God raised up Pharaoh (9:17), and has mercy on whomever he chooses and hardens whomever he chooses (9:18) – provide the basis for arguing for double predestination. Paul's theological objective in this context, however, is not to deliberate on predestination of individuals.[17] The emphasis falls on Israel's corporate election as evidenced by Paul's use of terms that refer to groups instead of individuals: 'my people', 'the remnant', 'the disobedient', 'Israel'. Election in the individual cases he mentions in this passage refers to those persons whom God selected as agents to advance God's historical purposes in the plan of salvation.[18]

God's choice of these individuals reveals that God does not put up a 'help wanted' sign and wait for applications. Instead, God raises up persons to achieve his objectives. Paul's citation of God's statement in Exodus 9:16 that he raised up Pharaoh 'for the very purpose of showing my power in you, so that my name may be proclaimed in all the earth' (9:17) is a case in point. God's use of Pharaoh is comparable to God's raising up Cyrus, the king of Persia (Isa. 45:1). While Pharaoh oppressed Israel in its Egyptian captivity, Cyrus delivered Israel from its Babylonian captivity. Shalom M. Paul's interpretation of God's reasons for choosing Cyrus are relevant for understanding God's election of persons. He argues

---

16. Gaventa, 'Romans 9:6–29', p. 257.

17. Cf. the debate between Abasciano, 'Corporate Election', and Schreiner, 'Corporate and Individual Election'.

18. On individual election in respect of salvation, see the comments on 8:29.

that the reasons behind the choice of Cyrus were threefold: 'personal – that he will come to know the God of Israel; national – for the sake of Israel; and universal – to be the means whereby the entire world will acknowledge God's uniqueness'.[19] One can infer from the apostle Paul's arguments in this unit that he understands God's election of individuals to have a 'national' purpose for Israel and a 'universal' purpose for the world. God's unilateral choice of Abraham, Sarah's son Isaac and Rebecca's son Jacob has national implications for Israel in that God creates Israel through them. God's preservation of a remnant in Israel's history and in the present also has national implications for Israel. God's preservation of a remnant in Israel kept Israel from being snuffed out like Sodom and Gomorrah.

God's election of persons and groups has universal ramifications in that God intends to show his power that his 'name may be proclaimed in all the earth' (9:17) and 'to make known the riches of his glory for the objects of mercy' (9:23). That is why Paul concludes his arguments in this entire section with a doxology, 'To him be the glory for ever', in anticipation that God will soon achieve the majestic purpose of redeeming both Jews and Gentiles (11:36). Therefore, the focus of election in this section is theocentric and not anthropocentric. It is about how God is directing history and is not about who will receive salvation. The 'personal' implications of God's election – what it meant personally, for example, for Jacob to be loved and Esau to be hated – are therefore not prominent in this unit. The focus of election is how God inscrutably (11:33) fulfils his purposes through the choice of various persons and groups. That is why the question that someone might ask, 'If there are elect, is there any point to evangelism?' is based on a flawed premise. It mistakenly assumes that the elect are those chosen to be saved and the un-elect are those chosen not to be saved. God says that the ultimate purpose in electing Israel was for it to be 'a light to the

---

19. Paul, *Isaiah 40 – 66*, p. 251. He notes that repetition of the formula 'I am the LORD' in Isa. 45:3, 5, 6, 7, and in the next pericope, Isa. 45:8, 18, 19, 21, 22, emphasizes God's purpose in making himself known to the entire world.

nations / that my salvation may reach to the end of the earth' (Isa. 49:6; 42:6; Acts 13:47).

Does God treat humans as if they were simply utilitarian pots, making from the same lump of clay 'one piece of pottery for honor and another for dishonor' (9:21, CSB)? It is important to understand the point that Paul makes from his analogies in the context before drawing theological tenets from them. The key word in this unit that surfaces in 9:15, 18 is 'mercy'. It is also the concluding word in 11:31−32 at the end of this large section. Paul seeks to show that God's purpose is to save, and that one can be saved only by God's mercy. Paul is not deliberating whether persons are predestined to be saved or damned. His argument continues a theme that courses through the letter. Salvation does not depend on human exertion or worthiness but only on the merciful grace of God. Paul's specific purpose in this unit is to make the case that Israel is not saved by race alone but by grace alone. From this fundamental truth he will argue that if God saves 'privileged' (9:3−5) Israel by grace alone, then God can also save unprivileged Gentiles by grace alone.

Paul makes the important theological argument that God's word powerfully fashions a people from nothingness according to God's purposes. God's election reverses conventional human values 'in the same way as the cross of Christ turns the values of this world upside down. God's elect have been given an invisible status that contradicts their visible status.'[20] God chose Jacob before he was born and had done anything good or bad. The 'no people' who had an idolatrous heritage and were unloved have now become loved as God's people (9:25−26). Those who did not strive for righteousness attained righteousness through faith (9:30), but Israel who did strive for righteousness utterly failed to attain it because they went all out to achieve righteousness that is based on the law and they could not fulfil the law (9:30−31). Those who were not seeking after God found God when God revealed himself to them (10:20). Since Israel is established by divine mercy alone, Paul has hope that God will save 'all Israel' (11:26) and not just a limited remnant. God also

---

20. Grindheim, *Election*, p. 196.

intends to save Gentiles. This unit, then, lays the foundation for Paul's argument that Wagner summarizes well:

> These once-hated scions of Esau are now called children of the living God for precisely the same reason that Jacob and his descendants have always been, and ever will be, God's beloved: because of the gracious, loving embrace of a merciful and sovereign God. Like Israel, their identity as God's people is determined 'not by works, but by the one who calls' (Rom 9:12).[21]

B. Righteousness through faith for Jew and Gentile has been made known to all Israel (9:30 – 10:21)

Context

In 9:30 – 10:21, Paul provides a deferred explanation for why he feels the sorrow over Israel's current spiritual malaise that he expressed in 9:1–3. Gentiles have attained the standing of righteousness from God without having sought it (9:30) while the majority in Israel have failed to attain it despite their zeal for the law. Paul tackles the current status of the majority in Israel, an anguishing question for Jewish Christians in the first century. If God's word did not fail (9:6), why is it that most Jews have rejected their Messiah? They were the very people who should have been prepared for his coming by 'the law of Moses, the prophets, and the psalms' (Luke 24:44–47).

Israel's problems are rooted in its refusal to accept theological assertions found in chapters 1–8. God reckons righteous only those who have faith in Christ. Consequently, ethnic Israel cannot rest on its God-given privileges. They do not guarantee salvation. Israel's salvation depends on confessing that Jesus is Lord and believing that God raised him from the dead (10:9). Those who do not do so will be lopped off from God's people. This reality leads to the central question in this unit: why did Gentiles who did not pursue righteousness obtain it, but Israel who pursued the law of righteousness did not (9:30–32)? If only those who believe the

---

21. Wagner, *Heralds*, p. 422.

gospel, including those who are uncircumcised, are the true heirs of Abraham (4:11–17) and the children of God (8:14–17), where did the majority of Jews go wrong? If the gospel is 'the power of God for salvation to everyone who has faith, to the Jew first and also to the Greek' (1:16), why is it that Jews who were the first to hear it do not believe?

To answer this question, Paul sets up a chain of evidence to find the missing link where Israel went wrong. Gentiles attained righteousness because it can be attained only by faith. Israel pursued its own righteousness based on works and did not attain God's righteousness. Paul asserts that Christ is the end of the law, which means that the law does not offer righteousness or salvation; all must be saved through faith in Christ. If that is the case, where is he (10:6–11)? Paul avows that Christ is not a dead prophet such that they must round up a committee to send up to heaven or down to the abyss to get hold of him. He is present, as near as the confession on one's lips and the trust in one's heart (10:8). What holds Israel back is this lack of trust.

Perhaps Israel has not heard, and, consequently, it has had no opportunity to make this confession of faith (10:18). Paul responds that the gospel has gone out everywhere and was preached to Israel first. It has heard the gospel and rejected it. Perhaps it was too hard to understand. Paul responds that a 'no nation', according to Israel's standards, has heard, understood and believed. Where does that leave Israel?

The crux of Israel's problem emerges in 10:20–21 where Paul quotes Isaiah 65:2: 'But of Israel he says, "All day long I have held out my hands to a disobedient and contrary people"' (10:21). Israel's problem is rooted in disobedience that rebuffs God's offer of salvation through Christ. Israel is lost because it stubbornly pursues its own ways of establishing a righteous standing with God and withholds the only thing God requires of it: faith and obedience. This failure of the majority of Israel to believe in the Messiah fits a long-established pattern of unfaithfulness to God. As Seifrid puts it,

> Israel for its part seems hell-bent on frustrating the divine purpose at
> nearly every step of the way. The faithfulness of God is met repeatedly

with the faithlessness of his people, to which God then responds with
all the wrath of a betrayed spouse.[22]

Comment

i. Gentiles have obtained righteousness by faith; Israel has not because it seeks to establish its own righteousness (9:30–33)

30–31. For the sixth and final time in the letter Paul asks the
rhetorical question *What then are we to say?* (4:1; 6:1; 7:7; 8:31; 9:14) to
introduce his discussion. The question concerns the contemporary
situation of non-believing Israel and believing Gentiles. Gentiles
have obtained the status of righteousness though they did not
pursue it. Paul takes for granted from his previous discussion (3:22;
4:13; 5:1) that Gentiles who have faith and confess Jesus as Lord
have been granted this righteous status. His purpose is to set up
the contrast between these Gentiles who had no divine privileges
and no expectation that God would reckon them as righteous and
Israel who with all its divine privileges has failed to attain this
status with God despite its zealous efforts.

One of the distinguishing benefits Israel received from God
was the law (9:4). The people of Israel failed to attain the righteous status they sought because they 'pursued the law' (NIV),
assuming that it was the sure-fire pathway to righteousness and
failing to acknowledge that God has sent Jesus as their Messiah,
whose death and resurrection alone procures righteousness. This
interpretation takes the Greek phrase literally translated 'law of
righteousness unto law' to mean 'pursuing the law for righteousness', for the prize of attaining a right relationship with God
(Schreiner, p. 525). This pursuit of righteousness was unproductive
because of the manner in which they chased after it (9:16, 32).
Some thought that by conforming their lives to the external
details of a written code without it penetrating and transforming
their hearts (Matt. 23:23–28) they could attain the status of righteousness. They did not fully recognize that 'uprightness before
God depends not on human will or exertion; it depends on God's
mercy' (Fitzmyer, p. 578). They also misguidedly pursued the law

---

22. Seifrid, *Justification*, p. 253.

as an end in itself. They ran after the law instead of running with God. In doing so, they misunderstood God's purpose in giving the law (5:20; 7:7; Gal. 3:19).

32a. Paul diagnoses Israel's problem as 'pursuing' righteousness *as if it were based on works*.[23] Once again, the contrast between faith and works arises in the letter (cf. 3:20–22), and here Paul specifically denies that works can lead to righteousness. To insist that *works* refers simply to boundary markers that maintain one's participation in Israel's covenant community utterly fails to make sense in this context. Paul portrays *works* as deeds that obey the law's commands and that are presumed to produce a righteous standing before God.[24] Galatians 3:10–12 provides an important parallel to understand Paul's assumptions about the law. Under the law, receiving life does not depend on faith but on doing the works of the law (Lev. 18:5; Gal. 3:12). Failure to do everything written in the law puts one under a curse (Deut. 27:26; Gal. 3:10). By contrast, Paul argues from Habakkuk 2:4 that the righteous are those who live by faith (Gal. 3:11; cf. Rom. 1:17). After the coming of Christ, the people of Israel continued imprudently to place their trust in works for righteousness. It contributed to their refusal to trust in the righteousness that God offers to everyone through faith in Christ. Paul contends that they took off from the starting blocks, thought they were in reach of the finish line, but they were on the wrong track. That Gentiles attained righteousness and Israel did not is not a matter of the Gentile tortoise passing an overconfident Jewish hare in a race. God never intended it to be a race at all. Salvation comes as a gift that is offered to all and received on the basis of faith (1:17; 3:21–22; Phil. 3:9).

32b–33. Paul cites Isaiah to add another factor that contributed to Israel's failure. In their race after the law, Israel tripped over a stumbling block that God placed in the middle of the track. Paul

---

23. No verb occurs in the Greek text, and the verb 'pursue' (*strive*, 'seek') is supplied.

24. Sanders, *Paul, the Law*, p. 36, concedes this point yet claims, 'Paul did not say precisely what he meant' (p. 42).

inserts *a rock that will make them fall* from Isaiah 8:14 into the middle
of his citation of Isaiah 28:16:

> *See, I am laying in Zion a stone that will make people stumble . . .*
> *and whoever believes in him will not be put to shame.*

The combination of these two texts makes the stone an image of
salvation as a refuge against a deluge and an image of judgment as
something that causes one to crash headlong to the ground (cf.
Dan. 2:34–35, 44–45). Paul follows the LXX that reads 'the one who
puts his trust in him will not be put to shame' instead of 'will not
panic'. He interprets not being put to shame eschatologically as a
reference to not being condemned at the final judgment. This
statement parallels 10:13: 'Everyone who calls on the name of the
Lord shall be saved.' The decisive factor that determines one's salvation is whether one puts one's trust in this stone or whether one
trips over it by refusing to put one's trust in it.

The Greek pronoun *autō* as the object of *believes* could be
translated as 'it' or 'him'. If it is translated 'it', the stumbling
block could refer to the law. The people of Israel put their faith
in the law that led them to stumble and fall because they misunderstood the law's purpose.[25] That may explain why Paul omits
the positive description of the stone as 'a foundation stone, a
tested stone, a precious cornerstone, a sure foundation' from his
citation of Isaiah 28:16. He does not believe that these metaphors
apply to the law. The verb 'believe', however, would more naturally lead the audience to assume that Christ is the object of belief
and that he is the cause of stumbling. This reading is most likely
since Christ is the object of faith in 10:11, where Paul cites Isaiah
28:16 again. The context is confessing Jesus as Lord and believing
that God raised him from the dead (10:9) and calling on the
name of the Lord (10:13). Therefore, Paul must understand Christ
to be the stumbling block and rock of offence (*petran skandalou*)
that has caused a majority of Jews to fall. This interpretation has
affinities with Simeon's words to Mary that the newborn Jesus 'is

---

25. Barrett, 'Romans 9.30 – 10.21'; and Meyer, 'Romans 10:4.'

destined for the falling and the rising of many in Israel' (Luke 2:34).

Paul identifies 'Christ crucified' as the major impediment (*skandalon*) that prevents the Jews from believing (1 Cor. 1:23). He also ties the offence (*skandalon*) of the cross to eliminating the requirement of circumcision, which imposes the obligation 'to obey the entire law' (Gal. 5:3), for attaining 'the hope of righteousness' (Gal. 5:5). Since Paul believes that righteousness cannot come through the law since the law does not 'impart life' (Gal. 3:21, NIV), the chief obstacle that prevents many Jews from receiving the status of righteousness, therefore, is their failure to believe in Christ crucified and their mistaken belief that righteousness and life can come from the law. The stone of stumbling that caused so many in Israel to fall was not an accidental hazard. God deliberately placed the stone in Zion, in the very midst of Israel. It did not cause people to trip because it was hidden from view. Paul agrees with the interpretation of other believers who add the testimony of Psalm 118:22 that this stone was deliberately rejected. God made it, however, the foundation upon which all believers are saved through their faith (cf. Mark 12:10–11; Acts 4:11; 1 Pet. 2:6–8).

ii. Christ has brought an end to the law as the basis for a righteous standing before God (10:1–4)

1. Paul addresses the Romans in the letter as *brothers [and sisters]* as he reiterates his fervent wish that Israel might be saved (9:3). Again, this wish assumes that the majority in Israel currently are not saved and that their salvation hangs in the balance. They do not believe and confess Jesus as Lord (10:9). If Paul believes that 'all Israel will be saved', as he affirms in 11:26, his confidence in God's providence does not make prayer for their salvation superfluous (Schreiner, pp. 529–530). He still appeals to God that this majority might make the same about-turn that he did in their attitude towards Christ. The desire to see this happen is one of the motives that causes him to return to Jerusalem. His goal is not simply to deliver a love offering from Gentile Christians for destitute Jewish Christians. Paul hopes that the tangible sign of the Gentiles' faith in the Jewish Messiah and their gratitude to Jews that this offering represents might cause other Jews to rethink their rejection of Christ and repent and believe.

2. Israel's lost condition is not due to a lack of zeal or moral seriousness.[26] As a former Pharisee, Paul knows of the impassioned resistance to pagan influences during the period of the Hasmonean persecution (1 Macc. 2:26–27) that continued in the Pharisaic movement as they tried to build a fence around the law (m. 'Abot 1:1; 3:14) and a fence around Israel to forestall assimilation. Nurtured by these values (Acts 23:6), Paul was formerly zealous to guard the traditions of the elders' interpretation of the law and to keep Israel faithful to the covenant (Acts 22:3; Phil. 3:6; Gal. 1:14). He made great efforts in pursuing the law and hounded the burgeoning church, but Christ revealed to him that he was running in vain and was like a stubborn ox kicking against the farmer's goads and worsening his discomfort (Acts 26:14). He learned that what counted with God was not his enthusiasm, devotion or gusto in the pursuit of the law, but accuracy in submitting to God's righteousness offered through Christ. His zeal was misaimed. Isaiah also reports God's displeasure with Israel's misguided zeal:

> Yet day after day they seek me
>   and delight to know my ways,
> as if they were a nation that practised righteousness
>   and did not forsake the ordinance of their God;
> they ask of me righteous judgements,
>   they delight to draw near to God.
> (Isa. 58:2)

Isaiah goes on to say that they fast and deny themselves but fail to feed the hungry and act with compassion towards the afflicted, so God rejects their outward show of piety as only window dressing that shrouds their true wickedness (Isa. 58:1–12).

---

26. Smiles, 'Concept of "Zeal"', p. 291, shows that the zeal Paul has in mind is not nationalistic fervour but an ardent commitment 'to keep the covenant by obeying the Law'.

Israel's zeal for God was off-target because it was *not enlightened*. That is, they did not correctly perceive the will of God in the law. The noun 'enlightenment' ('knowledge', *epignōsis*) appeared first in 1:28 to characterize the pagan refusal to see fit to have God in their knowledge. For Israel, the failure is due not to a want of theoretical knowledge of God or a philosophical misreading of God's will, but to rebellion against God's will, which makes the people's spiritual condition akin to that of the pagans. Gentiles are alienated from God because of their 'ignorance and hardness of heart' (Eph. 4:18). Israel is now alienated from God because of the people's ignorance of God's purposes and hardness of heart (11:7) and because they seek to establish their own way of salvation.

3. Paul supports his accusation that Israel's zeal is unenlightened, which echoes an earlier accusation that those who claim to have knowledge (2:17–20) are clueless. The problem is that they are ignorant of 'the righteousness of God' (NIV), a genitive of source that is correctly translated as *the righteousness that comes from God*. Consequently, they do not submit to it. Paul knows this error full well because he once could boast in his stellar Jewish heritage and performance as one 'circumcised on the eighth day, a member of the people of Israel, of the tribe of Benjamin, a Hebrew born of Hebrews'. His zealous pursuit of the law as 'a Pharisee' led him to become 'a persecutor of the church' and to perceive himself as 'blameless' when it came to righteousness prescribed by the law (Phil. 3:5–6). The parallels between 10:3–6 and Philippians 3:9 are significant (see Table 4 on p. 330).

Paul now knows that saving righteousness comes only as a gift of God's grace that cannot be inherited or earned. He sees Israel as persisting in this same error in seeking to stand on the rickety scaffolding of their own righteousness and forgetting the biblical warnings never to trust in their own righteousness (Deut. 9:4–6; Ezek. 33:12–13). How could they believe that they are justified freely by God's grace 'through the redemption that is in Christ Jesus' (3:24) when they are so busy trying to justify themselves on the basis of their works?

Paul judges their ignorance to be wilful snubbing of the truth about 'the righteousness of God' through which God has acted to bring people into right standing with himself. This right standing

Table 4: Parallels between Romans 10:3–6 and Philippians 3:9

Romans 10:3–6	Philippians 3:9
'the righteousness that comes from God' ('righteousness of God') (10:3)	'the righteousness from God'
'the righteousness that comes from [observing] the law' (10:5) versus 'the righteousness that comes from faith' (10:6)	'a righteousness of my own that comes from [observing] the law' versus 'the righteousness from God based on faith'
Israel 'seeking to establish their own' righteousness (10:3)	Paul seeking to establish 'a righteousness of my own that comes from the law'

is received only through 'faith in Jesus Christ' (3:22). Refusing to submit to God's righteousness, which is freely offered to all, is far more serious than simply making 'an intellectual miscalculation. It is tantamount to "spiritual apostasy".'[27]

4. They did not submit to God's righteousness because they did not realize that *Christ is the end of the law*. *Christ* is shorthand for the person of Jesus the Messiah and the message about his death and resurrection and its saving effects for all who believe. The word *telos*, which is placed first in the Greek construction for emphasis, can mean *end* in the sense of 'goal' (1 Tim. 1:5; 1 Pet. 1:9) or 'termination' (2 Cor. 3:13). Though Paul uses the word primarily in the sense of termination, more often than not with eschatological implications,[28] its translation in this context is debated. If it means 'goal', then Christ is the one to whom the law pointed as the source of righteousness. The law is not eliminated but fulfilled by Christ (3:31; cf. Matt. 5:17–20), and its just requirement is fulfilled by those walking according to the Spirit (8:4). In the context of the racing image (9:30–31; cf. Phil. 3:12–14), however, Christ marks the finish line of the race.

---

27. Gathercole, *Boasting*, p. 208.
28. Cf. Rom. 6:21, 22; 1 Cor. 1:8; 10:11; 15:24; 2 Cor. 1:13; 3:13; 11:15; Phil. 3:19; 1 Thess. 2:16.

If Christ is the finish line, it indicates that Christ marks the 'end' of the law whose role was only temporary (Gal. 3:21–25). In what sense is Christ the end of the law? It is important to read the whole clause to understand what Paul means. It can be translated: 'Christ is the end of the law for righteousness [that is, as a means for attaining righteousness] for everyone who believes.' If the Gentiles obtained righteousness though they did not pursue it, and the people of Israel pursued righteousness by works and did not obtain it, then keeping the law does not bring about righteousness as the people of Israel presumed it did. By saying that Christ is the end of the law Paul means, 'Christ has been proved as the better and proper way through whom humanity may find righteousness, so the soteriological function of the law has been brought to an end.'[29] The citation from Leviticus 18:5 in the next verse provides the context for understanding what Paul has in mind. The law of Moses stipulates that one shall live by keeping its statutes and ordinances. Christ is the end of the law as the way to life because the law provides not life but death, because it cannot overcome sin (7:9–10, 13). Christ provides life (5:10, 21) because God condemned sin in the flesh through his death (8:1–4). Jews and Gentiles alike can find righteousness only through faith in Christ, not through obedience to the law.

The end of the law for Paul is evident from his account of the various strategies he adopts to win others to Christ. When he says that he became '*as* a Jew' and '*as* one under the law' to win Jews and those under the law and 'as one outside the law (though I am not free from God's law but am under Christ's law)' to win those outside the law (1 Cor. 9:20–21, emphasis added), he takes for granted that as a Christian he no longer is required to live like a Jew or like one under the law (cf. Gal. 2:11–21). He understands himself to be under a different covenantal regime than that of the Mosaic law.

Christ's coming also means the end of the law's role as a *paidagōgos*, a slave childminder (Gal. 3:24–25) who carries a rod to keep his charges in line. Paul writes, 'But now that faith has come',

---

29. Chae, *Paul*, p. 242.

we no longer need the supervision of a 'disciplinarian' (NRSV), 'guardian' (NIV, CSB) or 'slave looking after us' (NJB). Those who are in Christ have reached maturity (Gal. 4:1–7). In the same vein, he has argued that Christ marks the end of slavery under the old written code that held us captive. Faith in Christ has set believers free for the new life of the Spirit (7:6).

Christ's death and resurrection also ends the law's power to curse the sinner (Deut. 27:26) who is now 'in Christ'. To believe in Christ crucified is to believe in someone who came under the curse of the law (Deut. 21:23; Gal. 3:13). Either the law's verdict is right, and he is permanently cursed, or God overturned that curse in the resurrection. The declaration that there is no condemnation in Christ (8:1) signifies that the law's jurisdiction has come to an end. It means that Christ's atoning sacrifice on the cross (3:21–25) marks the end of the system of animal sacrifices in the temple that bring only temporary forgiveness for only certain classifications of sins. Righteousness now comes to people like the tax collector in Jesus' parable. He simply cries out, 'God, be merciful to me, a sinner!' (or 'God, make an atonement for me, the sinner'). He 'went down to his home justified' instead of the Pharisee who exalted himself with an impressive list of works to his credit (Luke 18:10–14). Justification is available to *all* who believe since grace is the foundation of the new covenant, not works. Righteousness and salvation depend on faith, which encompasses the willingness to respond to God's invitation in Christ and to modify one's way of life so that it is now oriented towards the will of God. Christ sounds the death knell for all human efforts to earn God's favour and consequently also silences all human boasting based on the law. Christ also puts an end to the idea that possessing the law makes Israel superior to all other nations.

Paul understands that Christ brings an end to the old order of the Mosaic covenant (2 Cor. 3:13) and begins the new order of the Spirit (Bruce, p. 200). Christ's death and resurrection inaugurate a new covenant for how God and humans relate to each other.[30]

---

30. One can easily see why Paul would have been ill-treated in the synagogues for teaching his perspective on Christ and the law since his

That Christ has terminated the law as a way to righteousness does not mean that the law is now entirely revoked. Paul's citation of a sampling of commandments in 13:9 reveals the law's continued validity: 'You shall not commit adultery; You shall not murder; You shall not steal; You shall not covet.' They are summed up by the commandment to love your neighbour as yourself. One cannot claim, however, that by keeping these commandments one is righteous before God. Righteous standing with God comes only from submitting to God's righteousness through faith in Christ. Righteous living flows from 'the law of the Spirit of life in Christ Jesus' dwelling in the believer. In Christ, 'God has done what the law, weakened by the flesh, could not do' (8:2–3).

iii. How all can receive righteousness and salvation, and Israel's failure to do so (10:5–13)

5. Paul cites Leviticus 18:5 and Deuteronomy 30:12–14 to show that the law itself gives witness to these two different kinds of righteousness: the righteousness that comes from the law and the righteousness that comes from faith. Leviticus 18:5 declares that the law demands obedience to receive the promise of life. This perspective undergirds Israel's chasing after the law on the basis of works. The people of Israel think that obedience to the law is the condition for a righteous status with God and receiving life and that they can generate their own righteousness from obeying all the law's ordinances. The zealous efforts to obey the law have only sped Israel along the wrong track that leads to a dead end. Their goal is unattainable and creates only a self-righteousness that is fabricated from one's own or others' definitions of what counts with God.

---

view collides with Jewish assumptions about the law's eternal nature. Philo claims that the law is 'immortal as long as the sun and moon and heaven and the whole heaven and universe exist' (*Mos.* 2.3 [Colson, LCL]). Bar. 4:1 refers to 'the law that endures for ever', and Wis. 18:4 to 'the imperishable light of the law'. According to 2 Bar. 77:15, even when humankind disappears, the law will abide.

6–8. Paul cites Deuteronomy 30:12–14 to show that the law *also* speaks of a second kind of righteousness that is based on faith. He personifies *righteousness* as the speaker and interprets this passage as pointing to the gospel and to faith in Christ that has nothing to do with the law and obedience to it. Paul omits the threefold repetition of 'to observe [follow, obey, do] it' from his citation (emphasis added):

> It is not in heaven, that you should say, 'Who will go up to heaven for us, and get it for us so that we may hear it and *observe* it?' Neither is it beyond the sea, that you should say, 'Who will cross to the other side of the sea for us, and get it for us so that we may hear it and *observe* it?' No, the word is very near to you; it is in your mouth and in your heart for you to *observe*.

In omitting these references to observing the law, Paul replaces the commandment that needs to be obeyed with Christ who needs to be 'confessed'. It is Christ who is near, not the commandment.

Paul refashions Deuteronomy 30:11–14 further by having 'righteousness' speak prophetically about Christ as the near *word* of God. The *word* is the message about faith that proclaims that salvation is entirely unearned and undeserved and 'depends solely on God's act of raising Christ from the dead and exalting him as Lord (10:6–9)'.[31] Paul's interpretation of this passage makes the point that this second kind of righteousness is not so far away that one has to send a task force to heaven to procure it. What is preached is in reach of any who hear it.

Paul's method of interpretation would not have been considered so unusual or strained in first-century Jewish circles. Other Jewish interpreters applied Moses' declaration in Deuteronomy 30:11–14 in a comparable way. Baruch 3:29–30, for example, interprets this passage as referring to the special, divine wisdom that Israel possesses from the law, and maintains that Israel does not have to ascend into heaven or cross the sea to acquire wisdom. It concludes,

---

31. Wagner, 'Not from the Jews Only', p. 423.

Happy are we, O Israel,
> for we know what is pleasing to God.

(Bar. 4:4)[32]

Alas, from Paul's perspective, apart from Christ they are ignorant of 'what is pleasing to God'.

Interpreting the text through the lens of Christ also allows the audience to make the connection that they do not need to ascend into heaven to find Christ. Christ has already come in the flesh. Paul does not include the image of 'crossing the sea' but has *descend into the abyss* (cf. Ps. 107:26). The 'sea' and *the abyss* were sometimes transposable concepts in Judaism (Moo, p. 674). *The abyss*, however, provides more than just a fitting contrast with an ascent into heaven, something it is impossible for humans to do. Believers understand that it is fruitless to descend into the abyss to find Christ since he has been raised from the dead.

9–10. Paul asserts that all that is necessary for salvation is the confession that Christ is Lord and faith that God raised him from the dead. Those who genuinely believe and are obedient from the heart (6:17) confess their faith in public. Confessing Christ as Lord is far more than a politically provocative statement that Christ is Lord and Caesar is not. Since 'Lord' is used over 600 times in the LXX to translate the Hebrew YHWH, it is a provocative theological assertion. It assumes 'that Jesus shares the name and the nature, the holiness, the authority, power, majesty and eternity of the one and only true God' (Kruse, p. 410).

Paul clarifies the meaning of the phrases *with your lips* and *in your heart* to prevent anyone from mistakenly imagining that God requires only the miming of a pietistic, stock phrase as if it were a mystical 'open sesame' that magically opened the doors to heaven. Believing in one's heart is a more driven and aroused faith than simply believing in one's head. The heart is the seat of the

---

32. Philo applied Deut. 30:11–14 to assure his readers that they could keep 'the divine commandments' (*Praem.* 79–80), attain 'the good' (*Post.* 84–85; *Mut.* 236–237; *Praem.* 80) and refit their lives through 'repentance' (*Virt.* 183 [Colson, LCL]).

comprehension and desires that dictates one's direction in life. That is why Paul prays that the Lord 'so strengthen your hearts in holiness that you may be blameless before our God and Father at the coming of our Lord Jesus with all his saints' (1 Thess. 3:13), and that God will 'comfort your hearts and strengthen them in every good work and word' (2 Thess. 2:17) and 'direct your hearts' (2 Thess. 3:5). It is also why God 'tests our hearts' (1 Thess. 2:4). The confession that *Jesus is Lord* (1:4; 1 Cor. 12:3; 2 Cor. 4:5; Phil. 2:11) and that he was *raised from the dead* (4:24; 6:9; 8:34; 1 Cor. 15:4; Gal. 1:1) requires more than offering lip service to God. The reference to *heart* would recall for Jews the Shema:

> Hear, O Israel: The LORD is our God, the LORD alone. You shall love the LORD your God with all your heart, and with all your soul, and with all your might. Keep these words that I am commanding you today in your heart.
> (Deut. 6:4–6)

What one confesses, then, must match what is in one's heart. The mouth that utters 'cursing and bitterness' (3:14) is ruled by a 'senseless' and 'darkened' heart (1:21, CSB). The mouth that utters the confession that Jesus is Lord is ruled by a heart into which God has poured his love (5:5).

11–13. Paul cites the last part of Isaiah 28:16 again (cf. 9:33) and broadens the application from 'the one who believes shall not be put to shame' (LXX) to 'everyone who believes' (CSB). It is consistent with the citation from Joel 2:32 (3:5, LXX), *Everyone who calls on the name of the Lord shall be saved*, which Paul applies to the redemption offered in Christ (10:13). This statement applies to every person 'who believes' (10:4). All who believe are saved through their faith because Christ is 'over all' (9:5) and God makes no distinction between the peoples of the earth. They may have differences, but there are 'no distinctions of rank or privileges before God'.[33] God 'richly blesses all who call on him' (10:12, NIV). Calling on *the name of the Lord* refers to God in Joel's

---

33. Motyer, *Israel*, p. 106.

context, but again Paul expects his audience to understand that *the Lord* is 'the Lord Jesus Christ' (1:4, 7; 5:1, 11, 21; 6:23; 7:25; 8:39; 13:14; 14:14; 15:6, 30; 16:20).

It is a fundamental point of Christian theology that after Christ humbled himself in obedience on the cross, God raised him from the dead and 'highly exalted him / and gave him the name / that is above every name' (Phil. 2:6–11). Believers are those who call upon 'the name of our Lord Jesus Christ' (1 Cor. 1:10).

iv. Israel is without excuse for its unbelief (10:14–21)

14–15. With four rhetorical questions Paul sets up his refutation of any objection that Israel cannot be held accountable for failing to believe. The first three questions pick up the verbs *call on* (10:12–13), *believe* (10:9–10) and *proclaim* (10:8) in reverse order from the previous verses. The fourth question adds the idea that the proclaimer needs to be *sent* (cf. 1 Cor. 1:17). Paul then applies the questions to Israel's current situation to show that it is without excuse for its unbelief.[34]

In 10:15, Paul cites the gist of Isaiah 52:7: *How beautiful are the feet of those who bring good news!* He omits the phrases 'upon the mountains', 'who announces peace' and saying to Zion, 'Your God reigns!' that are in Isaiah's text and thereby removes any idea that the good news was intended to be proclaimed only to Zion or that God is the God only of Israel. He also changes the reference to a single herald proclaiming the good news to an array of heralds proclaiming the good news. Therefore, Paul applies the citation to those preaching the Christian gospel worldwide to all unbelievers.[35]

Paul gives primacy to the oral proclamation and aural reception of the gospel. The message takes effect only when it is preached, heard and received. The text literally reads, 'How can they believe [the one] whom they have not heard?' This does not mean that they can be excused if they have not heard Jesus in person, but presumes that Christ speaks through the one preaching the gospel. Preaching

---

34. Bekken, *Word*, 49.
35. Bell, *Jealousy*, p. 89.

is not simply passing on information about God and Christ jazzed up with the eloquence of human wisdom. That only empties the cross of its power (1 Cor. 1:18). Rather, preaching is the communication of God's wisdom in the cross through which the power of the Holy Spirit convicts human hearts and the audience hear Christ speak to them. The required response of faith results from the word progressing from the mouth of the preacher to the ear of the hearer to the heart of the hearer and then to the mouth of the hearer in a public confession. Paul adds that the preacher must be sent, which implies that God has commissioned the proclaimer and furnished the proclaimer's message through divine revelation. Like the prophets of old, the proclaimers of the gospel have not fashioned their message through their 'inquiry and research'. They have been prepared by God and have been given their message by God (Middendorf, II, p. 1025).

16. The previous questions set up a transition in which Paul sketches out Israel's culpability for failing to believe the message that has been preached. The citation from Isaiah 53:1a, which introduces the account of the despised, oppressed, suffering servant who is wounded for our transgressions and crushed for our iniquities, opens the indictment. The context of the quote summarizes the good news that the gospel proclaims:

> the LORD has laid on him
>   the iniquity of us all.
> (Isa. 53:6)

The citation from Isaiah implies that the situation of the prophet and his word to Israel about the suffering servant (Isa. 53:2–12) is no different from the current situation of the proclaimers of the gospel to Israel. Israel does not believe. John 12:35–38 uses the same passage from Isaiah 53:1 to condemn with amazement the people's refusal to believe despite the many signs Jesus did in their presence. The Isaiah passage can be applied generally to all who reject the gospel, but Paul focuses only on Israel's unbelief. As in the days of Isaiah when the people closed their ears to the good news, the Jewish majority in Paul's day do not believe the report about Christ. Paul laments that nothing has changed in Zion.

17. Faith comes through hearing, but Israel has been deaf to the word about Christ. Israel's refusal to believe the word of Christ confirms that the people are trying to establish their own righteousness and are draped in ignorance. They do not comprehend that Christ is the end of the law with respect to righteousness.

18. Paul adds more scriptural testimony to eliminate any alibi that Israel might offer for failing to heed the message. The question *have they not heard?* is phrased in Greek to expect the answer 'Yes, they have.' Their ignorance of the righteousness of God (10:3) is not because they have not heard the gospel. The proclamation of the gospel began in Israel and is spreading from it to the rest of the world. Israel cannot claim to have never heard these things (Luke 24:18; Acts 2:1–47). The appeal to Psalm 19:4 (18:5, LXX) confirms it. Paul applies *their voice* in the psalm to the voice of those preaching the good news about Christ (10:15). The word going *out to all the earth* does not mean that the message has already spread to all the inhabited earth since Paul plans to go to Spain as part of his project to take the gospel to places where Christ has not been named (15:20). As the light of the heavenly bodies covered Israel (Ps. 19:1), so the word of the gospel has covered Israel. Israel has heard but has a long history of ignoring and persecuting those sent to it with God's word (2 Chr. 36:15–16; Matt. 23:29–31, 34–37; Acts 7:51–52).

19. Paul answers another potential objection: perhaps the message was unintelligible, and Israel can be forgiven for not understanding. Paul cites Moses (Deut. 32:21) and relates it to the contemporary situation to chip away at this excuse. A non-nation has understood the message and believed. If a *foolish nation* has done so, then what does that say about Israel? If it was not too obscure for a *foolish nation* to understand, it is not too obscure for Israel with its rich spiritual heritage to understand. Nothing is more straightforward than the gospel of grace. The problem, which is true for many besides Israel, lies in the disinclination to accept the bad news of the gospel that in their current condition they are unacceptable and need God's mercy. Also, they are unwilling to recognize that God has accepted and shown mercy to those they spurn as unacceptable and deserving only of God's wrath. Paul believes that Israel understood the gospel – the message of a

crucified Messiah who takes away the iniquities of all who believe
– well enough to reject it. They also reject the consequence of this
message: Gentiles who believe have become children of Abraham
and co-heirs of the promises without first having to become Jews.
Israel disavows a central item of the gospel: one is reckoned righteous only by faith whether one is circumcised or not (4:1–25).

The context of this citation from Deuteronomy 32:21 is important for Paul's understanding of Israel's future. It is part of the
Song of Moses that contains Moses' fierce warnings that Israel will
face disaster in the future for doing what is evil in the Lord's sight
(Deut. 31:20). Moses complains that 'his degenerate children have
dealt falsely with him, / a perverse and crooked generation' (Deut.
32:5), which is no way for them to repay their Father and Creator
who made and sustained them (Deut. 32:6). Moses' tirade against
Israel, however, is mitigated by God's promise to vindicate his
people. Vengeance belongs to God, and their doom is coming
quickly (Deut. 32:35), but

> Indeed the LORD will vindicate his people,
>   have compassion on his servants,
> when he sees that their power is gone,
>   neither bond nor free remaining.
> (Deut. 32:36)[36]

After Israel has been brought low, God will raise them up once
again. The great irony is that God will raise them up *after* they have
become jealous and angry at those (the Gentiles) they regard as *not
a nation* and a people that 'has no understanding' (NIV). The verb
I will make you jealous means that everything is being directed by
God towards a predetermined end. The same Greek word (*zēlos*)
can be translated as 'zeal' (10:2) or 'jealousy' (13:13). In provoking
Israel to jealousy (*parazēlosō*), God miraculously will turn the zeal
into a jealousy that zealously seeks to emulate those whom they
currently despise so that they will accept the gospel. Paul will
expound further this incongruous turn of events in 11:11–31.

---

36. Grindheim, *Election*, p. 163.

20. Paul understands Isaiah to have prophesied the Gentiles' positive response to the gospel and again cites Isaiah who 'dares' to say with God's voice,

> I was ready to be sought out by those who did not ask,
>> to be found by those who did not seek me.
> I said, 'Here I am, here I am',
>> to a nation that did not call on my name.
> (Isa. 65:1)

Those who neither sought nor enquired after God is an apt description of Gentiles who are also 'a rebellious people' (Isa. 65:2) awash in idolatry. As he did in 9:25–26 with the citations from Hosea 1:10 and 2:23, Paul dares to apply this Isaiah text to the Gentiles. God showers the rebellious with both judgment and grace and extends the same elective grace to Gentiles that was extended to Israel when God created it. Israel may have been tirelessly seeking the Lord (9:30) but it was looking in all the wrong places. The theological lesson is clear. Salvation for Jews and Greeks comes solely from God's initiative and merciful action in Christ, not from human initiatives and efforts.

21. Paul finally pins down the root of Israel's failure with the continued citation from Isaiah 65:2. They have been and remain *a disobedient and contrary people*. The description of God's forbearance – *All day long I have held out my hands* (cf. 2:4; 9:22) – heightens Israel's guilt in defying God. Their unfaithfulness contrasts with God's faithfulness, and the consequence is that Israel cannot hold God to a contract that they themselves have broken. The next chapter, however, reveals that God has not thrown up his hands in exasperation over wayward Israel and disowned them. God still holds out his hands to Israel.

Theology
Some of those who propose 'new perspective' interpretations of Paul argue that he does not challenge a Jewish view that keeping the 'works' of the law merits salvation, but instead attacks 'works' such as circumcision, dietary laws and observance of special days as boundary markers erected to bar the Gentiles from sharing their

elected status with God. Even if it were true that Jews viewed living in conformity to the law as a way not of entering the covenant but rather of staying within the covenant, keeping the law was vital for maintaining that covenant relationship with God. Paul's assertion in 10:3, however, reveals that he thinks the problem is that the people of Israel seek to establish 'their own' righteous standing with God through their obedience to the law, rather than to maintain boundary markers of covenant membership that exclude Gentiles (Schreiner, p. 531). Paul denounces the unbelievers in Israel for substituting their own righteousness from obedience to the law for the righteousness that comes through faith in Christ. Forgiveness does not come from the law but only through Jesus' death on the cross. Righteousness that is based on obedience to the Mosaic law is impossible to attain and intentionally or unintentionally excludes Gentiles who do not become Jewish proselytes. Righteousness that is based on faith in Christ is possible to attain and embraces both Jews and Gentiles.

Therefore, Paul radically disagrees with the sentiment expressed in Sirach 27:8:

> If you pursue justice [righteousness], you will attain it
> and wear it like a glorious robe.

Paul believes that the pursuit of the law for righteousness is always doomed to fail. First, human efforts to obey the law, despite the resolve to do so, always fall short. In chasing after the law, Israel could never overtake it. Persons may think that they have earned a superior grade in righteousness because of what they have done, but the failure to obey *all* the law results in a failing grade and produces wrath (4:15). That is why Paul says that one key purpose of the law is to identify sin as sin (3:20; 5:20; 7:7; Gal. 3:19), not to generate righteousness through obedience to it.

Second, the pursuit of the law as a means of attaining righteousness fosters self-deception (cf. Matt. 23:15–31). As a zealous Pharisee, Paul understood himself at one time to be 'blameless' when it came to righteousness under the law (Phil. 3:6). As a believer, he understands this presumption to have been a delusion. Following his encounter with Jesus Christ, he now regards his 'self-made righteousness' as 'dung' (CSB) in comparison to 'the surpassing value of knowing Christ' (Phil. 3:8). He recognizes that his boasting in his religious heritage and performance was a great effrontery to God because he could never do anything to put God in his debt (3:28; 11:35; Gal. 2:16).

Since the law has come under the power of sin and death (7:23; 8:2), attempts to achieve righteousness through the law bring only death because of the down-drag of sin (7:10–11). The righteousness of God comes as a gift that we do not need to chase down. As God's election does not depend on 'human will or exertion' (9:16), so a right standing with God does not depend on human will or exertion. It comes as a gift from God on account of Jesus' death on the cross and therefore is something that cannot be earned (4:2).

Third, pursuing the law to attain a righteous standing before God makes it a race with winners and losers. From a Jewish perspective, Gentiles are automatic losers because they never entered the race. This perspective fails to recognize that everyone is a loser in such a race. Attempts to obey the law down to the last jot and tittle and through tangible acts of piety might make one a good Jew and strengthen the boundaries around a community that supposedly prevent contamination by the impious, but they do not make one righteous before God. Paul lumps Israel together with the rest of humanity as falling under the power of sin (3:9), falling short of the glory of God (3:23) and desperately needing God's gracious offer of atonement through Christ (3:24–25). Paul believes that his fellow Jews fatally ignore the fact that Israel's existence depends entirely on the sovereign will of God who called it into existence by grace. God can and has extended that call also to Gentiles. That is why Paul addresses Gentile Christians as his 'brothers and sisters' (10:1; 11:25; 12:1; 15:30; 16:17).

The Gentiles may have had a surprising advantage over Israel. They were not pursuing righteousness as Israel was with its zeal for God. Byrne comments, 'Nothing can be more inhibiting of the creative operation of God's grace than a religious zeal that masks real need for God's mercy' (Byrne, p. 311). Gentiles did not have righteousness in their sights as a goal that they thought they could achieve by their own strength. Consequently, they were more open to receiving God's unmerited grace as 'little children' (Matt. 18:2–4).

Paul emphasizes in this unit that faith arises only in response to the preaching of the gospel in which God's grace through Jesus Christ and our need for grace confront us. Faith surrenders to God's verdict that we are sinners and accepts God's solution to our sinful condition that nullifies all our attempted self-help cures. The stress on hearing the message implies that it needs to be articulated in words and that it is not communicated simply by deeds. The popular quote 'Preach the gospel at all times. Use words if necessary' is not only wrongly attributed to Francis of Assisi, but it is misleading if it is taken to mean that proclaiming the gospel by example is more creditable and effective than proclaiming it with words. It is simply impossible to preach the gospel without words that convict, and the church exists to proclaim this message. It is important, however, that one's deeds do match one's words. Being saved by grace brings with it the requirement and the power to live a life that has been transformed by God's grace.

Believers will sometimes ask after reading Paul, 'If God has his elect, do I belong to the group?' The question really is asking about election as it relates to salvation. Will I belong to the elect who are saved? The answer to this question comes in 10:9–13 (emphasis added):

> if you confess with your lips that Jesus is Lord and believe in your heart that God raised him from the dead, *you will be saved*. For one believes with the heart and so is justified, and one confesses with the mouth and *so is saved* . . . For there is no distinction between Jew and Greek; the same Lord is Lord of all and is generous to all who call on him. For, 'Everyone who calls on the name of the Lord *shall be saved*.'

Believing with one's heart involves more than simply confessing with one's mouth. Salvation in the life of a believer is a process and a lifelong discipleship. Marshall describes discipleship as portrayed in Mark's Gospel as beginning with conversion that is tied to faith. He writes,

> Conversion is marked by the spontaneous forsaking of all existing forms of security, and faith consists in embarking on a lifelong relationship of believing trust in Jesus involving material dependence,

reliance on him for eschatological salvation, and a submission to a process of learning and personal transformation.[37]

C. God's mercy for all: the interconnection of the salvation of Gentiles and the salvation of Israel (11:1–36)

Context

The conclusion in 10:21 that God has constantly dealt with a 'disobedient and contrary people' leads to the next question that governs the third unit (11:1–32): 'has God rejected his people?' (11:1). Again, Paul's answer is a ringing 'No!' To confirm that God has not swept Israel into history's dustbin, Paul picks up the fibres of hope hinted at earlier in 9:29 and weaves a panorama of Israel's future salvation. Had the Lord not left a seed ('survivors'), Israel would have ceased to exist, like Sodom and Gomorrah. God preserved a remnant of believing Jews with circumcised hearts (Deut. 10:16; 30:6; Jer. 4:4). As in Jesus' seed parables where the seed sprouts and grows into a harvest, this remnant seed that God has preserved foreshadows the salvation of all Israel.

Before jumping to the glorious conclusion of the salvation of all Israel, Paul develops the remnant and hardening motifs to show how God is using Israel's hardening to serve his redemptive purpose. God has utilized ethnic Israel's unbelief to pave the way for the salvation of Gentiles. Israel's hardening has resulted in the saving message of the gospel spreading into the Gentile world where scores have renounced their idolatry and turned to God. Paul then must make the case that 'God's inclusion of Gentiles in the people of God does not mean the exclusion of Jews'.[38] Despite the persistent waywardness of the majority in Israel, God has not severed the covenant relationship with Israel and created a new people of God. Gentile believers have not supplanted Israel. God has attached them to the people of God.

Paul goes on to make the case that ethnic Israel does not have to be lost. If their rejection of the gospel has brought blessings to

---

37. Marshall, *Faith*, p. 139.
38. Johnson, 'Covenant Faithfulness', pp. 160–161.

the Gentiles, how much more will their acceptance of the gospel bring even greater riches for the Gentiles and enhance his mission among them (11:12, 15)! Since the divine promises to Israel are not null and void, God has not terminated his purposes for Israel. That Gentile believers now share the blessings of Israel is intended, by God's design, to make the unbelievers in Israel jealous and to cause their softening so that they might reattach to the people of God who confess Christ as Lord. God's mercy can overcome all disobedience, and God continues to work in mystifying ways to accomplish the salvation of both Israel and Gentiles that will ultimately manifest God's glory. God's greater purpose is to save the fullness of Gentiles and all Israel.

Comment

i. Israel's hardening is not total; God has preserved a remnant (11:1–10)

1–2a. Paul comes back to the issue raised in 9:6. The word of God has not failed, which means that God has not *rejected his people*. It might be a reasonable assumption from God's righteous reaction to Israel's persistent waywardness (10:21) that God has rejected his people. God has threatened to reject his rebellious people in the past (2 Kgs 21:14; Jer. 7:29; 12:7), and Israel dreaded this possibility (Jer. 23:33). Paul's categorical denial, however, that God has rejected his people (*By no means!*) is the central point of this entire section. He phrases the question in Greek to expect the answer 'no': 'God has not rejected his people, has he?' (author's translation). Paul echoes the psalmist's declaration that God will not forsake his people or abandon his heritage but will persistently seek to save Israel (Ps. 94:14; cf. 1 Sam. 12:22; Lam. 3:31). He does not promise that God *will not* reject Israel but declares that God *has not* rejected Israel. As an Israelite and descendant of Abraham from the tribe of Benjamin, Paul is living proof that God has not cast off his people.[39] He is, however, only part of a remnant. He has made the

---

39. Benjamin was one of Jacob's sons, the only one born in the land of Israel, and is identified as the 'beloved of the LORD' who rests in God's safety (Deut. 33:12).

point that not all those claiming to be Israel belong to the true Israel (9:6), which is determined by God's sovereign choice, and that God has whittled down Israel's numbers (9:27–29). Israel consists of those 'chosen by grace' and not by works (11:5–6). Consequently, Paul had to re-evaluate his boasts about his Jewish heritage and his fantasy of his righteousness 'that comes from the law' (Phil. 3:5–9).

He describes God's people as those *whom he foreknew*. That verb appears in 8:29 to refer only to believers 'predestined to be conformed to the image of his Son'. The key to being among God's people is having faith in God's Son. Paul argues, however, that even hardened Israel has not been written off by God. Israel will still play a part in fulfilling God's sovereign aims in redemptive history, and Paul's expectation, expressed at the climax of this section, is that they too will be saved and will be 'conformed to the image of his Son'. Their hostility to the gospel makes that prospect seem impossible, but God's grace and faithfulness to Israel are at work even when traces of it seem imperceptible.

2b–4. The assertion that God has not rejected his people introduces the recollection of Elijah's woebegone complaint about Israel's widespread apostasy during the reign of King Ahab and his wife Jezebel (1 Kgs 18:1–46). After Elijah had triumphed over the prophets of Baal and braved Israel's continued enchantment with false gods, his situation became desperate. He was on the run. The Lord found him hiding in a cave on Mount Horeb and asked him what he was doing there. Elijah moaned that the Israelites had 'thrown down your altars, and killed your prophets'. He presumed that he was the last of the faithful left in all Israel, and God's enemies now were hunting him down. He implied that when he was gone, it would be game over for Israel. He bitterly pleaded with God *against Israel*, assuming that if God had not already given up on them, God should do so (1 Kgs 19:10, 14).

The word translated *divine reply* (*chrēmatismos*, v. 4) occurs only here in the New Testament and announces a divine oracle that reveals what is otherwise hidden. Oracle language in the Old Testament is connected almost exclusively to Sinai and God's words spoken to Moses (Dunn, II, p. 637). Paul uses this word here to highlight that this is the word of God, not a human reflection. God

declares to Elijah that all is not lost. God has *kept* for himself a
remnant. Paul emphasizes that God took the initiative in choosing
and preserving this remnant. Therefore, the seven thousand who
did not bow the knee to Baal do not merit commendation for
valiantly resisting the pressures to worship false gods. Their
faithfulness issues entirely from God's gracious choice of them, not
from their own valour.

God's preservation of a remnant rules out the false inference
that God has rejected Israel. The Elijah story's mention that only
a meagre *seven thousand* were left also rules out another false
inference. Some might dismiss the small group of Jews who
presently believe in Jesus as their Messiah and Lord as only an
insignificant, misguided sect who have fallen for the blasphemous
fabrications of Christian fanatics. Israel's history reveals, however,
that God has a predilection for working with only small, marginal
clusters of the faithful. Jewish Christians are the latest and most
significant embodiment of the remnant of Israel.

5–6. Paul cites the Elijah story as an example of how God
preserves for himself a remnant during times of Israel's disobedience when their future as a people looks bleak. He reminds his
audience that God is doing so again as the majority in Israel remain
sunk in unbelief. Those who belong to this holy remnant, however,
have not earned this standing. It is only because God has chosen
them by grace, and not because of their stellar zeal for the Lord.
The emphasis on grace resounds through this letter.[40] Works are
contrary to grace because humans use them to boast before God
(4:2), to seek to make God indebted to them (4:4) and to try to earn
righteousness by their own merits (4:5). *By grace* harks back to the
very creation of Israel and God's choice of Jacob over Esau before
they had done anything good or bad (9:11–12). As salvation comes
only by grace and not by works, the outworking of God's saving
purposes in history through God's initiative in electing different
groups and individuals is determined solely by God's gracious call
(9:16). Therefore, the remnant at *the present time* cannot boast of their
faithfulness amid a crooked generation. They exist because of

---

40. Rom. 3:24; 4:16; 5:2, 15, 17, 20–21; 6:14; 11:6.

God's faithfulness to Israel, not because of their faithfulness. They are not heroic survivors who have toughed it out, but those whom God has selected and empowered to tough it out.

7–8. Paul understands *the elect* among the people of Israel to be the Jewish Christians. Unbelieving Jews are simply *the rest* or 'the others'. What they earnestly sought and did not obtain is the 'righteousness' that comes from obeying the law (9:30–33). In seeking a righteousness based on works, they also did not obtain the saving righteousness that comes only through faith in Christ. Paul contrasts the *elect* who have obtained this saving righteousness with *the rest* who *were hardened*. The Jewish Christian remnant now continues Israel's role as a light to the nations so that God's salvation might reach to the ends of the earth (Isa. 49:6). *The rest* stubbornly spurn the righteousness based on faith and doggedly pursue the pipe dream of earning their own righteousness, while also excluding Gentiles whom they scorn as cursed and irredeemable. Consequently, they cannot fill the role of being a light to the nations because their reliance on works of the law excludes Gentiles from salvation.

The majority in Israel are beset by a 'spirit of stupor' (NIV), an unresponsiveness towards spiritual things. In 11:8, Paul combines citations from Moses (Deut. 29:4) and Isaiah (Isa. 29:10) that comment on Israel of old and applies them to the Israel of his day. What God has done through Christ in their midst has met with either hostility or coma-like vacant stares. The passive verb *the rest were hardened* in 11:7 implies that God is not only the agent in choosing the remnant, but also the agent in hardening *the rest*. It is not that God makes them unresponsive, but God hardens them in their own inclination to rebel. Calcified hearts caused Jesus' enemies to reject him during his ministry (Mark 3:5; John 12:40), to reject God's offer of grace after his crucifixion and resurrection, and to reject the inclusion of Gentiles in the people of God without their first being required to come under the law and become Jews.

Paul argues next that just as Pharaoh's obstinacy served God's purposes and created an opportunity for God to demonstrate his power to save Israel (9:17–18), so Israel's obstinacy serves God's larger purposes by creating an opportunity for God to demonstrate his power to save the Gentiles. The difference between Pharaoh and Israel, however, is that Israel at least is aiming at a positive goal, righteousness, but proceeding in the wrong way. Pharaoh was not. As Paul develops his argument, he lays out the expectation that though God has hardened Israel in its misguided pursuit of its own righteousness, the hardening that blinds Israel to the truth in Christ will eventually soften (11:25), their stiff necks will become pliable, and their uncircumcised hearts and ears will become receptive to the Holy Spirit's transforming power (cf. Acts 7:51).

9–10. Paul cites Psalm 69:22–23 (68:23–24, LXX) in which David asks God to punish his enemies who hate him without cause by blinding them in their sin:

> Let their table be a trap for them,
> a snare for their allies.
> Let their eyes be darkened so that they cannot see,
> and make their loins tremble continually.

Paul, possibly influenced by Psalm 35:8 (34:8, LXX), adds the words *stumbling-block* and *a retribution for them*. He understands Christ to be the stumbling block (9:33; 1 Cor. 1:23), and hardened Israel is unaware that it faces God's retribution for rejecting him.

The meaning of *their table* in Paul's context is uncertain. The *table* generally exemplifies a setting where people feel a sense of well-being and give thanks for God's goodness in providing the nourishment to be received. It would be startling for it suddenly to become a cause of ruin (Morris, p. 404). The table is also a place where persons gather together to celebrate with a banquet. The table could picture a feasting army that falsely believes it has everything under control and is caught off guard by a surprise attack amid its merriment.

Applied to the current situation of Israel, *their table* could be understood in different ways. (1) It could be a reference to the table fellowship that was so vital to the practices of Pharisaic Judaism. It would pass judgment on this tradition as evidence of Jewish self-righteousness that is confident of their salvation and excludes others as hazardous pollutants (Dunn, II, pp. 643, 650). (2) Another possibility is that it represents the cultic table in the holy place in the temple on which the bread of the Presence was placed (Exod.

25:23–30; Heb. 9:2). Using a figure of speech in which the part stands for the whole (synecdoche), the table could represent the temple sacrifices by which Jews sustained a right relationship with God. It would assail their misplaced devotion to the law and works righteousness (and their trust that forgiveness of sins can come from the temple cult). That confidence is a trap.

Paul follows the LXX version of their backs being bent, resulting in them being stooped over, rather than the Hebrew text that refers to their loins trembling. The darkened eyes and bent backs argue for this second interpretation of the table. David hoped his enemies would have to stoop over as slaves. For Paul, the law veils the minds of the people of Israel so that they cannot see the truth in Christ (2 Cor. 3:15), and as a result they live as slaves to the law of sin and death (6:14; 8:2). Hunched over, they also cannot see God's horizon and the truth that forgiveness of sins comes only through Christ's atoning death and not through the obsolescent temple cult (Schnabel, II, pp. 436–437).

ii. Israel has not stumbled so as to fall; the fullness of the Gentiles will lead to Israel's salvation (11:11–24)

11. Just as Paul took up the questions of a fictional Jew in 2:1–29, he now takes up the questions of a fictional Gentile believer. His answers clarify the central topic of chapters 9–11. God's plan to show mercy to all that is being worked out (9:27; 10:1, 9, 11, 13; 11:14, 26) entails that the salvation of Israel and the salvation of the Gentiles are interdependent. He begins his explanation of how this is so by classifying the people of Israel's stumbling and falling as 'transgression' (NIV). Their rejection of the gospel is intentional disobedience. They have been ensnared in a trap of their own making, blinded and caused to stumble. This transgression, however, does not mean the end for Israel. They have not fallen into a bottomless abyss from which there is no escape. Israel's 'no' to the gospel is only a temporary phase. As is true for everyone, their salvation is as near as the confession on their lips and the belief in their hearts.

If Israel had fallen beyond recovery, it would mean that God's promises had failed. Instead, Paul makes the startling assertion that Israel's hardening and stumbling is part of God's redemptive purpose to save the Gentiles.⁴¹ Israel's recalcitrance unexpectedly carved a pathway for Gentiles to enter as full members of God's covenantal people through their faith in Christ. Paul wrestled throughout his ministry with hard-line Christian Judaizers who baulked at including Gentiles without requiring them to be circumcised and to come under the law of Moses. One wonders how much worse it would have been if the majority of Israel, who were zealous for the law, were won over to the faith. They may have created a critical mass of resistance that would have ruinously stymied the offer of salvation to the Gentiles that is based on faith and not works.

Paul says that God hardened Pharaoh so that God's name might 'be proclaimed in all the earth' when God miraculously delivered Israel from Egypt (9:17). The great irony is that the current catalyst for God's name to be proclaimed in all the earth is now hardened Israel. What now brings glory to God is not Israel's redemption from the clutches of Pharaoh but the redemption of all humanity from the clutches of sin and death (11:32–36). It is even more ironic that Paul insists that God intends the Gentiles' conversion to stir Israel to such jealousy that it will open their eyes and lead them to faith in Christ.

Paul sees his own calling as part of God's larger plan foretold in Deuteronomy 32:21, which Paul cites in 10:19:

> I will make you jealous of those who are not a nation;
>   with a foolish nation I will make you angry.

This expectation explains why Paul devotes himself to his ministry among the Gentiles to set in motion this outcome. It also explains why he devotes so much attention to the collection and again postpones a visit to Rome so that he can present the gift and

---

41. It is not a completely foreign idea for Jews to think that evil has befallen Israel to serve God's purposes to save Gentiles. For example, Sanday and Headlam (p. 438) note the rabbis' use of Hosea: 'R. Eleazar also said: The Holy One, blessed be He, did not exile Israel among the nations save in order that proselytes might join them, for it is said: "And I will sow unto Me in the land"' (b. Pesaḥ. 87b).

interpret it to the saints in Jerusalem. He must be aware that when he and the representatives from the Gentile churches arrive in the holy city the thousands of Jewish believers will hear that they have come (Acts 21:20–22). So will the greater numbers of unbelievers. Paul anticipates the Jewish Christians reacting to this offering from Gentile Christians by glorifying God for their 'obedience to the confession of the gospel of Christ', their 'generosity' and this tangible manifestation of 'the surpassing grace of God' (2 Cor. 9:13–14). He hopes that some of the unbelieving Jews might react by being provoked to jealousy when they see the Gentiles' obedience of faith (1:5; 16:26) evident in this gracious gift. They may come to see that because of the Gentiles' faith in Jesus as the Messiah, the fulfilment of the promises spoken to Israel (9:5), Gentiles now enjoy God's favour that once was bestowed on Israel. Paul yearns for them to want to follow the Gentiles' lead and also embrace the gospel.

Paul contends that those in Israel who failed to be part of its calling to be a light to the nations are the ones who are lost. Gentile believers are saved because of their faith in the gospel and thereby become a light to Israel. Bell writes: 'This exchange of roles is the great surprise in salvation history.' Gentile Christians have received Israel's covenant privileges and are 'playing *her* role in history'. Paul believed that Israel would be provoked to jealousy when seeing that Gentiles are saved by the grace of God through their faith in Jesus.[42] Therefore the 'jealousy' in this context is not the green-eyed monster that resents rivals and provokes violence (cf. Acts 13:44–45; 17:1–5). It is the kind that fears permanently losing God's favour to others and losing their calling as the chief standard-bearers of God's revelation to the world. Jealousy, in this context, wants to protect something,[43] and therefore is quite different from envy that begrudges the success of another. The vision is that Israel will emulate the Gentiles by turning to the Lord in faith to avoid completely losing God's favour that it formerly enjoyed.[44]

---

42. Bell, *Jealousy*, p. 199.

43. Esler, *Conflict*, p 290.

44. Grindheim, *Election*, p. 163.

Therefore, Paul wants his Gentile audience to understand that Israel's hardening has a salvific purpose for them and that their acceptance of the gospel has a salvific purpose for Israel. It may seem from a human vantage point that such a plan is rather convoluted, but Paul is sure that God will remove Israel's hardness and take away their sins as God once miraculously did in his own life.

12. Paul continues that Israel's transgression in rejecting Christ has resulted in a twofold loss or *defeat*. Israel has suffered a loss in numbers and is reduced to a remnant, and it has lost the race it ran to attain righteousness. It is not a catastrophic defeat, because God has used it to bring rich results among the Gentiles. When Jewish Christians were driven out of Judea and were kicked out of the synagogues across the world, their zeal for the gospel did not flag. They continued to preach the gospel, but now their audience became Gentiles. Many Gentiles responded with faith (Acts 8:1–4; 13:44–49; 18:5–8; 19:8–10; 28:17–28).

Israel's loss, however, is not final but only a temporary phase that serves God's ends that everyone 'be saved' and 'come to the knowledge of the truth' (1 Tim. 2:4). Paul argues from the lesser to the greater. If Israel's defeat has brought *riches* to the nations, how much more will *their full inclusion* in the community of faith bring riches to the nations? This conclusion anticipates and attempts to forestall Gentile Christians in Rome possibly finding fault with his decision to delay coming to Rome and risk derailing his Gentile mission by turning back to Jerusalem. Paul wants to make clear that when he turns his attention to the Jews in returning to Jerusalem, he is not abandoning his calling as an apostle to the Gentiles. If he were to provoke more in Israel to jealousy so that they believe the gospel, their conversion with their rich heritage in the Scriptures will only enhance the enterprise of taking the gospel to the uttermost parts of the world.

Paul mentions here Israel's *full inclusion* (*plērōma*). The word refers to 'fullness', 'full measure' or 'full complement' (11:25; 15:29; Gal. 4:4; Eph. 1:23; 3:19; 4:13; Col. 1:19; 2:9; cf. Mark 6:43; 8:20; John 1:16). Paul uses the verb form of this noun in 13:10 to refer to the action of completing something: 'love is the fulfilling of the law' (13:10). He cites Psalm 24:1 in 1 Corinthians 10:26 in which the noun refers to what completely fills: 'the earth and its fullness are the Lord's'. The 'full inclusion of Israel' parallels 'the full number of the Gentiles' in 11:25 where Paul uses the same word in Greek (*plērōma*). In both passages, Paul refers to the full number of those destined to believe (Jewett, pp. 677–678; Thielman, p. 536). This 'fullness' is not a fixed number that marks a cut-off point when it is reached. It is like the symbolic number of 144,000 in Revelation 7:4–8. That number represents the completed number of the faithful, which is next identified as a vast multitude that no-one could count, from every nation, tribe and people, symbolizing the universality of those saved standing before God's throne and singing praise. It is a number that only God can know.

13–14. Paul directly addresses Gentiles for the first and only time in the letter. They should pay careful attention to what he is about to say about Israel's fall and how it has functioned in spreading the gospel to the nations. Paul also refers to himself for the first time as *an apostle to the Gentiles*. He does not consider himself to be *the* apostle to the Gentiles. He puts himself alongside others (Jewett, p. 678). As an apostle to the Gentiles, he wants his Gentile audience to know how his work among Gentiles has consequences for the salvation of Israel. Stagg comments, 'Paul is fighting desperately to hold on to his own people without jeopardizing the mission to the Gentiles.'[45] Gentiles dare not forget Israel, because God has not forgotten Israel.

By 'glorifying' his ministry, Paul means more than taking 'pride' in it (NIV) or 'publicizing' it (CEB). His ministry's glorification is related to the word of the Lord being glorified when it is proclaimed, and when Gentiles believe (Acts 13:48; 21:20; 2 Thess. 3:1). The conversion of the Gentiles will lead to the eventual conversion of the unbelievers in Israel, and so Paul cautions Gentile believers against ruling out the Jews. His work among the Gentiles has a special function in God's plan as a factor in provoking the Jews to jealousy. That is why he so urgently preached the gospel from Jerusalem to Illyricum and is driven to preach the good news where Christ has not already been named (15:19–20). His aim is not just to

---

45. Stagg, *Galatians, Romans*, p. 107.

save Gentiles but 'somehow' (NIV) to save *some* of his own people
by making them jealous. The *some* is an indefinite number and
acknowledges that he is not the only one preaching to the Jews (cf.
Gal. 2:9). He knows that since only God saves, whatever success he
might see depends entirely upon God's will.

The idea of Gentiles provoking Israel to jealousy differs dramatically from the Jewish expectation that God would restore the
fortunes of Israel and then Gentiles would flock to Zion, saying,

> God is with you alone, and there is no other;
> there is no god besides him.
> (Isa. 45:14–17; cf. 60:5–17; 61:6; Mic. 4:13; Tob. 13:11; 14:5–7)

In delivering the collection from Gentile churches to the believers
in Jerusalem, Gentiles are able to spread the news that they have a
share in God's salvation because of their belief in the Jewish Messiah.
Their emissaries do not come to Zion bearing gifts as supplicants but
as those who are full members of God's people in Christ and who
come to offer help to Jews as their spiritual brothers and sisters. Paul
hopes that when Jewish unbelievers see these Gentiles' faith it might
spur them to recognize that God's promises to Israel find fulfilment
in the gospel. They might become jealous to see that Gentile
believers are not eating the crumbs that the children might drop
from the table but are partaking of the full meal (Mark 7:27–28).
They also might see that Gentile Christians not only have gained the
blessings promised to Israel but also have a closer relationship to
God through Christ and the Spirit than they do (8:15).[46]

15. *Their rejection* refers to Israel's rejection of God, not God's
rejection of Israel. It means that in rejecting Christ and the truth
of the gospel, Israel has rejected God. *Their acceptance* is their acceptance of the gospel that leads to their acceptance by God who offers
salvation to all based on faith alone. It will mean *life from the dead*,
which is not a reference to the resurrection of the dead but a metaphorical portrayal of their spiritual revitalization (Eph. 2:5; Col.
2:13; cf. Luke 15:24, 32). It parallels Paul's exhortation for believers

---

46. Bell, *Jealousy*, pp. 103–104.

to offer themselves to God 'as those who have been brought from death to life' (6:13).

16a. Paul uses two metaphors, first fruits and the olive tree, to emphasize the Gentiles' dependence on Israel in the history of salvation. The *first fruits* metaphor draws on the law related to the ritual dedication of produce from the farmstead outlined in Numbers 15:20–21. The first portion that is offered to God consecrates the whole class of food so that people can eat it.[47] It is unlikely that Paul has Abraham and the patriarchs in mind as the first fruits. In the context, it refers to the elect remnant of Jewish Christians chosen by grace (11:5–6) and the inclusion of the Gentiles in the people of God. The point of this first metaphor is that the sacred offering of first fruits sanctifies the batch when mixed with the ordinary dough. This analogy explains how Gentiles who are mixed into this batch of dough do not adulterate the holiness of the people of God. Instead, they have been sanctified by their believing Jewish brothers and sisters. The consecration of unsacred Gentiles 'is assured by virtue of their association with the Jewish members of the holy community'.[48] Paul applies the first fruits metaphor elsewhere to distinguish the first converts in an area, Epaenetus in Asia (Rom. 16:5) and the household of Stephanas in Achaia (1 Cor. 16:15), who prefigured that God's redemptive work would lead to more converts. The sanctifying remnant in this batch of dough may also foreshadow the eventual reclamation of the rest of unbelieving Israel (11:12, 15), but that is not the main point here.

16b–17. The *olive tree* as a metaphor for Israel appears in the Old Testament only in Jeremiah 11:16–19 and Hosea 14:6–7. Paul

---

47. Paul uses 'first fruits' also to refer to Christ's resurrection from the dead as guaranteeing the resurrection of all those who belong to Christ (1 Cor. 15:20, 23). He has already used the metaphor in asserting that the gift of the Spirit is the 'first fruits' of believers who await the redemption of their bodies (8:23; cf. 2 Thess. 2:13).

48. Gordon, 'Sanctity', p. 363; cf. the parallel in 1 Cor. 7:14 where the unbelieving husband is made holy through the believing spouse with the result that the children are holy.

utilizes this metaphor to portray the salvation story of Israel in a nutshell. The olive tree's holy *root* represents Abraham and the patriarchs,[49] which accords with the statement in 11:28 that Israel is 'loved on account of the patriarchs' (NIV). The *branches* that have been *broken off* from the root that sustains their life represent unbelieving Israel. The branches that are *not* cut off represent the Jewish Christian remnant. The *wild olive shoot* that has been grafted onto the tree represents a Gentile believer. This wild olive shoot can now enjoy with the remnant the rich 'sap' (NIV) of the cultivated olive tree's life (cf. Judg. 9:9). That rich sap may represent multiple things: the spiritual sustenance of God's promises, the faith of Abraham that God credited to him as righteousness and also credits to others with faith like his (4:22–23), the nourishment of the Jewish Scriptures, and/or the gospel of Christ Jesus. The wild olive shoot *does not* replace all the branches. It is grafted in 'among them' (*en autois*; cf. NIV), that is, among the branches that are not broken off. It also is not a replacement for the branches that have been broken off since they can be regrafted onto the tree (11:23).

From Origen onwards, many have thought that Paul's olive tree allegory reflects his citified ignorance of farm practices. Dodd writes: 'Paul had the limitations of the town-bred man . . . and he had not the curiosity to inquire what went on in the olive-yards which fringed every road he walked' (Dodd, p. 189). He assumes that no sensible arborist would graft wild olive cuttings onto the stock of a cultivated tree, because they would produce only smaller, poor-quality, wild olives that would never yield useful oil. Instead, the shoots from an older cultivated olive might be grafted onto a wild olive and produce cultivated olives (cf. Theophrastus, *Caus. plant.* 1.6.10).

Paul admits that grafting wild olives onto a cultivated olive tree is 'contrary to nature' (11:24), and this abnormal action may be just the point he wants to make. Throughout Israel's history, God

---

49. Philo (*Her.* 279 [Colson and Whitaker, LCL]) writes that Abraham 'is indeed the founder of the nation and the race, since from him as root sprung the young plant called Israel'.

consistently has done what was unconventional, beginning with the choice of the younger Jacob over the elder Esau. It is odd for God to lop off the spiritually dead branches of Israel despite their rich heritage and to graft in Gentiles despite their abhorrent heritage of idolatry. By themselves, wild olives are of no value. Even when they are affixed to the cultivated olive, they 'do not sustain the root' (11:18, CSB) and seem to contribute nothing to the tree. This image fits the Jews' low esteem of Gentiles (cf. 1:18–31) that Paul expresses in Galatians 2:15: 'We being Jews by nature, and not sinners of the Gentiles' (ASV). This metaphor clearly implies that the salvation of Gentiles goes against nature, but it also reveals God's power to do the impossible and make the wild olive become part of the good olive. The analogy is aimed at deflating any spiritual vanity that might be budding among Gentile believers. Their addition to the people of God is not due to their suitability. They were not suitable, and, once again, God does the opposite of what might be expected. Introducing a wild, uncultivated olive sprig to the cultivated tree confounds traditional wisdom as something utterly incongruous.

Another interpretation contends that Paul's image is not horticulturally inaccurate. The practice of grafting scions of the wild olive onto a cultivated olive was not unheard of and was done to rejuvenate an unproductive diseased or ageing tree even though the olives were not as good.[50] This image suggests that God grafted a wild olive shoot onto the tree to revitalize Israel (11:26).

Both of these interpretations fit Paul's primary purpose to torpedo Gentile arrogance towards Israel. The first interpretation, however, makes the best sense. The Gentiles are described unfavourably as *a wild olive shoot* that shares 'in the rich root of the cultivated olive tree' (CBS). They do not sanctify the root (11:16) or support the tree. Instead, they are sustained by the root (11:18). The problem for the olive tree is not with the root, which is described

---

50. Baxter and Ziesler, 'Paul', cite Columella, *De re rustica* 5.9.16; Palladius, *De insitione* 53–54; Varro, *Rerum rusticarum* 1.40.5–6. This interpretation is convincingly refuted by Esler, 'Ancient Oleiculture', pp. 103–124; and Havemann, 'Cultivated Olive', pp. 96–97.

as already in a state of 'oily fatness' (*piotētos*, 11:17), but with some of the branches. Dead branches can be removed and replaced. The root, which was believed to be the source of the prized oil, cannot. Therefore, the addition of the Gentiles does not benefit the tree. They were added purely because of God's 'kindness' (11:22), and the allegory presents God as a strange arborist who does what goes against nature. This olive grower is like the eccentric vineyard owner who disregards the number of hours the labourers have toiled in his vineyard and pays them all the same wage (Matt. 20:1–15).

18–21. Paul now expresses the main point his Gentile audience should gather from the two metaphors. Gentiles have been grafted into Israel's rich heritage. This means that Gentile and Jewish believers are not separate trees but belong to the same tree. In 11:20, Paul concedes the truth of the statement in verse 19 that branches were broken off so that Gentile Christians might be introduced into the olive tree. Gentiles, however, should not become haughty. They have no grounds for boasting. God did not add them because God considered them an upgrade or loved them more than the Jews. They are included only by God's mercy, and, like all recipients of God's mercy, they are unworthy.

Paul's grafting image differs significantly from a similar one attributed to Rabbi Eleazar who comments on two women from idolatrous nations who were grafted into Israel. Ruth, a Moabitess, became the ancestress of David (Ruth 4:13–20). Naamah, an Ammonitess, became the mother of Rehoboam (1 Kgs 14:31) who had even more distinguished descendants, Asa, Jehoshaphat and Hezekiah. Rabbi Eleazar describes these Gentile women as worthy of this honour because they were 'goodly shoots to engraft on you' (b. Yebam. 63a).[51] In Paul's allegory, the Gentiles are *not* goodly shoots. They are wild olives that by nature do not produce good oil. Yet God slotted in these believing Gentiles, not because of their noble character but because of God's twofold purpose to save Israel by making it jealous and to create a new covenant community in which one's ethnic origin is irrelevant. Philo notes that shoots

---

51. Epstein, *Soncino Talmud*, p. 420.

from a productive tree are grafted onto an unproductive tree 'so that they grow together as one'. He continues, 'The same thing happens . . . in the case of men, when adopted sons become by reason of their native qualities congenial to those who by birth are aliens from them, and so become firmly fitted into the family' (*Agr.* 6 [Colson and Whitaker, LCL]). Paul inverts this image. Gentile followers of Christ have not been fitted into Abraham's family because 'their native qualities' were 'congenial', which Philo identifies as the basis of good practice. Gentiles had no prior merit. Therefore, God was going against best practice in showing unmerited mercy on them in the same way God did when God mercifully elected Israel (9:10–12).

The question Paul asks in 3:27, 'Where, then, is boasting?' (NIV), gets the same answer for both Jews and Gentiles: 'It is excluded.' The addition of the Gentiles to the people of God is intended to make hardened Israel jealous. Therefore, Gentile believers should not become arrogant (11:20) or boast (11:18). They are not to disdain either unbelieving Israel or the believing remnant. Paul puts Gentile Christians on alert that if God did not spare Israel, God's beloved, God surely will not spare them when they also warrant harsh judgment. They are not to think of themselves as God's enduring favourites the way Israel did. They are only branches, and since they do not support the root but are supported by the root, they are expendable if they are unproductive.

The emphasis on faith so central to the teaching in Romans (4:16) resurfaces. Those who were hardened in Israel were cut off because they did not have faith. Gentiles have also been cut off (11:24), but they were cut off from a legacy of paganism in which they had 'no hope', were 'without God in the world' (Eph. 2:12) and were ruled by 'the passions of our flesh' (Eph. 2:3). They have been saved by grace through faith (Eph. 2:8) and stand only because of their faith (Rom. 5:2; 2 Cor. 1:24). Just as Paul warned the Corinthians 'if you think you are standing, watch out that you do not fall' (1 Cor. 10:12), so he warns the Gentile Christians in Rome.

22. *Kindness* and *severity* belong together as inseparable parts of divine righteousness (Michel, p. 277). Belief meets with God's kindness. Unbelief meets with God's unyielding severity. God manifests kindness by loving (9:25; 11:28), electing (11:5, 28), giving gifts (11:29), calling (9:24; 11:29) and showing mercy (11:30–31). God's sternness is manifested in 'wrath' (9:22), 'hardening' (9:18; 11:7, 25), 'failure' ('defeat', 11:7); 'retribution' (11:9), 'rejection' (11:15) and cutting off (11:17, 19, 20). If Gentiles are in danger of arrogance, then being conscious of God's severe judgment on those in Israel who refused to believe and failed to submit to God's righteousness should keep them humble. If Gentiles flaunt their salvation as if they now ruled the roost as God's chosen, they can be severed from the tree as well. Remaining in God's kindness rules out both egocentrism and ethnocentrism and requires a kindly attitude towards Jews, both the believers and the hardened in Israel.

23. While God may have chopped off branches from the cultivated olive tree, God did not set them ablaze. Instead, God temporarily set them aside and is ready to regraft them onto the tree if they do not persist in their unbelief. We might assume that the branches cut off are now long dead and dried up. It would seem to be impossible that dead branches could be brought back to life and grafted onto the tree again. God, however, 'gives life to the dead' (4:17) and, according to John the Baptist, can raise children to Abraham from the lifeless stones in the wilderness (Matt. 3:9; Luke 3:8). In Ezekiel's vision in the valley of dry bones (Ezek. 37:1–14) the lament rises, 'Our bones are dried up, and our hope is lost; we are cut off completely' (Ezek. 37:11). God answers the lament with a promise: 'I will put my spirit within you, and you shall live' (Ezek. 37:14). In the same manner God is able to breathe new life into these dead branches, and it indeed would be life from the dead (11:15). The one condition for this revitalization is that they believe in Christ Jesus and accept his gospel of grace.

24. Israel's current disobedience in spurning the righteousness of God that is revealed in Christ means that they are in the same situation that the Gentiles were in before they heard and responded to the gospel. They have an advantage over the Gentiles, however, in that they are the *natural branches*. They naturally belong to the olive tree. Their rich heritage and privileges (9:4–5) mean that they have a closer connection to the gospel than Gentiles had, with their pagan heritage. Again, Paul holds out the assurance that all is not lost.

iii. The fullness of the Gentiles leads to all Israel's salvation and the fulfilment of God's promises (11:25–32)

25. Paul wraps up his argument with an attention-grabbing announcement: 'I do not want you to be ignorant of this mystery' (NIV). He wants to make sure that the Gentile Christians understand the full implications of his argument that the Gentiles' salvation and Israel's salvation are intertwined (11:12–13, 15, 16, 17–18). As a *mystery*, the interlinking of the destinies of the Gentiles and Israel is something that God has revealed to Paul and not something he unearthed searching through the Scriptures. It is quite possible that God revealed this mystery to him when God called him to become an apostle to the Gentiles (Gal. 1:15–16; cf. Acts 9:15; 13:2). This calling caused him to search the Scriptures that both constitute a crucial part and confirm the truth of his argument throughout chapters 9–11.[52] The mystery reveals to the Gentiles in his audience that their conversion is not God's ultimate objective. God's purpose in Israel's partial hardening was to save Gentiles. God's purpose in saving Gentiles is to save all Israel. Paul does add a new detail to his discussion. Israel's partial hardening will not be removed *until* (*achri hou*) the 'fullness' (CSB) *of the Gentiles* is reached.[53] Reaching the fullness of the Gentiles is the necessary condition that sets in motion the salvation of all Israel.

The 'fullness' or *full number* (*plērōma*) does not mean a preordained, quantitative number (cf. Rev. 6:11; 2 Esd. 4:36–37; 2 Bar. 23:4–5). As noted in the comments on its meaning in 11:12, it refers to what has been brought to completeness. It is better translated as 'fullness' (CSB) to avoid the implication that God

---

52. Kim, 'The "Mystery"', p. 419, argues, 'For a well-trained Jewish theologian like him [Paul] who was in the habit of substantiating a theological conviction or religious act from the Scriptures, is it not much more plausible to think that for the truly revolutionary decision to participate in the gentile mission he began immediately to think through its theological and salvation–historical implications and to seek its scriptural justification?'

53. The Greek phrase *achri hou* literally means 'until which [time]'.

operates with quotas. Paul refers to the entirety of Gentiles who respond to the gospel with faith.

This conviction goes against the grain of the common Jewish expectation that God would first restore and glorify Israel and then the Gentiles would flock to Jerusalem to pay homage to God.[54] God has reversed this expected eschatological sequence. The staggering reality is that God has glorified the Gentiles through their salvation to bring Israel to salvation. While Paul understands the gospel to be 'the power of God for salvation to everyone who has faith, to the Jew first and also to the Greek' (1:16), the situation is now reversed. The fullness of the Gentiles occurs first and then comes the fullness of Israel (11:12). The grounds for the conversions of Gentiles are also reversed. The Gentiles have not responded because God has glorified Israel, but because unbelieving Israel has been brought low and has become spiritually sluggish and cut off from its glorious root. It is not that Gentiles are made jealous of the Jews and flock to Zion to pay them homage; it is the Jews who will become jealous of the Gentiles, fulfilling God's declaration in Deuteronomy 32:21 that Paul cites in 10:19.

26. The Greek phrase translated *and so* (*kai houtōs*) describes the mode by which Israel will be saved, 'in this way' (NIV), which also implies that it occurs after the fullness of the Gentiles has come in so could also be a temporal reference that means 'only then will Israel be saved'.[55] It points to the stages of Israel's salvation. The Gentiles' salvation 'will take place prior to and will be a condition for the salvation of all Israel'.[56]

Who does *all Israel* who are destined to be saved include? (1) Paul has divided historical–empirical Israel from the elect in 9:6, 'not all Israelites truly belong to Israel', 'not all who are descended from Israel are Israel' (NIV), which seems to dissociate the term 'Israel' from its traditional ethnic connotation. Consequently, some believe that *all Israel* refers to a multi-ethnic Israel comprising the Jewish

---

54. Cf. Isa. 2:2–3; 56:6–7; 60:3–14; Mic. 4:1–2; Zech. 14:16–17; Tob. 13:11–13; Pss Sol. 17:26–46; Sib. Or. 3.710–726.

55. Van der Horst, 'Only Then', pp. 521–539.

56. Hvalvik, 'Sonderweg', p. 99.

remnant (11:5), the fullness of Gentiles (11:25) and those in Israel whose hardening will be removed and who come to believe in their crucified Messiah. If this is Paul's meaning, it would seem to state the obvious: all Christians will be saved. Paul's ten uses of the term 'Israel' in this section (9:6 [2x], 27 [2x], 31; 10:19, 21; 11:2, 7, 25), however, refer only to ethnic Israel. It is unlikely that he would now expand its meaning to include Gentiles without any explanation. Gentiles do not become Jews when they become believers but are incorporated into the body of Christ as Gentiles. If Paul were identifying the church as 'Israel' here, it would only 'fuel the fire of the Gentiles' arrogance by giving them grounds to brag that "*we* are the true Israel"' (Moo, p. 736).

(2) A second option is that *all Israel* does not include the Gentiles but applies only to remnant Israel (9:6, 27), which is a continually swelling entity but still a minority of Jews. But why would Paul need to say that all the remnant who believe in Christ and whom God has chosen by grace will be saved? If only a remnant from Israel is to be saved, it would hardly assuage his grief over 'his people' (9:2–3; 11:1). It is unlikely that Paul would suddenly shift the meaning of 'Israel', which in verse 25 is partially hardened and must refer to national Israel, to remnant Israel without further clarification.

(3) A third option assumes that *all Israel* refers to all the Jews alive in the last generation at the second coming of Christ. This view assumes that *Out of Zion will come the Deliverer; / he will banish ungodliness from Jacob* refers to the parousia, but that is not what Paul has in view as interpreted below.

(4) A fourth option understands *Israel* to be all the Jewish people, and the adjective *all* to mean that God will eliminate the divide between the remnant of believers in Israel and the hardened unbelievers in Israel. While God can do whatever God wants, this option does not mean that Paul thinks that Israel will be saved based on anything other than faith in Christ (10:4–6). If God were to save Israel by some alternative means that does not also apply to the Gentiles, it would be inaccurate to characterize God as impartial (2:11; 10:12). Paul does not believe that the Jews will get an automatic bye in the judgment because of their 'election' or for the sake of the patriarchs (11:28). If he did believe that all Israel would

be saved no matter what, why would he agonize over the current unbelief of his kinsfolk (9:1–3)? In 11:23, he asserts that the severed branches will be regrafted onto the olive tree *only* 'if they do not persist in unbelief'. This regrafting will not happen on the basis of God's faithfulness to a now obsolete Mosaic covenant based on works (10:4–5), but on the same basis that the Gentiles are grafted onto the tree – namely, faith in Christ Jesus. Throughout Romans, Paul asserts that God treats 'Jews and Gentiles . . . alike in the matters of sin, judgment, and salvation' (Kruse, p. 451).

Therefore, *all Israel* does not include every Israelite who has ever lived. Mishnah Sanhedrin 10:1 states: 'All Israelites have a share in the world to come, for it is written, "Thy people also shall be all righteous, they shall inherit the land for ever; the branch of my planting, the work of my hands that I may be glorified"' (Isa. 60:21). The discussion of this statement, however, adds several disclaimers:

> And these are they that have no share in the world to come: he that says that there is no resurrection of the dead prescribed in the Law, and [he that says] that the Law is not from Heaven, and an Epicurean [a general epithet for one who is licentious and sceptical]. R. Akiba says: Also he that reads the heretical books or that utters charms over a wound and says, 'I will put none of the diseases upon thee which I have put upon the Egyptians: for I am the Lord that healeth thee' [Exod. 15:26]. Abba Saul says: Also he that pronounces the Name with its proper letters. (m. Sanh. 10:1).[57]

The debate among the rabbis continues. Some exclude three kings, Jeroboam, Ahab and Manasseh, though Rabbi Judah defends Manasseh from 2 Chronicles 33:13, and four 'commoners', Balaam, Doeg, Ahithophel and Gehazi. Others also exclude the generation of the flood, the generation of the dispersion, the men of Sodom, the spies who brought an evil report and the generation of the wilderness (m. Sanh. 10:2). The rabbis did not believe that the statement 'all Israelites have a share in the world to come' included every Israelite. In the same way, Paul's statement that *all Israel will*

---

57. Danby, *Mishnah*, p. 397.

be saved does not include every Israelite who has ever lived. The use
of the term 'all Israel' elsewhere in Scripture confirms the view that
it does not mean every person in Israel but refers instead to a broad
and not exhaustive distribution of the nation (cf. Judg. 8:27; 1 Sam.
7:5; 13:20; 25:1; 2 Sam. 3:37; 16:22; Dan. 9:11; Acts 4:10; 13:24). Paul,
therefore, has in mind only the full complement of Israel (11:12),
whatever number that might be. It is composed of 'all Israelites'
who 'truly belong to Israel' (9:6) because they 'do not persist in
unbelief' (11:23).

Paul connects the Gentiles' salvation to Israel's hardening and
all Israel's salvation to the fullness of the Gentiles coming in (11:25).
Motyer contends that 'the hardening grows less and less as more
and more Jews are made "jealous" and believe'.[58] Paul sees reaching
the full complement of Gentiles and the salvation of all in Israel as
two converging lines. As Gentiles come to faith and it creates
jealousy among the Jews (11:14), it strips away a portion of the
tough carapace of the Jews' unbelief. More and more Jews will
regard the cross no longer as a stumbling block but as 'the power
of God and the wisdom of God' (1 Cor. 1:24) and will believe that
the gospel is 'the power of God for salvation to everyone who has
faith' (1:16). This process continues until eventually the two lines
intersect.[59] This conviction drives Paul to bring the fruit of his
success in preaching the gospel among the Gentiles to the saints in
Jerusalem. It is a return on their sharing their spiritual blessings
with the Gentiles. But he also must hope that some unbelieving
Jews might see it as 'alms' to the nation (Acts 24:17) and become
jealous, and that their hardening is removed so that they might be
saved. It also drives him to want to proclaim the gospel as far as
Spain to swell the ranks of Gentiles obedient to the faith in the
march towards reaching the full number of Gentiles that will lead
to Israel's salvation.

To substantiate this assertion about Israel's salvation, Paul cites
Isaiah 59:20–21a. His citation has it that *the Deliverer* will come *out
of* Zion rather than '*to* Zion', as in the Hebrew text. Neither does it

---

58. Motyer, *Israel*, p. 159.
59. Ibid.

include the statement '*for the sake of* Zion' or '*because of* Zion' as in the LXX version. If Paul did not deliberately alter the text, he cites a version he knew that supported his argument.

What does it mean for the Deliverer to come *out of* Zion? If the Deliverer is understood to be God, is it possible that Paul envisages God saving Israel apart from Christ, since Christ is not specifically mentioned? If so, it is odd that he would not then cite the reading in the Hebrew or the Greek text. It would make sense that God will save 'all Israel' by coming as the Deliverer *to* Zion or *because of* Zion. It does not make sense that God brings salvation to Israel by coming 'out of Zion' unless Zion is understood as heavenly Zion (cf. Heb. 12:22).[60] Some interpreters do understand Paul to refer to Christ as coming from the heavenly Zion at the time of the parousia. The only other time that Paul uses the word 'Zion', however, is in 9:33, where it refers to God placing a stone of stumbling in Zion. He understands Zion to refer either to the city of Jerusalem or to the people of Israel. Paul would need to give the audience some clue that he now uses Zion to refer to the heavenly Zion. In 1 Thessalonians 1:10, Paul writes that we 'wait for his Son from heaven, whom he raised from the dead – Jesus, who rescues us from the wrath that is coming'. In referring to the parousia, he specifically refers to Jesus coming out of heaven, not Zion (1 Thess. 4:16).

More critical are the theological problems that this interpretation raises. If Paul refers to a mass conversion of Israel at the parousia, presumably in the blink of an eye, from 'a large-scale last minute fresh act of salvation' (Wright, p. 691), it contradicts what he says in 10:6–21. Israel will be saved if they confess that Jesus is Lord and believe that God raised him from the dead. Paul believes that they can do that now in response to hearing the word and can be restored if they do not continue in their unbelief. It does not require Christ's descent from heaven for that to happen. Since

---

60. It is possible that the phrase *out of Zion* refers to God delivering the Jews scattered in the diaspora awaiting their salvation that goes forth from Zion (Wagner, *Heralds*, p. 284). A reference to diaspora Jews, however, is extraneous to the context.

there is no mention of faith in Christ in this verse, this interpretation implies that the salvation of all Israel has nothing to do with the preaching of the gospel. It makes the thematic statement in 1:16–17 that refers to the gospel as 'the power of God for salvation to everyone who has faith' not applicable to the Jews.

The phrase *out of Zion will come the Deliverer* is best construed as a reference to Christ as the Deliverer (*ho ruomenos*), and Paul believes that the Deliverer has already come. The verb *will come* is then a prophetic future *from Isaiah's standpoint* (Schnabel, II, pp. 511–514), not Paul's. He interprets Isaiah's prophecy as applying to the message of Christ's death and resurrection that went out from Zion (Jerusalem or Israel) 'to all the earth' and 'to the ends of the world' (10:18). Paul has argued that Christ is already present (10:8–9), and faith in him is not triggered by some miraculous *deus ex machina* to bring a happy ending to the story for Israel. He outlines the sequence of how God brings salvation to Gentiles and Israel. God placed a stone of stumbling in Zion (9:33), and Israel stumbled (11:11). Israel's stumbling, however, caused the message of salvation that requires the confession of faith (10:8–10) to come to the Gentiles (11:11a, 12). The Gentiles' salvation provokes Israel to jealousy that will lead to their salvation (11:11b, 14) when they no longer persist in their unbelief. God regrafts them into the people of God. Since Paul argues that Israel's salvation is to be driven by their jealousy over the blessings that have come to the Gentiles (11:11–15), he expects that their turning to faith in Christ will occur *prior* to the parousia. As the fullness of the Gentiles comes in, the partial hardening of many in Israel is removed. The second advent of Christ does not offer persons a second chance or Jews a preferential free pass because of their ethnic heritage. It is then too late for those who have remained steadfast in their rejection of Christ Jesus.

27. The *covenant* God will make with Israel may refer to the new covenant when God will put his law within them and write it on their hearts (Jer. 31:33). *Tak[ing] away their sins* alludes to Isaiah 27:9. After reciting a litany of sins, Isaiah then says that God will expiate 'the guilt of Jacob'. The shift from the use of the third-person verb in verse 26 to first person in this verse reveals that Paul makes a distinction between the Deliverer who comes from Zion and God who takes away the sin. It is God who takes away sin. As God elected Jacob by grace, so God will save Jacob, that is, Israel, by grace.

Paul has charged that both Jews and Greeks are under the power of sin (3:9, 20–23). It is not that Israel must wait for God to do something else to take away their sin. God has already dealt with the sin problem by sending his Son as an atoning sacrifice (3:25; 8:2–3). They must submit to the righteousness of God and accept with faith that their sin has been taken away through Christ (3:25–26).

28. Paul bluntly describes unbelieving Israel as *enemies of God* because of their rejection of the gospel, but he adds that this rejection is *for your* [Gentile believers'] *sake*. It has providentially facilitated the Gentiles' reception of the gospel. The attempt by the Hellenistic Jews in Jerusalem to kill Paul, for example, drove him out into the Gentile world where he would preach the gospel (Acts 9:29–30) from Jerusalem to Illyricum (15:19). Paul is confident that being God's enemy does not mean that Israel is now a lost cause. Through the death of God's Son, Jewish and Gentile believers were reconciled to God when they also were God's enemies (5:10). God proved his love for them in that Christ died for them while they were still sinners (5:8). Being sinners and enemies of God does not slam the door to the possibility of redemption, particularly since God's prior love for Israel has not grown cold. God ratified the promise to Abraham with an oath (Gen. 12:1–3; 22:15–18; Heb. 6:17), and God will not reject Israel for ever. Israel retains its advantages (9:4–5) because God still delights in its patriarchs (Deut. 4:37; 10:15; Rom. 9:13). The people of Israel need only to take advantage of their advantages by coming to faith in Messiah Jesus. That assurance entails that Israel will not reject the gospel for ever. Israel's future salvation will fulfil the promise of Micah 7:18–20:

> Who is a God like you, pardoning iniquity
>   and passing over the transgression
>   of the remnant of your possession?
> He does not retain his anger for ever,
>   because he delights in showing clemency.

He will again have compassion upon us;
  he will tread our iniquities under foot.
You will cast all our sins
  into the depths of the sea.
You will show faithfulness to Jacob
  and unswerving loyalty to Abraham,
as you have sworn to our ancestors
  from the days of old.

What Micah did not fully recognize is that Israel's sins will be for-given through Christ's faithfulness in dying for others, and Israel's salvation will come through their faith in Christ (11:20, 23).

29. Paul asserts that God's gifts and call are *irrevocable*, which translates a word (*ametamelēta*) that primarily is used to mean 'without regret' (2 Cor. 7:10). God does not regret the past decision to call Israel into being, and God has not discarded them and replaced them with Gentile Christians and a handful of Jewish Christians. Humans might renege on their promises when events take a turn for the worse. God's faithfulness to the covenant, however, surmounts the snag of Israel's unfaithfulness.[61] This affirmation of God's righteous character repeats the theme that runs through the letter. God's covenant with Israel remains binding despite Israel's continual violation of it.

Paul shared the theological presuppositions found in Psalm 78 and Nehemiah 9:1–37 that rehearse Israel's long record of waywardness. Each concludes that God is both righteous in being faithful to the covenant with Israel and also merciful. Furthermore, God's love for Gentiles does not diminish God's love for Israel, as if there were only a limited supply of God's love to go around. The boundless love 'by which God has embraced all humanity in Jesus Christ does not invalidate the first love which he bestowed on the people of Israel'.[62] Therefore, God does not love Israel less by adding Gentiles to the people of God, and Israel is not the poorer for it but will be the richer for it. Jesus illustrates this love in his parable about

---

61. Wagner, *Heralds*, p. 219.
62. Baum, *Anti-Semitic*, p. 243.

the father who had two sons. The father loved both sons: the younger, who was prodigal in body and abandoned him to venture to a far country, and the elder, who stayed at home to work the farm but was prodigal in spirit and served his father with the heart of a slave. After graciously receiving and forgiving the disgraced son when he came to himself and returned home, the father graciously goes out to plead with his elder son to join in the celebration of his brother's return to the family (Luke 15:28–30). The elder son may be jealous that his prodigal brother has received such a lavish reception, but he should realize that the father's merciful love extends also to him: 'Son, you are always with me, and all that is mine is yours' (Luke 15:31). In the same way, Israel must accept the invitation of salvation that Gentile believers have accepted, but they can do so only on God's terms. God's love is now defined by the grace extended to sinners through the self-giving sacrifice of Jesus that atones for sin (8:34, 37; Gal. 2:20).

30–31. For the people of Israel to receive God's mercy, they must recognize they have done something that requires forgiveness. With the coming of its Messiah, Israel has become blatantly disobedient. The Greek construction has it that Israel 'disobeyed your mercy', that is, they challenged the undeserved mercy that God showered on sinners like the Gentiles. They did not submit to God's righteousness, which comes through faith apart from the law (Keck, p. 285; 10:3–4). Now they find themselves in the same position as the Gentiles before Christ's coming: 'dead through the trespasses and sins' in which they once lived, 'following the ruler of the power of the air', 'following the desires of flesh and senses' and being 'children of wrath' (Eph. 2:1–3). If God showed mercy to disobedient Gentiles who are saved by faith (Eph. 2:8), then God will surely show mercy to disobedient Israel when they come to faith (11:23). When they shut their eyes to the light of the gospel, thereby forsaking their commission to be the light to the world, God shut them up in darkness but did not abandon Israel. Paul does not detail how God's mercy will manifest itself, but the promise is that a national awakening will occur when God removes their spiritual stupor and gives them eyes to see and ears to hear (Isa. 29:9–10, 18) as God once did with Paul (Acts 9:1–21). Since God repeatedly has forgiven the sins of those in Israel throughout their history together, it is improbable that God would so harden them that they would have no chance to repent.

32. Paul has argued that God is impartial (2:11) and now expresses most clearly what that impartiality entails: *God has imprisoned all in disobedience so that he may be merciful to all*. Paul earlier cited God's word to Moses, 'I will have mercy on whom I have mercy, / and I will have compassion on whom I have compassion' (9:15), and it turns out that God wants to have mercy on all, Jews and Gentiles, without distinction (10:12). God has plunked all Israel along with all the Gentiles into the same sinking boat (3:9). All are sinners (3:23), and no-one will get red-carpet treatment before God's throne of judgment. All must cast themselves entirely on God's mercy. None deserve it, but it is offered to all through Christ. Israel has been brought low, but God's love will exalt Israel again. The catch is that they must accept that they will be exalted *with* Gentile believers (15:8–11).

The second *all* in this statement, [*God*] *may be merciful to all*, does not apply to every person. The *all* refers to Jews and Gentiles without distinction as 'the beneficiaries of God's saving grace' (Schreiner, p. 613). While the divine plan is to gather the disobedient, God does not force anyone to repent (2:4) and to turn to Christ. The parallel in Galatians 3:22 proves that one should not interpret Paul's statement here to imply universalism: 'But the scripture has imprisoned all things under the power of sin, so that what was promised through faith in Jesus Christ might be given to those who believe.' God's offer of mercy can be turned down by refusing to have faith in Christ.

iv. Hymn of praise for the riches of God's wisdom and knowledge (11:33–36)

33. Paul concludes this section with a song of praise that describes God's judgments as *unsearchable* and God's ways as *inscrutable* (cf. Job 11:7–8; 37:5). If we do not fully fathom how the world around us works, how can we possibly begin to understand how God is working out his purposes for us and others in history? Naselli employs the imagery from Psalm 77:19 in saying, 'Trying to track God's ways in salvation history is like trying to track an unseen person by following their footsteps on the beach right into the water where they disappear into the shallowest part of the ocean.'[63] Paul could have searched the Scriptures night and day, but his rigorous study never would have figured out what God intended in Christ. It had to be revealed to him (Gal. 1:11–12; Eph. 3:3). Even when that mystery is revealed, as Paul reveals it here in expounding the interlocking destinies of Israel and Gentiles in God's plan of salvation, it remains perplexing. God's election and mercy have been manifested in history in ways that no human could anticipate, and few would appreciate. We see in a mirror dimly. We can barely make out what God has done in the past, are often unaware of what God is doing in the present, and cannot foresee what God will do in the future. The only resources we have for understanding what God has done are the Scriptures and the Spirit who 'searches everything, even the depths of God', and reveals things to us (1 Cor. 2:10–11). Even then, we cannot boast that we understand all mysteries (1 Cor. 13:2), but can only respond, as Paul does here, with reverent awe and hymnic doxology.

34. Paul inserts two Old Testament passages between the exclamation in 11:33 and the doxology in 11:36. The first citation, from Isaiah 40:13, *who has known the mind of the Lord? / or who has been his counsellor?* (cf. Job 15:8; Jer. 23:18), assumes that no human has ever been invited to counsel God on how to govern the world. Paul also cites Isaiah 40:13 in 1 Corinthians 2:16 but there gives it a Christological twist by adding, 'But we have the mind of Christ.' Everything we might know about God's intentions regarding salvation and how God is working it out in history comes only through the lens of knowing Christ (cf. John 15:15).

35. The second citation partially quotes Job 41:3 (in the Hebrew and LXX versification; 41:11 in English translations):

Who has first given to me, that I should repay him?
   Whatever is under the whole heaven is mine.
   (ESV; cf. Job 35:7)

---

63. Naselli, *Doxology*, p. 32.

It asserts that the relationship between God and humans is not based on balanced reciprocity. Humans can never give to God with the expectation that God is obligated to return the favour. All things arise from God's initiative and are swathed in undeserved grace. Since God owes humans nothing, God can do as he pleases in bestowing grace on whomever he chooses.

Naselli contends that Paul employs Isaiah 40:13 and Job 41:3a as the scriptural climax of his arguments in 9:1 – 11:32 because he sees the larger contexts of these passages about Israel's exile and Job's saga as typologies. These accounts reveal the script for what is happening now to Israel and what God will fulfil in culminating salvation history.[64] Both Israel before the exile and Job experienced God's magnanimous blessings, but Israel and Job were stripped of their blessings – Israel by the exile, and Job by his many travails. They were brought low to such an extent that restoration seemed impossible. In exile, Israel begins to question God's power and fairness. For most of the book, Job refuses to question God, but he becomes so vexed by his suffering that he confronts God for being unjust. Israel and Job sought to assert their own righteousness. To receive God's restored blessing, both the Israel of Isaiah's day and Job had to revise their mistaken views of God and restore their trust that God would deliver them through suffering. When they changed their attitudes, they experienced God's blessings in ways that far surpassed the blessings they had before.

The typological pattern of the stories of Israel's history in exile and of Job provides hope for hardened Israel. Paul describes the majority of Israel as being stripped of God's blessing and given 'a spirit of stupor, / eyes that could not see, / and ears that could not hear' (11:8, NIV). 'Their table' has become 'a snare and a trap, / a stumbling-block and a retribution for them' (11:9–10). This situation leads to questioning God's righteousness (9:6, 14, 19), refusing to submit to God's righteousness, and attempting to establish their own righteousness (10:3). Paul insists that Israel must change their views of God and his Son and not remain stuck in their unbelief (11:23). If they do not remain in their unbelief,

---

64. Ibid., pp. 131–141.

they will receive not the restoration of material bounty, as Job did, or national salvation, as Israel did when they returned from exile, but the glory of eternal salvation.

36. Paul has inserted praise to God throughout the letter (1:25; 9:5; 15:33; 16:27), and as he began this section with a doxology in 9:5b, he ends it with a doxology. The bottomless depths of God's knowledge, wisdom and riches (9:23; 11:22) defy the human capacity to plumb them. It confirms that God does not need or want human counsel and that God owes humans nothing since they have added nothing to the endless store of God's riches. All that humans can do in the presence of God's mysterious sovereignty, righteousness and mercy is to give glory to God as the source of all things, the agency by which all things come into being and the goal towards whom all things are directed. The phrase *all things* are *to him* means that what God has created will return to him. That statement is the ground for believers' assurance. Paul could also ascribe to Christ the same agency in creation in 1 Corinthians 8:6 and Colossians 1:16–17, which indicates his high Christology (9:5), since he 'saw no conflict whatsoever' between the two (Dunn, II, p. 704).

Theology

Paul has reached the crowning point of his doctrinal arguments that began in chapter 1. He has covered the arrival of the Messiah promised by the prophets (1:2–4), his atoning death (3:25) and resurrection (1:4), the hardening of Israel and the preservation of a remnant that is instrumental in gathering Gentiles (9:23–30; 10:12–13; 11:1–8, 25), and, finally, the regathering of Israel into the new messianic community (11:24–26). These are not random events. All history moves towards God's predetermined goal of showing mercy to all who are imprisoned in their disobedience (10:12; 11:32). The prospects for Israel's salvation may seem poor since the mass of Israel in Paul's time rejected the gospel. Paul's primary point in chapters 9–11 is that the Gentiles' justification by faith does not negate God's election of Israel but is integral to God's plan of salvation for Israel. God took the initiative in creating Israel purely out of mercy and has responded to Israel's headstrong disobedience throughout its history with judgment by cutting it down to a remnant. Hardened (11:7) and stumbling (11:11), Israel now experiences God's severity (11:22), retribution (11:9) and rejection (11:12, 15). Many have been broken off from the olive tree (11:17) and have become enemies regarding the gospel (11:28). Gentile Christians should never forget, however, that they also were once enemies of God but received God's mercy and reconciliation (5:10). Stowers notes that Paul argues,

> In God's way of shaping the larger course of history he chooses some and rejects others not because of the works of the chosen or the rejected but for the sake of his larger purposes; God sometimes allows (or causes) individuals or groups to rebel against him in order to bring about the greatest good for all.
>
> (Stowers, p. 40)

A remnant of Israel remains, which is a seed of hope that mainstream Israel will no longer 'despise the riches of his kindness and forbearance and patience' and will repent (2:4). It all hinges on Israel accepting the gospel. Their acceptance (11:15) will result in their being regrafted into the olive tree (11:23), being saved (11:26), having their sins taken away (11:27) and being loved in fulfilment of the promises to the patriarchs (11:28).

The sad picture of Israel that Paul presents in 11:7–10 closely resembles what he outlined in 1:18–31 about humanity's situation under God's wrath. Gentiles 'suppress the truth' (1:18), claim 'to be wise' (1:22) and 'did not see fit to acknowledge God' (1:28), and as a result in God's wrath they 'became futile in their thinking', 'their senseless minds were darkened' (1:21) and they 'became fools' (1:22). In like manner, Israel did not properly acknowledge God or submit to God's righteousness (10:2–3) and were 'disobedient and contrary' (10:21), and as a result in God's wrath they became 'hardened' (11:7; cf. John 12:40). 'God gave them a sluggish spirit', and they became darkened in their vision and dull in their hearing (11:8).[65] Paul attests that God is sovereign even over this disobedience. Their downfall leads to mercy for others (11:11). God's wrath on this

---

65. Dixon, 'Judgement', pp. 576–578.

disobedience, however, is only provisional. Israel's hardening is not final (11:25–26), and the castaways will be recast as Abraham's true descendants (9:7) if they do not persist in their unbelief (11:23) and if they 'follow the example of the faith that [their] ancestor Abraham had' (4:12).

Therefore, Gentile Christians should know that, despite appearances, God has not dumped Israel and replaced them with a new, improved Israel now composed mostly of Gentiles. Israel's obduracy in rejecting God's Messiah and the gospel of grace is not a permanent condition. God may have cut off the spiritually dead branches of Israel from the life-giving root of the olive tree and grafted in Gentile wild olive shoots, but Gentiles should not pour scorn on the severed branches. Nor should they flatter themselves into thinking that God grafted them in because of their merit. They should be mindful that as the tree surgeon God can pick up the pruning shears again if necessary. Instead of becoming arrogant, they should marvel at what God has done, is doing, and promises to do to save both Gentiles and Israel. Paul wants his Gentile audience to recognize that the salvation of Gentiles and the salvation of Israel are interconnected because God's objective is to show mercy to all. This plan moves forwards in three stages: (1) Israel's hardening and unbelief lead to the grafting in of Gentile Christians to enjoy the rich sap of the olive tree. (2) Israel is provoked to jealousy when it sees that God's blessings have been bestowed on Gentiles. (3) Israel will be saved when the fullness of Gentiles has entered. God's 'wrath on disobedience becomes mercy on the disobedient' as 'God turns tragedy to good'.[66] Isaiah 60:10 expresses Paul's vision of how God deals with Israel: 'for in my wrath I struck you down, / but in my favour I have had mercy on you' is also the same way God deals with the world.[67]

Paul's conviction that Israel's salvation is tied to their being provoked by the Gentiles' salvation propels his apostolic work 'to bring about the obedience of faith among all the Gentiles' (1:5; 16:26) and compels him to go to places where Christ has not been

---

66. Ibid., p. 574.
67. Ibid., p. 581.

named to proclaim the gospel (15:20). His arguments in this section provide the theological background that explains the plans he lays out in 15:22–32 to postpone his trip to Rome and break off temporarily his ministry that focuses on Gentiles and journey back to Jerusalem with the offering for the poor of the saints from his Gentile churches. Fitzmyer is correct: 'what Paul says in [chapters] 9–11 is intimately bound up with his personal missionary activity' (Fitzmyer, p. 541). Paul also seeks to prevent the anti-Judaism that was endemic in the Graeco-Roman pagan world from rearing its ugly head among Gentile Christians in Rome.[68] He is mindful that some Gentile Christians might find it surprising and perhaps offensive that an 'apostle to the Gentiles' (11:13) would veer off from his work among them and turn his attention to the Jews in Jerusalem. That explains why he stresses that if Israel's failure has resulted in the riches of the gospel coming to the Gentiles, how much greater riches will their conversion to the gospel bring to the world (11:12). He seeks to ward off any potential criticism that he is turning his back on the Gentiles by going to Jerusalem. Instead, he hopes that it will augment his ministry to the Gentiles. Paul hopes that this evidence of the fruit of his evangelistic work among the Gentiles, which he regards as proof of the Gentiles' obedience of faith (2 Cor. 9:13), might somehow make his people jealous and save some of them (11:14). He may not expect the mass conversion of all Israel from this visit to Jerusalem but adding 'some' to the faith would nevertheless bring an abundance of benefits for Gentiles and bring the moment nearer when 'the partial hardening' of Israel will be removed (11:25). Should this hope not come to fruition, Paul still wants to instil a shared Christian identity and ethos among Jewish and Gentile believers before undertaking to preach the gospel in the virgin territory of Spain. This resolve underlies the ethical exhortations that begin in chapter 12.

The question remains, however, as to what will be the catalyst that softens Israel's hard-edged opposition to faith in Christ. Paul does not envision that Israel's transformation will be brought about by Christ's return. First, when that event occurs, it will be too late

---

68. Davies, 'Paul and the People of Israel', p. 22.

for the disobedient Jews (and Gentiles) to decide to change their minds about Christ. Second, if Israel's mass salvation were to be brought about miraculously at the parousia, it would call into question God's impartiality (2:11). Why would the rest of the Gentile world not also be miraculously saved? This view imagines that Israel's salvation derives from their ancestral privilege apart from their faith in Christ. It cuts the ground from under Paul's insistence that salvation is not based on ethnicity. If God's even-handed justice and mercy will treat Jews and Gentiles exactly the same (11:30–32), then there cannot be an eschatological event in which 'all Israel' and only all Israel is saved.

God justifies the ungodly (4:5); God can also justify the ungodly in Israel and cover their sins (4:7). When Paul emphasizes that God has the power to graft Jews again into their natural tree (11:23b), it comes from 'the power of God for salvation to everyone who has faith', for both Jew and Greek (1:16). Therefore, God will not do so through a separate path to salvation that excludes the confession that Jesus is the promised 'Messiah, who is God over all' (9:5, NIV) and is 'Lord' (10:16). Israel can be saved only on the same basis as Gentiles are saved: by faith in Christ. That implies that 'Israel's salvation does not take place apart from the preaching and acceptance of the gospel of Christ.'[69] Jakob Jocz, a third-generation Jewish Christian, argues that Christians can only present the gospel to Jews with humility, having repented of the past sins committed against the Jews. Yet, as much as Christians may wish not to offend Jews today, he insists that they cannot budge on the critical issue of the lordship of Jesus Christ. He writes, 'For the Church to reduce her high christology in order to accommodate the Synagogue would spell dissolution. She stands or falls with the confession that Jesus is Lord.'[70] Wright boldly recognizes the temptation to make the text say something else that does not censure unbelieving Israel, so that

> we do not (dreaded thought!) have to be so politically ignorant, naïve, or simply incorrect as to say that Jesus was and is the promised Messiah

---

69. Hvalvik, 'Sonderweg', p. 91.
70. Jocz, *Christians and Jews*, p. 33.

and that Paul envisages salvation coming only by the route of confessing him as Lord and believing that God raised him from the dead.

This approach, he writes, abandons the text to win

> the relieved smiles of the congregation, who no longer need be shocked by attitudes that modern and postmodern thought are eager to label as arrogant, imperialistic or exclusive – not noticing, of course, that to treat texts in this way is to be guilty, oneself, of all those things. (Wright, p. 697)

During the time when some German theologians wanted to purge Jewish influence from German ecclesiastical life, Ernst Lohmeyer wrote a letter to Martin Buber, a noted Jewish scholar and author of *I and Thou*. In this letter dated 19 August 1933 he said,

> The Christian faith is Christian only insofar as it bears the Jewish faith in its heart; I do not know if you will be able also to affirm the reverse, that the Jewish faith is Jewish only insofar as it preserves within itself a place for the Christian faith.[71]

I believe that this statement, bold for its time, captures Paul's conviction.

The conclusion of this section reveals that God did not choose Israel only to serve as a warning example for Gentiles (cf. 1 Cor. 10:6). God's unshakeable love for rebellious Israel can inspire a sense of security for Gentile believers as well. Achtemeier comments, 'If God's word can be defeated by Israel's rejection, then what assurance do we have that God's redemptive word, spoken in Christ, may not also finally fail for us?' (Achtemeier, p. 154). Believers can draw comfort from the fact that God has not forsaken and does not forsake his people (Ps. 94:14), but they must not take it for granted. Paul warns Gentile believers not to confuse their salvation with divine favouritism as Israel did. Consequently, they are not to

---

71. Edwards, *Between the Swastika and the Sickle*, p. 120.

become arrogant over Israel's stumbling. Believers throughout the ages must be careful never to suppose that God's redemptive history centres only on them and presume that God cares only about them. Paul contends that the Gentiles' role in God's redemptive plan is to spur Israel to jealousy. Believers may not shrug their shoulders over Israel's unbelief and wait for God to save them at the parousia.[72] Israel's salvation will occur over time in the course of the Christian witness to Israel (11:13–14). After the fullness of the Gentiles has been added to the people of God, the fullness of Israel will be saved (11:25–26). If Gentiles who go by the name 'Christian' are too haughty, self-important, arrogant and prejudiced, or worse, if they persecute the race to whom they owe so much, they will sabotage provoking Israel to jealousy and will face God's judgment. The early history of Christianity reveals, however, that Gentile Christians did not understand or take to heart Paul's word in these chapters. The Epistle of Barnabas is a prime example that assumes that Israel has been completely abandoned by God. Paul's optimistic picture differs in its emphasis from Jesus' warning to his contemporaries in the parable of the man who invited many to a large banquet. When those invited made feeble excuses to bow out from their previous commitment to attend, he angrily determined to fill up the places with outcasts from 'the streets and lanes' so that 'none of those who were invited will taste my dinner' (Luke 14:16–24). Paul considers the invitation to salvation to be still open and expects that eventually an indifferent Israel will accept the gospel. The message of salvation from the Deliverer (11:26) that fulfils the promises of Scripture (1:2; 15:8) and reveals God's righteousness (3:21–26) has gone out from Zion and has reached the Gentiles who have responded to its proclamation (15:19). According to God's plan, their witness somehow and at some time in history will provoke Israel to jealousy and melt their hardening.

---

72. Wright, *Paul*, p. 1251.

6. THE LOVE-ETHICS OF THE PEOPLE OF GOD (12:1 – 15:13)

In all his letters, Paul seeks to form communities whose attitudes and behaviour give visible evidence of their faith as they follow God's way and not the ways of the world. Even though he was not the founder of the church in Rome, through this letter he wants to strengthen them by imparting to them his spiritual gift as an apostle (1:11). At the beginning and end of the letter, he says his purpose as an apostle is to 'bring about the obedience of faith among all the Gentiles for the sake of his [Christ's] name' (1:5; 16:26). It is faith that generates 'obedience' or 'work' (1 Thess. 1:3; cf. 2 Cor. 9:8; Eph. 2:10; 2 Thess. 1:11) and stamps the believers' identity as Christ's body. Consequently, he follows his exposition of theological issues related to salvation (1:16 – 11:32) with this lengthy discourse on the ethical obligations incumbent on those who have accepted God's offer of salvation through faith in Christ. A similar pattern is found in Galatians (1:6 – 5:12 / 5:13 – 6:10), Ephesians (2:1 – 3:21 / 4:1 – 6:20), Colossians (1:13 – 2:23 / 3:1 – 4:6) and 1 Thessalonians (2:1 – 3:13 / 4:1 – 5:22). The thirty-two imperatives in this section (12:1 – 15:13) corroborate his insistence that his gospel does not foster doing 'evil so that good may come', as some slanderously charge (3:8). The gospel of justification by faith introduces and leads to a righteous life (Stuhlmacher, p. 186).

After stating the overarching principle that Christians are to be set apart to God and not conformed to the corrupt conventions of this world (12:1–2), the section divides into three units: (1) how believers are to treat one another in the community of faith (12:3–16); (2) how believers are to interact with outsiders and navigate the perils of living in a fallen and hostile world (12:17 – 13:14); and (3) how believers are to instil peace in the faith community that has brought people from diverse backgrounds into union with Christ (14:1 – 15:13). The commands throughout this section give concrete expression to what it means for faith to work through love (Gal. 5:6).

A. The transformed life in the body of Christ (12:1–21)

Context
The 'therefore' that begins this section draws the necessary conclusions from all that Paul has written to this point that culminates in the praise of God in 11:33–36. Singing God's praise is not enough. God's merciful justification of sinners by faith requires them to offer thankful praise to God *and* to offer their bodies as a living sacrifice to God. The opening commands in 12:1–2 undergird all the exhortations that follow. They also contrast the attitudes and actions of believers moored by their faith in Christ with those who suppress the truth and evoke God's wrath with their idolatry and unrighteous conduct (1:18–32). Idolaters fail to give glory to God (1:21); believers glorify God (11:36). The worship of idols is irrational (1:22–23, 25); Christian worship of God befits the Creator–creation relationship and conforms to reason (*logikos*). The refusal of non-believers to 'see fit to acknowledge God' has resulted in God handing them over to their worthless minds that keep them from discerning or doing what is right (1:28). Giving free rein to their debased passions gives rise to degraded bodies (1:24) and a descent into a moral morass of 'envy, murder, strife, deceit and malice' (1:29–31, NIV). By contrast, the minds of believers are renewed so that they offer their bodies in holy service to God. With minds

renewed by the Holy Spirit they can discern 'the will of God – what is good and acceptable and perfect' (12:2; see Phil. 4:8), and through the Holy Spirit they also can do it (8:4–14). Paul guides his audience on how Christians are to offer their bodies as living sacrifices in their relations with those within and without the church body.

The moral commands in this section arise out of Paul's lengthy ministry experience in establishing communities of faith in whom Christ is formed (Gal. 4:19). It is, therefore, no surprise that these exhortations echo those he has given to other churches (see 1 Cor. 12:1–28; Phil. 2:1–11; 1 Thess. 4:9–10; 5:12–22). They cover what 'he knows to be significant in the life of Gentile Christian communities trying to live out the gospel in the wider Mediterranean world' (Byrne, p. 362). Neither is the emphasis on unity surprising since Paul has stressed how the gospel brings together into the body of Christ persons from different cultures and walks of life – Greeks and barbarians, the wise and foolish (1:14), Jews and Gentiles (1:16). Their reconciliation to God should be evident in their harmonious relationships with 'one another'. The word 'one another' (*allēlōn*) appears in 12:5, 10 (2x), 16; 13:8; 14:13, 19; and 15:5, 7, 14. Factions and struggles for dominance can develop wherever humans gather, and the Roman Christians would have been no exception. The multiple house churches with members from differing backgrounds, social status and even zones of this large city would make it a challenge to maintain harmony. As they are 'one body in Christ' (12:5), Paul insists that they must live in harmony with one another (12:16; 15:5), which is often neglected as a way in which believers offer their bodies as living sacrifices to God.

Unity does not mean uniformity. In 14:1 – 15:13, Paul urges fellow Christians with contrasting convictions to accept one another. They are not to disparage fellow believers for observing different customs in honour of the Lord, nor are they to try to coerce them to conform to their practices. To create a harmonious community that embraces diversity (15:2), Paul implores them to show love (12:9, 10; 13:8, 9, 10; 14:15), to accept (welcome) one another (14:1, 3; 15:7), to tolerate differences (15:1), to seek to please their neighbours (15:1–3), and to do things that promote peace and build up fellow believers (14:19). In brief, they are to 'accept one another, just as Christ also accepted us, for the glory of God' (15:7, NASB).

Comment

i. Present your bodies as living sacrifices to God (12:1–2)

1. Paul uses the address *brothers [and sisters]* throughout the letter to open or to conclude a unit (1:13; 7:1, 4; 8:12; 10:1; 11:25; 15:14, 30; 16:17). Here this direct address begins the last large section in the letter. The word *therefore* introduces the consequences God expects of believers as the recipients of God's mercy (11:30–32). Receiving the bounty of God's mercies – forgiveness, peace, reconciliation, hope, assurance and new life through the power of the Holy Spirit – brings the obligation to live a certain way. It is not enough that Christians believe the doctrine set forth in the previous chapters. They must demonstrate their complete dedication to God through their holy living and the obedience that true faith generates (1:5; 6:16; 15:18; 16:19, 26). This is what it means to 'offer yourselves to God, and all the parts of yourselves to God as weapons for right-eousness' (6:13, CSB). He switches from this military imagery to sacrificial imagery to exhort them to offer their bodies *as a living sacrifice* to God.

Why present our *bodies*? It is because the body is for the Lord (1 Cor. 6:13), and the Spirit of God/the Spirit of Christ/the Spirit dwells in our bodies (8:9–11). It is in our bodies that we visibly live out the will of God through our actions. It is a pious bromide nowadays to say to those who have faced tragedy, 'Our thoughts and prayers are with you.' Service to God and to others requires more than offering thoughts and prayers. It requires actions. It is in our embodied faith that others can see God's extraordinary power at work (2 Cor. 4:7–9). As Paul says, '[We are] always carrying in the body the death of Jesus, so that the life of Jesus may also be made visible in our bodies' (2 Cor. 4:10). We present our bodies to God also because the body will be resurrected (1 Cor. 15:53–54). Christians, therefore, are not asked to present to God some nebulous spirituality but the entirety of their lives, since a sacrifice belongs wholly to God (see Philo, *Spec.* 1.221).

Throughout the ancient world sacrifices were the fundamental method of honouring deities. A *living sacrifice*, however, might seem to be an oxymoron since sacrifices were either lifeless objects or ritually slaughtered animals, birds or fish. A living sacrifice has several distinguishing characteristics. (1) Customary sacrifices offer an object on the altar that is distinct from the worshipper. In a living sacrifice, the worshippers offer themselves, not things, to God. (2) Sacrifices of living things are ritually slaughtered and burned up and can therefore be offered only once. Believers, as living sacrifices, offer their entire existence to God day after day. What is put to death are the sinful, self-absorbed and self-indulgent passions and deeds of the body (8:13; Gal. 5:24). The altar becomes a cross on which, as Paul says, 'the world has been crucified to me, and I to the world' (Gal. 6:14; Leenhardt, p. 302). (3) The word *worship* (*latreia*) is applied to the regulated rituals required in the temple's cult (Heb. 9:1, 6). Paul modifies this usage. It no longer applies to the altar. The living sacrifice that is well pleasing to God is not a sacred ritual performed in a sacred space at a prescribed sacred time (Käsemann, p. 329). The temple in which believers offer their living sacrifice is every sphere of life in the world, and they offer it to God every day through their righteous living. Paul does not want to separate worship in a religious service from everyday service as if one were more holy than the other. (4) The living sacrifice shows love and mercy towards others. The prophets and Jesus declare that sacrifices are worthless to God if they do not synchronize with the way the worshippers conduct themselves in their daily lives (1 Sam. 15:22; Pss 40:6; 51:6–7; Isa. 1:10–17; Hos. 6:6; Matt. 9:13; 12:7). They cannot act unjustly towards others, oppress the resident alien, the fatherless or the widow, shed innocent blood, follow other gods, steal, murder, commit adultery and swear falsely, and then come into the temple chanting, 'This is the temple of the LORD, the temple of the LORD, the temple of the LORD.' They cannot dare to presume that they are 'rescued' by their sacrifices so that they 'can continue doing all these detestable acts' with impunity (Jer. 7:1–15, CSB; see Mark 11:15–17). As Paul declares in Galatians 5:6, 'For in Christ Jesus neither circumcision nor uncircumcision counts for anything; the only thing that counts is faith working through love.' (5) The use of plurals (*brothers and sisters, you, your bodies, your spiritual* [or 'true'] *worship*) indicates that Paul understands this living sacrifice to be a communal offering.

The whole community, not an assortment of separate individuals, present themselves on the altar. This image accords with Paul's hope as 'a minister of Christ Jesus to the Gentiles, serving as a priest of the gospel of God', to present the Gentiles to God collectively as 'an acceptable offering, sanctified by the Holy Spirit' (15:16, CSB).

The Greek word *logikos* that modifies *worship* is rendered as *spiritual* (NRSV, NASB, ESV), 'true' (CSB), 'true and proper' (NIV), 'rational', 'thoughtful', 'reasonable' (KJV) and 'speaking'. Since the minds of believers have been renewed through the Holy Spirit so that all their aspirations and actions become rightly oriented towards God, it is likely that the worship pertains to reason. This rational worship is the antithesis of the senseless worship offered by darkened minds of idolaters (1:21) who 'by their wickedness suppress the truth' about God (1:18). The connection to discerning 'the will of God – what is good and acceptable and perfect' (12:2) suggests that this worship is performed with a new moral consciousness that decides to live in obedience to God's will. Schnabel plausibly contends that the *logikos* is related to *logos*, which has to do with speech. Since believers are to present their bodies, something that is evident to others, it is plausible that Paul has in mind worship that communicates to others their commitment to God and that the gospel 'is the power of God for salvation to everyone who has faith' (1:16).[1] One might say, then, that it is worship 'in spirit and truth' (John 4:24) that proclaims to others the truth of the gospel through their pattern of living. Paul describes what that pattern demands in the rest of this section.

2. Humans are easily shaped by the cultural forces surrounding them. *This world* ('this age') refers to a worldview that fashions into warped replicas of humanity those who take no account of God and who do not consider themselves accountable to God. J. B. Phillips memorably paraphrases this verse:

> Don't let the world around you squeeze you into its own mould,
> but let God re-mould your minds from within, so that you may

---

1. Schnabel, *Jesus, Paul*, p. 187.

prove in practice that the plan of God for you is good, meets all his
demands and moves towards the goal of true maturity.

(JBP)

The renewed mind is liberated from this age enslaved under the
power of sin (Gal. 1:4) and is 'renewed in knowledge according to
the image of its creator' (Col. 3:10). It is no longer swayed by this
world's fleeting trends, debased standards and godless notions of
reality. Only a renewed mind that is receptive to the illumination
of God's life-giving Spirit can distinguish between what is the will
of God – what is *good* (2:10), *acceptable* (Eph. 5:10) and *perfect* (Phil.
1:10; Jas 1:25) – and what is not. The mind charmed by this world
and its pursuits cannot do so. It becomes depraved by excluding
God, which then gives rise to all sorts of depraved behaviours
(1:28–31; 3:10–18). A mind that Christ continually shapes (1 Cor.
2:16) wins the war raging in the mind by defeating the law of sin
that would take the mind captive to do what is evil (7:18–25). It
throws off the 'former way of life' 'corrupted by deceitful desires'
(Eph. 4:17–24, CSB). What Paul pictures here is not a minor
cosmetic makeover but a radical transformation. As God's power
transforms believers into the glorious image of Christ (8:29; 2 Cor.
3:18), it is like life from the dead (6:11, 13; 11:15). This inner transformation that is now oriented towards God becomes outwardly
evident in the way Christians live.

ii. Unity and diversity in the body of Christ (12:3–9a)

3. With the phrase *by the grace given to me* Paul delicately reminds
his audience that he instructs them through his gift as an apostle
called by Christ (1:5; 15:15; 1 Cor. 3:10; 15:10; Eph. 3:2, 7–8). In
12:3–9a he crisply reworks similar appeals he delivered to the Corinthians that warned them against becoming puffed up and
arrogant (1 Cor. 4:6, 18–19; 5:2; 8:1; 13:4) and portrayed the faith
community as a body, with its varied members, united in Christ (1
Cor. 12:1–31). As in Corinth, he seeks to root out the pride that
creates divisions, a common problem wherever humans come
together (Phil. 2:1–4). Christians are not to have inflated estimates
of themselves that cause them to assess others negatively because
they do not seem to measure up to their high standards. Those

whose gifts are prominently displayed for all to see and admire may develop a false sense of their importance. Their conceit will lead them to sort others into categories: valuable (like me), of middling value, and of no value; or honoured (like me), undistinguished, and shamed. This attitude inevitably foments discord.

The *measure of faith* does not refer to how they carry out their gifts in the community, as if there were different proportions of faith required for each function. In the context, it refers to how they should measure themselves and others (see Matt. 7:2). Paul has argued that every believer alike was under sin (3:9) and that every believer alike is justified through Jesus Christ (4:25; 5:1, 9). Justification by grace becomes the measuring rod that 'should provide the basis for a true estimation of oneself, since it reveals that one is dependent, along with other believers, on the saving mercy of God in Christ' (Harrison and Hagner, p. 186). Therefore, the measure of faith 'is the same for all' (Wright, p. 709). If they are to do any measuring, Christ is the only standard by which they can truly measure themselves. Their faith in Christ reminds them that they were formerly God's enemies who are now reconciled to God only because of grace offered through the death of his Son (5:10). Their renewed minds should keep them from having too high an opinion of themselves and too low an opinion of others.

This standard promotes sober-mindedness that does not give way to flights of fancy about oneself nor crush one with an acute sense of inferiority. Paul models this sober-minded self-assessment when he describes himself as 'the least of the apostles, unfit to be called an apostle . . . But by the grace of God I am what I am' (1 Cor. 15:9–10), and when he compares himself and Apollos to farmhands, the seed planter and the water boy, carrying out the roles God has given them. They work together for God in the field where only God gives the growth and only God is to get the glory (1 Cor. 3:5–9).

4–6a. Paul's goal as an apostle is to sculpt the social identity of churches as the body of Christ. Paul develops the metaphor of the body to make the point that as the body has many parts, each of which is essential and depends on other parts for the body to be healthy, so the many different parts in the body of Christ, one by one, contribute to the body's flourishing. The implication is that every believer who has received grace also has received a gift (or gifts) intended to contribute to the body of Christ. The gift given to one member is therefore given to the whole body. No member has every possible gift. Different members fill different roles that augment those of others and create a balance. They should not overreach into another's sphere any more than an ear should try to walk.

Consequently, different gifts may distinguish one member from another, but they do not make one superior to another. The various gifts, then, do not create a pecking order in the community, any more than the ear's gift of hearing or the eye's gift of seeing in a physical body makes them superior to the feet or the hands (1 Cor. 12:14–24). God does not give gifts to build up an individual but to build up the body and promote its health. If all believers recognize that they function as members of the *body* of *Christ*, they cannot consider themselves so important that they receive more glory than the One to whose body they belong.

Members of Christ's body come from different backgrounds and have different preferences and aptitudes. They have been knitted together in Christ for the mutual benefit of the whole, and they must recognize that they are interdependent and not self-sufficient. They cannot survive if separated from other parts of the body. They cannot thrive if one member is neglected.

6b–9a. Paul gives a sampling of the gifts in Christ's body. He does not intend to provide a definitive list, since he includes different gifts in the lists in 1 Corinthians 12:8–10, 27–31 and Ephesians 4:11. His goal is to exhort those who have gifts to use them with all diligence 'to strengthen the body's unity and to help it to flourish' (Moo, p. 782).

The gift of *prophecy* is the ability to convey revelations given by the Holy Spirit to others. It may occur first in this list because Paul told the Corinthians to 'pursue love and strive for the spiritual gifts, and especially that you may prophesy' (1 Cor. 14:1). Paul defines it as speech for the community's 'building up and encouragement and consolation' (1 Cor. 14:3) so that they 'may learn' and 'be encouraged' (1 Cor. 14:31). It is also speech that might convict unbelievers and prompt them to worship God (1 Cor. 14:24–25). In the context of public worship, it is not restricted to foretelling (Acts 11:28; 21:10–11) but refers to inspired speech that 'builds up the church' (1 Cor. 14:4). According to Revelation 19:10, prophets 'hold the testimony of Jesus', and the words of prophecy must be obeyed (Rev. 1:3; 22:7). Paul assumes that all could prophesy (1 Cor. 14:31) because he encourages the Corinthians to 'pursue' prophecy (1 Cor. 14:1) and 'be eager to prophesy' (1 Cor. 14:39) and limits their speaking in worship to two or three (1 Cor. 14:29–31a).

Prophecy *in proportion to faith* may refer to the individual's personal faith. That might imply that persons will speak from their different levels of faith, some greater, some lesser. It is more likely that the phrase means that what they say should be in keeping with the standard of the Christian faith 'once for all entrusted to the saints' (Jude 3; cf. 2 John 5–11). It implicitly cautions against the deviant interpretations of those who might claim to be inspired (1 Cor. 12:3). His caution 'If anyone thinks he is a prophet or spiritual . . .' (1 Cor. 14:37, CSB) implies that someone might be self-deceived and untrustworthy. That is why the community is to evaluate what a person says (1 Cor. 14:29; 1 Thess. 5:20–21a; cf. Acts 18:25–26). Paul, however, does not mention the gift of 'the discernment of spirits' that follows 'prophecy' in the list of gifts in 1 Corinthians 12:10. Its use is implied, however, in his command to 'watch out for those who create divisions and obstacles contrary to the teaching that you learned' (16:17, CSB).

Paul uses the word translated *ministry* or 'service' (*diakonia*) for his own work as an apostle (11:13; 2 Cor. 3:6–9; 4:1; 5:18; 1 Tim. 1:12; cf. Acts 20:24; 21:19). But he says, 'There are different ministries' (1 Cor. 12:5, CSB). He identifies one of the tasks of the apostles, prophets, evangelists and teaching pastors who are given to the church as 'to equip the saints *for the work of ministry*, for building up the body of Christ' (Eph. 4:11–12, emphasis added). *Ministry*, therefore, pertains to a wide variety of services that many in the church can render. In Acts 6:1; 11:27–30; 12:25, *diakonia* ('ministry') refers to providing charity to meet the material needs of poverty-stricken believers. Paul also uses the noun and verb form to refer to the collection taken up to help the poor of the saints in Jerusalem (15:25, 31; 2 Cor. 8:4, 19–20; 9:1, 12–13). Since he writes this letter on the eve of his departure to Jerusalem with that collection, he may be especially mindful of this responsibility in the service of the saints (12:13).

Teaching firms up the faith of believers. It passes on the truth of the gospel preserved by the church (1 Cor. 11:2, 23; 15:3), expounds the Scriptures that he says are written for our instruction (15:4), and applies theological instruction to the lives of the hearers (1 Cor. 10:6, 11).

Exhortation urges others to action as Paul does throughout his letters (12:1; 15:30; 16:17; 1 Cor. 1:10). It also can refer to giving encouragement (2 Cor. 13:11; 1 Thess. 4:18; 5:11, 14). The exhorter spurs those struggling to stay in the race and reaches out to help the stragglers.

All Christians regardless of their means are commanded to give *in generosity* (2 Cor. 9:7). The sacrificial giving of some can only be understood as a spiritual gift. Some, like Philemon (Phlm. 7) and Phoebe (16:2), are specially gifted in sharing their resources with others. They do not give as a chore but as a joy. Paul celebrates the contributions of the Macedonian churches to the collection for Jerusalem. They gave out of abundant joy despite their severe trials and extreme poverty, which Paul takes to be clear evidence of the grace of God given to them (2 Cor. 8:1–5).

The participle in Greek rendered *the leader* relates to standing up before and presiding over a group (1 Thess. 5:12). This gift enables a person to take charge, manage and guide the group in a positive, productive direction. Such leaders do not lead out of their own strength but out of the strength that God imparts to them. People with this gift should do their work eagerly, gladly, with energy and full commitment. The word can also mean 'to apply oneself in giving aid' (cf. Titus 3:8, 14), and this may be its meaning here since it is followed by 'showing mercy' (CSB). Showing mercy to others means to reach out with the compassion of Christ to those who are hurting in a myriad of ways (see Matt. 9:27; 15:22; 17:15). Since this work is carried out in grim situations, it must be done with gladness.

The exhortation to love in verse 9a (literally, 'love, without hypocrisy') concludes the sentence that began in 12:6. A new series begins in 12:9b with the commands now presented using participles in Greek. As the conclusion to this first series of exhortations related to gifts, it means that all the spiritual gifts listed should be carried out in a spirit of love, which appears first in Paul's list of the fruit of the Spirit (Gal. 5:22), and without ulterior motives. This fits the pattern found in 1 Corinthians where Paul caps his listing of spiritual gifts (1 Cor. 12:1–31) with an exhortation to love, which he considers to be 'a still more excellent way' (1 Cor. 12:31 – 13:3). Here he does not describe in detail what love does as he did in 1 Corinthians 13:4–7, which contains a list that applied to identifiable difficulties that had arisen in that church, but only says it is to be without hypocrisy. It means that the gifts are to be discharged with love, which does not seek to gain advantages over or to receive accolades from others. They are not to engage in a dishonest charade that intends only to show others how loving they are. Love is to be sincere, which is exactly how Paul says he has carried out his ministry among the Corinthians: 'by purity, knowledge, patience, kindness, holiness of spirit, genuine love [lit. 'in love unhypocritical']' (2 Cor. 6:6). As an example of the opposite, one might think of Ananias and Sapphira and their deceitful donation to the apostles. They made an exhibition of the gift of loving 'generosity' (12:8) with hypocrisy (Acts 5:1–11).

Since many interpreters consider the exhortation to love as the beginning of the next series of commands (12:9–14), it can also serve as a bridge that covers both series. The first mention of 'love' in Romans sets the highest standard for what it requires: 'God proves his love for us in that while we were still sinners Christ died for us' (5:8). Love obliges Christians to put the needs of others ahead of their own (13:8, 10; 14:15).

iii. The believer's obligations towards fellow believers (12:9b–13)

9b–10. Believers must abhor *evil* (Amos 5:15). Detesting evil is stronger than disliking it and implies fleeing from it in horror (1 Thess. 5:22). They are to despise that which is evil rather than persons who do evil things. *Hold[ing] fast to what is good* means doing what is good.

The theme of love resurfaces in Paul's urging devotion to brotherly love (*philadephia*). In secular Greek that word was 'confined to the love of those who are brothers by common descent' (MM, p. 668). New Testament writers expand brotherly love beyond blood ties to the adoptive family of Christian brothers and sisters (1 Thess. 4:9–10; Heb. 13:1; 1 Pet. 1:22; 3:8; 2 Pet. 1:7). The word translated as *mutual affection*, a deep, tender devotion to others (*philostorgos*), was also used for 'active beneficence, devotion, and generosity' towards strangers.[2]

Acquiring *honour* in the public sphere, particularly in ancient Rome, was like an addictive drug. Competing for honour was almost a blood sport. Persons sought to outclass others by destroying their honour. Most Christians could not compete for honours in the public arena because of their lower social status, but they might employ the same ruthless stratagems of their pagan neighbours to gain honour and influence in the smaller gatherings of believers. Paul reverses the objectives in the competition for honour. Christians are not to *outdo* others in acquiring honour for themselves, but become leaders in showering other believers with honour. When one member of the body is honoured, the result is that 'all the members rejoice with it' (1 Cor. 12:26, CSB).

11. What it means to *lag in zeal* or to 'lack diligence' (*oknēroi*) is illustrated by the word's use in Jesus' parable of the talents. The master accuses the slave who received one talent and buried it in the ground of being 'wicked' and 'lazy' even though he knew he served a hard taskmaster (Matt. 25:18, 24–28). Paul uses the same word when telling the Philippians that he is not reluctant to write the same things to them (Phil. 3:1). It means that he knows his responsibility to bolster their spiritual security, not letting things slide or hesitating to confront issues that might be troublesome.

Instead of being lackadaisical in exercising their gifts, they are to be *ardent in spirit* or 'fervent in the Spirit' (CSB). Either they are to serve the Lord with burning zeal, or the Spirit inflames their zeal to serve the Lord. Apollos is described as being filled with fiery zeal (Acts 18:25). Since he 'knew only the baptism of John', he apparently did not know the baptism of the Spirit and fire that John promised that the Messiah would bring (Luke 3:16). Therefore, it seems unlikely that Apollos is portrayed as speaking ardently in the Spirit. This account does suggest that a sound ministry requires more than simply enthusiasm; it also needs doctrinal accuracy.

---

2. *TLNT* III, p. 464.

Since Paul uses the word *pneuma* elsewhere not to refer to the internal emotions of humans but nearly always to refer to the Holy Spirit, it is more likely that he refers to the Holy Spirit here.[3] His command not to 'quench [extinguish] the Spirit' (1 Thess. 5:19) would support this interpretation. Like the tongues of fire that rested on the disciples at Pentecost when they were all filled with the Holy Spirit (Acts 2:3–4), Paul thinks of being aglow from the power of the Holy Spirit who sets hearts afire to serve the Lord passionately and keeps them from frittering away opportunities to do so.

12. *Rejoic[ing] in hope* and *be[ing] patient in suffering* recalls 5:2–5. Believers can endure afflictions (8:35–39) because they have the assurance of their hope in Christ that nothing the enemies of God might unleash against them can ultimately hurt them or separate them from God's love. In the context of such suffering, devotion to *prayer* (Luke 18:1; Eph. 6:18; Col. 4:2; 1 Thess. 5:17) becomes even more important in interceding for others (15:30–31) and receiving the Holy Spirit's intercession for oneself (8:26–27).

13. *Contribut[ing] to the needs of the saints* is precisely what Paul is doing in organizing and delivering the gifts from the churches in Macedonia and Achaia for 'the poor among the saints at Jerusalem' (15:25–26; cf. Gal. 2:10). The transliteration of the Greek noun *koinonia* into English connotes for many the idea of sharing fellowship. Paul, however, can use both the noun and its cognate verb to mean 'to share financially' (15:27; 2 Cor. 8:4; 9:13; Gal. 6:6; Phil. 1:5; 4:15). For him, this sharing involves more than making an impersonal donation. It involves entering into a mutual relationship between the donor and the recipient.

Paul does not merely command to *extend* or 'practise' (NIV) hospitality but uses the verb 'pursue' (*diōkō*, CSB; cf. 9:31; 14:19). They are to seek opportunities to show hospitality. This entails not just offering a night's rest but entering a mutual relationship with strangers, not just a friend or a friend of a friend (Job 31:32). Hospitality was vital to itinerant preachers like Paul (see 3 John 5–8) since inns were disreputable, dangerous, uncomfortable and

---

3. Thiselton, *Holy Spirit*, pp. 76–78.

imposed extra costs. The author of Hebrews admonishes his audience not to neglect showing hospitality and connects this virtue to the story of entertaining angels (Heb. 13:2; cf. Gen. 18:1–3; 19:1–3). Showing hospitality is also one of the criteria for leaders in the church (1 Tim. 3:2; Titus 1:8). The early Christian mission would have been stymied had Christians not offered hospitality to travelling fellow believers, whom they received as brothers and sisters in Christ. Most important, whether or not one has taken in strangers will be a decisive factor in the last judgment, according to Jesus' parable of the sheep and the goats (Matt. 25:35, 38, 43–44). Some of Paul's many hosts are mentioned in Acts: Lydia (16:15); the Philippian jailer (Acts 16:32–34); Aquila and Prisca (Acts 18:3); the disciples at Tyre (Acts 21:4–6); and Publius (Acts 28:7). Gaius currently hosts him in Corinth (16:23; cf. Phlm. 22).

iv. The believer's obligations to others, whether fellow believers or enemies (12:14–16)

14. Blessing one's tormentors and not cursing them echoes the teaching of Jesus (Matt. 5:44; Luke 6:28) and what Paul says he does in his work as an apostle: 'When reviled, we bless; when persecuted, we endure; when slandered, we speak kindly' (1 Cor. 4:12–13a). To *bless* does not mean to wish them well but to call down God's gracious power on them (BDAG, p. 408). Likewise, while one must 'hate what is evil' (12:9), one may not hate or *curse* those who do evil. Outsiders persecute Christians because of their allegiance to the exclusive sovereignty of Christ, intolerance of immorality and inclusivity. They perceive Christians as threatening their national identities, social customs and deities. Since God uses kindness and restraint to prod sinners to repentance (2:4), the Christians' response in blessing their persecutors may lead their enemies to faith. That is not, however, the primary motivation behind this command. Paul addresses those who have experienced God's gracious love, forgiveness and blessings. Imitating Christ in their interactions with enemies displays their love for the one who has saved them.

15. *Rejoic*[*ing*] *with those who rejoice* and *weep*[*ing*] *with those who weep* reveals the interconnectedness of members of the faith body (1 Cor. 12:26). We are easily moved to pity and weeping with those who suffer, and not so easily moved to rejoice with those who have received a windfall of good fortune. Rejoicing with others derails the impulse to become jealous when things go well for them. Weeping with those who weep may be easier to do with fellow Christians. The impulse to revel in the sorrows of enemies, however, must also be derailed. Rejoicing and weeping with others acknowledges our shared humanity.

16. Paul returns to the overarching theme of harmony in using three times the Greek verb 'to think' (*phroneō*) and its cognate (*phronimos*) that are related to one's mindset. A literal translation would be as follows: 'Be likeminded towards one another' – that is, *Live in harmony with one another* (15:5; Phil. 2:2; cf. 2 Cor. 13:11); 'do not set your mind on exalted things' – that is, do not be uppity or haughty (11:20; 12:3; 1 Tim. 6:17); 'do not become wise in your own mind' – that is, do not become pretentious (Prov. 3:7; Isa. 5:21). Paul had his fill of those puffed up with their own sense of self-importance and wisdom in the discordant church in Corinth (1 Cor. 4:10; 2 Cor. 11:19). He has already warned the Gentile believers in Rome not to become haughty over the Jews broken off from the olive tree because of their unbelief. God might break off Gentiles too if it is warranted (11:19–21). They must recognize that the danger of claiming to be wise is that it makes them more apt to being exposed as fools (1:22).

Associate with the lowly reads literally in the Greek 'be carried away to the lowly'. *Lowly* can be read as a neuter and refer to 'lowly things'. This would urge believers not to shun doing menial tasks in the faith community that they might regard as beneath their dignity. The context of living in harmony, however, favours reading *lowly* as masculine to refer to those of lower social status. Humans have a natural proclivity to want to curry favour with those who are in a high position to gain their patronage. Believers are to have a realistic appraisal of themselves before God so that they no longer regard themselves or others from a 'worldly perspective' (2 Cor. 5:16–17, CSB). Being in Christ eradicates all the honour–shame distinctions that carve up the world into the high and the lowly.

Consequently, believers must not shun or treat with indifference those whom the world regards as of no account and who, because of their humble station, do not seem able to offer any return on the attentions paid to them. Believers are to follow the example of Christ who had meal fellowship with tax collectors and sinners (Luke 15:1–2; 19:5–7) and to make the effort to draw the little ones and the downtrodden into their lives. The upshot of these directives? Harmony requires being humble, honouring those of low rank, and recognizing that wisdom comes only from God, not from the world or themselves (11:33).

v. The believer's response to evil and adversaries (12:17–21)

17–19. The exhortation not to return evil for evil, found also in 1 Thessalonians 5:15 and 1 Peter 3:9, derives from the Jewish wisdom tradition (Prov. 17:13; 20:22; 24:29; cf. Lev. 19:18a) and, most importantly, from Jesus' teaching (Matt. 5:38–48; Luke 6:27–36). Instead of resorting to violence when wronged, Christians are to respond in ways that even the unbelieving world recognizes as good and noble (Matt. 5:16; 2 Cor. 8:21; Phil. 4:5). Conversely, every time we return evil for evil, we extend its life, reinforcing the hatreds and fears of the other and setting in motion a chain reaction of retaliation. Vengeance is a Petri dish that breeds the pathogens that launch pandemics of violence. Also, when persons seek to overcome evil with their evil actions, evil inevitably engulfs them. Paul therefore insists that since God is the God of love and peace (2 Cor. 13:11), Christians must seek to *live peaceably with all*. *If it is possible* is a dose of realism. Not all will allow Christians to live peaceable lives. Pedersen, reflecting on Israel, wisely comments,

> Violence is apparently an expression of strength, but the Israelite considers this strength a delusion, which can only exist for a time, because it does not draw directly from the source of strength, peace and its blessing, which rests in the divine forces.[4]

Since Paul classifies the wrongdoer's deed as *evil*, it means that God will handle this person in due time. Vengeance belongs only to God (Deut. 32:35). Leaving God's justice to deal with human injustice places Christian ethics in the framework of God's

---

4. Pedersen, *Israel*, p. 419.

end-time judgment (2 Thess. 1:6–8). All will have to give an account before God's judgment seat (14:11–12), and only God can mete out true justice since only God knows the heart of every person and is not capricious. Our human penchant for revenge understandably may be frustrated by the fact that a loving God wants to restore sinners rather than destroy them and that the divine mill of justice grinds slowly waiting for their repentance. Believers do not need to seethe in bitter silence, however. The vengeance psalms, such as Psalm 109, allow victims of evil to yell their desire for vengeance to God (see Rev. 6:10). Turning retribution over to God can keep a hell-broth of bitterness from flooding our lives.

20. Feeding enemies when they are hungry or giving them something to drink when they are thirsty recalls Jesus' teaching in Matthew 25:31–46. The difference is that they are not caring for 'the least of these', who are downtrodden, but enemies, who are out to tread on them. In these actions, they embody the love of God for enemies (5:5–10).

The meaning of proverbial expressions such as to *heap burning coals* on your enemy's head (cf. Prov. 25:21–22) has a way of morphing over time in different contexts, and this saying is no exception. What it means is not clear. Many consider that it meta-phorically refers to the goal of responding to hostility with kindness. Loving actions burn away the hatred within enemies (Achtemeier, p. 202). Killing them with kindness may soften their hostility. As the ashes of shame fall from their heads, enmity is turned into friendship. The focus in this context, however, falls on the responsibility of the Christian to respond to enmity always with love. The focus is not on how to change the enemy and create contrite repentance through loving acts. In fact, trying to shame another with kindness is a variant way of avenging ourselves.

Another option takes the 'coals of fire' as a reference to how the (future) punishment of the enemy will take place. The metaphor of *burning coals* appears in the context of God's judgment in Psalm 140:10, 'Let burning coals fall on them! / Let them be flung into pits, no more to rise', and in 2 Esdras 16:53: 'Sinners must not say that they have not sinned; for God will burn coals of fire on the head of everyone who says, "I have not sinned before God and his glory."' ⁵ *On their heads* is also used as a judgment metaphor (1 Kgs 2:32–33, 37; Joel 3:4, 7; Obad. 15; Acts 18:6). Therefore, Paul may be using the saying to reinforce the point that judgment and vengeance are to be left to God. It is God, not the believer, who heaps hot coals on the heads of sinners.

This interpretation may explain why Paul leaves out the reference to reward from the citation of Proverbs 25:22: 'and the LORD will reward you' (Luke 6:35; cf. Matt. 5:44–47). The goal of these actions is not to receive a reward; it is the fundamental way that Christians are to treat everyone with love. They do so because they understand that God is the judge of both Christians and those they regard as enemies. Christians will be judged by how they treat others. The enemies will be judged by how they respond to this kindness (Bird, p. 436). They might repent and receive God's grace instead of God's retribution, but that is out of the believer's control.

21. Paul concludes these instructions by insisting that the only means that Christians have for conquering evil is with good. Micah 6:8 is a fitting commentary:

> He has told you, O mortal, what is good;
>   and what does the LORD require of you
> but to do justice, and to love kindness,
>   and to walk humbly with your God?

Christ-followers are to rely on the power of God that enables them to abound in every good work (2 Cor. 9:8; 2 Tim. 3:17; Titus 3:1).

Theology

Paul has made it clear in the preceding sections of his letter that no-one is saved by meritorious works or ritual performances alone. Neither does Paul believe that one can be saved by faith alone. He never dreamt that one could be righteous in God's sight without the Spirit also transforming and renewing one's mind so that one lives according to the Spirit (8:1–13). 'Faith alone' is not a Pauline phrase. It occurs only in James 2:24. For Paul, like James, faith and

---

5. Cf. Pss 18:8, 12; 120:4; Sir. 8:10; 28:10.

works go together. Faith is not a sterile, intellectual nod of approval to various theological propositions. It comes to fruition in fulfilling 'the law of the Spirit of life in Christ Jesus' (8:2). This section gives examples of what that involves.

Trusting that God saves by grace apart from the law does not mean that God requires less of the followers of Christ than God requires of those who live under the law. The Christian faith requires that one offer oneself wholly to God. Receiving God's offer of salvation by grace incurs the responsibility to live out one's faith through loving acts of kindness towards others, including enemies. Doing so is not calculated to secure salvation or to win kudos from God or humans. It is the natural result of the spiritual overhaul of a believer's life. The believer responds to an *is* – this is who he or she is. Obeying the commands in this section is evidence of the change in one's life as the fruit of salvation, not its root.

Those who remain in bondage to sin cannot respond positively to these ethical exhortations because obedience is worked only through the power of the Holy Spirit. These are demands made of believers whose minds have been renewed by God. People with a secular mindset would sooner remodel their homes than allow God to renew their minds. They have every product imaginable to renew the outsides of their heads but ignore renewing the internal spirit. Paul exhorts believers to allow the Holy Spirit to shape them from the inside out so that they emulate Christ. This does not mean that everyone becomes a duplicate. Many different members make up the body of Christ and they vary from one another, but they all are to be conformed to the mind of Christ who regulates their thoughts and actions.

How are they to live in the social context of the church that is diverse and a world that is often hostile? Paul assumes that a believer's relationship to Christ will affect his or her relationship with others. The key to positive Christian relationships is humility that comes from an honest evaluation of oneself as a beggared debtor saved only by God's improbable grace (12:3). Humility is fundamental. Outsized egos must be constrained. Personal ambitions must be checked. The desire for recognition must be curbed. The drive that pushes individuals to achieve must be prevented from becoming so relentless that it flattens everyone in its path. A healthy church body has members who know their roles and limitations. They do not think that they are so gifted that they try to do and to control everything. They do not squander their time trying to do what they cannot and should not do, which gives them time to do what God gifted them to do. They recognize that their gifts have been given to them to build up the body of Christ for the glory of God, not their personal glory. A healthy church body has everyone exercising his or her gift in cooperation with others. Individuals are not to waste their gifts from God by letting them atrophy from lack of use. Individuals are not lionized for having gifts that are more conspicuous than others. All contribute. Schweizer's comments on Paul's lists of gifts in 1 Corinthians 12:4–11 and 28–30 are apropos:

> The Corinthians did not think there was anything religious about social service or leadership. To prepare a meal for the sick, you don't need the Spirit but a cooking pot, and to sweep a church you need a broom. And to chair a meeting all you need is a little talent for organization. But Paul knows that care of the sick and institutional administration are just as much gifts of the Holy Spirit as speaking in tongues, prophecy and prayer . . .
>
> If out of love for his church a trained bookkeeper straightens out its accounts, the Holy Spirit is just as much at work as if the bookkeeper had given an inspiring sermon, gone out full of enthusiasm as a missionary, prayed with great emotion, or even spoken in tongues.[6]

B. The believer's obligations to governmental authorities (13:1–14)

Context

Paul continues the instructions that begin in 12:17 on how Christians are to relate to others in their world who are not believers. He addresses how Christians are to coexist peaceably with governmental authorities and why they should do so. The chapter division at the end of 12:21 is unfortunate, because it might suggest that Paul goes off on a tangent. This passage does not address an

---

6. Schweizer, *Holy Spirit*, pp. 93–94.

extraneous subject, nor is it a later interpolation. Many words that appear in the previous section resurface in this unit: 'good' (12:2, 9, 21; 13:3, 4); 'evil' (12:9, 17), also rendered as 'bad' and 'wrong' (13:3–4, 10); 'wrath' (12:19; 13:4, 5); showing 'honour' (12:10; 13:7); and the concept of vengeance (12:17, 19; 13:4). Paul applies being renewed in mind 'so that you may discern what is the good, pleasing, and perfect will of God' (12:2, CSB) and the admonition 'If it is possible, so far as it depends on you, live peaceably with all' (12:18) to believers' relations with civil authorities. They might be free from the law, but they are not free from civil law, which is designed to promote order in society.

The battery of loosely connected terse commands found in 12:1–21 changes in 13:1–7 to a more reflective style that provides theological and practical reasons for the exhortations. In 13:8–10 Paul provides the overarching code of behaviour that should govern the Christians' relationships with everyone: 'Love your neighbour as yourself' (13:9). In 13:11–14 he affixes an eschatological rationale and encouragement for not only discerning but doing 'the good, pleasing, and perfect will of God' (12:2, CSB): 'salvation is nearer to us now than when we became believers' (13:11).

Comment

i. Submitting to governmental authorities (13:1–7)

1. The command for *every person* to *be subject to the governing authorities* means that Christians, despite having their citizenship in heaven (Phil. 3:20), must be subject to those who hold various levels of political power.[7] What may have elicited this admonition is debated, and the attempts to reconstruct the setting in Paul's or the Romans' circumstances are entirely hypothetical.[8] Paul's religious convictions and concern for the church's continuing mission shape

---

7. Spiritual powers are not in mind. Christians are set free from these powers (Col. 1:13), struggle against them (Eph. 6:12–13; Col. 2:10, 15), and certainly do not pay them taxes (13:6–7).

8. Krauter, *Röm 13,1–7*, rigorously examines the historical sources and doubts that the different proposed scenarios or anti-imperial readings based on them are useful.

his arguments, not the political and social circumstances that the Roman church may be facing or the stirrings of insurgency in Judea.

Paul commands them to *be subject to the governing authorities* because all authority is from God, and God has instituted the ruling authorities to govern the social order. It is possible to read Paul to mean, 'For authority does not exist *if it is not* from God' (cf. Hos. 8:4). This interpretation might provide a pretext for resisting authorities that one judges not to have been instituted by God because of their policies and actions.[9] Paul, however, does not leave it open for believers to decide on the legitimacy of any secular authority. His view that God has put these ruling powers in place accords with both Jewish and biblical assessments of government (Prov. 8:15–16; Isa. 45:1–7; Jer. 27:5–7; Dan. 2:21, 37–38; 4:17, 25, 32; 5:21; Wis. 6:1–11; Josephus, *J.W.* 2.140; 5.367) and Graeco-Roman perspectives (Schnabel, II, pp. 666–669).[10]

Paul's own positive experiences of the Roman authorities do not colour his views of the authorities. Gallio, the proconsul of Achaia, may have dismissed the charges that Jews raised against him in Corinth (Acts 18:12–16), but that positive outcome is offset by Paul's many other negative experiences of Roman justice. Paul was beaten with rods at least three times by Roman magistrates (2 Cor. 11:25; cf. 2 Cor. 1:8–10; 1 Thess. 2:2), and Acts 16:22, 36–39 emphasizes how unjust this punishment was when it was administered in Philippi. Paul is not engaged in doublespeak by encouraging believers only to feign loyalty to the empire. His command is theologically grounded in his view of creation: 'there is one God, the Father, from whom are all things and for whom we exist, and one Lord, Jesus Christ, through whom are all things and through whom we exist' (1 Cor. 8:6). Governments are simply a part of

---

9. Mukuka, 'Romans 13:1–7', p. 126.

10. Seneca writes to the young Nero urging him to reflect on how he will use his great power, having been favoured by heaven 'to serve on earth as vicar of the gods' and to be 'the arbiter of life and death for the nations' (*Clem.* 1.1.2, noted by Engberg-Pedersen, 'Paul's Stoicizing Politics', pp. 167–169).

God's ordered creation that are tasked by God to preserve the social order. When he tries to bring order to the Corinthians' worship, Paul says that 'God is a God not of disorder but of peace' (1 Cor. 14:33). Paul would also apply this saying to the social order.

Paul's instruction in some measure subverts the supremacy of the powers that be. The authorities belong to the 'undifferentiated, finite political powers that derive their existence from God'.[11] Since they are *from God*, they are not supreme. Paul mentions three times in verses 4–6 that they are only God's servants, whether they acknowledge it or not. God remains in sovereign control over even the most potent authorities that seem invincible. They are all dependent on, subordinate to and answerable to God.

2. Paul bolsters this mandate by saying that resisting or rebelling against the authorities that God has established will meet with *judgment* (*krima*), not 'damnation' (KJV). The judgment might come from the rulers who can ruthlessly quell rebellions (cf. Luke 21:20; Acts 5:36–37) and/or from God at the final judgment (2:2–3; 3:8; 5:16). Paul knows that God has used earthly powers as instruments to vent God's wrath in history (Isa. 13:5; Jer. 50:25), but the ultimate punishment comes from God's judgment at the end of the age.

3. God desires order and justice in the world over anarchy and lynch mobs. Paul assumes that the governing authorities have the ability and the responsibility to distinguish between good and evil so that they can act to foster a civil society and to protect it. The government can perform a positive role as a dyke against evil. To maintain order, authorities punish what is evil and reward what is good. Wishing *to have no fear of the authority*, however, suggests that it was not unusual to live in fear of authorities who might unjustly inflict harm. Paul is not naïve. The authorities can be brutal, and few could appeal to Roman citizenship as Paul did to seek justice (Acts 22:25–29; 23:27; 25:1–12). Consequently, he advises a misunderstood and maltreated minority to avoid doing anything that might justifiably cause the authorities to mete out punishment and to perceive them as threats to the order and well-being of the state.

---

11. Pinter, 'Josephus', p. 148.

What is the *good* they might do to receive approval? It may not refer simply to good behaviour but to undertaking good works that benefit the city and receive public honours. One wonders, however, how many in the churches had the resources to undertake public works. If Paul had this in mind rather than private morality, he could have cited Jeremiah's admonition to pursue the welfare of the city (Jer. 29:7). Since Paul addresses private morality in 13:8–10, it is more likely that he exhorts his audience to behave in ways that are plainly perceived as good and as good for others (12:21; Gal. 6:10; 1 Thess. 5:15; 1 Pet. 3:13–14). Doing what is good not only heads off unwanted, negative attention from the authorities, it might also open the door for others to come to faith.

4. The assertion that only *wrongdoers* need fear the governing authorities envisages 'a civil government properly fulfilling its functions' (Fitzmyer, p. 668). Believers are to leave room for God's wrath and are forbidden to avenge themselves (12:19). God has given the task of redressing crime and inflicting wrath on evildoers to the authorities (Bruce, p. 238). Paul expresses a truism that the fear of retribution for wrongdoing can preserve civil order. Rabbi Hanina, the Prefect of the Priests, said: 'Pray for the peace of the ruling power, since but for fear of it men would have swallowed up each other alive' (m. ʾAbot 3:2).[12] The *sword* may refer to the supreme right to absolve or to condemn a person to death (*ius gladii*). Herod Antipas, for example, put James to death by the sword (Acts 12:1–2; cf. Rom. 8:35; Heb. 11:37). Paul is not making a case for the state's right to carry out the death penalty. Papyrus documents use the term 'sword-bearers' for policemen who carry out their duties, particularly in collecting taxes.[13] 'The *sword* serves as a metonym for the government's power to punish the violators of the law in various ways.

5. Paul restates the fundamental admonition that one must be subject to the secular authorities and provides an additional reason for doing so. They not only must be wary of the *wrath* (of the state) but also must submit *because of conscience*. Christians do not submit

---

12. Danby, *Mishnah*, p. 450.
13. E. Plümacher, 'μάχαιρα', *EDNT* II, p. 397.

solely out of fear of retaliation or from a desire to gain advantages or praise from the rulers, but because they know in their conscience that such conduct is good. Paul's use of *conscience* corresponds to Stoic thought that understood it to apply to 'the individual's sense of right and wrong, his moral judgement, his recognition of the inherent claims of the good, and the grounds for rejecting what is wrong' (Black, p. 160). A 'clear conscience' leads one to 'act honourably in all things' (Heb. 13:18), but one acts honourably because of a consciousness of God and God's will (1 Pet. 2:19). The conscience recognizes that rulers have received their authority from God, and it persuades one to obey them. One does not cower before the ruler's sword but defers to the governing authorities out of deference to God.

Introducing the conscience, however, also allows for the possibility that one might resist the authorities since earthly rulers are not the final arbiters of right and wrong, good and evil. Obedience is not intrinsically a virtue (Leenhardt, p. 324), since one can obey what is wrong. Since obedience is motivated by conscience it is not to be carried out in a spirit of fawning servility. Out of conscience Peter and John defied the demands of the Sanhedrin to cease speaking or teaching in the name of Jesus: 'Whether it is right in God's sight to listen to you rather than to God, you must judge; for we cannot keep from speaking about what we have seen and heard' (Acts 4:18–20). Later, Peter and the apostles persisted in disobeying the high priest's order to stop preaching and insisted, 'We must obey God rather than any human authority' (Acts 5:27–32, 40–42). They refused to comply, knowing full well that the authorities would unleash persecution for their disobedience. The early Christians continued to proclaim their faith because they were persuaded, 'It is through many persecutions that we must enter the kingdom of God' (Acts 14:22). Believers follow the 'Lamb' of God who has been slaughtered (Rev. 5:6), knowing that he is also 'the Lion of the tribe of Judah' (Rev. 5:5) who will triumph (Rev. 19:11–16). He will come to conquer and destroy 'the beast and the kings of the earth with their armies' (Rev. 19:19–21) who are 'drunk with the blood of the saints and the blood of the witnesses to Jesus' (Rev. 17:6). They are not to rise to try to conquer the oppressor by their own strength but must wait patiently for God to 'judge and avenge' (Rev. 6:9–11), as God assuredly will.

6–7. Paul explains further why they should submit to the authorities by introducing the reason behind paying the tributes they demand. He does not tell his audience that they should pay tributes but assumes that they do so 'because of conscience'. He does not address an imagined unhappiness with the Roman taxation system that led to the later tax protests under Nero (Tacitus, *Ann.* 13.50–51). The noun translated *taxes* or 'tribute' (*phoros*; Luke 20:22; 23:2) designates something directly levied on subject peoples as a token of their subjugation to a foreign ruler (cf. 1 Macc. 8:4, 7). It was not required of the inhabitants of Rome, but it is unclear what the obligations were for Jews or immigrants or those outside the city boundaries. Paul simply assumes that his audience pays taxes. The noun translated *revenue*, 'tolls' or 'customs' (*telos*), in verse 7 denotes a wide variety of indirect taxes on goods, sales and property. He uses the word 'pay back' (*apodote*) rather than simply 'pay', which recalls Jesus' response to the question whether it was 'lawful to pay [*dounai*] taxes to Caesar or not' (Mark 12:14, CSB). Jesus' reply is, 'Give ['Pay back', *apodote*] to Caesar the things that are Caesar's' (Mark 12:17, CSB).

Christians do not reject the obligation to pay these various tributes and taxes because they recognize that the secular authorities require the financial resources to carry out their task of governing by maintaining civic order and performing public services. This letter was first carried and later disseminated by those using the Roman transportation system, the product of resourceful Roman engineering. While the highways facilitated Roman conquest and the administration of the growing empire, they also hastened the spread of the Christian faith. Paul's rationale for paying taxes is quite different from Josephus's account of the warning Herod Agrippa gave to crowds who were on the verge of revolt and of withholding tribute to Caesar because of the wrongdoings committed by Florus, the Roman governor. The failure to pay tribute, he says, would be considered by the Romans to be an act of war. His counsel is direct: 'If you wish to clear yourselves of the charge of insurrection . . . pay the tax', or face the vengeance of Rome (*J.W.* 2.403–406 [Thackeray, LCL]). Paul instead ties paying taxes to the higher obligation to pay everyone what is due to him or her.

Paul does not mention the challenges presented by the emperor cult to Christians, but he does imply that the authorities deserve only *honour*, not worship. While leaders deserve honour (1 Pet. 2:17), so do wives (1 Pet. 3:7) and fellow believers (12:10; Phil. 2:3), especially the less-honoured members of the church body (1 Cor. 12:22–26). Even Moses honoured Pharaoh (Exod. 8:9). The respect that Christians show to leaders is the same respect that they are to show to all persons because of the command to love their neighbour, which Paul spells out in the following verses. Polycarp tells the proconsul of Asia, 'We have been taught to give honor to magistrates and authorities appointed by God, as is fitting' (*Mart. Pol.* 10.2 [Lake, LCL]). The authorities, from lowly magistrates to exalted emperors, are owed only honour, not absolute obedience. Only God is owed utmost allegiance.

ii. The theological rationale for acting this way: fulfilling the command to love the neighbour (13:8–10)

8–10. The admonition to *owe no one anything* is not merely conventional advice forewarning that 'the borrower is the slave of the lender' (Prov. 22:7); it sets up the exception that they are to love one another. The object of love that begins with *one another* (13:8a), namely, fellow believers (cf. 12:9; 14:15), is then expanded to include *another* (13:8b) and the *neighbour* (13:9–10). Believers are also to love those who are outside the community of faith. The obligation to love is not limited to a closed circle of like-minded intimates, but it begins with fellow believers. One can hardly expect believers to show love to strangers (12:13), persecutors (12:14) and enemies (12:20) if they do not show love to their fellow believers.

This unit is not to be detached from the instructions to be subject to the governing authorities. Love is to guide believers' relationships with everyone. Since love detests evil (12:9), does not repay anyone evil for evil (12:17) and *does no wrong to a neighbour* (13:10), it is possible that rulers, who are not a terror to good conduct, will commend such behaviour (13:3). Believers, however, are not simply trying to please the authorities who seek to preserve civil order and often are only interested in their self-preservation. They are striving to please God. Their love for others 'takes its cue from somewhere other than civil obligations and is played out in a different key altogether, often going far beyond the demands of civic decency'.[14] Love originates from God, and loving the neighbour emulates God's rule and wins God's commendation. Unlike the taxes owed to rulers, love is a debt that never can be paid in full, but loving others does fulfil the law.

For Paul, doing the law (10:5; cf. Gal. 3:10, 12; 5:3) is different from fulfilling the law (cf. Gal. 5:14; 6:2). Doing the law means obeying commands. Fulfilling the law means living out the divine intention of the commands. The command to love one's neighbour in Leviticus 19:18 breathes life into all the commands. Loving one's neighbour means not committing adultery and not murdering, stealing, coveting or doing anything else to harm a neighbour. Paul can equate this with fulfilling 'the law of Christ' (Gal. 6:2), which entails acting with another's best interests at heart. The love that fulfils the law is now defined by the self-giving sacrifice of Jesus (Gal. 2:20; cf. Rom. 8:34) and God's action on behalf of enemies (5:5–8). Believers are enabled to fulfil the law's intention through the power of the Holy Spirit (8:4) who has poured out God's love in their hearts (5:5).

iii. The theological rationale for acting this way: the nearness of the end (13:11–14)

11. The phrase translated *besides this* (*kai touto*) intends to link Christian ethics to eschatology (cf. 1 Cor. 7:25–31). The *time* is God's appointed time for the end that does not show up on human calendars. Paul assumes the audience knows that the end will come suddenly and unpredictably like a thief in the night (1 Thess. 5:2, 4). He also assumes the believers know that their salvation hinges on their faith. This means that they must await the time when all will be fulfilled. The theme of waiting and hoping reverberates through the biblical stories. Rabbi Isaac interprets Jacob's statement in Genesis 49:18, 'I wait for your salvation, O LORD', by combining it with Isaiah 26:8, where the word 'wait' occurs, and Isaiah 33:2, where the word 'wait' and the phrase 'our salvation in the time of trouble' occur. He claims that Jacob was waiting for the Messiah

---

14. Bertschmann, 'The Good', p. 248.

and concludes, 'everything is bound up with waiting [hoping]. Suffering is bound up with waiting, the sanctification of the Divine Name with waiting, the merit of the Fathers with waiting, and the desire of the World to Come with waiting' (Gen. Rab. 98:14).[15] Paul insists that with the coming of Christ the wait-time has narrowed. The alarm to awake from *sleep*, a metaphor for sluggishness and dullness that ignore the urgency of the hour and the need to keep watch (cf. Mark 13:35–37; 1 Thess. 5:6; Rev. 16:15), has sounded.

What Paul says about the nearness of the end (cf. Luke 21:28, 31) matches what he wrote in 1 Thessalonians 5:1–11, his earliest letter. His eschatology has not changed. He asserts that the end is imminent (1 Thess. 5:2; cf. Jas 5:8; 1 Pet. 4:7) and juxtaposes sleeping and waking (1 Thess. 5:6), night and day (1 Thess. 5:5, 7–8), light and darkness (1 Thess. 5:4–5) and drunkenness and sobriety (1 Thess. 5:7; cf. Rom. 13:13) to stress the need to be ready. He also refers to 'putting on' armour, 'the armour of light' (13:12), and 'the breastplate of faith and love, and for a helmet the hope of salvation' (1 Thess. 5:8).

Knowing *what time it is* means that believers must be conscious that they live in two different time zones: the time zone of this world that is passing away (1 Cor. 7:31; 1 John 2:17), and the time zone of the new age that has broken into our history through Christ. It requires believers to live in this present time in ways that befit the new age. As Käsemann asserts, 'Christian ethics is lived-out eschatology' (Käsemann, p. 185). Cottrell draws attention to the fact that Paul does not say,

'Live right, so that you will be ready for Christ's return and so you will be rewarded in heaven.' He says rather, 'Live right, because this alone is consistent with the new age which was inaugurated by Christ's death and resurrection, and in which you are already participating by virtue of your conversion.'
(Cottrell, p. 489)

---

15. Freedman and Simon, *Midrash Rabbah*, p. 964.

12. With the dawning of a new and eternal day, 'the night is nearly over' (NIV). That is a cause for rejoicing, but Paul uses it as a warning. The day's light dispels the darkness and exposes deeds done under the cover of darkness (Eph. 5:1–14). That is why the wicked are 'those who rebel against the light' and do not recognize 'its ways' or 'stay in its paths' (Job 24:13). Jesus said, 'For all who do evil hate the light and do not come to the light, so that their deeds may not be exposed' (John 3:20). For Christians, it is time to throw off the reassuring mantras of 'peace and security' (1 Thess. 5:3) that lull them to sleep. They must get ready for the new day by putting on the *armour of light* and living as those who belong to the light (Eph. 5:8; Col. 1:12–13). The metaphor of light as armour may seem curious since armour normally consisted of metal coverings worn to protect the body in battle. The armour of light is not a lightsabre to destroy enemies in duels but a protective spiritual armament that is emitted when believers allow themselves to be bathed in the light of God's grace and then walk in the light. God supplies the armour, which 'consists of all goodness, righteousness, and truth' (Eph. 5:9, CSB), to repulse the deeds of darkness that might entice believers.

13. Some equate *liv[ing] honourably* or 'walking in decency' with simply what is culturally considered to be respectable behaviour and assume that all God requires of them is to be a 'good person'. Paul has far more in mind than following the rules of conduct that a culture considers worthy of public admiration. He exhorts his audience to follow God's rules of conduct and to walk worthily of God's calling (Eph. 4:1).

The warnings about *revelling and drunkenness* are in the plural, suggesting multiple incidents that are typical behaviours in the darkness of night and typical sins in Graeco-Roman culture (1 Pet. 4:3; cf. Jesus' warnings in Luke 21:34). They also serve as metaphors for all behaviours that dull and disorient the mind and keep one from being vigilant in preparation for the end. Paul adds 'sexual impurity and promiscuity' (CSB), which often accompany the revelry of night-time partying, and these behaviours can even afflict the church (2 Cor. 12:21). *Quarrelling* and *jealousy* occur night and day and can assail the church (2 Cor. 12:20).

14. *Put on the Lord Jesus Christ* restates with a different metaphor the basic call for believers to be transformed with a renewed mind that can 'discern what is the good, pleasing, and perfect will of God' that began this section (12:1-2, CSB). It may be a baptismal metaphor (Gal. 3:27; Eph. 4:24; Col. 3:10) that expects those who are baptized to live no longer as they once did but after the model of Christ. Putting on the Lord Jesus Christ means that they now have the power to overcome fleshly desires and can fashion their lives according to the model of Christ's love for others (15:1-3). It also means that at the abrupt coming of Christ they will not be found naked and subject to shame and judgment (Rev. 16:15).

Theology
The Christian community cannot withdraw to a secluded never-never land if it is to carry on its witness to the gospel in the world. Instead, it must continue to live as members of the wider society even when it faces intense animosity. In giving his advice on how to coexist with the governing authorities Paul provides only one side of the story: the Christian's responsibility. He speaks only to what he can influence and does not address the government's responsibility to the governed as God's servant. Unless one was born a member of the elite ruling circle, one had little hope of exercising power, let alone changing the power structures. Christians therefore could only live 'within the structures' (Dunn, II, p. 770). Therefore, Paul does not campaign for morality in government but for morality in Christians.

Paul gives no explicit criteria for deciding when the state has crossed its appointed limits and has become God's adversary rather than God's servant. Luther famously concluded in a marginal gloss of his lectures on Romans, 'Christians should not refuse, under the pretext of religion, to obey men, especially evil ones.'[16] He misinterprets Paul's intentions, but it affords an example of how easily this passage can be misused. Governing authorities have exploited such interpretations to pressure believers to turn a blind eye to their governmental abuse of power and reign of terror and to drub the church and its leaders into submission. Feldmeier cites as an example the Ansbach Memorandum written by a working party in

---

16. Luther, *Lectures*, p. 358 n. 1.

the National Socialist Union of Protestant Pastors in 1934 in response to the Theological Declaration of Barmen whose third point stated,

> We reject the false doctrine that the Church could have permission to hand over the form of its message and of its order to whatever it itself might wish or to the vicissitudes of the prevailing ideological and political convictions of the day.

The signatories of the Ansbach Memorandum emphasized their loyalty to the Führer, Adolf Hitler, and the new Nazi state with its fourth thesis: 'as Christians, we honor, with gratitude to God, every ordering of society, and thus every authority, even in disfigurement'.[17] The history of the Third Reich that followed shows how mistaken such a view of submission to the governing authorities can be.

Paul does not advocate blind obedience, but obedience directed by a vigilant and discerning conscience (cf. Acts 4:19–20). Identifying rulers as God's 'servants' presupposes that they are answerable to God and that God does not license them to do as they please. God has put them in place as a dyke against evil and an impetus for good. As God's servants, they are to emulate God's righteous rule, not compete with it. They overstep the line when they expect to be venerated as gods. Their delegated authority is limited only to this world, and it is time-limited. History again shows that human empires rise and seem unshakeably established, only to fall and give rise to other human empires. Since the believer owes ultimate obedience only to God, one can argue that the state is to be obeyed only as it functions within God's appointed limits (13:4).

Paul does not spell out when or how believers might resist an evil government. Since his instructions in 13:1–7 are framed by the renunciation of force (12:21) and the love command (13:9), believers

---

17. Feldmeier, *Power*, p. 54. Schlatter presciently warned in 1935 of the danger posed by 'the proximity of the palace to Christians' (Schlatter, p. 183).

are not to lead insurrections. Revolution is not the way forward. Paul would know that the armed rebellions of Theudas and Judas the Galilean against Roman rule had failed in Judea (Acts 5:36–37). He could have foreseen that the Jewish revolts against Rome in AD 66–73, 115–17 and 132–36 would beget utter disaster for Israel. The last revolt led by Simon Bar Kokhba ('son of the star', cf. Num. 24:17) met with vicious vengeance as the Romans sought to annihilate the Jewish population. The ruined city of Jerusalem became a Roman colony renamed Aelia Capitolina. Aelia was the family name (*nomen gentile*) of the Roman emperor Hadrian, and Capitolina meant that the city was now dedicated to Jupiter, king of the gods. A temple dedicated to Jupiter was erected on the temple mount, and Jews were banned from Jerusalem. Jews suffered almost universal disdain, their attempts to spread their beliefs through proselytism essentially ended, and Judaism became increasingly insular.[18]

Paul's thoughts here are influenced by one pivotal concern and three theological principles. First, Paul speaks strategically. His primary concern is missional. He wants to gain Roman toleration of Christians for the sake of the church's mission in the world. He knows that believers are highly vulnerable, subject to persecution, suffering, hardship and death (5:3–5; 8:18, 31–39; 12:14, 17). He wants the Roman authorities to view Christians as model citizens (Keener, p. 153). Attracting unfavourable attention from the governing authorities would only hinder the Christian mission. In Thessalonica, some years earlier, antagonistic Jews accused Paul and Silas and their converts of 'acting contrary to the decrees of the emperor, saying that there is another king named Jesus' (Acts 17:7). Shortly after writing Romans, he would be mistaken by Roman soldiers in Jerusalem for an Egyptian terrorist (Acts 21:38; cf. Acts 5:37). No Roman official could ignore the charges brought against Paul that he was a rabble-rouser or guilty of offending the majesty of the emperor, but, after investigating them, none gives them any credence. Their judgment is that he has done nothing deserving of death or imprisonment (Acts 18:14–16; 23:29; 25:25; 26:31). Paul is for government-imposed order and trying to live at

---

18. Segal, *Paul*, pp. 105–106.

peace with everyone (12:18) because it can facilitate the progress of preaching the gospel of Jesus Christ. Therefore, he desires that his audience not get caught up in actions that might bring their witness to the gospel into disrepute.

Second, Paul thinks theologically in terms of the love that believers owe to all (13:8–10). What he says in 13:3 about doing what is good resonates with admonitions in 1 Peter: 'For it is God's will that by doing right you should silence the ignorance of the foolish' (1 Pet. 2:15). Believers are to bear witness to the hope that is in them with 'gentleness and reverence' so that opponents cannot disparage their 'good conduct' (1 Pet. 3:15–16; cf. Rom. 12:9, 17). When believers encounter evil, are hated by everyone and are threatened with being killed by the sword, they are called to endure (Mark 13:13; Rev. 13:10), to love their enemies (12:17, 20–21) and to leave room for God's vengeance (12:19). Paul does not command mindless surrender to the governing authorities. He assumes that Christians whose minds are transformed (12:2) can discern what is good and pleasing to God in their various political circumstances. Their decisions must be piloted by the paramount demand to love others.

Third, Paul thinks eschatologically. He links the commands about submission to the governing authorities (13:1–7) to eschatology (13:11–14). Christians live in the present evil age under the thrall of Satan and sin (Gal. 1:4; cf. Rom. 12:2). He understands this age to be teetering on the edge of collapse as 'its current form is passing away' (1 Cor. 7:31, CSB). He insists that the 'time is short' (1 Cor. 7:29, NIV) and the 'day is near' (Rom. 13:12). All earthly governments, therefore, are lame ducks since their days are numbered. Paul concludes his letter by saying, 'The God of peace will shortly crush Satan under your feet' (16:20). Christ's parousia will render them null and void (1 Cor. 15:24–25). Tibullus was the first to refer to Rome as eternal (*Elegies*). Vergil has Jupiter proclaim in the *Aeneid* that Rome is 'an empire without end' (*imperium sine fine*). Both were wrong. Though Paul might submit to governing authorities out of respect for God's appointed servants and as a prudent way of staying under the radar of the imperial security apparatus, he knows that Rome is not 'the eternal city'. The adjective 'eternal' applies only to the heavenly Jerusalem (Gal. 4:26; Heb. 12:22; Rev. 3:12; 21:2, 10).

Submitting to these rulers in the meantime is qualified by the demand that absolute obedience is owed only to Christ, who 'will rule over the nations' (15:12, NIV). Nothing in this passage infringes on Jesus' lordship. As Saviour and Ruler of the world, Jesus is invested with divine authority that transcends the claims of Caesar and all other political and religious authorities yet to come. Morrison correctly observes,

> The eschatological character of Paul's thought excluded preoccupation with the concept of an 'ideal state'. So long as the world endured there would be a State, and there is no ground for believing Paul thought it would be any better or any worse, any more or less a servant of God, than it was when he wrote or had experienced personally . . . Paul's 'ideal' was the consummation of the Kingdom of God, and there was no place in that ideal for the work of Roman officials.[19]

Fourth, these instructions are steeped in references to God, which occur six times in verses 1–7, and in Paul's certitude in God's sovereignty. Bird comments,

> For Paul there is no authority *except from God*; the powers are *appointed by God*; those who resist his appointed political authorities oppose the *authority of God*; political authorities preserving social order with the sword are in effect the *agent of God*; and political authorities are even *servants of God*.[20]

Paul knows that Jesus had suffered and was executed at the hands of the state. Paul also had been its victim, but he was peculiarly impressed by the hand of God in it all. Jesus responded to Pilate that he would have no power over him if it had not been given to him from above (John 19:11). Even pagan authorities from Cyrus to Pilate can serve an ordained role in God's purposes. The mysterious hand of God that 'raised up' Pharaoh (9:17) can use other evil authorities to display God's power. They are no better than the

---

19. Morrison, *Powers That Be*, p. 106
20. Bird, 'One Who Will Arise', p. 159.

client-kings in the Roman Empire who existed under the higher power of Rome and whose delegated authority could be revoked at any time. All earthly rulers stand under the higher power of God who permits them to rule for a time. They are all transitory. In the end, only the name of God, who forms light and creates darkness, makes success and creates disaster (Isa. 45:7), will be proclaimed in the whole earth.

C. Dealing with conflict in the body of Christ (14:1 − 15:13)

Context
Some recent studies ground the occasion of Paul's writing to the Roman community of believers on the supposition that Jewish Christians returned to Rome at the beginning of the reign of Nero in AD 54, after Emperor Claudius expelled them in AD 49, and found a community that was controlled by Gentile Christians. These interpreters see in 14:1 − 15:7 the reflection of an acute schism in the church between Jewish and Gentile believers. They contend that Paul wrote this letter to try to unify these fractured groups. Anti-Jewish attitudes were notorious among the Roman cultural elites. For example, Tacitus, in his jaundiced account of the Jews and their history, says that they 'are extremely loyal toward one another, and always ready to show compassion, but toward every other people they feel only hate and enmity' (*Hist.* 5.5 [Hutton et al., LCL]). It is imagined that Gentile Christians, infected by such views, discounted the Jewish Christians' religious heritage and disdained their desire to retain their cultural identity as Jews by continuing to follow the Mosaic law's strictures related to food. These interpreters claim that Paul writes to persuade the law-free majority consisting of Gentiles to show tolerance towards the hidebound Jewish Christian minority and to persuade the strict Jewish Christians to stop denouncing the emancipated Gentile Christians.[21]

---

21. Fowler, *Structure*, p. 142, wonders if the disagreement over food was only 'a surface issue that betrayed a deeper problem of antisemitism'. If that were true, the Gentile majority would be no more likely to listen

This hypothesis is the product of mirror-reading, which pores over one side of the conversation, what Paul says, and conjectures what is being said by the addressees or is transpiring in their midst. Mirror-reading is an unreliable but often necessary method for interpreting Paul's letters.[22] It is even more undependable for interpreting Romans since Paul had no direct contact with this community and has received no direct communication from them asking for his counsel. It is unwise to claim that what he writes in 14:1 − 15:7 unveils his main purpose for writing this letter, for the following reasons.

(1) If Claudius's expulsion of the Jews from Rome and their later return after Nero became emperor provides the backdrop for understanding Romans, one wonders why Paul never alludes to it, particularly when he sends greetings to Prisca and Aquila who were among those forced to leave (16:3; cf. Acts 18:2).

(2) This view is at odds with the celebratory tone of the letter. Paul praises the Romans immediately following this section: 'My brothers and sisters, I myself am convinced about you that you also are full of goodness, filled with all knowledge, and able to instruct one another.' He says that he has written only 'to remind you more boldly on some points because of the grace given me by God' (15:14–15, CSB). He concludes the letter by praising their obedience: 'The report of your obedience has reached everyone. Therefore I rejoice over you' (16:19a, CSB), which reiterates how he began the letter by giving thanks to God 'through Jesus Christ for all of you because the news of your faith is being reported in all the world' (1:8, CSB).

(3) His explanation in 16:19b that he wants them 'to be wise about what is good, and yet innocent about what is evil' (CSB) reveals that his moral exhortations are intended to prevent problems rather than to correct them. Paul knows that factionalism can surface anywhere humans gather. His warning about it does not

---

(note 21 *cont.*) to Paul, the Jewish apostle whom they had never met, than white churches in the American South listened to the appeal of Martin Luther King, Jr, 'the outsider', in his 'Letter from a Birmingham Jail', also known as 'The Negro Is Your Brother'.

22. Cf. Barclay, 'Mirror-Reading'; and Gupta, 'Mirror-Reading'.

mean that it was a burning issue in Rome. Paul warns against the vices of 'debauchery and licentiousness' as well as 'quarrelling and jealousy' (13:13), but that does not mean that sexual sins (cf. 1:24–27; 2:22; 7:5, 7–8) were a rampant problem in Rome that he seeks to correct. One can assume that the Romans already share the values he espouses and that the warnings are only precautionary. They should be interpreted as 'a paradigm for Christian conduct in general'.[23] Wolter contends that Paul does not discuss conflict 'on the level of an *actual problem* . . . but rather on the level of the *dealings* of the congregation with such conflicts'.[24]

(4) The issue of discord is not addressed at key points elsewhere in the letter unless the interpreter begs the question and reads it into the text. Reading Romans backwards from this chapter is an example of this approach.

(5) Much of what Paul says in 14:1 – 15:13 can found in 1 Corinthians 8:1–13 and 10:1 – 11:1. The issue in 1 Corinthians was specifically over food sacrificed to idols, and Paul adapts the principles introduced in that context and makes them more broadly applicable. His discussion in this section is marked by a degree of generality, and he does not explicitly set up the conflict as a flare-up between Jewish and Gentile Christians. He understands that any social group will contain a broad spectrum of maturity in faith and have differing views and practices. He pictures a split between the weak who eat only vegetables (14:2), judge one day to be more important than another (14:5) and abstain from wine (14:21), and the strong who do not. The strong are in danger of disdaining the weak (14:3, 10). The weak are in danger of condemning the strong (14:4, 10, 13). The divisions between the weak and the strong are so blurred that scholars disagree over the identity of the weak and strong. Interpreters identify 'the weak' as law-observant Jewish Christians, law-observant Gentile Christians, or non-Christian Jews. They identify 'the strong' as non-observant Gentile Christians or as Jewish and Gentile Christians. The weak need not be only Jews, and the strong need not be only Gentiles. Gentiles could

23. Dahl, *Studies*, p. 87.
24. Wolter, *Paul*, p. 316.

be vegetarians for a variety of reasons, regard one day as more auspicious than another,[25] and be identified as weak in conscience (1 Cor. 8:7–13). Paul was a Jew who identified with 'the strong' (15:1), and he says he could live 'as one outside the law (though I am not free from God's law but am under Christ's law) so that I might win those outside the law' (1 Cor. 9:21).

Glad concludes that when Paul speaks of some as the 'weak in faith' (14:1, 2; 15:1) and others as the 'strong' (15:1), he is describing a 'psychological disposition' or 'character type' rather than an ethnic identity. Such classifications presuppose that people have different aptitudes and maturation.[26] These 'weak' and 'strong' 'are not fixed roles but relative categories that would differ for an individual at various times and in regard to the particular behavior or aspect of character in question'.[27] Paul argues that the strong should not try to reform the weak and 'dispel their false beliefs by rational arguments and by means of a forceful example', and that they should avoid 'inconsiderate harshness' that might wound the weak and destroy them. Glad claims that these arguments reflect the debate between Paul and the 'wise' in Corinth on issues of pedagogy that centre on questions of maturation and harsh and gentle means of persuasion.[28] These principles are applicable to a wide variety of situations.

(6) Paul's use of the word translated 'unclean' (*koinos*, 'common') in 14:14 does suggest that he is thinking of Jewish religious sensitivities, since that word can be used to refer to food that Jews regarded as ceremonially impure (Mark 7:2; Acts 10:14, 28; 11:8; 1 Macc. 1:47, 62). Judging one day to be 'better than another' (14:5) is most likely a reference to the Sabbath and days of fasting that are specific to Judaism. The avoidance of wine (14:21) also could become a concern when Jews were in contact with Gentiles. Such Jewish scruples go back to God's demand that Israel be holy and must avoid what God declares to be unclean (Lev. 20:25–26; Deut.

---

25. Stowers, 'Use and Abuse', pp. 280–281; Talbert, pp. 313–315.

26. Glad, *Paul and Philodemus*, p. 289.

27. Ibid., p. 333.

28. Ibid., p. 334.

12:15–18, 20–28; Isa. 52:11) and anything that would seem to lend support to worship of another God. From the time of Ezra, pious Jews made a serious attempt to make their separation as a holy people a reality. So it seems that Paul does pose a conflict with Jews who are law-observant.

Divisions between Jewish and Gentile believers had surfaced in communities where Paul had ministered and were not confined to Rome. According to Galatians 2:12, 'certain men from James' arrived in Antioch and caused Cephas and even Barnabas to separate themselves from eating with Gentiles. This caused Paul to lay into Peter and Barnabas publicly for straying from the truth of the gospel by their withdrawal from Gentile Christians (Gal. 2:11–21). He does not respond with such vehemence here or betray a sense of urgency. He is concerned that Christians should neither disdain nor judge fellow Christians who have different convictions about how they honour God. They should all follow the example of Christ in not seeking to please themselves.

Without knowing specific details, Paul might suspect that these issues could have arisen because of the mixed ethnicity of the Roman house churches. More likely, Paul constructs 'imaginary opponents, "the weak" and "the strong", to make a case study of persons in conflict that has implications for any community that is divided over matters that some consider important and others consider indifferent' (Hultgren, p. 510). In his case study, he uses hyperbole by saying that the weak eat only vegetables and the strong eat anything, to make his point that dividing over such issues is ludicrous.

Paul does not admonish the Romans because he has heard that they are torn asunder by a Jewish–Gentile conflict (14:1 – 15:13). While he warns Gentile Christians not to be arrogant towards Israel (11:13–24), that arrogance is directed towards Jewish unbelievers, not Jewish believers. Paul writes from his experience of preaching the gospel from Jerusalem to Illyricum (15:19), 'with the controversies of Galatia and Corinth behind him and the meeting with the Jerusalem apostles before him'.[29]

---

29. Sanders, *Paul, the Law*, pp. 30–31.

He soon will embark for Jerusalem with the offering that symbolizes the unity of Gentile believers and Jewish believers. There he will face the ultimate test of Christian unity, and he worries that this material demonstration of fellowship from uncircumcised, law-neglecting Gentiles might not be 'acceptable to the saints'. Therefore, he asks the Romans to pray that it will be welcomed (15:25–27, 31). The account in Acts 21:17–26 suggests that the principles outlined in this section would also be relevant for the situation in Jerusalem. The instructions in this section apply to Jerusalem, Rome, and churches across the world today. That Paul wants to secure a harmonious base in Rome for his Spanish journey does not imply that he knows they are riddled with disharmony. Meeks is correct:

> there is no evidence, despite the many attempts at 'mirror-reading' by commentators, of any present crisis around this issue in the Roman groups. Paul takes up the topic out of his experience, not theirs, because it is well suited to show in behavioral terms the outworking of the main themes of the letter.[30]

Paul knows that the unity of believers is found in Jesus Christ alone and not in the uniformity of their practices. He wants to combat disunity wherever it might surface and insists that Christ-followers are to be set apart by a mindset modelled by Christ that is distinguished by love, humility and acceptance of others. Paul has made it clear in this letter that Jews and Gentiles have equal status in Christ. While they may have different convictions from their different life experiences, only when they appreciate their equal status in God's eyes will each also appreciate the other's distinctive contribution to the community of faith and 'believe they will benefit from the presence of the other'.[31]

---

30. Meeks, 'Judgment', p. 292.
31. Esler, *Conflict*, p 144.

i. Believers should accept those accepted by God (14:1–12)
Comment

1. Paul provides minimal information to identify the weak and the strong. Being *weak in faith* is not a characteristic of Jewish Christians as a group but refers 'to individuals and their *inability to do something in good conscience*'.[32] In his arguments about food offered to idols, Paul refers to former idolaters as those so used to idolatry up until now that when they eat food that has been sacrificed to an idol, 'their conscience, being weak, is defiled' (1 Cor. 8:7).[33] Cicero defined 'weakness' as an 'unwholesome aversion and loathing for certain things'; 'The product of aversion moreover is defined as an intense belief, persistent and deeply rooted, which regards a thing that need not be shunned as though it ought to be shunned' (*Tusc.* 4.10–11 §§23, 26 [King, LCL]). Paul's statement 'to someone who considers a thing to be unclean, to that one it is unclean' (14:14, CSB) confirms this understanding of weakness. It refers to individuals with a conscience-driven aversion to something, and it does not designate a rigidly defined ethnic group such as Jewish Christians. Since Paul does not urge the weak in faith to grow in maturity and change their views, he rejects any attempts by the strong to compel them to change. He does not view them or their views as a theological danger to the community. They are simply not far enough along in their faith to believe that they can safely risk breaking what they regard as taboos without breaking their relationship with God. Some argue, however, that they are Jewish Christians who do not want to risk breaking their relationship with non-believing Jews. This approach is little different from Paul's statement 'To the Jews I became as a Jew, in order to win Jews' (1 Cor. 9:20). While they may be motivated to practise Jewish customs to maintain access to the Jewish community rather than to win them, such a course of action does not fit the category of being weak in faith. It is pragmatic.

The adjective 'strong' (15:1) equally does not refer to Gentile Christians as a group but refers to the ability of individuals '*to do*

---

32. Glad, *Paul and Philodemus*, p. 333.
33. Garland, *1 Corinthians*, p. 384.

something without self-condemnation.[34] They have the confidence 'in the Lord Jesus that nothing is unclean in itself' (14:14) and are 'blessed' because they 'have no reason to condemn themselves because of what they approve' (14:22). The weak in faith are presumed to be in the minority, since Paul insists that they should be welcomed and not refused hospitality (12:3; cf. 1 Tim. 3:2; 1 Pet. 4:9), presumably at the communal meal. The word translated 'accept' (NIV) or 'to extend a welcome' (*proslambanō*; cf. NRSV) reappears in 15:7 and summarizes the thrust of this section. Acceptance requires more than toleration. It is the key to creating a harmonious community of people from diverse backgrounds and inclinations because it demands receiving others without conditions. Christ-followers are to do so because God has accepted them without conditions (14:3). Before God they are equals. Consequently, Paul stipulates that when they (presumably 'the strong') welcome the weak in faith they are not to use that welcome as a pretext for hammering them with arguments to bring them round to their way of thinking or to coerce them to act against their convictions.

If Paul expects the strong to welcome the weak in faith, he assumes that the weak in faith want to join the community gatherings for meals. It suggests that he does not think that the church is so wracked by acrimony that they recoil from eating together.

2. Eating *only vegetables* might allude to the Jewish aversion to eating meat that was improperly butchered (Lev. 7:22–27; 17:10–16) or potentially defiled by its associations with pagan sacrifices. The dietary prohibitions in Scripture made Jewish associations with Gentiles problematic because Gentile food may have been sacrificed to an idol (Exod. 34:15; 1 Cor. 10:28), been a forbidden animal (Lev. 11:1–20) or been slain in ways that violated ritual restrictions (Exod. 23:19). Daniel is held up as a hero precisely because he would not defile himself with the pagan king's rich food and wine and instead insisted on only eating vegetables and drinking water. Because of his fidelity to the bounds of the covenant, God delivered him (Dan. 1:8–16). Tobit was also a hero

---

34. Glad, *Paul and Philodemus*, p. 334 (emphasis original).

because of his scrupulous concern for food laws: 'After I was carried away captive to Assyria and came as a captive to Nineveh, everyone of my kindred and my people ate the food of the Gentiles, but I kept myself from eating the food of the Gentiles. Because I was mindful of God with all my heart' (Tob. 1:10–12). Judith was a heroine because she would not eat or drink pagan food and wine lest it be an offence to God. Her victory over the enemy is ascribed to her scrupulous observance of dietary laws (Jdt. 10:5, 12:1–4, 19). The heroes in 1 Maccabees are those who 'stood firm and were resolved in their hearts not to eat unclean food' (1 Macc. 1:62). Peter declares in his vision in Acts 10 that he had 'never eaten anything impure and ritually unclean' (Acts 10:14, CSB; 11:8). Not all Jewish Christians had received such a vision from God pronouncing all things clean. They would abstain from meat because obeying the law's restrictions had been so deeply engrained from years of practice that their consciences would not allow them to abandon their long-held principles, and because they felt it necessary to dispel any appearance of supporting idolatry, however remote it might be (1 Cor. 10:14). Those who eat *anything* do not worry that they might violate the commands of God regarding food.

Since Jews did not normally abstain from meat or wine, it is quite possible that Paul constructs a fictive situation and speaks hyperbolically about those who eat only vegetables and those who eat everything (Wolter, II, pp. 354, 356). Jewett paraphrases the exaggerated depiction: 'The weak only eat lettuce' (Jewett, p. 838). Paul does not suggest the food had any prior associations with idolatry. He presents an exaggerated case to illustrate a principle.

3. It is not uncommon in religious circles for those who regard themselves as liberated to *despise* others because they are sticklers about issues that the liberated consider to be matters of theological indifference that have no bearing on salvation. The sticklers, however, do not regard these issues as matters of indifference. They are likely to respond by condemning the liberated who violate rules they consider sacrosanct. What to do? Paul does not want to settle an imagined dispute over food as he does in 1 Corinthians 8 – 10 in forbidding idol food that is known to be idol food (1 Cor. 10:14,

25–28). His primary concern is to impart standards for how fellow believers must treat one another when, in good conscience, they make different lifestyle choices. When disagreements arise, it is unacceptable for believers to cast aside other believers or try to ride roughshod over them to get them to give in. The weak and strong are brothers and sisters (14:10, 13, 15) accepted by God (14:3) and servants belonging to the Lord (14:4, 8; cf. 1:6; 7:4). Both were bought with a price (1 Cor. 6:20). Since believers should not think more highly of themselves than they ought (12:3) or be proud (12:16), they should not despise, treat as nothing (14:10) or castigate other believers.

4. Paul's switch to the second-person singular verb makes his appeal more personal as he addresses the weak who judge and condemn others. He does not expect believers to withhold all judgment of others. One may condemn those beliefs and practices that do not harmonize with 'what is known of God through Jesus' (Best, p. 156). He expects the Roman Christians to admonish one another (15:14), which entails constructive criticism (1 Cor. 4:14) that leads others to a healthier grasp of the faith. Admonition consists of cautioning, reproving, guiding or instructing others in their duties and how to interpret the prohibitions and positive commands in Scripture. Condemnation in this case is destructive. It passes sentence on others.

To make this point Paul introduces the analogy of judging another's slave to illustrate how presumptuous they are in judging fellow believers. He uses the word for 'household servant' (*oiketēs*) – one who would have a closer relationship with the master – think of Cicero's slave, Tiro, who later became his freedman and published his master's collected works. In Paul's historical context, one would never think it permissible to encroach on a master's relationship to a slave by passing sentence on the slave. To do so would only incur the master's indignation (cf. how delicately Paul addresses Philemon concerning his slave Onesimus). In our context, one would not encroach on a parent's charge over his or her young child by announcing that the child's behaviour deserved a failing grade. This action would justifiably incur the parent's indignation. The argument is this: masters alone have the right to judge their slaves; how others might assess them has no force.

The lordship of Christ is the fundamental premise that grounds Paul's comments. The twelve uses of *kyrios* (*Lord*) in this section (14:4 [2x], 6 [3x], 8 [3x], 11, 14; 15:6, 11) refer to the Lord Jesus Christ. The gravity of condemning other believers is heightened by the reality that they all are the Lord's slaves. Since only the Lord has the right to pass judgment on them, and his judgment alone carries weight, how much more is it true that our judgment of Christ's servants is of no consequence? Worse, such judgments brazenly infringe on the Lord's authority.

Paul understands 'the judgement seat of God' in 14:10 to be equivalent to 'the judgement seat of Christ' in 2 Corinthians 5:10. He assumes that Christ's servants will not fall at the final judgment but will stand. They 'stand only through faith' (11:20), and because Christ is the only one who has the power to save and enable them to stand (Jas 4:12).

5–6. One legitimately may make judgments on whether to observe different days or not or to eat or abstain from food in honour of the Lord. *The day* in 14:6 is probably the Jewish Sabbath. Since it is 'to the Lord' (NIV; or 'to honour the Lord'; cf. NRSV), it rules out an auspicious day venerated by pagans. Those who observe the day believe that they are obeying God's direct command (Exod. 20:8). Paul does not say that those who pay no heed to special days do so in honour of the Lord. He simply assumes they do not believe that honouring the Lord requires observing special days on a religious calendar. They may interpret Psalm 118:24, 'This is the day that the LORD has made; / let us rejoice and be glad in it', to mean that each day we have is a day created by God for us to honour God (12:1–2; cf. 1 Cor. 10:31, 'do everything for the glory of God').

One need not presume automatically that Paul refers here to Jewish Christians. Gentile converts, for example, who heard Isaiah 56:6–7 might well assume it applied to them:

> And the foreigners who join themselves to the LORD,
>> to minister to him, to love the name of the LORD,
>> and to be his servants,
> all who keep the sabbath, and do not profane it,
>> and hold fast my covenant –

> these I will bring to my holy mountain,
>   and make them joyful in my house of prayer;
> their burnt-offerings and their sacrifices
>   will be accepted on my altar;
> for my house shall be called a house of prayer
>   for all peoples.

As believers joined to Israel, they may come to believe that they must keep the Sabbath and keep the covenantal requirements of purity. What is important, however, is not the identity of those who observe different days but the two criteria that Paul gives for making authentic decisions about how one lives out religious devotion to God.

First, one must be fully convinced in one's own mind how one expresses this devotion to God and not just yield to external pressure from others to conform. This principle does not mean that whatever one might decide is acceptable. Some practices are directly contrary to God's purposes in creation and doing them is an expression of self-will rather than devotion to God's will. Paul assumes that the convictions come from a mind that has been transformed and informed by faith.

Second, one must determine if these activities are carried out *in honour of the Lord* and are appropriate ways of giving thanks to the Lord. The criterion is the desire to honour God, not to advertise one's piety. God is most honoured when one loves and respects the dignity of others who have done the same thing in deciding how they honour God. Therefore, one may not condemn them for reaching different conclusions on how to express their devotion to God.

7–9. Paul now provides the theological foundation for his exhortations by revisiting the essence of the gospel. First, as Christians, 'none of us lives for ourselves alone, and none of us dies for ourselves alone' (NIV). Believers have a new collective identity as part of the body of Christ (12:5; 1 Cor. 12:27). Faith binds the individual believer to the community and the community to the individual. Also, believers are not their own because they have been bought with a price and belong to the Lord (1 Cor. 6:19–20). Therefore, they cannot do whatever they want. Some who consider individual rights to be the bedrock of a free society might find Paul's advice objectionable. Insisting on exercising one's rights, however, does not provide guidance for doing what is right for those around us. It easily can degenerate into extreme individualism that thinks only about what is best for me, what I want that will make me happy, and what will bring me honour. Paul understands that believers have died to self (Gal. 2:20–21); they therefore cannot make the self their priority. Demanding to exercise one's rights while looking through others as if they did not exist destroys community.

Second, whether we live or die, we belong to the Lord. Christ's lordship is established by his death and resurrection. Only those devoted to themselves and asserting their rights would consider as unreasonable Paul's call to sacrifice the right to express one's freedom however one wants. Christ's sacrifice on the cross serves as an example of a far more extreme sacrifice. The unusual expression *Christ died and lived*, instead of 'he died and was raised', conveys two things. First, Christ's lordship is universal, covering the dead and the living (Acts 10:42). Christ rules every part of our existence, whether in our present life or in our death. As Paul says, neither death nor life can separate us from 'the love of God in Christ Jesus our Lord' (8:39). Second, Christ's sacrifice teaches believers something about living. As Paul writes in 2 Corinthians 5:15, Christ 'died for all, so that those who live might live no longer for themselves, but for him who died and was raised for them'.

10. Paul now poses the prohibitions against condemning and despising others as warning questions. Why condemn a brother or sister since each of us has to stand before God's judgment seat and answer for our own conduct and not that of another (1 Cor. 4:3–4; 2 Cor. 5:10)? We will not be judged based on how we judged the errors of others. God also will not ask for our opinions about them. If we are to do any judging, we should first examine ourselves (1 Cor. 11:28, 31; 2 Cor. 13:5; Gal. 6:4). If we are to do any despising, it must be of our wretched selves who do not do the good that we want to do but the evil we hate (7:15–24; cf. 2:1–16). When believers stand before God, they will stand as peers with none elevated over another. God will uncover the secrets of the heart of each person and judge impartially (2:16; 1 Cor. 4:5).

11. To conclude this first unit, Paul applies Isaiah 45:23 to what will happen at the last judgment. Paul replaces the first words in Isaiah 45:23, 'By myself I have sworn', with the explicit oath formula that God utters in Isaiah 49:18: *As I live, says the Lord.* With this oath 'God promises and guarantees fulfillment by putting His own name, so to speak, on the line.'[35] The promise in Isaiah 45:23 that *every knee shall bow to me, / and every tongue shall give praise to God* is momentous. Every tongue will openly acknowledge God's rule, and praise God because of this acknowledgment. The Isaiah passage occurs in the setting of a mock trial scene in which the idolaters and their gods, the enemies of God and Israel, are arraigned before God. God declares that he alone is the Lord and has threatened to punish and utterly destroy them (Isa. 41:1–3, 11–12; 42:13; 43:14; 45:1–3; 47; 49:26; cf. Isa. 51:22–23; 59:17–19; 60:12; 63:1–6; 66:15–16). Childs comments,

> What now occurs in [Isa. 45:]22–25 is astonishing and unexpected, going beyond anything so far seen in Second Isaiah. Instead of the disputation with the nations ending in a resounding pronouncement of judgement (cf. 41:21–24), the widest possible invitation to salvation is extended by God.[36]

It sets up Paul's 'climactic vision in 15:6, 9–12 of a global participation in the praise of God' (Jewett, p. 852).

12. This unit ends with a reiteration of the theme in 14:3–4. Each of us must give an account to God, and therefore we must examine our own attitudes and actions (Matt. 12:36; 16:27; 1 Pet. 4:5) rather than weighing the merits of others.

ii. The strong should forgo exercising their freedom to avoid injuring the faith of others (14:13–23)

13. Paul sums up what he has just argued with the exhortation not to pass judgment on others. He now adds reasons why those who believe they have the freedom to eat anything should not be

---

35. Paul, *Isaiah 40 – 66*, p. 337.
36. Childs, *Isaiah*, p. 355.

indifferent to the scruples of those fellow believers who might be offended by their actions. Their freedom is to be restricted whenever their behaviour imperils the faith of a Christian brother or sister. It makes no difference if their views are right. They may not do as they please if it puts a stumbling block in front of another. Paul states this principle more sharply in 1 Corinthians 8:9–12 regarding idol food:

> But take care that this liberty of yours does not somehow become a stumbling-block to the weak. For if others see you, who possess knowledge, eating in the temple of an idol, might they not, since their conscience is weak, be encouraged to the point of eating food sacrificed to idols? So by your knowledge those weak believers for whom Christ died are destroyed. But when you thus sin against members of your family, and wound their conscience when it is weak, you sin against Christ.

Paul does not mention 'conscience' in his arguments here, but he assumes that the strong may cause others to act against their inner persuasion that an action is wrong. These others may be sensitive to ridicule or taunting, but if they do something that they regard as a sin to avoid derision, their faith loses its footing. They might feel compelled to leave the community entirely to escape contamination, temptation or recrimination. Their faith also might become so diluted that they eventually lose it altogether. What is at stake is their 'security as a Christian' (Ziesler, p. 331), which is cause for serious concern and sensitivity.

The phrase *no longer* may mean that Paul is aware that 'such divisions existed in Rome and wrote Romans, in part, to help heal these wounds (cf. 1:11; 15:15–16)' (Thielman, p. 643). But it also may mean that the gospel has created a new reality (6:6; 2 Cor. 5:15). The command in Ephesians 4:17, 'you must no longer live as the Gentiles live, in the futility of their minds', does not mean that the recipients of the letter have let themselves go by indulging in pagan immorality and have lost touch with God. It means that from now on these things are unthinkable for believers fashioned by Christ. The phrase *no longer* reflects a new eschatological reality that is equivalent to 'but now' in 3:21.

14. Paul has no interest in deliberating the pros and cons of each position but only wants those who hold strong views on matters of indifference to show consideration for those who hold opposing views. He thinks the strong are right: *nothing is unclean in itself*. This statement is a stunning about-turn for a former Pharisee (Phil. 3:5). Pharisees were especially known for their purity rules that classified things, times and persons as pure and impure. Their purity concerns were especially focused on agricultural rules, which specified not only what might be eaten, but which vessel could be used and with whom one could eat. To say *nothing is unclean in itself* is an ontological statement. Nothing is inherently unclean. This statement is not all-embracing. In the context, Paul refers only to food laws that designate different foods and drinks as permissible (pure) or impermissible (defiled). Food laws no longer carry any weight for those who have died with Christ (6:8; 7:4, 6).

Paul makes no effort to argue why this assertion is true except to say that he is *persuaded in the Lord Jesus*. It does not mean that he is persuaded as one who is 'in the Lord Jesus'. That might imply that those who are persuaded otherwise are *not* 'in the Lord Jesus'. He must mean that he was persuaded '*by* the Lord Jesus'.[37] It is plausible that he knows Jesus' teaching about food laws reflected in Mark 7:18–20 (Matt. 15:11) in the same way that he knows his teaching on divorce (1 Cor. 7:10; cf. Mark 10:11), and his views are grounded in that tradition. Implicit in this personal conviction, however, is the theological certainty that if the Lord justifies (4:5) and is able to make stand in the final judgment (14:4) those who were formerly godless and unrighteous (1:18; 5:6) and who did not have the law (2:14), then he also must have the power to revolutionize the purity and food regulations as conditions for life as the holy people of God (Schnabel, II, p. 745).

Others, however, may not know Jesus' teaching nor have received a divine vision as Peter did that declared, 'What God has made clean, you must not call profane [impure]' (Acts 10:15; 11:9). Paul might disagree with those who believe that certain foods and drinks are taboo. But he insists that if they believe they dishonour

---

37. Campbell, *Union with Christ*, pp. 167–168.

God in some way by partaking of forbidden foods, it is wrong for them to compromise their convictions by playing the game of conformism and following the crowd. It is also wrong for others to pressure them to go along. If this principle is applied to Jewish Christians, then it means that Jews who become Christians do not need to jettison their Jewish identity. While a Gentile need not become a Jew to be accepted by God, a Jew need not become a Gentile and flout the purity laws to become accepted by the Christian community. Both must concede that one can honour the Lord whether one ignores purity laws or obeys them.

15. The shocking notion of destroying another for whom Christ died because of what one eats is also found in 1 Corinthians 8:8–13. Believers should never allow their enlightenment to injure a brother or sister. If they do so, it is not a matter of honouring God; when it is done 'without consideration to the sensibilities of others' it has become 'mere self-indulgence' (Westerholm, p. 124). To refrain from eating does not jeopardize one's convictions or Christian faith but ignoring the brother or sister by insisting on exercising one's freedom does serious harm. Paul uses strong language with the verb *cause the ruin of* (*apollymi*) which he applies to perishing and eternal damnation (2:12; cf. 1 Cor. 1:18; 15:18; 2 Cor. 2:15; 4:3; 2 Thess. 2:10). Paul is addressing the strong and agrees with them that everything is clean and therefore permissible to eat. But if one lives out those convictions in such a manner that it distresses and ruins another for whom Christ died, then it has become evil (1 Cor. 10:23). It tears down rather than builds up. If they are rooted in love, they can tolerate differences of opinion over matters of indifference.

16. The *good* that should not 'be slandered' (csb; *blasphēmeisthō*) may refer to the freedom that the strong believe they have in Christ. In that case, the ones who slander them are 'the weak'. The strong may then ask, 'If I partake with thankfulness, why should I be denounced [*blasphēmoumai*] because of that for which I give thanks?' (1 Cor. 10:30).

The *good*, however, may refer instead to the blessings both the strong and the weak possess, namely, their identity as Christ-followers (Wolter, II, pp. 379–380). Those who slander them are outsiders (cf. 2:24) who would malign them over the jabber and babble of their discord. Disharmony does not convey to unbelievers that 'the kingdom of God' brings 'peace and joy in the Holy Spirit' (14:17). Outsiders will be disinclined to join such a quarrelsome group.

17. The phrase *the kingdom of God* appears less frequently in Paul's letters than in the teaching of Jesus. In this context, it refers to God's reign that is experienced in the present (cf. 1 Cor. 4:20; Col. 1:13); elsewhere, to the eschatological kingdom that the worthy inherit (1 Cor. 6:9–10; 15:24, 50; Gal. 5:21; Eph. 5:5; 1 Thess. 2:12; 2 Thess. 1:5; 2 Tim. 4:1, 18). He asserts that one's relationship to God is not determined by one's practices related to food and drink. Again, this thought is found in his earlier discussion in 1 Corinthians: 'Food will not bring us close to God. We are no worse off if we do not eat, and no better off if we do' (1 Cor. 8:8).

Those who come under God's reign are marked by *righteousness*, uprightness as opposed to lawlessness (2 Cor. 6:14); *peace* brought about by being made right with and reconciled to God (5:1–11), which generates reconciliation with others (Eph. 2:15–17); and *joy*, which is the fruit of the Holy Spirit (8:6; Gal. 5:22; 1 Thess. 1:6). This assertion is a subtle critique of the position of the weak and encouragement for them to reassess their views on what is forbidden. Righteousness, peace and joy far exceed and make irrelevant any matters related to food and drink. Such things can no longer be considered the benchmarks of holiness nor pertinent for coming under God's reign.

18. Serving Christ 'in this' makes one *acceptable* ['well-pleasing'] *to God*, but to what does 'in this' refer? Does it mean 'in this way' or 'in this matter'? Most likely, it refers in the context to the issue of not destroying another by what you eat (14:15) and instead pursuing what promotes peace and builds another up (14:19). One may think that one serves Christ by hailing and living out one's freedom in Christ or by holding the line on purity. When doing so rebuffs others and creates strife, however, it is anything but service to Christ. Serving Christ involves following the pattern of Christ's self-denial for the benefit of others and not insisting on one's rights. It is 'pleasing to God' (12:1, CSB) and receives 'human approval' or 'esteem' (12:17) that shows the believer to be 'genuine', 'tried and true' (BDAG, p. 256). Paul expects that Christians' love for one another will win human approval (1

Thess. 4:9–12) instead of slander and will validate their witness
to the truth of the gospel.

19. The exhortation to *pursue what makes for peace* is not unique to
the Roman situation. Jesus commanded his disciples to be at peace
with one another (Mark 9:50), and Paul commanded the Thessalonians (1 Thess. 5:13) and the Corinthians (2 Cor. 13:11) to be at peace
among themselves. Pursuing peace among believers is a concern
throughout the New Testament (Eph. 4:3; Jas 3:18; Heb. 12:14),
because Christ's disciples have a penchant for disputing among
themselves (cf. Mark 9:34; Luke 22:24). The goal of mutual
upbuilding recognizes that no-one in the faith community is a
finished product. Every member can increase his or her faith (2
Cor. 10:15), and every member, according to his or her various gifts,
can help others in working towards this goal (1 Cor. 14:26; Eph.
4:12; 1 Thess. 5:11). In doing so, believers shelve their own wishes
and resolve to contribute to the greater good of the community by
boosting others rather than themselves. They recognize their
commonality and do everything they can to preserve it and thereby
promote peace.

20. The one who believes in Christ and accepts his atoning
death on the cross becomes a *work of God* and a new creation (2 Cor.
5:17; Gal. 6:15; cf. John 6:29). Consequently, it is not an indifferent
matter to demolish God's work over such trivial issues as the food
one eats even when one knows that the orderings of what is pure
and impure have been abolished in Christ (10:4). Any action that
topples the faith of a fellow Christian is wrong.

One wonders, though, how eating meat, which Paul asserts is
clean, destroys the work of God. This argument seeps in from his
treatment of idol food in 1 Corinthians 8. He says there that we
know 'an idol is nothing' (1 Cor. 8:4, NIV), which would seem to
support the position of those in Corinth who eat food that may
have been sacrificed to idols. The problem is that 'not everyone . . .
has this knowledge' (1 Cor. 8:7). Those who were accustomed to
eating food sacrificed in honour of an idol before they became
Christians may be encouraged to do so again but will still believe
in their hearts that doing so honours an idol. Their weak conscience
is defiled, which makes them susceptible to being swept back into
the mire of their former idolatry. The knowledge of the wise causes

this ruin, which is a sin against Christ (1 Cor. 8:7–12). While those with the knowledge that idols do not exist may not cause this collapse deliberately, God will hold them accountable for their lack of care and attention to the needs of their brother or sister. This interpretation of the context challenges the view that Paul is addressing solely the divide between Jewish and Gentile Christians in Rome.

21. The avoidance of *wine* has nothing to do with abstinence from intoxicating drink. Later rabbinic tradition forbade Jews from consuming or gaining benefit from the wine of heathens (m. 'Abod. Zar. 2:4; 5:2; b. 'Abod. Zar. 29b) and identified three kinds of wine that Jews must not drink: libation-wine, which caused grave defilement; ordinary wine of heathens that might have been used in libations; and wine that an Israelite had deposited with an idolater (b. 'Abod. Zar. 31b). Jews therefore were wary of purchasing wine and meat in pagan cities in case they were defiled by any contact with idolatry. The combination of *meat* and *wine*, however, is associated with feasting and may have only an 'exemplary meaning' that illustrates a general rule (Wolter, II, pp. 387–388). One's indulgence can cause others to stumble.

If the verb translated *stumble* (*proskoptei*) simply means to cause offence, then the caution is not to offend others by feasting in their presence. But Paul warns that their actions might destroy God's work by causing them to fall away. He cautions against careless feasting that can lead to the unhappy result of causing a brother or sister's spiritual downfall.

22. Paul again asserts that convictions about these things must be rooted in *faith*. *Faith* is connected in this context to a sense of assurance in their relation to God that they do not dishonour God in exercising their freedom to eat or drink anything. They have conscientiously examined their motivations before God and do not *condemn themselves because of what they approve*. The meaning of this statement is illuminated by 1 Corinthians 4:3–4:

> With me it is a very small thing that I should be judged by you or by any human court. I do not even judge myself. I am not aware of anything against myself, but I am not thereby acquitted. It is the Lord who judges me.

They should not let anyone condemn them 'in matters of food and drink or of observing festivals, new moons, or sabbaths' (Col. 2:16), because they understand themselves already to be blessed by God.

23. *Those who have doubts* about whether, if they eat, they might dishonour God are not 'blessed' but are *condemned* by their deeply held convictions. Their doubts reveal that they think an action is wrong. They are not doing what they believe in their hearts is pleasing to God (12:2) but are taking a course of action that they believe is at odds with what God expects of them. By eating they do not obey God but surrender to the majority's preferences by doing the accepted thing.

iii. Christ, the model of believers' relationships with others (15:1–6)

1. For the first time Paul identifies those who are convinced that 'nothing is unclean in itself' (14:14) and believe that they can eat anything in honour of the Lord (14:2, 6) as the *strong*. He also identifies himself as belonging to this group: *we who are strong*. This may help make it easier for the strong to accept his directions to forgo eating whatever they want to avoid causing the weak to stumble. The strong, with their more resilient faith, are under obligation 'to bear the weaknesses of those without strength' (csb). The nrsv's translation *to put up with the failings of the weak* is misleading. The verb (*bastazein*) means 'to take up in order to carry' something (cf. Gal. 6:2, 5). The same verb is used in 11:18 to describe the root of the olive tree bearing the branches. In addition to not despising the weak (14:3, 10) or inducing them to do something that goes against their principles (14:13, 15, 21), the strong are to shore up those who are weak (cf. Col. 3:13; 1 Thess. 5:14).

The noun translated 'weaknesses' does not connote 'failings' or 'shortcomings' since Paul has ruled out such judgmental assessments of the convictions of the weak. Simply tolerating the weak is not enough. Love demands that one do much more and take responsibility for their spiritual welfare. This demonstration of love is not to be a hypocritical show (12:9). Barth aptly warns against 'patronizing dissimulation':

Should we, whilst appearing to bear their infirmities, secretly rejoice in our strength and freedom? But that is not to *bear* infirmity. After all, the New Testament is not a theatre. The bearing of infirmity is a wholly existential occurrence; it is a genuine being weak with the weak. (Barth, p. 524).

2. *Each of us* refers in the context to the strong since they are the ones who must make concessions and forgo their rights. Instead of pleasing themselves, they must *please* their *neighbour*, their fellow Christian who has scruples. Paul's choice of the word *neighbour* rather than 'brother', which he has used in 14:10, 13, 15, 21, recalls his comment that loving one's neighbour 'is the fulfilling of the law' (13:9–10). Loving one's neighbour is commanded of all Christians, but in this situation the strong are the ones who are expected to act out of love and hold back on living out their freedom if doing so might harm the faith of the weak believer. Love limits liberty. Paul applied the same principle of not pleasing oneself in his discussion of idol meat in 1 Corinthians. He concedes that everything may be permissible, but it becomes impermissible when it fails to build others up and instead tears them down (1 Cor. 10:23–33). They are not to please themselves by insisting on their freedom and doing whatever they like while shrugging off its detrimental effects on others (1 Cor. 10:24, 33).

When the strong do not seek to please themselves by satisfying their own desires, they follow the example of Christ, who did not please himself but 'took our infirmities and bore our diseases' (Matt. 8:17, citing Isa. 53:4). The purpose behind pleasing one's neighbour is to act for the neighbour's good and do what edifies him or her, rather than do what might confuse or might push the neighbour's precarious faith over the edge (1 Cor. 10:33). The goal is not to keep the weak happy at all costs but to help their growth and development. Paul does not expect the strong to cater to every quirk or to give in to every possible complaint. The grievances of the weak also have their limits because they also are not to please themselves and seek to dominate. While all believers can expect others in the fellowship to take their views into consideration and seek to please them (Phil. 2:4), at the same time they are to take the views of others into consideration and seek to please them, embodying the 'principle of egalitarian reciprocity'.[38]

3. In concluding his arguments about food offered to idols, Paul tells the Corinthians, 'Give no offence to Jews or to Greeks or to the church of God' (1 Cor. 10:32). He then offers himself as an example that they should imitate: 'just as I try to please everyone in everything I do, not seeking my own advantage, but that of many, so that they may be saved. Be imitators of me, as I am of Christ' (1 Cor. 10:33 – 11:1). He can make this appeal for the Corinthians to imitate him because they have first-hand experience of his ministry. The Romans do not know him, and therefore he cannot use himself as an example. He can only appeal for them to imitate what they know of Christ. Christ's self-denying sacrifice on the cross sets the standard for the mindset of all Christians (Phil. 2:5–11), but here he expects the strong particularly to be exemplars of it.

Paul quotes only the second half of Psalm 69:9 (68:10, LXX) and reads it as if it were spoken by Jesus. The reference to him bearing the shame of insults directed at God brings up a host of associations connected to the passion narrative.[39] On the cross, Christ passively suffered his fate and bore the insults of the insolent (Matt. 27:44; Mark 15:32; Luke 23:39) in dying for those who are weak (Rom. 5:6). God, however, made this one who was the object of widespread scorn the object of humanity's hope. His death brings forgiveness, which requires those who receive this forgiveness to forgive others (Col. 3:13). His death enabled the reconciliation of both Jews and Gentiles to God, uniting them in one body and putting to death the relentless hostility that walled them off from each other (Eph. 2:13–16). Believers who receive this reconciliation must for their part be reconciling. Rather than reproaching other believers with whom they disagree, they are to accept reproaches. When they do so for the name of Christ, they can be called 'blessed,

---

38. Wolter, *Paul*, p. 313.

39. The detail of being given vinegar to drink (Ps. 69:21 [LXX 68:21]) is taken as prefiguring Jesus' humiliating death on the cross elsewhere (Matt. 27:34, 48; Mark 15:23, 36; Luke 23:36; John 19:28–29).

because the spirit of glory, which is the Spirit of God, is resting on you' (1 Pet. 4:14).

4. Paul supports his citation of the psalm by affirming that all the Scriptures were written for *our instruction*, that is, for the instruction of believers who read the Scriptures as pointing to Christ (1 Cor. 10:11; 2 Tim. 3:16). The Scriptures deepen their faith in Christ and provide *encouragement* that bolsters their endurance and nourishes their *hope*. Relying on the Scriptures prevents believers from being 'tossed by the waves and blown around by every wind of teaching, by human cunning with cleverness in the techniques of deceit' (Eph. 4:14, CSB). The Scriptures can also lead them to recognize that decrees such as 'Do not handle, Do not taste, Do not touch' are mere human commands and doctrines (Col. 2:21–22).

5. Paul's command in 12:16, 'Live in harmony with one another', now becomes a prayer to God that they will live in harmony to glorify God. Those who may be of two minds regarding food must be of one mind in their common commitment to Christ. Having the same mind does not mean that they will come to agreement over every disputable matter, but that God will help them to put aside their differences for the good of the whole body of Christ (1 Cor. 1:10; 2 Cor. 13:11; Phil. 4:2). Paul recognizes that only God can create the desired harmony as the Holy Spirit melts away any arrogance (11:20; 12:3, 16) and selfishness. *In accordance with Christ Jesus* refers to his example in not seeking to please himself (15:3). Those who serve Christ (14:18) should model Christ's service to God (15:8).

6. The word translated *together* (*homothymadon*) occurs in Acts to describe the early Jewish believers as being of 'one accord' in prayer (Acts 1:14, ASV), in worship and breaking bread (Acts 2:46; 5:12), and in praising God, speaking the word boldly and sharing possessions (Acts 4:24–35). That harmony was challenged when Greek-living Jewish Christians, identified as Hellenists, joined with Jewish-living Jewish Christians. The church struggled to overcome the cultural and ethnic differences that created the inequality in the treatment of the Hellenistic widows (Acts 6:1–7). Because both Jewish and Gentile believers have a common hope (15:4), they can lift up their voices together to worship the one God and their Lord

Jesus Christ. When they do so, it is evidence that there is no partiality with God and that all discrimination has faded away (Acts 11:18; 21:19–20). Paul is not calling believers simply to be nice to one another but to magnify *the God and Father of our Lord Jesus Christ* (cf. Eph. 1:17) through their unanimity based on their shared commitment to Christ. They become like a choir that need not sing praises to God in unison but sings different notes and pitches in harmony. Glorifying God is what God intends all creation to do (1:21). When believers together glorify the Father of our Lord Jesus Christ in response to what he has done through Christ, it gives witness to how the gospel transforms the venomous cursing and bitterness that formerly came out of their mouths (3:13–14) into adoring praise and mellifluous interpersonal relations.

iv. The unity of diverse believers praising God together (15:7–13)

7. The command to 'accept one another' (NIV) picks up the verb used in 14:1, 3. The structural parallels with 15:1–6 suggest that 15:7–13 may serve as a second conclusion to the argument that began in 14:1.

Exhortation	15:1–2	15:7
Example of Christ	15:3a	15:8–9a
Appeal to Scripture	15:3b–4	15:9b–12
Exhortatory prayer to God	15:5–6	15:13

Both passages include majestic trilogies: 'hope', 'steadfastness' and 'encouragement' (15:4b); and 'hope', 'joy' and 'peace' (15:13). Paul closed the previous long section in 9:1 – 11:36 on the inter-dependence of the Gentiles' salvation and Israel's salvation with scriptural citations (11:32–36). He repeats that pattern by concluding the larger section of moral exhortations that began in 12:1 with four promises from Scripture that emphasize the salvation of the Gentiles (15:9–12).

These verses also may be interpreted as offering a conclusion to 12:1 – 15:6 as well as the entire letter (Wright, p. 744). The parallels with Paul's salutation in 1:1–7 are noteworthy. (1) The 'gospel of God' was 'promised beforehand through his prophets in the holy scriptures' (1:1–2; 15:8). (2) Paul is called 'to bring about the obedience of faith among all the Gentiles *for the sake of his name'* (1:5, emphasis added), and the Gentiles will praise his name for his mercy (15:9–11). (3) The gospel concerns God's Son, Jesus Christ our Lord, who is a descendant of David (1:3) from 'the root of Jesse' (15:12). (4) The gospel brings grace and peace to all who believe through the power of the Holy Spirit (1:4, 7; 15:13). One might also note that Christ becoming 'a servant of the circumcised on behalf of the truth of God' (15:8) parallels Paul becoming 'a servant of Jesus Christ . . . set apart for the gospel of God' on behalf of the Gentiles (1:1, 5). The Jerusalem pillar apostles recognized that Paul had been 'entrusted with the gospel for the uncircumcised' (Gal. 2:7), and this calling is the cornerstone of the next section (15:14–33) where Paul discusses his itinerary as a minister and apostle to the Gentiles (15:16) and his vision of going to Spain.

To interpret the command to *welcome* ['accept'] *one another* at their common meal as building a bridge across the Jewish-oriented and Gentile-oriented tendencies that had created the Roman believers' imagined factionalism[40] unduly restricts it to the Roman situation. The command to accept (welcome) one another is the foundation of Paul's understanding of what God's grand vision for the world intends. It should not be restricted to an attempt to remedy a localized problem in Rome. God's intention is to eradicate the human divisions of Jews and Gentiles, Greeks and barbarians, wise and foolish, and strong and weak, so that all might praise him with one voice. Since Christ's death lays out the welcome mat for all the ungodly, Paul notably shifts the grounds for welcoming one another from God who welcomed them (14:3) to Christ who welcomed them. Welcoming persons from different cultures and ethnicities into the church's fellow-ship, which is most evident when they celebrate common meals together, testifies to God's righteous impartiality and to their justification by faith through Christ's death. The unified church becomes a visible microcosm of God's redemptive intention to unite all humankind in Christ to the glory of God. The ethical injunctions in 12:1 – 15:7 are about shaping the church's identity

---

40. Casson, *Textual Signposts*, p. 258.

for its witness in the world. Only a church bathed in peace can authentically proclaim the message of God's peace to the world that does not know 'the way of peace' (3:17). Welcoming one another also applies to Paul's intent to take the gospel to Spain to win more converts who will need to be welcomed in Christ.

8–9a. *For I tell you* solemnly introduces a momentous declaration. Paul may be identifying two parallel purposes of Christ's incarnation and ministry. First, Christ became a servant of the circumcised for the sake of God's truth *in order that he might confirm the promises given to the patriarchs* and, second, *in order that the Gentiles might glorify God for his mercy*. Alternatively, Paul could be saying that Christ became the servant of the circumcision for the sake of God's truth, 'to confirm the promises of the fathers, that the Gentiles would glorify God for his mercy'. It is difficult to decide between the two options based on the Greek grammar. Both translations recap the pattern introduced at the beginning of the letter, 'to the Jew first and also to the Greek' (1:16). God's promise to Abraham that he would become the father of many nations (4:18; cf. Gen. 12:2–3; 18:18; 22:18; 26:4; 28:14; Gal. 3:8, 14, 22, 29) required that the Messiah belong to the circumcised line of Abraham for that promise to be fulfilled. Therefore, Paul graphically asserts Jesus' Jewish identity as belonging to the circumcised (3:30; 4:9, 12; Gal. 2:7–9). He became their servant (Mark 10:45) on behalf of God's truth or truthfulness, which Paul connects to God's fidelity to the covenant with Israel (3:3–4). Christ performed his salvific mission as a Jew to whom belong the promises, the patriarchs and the Christ by physical descent (9:4–5). That which God 'promised beforehand through his prophets in the holy scriptures' (1:2) was thus fulfilled. What is most important: were it not for God's mercy, none would be saved (11:30–32).

Christ's ministry among the circumcised also has resulted in God's mercy being showered on all the nations, which explains Paul's expression 'and also to the Greek' (1:16; 2:10). God's truthfulness is also closely tied to 'the glory of . . . God' (1:23, 25). The Scripture quotations that follow reveal that Jesus' incarnation, death and resurrection bring glory to God when the Gentiles accept God's mercy and join Israel in praising the Lord. Those among the nations who now glorify God have turned from their former sin of knowing God but failing to honour or give thanks to him as God (1:21). God then becomes the Father of all who believe from 'the circumcised' and 'the uncircumcised' (4:9–17).

9b–12. The series of citations that follow confirm from the 'law of Moses, the prophets, and the psalms' (Luke 24:44) that the inclusion of the Gentiles in salvation as part of the people of God is divinely willed. They sound the theme of glorifying God with singing, praising and rejoicing because the recipients of God's mercy now have in Christ the full assurance of hope.

The first citation comes from Psalm 18:49 (17:50, LXX; 18:50, MT):

> For this I will extol you, O LORD, among the nations,
> and sing praises to your name.
> (Cf. 2 Sam. 22:50)

The setting for the psalm is David praising God for delivering him from the hand of his enemies (2 Sam. 22:1, 50), but by omitting the address 'O LORD' in the citation, it is likely that Paul understands the speaker to be Christ. He envisions either 'the pre-existent Christ declaring in advance the purpose of his impending incarnation',[41] or the risen Lord becoming 'the "choirmaster"' in leading this chorus of praise to God (Byrne, p. 432). The next verse of the psalm (18:50) affirms God's 'steadfast love to his anointed, / to David and his descendants ['seed'] for ever' (Ps. 18:50). God has indeed fulfilled 'the promises given to the patriarch' in Christ (1:3).

The second citation in 15:10, from Deuteronomy 32:43, summons all the nations to rejoice together. The Hebrew text has

> Praise, O heavens, his people,
> worship him, all you gods!

Paul chooses to cite and abbreviate the Septuagint version that reads, 'Heavens, rejoice with him, let all the children of God pay him homage! Nations, rejoice with his people, let God's envoys tell

---

41. Keck, *Why Christ Matters*, p. 102.

of his power!' He omits the harsh references to God taking vengeance on his adversaries, repaying those who hate him and purging the land for his people, that would cancel out the positive force of the citation.

The third citation in 15:11, from Psalm 117:1 (116:1, LXX), directs *all* the nations to sing praises to God. The gospel produces praise to God, which is the exact opposite of what Paul claims his Jewish interlocutor produces: 'The name of God is blasphemed among the Gentiles because of you' (2:24).

The fourth citation in 15:12 melds together Isaiah 11:1 and 10 and states that the promise to David has been fulfilled and the Gentiles' hope is established by a Jewish Messiah who also fulfils the hopes of Israel. The Lord's anointed was to come from *the root of Jesse* (1 Sam. 16:1–13; Matt. 1:5–6; Acts 13:22), and he has appeared (1:3). The participle, which translated literally means 'the one who appears' or 'comes', can also mean 'the one who rises up' (*ho anistamenos*; cf. NRSV). Paul probably understands it as an allusion to Christ's resurrection that results in his universal lordship. Paul omits the phrase 'on that day' because he reserves it for the day of judgment (Dunn, II, p. 850). Christ's rule does not lead to the Gentiles' subordination to Israel but to sharing the hope of salvation *with* Israel. The crucified and resurrected root of Jesse is not only the Messiah of Israel but also the Gentiles' risen Lord in whom they have hope.

13. Paul does not refer to God as *the God of hope* elsewhere, but hope is prominent throughout the letter (4:18; 5:2, 4–5; 8:17–30; 12:12; 15:4; also 13:11–14). God is the fountainhead of our hope, and those who are without God are also without hope. Those who have been justified by God live in hope for the glory of God for which they have been divinely predestined. This hope is made possible by divine love and secured by divine power. This hope enables believers to bear up under suffering. It enlightens the heart so that it sees the good in others who might otherwise be disregarded as hopeless. Experiencing the *peace* of God (1:7; 5:1; 8:6; 15:13) requires believers to 'live peaceably with all' (12:18) and to 'pursue what makes for peace and for mutual edification' in the church (14:19). The phrase *by the power of the Holy Spirit* implies that Christians live in a supernatural power sphere (5:5; 8:2–27).

Theology

One of Paul's primary interests is to reveal God's eschatological plot to unify humanity in Christ and for this unity to be manifest in the church. He wants his audience to join with him in his resolve to broaden 'the obedience of faith' among every nation that will bring glory to God (11:36; 16:27). That goal requires that those who are different from one another recognize that they are merged in one body in service to Christ. 'In Christ', the different ascriptions of status of the everyday world are annulled and 'all who believe in Christ and are baptized into him are one'.[42] Therefore, cultural preferences cannot be used to define insiders and outsiders (Jackson W., p. 36). Jewish and Gentile Christians both are 'beloved of God' (1:7), 'children of God' (8:16) and 'heirs of God and joint heirs with Christ' (8:17) because Christ died for them (5:6, 9; 14:15). Each believer is the work of God who in Christ belongs to the 'elect' of God (8:33), belongs to the branches in the one olive tree (11:17–24), is predestined for glory (8:29–30) and will join in a chorus of praise to God with one mind and one voice (15:5).

The gathering of believers that embraces diversity while embodying unity testifies to the transforming power of God's gospel that breaks down ethnic and cultural barriers that otherwise separate people from one another. Paul is not a daydreamer, however. He knows that divine impartiality in saving Jews and Gentiles, Greeks and barbarians, the wise and foolish, and the strong and weak creates social complications. Unity, however, is to be an essential characteristic of the church for its mission to bring all people to Christ so that they may sing praises to God for his mercy. Paul knew that believers exhibiting concord among themselves rather than strife would elicit 'human approval' (14:18). Feldman points out that Josephus was mindful of this in his defence of Judaism to his Gentile audience. He notes,

> When Josephus (*Against Apion* 2.170) says that Moses made the various
> virtues – justice, temperance, bravery, and harmony among the

---

42. Wolter, *Paul*, p. 313.

members of the community – departments of religion, he substitutes harmony (*symphonian*) for wisdom as one of the cardinal virtues; and we are indeed reminded of Plato's question (*Laws* 3.689D), How can there be the least shadow of wisdom when there is no harmony (*symphonia*)? Similarly Plato (*Republic* 3.401D) speaks of the ideal state as one in which people live in harmony (*symphonia*) and friendship with beauty and reason.[43]

In this section, Paul is not simply trying to tamp down the fires of ethnic conflict among the Roman Christ-followers. Instead, he provides the equivalent of a spiritual fire extinguisher to keep sparks of dissent in congregations from exploding into conflagrations. Differences of opinion are to be expected among gatherings of diverse people. Living at peace with God in the context of the believing community means that believers are not to be stratified into ethnic, caste or rival theological groups. Paul's basic concern is forming inclusive communities of believers and maintaining harmony despite differences. He presents principles to promote unity that apply universally when it comes to disagreements over inconsequential issues. This section contains twelve directives that are universally applicable for forming a church marked by peace. Ten (two of which are repeated) concern how one is to relate to other believers: welcome or accept one another (14:1; 15:7); do not look down on another (14:3); do not pass judgment on another (14:3, 13); determine never to put a stumbling block or pitfall in another's way (14:13); do not destroy another by your actions (14:15); do not let your good be slandered by provoking strife (14:16); pursue what makes for peace and building others up (14:19); and seek to please your neighbour (15:2). The other two concern the individual: each one is to be fully convinced in his or her own mind in deciding what honours God (14:5); and whatever each one believes about these things is to be kept between oneself and God (14:22). All these commands entail walking in love (14:15) and faith (14:22–23) and following the example of Christ in not seeking to please oneself.

---

43. Feldman, *Jew and Gentile*, p. 147.

Paul's discussion concerns matters of opinion over disputed things that do not affect one's salvation. To use hyperbole, as I believe Paul does in his example, one is not saved by eating what one considers a pious diet, and one is not condemned for not doing so. The way Christians handle disputes with one another, however, is not a matter of indifference and does have an effect on salvation for oneself and others. Paul gives five basic principles for how to handle disputes over indifferent matters.

First, each must be convinced in his or her own mind about what is allowable because each will have to answer to God for what he or she has done. This principle assumes that one has carefully thought through one's decisions and is not bowing blindly to tradition. Those with scruples about taboos should therefore hold onto them until they are edified and believe they should abandon their convictions (14:4). Giving up convictions without understanding the scriptural and theological whys and wherefores that justify changing them only leads to moral erosion. For Paul, whatever is done against the conscience is wrong (14:23). Most of the time, actions are neutral. It is the motive or attitude behind them that makes them evil or good. Paul knows and is 'persuaded in the Lord Jesus' that nothing in itself is unclean, but for those who consider something to be unclean then, for them, it is unclean (14:14).

Second, one should acknowledge that the brothers or sisters who have been accepted by God and who have reached different conclusions about what is allowable also have carefully thought through their decisions and are convinced in their minds. Respect their convictions and do not belittle them as pathetically out of touch.

Third, one should not make one's own convictions a yardstick by which to measure others. The Christian faith is larger than one's personal definition of it. For one to be right does not mean that the other must be wrong and subsequently excluded or demeaned. Do not pronounce judgment on others. Christ-followers are not the masters of God's house, and they are not entitled to judge God's servants or engage in witch-hunts. Believers do not get to define the limits of acceptability and cannot dictate to God the terms by which others are to be accepted. They cannot make a test of fellowship what God does not make a condition of salvation. Therefore, believers should guard against the temptation to impose their understanding of the Christian lifestyle on all others. The person who is constrained by taboos must not be censorious, and the emancipated person must not be provocative and pugnacious.

Fourth, one should recognize that each acts in honour of the Lord, whether observing a day or not, or eating or abstaining (14:6). The vegetarian says grace over the Brussel sprouts and beets; the meat-eater, over the hamburger. If something is done to honour God, it should not be condemned by those who would choose to honour God in a different way. Since each intends to honour the Lord by giving thanks, each should accept as their brothers and sisters those who confess Christ as Lord and give thanks to God.

A caveat needs to be added here. Desiring to respect the dignity of others who differ does not mean that all differences should be embraced. Paul does not validate another's opinions and practices simply because they are 'sincerely held' (Best, p. 156). Sincerity is not the litmus test for truth. He does not propose a personal morality where one gets to choose what is right regardless of what others might think. He urges the Romans 'to watch out for those who create divisions and obstacles *contrary to the teaching that you learned*' and to 'avoid them, because such people do not serve our Lord Christ but their own appetites. They deceive the hearts of the unsuspecting with smooth talk and flattering words' (16:17–19, CSB; emphasis added). When it comes to what the Scriptures pronounce as immoral behaviour, a line must be drawn. Such matters are not indifferent. While others might complain that the church has no right to impose its values and tell them that their choices are immoral, they need to examine their motives to see if their views and behaviour are truly God-honouring.

Fifth, those who live out the freedom they have in Christ must recognize that that freedom is to be moderated by love. Christians do not live for themselves. They should ask: how do others benefit from what I do, and who might be hurt by it? Insisting on one's own rights and foisting one's own views on others never contribute to the building up of the community. The limit of one's freedom is what is good for one's brother or sister (Achtemeier, p. 221). Paul believes that if one is free, then one must be radically free by being willing not to exercise that freedom out of concern for the good of a fellow believer. He will do nothing, however, that might cause another's spiritual downfall. Paul disagrees with the views of those identified as weak, but he does not regard their views as dangerous and does not think it important to change them. The issue in Galatians 2:11–21 was quite different. The problem that arose in Antioch had to do with deviating from the truth of the gospel and, in effect, denying justification by faith and requiring justification by works. The problem that requires guidance from the Holy Spirit arises when one must discern what is a matter of indifference which permits compromise and what is a matter on which one cannot compromise.

7. THE LETTER CLOSING (15:14 – 16:27)

A. Paul's calling as a minister of Christ Jesus to the Gentiles and his travel plans (15:14–33)

Context

This section forms an inclusio with 1:8–15 as Paul revisits his longstanding desire to come to Rome (1:10, 13; 15:22–24, 28, 32) and to take part in mutual spiritual encouragement with the Roman Christians (1:11–13; 15:24, 29). In both sections, he highlights his commission as an apostle to the Gentiles and his goal to bring about their obedience of faith and to present them as an 'acceptable offering, sanctified by the Holy Spirit' to God (1:5, 14; 15:15–16, CSB). The two sections display a chiastic structure (Toews, p. 45):

> A 1:8 Paul gives thanks to God for the Romans' faith
> > B 1:9 Paul prays for the Romans
> > > C 1:10–11 Paul's longstanding desire to visit Rome
> > > > D 1:13 Paul has been hindered from visiting Rome

E 1:14–15 Paul's commission related to the
   Gentiles
   E' 15:14–16 Paul's commission related to the
      Gentiles
      D' 15:17–22 Paul again is hindered from visiting
         Rome
      C' 15:23–29 Paul's plans to fulfil his longstanding desire
         to come to Rome (after going to Jerusalem)
   B' 15:30–32 Paul exhorts the Romans to pray for him
A' 15:33 Paul invokes God's peace on the Romans

The theme of indebtedness also appears in both sections: Paul's indebtedness to bring the gospel to Greeks and barbarians and to the wise and the foolish (1:14), and the Gentiles' indebtedness to the saints in Jerusalem for sending the gospel their way (15:25–27).

The summary of Paul's successful ministry to the Gentiles in the East and his ambition to preach the gospel in unevangelized Spain fittingly follows the previous unit with its citations of Scriptures prophesying that the Gentiles would glorify God for his mercy (15:7–13). More Gentiles need to hear the invitation to join this chorus, and this drives Paul's ambition to proclaim the gospel in Spain. Paul's appeal to 'accept one another, then, just as Christ accepted you, in order to bring praise to God' (15:7, NIV) also fits his appeal that the Romans pray that the offering from Gentile Christians to the poor among the saints in Jerusalem might be 'acceptable' to them (15:31). If Jewish Christians accept a Gentile offering that conveys love and the offer of fellowship, then they also accept these Gentiles as their brothers and sisters in Christ.

This section is much longer than 1:8–15 because it introduces two new topics that are of central importance to Paul: his trip to Jerusalem with the collection, and his aspiration to be sent on by the Roman believers to carry out a mission in Spain. The focus in both 1:8–15 and this section is on Paul himself, his calling and travel itinerary, and not on the Romans and their situation. This focus is particularly relevant for understanding the letter's purpose. What are only subtle hints in 1:8–15 become very specific in 15:24–29. The contingency that prompts him to write this letter resides in his own circumstances and calling. He explains why he will delay his visit to Rome. He must first go to Jerusalem to deliver the Gentiles' charitable gifts to Jewish believers and then to interpret their theological significance for them. After he has completed this undertaking, he will travel to Rome, and he unveils his long-range plan to be sent on by them to Spain. It is this purpose, and not what he might have heard about the situation in Rome, that impels him to write this letter. He focuses on his own ministry work and how his obligation to serve the gospel of God as a minister of Christ Jesus connects to his future visit to Rome. Paul does not provide this reflection on his ministry in the East or the details of his travel itinerary merely to satisfy their curiosity. He wants to predispose them to accept the role he hopes they will play in his aim to preach the gospel in Spain.

This hope that they will support this mission effort is one of the reasons why Paul has written at such length laying out the gospel he preaches with theological arguments and scriptural support before broaching his request at the end of the letter. He cannot avail himself of the privileges of an apostle before he has earned it. He therefore commends himself to them by presenting a 'theological résumé' to persuade them that he and his mission to Spain are worthy of their support.[1]

Comment

i. Paul's calling as a minister of Christ Jesus to the Gentiles (15:14–22)

14. With the address *brothers and sisters*, Paul switches to the topic of his calling to preach the gospel among the Gentiles and how that has an impact on his future plans. He begins by lauding the Romans for being *full of goodness, filled with all knowledge, and able to instruct* ['admonish'] *one another. Goodness* is the opposite of Paul's description of those who have debased themselves in turning away from God and who do nothing good (3:9–18). 'Goodness' is a fruit of the Spirit (Gal. 5:22, NIV) and a sign that 'the Spirit of life in Christ Jesus has set you free from the law of sin and of death' (8:2).

---

1. Williams, 'Righteousness', pp. 249, 254.

Filled with all knowledge applies to their understanding of God's saving purpose in Christ (Col. 2:2–3) that contrasts with those who are 'filled with every kind of wickedness' (1:29). Their minds are no longer corrupted (1:28) but have been renewed (12:2). That is why they can instruct, chide and correct one another, even when such speech might sting and offend, so that they may build one another up into maturity in Christ.

If one assumes that Paul wrote to correct a desperate situation in Rome, this commendation may seem insincere flattery. When he says elsewhere in Romans that he 'is convinced' or 'persuaded' (8:38; 14:14), however, it refers to something he genuinely believes. Here, he is most emphatic: *I myself feel confident*. He is not, therefore, trying to cajole the Roman believers. He may assume that these qualities mark them from his direct acquaintance with the noble character of those persons mentioned in his final greetings. Alternatively, he has heard that these things are true since their 'faith is proclaimed throughout the world' (1:8; 16:19). This does not mean that he does not also praise them as a means to exhort (cf. Gal. 5:10; 2 Thess. 3:4; 2 Tim. 1:5). Pelagius comments, 'As a good teacher Paul rouses the people to further progress by praising them, so that they might blush for not being the sort of people the apostle thought they were' (cited by Kruse, pp. 536–537). Paul's praise of the Romans is part of a rhetorical strategy to prime them to respond positively to the implicit (15:24) and explicit (15:30–32) requests that follow.

15. Paul concedes that he has written *rather boldly*. Does the phrase *on some points* (*apo merous*), often translated 'in part', go with the verb 'written': 'there are parts of the letter that I have written more boldly'? If so, which parts? Those who think it applies to only parts of the letter usually identify 12:1 – 15:13 as the bold passage. In that section Paul may seem to take liberties by exhorting a church he had not founded nor visited to resolve their presumed divisions. Some might misconstrue it as audacious meddling even though he asserts he has apostolic authority to do so (12:3). The conventional moral exhortation in this section, however, need not be read as Paul's direct intervention in the affairs of the Roman community to bring peace to feuding factions. Other parts of the letter might better qualify as overbold;

for example, the statements in 3:5–9, 23 or 10:4, or his use of diatribe language: 'Are ye ignorant?' (6:3; 7:1, ASV); 'Do you not know?' (6:16; 11:2). Paul describes the words of the prophet Isaiah in 10:20 as bold speech:

> I have been found by those who did not seek me;
> I have shown myself to those who did not ask for me.
> (Isa. 65:1)

If this is an example of what Paul regards as bold discourse, it might apply to Paul's bold theological assertions throughout the letter, not simply his ethical exhortations. The gospel by its very nature is audacious, and the *grace given* to Paul *by God* as an apostle (1:5; 1 Cor. 3:10; Eph. 3:2) to proclaim that gospel among the Gentiles (Gal. 2:7–9) entails using bold speech (Acts 9:27–28; 13:46; 14:3; 19:8; Eph. 6:20).

A better option understands the phrase 'in part' (the noun is singular in Greek) as going with the verb 'to remind': 'I have written these matters in part to remind you.' This fits the context of his 'polite tone'. His 'discourse is "partially" a reminder of what the Roman converts already know and believe' (Jewett, p. 905). Paul proclaims the gospel boldly in this letter, reminding and admonishing both the Roman audience and later audiences. They may be filled with all knowledge about some things but not about all things. Therefore, he also boldly discloses things they do not know: 'I want you to understand this mystery: a hardening has come upon part of Israel, until the full number of the Gentiles has come in' (11:25).

16. Paul used cultic language in urging the audience to present their bodies 'as a living sacrifice, holy and acceptable to God' (12:1), and he again applies cultic terminology to describe how he carries out his commission from God. He pictures himself as an officiating minister (*leitourgos*; Heb. 8:2), serving as a priest (*hiergounta*) and presenting to God a sacrificial offering. As Christ's minister, he follows Christ's orders; Christ alone directs his mission work (Schnabel, II, p. 818). His work as an apostle is not plotted out by a community of faith, nor is it driven by his own visionary inventiveness.

From the parallel in 1:9 ('For God, whom I serve with my spirit
by announcing the gospel of his Son, is my witness that without
ceasing I remember you always in my prayers'), one can infer that
Paul understands his *priestly service of the gospel of God* as preaching the
gospel (2 Cor. 11:7; 1 Thess. 2:2, 8–9), which through the power of
the Spirit persuades persons to believe (1 Cor. 2:1–5). He then can
present the Gentiles' 'obedience of faith' (1:5; 15:18), holy living
(12:2) and praise for God's extravagant mercies (15:9–11) as an
offering to God. *The offering of the Gentiles* is not a reference to their
donations for 'the poor among the saints at Jerusalem' (15:26).[2]
Paul has not yet mentioned the collection, and the audience would
hardly understand this phrase as a reference to it. The phrase is a
genitive of apposition: 'the offering, which consists of the Gentiles'.
It is not the Gentiles' self-offering (12:1), since Paul serves in the
sacred capacity of a priest who brings them into the presence of
God through his preaching. The language of Isaiah 61:6 may have
shaped this notion of his work as an apostle as he applied it to his
context:

> but you shall be called priests of the LORD,
>   you shall be named ministers [*leitourgoi*, LXX] of our God.

The vocabulary in this verse does not overlap with Isaiah 66:18–20,
but Paul may have been influenced by it as well: 'They shall bring
all your kindred from all the nations as an offering to the LORD'
(Isa. 66:20).[3] Paul would understand it as a reference to the Gentiles as an offering rather than as a reference to the scattered Jews,
as it was in Isaiah's context.

Sacrifices to God must be ritually pure, and Paul confirms that
Gentiles, who are inherently impure according to Jewish standards,
have been *sanctified*, 'made holy' (1 Cor. 6:11; Eph. 5:25–27; 2 Thess.
2:13; Heb. 10:10). Their sanctification *by the Holy Spirit* ('the spirit of
holiness', 1:4) makes them an *acceptable* sacrifice to God. This is a
revolutionary assertion. It means that the distinction between Jews

---

2. Against Downs, *Offering*, pp. 40–60.
3. Whittle, *Covenant Renewal*, pp. 171–182.

as a holy people set apart to God (Lev. 11:45; 19:2; 20:26) and Gentiles as an unholy people 'without hope and without God in the world' (Eph. 2:12, NIV) has evaporated. Those who are in Christ, whether they be Jew or Greek, are consecrated, called out of the world, and brought near to God as one people.

17–19. Paul next gives a retrospective of his ministry in the East and asserts that he has accomplished the purpose for which Christ commissioned him: to bring Gentiles to the obedience of faith. 'Getting immoral idolatrous pagans to obey God is a key theme of the letter' (Bird, p. 506), and most would consider accomplishing such a reformation as one about which one might want to boast. Paul speaks the truth of the gospel daringly (15:15), but he dare not speak of his ministry success as something for which he could take credit. He can boast only about what Christ's power has worked through him (Col. 1:28–29), not what he has done through his own Herculean efforts. For his part, he did *fully* [*proclaim*] *the good news of Christ* (Col. 1:25; 2 Tim. 4:17). He planted seeds, but God gave the growth (1 Cor. 3:6). He laid foundations as 'a skilled master builder' by God's grace, but the foundation is Christ, which others may build upon if they do so faithfully (1 Cor. 3:10–11). He would therefore be horrified to learn that many churches today go by the name 'St Paul's'. It is not his name he proclaims (1 Cor. 1:13), and his ministry success is attributable to the gospel infused with divine power (2 Cor. 4:7; 1 Thess. 1:5), not to himself, cracked, earthen vessel that he is.

Paul does not mean by *fully* that he proclaimed the gospel in every imaginable place and exhausted all possibilities for winning converts in these regions. He established churches in urban hubs on important trade routes, and his co-workers and converts took the gospel to more remote areas. Acts reports that Paul preached and ministered in Ephesus for two years and that 'all the residents of Asia, both Jews and Greeks, heard the word of the Lord' (Acts 19:8–10). It was not because they heard him teach in private homes, the marketplace or the lecture hall of Tyrannus. It was because others, like Epaphras who evangelized in the Lycus Valley (Col. 1:7; 4:12–16), sowed the seeds of the gospel far and wide. Paul is confident that when the seed of the gospel is sown, it grows automatically to produce a harvest (Mark 4:26–29).

The grace that God gave to Paul when he was called to be an apostle (15:15) continued to manifest itself in his *word and deed*. Divine power revealed in *signs and wonders* (cf. Acts 14:3; 15:12) magnified his preaching to bring about conversions (1 Cor. 2:4; 1 Thess. 1:5). Harrison and Hagner define a 'sign' as

> a visible token of an invisible reality that is spiritually significant. The same act may also be a 'wonder', something that appeals to the senses and is recognized as a phenomenon that needs explanation . . . 'the power of the Spirit' (v. 19) was required to persuade people to make the connection between the miracles and the message and so believe the gospel and be saved.
> (Harrison and Hagner, p. 220)

The *signs and wonders* confirmed God's presence in the message and disquieted the witnesses so much that they submitted in obedience to the Christ.

Paul never mentions in his letters any specific miracles that he performed, but Acts does record some (Acts 14:8–10; 16:16–18; 19:11–12; 20:9–12; 28:8–9). He assumes that his audience understands what *signs and wonders* (miracles) means from the biblical accounts of Moses during the exodus and from their own experience of divine happenings (Heb. 2:4). They would know that they were 'the signs of a true apostle' (2 Cor. 12:12).

The territory where Paul proclaimed the gospel forms a partial arc that radiates out from the south-east, *Jerusalem*, to the north-west, *Illyricum*. This summary of his success through Christ and the Holy Spirit is intended to encourage the Romans to support his next undertaking that would extend the arc to Spain. Acts 9:26–30 briefly recounts Paul speaking boldly in Jerusalem after his first successful preaching in Damascus. In Damascus, his preaching was so bold that he had to be lowered in a basket through a window in the wall to be saved from the clutches of King Aretas who was seeking to arrest him (2 Cor. 11:32–33). In Jerusalem, he spoke boldly in the name of the Lord to the Hellenists, who attempted to kill him, and he had to escape to Tarsus for his safety (Acts 9:27–30; 22:17–21). He identifies Jerusalem as the starting point of his preaching, rather than Arabia (Gal. 1:17) or Damascus, because of the city's significance in the spread of the gospel. As the resurrected Jesus taught from the Scriptures:

> Thus it is written, that the Messiah is to suffer and to rise from the dead on the third day, and that repentance and forgiveness of sins is to be proclaimed in his name to all nations, beginning from Jerusalem.
> (Luke 24:46–47)

Paul uses the Latinized form *Illyricum* to refer to the Roman province across from Italy on the east coast of the Adriatic Sea. The Greek word translated *as far . . . as* (*mechri*) may mean that he went 'up to' but did not cross into that area. The departure of Titus for Dalmatia, which is in Illyricum, is recorded in 2 Timothy 4:10 and may provide evidence that Paul had worked in that area even though it is not mentioned in Acts.[4]

20. Paul's ambition is to please the Lord (2 Cor. 5:9), and part of his pleasing the Lord is to fulfil his calling to take the gospel to those who have never heard it. The urgency is great, and he does not want to waste time duplicating what others have done. He also does not want to create unnecessary rivalries by building on another's foundation (2 Cor. 10:15–16). Competition fails 'to reflect the message of oneness in the Christian gospel' (Longenecker, p. 1042).

21–22. Isaiah has influenced Paul's vision of what God has called him to do as an apostle to the Gentiles. He interprets Isaiah 52:15 as charting the next course of his apostolic ministry, to go to *those who have never been told* 'about him' (NIV), so that they will see. He cites the LXX version that has the phrase 'about him'. The Hebrew text does not. Paul takes *him* to be a prophetic reference to Christ as God's Suffering Servant,[5] in which Isaiah 52:13 forms the backdrop:

> See, my servant shall prosper;
>   he shall be exalted and lifted up,
>   and shall be very high.

---

4. Schnabel, *Paul and the Early Church*, pp. 1250–1257.
5. Allusions to Christ as the Suffering Servant are found in Matt. 8:17; Luke 22:37; John 12:38; Acts 8:26–35; and 1 Pet. 2:21–25.

Paul understands himself to be 'a servant of Jesus Christ, called to be an apostle, set apart for the gospel of God' (1:1–2) and sent to those who have not heard so that they may call on the name of the Lord to be saved (10:13). He has completed his work in the East that had prevented him from coming to Rome earlier; his calling from God now requires him to transfer the focus of his mission to the unreached regions in the West. Before he can do that, however, he must attend to a project that will take him back to Jerusalem.

ii. Paul's plans to visit Jerusalem, Rome, and Spain (15:23–29)

23. Paul shifts to a discussion of his travel plans to go to Jerusalem, then to Rome, and then to Spain. His extensive work in the East has so far prevented him from fulfilling his longstanding wish to go to Rome (cf. 1:13). Having planted and nourished churches in strategic locales in this region, he now can consider coming to Rome.

24. Paul unveils a surprise. His ultimate goal is to go to *Spain*. He starts, 'whenever I travel to Spain' (CSB), but breaks off his thought to state that he plans to 'pass through' (CSB) Rome. The visit will be brief because his aim is only 'to preach the gospel where Christ has not been named' (CSB), and he has no intention of settling down in Rome and building on another's foundation (15:20). He expresses his intention to go to an unevangelized Spain tentatively, 'whenever', because it depends on God's will. He does not know what his future circumstances will be or if the Romans will back this mission. He can only hope that they will receive him gladly and *send [him] on* (*propempein*). This verb implies more than laying hands on him and promising to pray for him. Prayer was needed for this endeavour to be successful, but so were money and co-workers. 'Sending someone on' involves providing material assistance for the journey (Acts 15:3; 1 Cor. 16:6; 2 Cor. 1:16; Titus 3:13; 3 John 6; Let. Aris. 172). Paul delicately requests the Roman Christians partner with him in the mission to Spain by supplying rations, equipment, funds, and travel companions who would be familiar with the area and who could serve as guides and translators. Recent research indicates that Spain may have lacked a significant Jewish support population at this time. If that is correct, Paul could not start by preaching in synagogues as he so often did in the East, according to Acts. He would need other avenues to reach people and help in doing so. By not making a direct request to recruit the Roman Christians to support him and by expressing it only as a hope, he avoids forcing them into a corner and bringing dishonour on them should they refuse.

Paul tactfully checks himself so as not to imply that he plans only to use them as a transit station on his way to Spain. He will stay with them for a period. A literal translation of the Greek can be amusingly misleading to English ears: 'if first in some measure I might have my fill of you'. He is saying that he looks forward to getting acquainted with them and hopes that the visit will be mutually satisfying as they share spiritually (1:11) and presumably discuss the logistics of the Spanish mission. The translation *once I have enjoyed your company for a little while* captures his meaning.

Why Spain? Paul apparently does not feel any need to explain to the Roman Christians why a mission to Spain is important, and we can only surmise why he felt compelled to go there. Jewett contends that Spain was 'a logical goal for the apostle to the Gentiles who felt "indebted both to Greeks and to barbarians"' (Jewett, p. 924). The Romans considered Spain to be barbarian. Its geographic location at the end of the Mediterranean also completes an arc that began in Jerusalem and reached Illyricum (15:19). One might infer that Paul sought to cover the northern half of the Mediterranean (Dunn, II, p. 872) and knew of others evangelizing the southern half. Spain also was regarded as the end of the known earth (Keener, p. 176 n. 26), and preaching there would, in part, fulfil Christ's prophecy in Acts 1:8 (Isa. 49:6). Schnabel correctly points out, however, that 'the strategy of the early Christian mission focuses on the conversion of people no matter where they live or who they are'.[6]

25. Paul unveils another surprise. He is not coming to Rome now. His statement *At present, however, I am going to Jerusalem* would seem to imply that he is already on the road. It is a futuristic use of the present tense that indicates he will be leaving soon, but it means that once again he will postpone his trip to Rome (Acts 19:21). He

---

6. Schnabel, *Paul and the Early Church*, p. 1473.

leaves for Jerusalem 'to serve' (CSB; 'minister to', *diakonōn*) the saints there. *Saints* is a normal reference to Christians (1:7; 1 Cor. 1:2; 2 Cor. 1:1; Eph. 1:1; Phil. 1:1; Col. 1:2; Phlm. 5).

26. This service involves bringing donations from Gentile congregations he has founded to aid the impoverished Christians in Jerusalem. *The poor among the saints* is a correct translation of the partitive genitive, though one wonders if all the Christians in Jerusalem were not in need after experiencing famine (Acts 11:27–30) and years of persecution (1 Thess. 2:14). Paul repeats twice that the churches in Macedonia and Achaia *have been pleased* (*eudokēsan*) to contribute (15:26–27), which makes it clear that this service was a freewill offering and not their payment of a tax levied on them. They 'contribute to the needs of the saints' (12:13) as 'cheerful givers' (2 Cor. 9:7; 8:1–5) and as those who share with believers in Jerusalem in the 'spiritual blessings' (15:27) of the gospel. It is puzzling that Paul mentions only Macedonia and Achaia as the donors when presumably churches in Galatia (1 Cor. 16:1) and Asia (Acts 20:4) also participated. The desire to fill in the blanks in Paul's statements presents many opportunities for fruitless guesswork. We simply do not know why Paul omitted them.

Why take up a collection only for the poor Christians in Jerusalem? Paul says that the Macedonians experienced 'a severe ordeal of affliction' and were weighed down by 'extreme poverty' (2 Cor. 8:1–2) but, as far as we know, he did not organize a charitable collection to relieve their poverty. Paul may be fulfilling what the pillar apostles, James, Cephas and John, asked of him long before. They acknowledged that 'he who worked through Peter making him an apostle to the circumcised also worked through [Paul] in sending [him] to the Gentiles' (Gal. 2:8). They then asked him to 'remember the poor', which he says he was eager to do (Gal. 2:10). This ministry that he is undertaking has far greater importance for him than simply offering aid for the poor. Its significance is tied to the predominant Gentile ethnicity of the donors and the Jewish ethnicity of the recipients.

The translation 'Macedonia and Achaia were pleased to make a contribution' (NIV) does not fully capture the nuance of Paul's wording. The noun, *koinōnia*, which also appears in 2 Corinthians 8:4 and 9:13 in describing the collection, is usually translated as referring to a 'monetary contribution'. The BDAG lexicon lists the following usages for the noun: (1) a close association involving mutual interests and sharing, *association, communion, fellowship*; (2) an attitude of goodwill that manifests an interest in a close relationship, *generosity, fellow-feeling, altruism*; and (3) a sign *of fellowship, proof of brotherly unity* (pp. 552-553). Translating *koinōnia* as 'gift' or 'contribution' is accurate, but Paul's use of this noun needs to be interpreted in the light of the conventions related to the giving and receiving of gifts in the Graeco-Roman world. Giving a gift was a recognized way of creating a social bond, an alliance. Paul uses this noun to accentuate that the Gentile Christians' gift to Jewish Christians desires to establish community with them from their common bond in Christ. They both share in the gospel's 'spiritual blessings', and these Gentile churches are giving back a portion of their blessings. If accepted in Jerusalem, it would be proof of their solidarity with Gentile believers that cuts across their sociocultural and ethnic differences.[7] The Gentile believers are uncircumcised and law-free. The Jewish believers in Jerusalem are circumcised and law-observant. Paul intends for this service to be an emblem of cross-cultural reconciliation between Gentile and Jewish Christ-followers. It is a tangible symbol of a reconciliation that has overcome the divisions so easily deepened by different judgments concerning the matters of indifference that Paul outlines in 14:1 - 15:13.

Furthermore, Paul had urged the Corinthians to give to this service because 'through the testing of this ministry you glorify God by your obedience to the confession of the gospel of Christ and by the generosity of your sharing with them and with all others' (2 Cor. 9:13). The collection presents confirmation to the Jewish recipients that Gentiles who confess Christ as Lord have received the mercies of God that obligate them to be merciful to their fellow believers.

27. Paul also emphasizes that this service repays a debt. Paul considers himself a 'debtor' to the entire Gentile world to preach the gospel (1:14), and he regards the Gentiles who have received the

---

7. Peterman, 'Contribution'; and Ogereau, 'Jerusalem Collection'.

gospel as 'debtors' (*opheleitai*, translated as *they owe it to them*) to the mother church in Jerusalem. They had sent emissaries into the world with the gospel (Luke 24:46–48; Acts 1:8; 8:1–4). Receiving a benefit from another made one obligated to reciprocate in some way. Seneca, writing on the conventions involving the giving and receiving of benefits, asserts, 'Not to return gratitude for benefits is a disgrace and the whole world counts it as such' (*Ben.* 3.1.1).[8] Paul applies this expectation to repaying spiritual benefits (cf. John 13:14; 1 John 4:11) with *material things*. He articulates this principle of a social quid pro quo in 1 Corinthians 9:11: 'If we have sown spiritual good among you, is it too much if we reap your material benefits?' (cf. Gal. 6:6). In 2 Corinthians 8:13–14, he applies it to the collection. Jewish believers shared their spiritual abundance, the gospel, with the world. Gentiles who have received the gospel by faith are obliged to give something back to the mother church from their abundance.

Paul describes the financial offering to the saints in Jerusalem in terms of 'a fair balance' (NIV 'equality', 2 Cor. 8:14). The gift, however, does not solely settle a debt. It is not simply an exchange of goods for services. Reciprocity in giving and receiving creates an alliance or partnership (*koinonia*) between these differing communities. Since Paul takes for granted that gifts come with strings attached, he would expect that the Jerusalem believers' acceptance of this gift obligated them to accept these Gentile donors as partners in the faith. In so doing, they would endorse the law-free mission to the uncircumcised and affirm the truth of his gospel that Paul proclaims among the Gentiles (cf. Gal. 2:1–10).

The verb in the phrase *to be of service* [*leitourgēsai*, 'to minister to'] *to them in material things* has the same cultic overtone as its cognate noun (*leitourgon*) in 15:16. Its use here provides another indication that in Christ the boundaries between pure and profane that separated Jews from Gentiles have collapsed. The Gentiles come to Jerusalem bearing gifts and 'ministering (as priests) to Jews' (Dunn, II, p. 876). Paul's picture of Gentiles performing a priestly sacrifice for Jews through their generosity is incongruous since Gentiles were not

---

8. Cited by Peterman, 'Contribution', p. 460.

allowed into the sacred precincts of the Jerusalem temple (Acts 21:27–29), let alone anywhere near the altar. The gospel, however, has toppled Jewish preconceived notions about Gentiles. Gentiles can make an offering that is 'acceptable' because it is 'sanctified by the Holy Spirit', and they can minister to Jews in their 'priestly service' to God (15:16; cf. 12:1). The gospel also overturns end-time expectations about Gentiles coming to Jerusalem. The Gentile envoys bearing the gifts for the Jews will not come in chains, bowing face down in 'supplication' (Isa. 45:14) and licking 'the dust of your feet' (Isa. 49:23). They come as benefactors extending the right hand of fellowship to their brothers and sisters in Christ.

28. Paul says that after he has completed this task and *delivered to them what has been collected*, he will come to Rome. The phrase reads literally in the Greek, 'when I have sealed to them this fruit', and many puzzle over why Paul uses this phrase and what it means (Jewett, pp. 874–875). It is an idiom used in commercial transactions that basically means 'signed, sealed and delivered'. In this case, the gift will arrive under Paul's seal. It is hard to imagine, however, that Paul understands this project only as a business transaction in which he simply hands over monies safe and sound to the Jerusalem Christians. He baptizes a secular idiom so that it takes on a different connotation in a Christian theological context. The funds are the 'fruit' of the Gentiles' sanctification (6:22, 15:16) upon which Paul puts his seal. He is not in the business of securely providing the international transferal of goods. He is conveying to Jews concrete evidence of the goodwill of Gentile Christians whose lives have been transformed by the power of the gospel. The gospel came to the Jew first and then to the Greek (1:16–17). The Greeks who now live by faith reciprocate by giving back to Jews a material token of the fruit of their righteousness.

Paul again makes it clear that he is coming to Rome on his way to Spain when he has completed this duty. Literally, it reads, 'I will go on through you to Spain.' He may mean that he will be coming 'through your city'. The preposition 'through' (*dia*) might, however, also be a marker of instrumentality. He will be able to go on to Spain through their help.

29. Paul remains confident that he will complete this initiative and will come to Rome. He knows that dangers lie in wait, but he does not know exactly what lies in the future. He indeed will come to Rome, but as a prisoner in chains. *The fullness of the blessing of Christ* that he mentions here will take a strange turn.

iii. Request for prayers for Paul's safety and the success of the Jerusalem offering (15:30–33)

30. Paul makes his second appeal in the letter, and it is possible that it, rather than the first appeal in 12:1, expresses his real intention in the letter.[9] If that is correct, his concern for the success of the offering for the Christians in Jerusalem is not a minor footnote unrelated to the purposes of Romans. Paul wants the Romans to pray for the success of this project because it has a bearing on his planned mission to Spain. If the Jerusalem church were to cut off relations with Gentile Christians, Jewish and Gentile believers would remain unreconciled. If that were the result, what hope would there be that Roman Christians would accept Spanish barbarians as their brothers and sisters in Christ? Perhaps this interpretation is too speculative, but the concern for reconciliation in 14:1 – 15:13 among fellow believers who are different from one another and who differ over inconsequential issues such as customs related to food and purity does not concern solely an imagined flare-up among Roman Christians; it has global consequences for the unity of the body of Christ. Paul sees himself as a minister of reconciliation: 'in Christ God was reconciling the world to himself, not counting their trespasses against them, and entrusting the message of reconciliation to us' (2 Cor. 5:19). When he pleads 'on behalf of Christ, be reconciled to God' (2 Cor. 5:20), he also pleads for Christians from different ethnicities and backgrounds to be reconciled to one another.

Therefore, Paul summons the Romans through the authority of Jesus Christ, whom they both worship as Lord, and through their love for one another, which the Spirit instils, to struggle together with him in intercessory prayers to God on his behalf. The Greek verb (*synagōnisasthai*) implies grappling or wrestling in prayer (Col. 4:12), and the translation *join me in earnest prayer* does not quite

---

9. Bjerkelund, *Parakalō*, p. 158.

capture how intense this prayer should be. The plural 'prayers' suggests that he wants them to pray continually for him and for his purpose in going to Jerusalem.

31. Paul cherishes the prayers of his fellow believers for his ministry (2 Cor. 1:10–11; Phil. 1:19) and specifies that he wants the Romans to pray for two things. First, he asks them to pray that he might be rescued from the malice of *unbelievers in Judea* during this mission. *Unbelievers* might be better translated as 'disobedient' to connect it to the use of the word in 10:16, 21; 11:30, 31. These Jews should believe the message of good news but have disobeyed and as a result persecute the church. According to 1 Thessalonians 2:14–16, they are particularly concerned about keeping Jewish Christians 'from speaking to the Gentiles so that they may be saved'. The rising tide of nationalistic fervour in Judea and the upsurge in militant fanatics who condemned as traitors Jews who fraternized with Gentiles was a worry. Dangers from Jews, in fact, will dog Paul and his companions in Greece long before they reach Judea. It will require them to make a detour by land through Macedonia instead of setting sail for Syria (Acts 20:2–3). Luke records others along the way forewarning Paul of the peril he faces in Jerusalem (Acts 21:4, 11–13). He acknowledges that the Holy Spirit warned him that 'imprisonment and persecutions are waiting for me', but it does not deter him. His purpose, he says, is to 'finish my course and the ministry that I received from the Lord Jesus, to testify to the good news of God's grace' (Acts 20:22–25).

Second, he asks them to pray that his *ministry to Jerusalem may be acceptable to the saints.* Why would one need to pray for those who are impoverished to accept money? The problem is that it is Gentile money. Paul fears that Jewish believers in Jerusalem might condemn Gentile believers who are not circumcised and do not obey the law's dietary regulations, and therefore decline their generous gesture of fellowship. The Gentiles, sanctified by the Holy Spirit, might be an acceptable offering to God (15:16), but Jewish Christians may not find their love offering acceptable since it symbolizes their equal status before God as brothers and sisters in Christ. The faction of 'false brothers' who slipped into the conference with the pillar apostles in Jerusalem to stifle the freedom from the law that Gentiles have in Christ (Gal. 2:4; cf.

Acts 15:1–2) and those who caused Peter and Barnabas to withdraw from meal fellowship with Gentiles in Antioch (Gal. 2:11–21) might still be around to sway others to reject this offering. They also may be behind the false rumours that Paul's law-free gospel incited Jews living among the Gentiles to forsake Moses, abandon circumcising their children and quit observing Jewish customs (Acts 21:20–21). Josephus reports that Eleazar, the son of Ananias the high priest, and captain of the temple,

> persuaded those who officiated in the Temple services to accept no gift or sacrifice from a foreigner. This action laid the foundation of the war with the Romans; for the sacrifices offered on behalf of that nation and the emperor were in consequence rejected.
>
> (*J.W.* 2.409 [Thackeray, LCL])

Such anti-Gentile sympathies may have infected members of the Jerusalem church, or the Jews could have feared being denounced as turncoats if they accepted this sign of fellowship with Gentiles.

Paul's apprehension that this offering might be rejected is why he now feels compelled to go with the envoys from the various churches to interpret the gift. He said that he would go with them only if he thought it 'advisable' or 'suitable' (1 Cor. 16:4). It is not only 'advisable' for him to go; he believes that it is mandatory. He is willing 'to put his life on the line' to carry out this task.[10] It is very likely that 'Paul wanted to go to Jerusalem to present the Jewish believers of that city the essence of what he had been writing in his letter to the Christians at Rome' (Longenecker, p. 1045). What he wrote in 14:1 – 15:13 about judging and condemning fellow believers over food would also be apropos for those in Jerusalem still influenced by ritual purity imperatives that would incline them to condemn the Gentiles.

If they do accept the Gentiles' offer of fellowship, they accept uncircumcised, law-free Gentiles as co-heirs to the promises and spiritual blessings of Israel. For unknown reasons, Acts never mentions the collection project and its vital importance to Paul.

---

10. Longenecker, *Remember the Poor*, pp. 311, 315.

There is only a passing reference when, in his defence before Felix the governor, Paul says that he came 'to bring alms to my nation' (Acts 24:17). We know only that when Paul reported to James and the elders 'one by one the things that God had done among the Gentiles through his ministry', 'they praised God' (Acts 21:19–20).

32. Paul mentions for the third time his plan to come to Rome, but he understands that the fulfilment of even the best-thought-out plans depends entirely on *God's will* (see Jas 4:13–15). If it is God's will, he will come to Rome *with joy* and *be refreshed* with them after all his labours. Until then, this letter serves as a substitute for his presence. It imparts his spiritual gift to them that will strengthen and deepen the maturity of their faith and inspire them to reach out to those in unreached lands.

Did Paul succeed in going to Spain? Clement, whom Irenaeus and Tertullian identify as the bishop of Rome from AD 88 to his death in 99, extols Paul as a 'herald both in the East and in the West', 'teaching righteousness to all the world' and going to 'the limits [*terma*] of the West', which, from his standpoint in Rome, would suggest Spain as the final frontier or turning point (1 Clem. 5:5–7). Schnabel comments,

> The assertion of Clement cannot be dismissed as a later fictional projection on the basis of Romans 15:24, designed to enhance the reputation of the apostle; if Paul's letter to the Romans was the only source for Clement's comment, he would probably not speak in general terms of Paul having reached the 'limits of the West' but more specifically of 'Spain'.[11]

33. Paul concludes this section with a favourite benediction that the *God of peace be with all of* [*them*], but it does not conclude the letter. God is the source of peace (Num. 6:26; Isa. 26:12), and if peace is to exist between Jews and Gentiles it is because Christ, 'our peace', 'tore down the dividing wall of hostility' in his sacrificial death on the cross and 'made both groups one' 'so that he might create in himself one new man from the two, resulting in peace' (Eph.

---

11. Schnabel, *Paul the Missionary*, pp. 116–117.

2:14–15, CSB). Peace comes when believers respond in faith and understand that God has called us to live in peace with one another (1:7; 12:18; 14:19; 15:13; 1 Cor. 7:15).

Theology

In an age when long-range planning is highly prized, we see Paul as a skilled administrator organizing the collection and a long-range planner projecting a mission to Spain. He is completely mindful that everything depends on the will of God and not on the imaginative strategies and devices of humans. If it is God's will, Paul hopes to come to Rome with joy after completing his task in Jerusalem. He expects to be refreshed by them before tackling a new venture (15:32). The will of God, however, will take him down a different and stranger path. In Jerusalem, he will barely escape being lynched by a mob in the temple (Acts 21:27–36; 22:22–23), will narrowly evade being flogged by Roman soldiers (Acts 22:24–29) and will have a face-off with bitter opponents in a trial before the Sanhedrin (Acts 23:1–10). He then will dodge an assassination attempt when transported under guard to Caesarea (Acts 23:12–32) and will endure at least two years of imprisonment at the hands of two indifferent and corrupt Roman governors (Acts 23:33 – 26:32). On his way to Rome, he will survive a shipwreck and a murderous plot by sailors (Acts 27:39–44) and then a venomous snakebite on the island of Malta (Acts 28:3–6). He arrives in Rome in chains.

Joy and refreshment, however, always come to those who are in Christ (Phil. 4:8). There is the joy that comes to Paul when brothers and sisters meet him in Puteoli and when those who have travelled from Rome come to greet and comfort him at the Forum of Appius and the Three Taverns (Acts 28:14–15). If Philippians 1:12–14 is a reference to his Roman imprisonment, he will experience the joy that his imprisonment has unexpectedly advanced the gospel. The whole Praetorian Guard has heard about Christ, and most of the believers 'dare to speak the word with greater boldness and without fear'.

Dodd claims,

> The course of history . . . has given a deep color of tragic irony to this section of the letter. The man who writes to Rome, full of far-reaching

> schemes, who is planning to visit the capital on his way to remoter fields
> of enterprise, was brought to Rome worn by years of imprisonment, in
> chains, his hopes disappointed, his active career at an end.
> (Dodd, p. 236)

Perhaps not. As noted in the comments on 15:32, 1 Clement, written from Rome to Corinth around AD 96, describes the ministry and martyrdom of Paul and suggests that in teaching 'righteousness to the whole world' he 'came to the limits of the West', an apparent reference to Spain (1 Clem. 5:5–7; cf. Acts Pet. 1). We do not have any further information since Acts stops with Paul still imprisoned. Paul would agree that the story is not about what happened to him but about the gospel that is proclaimed 'boldly and unhinderedly' (Acts 28:31 [author's translation]; the last word in Acts is an adverb in Greek).

Paul understands all mission success to be a work of God's grace and the power of miraculous signs and wonders. On the human side, it needs those willing to serve and give of their lives, a network of partners, and intense intercessory prayers. The Romans' prayers for Paul's safety and that the Jews would accept the collection from Gentile churches acknowledge their own indebtedness to Israel's Christian remnant for sending the gospel their way. It means that they understand the mystery of God's grand purpose to put ethnic hostilities to death through the cross and to reconcile Jews and Gentiles to God and each other, knitting them together in one body in Christ. Their prayers also mean that they join Paul in proclaiming 'the good news of peace to you who were far away and peace to those who were near' (Eph. 2:16–17, CSB). As a mission church who were the recipients of the spiritual blessings from Jewish Christians, Paul hopes that the Romans will glean from his own mission itinerary that they need to become a mission-sending church.

B. Final greetings (16:1–27)

Context
The closing of the letter to the Romans differs from the closings of Paul's other letters by its disproportionate length. Romans closes

with a brief commendation of Phoebe (16:1–2), a request to give greetings to twenty-six persons and two households (16:3–16), a sharp warning about troublemakers and praise for the Romans' obedience (16:17–20), greetings from eight individuals (16:21–23) and a concluding doxology (16:25–27). The extensive list of persons whom Paul asks them to greet is exceptional. He does not send lengthy greetings to named individuals in his letters to churches he has founded and with which he has had a long-term relationship; he salutes the entire church by wishing that grace might be with 'all of you'. Attempting to mention every person would take up a page or more of precious papyri and increases the likelihood of unintentionally overlooking someone (1 Cor. 1:16) and causing offence. This fact alone makes it very unlikely that this section was a portion of a letter sent to Ephesus, as some claim, since Paul had stayed in Ephesus for a long time. He is far more likely to name all the people he might know in a letter to a faith community he has never visited in order to establish relations with those he does not know.

It is tempting to try to weave backstories from the small threads of information that can be gleaned from the names and occasional details Paul includes plus inferences from mentions of the persons in Acts or clues about the names in extra-biblical sources. The truth is that we know very little about these people, and such speculation, while fascinating, should not distract us from discerning Paul's purpose in this section. These persons he lists serve as unofficial 'character references' and 'living proof of the genuineness and effectiveness of Paul's gospel' to those in Rome he does not know.[12] His praise of these persons with whom he is connected augments his trustworthiness as a minister of the gospel that he expects will incline them to support his mission to Spain. These public tributes also promote a sense of solidarity because the community can take pride in the praise directed towards their fellow believers. Their work for Christ is a communal fount of joy.

---

12. Weima, *Neglected Endings*, p. 29.

Comment

i. Commendation of Phoebe (16:1–2)

1. In concluding the letter, Paul introduces *Phoebe* to the Romans with a warm commendation. It was an ancient epistolary practice to commend the carrier of the letter (Jewett, pp. 942–943). Paul identifies her as *our sister*, a term that reflects the family intimacy that Christians felt for one another as the spiritual children of God, which transcends biological kinship. She must be a converted Gentile since Jewish parents would hardly name their child after one of the Titans in Greek mythology. Paul also commends her as a *deacon* or 'servant', depending on whether one regards the word *diakonos* as a reference to a church office or not. By itself, the term *diakonos* need only denote servanthood (13:4; 15:8; 1 Cor. 3:5; Col. 1:7; 4:7; cf. Mark 9:35; 10:43). In 12:7, Paul refers to service in general terms as one of the spiritual gifts: 'if service, use it in service' (CSB). But he does not identify Phoebe in general terms as one 'devoted . . . to the service of the saints' (1 Cor. 16:15). Instead, he specifically distinguishes her as a *diakonos* of the church in Cenchreae. This is the first time Paul uses the word *church* in the letter, and it seems to imply that she holds some official position as a leader in that congregation (Phil. 1:1).[13] It is impossible to define precisely her role because Paul applies the term *diakonia* to all the ministries of the church: 'There are different ministries [*diakoniōn*], but the same Lord' (1 Cor. 12:5, CSB). One can reasonably infer, however, that she is a leader in the church.

Cenchreae was the eastern port of Corinth, which was an important hub for transporting goods from the East to Rome. It is possible that Phoebe was a merchant like Lydia in Philippi (Acts 16:14–15), who possessed independent means and freedom to travel. Paul's commendation of her at the head of these greetings before naming such important persons as Prisca and Aquila and Andronicus and Junia indicates her prominence in his eyes. Some

---

13. The Greek word *diakonos* is a second declension feminine noun – feminine because of the context, since Phoebe is a woman. It should not be translated as 'deaconess', however, because that can be mistaken for an office that developed centuries later in the church.

think that she happened to be going to Rome to attend to some business, which afforded Paul the opportunity to use her as a courier. The necessity of the letter's oral delivery is usually neglected in the commentaries. Paul did not leave it to chance that the audience would understand his letters and could figure things out on their own. He sent trusted co-workers who knew his mind and the contents of the letters to deliver them and also to read, interpret and answer questions. Therefore, it is likely that Paul chose Phoebe as one who was mature in faith not only to deliver the letter but also to deliver 'an oral performance in reading and explaining the long and difficult text'.[14] She probably read it aloud multiple times in multiple settings in Rome. Cadwallader points out 'the crucial importance of the work passing oral muster', citing Pliny who would have a public reading before friends as part of revising the work before sending it off (Pliny, *Ep.* 7.17). He concludes, 'If her delivery of the letter was oral, not merely as Paul's mule, her contribution becomes crucial to the production of the "Epistle to the Romans".'[15] Longenecker reasonably surmises, 'Probably Phoebe should be viewed as the first commentator to others on Paul's letter to Rome' (Longenecker, p. 1064).

2. Paul commends Phoebe so that the Romans will *welcome her in the Lord as is fitting for the saints*. That welcome implies offering lodging and support. Such hospitality was second nature to Christians who took in and embraced strangers because they also belonged to Christ. Paul notes that she is especially deserving of hospitality. She has a leadership role in the church, and she has welcomed and offered assistance to many where she lives (cf. 12:17). He identifies her as a *benefactor*, a 'patroness' and 'protectress'. She is not a 'benefactor' in the sense that she seeks to create an entourage of clients through her patronage. Her generosity (cf. 12:8) in 'sharing with the saints in their needs' (cf. 12:13, CSB) expects nothing in return as we might imagine would also be the case with Rufus's mother for mothering Paul (16:13). That she could be generous to *many* suggests that she possessed some measure of

---

14. Cadwallader, 'Phoebe', p. 448.
15. Cadwallader, 'Tertius', p. 396.

wealth and high social standing. She also has supported Paul. He does not spell out what she did, but she may have covered the costs of the production of this letter by providing a skilled secretary in Tertius, who could have been either her slave or employee (16:22; Jewett, pp. 22–23, 979).

Besides the request to offer Phoebe hospitality, Paul asks them to *help her in whatever she may require from you* or to 'assist her in whatever matter she may require your help' (CSB). Paul leaves the 'matter' up in the air; she would explain what it was when she arrived. Because Paul is single-mindedly focused on the work of the gospel (16:3, 6, 9, 12), it is unlikely that he asks the Romans to help Phoebe with a mundane legal matter – what influence would they have in the courts? Nor is he asking them to help with her routine business affairs. It is more likely that he wants them to help her in the work of the gospel. Jewett sensibly claims that her task was to make preparations for Paul's arrival in Rome and to gain support for his mission to Spain (Jewett, p. 948).[16] If this view is correct, Phoebe's mission would have been similar to the role that Titus and the brothers were to play in Corinth when Paul sent them to help the church get their contribution to the collection ready before he arrived (2 Cor. 8:16–24). Phoebe is to help the Romans make ready for Paul's arrival and the hopefully ensuing expedition to Spain. He leaves 'the matter' ambiguous at this point because he wishes to clarify what it is after he extends the greetings.

ii. Greetings to various individuals and groups (16:3–16)

3–5a. *Prisca and Aquila* understandably come first in the greetings because of Paul's close association with them. According to Acts 18:1–3, he joined up with them in Corinth where they had landed after the Emperor Claudius ordered Jews to leave Rome. It is not surprising that they became co-workers in the gospel since they were fellow believers, fellow Jews and fellow leather workers. They travelled with him when he left for Ephesus (Acts 18:18–19), and hosted a church gathering in their home there (1 Cor. 16:19) as they

---

16. Cf. Jewett, 'Paul, Phoebe'.

are also now doing in Rome. Paul makes no mention of their expulsion from Rome (Acts 18:2) nor of why they have since returned to Rome.

At some point, they *risked their necks* to save Paul. He may not be speaking figuratively but alluding to the penalty of beheading, an alternative reserved for Roman citizens to avoid more terrible forms of execution. Paul does not go into details, and Acts does not record the event. We can guess that this incident occurred when Paul said he 'fought with wild animals at Ephesus' (1 Cor. 15:32) or when he suffered such affliction in Asia that he despaired of life and felt that he had 'received the sentence of death' (2 Cor. 1:8–10). Perhaps these allude to the same event. Paul noted earlier that few would endanger their lives for another (5:7), so Prisca and Aquila's readiness to sacrifice their lives for him reflects their deep love for Paul and their strong bond. That all the Gentile churches are thankful along with Paul for their willingness to lay their lives on the line for him also reflects the strong love that the Gentile Christians have for this Jewish apostle.

5b–15. Paul offers others friendly words of approbation related to their ministry service or relationship to him and, in doing so, he strengthens his ties to the Roman community. *Epaenetus* (16:5), *Ampliatus* (16:8), *Stachys* (16:9) and *Persis* (16:12) are identified as *my beloved* ('dear friend'). Prisca and Aquila (16:3) and *Urbanus* (16:9) are recognized as his *co-workers*. *Mary* (16:6), *Tryphaena, Tryphosa* and *Persis* (16:12) are commended for working very hard *among you* or *in the Lord*. These women did not labour away in the kitchen. Paul uses the verb 'worked very hard' (*ekopiasen*) to refer to his own apostolic ministry in evangelism and church-building (1 Cor. 15:10; 16:16; Gal. 4:11; Phil. 2:16) and to the labours of his associates (1 Thess. 5:12). One can presume that he uses the verb here to commend these women for toiling in the work of the gospel.

Others are identified simply as believers: *Asyncritus, Phlegon, Hermes, Patrobas, Hermas, and the brothers and sisters who are with them* (16:14); and *Philologus, Julia, Nereus and his sister, and Olympas, and all the saints who are with them* (16:15). They may be representatives of different house churches, but we cannot be certain.

Paul adds personal details to some who are named. *Epaenetus* was the first convert to Christ in Asia (16:5). *Apelles* was *approved* [tested and proven true] *in Christ* (16:10). *Rufus* was *chosen* [elect] *in the Lord* (16:13). Does that mean he was chosen as all Christians are (8:33), or chosen for a particular role? Also, is he the same Rufus whom Mark, alone of the Evangelists, identifies as one of the sons of Simon of Cyrene who was forced to carry Jesus' cross to Golgotha (Mark 15:21)? It is possible that Mark adds this anomalous detail in identifying Simon because Rufus had a prominent role among the Christians of Rome. Rufus's mother also became Paul's mother (16:13). Paul does not fill in this tantalizing detail and leaves us wondering why, when, where and how?

Paul uses the word translated as 'kinsmen' or *relatives (syngeneis)* only for his fellow Jews (9:3). His fellow Jews are Prisca and Aquila (as we know from Acts 18:2), *Andronicus and Junia* (16:7), *Herodion* (16:11) and those co-workers sending greetings to the Romans: Timothy, Lucius, Jason, and Sosipater (16:21). If *Mary* is a translation of Miriam and not the feminine form of the Latin family name Marius, then she is probably also a Jew. Could she be one of the Marys mentioned in the Gospels or in Acts who somehow wound up in Rome? *Andronicus and Junia* are also distinguished as his fellow prisoners. Two households are greeted: those belonging to *Aristobulus* (16:10) and those to *Narcissus* (16:11). *Aristobulus* and *Narcissus* are not Christians, since Paul does not send them greetings; he greets those Christians who belong to their households. It is speculated that this *Aristobulus* could be the grandson of Herod the Great and the brother of Herod Agrippa I. From Josephus we learn that Aristobulus lived in Rome and was a friend of Emperor Claudius (*J.W.* 2.221–222; *Ant.* 18.273–276; 20.13). Aristobulus died in the late 40s, but his household would have continued to exist and would have included several Jews (Cranfield, II, pp. 791–792). Cranfield thinks it likely that *Narcissus* is the 'notorious freed man of Emperor Claudius'. He had considerable influence over the emperor and his wealth was proverbial (Juvenal, *Sat.* 14.329). As often happened in the unpredictable politics of Rome, however, he was forced to commit suicide at the instigation of Nero's mother, Agrippina, shortly after Nero's accession. That would have occurred only a year or two before Paul wrote this letter (Cranfield, II, p. 792).

The mention of *Andronicus and Junia* (16:7) has drawn special attention from interpreters. They are Paul's 'fellow Jews'. Some translations (ASV, RSV, NJB) have the name Junias instead of Junia. The lack of accent marks in the early Greek manuscripts (these being added by much later editors of the text) creates the confusion. If the name *IOUNIAN* in the Greek receives a circumflex accent on the last syllable, it would be a masculine name, Junias. If it receives an acute accent on the penultimate syllable, it would be a feminine name, Junia. The consensus among the early church and modern interpreters is that it is a feminine name.[17] Abundant examples of the name Junia have been found in more than 250 Latin and Greek inscriptions in the Rome area alone, but not one has surfaced anywhere for the masculine name Junias (Jewett, p. 961).[18] Junia is the wife of Andronicus as Prisca is the wife of Aquila.

Later interpreters and translators changed her gender because they assumed that a woman could not be 'esteemed' *among the apostles*. This leads to a second translation issue in the text. Are Andronicus and Junia 'prominent [noteworthy] *among* the apostles' – an inclusive sense meaning that they are apostles? Or are they 'noteworthy *to* the apostles' – an exclusive sense meaning that they are not apostles? Searching ancient Greek literature for examples of Paul's phrasing yields evidence for both possibilities. Some conclude that Paul meant that the couple were 'noteworthy in the eyes of the apostles' (CSB).[19] Others have reached the opposite conclusion from their examination of the grammatical evidence.[20] The debate over the grammar, therefore, has not settled the matter. Paul's ambivalence about the value of being esteemed by the apostles (Gal. 2:6), however, makes this interpretation of the phrase questionable. Lin argues from Paul's reference to *apostles* and the

---

17. From the thirteenth century until the middle of the twentieth century, it was regarded as a masculine name.
18. See Epp, *Junia*, for an exhaustive, technical treatment of the issues.
19. Burer and Wallace, 'Junia'; supported by Curtis, 'Female Apostle.'
20. Belleville, 'Ἰουνίαν', offers significant counter-arguments to Burer and Wallace.

phrase *they were in Christ before I was* that he understands Andronicus and Junia to be 'apostles before him', not those who became Christians before him. The only other time Paul uses the phrase 'before me' is in Galatians 1:17. He says that after God 'was pleased to reveal his Son to me, so that I might proclaim him among the Gentiles' (Gal. 1:15–17), he did not 'go up to Jerusalem to those who were already apostles before me'.[21] He later identifies himself as 'the last' and 'least' of all the apostles (1 Cor. 15:8–10). If Andronicus and Junia were apostles, they may have been one of the apostle couples whom Paul mentions as travelling together (1 Cor. 9:5). Bauckham makes the intriguing suggestion that Junia is the conversion of Joanna into Latin. Joanna is mentioned as one of the women who used their possessions to support Jesus' ministry (Luke 8:3), and one of the women who discovered the empty tomb and reported to the disciples the angels' message that Jesus was risen (Luke 24:10). She also could have been one of the sources for Luke's Gospel.[22] She and her husband could very well have been among the more than five hundred to whom the resurrected Jesus appeared (1 Cor. 15:6). Paul considered them to be among the apostles because his definition of an apostle was not limited to the Twelve.

Paul does not say when or where Andronicus and Junia were imprisoned with him (Col. 4:10; Phlm. 23). They did not go to prison as the sentence for a crime. They were locked up to keep them secure until they could be tried (Acts 21 – 28). Why did Paul mention their imprisonment, since chains were something that one would be ashamed of in Roman society (2 Tim. 1:16)? It is Paul's conviction that faithfully preaching the gospel brings suffering in its wake. It is the norm for apostles to suffer. Since their preaching the gospel inflamed hostility, they are not the same as the

---

21. Lin, 'Junia.'

22. Bauckham, *Gospel Women*, pp. 109–202. According to Luke 8:3, Joanna was the wife of 'Herod's steward Chuza'. Chuza may have changed his Nabatean name to Andronicus as a more fitting name in a Graeco-Roman context, or he may have died, and Joanna remarried Andronicus. Cf. Schnabel, II, pp. 888–889.

'messengers' (literally, 'apostles') of the churches from Asia (2 Cor. 8:23) or Epaphroditus, the 'messenger' ('apostle') from the Philippian church (Phil. 2:25). Paul thinks of their apostleship in terms of their missionary work.

One's predilections probably will determine how one evaluates the evidence whether Andronicus and Junia were apostles or not. John Chrysostom's comments, however, should be noted: 'Think what great praise it was to be considered of note among the apostles. These two were of note because of their works and achievements. Think how great the devotion of this woman Junia must have been, that she should be worthy to be called an apostle!'[23]

16. The *holy kiss* was a common greeting in early Christian communities (cf. 1 Cor. 16:20; 2 Cor. 13:12; 1 Thess. 5:26; 1 Pet. 5:14). This visible gesture of love symbolized their sense of a familial relationship (Gen. 27:26; Luke 15:20) and their honour of one another. Paul never conveys greetings from *all the churches of Christ* in other letters. These must be the churches he has founded and ministered in throughout the East. This greeting also implies that they 'are behind him in his mission as articulated both in theological and political terms in the preceding chapters', and that all these churches should be as one with the Roman church (Dunn, II, p. 899).

iii. Concluding admonitions and a blessing (16:17–20)

17–18. The sharp tone of the warning in 16:17 against dangerous external influences contrasts with what precedes. Paul fires off a similar, surprisingly vehement warning shot at the end of his letter in 1 Corinthians 16:22: 'Let anyone be accursed who has no love for the Lord.' That Paul calls for them to watch out for *those who cause dissensions and offences* rather than 'anyone who causes dissensions' suggests that he might have particular false teachers in mind. But he does not give any detailed information about them. The warning may, therefore, be pre-emptive because enemies of the gospel are always on the prowl, trying to infiltrate and disrupt

---

23. Bray, *Romans*, p. 372.

communities of faith. He characterizes them as creating schisms, fabricating obstacles to draw believers away from received teaching, serving *their own appetites* (literally, 'the belly') rather than Christ, and hoodwinking the naïve with their charming way with words. Many throughout the history of the church fit these characteristics, and the warning is pertinent for multiple contexts (Acts 20:28–30; Eph. 4:14; Col. 2:4).

'Serving the belly' was a phrase applied to those devoted to gratifying their bodily lusts, and Paul also applied it to the danger of 'the enemies of the cross' deceiving the Philippians (Phil. 3:18–19). Philo connected the belly to God's cursing the snake in the Garden of Eden, condemning it to slither on its belly and eat dust all the days of its life (Gen. 3:14), and compared it to 'a person who loves pleasure and who cannot lift his head. Such a person grovels in dirt and feeds on the earth rather than on the heavenly nourishment of wisdom'. Philo notes another aspect of this snake: 'It has venom in its teeth', 'looks for a victim' and uses 'a human voice to deceive'. It teaches a lifestyle of drunkenness, gluttony and greed.[24] The implication from this parallel is that Paul sounds the alarm for the Romans to be on the watch for smooth talkers whose minds are 'set . . . on the things of the flesh' (8:5), who are given to quarrelling, and who contradict the teaching committed to them (6:17; 2 Tim. 3:14–17).

19. Paul expresses confidence in the Romans because their obedience to Christ is widely known. Nevertheless, they should be vigilant. Knowing what is good will prevent their being deceived so that they become conformed to this age (12:2). His desire that they be wise about what is good and innocent about what is evil is less direct than the command to 'hate what is evil, hold fast to what is good' (12:9).

20. The benediction in 15:13, 'May the God of hope fill you with all joy and peace', has been shortened to 'the God of peace' in 15:33

---

24. Das, *Romans Debate*, pp. 45–46, citing Philo, *Opif.* 55–59 §§156–166; and *Leg.* 3.26 §76; 3.47 §§138–139; 3.49 §145; 3.51 §149. Paul may not be applying this metaphor to 'the strong' in Rome, however, as Das contends.

and in this verse. It marks the conclusion of the respective units. Crushing Satan is a bellicose, unpeaceful act, but Satan is the lord of all that opposes peace. For there to be peace, God must destroy Satan, God's supernatural antagonist, ruler of all evil spirits and chief deceiver and accuser of humans. Paul draws on the apocalyptic image of the battle with the dragon (Rev. 12:7, 12; 20:1–3; cf. Matt. 25:41) and singles out the community of believers as the beneficiaries of the final cosmic victory over Satan. *Under your feet* may be an allusion to the serpent being trampled underfoot in Genesis 3:15, but God does the crushing, not the offspring of Adam and Eve. Therefore, Paul may allude instead to Psalm 110:1, where God promises to 'make your enemies your footstool'. Whatever the allusion, Paul assures his audience that Christ's victory over Satan achieved at the cross and confirmed in the resurrection will be evident to all when their salvation that is drawing near (13:11) is fully accomplished. It is not a second event but the same event. The defeat of Satan may be compared to seeing a flash of lightning and hearing the thunder from that burst of energy only later, or seeing a volcano erupt and then watching the sound waves hurtle through the cloud of ash before hearing the noise from the explosion. The victory has already been won.

Paul prays, 'The grace of our Lord Jesus be *with* you.' He concludes his long salutation at the beginning of the letter with the prayer, 'Grace *to* you and peace from God our Father and the Lord Jesus Christ' (1:7). Why does he switch preposition from 'grace *to* you' at the beginning of the letter to 'grace *with* you' at its end? Piper suggests that Paul believes his letter to be a channel of God's grace that comes *to* them in and through the hearing of God's authoritative word ('the word of his grace' in Acts 14:3; 20:32) that is contained in this letter. 'This letter is the channel of God's grace to you.' After hearing this word, they will be going out into a hostile world where Satan still lies in wait. The papyrus will be put away until its next reading, but God's grace is not locked away with the letter; it goes with them because Christ goes with them.[25]

---

25. Piper, 'Grace'.

iv. Greetings from those with Paul (16:21–24)

21. *Timothy* has been Paul's long-term co-worker (God's co-worker in 1 Thess. 3:2) and is also Paul's 'beloved and faithful child in the Lord' (1 Cor. 4:17). Paul mentions him in the salutations of other letters as the co-sender (2 Cor. 1:1; Phil. 1:1; Col. 1:1; 1 Thess. 1:1; 2 Thess. 1:1; Phlm. 1), but not for this letter. The focus of Romans is only on Paul and his gospel.

Paul identifies *Lucius, Jason* and *Sosipater* as his kinsmen, fellow Jews, not his blood relatives. *Lucius* (*Loukios*) may be the Lucius mentioned in the list of prophets and teachers in the church at Antioch (Acts 13:1) who hails from Cyrene. Or is Paul using the formal name for Luke instead of the nickname Loukas? *Jason* is possibly the same Jason mentioned in Acts 17:5–7, 9 who was Paul's host in Thessalonica and was attacked by Jews for harbouring him. Sopater, a shortening of the name *Sosipater*, is mentioned in Acts 20:4 as one of the seven persons accompanying Paul to Jerusalem, which would have occurred soon after the writing of Romans. He is said to be the son of Pyrrhus from Berea.[26]

22. *Tertius* is not the co-author of this letter but simply its transcriber at the end of the production line. He did not do any editing or critical assessment of the letter, and his greeting may have been written in the margin of the text.[27] Why he inserted himself is unclear.

23. *Gaius*, who hosts Paul and *the whole church*, either by welcoming into his home every member of the church or by providing space in his home for them to worship, is a model of the hospitality that Paul hopes the Romans will show Phoebe. Since Paul writes from Corinth, this Gaius is probably the one Paul mentions having baptized (1 Cor. 1:14; cf. Acts 18:7).

Erastus is recognized as *the city treasurer* or 'director of public works' (NIV), but it is unclear what this means. The name Erastus appears in an inscription, datable to the reign of Nero, that was

---

26. From Acts 20:4 and Rom. 16:21, Schnabel, II, p. 916, identifies twelve delegates, including Paul, who are going to Jerusalem with the collection.

27. Cadwallader, 'Tertius'.

found in front of the stadium in Corinth: 'Erastus, in return for his aedileship, laid [the pavement] at his own expense.' The infrequency of this name in this era in Greece makes it almost certain that Paul refers to one and the same man (cf. 2 Tim. 4:20).[28] He either was promoted from city steward to aedile, was running for the office and showed by his public service that he would make a good aedile; or the Greek term *oikonomos* that Paul uses is equivalent to the Latin 'aedile'.[29] Cicero defines the role of one elected for the one-year term of aedile in Rome as 'care of the city', superintending repairs of streets, sewers, aqueducts and buildings, and supervising the public baths, taverns and public morals; 'care of provisions', supervising the public markets; and 'care of the public games' (*Leg.* 3.3, 7 [Keyes, LCL]). Paul probably mentions Erastus's position in the city to convey that influential persons in civic life also support him.[30] It also conveys the fact the Christian faith is a missional movement, not a protest movement. One can be a Christian and hold high public office in a Roman colony.

Quartus is mentioned last as sending greetings almost as an afterthought as 'the brother', translated as *our brother*. Is he the brother of Erastus sending his greetings with Erastus, or is he simply identified as a Christian 'brother'?

v. Benediction: glory to the God of wisdom through Jesus Christ (16:25–27)

25. The roaming location of this doxology – after 14:23; 15:33; and here – in the manuscript tradition has caused some to argue that it was composed and inserted by a later redactor of Romans. Nevertheless, its location here has strong support from the manuscript evidence. Furthermore, Childs comments, 'Romans closes with a doxology which has been patterned after the praescript and

---

28. Brookins, '(In)frequency'.
29. Mason, *Greek Terms*, pp. 71, 91, 175–176.
30. Goodrich, *Paul*, pp. 50, 75, and 'Erastus', pp. 583–593, demonstrates that municipal *oikonomoi*, as opposed to private ones who were generally slaves, 'possessed considerable socio-economic status within their respective communities'.

which serves to encompass the entire book within the same consistently christological context.'[31] It sums up important themes in the letter.[32] First, Paul expects that God will use the proclamation about Jesus Christ he articulates in this letter to strengthen the Roman Christians. This recalls what he states in the letter opening that he hoped would happen when he arrived in Rome: 'I am longing to see you so that I may share with you some spiritual gift to strengthen you' (1:11). This letter, which would have been presented orally, serves as a substitute for his preaching the gospel to them in person.

Second, the ancient divine plan that has come to fruition (1:1b–2), *the mystery that was kept secret for long ages* but has now been revealed and 'made known' (16:26), is the mystery of how the salvation of Jews and the salvation of Gentiles are interwoven (11:25). A partial hardening has come upon Israel that has opened the door for Gentiles to be evangelized, and when the fullness of the Gentiles comes in, all Israel will be saved. God will be shown to have been righteous and faithful to the promises in imprisoning 'all in disobedience so that he may be merciful to all' (11:32).

26. Third, the mystery has been 'revealed and made known through the prophetic Scriptures, according to the command of the eternal God' (csb). Paul's gospel is rooted in the prophets, which he underlines in his salutation: '[the gospel] which he promised beforehand through his prophets in the holy scriptures' (1:2–4). The multiple citations from the prophets, particularly Isaiah, in chapters 9–11, where Paul unravels the mystery of God's sovereignty and mercy in saving Jews and Gentiles through their faith in Christ, support this assertion. Since the previous epochs of silence occurred when Israel possessed the oracles of God, the study of the Scriptures by itself, however, does not unveil the mystery. These Scriptures must now be read through the lens of Paul's 'gospel and the proclamation of Jesus Christ' (16:25). Only then do they become divinely rebooted and newly prophetic so that

---

31. Childs, *New Testament*, p. 254.

32. Verse 24 is absent from the earliest and most reliable copies of Romans.

this mystery becomes plain to any believing reader (1 Pet. 1:10–12). Only then may we see that 'whatever was written in former days was written for our instruction' and points us to the ground of our 'hope' (15:4).

Fourth, the goal of the revelation of this mystery is *to bring about the obedience of faith* among *all the Gentiles*, which, Paul states, is the purpose behind God calling him to be an apostle (1:5; 15:18). The benediction reveals that Paul's central concern is fulfilling the call to global mission among the Gentiles and not to settle an internecine conflict among the Christians in Rome.

27. Fifth, *to the only wise God* recalls what Paul says about 'the depth of the riches and wisdom and knowledge of God' (11:33). Those who claim to be wise in this world (1:22) cannot fathom God's wisdom that comes only from believing in Jesus Christ. By dismissing it as foolishness, they consign themselves to perdition.

Sixth, the concluding exclamation, *to whom be the glory for ever!*, is the final chiming of the theme of God's glory that runs through the letter (1:23; 3:7, 23; 4:20; 5:2; 6:4; 9:23; 11:36; 15:6–9). The doxology in 11:36 glorifies God for the plan to save all Israel (11:26). The doxology here that glorifies God for saving Gentiles through their obedience of faith (15:9–11) is its counterpart.[33] It serves as a fitting finale to this glorious letter.

Theology

Paul asks the Roman Christians to greet twenty-six persons, two of whom are unnamed – Rufus's mother and Nereus's sister. Also included are anonymous persons connected to two households and those connected to named persons and identified only as 'the brothers and sisters who are with them' (16:14) and 'all the saints who are with them' (16:15). He exudes a generosity of spirit in the way he characterizes those he knows well. The request for others in the community to greet these persons on his behalf reveals his concern for their unity. Extending these laudatory greetings to others in the community can only reinforce their goodwill towards one another.

---

33. Hurtado, 'Doxology', p. 198 n. 55.

While we do not know much about the persons named other than what Paul says about them or what might be supplemented by Acts, the list of names gives us clues about how the Christian faith transforms relationships and surmounts the barriers society has erected between male and female, Greek and Jew, slave and free, and those of different social rank (Gal. 3:28; Jewett, p. 956). The striking diversity of names that are Greek and Latin, and persons specifically identified as Jews, reveals that the church is not a homogeneous society from one nation but a conglomeration of persons from various cultures. They also come from different family situations. Paul lists husband-and-wife teams, single persons, widows and whole households. Some names are typical or possible slave names: Ampliatus, Urbanus, Hermes, Philologus, Persis, Stachys, Herodion and Phlegon. Lampe claims that more than two-thirds of the people listed 'have an affinity to slave origins'.[34] Some are connected to high social class. Those belonging to the households of Aristobulus (16:10), if he is the Aristobulus who was the grandson of Herod the Great and friend of Emperor Claudius, or Narcissus, if he is the well-known, powerful freedman who was Claudius's secretary, would have been regarded as belonging to a higher social class. Whether they were freedmen or slaves in these households, their connection to powerful families gave them their identity. Some on the list are wealthy enough to provide financial support to others. A few can host house churches. The majority are certainly less wealthy. There is no evidence of rank among the persons listed. They are identified as 'benefactor' (16:2), one who gives to help others; 'workers' (16:3, 6, 9, 12); fellow prisoners (16:7); 'approved in Christ' (16:10); and 'mother' (16:13). No-one is an overlord. One is identified as a deacon (16:1) and two as apostles (16:7), but it is not their echelon in the church that Paul praises. It is their sacrificial service for others.

The mistaken opinion that Paul had a low view of women and wanted to stifle them is contradicted by the warm-hearted references to the nine women greeted in this section: Prisca, Junia, Mary, Tryphaena, Tryphosa, Persis, Rufus's mother, Julia and Nereus's

---

34. Lampe, *From Paul to Valentinus*, p. 228.

sister. They are warmly honoured for their value and contribution to the cause of Christ. Adding the strong commendation of Phoebe, the total of women mentioned is ten. Phoebe and Prisca stand out for their close relationship to Paul, and both have leadership roles. Junia, hidden for so long by the attempt to change her gender, may be the biggest surprise. If she is recognized as belonging to the group of apostles before Paul, she is certainly admirable, even more so if she is the Joanna mentioned in Luke's Gospel. The four women who are commended for their wearying labour 'in the Lord' is telling. Paul understands them to be doing ministry and uses the same verb to describe their work as he does to describe his own labours. Keener observes, 'Although Paul greets over twice as many men as women, he commends more women than men for ministry, perhaps partly because even in Rome their ministries faced more challenges than men, hence invited more affirmation' (Keener, p. 185). Paul understands that the progress of the gospel involves a large network of men and women serving Christ, exercising their spiritual gifts for the faith community, and proclaiming the gospel to others in word and deed.